Lineberger Memorial
Library

ARISTOTLE

XXII

LCL 193

ARISTOTLE

THE "ART" OF RHETORIC

WITH AN ENGLISH TRANSLATION BY

JOHN HENRY FREESE

HARVARD UNIVERSITY PRESS

CAMBRIDGE, MASSACHUSETTS

LONDON, ENGLAND

First published 1926
Reprinted 1939, 1947, 1959, 1967, 1975, 1982, 1991, 1994

ISBN 0-674-99212-1

Printed in Great Britain by St Edmundsbury Press Ltd,
Bury St Edmunds, Suffolk, on acid-free paper.
Bound by Hunter & Foulis Ltd, Edinburgh, Scotland.

CONTENTS

THE TRADITIONAL ORDER of the works of
Aristotle as they appear since the edition of
Immanuel Bekker (Berlin, 1831), and their
division into volumes in this edition.

THE TRADITIONAL ORDER

THE TRADITIONAL ORDER

THE TRADITIONAL ORDER

INTRODUCTION

The beginnings of rhetoric—the Homeric poems—Themistocles and Pericles—the influence of the Sophists—Sicily the birthplace of rhetoric as an art—the *Western* or *Sicilian school* (Corax—Tisias—Gorgias—Agathon—Polus—Licymnius — Evenus — Alcidamas — Lycophron — Polycrates — Callippus — Pamphilus) — Thrasymachus — the *Eastern* or *Ionic school* (Protagoras—Prodicus—Hippias—Theodorus—Theodectes)—decay of rhetoric—Demetrius of Phalerum—treatment of rhetoric in Plato's *Gorgias* and *Phaedrus*—other rhetorical works by Aristotle—date of the *Rhetoric*—Aristotle and Demosthenes—Aristotle and Isocrates—the *Rhetorica ad Alexandrum*—text of the *Rhetoric*.

RHETORIC, in the general sense of the use of language in such a manner as to impress the hearers and influence them for or against a certain course of action, is as old as language itself and the beginnings of social and political life. It was practised and highly esteemed among the Greeks from the earliest times. The reputation of Odysseus and Nestor as speakers, the reply of Achilles to the embassy entreating him to take the field again, the trial-scene represented on the shield of Achilles, bear witness to this, and justify the opinion of the ancient Greeks that Homer was the real father of oratory. After the age of Homer and Hesiod and the establishment of democratic institutions, the development of industry and commerce and the gradually increasing naval power of

xi

INTRODUCTION

Athens compelled statesmen to become orators. Themistocles and Pericles were the foremost statesmen of their time. The former, although not specially distinguished for eloquence, was regarded as a most capable speaker ; the latter was a great orator. It is much to be regretted that none of his speeches has survived ; but some idea of their lofty patriotism may be gained from those put into his mouth by Thucydides, while the genuine fragments, several of which have been preserved in Aristotle, are characterized by impressive vividness.

The next step in the development of Greek prose and Rhetoric must be set down to the credit of the Sophists. Whatever opinion may be held, from a moral standpoint, of the teaching of these much-discussed professors of wisdom and of its effects on the national life and character, it is generally conceded that they have a claim to be considered the founders of an artificial prose style, which ultimately led to the highly-finished diction of Plato and Demosthenes. It is usual to make a distinction between eastern (Ionic) and western (Sicilian) sophistical rhetoric, the representatives of the former paying attention chiefly to accuracy (ὀρθοέπεια), those of the latter to beauty (εὐέπεια), of style.

The birthplace of Rhetoric as an art was the island of Sicily. According to Cicero,[a] Aristotle, no doubt in his lost history of the literature of the subject (Συναγωγὴ τεχνῶν), gives the following account of its origin. After the expulsion of the " tyrants " (467 B.C.), a number of civil processes were insti-

---

[a] Cicero, *Brutus*, xii. 46.

INTRODUCTION

tuted by citizens, who had been previously banished and then returned from exile, for the recovery of property belonging to them which had been illegally confiscated by the tyrants. This made it necessary for the claimants to obtain assistance from others, and the Sicilians, " an acute people and born controversialists," supplied the want in the persons of Corax and Tisias (both of Syracuse), who drew up a system which could be imparted by instruction, and a set of rules dealing with such questions as were likely to arise. These two may therefore claim to have been the founders of technical Rhetoric, although Aristotle, in an early lost work called the *Sophist*, gives the credit to the philosopher Empedocles, whose pupil Gorgias is said to have been.

CORAX [a] was the author of the first of the numerous " Arts " (τέχναι, handbooks of Rhetoric), and to him is attributed the definition of it as " the artificer of persuasion " (πειθοῦς δημιουργός). The speech was divided into three parts—exordium (προοίμιον), arguments constructive and refutative (ἀγῶνες), and epilogue (ἐπίλογος), or into five, with the addition of narrative (διήγησις), which followed the exordium, and παρεκβάσεις.[b] It may be assumed that he also wrote speeches [c] for his clients to learn and deliver in the courts, as it was no doubt the rule in

[a] The sophists and rhetoricians here mentioned are limited (with the exception of Demetrius of Phalerum) to those whose names actually occur in the *Rhetoric*.

[b] Apparently not to be understood in the more usual senses of " perversions " (of forms of government), or "digressions " (in a book or speech), but in that of " auxiliaries," subsidiary aids to the speech (πρὸς ἐπικουρίαν τῶν λεγομένων, quoted in Stephanus, *Thesaurus*, from the Prolegomena to Hermogenes).

[c] Such writers were called " logographers " (see ii. 11. 7).

INTRODUCTION

Syracuse, as at Athens, that the litigant should at least create the impression that he was conducting his own case.

His pupil TISIAS, also the author of an " Art," is said to have been the tutor of Gorgias, Lysias, and Isocrates, and to have accompanied the first-named on his embassy to Athens. He laid even greater stress than his master on the argument from probability (εἰκός) which he regarded as more valuable than truth [a]

GORGIAS of Leontini (c. 483–375 B.C.) first attracted the attention of Greece proper when he visited Athens as an ambassador (427 B.C.) from his native place, with the object of obtaining assistance against Syracuse. His view of rhetoric was that it was only a means of persuasion, and he was careful to explain that his only object was to make his pupils skilful rhetoricians, able to speak on every subject, either for or against, and not, like certain other sophists, to teach them virtue or wisdom. This made him pay greater attention to the style than to the subject matter of his discourses. In addition to fragments of these, from which there are several quotations preserved in the *Rhetoric*, two extant orations (*Encomium of Helen* and *Defence of Palamedes*) are now generally considered to be his. An " Art " of Rhetoric has also been assigned to him. Regarded as the creator of artificial Greek prose, his writings were distinguished by flowery ornamentation, poetical colouring, unusual phraseology (as shown in the use of rare, compound, and poetical words), and many

[a] On the relation of a fragment in Doric (*Oxyrhynchus Papyri*, iii. p. 27) to the τέχναι of Corax and Tisias see W. R. Roberts in *Classical Review*, Feb. 1904.

INTRODUCTION

new rhetorical figures, for the employment of which the contemptuous term " to gorgiaze " was invented. He further introduced an artificial and symmetrical structure of sentences and periods, which gave the impression of metre. According to Diodorus Siculus (xii. 53), the Athenians were astounded at his uncommon style, his use of antitheses, his evenly balanced clauses of equal length, and the similarity of the (beginnings or) endings of words. Gomperz [a] remarks that the English counterpart of the style of Gorgias is euphuism. In the Platonic dialogue, in the first part of which Gorgias takes a prominent part, it is noticeable that he is treated more leniently than might have been expected, considering Plato's opinion of rhetoric as taught and practised by him and his successors.

AGATHON (c. 447–401 B.C.), an Athenian, was by profession a tragedian. His beauty and affected manners made him the butt of the comic poets.[b] A pupil of Gorgias, he imitated the flowery language, antitheses, and parallelisms of his master, and was fond of using the rhetorical figure antonomasia, the use of an epithet or patronymic instead of the name of a person. His first victory with a tragedy at the Lenaea is celebrated in the Platonic dialogue *Symposium*, in which he is one of the interlocutors.

POLUS, of Agrigentum, the favourite pupil of Gorgias, is one of the interlocutors in the Platonic *Gorgias*. In this he is attacked by Socrates, and the special attention paid by him to the ornamentation of his speeches and his affected style are severely criticized. He was the author of an " Art," of

[a] *Greek Thinkers*, i. 478 (Eng. tr.).
[b] Aristophanes, *Thesmophoriazusae*, 100.

which some fragments are preserved in Plato and Aristotle.

LICYMNIUS, pupil of Gorgias and a dithyrambic poet, was the author of an " Art." He invented a number of unnecessary technical terms,[a] and classified nouns under the heads of the proper, compound, synonymous or quasi-synonymous, and single words or periphrases intended to take the place of nouns (κύρια, σύνθετα, ἀδελφά, ἐπίθετα). By some he is considered to be a different person from the dithyrambic poet.

EVENUS, of Paros, elegiac poet and sophist, contemporary of Socrates, wrote an " Art " and rhetorical rules or examples in verse.[b]

ALCIDAMAS, of Elaea in Aeolis in Asia Minor, was the pupil and successor of Gorgias, the chief and last representative of his rhetorical school. A rival and opponent of Isocrates, against whom his treatise *On the Sophists* (now generally accepted as genuine), is directed, he lays stress upon the superiority of extempore speeches to those written out. His writings are characterized by a bombastic style, excessive use of poetical epithets and phrases, and far-fetched metaphors. They are drawn upon in the *Rhetoric* (iii. 3. 1) to illustrate the " frigid " or insipid style.

Another critic [c] describes his style as rather coarse and commonplace (κοινότερον). He was also the author of an " Art " and of a show-speech *Messeniacus*,[d] a reply to the *Archidamus* of Isocrates.

LYCOPHRON, pupil of Gorgias, and, like Alcidamas, condemned in the *Rhetoric* for the frigidity of his style.

---

[a] *Rhetoric*, iii. 12. 2 ; Plato, *Phaedrus*, 267 c.
[b] *Phaedrus*, 267 B.
[c] Dion. Halic., *De Isaeo*, xix. (*v.l.* κενότερον, " emptier ").
[d] *Rhetoric*, i. 13. 2.

He appears to have specially affected the use of periphrases. He declared that the accident of noble birth was utterly valueless, and described law as merely a compact, " a mutual guarantee among men that justice will be preserved." [a]

POLYCRATES, of Athens, sophist and rhetorician, contemporary of Isocrates, whose displeasure he incurred by his *Defence of Busiris* and *Accusation of Socrates.* The former is criticized by Isocrates in his *Busiris* and its defects pointed out. A *Panegyric on Helen*, formerly attributed to Gorgias, is by some considered the work of Polycrates. He also wrote eulogies on such trifling subjects as mice (*Rhetoric*, ii. 24. 6), pots, salt, pebbles. He appears to have at one time enjoyed a certain reputation as an orator, but Dionysius of Halicarnassus severely censures his style, describing him as " empty in things that matter, frigid and vulgar in epideictic oratory, and without charm where it is needed." [b]

Of CALLIPPUS and PAMPHILUS, each the writer of an " Art," nothing more seems to be known than the reference to them in the *Rhetoric.*[c] They are said to have paid special attention to skill in drawing conclusions.

THRASYMACHUS, of Chalcedon (*c.* 457-400 B.C.), sophist and rhetorician, was regarded as the inventor of the " mixed " style of oratory, half-way between the varied and artificially-wrought style of Antiphon and Thucydides and the plain and simple style of Lysias. Its excellence consisted in condensing the ideas and expressing them tersely, which was especially necessary in genuine rhetorical contests. Although he rounded off his sentences in periods,

[a] *Politics*, iii. 9. 8.   [b] *De Isaeo*, 20.   [c] ii. 23. 21.

marked by a paeanic rhythm[a] at the beginning and
the end, he by no means favoured the reduction of
prose to rhythmical verse. He was the first to direct
attention to the importance of delivery (ὑπόκρισις).
In addition to an " Art," and a work on commonplaces (ἀφορμαί, starting-points ; or, resources), he
wrote " Compassion speeches,"[b] intended to excite
the emotions of the hearers, a method of persuasion
to which he attached great importance.

The rhetoricians mentioned above, with the exception of Thrasymachus, may be regarded as representatives of the Sicilian or western school. A brief
account may here be given of the best known sophists
(the name by which they distinguished themselves
from the mere rhetorician) belonging to Greece
proper and the eastern colonies.

PROTAGORAS (c. 485-415 B.C.), of Abdera, was a frequent visitor to Athens and a friend of Pericles. He
was the author of the famous dictum, " Man is the
measure of all things," that is, there is no such thing
as absolute truth, but things are such as they appear
to one who perceives them. He was the first to
enter upon the scientific study of language, and
wrote on accuracy of style (ὀρθοέπεια)[c] ; he also
distinguished the genders of nouns,[d] the tenses and
moods of verbs, and the various modes and forms of
address (interrogation, response, command, entreaty).
He taught his pupils to discuss commonplaces from

[a] See *Rhetoric*, iii. 8. 4-6.
[b] *Rhetoric*, iii. 1. 7 ; cp. Plato, *Phaedrus*, 267 c.
[c] Others take this to mean that he adopted a simple or
straightforward style as contrasted with the affected Sicilian
rhetoric (Thompson on *Phaedrus*, 267 c).
[d] See iii. 5. 5 note.

INTRODUCTION

opposite points of view and the art of making the weaker (worse) cause appear the stronger, by which success in a case which otherwise appeared hopeless was frequently attained. The first to call himself a sophist, he was the first teacher who demanded a fee for his instruction. His character is severely handled in the Platonic dialogue called after him, and his theory of knowledge attacked in the *Theaetetus*.

PRODICUS, of Ceos, an island in the Aegean, is best known for his moral apologue of the Choice of Hercules (between virtue and vice). The date of his birth and death is uncertain, but he was at any rate junior to Protagoras. He paid special attention to the use of synonyms and the accurate distinction of words of kindred meaning.

HIPPIAS, of Elis, depicted in the two Platonic dialogues (of doubtful genuineness), was a veritable polymath. His numerous studies embraced grammar and the cultivation of a correct and elevated style of expression. He also interested himself in political matters, and, by comparing the forms of government and institutions of different states, laid the foundation of political science.

THEODORUS (*fl. c.* 412 B.C.), of Byzantium, is mentioned by Plato [a] as a most excellent " tricker-out " of speeches ($\lambda o\gamma o\delta a\iota\delta a\lambda o\varsigma$). He was the author of an " Art," and invented a number of new terms or " novelties " ($\kappa a\iota\nu\acute{a}$), introducing additional divisions of the speech. According to Cicero,[b] Lysias once gave lessons in rhetoric, but abandoned it for writing forensic speeches for others, on the ground that

[a] *Phaedrus*, 266 E ; Cicero, *Orator*, xii. 39.
[b] *Brutus*, xii. 48.

INTRODUCTION

Theodorus was more subtle than himself in technicalities, although feebler in oratory.

THEODECTES (c. 380–344 B.C.), of Phaselis in Pamphylia, Greek tragic poet and rhetorician, was the pupil of Isocrates and an intimate friend of Aristotle. He at first wrote speeches for litigants, but later turned his attention to tragedy. He is said to have written at least fifty dramas. The *Mausolus* was written at the request of Artemisia, widow of the prince of Caria, to be recited at his funeral. Theodectes was the author of an " Art " in both prose and verse, and is coupled by Dionysius of Halicarnassus [a] with Aristotle as to the author of the division of the parts of speech into nouns, verbs, and connecting particles (conjunctions). He agreed with Aristotle as to the use of the paeanic rhythm, and supported the view that prose should be rhythmical, but not metrical.[b] His extraordinary memory and skill in solving puzzles were celebrated.

After Greece had lost her freedom and Athens her independence as the result of the battle of Chaeronea (338), political oratory gradually declined, its place being subsequently taken by the rhetoric of the schools, characterized by a highly artificial and exaggerated style, the so-called Asianism. Mention may be made, however, of DEMETRIUS of Phalerum (c. 350–283 B.C.), appointed ruler of Athens by Cassander (317–307 B.C.). A versatile writer, he was the author of historical, political, and philosophical treatises, collections of the fables of Aesop and noteworthy moral maxims (χρεῖαι), and

---

[a] *Demosthenes,* 48 ; Quintilian, i. 4. 18.
[b] For the *Theodectea* (*Rhetoric,* iii. 9. 9) see later.

INTRODUCTION

of a lost treatise on Rhetoric in two books.[a] The
work *On Interpretation*, dealing with the different
kinds of style, the period, hiatus, and rhetorical
figures, which has come down to us under his name,
is really of much later date. According to Cicero,[b]
" he was the first who altered the character of oratory,
rendering it weak and effeminate, and preferred to
be thought agreeable rather than dignified. His
flow of language is calm and placid, embellished by
metaphor and metonymy. But his speeches seem
to me to have a genuine Attic flavour." Quintilian
says: " although he was the first to alter the style
of oratory for the worse, I must confess that he
was an able and eloquent speaker, and deserves to
be remembered as almost the last of the Attic orators
worthy to be called by that name." [c]

The writers of the " Arts " which preceded the
great work of Aristotle had almost entirely devoted
their attention to forensic oratory, adapted to the
requirements of the law courts, for which deliberative oratory, the language of the public assembly,
although the nobler of the two, was neglected. Epideictic or display oratory[d] may certainly be said to

[a] A list of his works is given in the life of him by Diogenes
Laërtius. [b] *Brutus*, ix. 38, lxxxii. 285 ; *Orator*, xxvii. 92.
[c] *Inst. Orat.* x. i. 80.
[d] The chief object of epideictic or show-speeches was to
give pleasure to the hearers, whose function in regard to
them is defined (*Rhetoric*, i. 3. 2) as that of " critics " of the
intellectual performance and ability of the speaker, rather
than that of " judges " of anything of serious importance,
as in deliberative and forensic oratory. Funeral orations
and speeches at the great public assemblies come under this
head (see also iii. 12. 5). Quintilian (*Inst. Orat.* iii. 8. 7)
says that the only result or gain in epideictic oratory is
praise, not anything of practical value.

xxi

have existed since the time of Gorgias, but it is not spoken of as being on an equality with the two other branches. The creator of a systematic and scientific " Art " of Rhetoric is Aristotle. The unsatisfactory character of previous productions, whose compilers had neglected the all-important subject of " proofs " and confined themselves chiefly to appeals to the emotions and things irrelevant to the matter in hand, induced him to attack the subject from the point of view of a philosopher and psychologist, not from that of the mere rhetorician, which assuredly Aristotle was not.

Two of the Platonic dialogues, the *Gorgias* and the *Phaedrus*, deal more or less with the subject of rhetoric, although they differ as to the manner in which it is discussed and in the attitude adopted towards it. In the *Gorgias*, the earlier dialogue, the discussion mainly turns upon the meaning of the term—the *nature* of rhetoric not its *value*, and various definitions proposed are critically examined, amended, or narrowed down. Rhetoric is the artificer of persuasion, and its function is to persuade the unintelligent multitude in the law courts and public assemblies in regard to justice and injustice. But the result of such persuasion is not the acquisition of knowledge ; it merely produces belief, which is sometimes false, sometimes true, whereas knowledge is always true. The time at the speaker's disposal is not sufficient for the thorough discussion of such important subjects that leads to truth. Nevertheless, the practised rhetorician will be more successful than the expert in persuading his hearers on any subject whatever, even such matters as the building of walls

INTRODUCTION

and dockyards, although he knows nothing about them. It is sufficient for him to have acquired the power of persuasion, which will enable him to convince an ignorant audience that he knows more than those who possess real knowledge. This is sufficient to show the great power of the rhetorician, which must not, however, be abused; but if it is, the teacher cannot be blamed.[a]

Socrates himself, being asked to give *his* definition of rhetoric, replies that it is not an art at all, but a mere knack of gratifying and pleasing the hearer. It is a species of the genus flattery, like cookery (the art of making dainties), cosmetic (of adorning the person), and sophistic. Mind and body have, each of them, a really healthy condition and a condition that is only apparently healthy. The art that is concerned with the mind is the political art, its branches are legislation and justice; that which is concerned with the body has no special name, its branches are gymnastic and medicine. Each of these true arts has a sham counterpart; sophistic corresponding to legislation, rhetoric to justice, cosmetic to gymnastic, cookery to medicine. The end of the true arts is what is good for mind or body; of the false, immediate gratification. Rhetoric is not a true art, and the power of the rhetorician is of the slightest, since he can only carry out what seems to him to be best, not what he really wishes to attain —happiness and well-being. The paradoxes, that it is *worse* to do wrong than to suffer wrong, and that it is *better* for the wrongdoer to be punished than to

---

[a] Aristotle (*Rhetoric*, i. 1. 13) points out that the objection that rhetoric may be abused is applicable to everything that is good and useful, except virtue.

INTRODUCTION

escape punishment, lead to the conclusion that the only use of rhetoric is, if we have done wrong, to enable us to accuse ourselves (and similarly our parents, children, friends, or country) and to bring our misdeeds to light, that we may be punished and healed ; but, if an enemy is the offender, to prevent his being punished, so that he may spend the rest of his life in misery.

The difference between Plato's treatment of rhetoric in the *Phaedrus* and in the *Gorgias* and his attitude towards it are obvious.[a] The latter dealt chiefly with various definitions of rhetoric and its nature as expounded by its professors ; the former is a philosophical *theory* of rhetoric as it ought to be, if it is to justify its claim to be considered a true art. It is not an out-and-out condemnation of sophistical rhetoric. Although the rules contained in the " Arts " of Thrasymachus, Theodorus, and others are rejected as absurd and useless, it is admitted that there is some practical benefit in its teaching.[b] But it is unsystematic and, not being based upon truth, cannot be properly called an art, but is merely a preliminary training.

The basis of the discussion is an erotic speech by Lysias (read by Phaedrus), which is criticized by Socrates with the object of showing the superiority of his own speech and method. According to him, this is chiefly shown in the due observation of the two great principles of generalization and division, which are effected by Dialectic, " the coping-stone of all learning and the truest of all sciences,"[c] to

[a] Cope, however, does not admit this.
[b] On this cp. *Rhetoric*, i. 1. 12.
[c] *Republic*, 534 E. On the relation of Rhetoric to Dialectic see Glossary.

INTRODUCTION

which rhetoric is indebted for nearly everything of value that it contains.

But the most important point is that the foundation of true rhetoric is psychology, the science of mind (soul), as already hinted in the definition here accepted by Plato (ψυχαγωγία διὰ λόγων, "winning men's minds by words," as contrasted with the vague πειθοῦς δημιουργός). The true rhetorician is assumed to have already settled the question whether all mind is one, or multiform. If it is multiform, he must know what are its different varieties ; he must also be acquainted with all the different forms of argument, and know what particular forms of it are likely to be effective as instruments of persuasion in each particular case. But a merely theoretical knowledge of this is not sufficient ; he must have practical experience to guide him, and must be able to decide without hesitation to which class of mind his hearers belong and to seize the opportune moment for the employment of each kind of discourse. A knowledge of the various rhetorical styles and figures of diction is also a useful accessory.

In view of these facts, the three (in particular the first two) books of Aristotle's *Rhetoric* have been described as " an expanded Phaedrus." [a] Thus, the first book deals with the means of persuasion, the logical proofs based upon dialectic ; the second with the psychological or ethical proofs, based upon a knowledge of the human emotions and their causes, and of the different types of character. The questions of style and arrangement (which are only cursorily alluded to in the *Phaedrus* in reference to

[a] Thompson, Introduction, p. xx.

INTRODUCTION

the superiority of oral to written instruction) are treated, but less fully, in the third book.

In addition to the *Rhetoric*, Aristotle was the author of several other rhetorical works, which have been lost. Six of these are mentioned in the Life of him by Diogenes Laërtius : (1) A collection of previous "Arts" of Rhetoric (Συναγωγὴ τεχνῶν), a kind of literary history of the subject [a] ; (2) a dialogue called *Gryllus*, written in commemoration of his friend of that name, who was the son of Xenophon and fell in the battle of Mantinea (362 B.C.) ; (3), (4), (5) simply called "Arts" of Rhetoric in two, one, and two books respectively ; (6) the *Theodectea* (*Rhetoric*, iii. 9. 9). There has been considerable discussion as to the authorship of the last, but it is now generally agreed that it is an earlier work of Aristotle, re-edited later, dealing mainly with style and composition, and that he named it after his friend and pupil. Its identification with the *Rhetorica ad Alexandrum* is rejected.

The date of the *Rhetoric*, which was written at Athens, is assigned to his second residence there (335–322), about 330 B.C. (at the earliest 335), although the exact year cannot be determined. The latest historical events which are referred to are : (ii. 23. 6) the embassy of Philip of Macedon to the Thebans, asking for a free passage for his army through their territory, so that he might attack Attica (Oct. Nov. 339) ; (ii. 23. 18) the peace concluded at Corinth soon after the accession of Alexander (autumn, 336) ; (ii. 24. 8) the attribution by

[a] Cicero, *De Oratore*, xxxviii. 160: *librum, in quo exposuit dicendi artes omnium superiorum.*

INTRODUCTION

Demades of the responsibility for the misfortunes of Greece to Demosthenes, but there is nothing to show whether the reference is to a time before or after Chaeronea. In this connexion it may be noted that the political opponents of Demosthenes declared that all that was best in his speeches was borrowed from Aristotle, whereas Dionysius of Halicarnassus [a] endeavours to show that the *Rhetoric* was not written until after the delivery of the orator's most important speeches.

It is remarkable that Aristotle, while freely drawing upon Isocrates, whose name is mentioned several times, to illustrate points of style, never once quotes from Demosthenes. The name of the latter occurs three times in the *Rhetoric* : in iii. 4. 3 it is suggested that the Athenian general, not the orator, is meant ; in ii. 24. 8 it occurs in reference to the fallacy of treating as a cause what is not really so ; in ii. 23. 3 it is also doubtful whether the orator is referred to. Nothing is known of Nicanor, and if necessary to connect Demosthenes with the affair, it has been suggested to read Nicodemus, in whose murder he was suspected of being concerned (Demosthenes, *Midias*, p. 549).

Isocrates is most highly spoken of in the *Phaedrus*, but his relations with Aristotle were, according to ancient authorities, the reverse of friendly. The chief reason for this seems to have been that Aristotle had started a school of Rhetoric, which threatened to endanger the popularity of that of his older rival. According to Cicero,[b] "Aristotle, seeing that Isocrates was prospering and had a number of distinguished pupils (the result of having removed his

[a] First Letter to Ammaeus (ed. W. R. Roberts), 1901.
[b] *De Oratore*, iii. 35. 141.

disputations from forensic and political causes and transferred them to an empty elegance of style), himself suddenly changed the form of his teaching almost entirely, slightly altering a verse in the *Philoctetes*.[a] The original has, ' It is disgraceful to remain silent and allow barbarians to speak,' where Aristotle substituted *Isocrates* for *barbarians*. And so he ornamented and embellished the entire system of teaching rhetoric and united a knowledge of things with practice in speaking.'' Further, Aristotle had attacked Isocrates, either in the *Gryllus* or the treatise on the different " Arts " of rhetoric, which called forth a lengthy reply from Cephisodorus, one of the pupils of Isocrates, in which various theories of Aristotle were criticized, and the philosopher himself stigmatized as a drunkard and a gourmandizer. Isocrates himself is said to have entered the lists ; for the reference to " three or four sophists of the common herd who pretended to know everything," [b] is supposed to be meant for Aristotle, who is also attacked in the fifth *Letter* of Isocrates. The numerous citations from Isocrates in the *Rhetoric* have been explained by the assumption that, in a revised edition of his work, Aristotle retained the examples of an earlier MS., dating from a time (347) when Isocrates held the field and Demosthenes had not yet made his name. But the view is generally held that the *Rhetoric* was not published till at least ten years later, and in any case there seems no reason why a writer should not quote from the works of an unfriendly rival, if they seemed best suited for his purpose.

A brief notice must here be given of the *Rhetorica*

[a] A lost play of Euripides.   [b] *Panathenaicus*, 20.

ad Alexandrum, which gets its title from the admittedly spurious letter of dedication to the great Macedonian. More than half the length of our *Rhetoric,* it was formerly printed with Aristotle's works as his. Its genuineness was first doubted by Erasmus, followed by the well-known commentator Vittorio (Victorius), who did not hesitate to ascribe it to Anaximenes (*c.* 380–320), an historian and rhetorician of the time of Alexander the Great, whose tutor and friend he was and his companion in his Persian campaigns. Anaximenes is said to have been the first to practise extempore speaking, to have devoted his attention to all three branches of Rhetoric, and to have written an " Art." The question of authorship is generally regarded as settled in favour of Anaximenes by the arguments of Spengel (who certainly is obliged to take considerable liberties in some passages of the text without MS. authority) and Wendland. Cope, whose *Introduction to Aristotle's Rhetoric* contains a detailed analysis of the work and its language, and a full discussion of the question, supports Spengel's view, while admitting that " the evidence for the authorship of Anaximenes is not quite all that could be desired." His opinion of the work itself, which he says may be fairly called " An Art of Cheating," is in the highest degree unfavourable.

Other views are : (1) That it is a genuine work of Aristotle. This is supported by the former President of Corpus Christi College, Oxford.[a] (2) That it is a compilation by two, or even three hands, dating

---

[a] Thomas Case (president 1904-1924), in his article "Aristotle" in the eleventh edition of the *Encyclopædia Britannica.*

INTRODUCTION

at the earliest from the first or second century A.D., and showing such numerous and striking resemblances to the *Rhetoric* of Aristotle that it must have been based upon it.[a] (3) That it is a hodge-podge of very much later date. Other critics, however, maintain that the author (or authors) was unacquainted with Aristotle's work, and that the resemblances between the two are not sufficiently strong to justify the theory of dependence. Further, the historical allusions in the *Ad Alexandrum* (regarded chronologically) are taken to show that it preceded the *Rhetoric* of Aristotle, and was written about 340 B.C. There is nothing about the relations of Athens with Philip and Alexander, but the Athenian naval league, Sparta, and Thebes are often mentioned. The latest event referred to is the defeat of the Carthaginians in Sicily by Timoleon (343). The beginning of the treatise is first definitely spoken of by Syrianus (*In Hermogenem Commentaria*, 133. 9) a Neo-Platonist of the fifth century A.D.[b]

Full information concerning the MSS. of our *Rhetoric* and other matters connected with the text and arrangement of the work is given by A. Roemer in his critical edition (Teubner Series, 1899). The oldest and by far the best of the first-class MSS. is the Paris A[c] of the eleventh century, which also contains the *Poetics* ; those of the second class are all inferior. Midway between the two in point of

[a] Barthélemy St. Hilaire, who includes it in his translation of the works of Aristotle, with a Preface in which he supports the above view.

[b] For another account of the work consult Brzoska's article *Anaximenes* in Pauly-Wissowa, *Real-Encyklopädie*. To the Bibliography P. Wendland, *Anaximenes von Lampsakos*, 1905, may be added.

INTRODUCTION

value is placed the old Latin translation by William
of Moerbeke (thirteenth century), which, being ex-
tremely literal, is frequently of considerable service
in determining the text of the original MS. from
which the translation was made. It is not, however,
to be taken for granted that this *vetusta translatio*
(Vet. Tr.) reproduces the text of only *one* MS. ;
further, it may represent in places a marginal gloss
or conjectural reading ; also, Moerbeke's knowledge
of Greek is said to have been very limited. The
conclusion arrived at by Roemer (p. lxix) is that the
present text represents the fusion of two copies of
unequal length, the shorter of which contains a
number of haphazard insertions by the copyist from
the longer recension or alterations of his own. The
original text has perished.

The genuineness of the whole of Book III., which
originally may have been an independent supple-
ment, has been disputed, but it is now generally
recognized as Aristotle's. The numerous gaps, lack
of connexion and arrangement [a] (a common feature,
indeed, of all the Aristotelian writings), and textual
errors have been attributed to the unsatisfactory
manner in which the reports of three different lectures
were made and put together by his pupils and to the
lecturer's own faulty enunciation.

The present text (which makes no pretence of
being a critical one) is based upon that of Bekker
(Oxford, 1837), but numerous alterations, suggested
by Roemer and others, have been incorporated.
Several of these are also mentioned in the Notes to
the Translation.

[a] Such as the position of ii. 18-26, which should properly
come before 1-17.

BIBLIOGRAPHY [a]

GENERAL.—L. Spengel, *Artium Scriptores*, 1828; A. Westermann, *Geschichte der Beredtsamkeit*, 1833–35; E. Havet, *Étude sur la Rhétorique d'Aristote*, 1846; E. M. Cope in the *Journal of Classical and Sacred Philology*, i., ii., iii., Cambridge, 1854, etc., and translation, with Introduction, of Plato's *Gorgias*, 1864; W. H. Thompson, editions of Plato's *Phaedrus*, 1868, *Gorgias*, 1871; G. Perrot, *L'Éloquence politique et judiciaire à Athènes*, pt. i. 1873; A. S. Wilkins, Introduction to his edition of Cicero, *De Oratore*, 1879; Grote's *Aristotle*, 1880; J. E. Sandys, Introduction to his edition of Cicero, *Orator*, 1885, and *History of Classical Scholarship*, i. pp. 76-82, ed. 3, 1921; Grant's *Ethics* of Aristotle, i. 104-153 (1885); R. Volkmann, *Die Rhetorik der Griechen und Römer*, ed. 2, 1885; F. Blass, *Die attische Beredsamkeit*, ed. 2, 1887-98; E. Norden, *Die antike Kunstprosa*, 1898; R. C. Jebb, *The Attic Orators from Antiphon to Isaeus*, 1893; Octave Navarre, *Essai sur la rhétorique grecque avant Aristote*, Paris, 1900; W. Suess, *Ethos. Studien zu der alten griechischen Rhetorik*, 1910; T. Gomperz, *Griechische Denker*, Eng. trans., i. pp. 412-490, iv. pp. 435-460 (1901-1912); Aristotle, *Politics*, ed. W. L. Newman, 1887-1902; W. R. Roberts, *The Literary Letters of Dionysius of Halicarnassus*, 1901, and *On Literary Composition*, 1910, Demetrius, *On Style*, 1902, Longinus, *On the Sublime*, 1907 (text, Eng. trans., notes, and glossaries); Aristotle's *Poetics*, ed.

[a] To most of the books here mentioned the translator, in one way or another, desires to acknowledge his obligations. He ought, perhaps, to mention that his translation was completed before he consulted those of Jebb and Welldon.

xxxii

BIBLIOGRAPHY

Bywater, 1909; Histories of Greek Literature: Müller and Donaldson, ii., 1858; M. Croiset, 1887–1899, abridged ed. (Eng. trans.), 1904; J. P. Mahaffy, ed. 3, 1895; Gilbert Murray, 1897; W. Christ, ed. 6, 1912, i. pp. 541-607; numerous articles in German periodicals, the most important of which are given by Roemer and Christ. In addition to the glossaries in W. R. Roberts' works, consult also J. C. G. Ernesti, *Lexicon Technologiae Graecorum Rhetoricae*, 1795, the only separate work of the kind; Bonitz, *Index Aristotelicus*, will also be found useful.

EDITIONS.—Text only: I. Bekker, Oxford, 1837; A. Roemer, ed. 2, 1898, with long critical Introduction and Notes, references to the source of quotations, and full Apparatus Criticus (see also *Zur Kritik der Rhetorik des A.*, an article by him in *Rheinisches Museum*, xxxix. 1884, pp. 491-510). With Notes: P. Victorius (Vittorio, Vettori), 1579; E. M. Cope, an exhaustive commentary in 3 vols., ed. J. E. Sandys, 1877. The last, together with Cope's *Introduction to the Rhetoric of Aristotle*, 1867, stands first and foremost (in fact, almost alone) as a help to the English reader of the original. It must be admitted, however, that the diffuseness, lengthy parentheses, and wealth of detail sometimes make it difficult " to see the wood for the trees," while many of the purely grammatical notes might have been shortened or omitted.[a] Spengel's edition, 1867, with notes in Latin and containing William de Moerbeke's old translation, is strongest on the critical side and in illustrations from the ancient orators, but less helpful exegetically; Variorum Edition, Oxford, 1820 (the name of Gaisford, the real editor, does not appear); F. J. Parsons, Oxford, 1836.

TRANSLATIONS.—Barthélemy St. Hilaire (including *Rhetorica ad Alexandrum*) in his translation of A.'s works;

---

[a] It may be noted that Prof. W. R. Roberts, of Leeds, well known for his work in kindred fields, in the Preface to his edition of the Literary Letters of Halicarnassus, promises a critical and annotated edition of the *Rhetoric* with notes.

BIBLIOGRAPHY

T. A. Buckley (including the *Poetics*), 1850 (Bohn's Classical Library) ; N. Bonafous, Paris, 1856 ; J. E. C. Welldon, 1886, with notes and full analysis ; R. C. Jebb (edited by J. E. Sandys with Introduction and additional notes), 1909.

The following abbreviations have been used in the Notes :

P.L.G.—T. Bergk, *Poetae Lyrici Graeci*, ii. (1915), iii. (1914).[a] *T.G.F.*—A. Nauck, *Tragicorum Graecorum Fragmenta*, 1889. *C.A.F.*—T. Kock, *Comicorum Atticorum Fragmenta*, 1880–88.

[a] Reference should also be made to *Lyra Graeca* (J. M. Edmonds, 1922, in the Loeb Classical Library).

ANALYSIS

BOOK I

(i) RHETORIC is a counterpart of dialectic, which it resembles in being concerned with matters of common knowledge, and not with any special science. Rhetoric is also an art; since it is possible to reduce to a system the means by which the rhetorician obtains success. Previous compilers of " Arts " of Rhetoric have neglected enthymemes, which are " the body " of proof, and have confined themselves to appeals to the passions, which are irrelevant and only have the effect of biasing the judge.

Although deliberative oratory is nobler than forensic, men prefer the latter, because it offers more opportunity for irrelevance and chicanery.

The rhetorical (as contrasted with the strictly scientific) method of demonstration is the enthymeme, which is a kind of syllogism. Therefore one who is thoroughly acquainted with the nature of the logical syllogism will be most likely to prove a master of enthymemes.

However, notwithstanding the unsatisfactory nature of previous " Arts," rhetoric is undoubtedly useful : (1) when truth and justice fail through inefficient advocates, the skilled rhetorician will set this right ; (2) it enables a man to state his case in

ANALYSIS

popular, not in scientific language, which would be unintelligible to some of his hearers ; (3) it enables him to prove opposites, and to refute an opponent who makes an unfair use of arguments ; (4) it provides an efficient defence. If it be objected that it does much harm when unfairly used, this applies to every good thing, except virtue.

(ii) Rhetoric may be defined as the faculty of discerning the possible means of persuasion in each particular case. These consist of *proofs*, which are (1) inartificial (see xv.) ; (2) artificial. The latter are of three kinds : (1) ethical, derived from the moral character of the speaker ; (2) emotional, the object of which is to put the hearer into a certain frame of mind ; (3) logical, contained in the speech itself when a real or apparent truth is demonstrated. The orator must therefore be a competent judge of virtue and character ; he must have a thorough knowledge of the emotions (or passions) ; and he must possess the power of reasoning. This being so, rhetoric must be considered as an offshoot of dialectic and of politics (including ethics).

There are two kinds of logical proof : (1) deductive—the enthymeme ; (2) inductive—the example. Enthymeme is a rhetorical syllogism, example a rhetorical induction.

Rhetoric does not consider what is probable for individuals, but for certain *classes* of individuals ; and derives its material from the usual subjects of deliberation, which are necessarily contingent, for no one deliberates about what is certain. Hence enthymeme and example are concerned with things which, generally speaking, admit of being otherwise than they are.

ANALYSIS

Enthymemes are formed from (1) probabilities; (2) signs. Signs are of two kinds: (1) necessary (*tekmēria*); (2) unnecessary, which have no distinctive name, and are related (*a*) as particular to universal, (*b*) as universal to particular. The example defined. Enthymemes are of two kinds: those which are deduced from (1) general truths, (2) special truths—from general or special " topics " or commonplaces.

(iii) There are three kinds of rhetoric, corresponding to the three kinds of hearers; for the hearer must be either (1) a judge of the future; or (2) a judge of the past; or (3) a mere " spectator " (critic) of the orator's skill. Hence the three kinds of rhetoric are: (1) deliberative; (2) forensic; (3) epideictic.

The business of the deliberative kind is to exhort or dissuade, its time the future, its end the expedient or the harmful: of the forensic to accuse or defend, its time the past, its end the just or the unjust; of the epideictic praise or blame, its time the present (sometimes the past or the future), its end the noble or the disgraceful.

All orators must, in addition, have ready for use a stock of propositions relating to the possible and the impossible; to the truth (or the contrary) of a past or a future fact; to the great and small, and the greater and less.

(iv) *Deliberative* oratory deals with contingent things, not with all, but only with such as are within our control; that which necessarily happens, or cannot possibly happen, is not a subject for consideration. Its most important topics are: (1) ways and means; (2) war and peace; (3) defence of the country; (4) imports and exports; (5) legislation.

ANALYSIS

(v) The aim of all men is happiness, which is the subject of all exhortation and dissuasion. Definition of happiness. Its component parts are : noble birth ; many and good friends ; wealth ; the blessing of many and good children ; a good old age ; health ; beauty ; strength ; stature ; athletic skill ; a good reputation ; good fortune ; virtue.

(vi) The special end of the deliberative orator is that which is expedient; and since that which is expedient is a good, he must establish the general principles of the good and the expedient. Definition of the good. Indisputable and disputable goods.

(vii) The greater and less degree of the expedient and the good.

(viii) The deliberative orator must also be acquainted with the different forms of government: democracy, oligarchy, aristocracy, monarchy, the ends of which are freedom, wealth, education in accordance with the constitution. An unrestricted monarchy is called a tyranny, and its end is personal protection.

(ix) *Epideictic* oratory deals with praise or censure, the objects of which are the noble and the disgraceful, virtue and vice. (In discussing these, incidentally the orator will be able to produce a certain impression as to his own moral character, the ethical kind of proof mentioned in ii.)

The component parts of virtue are : justice, courage, self-control, magnificence, magnanimity, liberality, mildness, wisdom (both practical and speculative).

For purposes of praise or censure qualities which are closely akin may be regarded as identical. We

should consider our audience, and praise that to
which they attach special importance; and also
endeavour to show that one whom we praise has
acted with deliberate moral purpose, even in the
case of mere coincidences and accidents.

Praise and *encomium* differ, in that the former com-
mends the greatness of a virtue, while the latter is
concerned with the things actually achieved.

Amplification also should be frequently made use
of, and the person whom it is desired to praise should
be compared with men of renown, or at any rate with
other men generally. Amplification is most suitable
to epideictic oratory; example to deliberative;
enthymeme to forensic.

(x) *Forensic* oratory, which deals with accusation
and defence, requires the consideration of (1) the
motives of wrongdoing; (2) the frame of mind of
the wrongdoer; (3) the kind of people to whom he
does wrong. Wrongdoing is defined as voluntarily
inflicting injury contrary to the law. A voluntary
act is one committed with full knowledge and without
compulsion, and as a rule with deliberate purpose.
The causes of wrongdoing are depravity and lack of
self-control. Its motives arise from human actions
generally, which are *voluntary* or *involuntary*. There
are four causes of voluntary action : habit, reason,
anger, desire ; of involuntary action, three : chance,
nature, compulsion. The motives of the first are
the good or the apparently good, and the pleasant or
the apparently pleasant. The good has been already
discussed (vi.), so that it only remains to speak of
the pleasant.

(xi) Definition of the pleasant and a list of
pleasant things.

(xii) The frame of mind of the wrongdoer, and the classes of people liable to suffer wrong.

(xiii) Laws being special or general, so also are just and unjust acts, according as they affect the individual or the community. Hence it is necessary to have an exact definition of acts of injustice, because it often happens that a person, while admitting the commission of an act, will deny the description of it and its application.

There are two kinds of rules in regard to just and unjust acts, *written* (prescribed by the laws) and *unwritten*. The latter refer to the excess of virtue or vice, involving praise or disgrace, honour or dishonour; or they supply the omissions, voluntary or involuntary, in the written law. This supplementary justice is *equity*, defined as justice independent of the written law. " Equitable " acts are such as may be treated with leniency, and equity considers the intention or moral purpose of the agent rather than the act itself.

(xiv) The degrees of wrongdoing.

(xv) *Inartificial* proofs, which are specially adapted to forensic oratory, are five in number : laws, witnesses, contracts, torture, oaths.

Book II

(i) Since, in both deliberative and forensic oratory, it is a question of a decision being reached, the orator should consider, not only how to convince or persuade, but also how to create a certain impression of himself, and to put the judge into a certain frame of

ANALYSIS

mind. The former is more important in the assembly, the latter in the law courts. The three qualities necessary to enable the speaker to convince the audience of his trustworthiness are : *practical wisdom, virtue, and goodwill.* How to obtain a reputation for wisdom and virtue will be clear from what has already been said concerning the virtues (i. 9) ; goodwill requires a knowledge of the emotions. Each of these falls under three heads : (1) the frame of mind which produces it ; (2) those who are the objects of it ; (3) the usual occasions of it.

(ii) Anger and Slight. There are three kinds of the latter : contempt, spite, and insolence. The frame of mind in which, and towards whom, men feel anger.

(iii) Mildness. The frame of mind and the situations in which, and the persons towards whom, men feel mildness.

(iv) Love or friendship. The persons for whom men feel friendship, and for what reason. Its opposite is hatred, the causes of which are anger, spite, and slander. Anger and hatred compared.

(v) Fear. Things which are objects of fear, and the feelings of those affected by it. Its opposite is boldness or confidence.

(vi) Shame and shamelessness. Persons in whose presence men feel shame, and the frame of mind in which they feel it.

(vii) Favour or benevolence. The means of disposing the hearer favourably or the reverse in regard to acts of benevolence.

(viii) Pity. Persons who are inclined to pity or the reverse. Things and persons that arouse pity. The difference between pity and horror.

ANALYSIS

(ix) The particular opposite of pity is virtuous indignation. Envy also is an opposite of pity, but in a different way, being a pain at the good fortune of others (not because they are undeserving of it) who are our likes and equals. Those who arouse virtuous indignation, those who are likely to feel it, and on what occasions.

(x) Envy defined more at length. Persons who are liable to be the objects of envy, and the things which excite it.

(xi) Emulation. How it differs from envy. Persons likely to feel it, and the things which arouse it. Its opposite is contempt.

(xii) The characters of men must be considered with reference to their moral habits (i. 9) and their emotions (ii. 1), and their ages : youth, the prime of life, old age. Character of the young.

(xiii) Character of the old.

(xiv) Character of those in the prime of life.

(xv-xvii) Character as affected by the goods of fortune, such as noble birth, wealth, power, and good fortune.

(xviii, xix) The *topics* common to all three kinds of rhetoric are : (1) the possible and the impossible ; (2) whether a thing has happened or not ; (3) whether a thing will happen or not ; (4) greatness or smallness, including amplification and depreciation.

(xx) The *proofs* common to all three kinds of rhetoric are : *example* and *enthymeme* (maxims being included under the latter). Examples are either (1) statements of things that have actually happened ; or (2) invented by the speaker, consisting of (*a*) comparisons, (*b*) fables.

(xxi) Maxims are general statements relating to

human actions, and teach what should be chosen
or avoided. Maxims are the conclusions and
premises of enthymemes, when the form of the
syllogism is absent ; when the *why* and the *wherefore*
are added, the result is a true enthymeme. The
four kinds of maxims. Directions for their use.

(xxii) Enthymemes must be neither too far-
fetched nor too general ; they must not be drawn
from all opinions, but from such as are defined (*e.g.*
by the judges) : and conclusions must not be drawn
only from necessary, but also from probable, premises. The speaker must also be acquainted with
the special elements of the case. Enthymemes are :
(1) *demonstrative*, which draw a conclusion from
acknowledged premises ; (2) *refutative*, which draw
a conclusion which is not admitted by the opponent.

(xxiii) Twenty-eight topics or elements (for the
two are identical) of demonstrative and refutative
enthymemes.

(xxiv) Ten topics of apparent enthymemes
(fallacies).

(xxv) Solution (refutation) of arguments may be
effected by (1) counter-conclusions, (2) objections.
The latter are obtained : (1) from the thing itself
(the opponent's enthymeme) ; (2) from an opposite ;
or (3) similar thing ; (4) from previous decisions of
well-known persons. There are four sources of
enthymemes : the probable ; the example ; the
necessary, and the fallible, sign. As the probable is
that which happens generally, but not always, an
enthymeme from probabilities and examples may
always be refuted by an objection, not always real
but sometimes fallacious ; fallible signs also may be
refuted, even if the facts are true (i. 2. 18). Infallible

signs cannot be refuted, unless the premises can be shown to be false.

(xxvi) Amplification and depreciation are not topics of enthymemes, but are themselves enthymemes, intended to show that a thing is great or small. Refutative and constructive enthymemes are of the same kind, for each infers the opposite of what has been demonstrated by another. An objection is not an enthymeme ; it consists in stating a generally received opinion, from which it appears either that the argument is not strictly logical or that a false assumption has been made.

Examples, enthymemes. and, generally speaking, everything connected with " the intellect " (διάνοια), the inventive part of rhetoric (*inventio*), having been discussed, there only remain the questions of style and arrangement.

Book III

(i) *Style.* It is not sufficient to know *what* to say ; we must also know *how* to say it. *Delivery* (declamation, oratorical action) is chiefly concerned with the management of the voice, and the employment of the tones and rhythms. It has hitherto been neglected, and has not yet been reduced to a system.

(ii) The two chief excellences of style are (1) clearness, (2) propriety. The first is attained by the use of terms in their proper sense ; the other terms enumerated in the *Poetics* (xxii.) contribute to elevation and ornamentation.

The language should have a " foreign " air, some-

ANALYSIS

thing removed from the commonplace. In prose—
and indeed, in poetry also—the appearance of arti-
ficiality must be concealed, and that of naturalness
maintained. In prose the only terms suitable are
those in general use and those used in their ordinary
meaning ; also metaphors, for all use metaphors in
ordinary conversation. They produce clearness and
a " foreign " air. They should be proportional, and,
if the object be adornment, taken from the better
things in the same class, if censure, from the worse ;
they should be euphonious ; not too far-fetched ;
and taken from things beautiful to the ear or other
senses. Epithets may be taken from the worse or
from the better side.

(iii) Frigidity of style is due to the use of (1) compound words ; (2) uncommon words ; (3) long, mis-
placed, or heaped up epithets ; (4) unsuitable metaphors—ridiculous, too pompous, or too tragic.

(iv) Simile is metaphor enlarged by a particle
of comparison prefixed. Simile is useful in prose,
but must not be used too frequently, for this gives
an air of poetry.

(v) In regard to *composition* (as contrasted with
the use of single words), the first consideration is
purity ; which is obtained by (1) the proper use of
connecting particles or of clauses ; (2) the use of
special, not general terms ; (3) of unambiguous
terms ; (4) correct use of genders ; and (5) of numbers.

Written compositions should be easy to read and
easy to utter ; they should neither contain too many
connecting particles, nor be badly punctuated ; if
there are two words referring to different senses,
connecting them with a verb which denotes the
operation of only one of these senses should be

ANALYSIS

avoided ; the meaning should be stated at the outset, if a number of parentheses are to be inserted,
otherwise obscurity results.

(vi) To secure *dignity* of style, one should (1) use
definitions instead of names, or *vice versa* for conciseness ; (2) if there is anything indecent in the definition, use the name, and *vice versa* ; (3) illustrate
by metaphors and epithets (but avoiding the poetical);
(4) use the plural for the singular ; (5) avoid joining
several terms with one article ; (6) use connecting
particles or omit them for conciseness, but without
destroying the connexion of ideas ; (7) amplify by
using negative epithets to describe anything.

(vii) *Propriety* of style consists in its being emotional,
ethical, and proportionate to the subject. The first
creates a feeling of sympathy ; the second expresses
character, because every condition of life and moral
habit has a language appropriate to it ; the third is
a caution against treating important subjects offhand
or trivial matters in the grand style ; nor should
voice and gesture agree too exactly, for then the
artifice is obvious. Compound words, a fair number
of epithets, and " foreign " words should only be
used by one who is under the influence of passionate
emotion.

(viii) Prose should not be *metrical*, but must have
rhythm. Metre distracts the hearer's attention,
while the absence of rhythm creates unpleasantness
and obscurity. The different kinds of rhythm are :
the heroic, which is too dignified ; the iambic, which
is too ordinary ; the trochaic, which is too like a
comic dance ; and the paean, which is of two kinds,
—one ($-\cup\cup\cup$) suitable to the beginning, the other
($\cup\cup\cup$ $-$) to the end of the sentence.

ANALYSIS

(ix) Style must be (1) continuous or (2) periodic. The former is unpleasing, because it has no end in itself; whereas in the latter the period has a beginning and end in itself and its length can be taken in at a glance, so that it is pleasant and easily imparts information. The period must end with the sense, and must not be cut off abruptly. Periods contain either several members (clauses) or one only (simple periods). But neither members nor periods must be too short or too prolix. The period of several members is (1) divided by disjunctives, or (2) antithetical; in which there is a contrast of sense (there are also false antitheses). *Parisosis* is equality of members, *Paromoiosis* similarity of sound, either at the beginning,[a] or end (Homoeoteleuton) of the sentence. All three (or four) may occur in the same sentence.

(x) Easy learning is naturally agreeable to all, and is the result of smartness of style and argument. Those arguments are most approved, which are neither superficial (obvious at once) nor difficult to understand, but are understood the moment they are uttered, or almost immediately afterwards. Smart sayings and arguments depend upon antithesis, metaphor, and actualization. Metaphors are of four kinds, the most approved being the proportional.

(xi) Actualization (putting things before the eyes) consists in representing things in a state of activity (*e.g.* representing inanimate things as animate). It is produced by metaphors and similes, which must be taken from things that are familiar, but not

---

[a] The technical term is *Homoeokatarkton*, not mentioned by Aristotle.

obvious. Apophthegms, well-constructed riddles, paradoxes, jokes, play upon words, proverbs (which are metaphors from species to species) and hyperbole are also smart and pleasant.

(xii) Each kind of rhetoric has its own special style. The written style is most refined ; the agonistic (that of debate) is best suited for declamation, and is ethical or emotional (pathetic). The deliberative style resembles a rough sketch ; the forensic is more finished ; the epideictic is best adapted for writing and, next to it, the forensic. Unnecessary classifications of style. This concludes the treatment of the subject of style.

(xiii) *Arrangement.* There are two necessary parts of a speech : (1) *statement* of the case ; (2) *proof*. To these may be added *exordium* and *epilogue*. Further divisions are absurd ; even the epilogue is not always necessary.

(xiv) *Exordium* is the beginning of a speech, resembling the prologue in poetry and the prelude in flute-playing. In an epideictic speech it resembles the musical prelude, and is connected with the body of the speech by the key-note ; it is derived from topics of praise or blame. In a forensic speech, it resembles the prologue of a play or epic poem ; hence it must declare the object of the speech. In a deliberative speech, the proems are derived from those of the forensic, but they are rarest in this kind of rhetoric (deliberative), being only needed (1) on account of the speaker himself, or (2) of his opponents ; (3) to impress the hearer with the importance or otherwise of the case ; (4) for ornament.

Other exordia are collective and general. They are derived (1) from the speaker, or (2) from the

opponent ; (3) from the hearer, to make him well-disposed towards us or ill-disposed towards the opponent ; (4) from the subject, making it out to be important or unimportant. Arousing the hearer's attention belongs to any part of a speech.

(xv) The topics that may be employed in dealing with slander or prejudice.

(xvi) *Narrative*, in epideictic speeches should not be continuous, but disjointed. In forensic, it must make the subject clear, and the speaker should narrate what tends to show his own good character or the opposite in the adversary, or is agreeable to the judges.

It is of less importance to the defendant, who should only give a summary of past events unless an account of them as actually taking place produces horror or pity. The narrative should also be ethical and show the moral purpose, and the various moral traits that accompany each particular character. The speaker should also use emotional features.

Narration finds least place in deliberative oratory.

(xvii) *Proof*, in deliberative oratory, has reference to (1) the fact, (2) the harm done, (3) the degree of harm, (4) the justification. In epideictic oratory, where there is little dispute as to the fact, *amplification* is the chief means of proof. In deliberative oratory, we must contend that what is predicted by the adversary will not take place ; or, if it does, that it will be unjust or inexpedient, for which the responsibility will rest with him ; or that it will be of less importance than he asserts. We must also look out for any false statement of his, for they are part of our proof.

Examples are best suited to deliberative, enthy-

memes to forensic oratory. Enthymemes should not be used in a series, nor on all subjects, nor to appeal to the emotions. Maxims may be used in both proof and narrative, for maxims are ethical.

Deliberative oratory is harder than forensic, for it deals with the unknown future, while forensic deals with the past, and has law for a foundation ; nor does deliberative oratory offer so many opportunities for digression. If you have enthymemes, you should speak both ethically and demonstratively ; if not, only ethically.

Refutative enthymemes are more highly thought of than demonstrative. In dealing with an adversary, the first speaker should give his proofs and anticipate the arguments of the other side ; the second speaker should attack the arguments of the first and draw counter-syllogisms.

The character of the speaker, since statements may be made by him that are tactless, offensive, or too favourable to himself, is best conveyed by putting them into the mouth of some other person.

Enthymemes may sometimes be stated in the form of maxims.

(xviii) *Interrogation* and *Ridicule*. The first should be used when the adversary has already made an admission of such a kind that, when one more question is asked, the absurdity will be complete ; when your conclusion will be established by it ; when his arguments are shown to be self-contradictory or paradoxical ; when he is reduced to giving sophistical answers. An ambiguous question should be answered by a regular definition, not too concise ; by a direct answer before the adversary has finished ; and by adding the reason for our action at the con-

l

clusion. Ridicule is of some use in debate, but the jokes must be such as befit a gentleman.

(xix) The *peroration* (epilogue) is composed of four elements : (1) making the hearer favourable to yourself and unfavourable to the adversary ; (2) amplification or depreciation ; (3) putting the hearer into an emotional frame of mind ; (4) recapitulation. The speaker must begin by asserting that he has done what he promised ; he must compare his arguments with those of the adversary, by irony or by interrogation. At the end of a speech connecting particles may be omitted, to show that it is not an *oration*, but a *peroration*.

ARISTOTLE'S
"ART" OF RHETORIC

ΑΡΙΣΤΟΤΕΛΟΥΣ
ΤΕΧΝΗΣ ΡΗΤΟΡΙΚΗΣ

Α

354 a [1] **1.** Ἡ ῥητορική ἐστιν ἀντίστροφος τῇ διαλεκτικῇ· ἀμφότεραι γὰρ περὶ τοιούτων τινῶν εἰσὶν ἃ κοινὰ τρόπον τινὰ ἁπάντων ἐστὶ γνωρίζειν καὶ οὐδεμιᾶς ἐπιστήμης ἀφωρισμένης. διὸ καὶ πάντες τρόπον τινὰ μετέχουσιν ἀμφοῖν· πάντες γὰρ μέχρι τινὸς καὶ ἐξετάζειν καὶ ὑπέχειν λόγον καὶ ἀπο-
2 λογεῖσθαι καὶ κατηγορεῖν ἐγχειροῦσιν. τῶν μὲν οὖν πολλῶν οἱ μὲν εἰκῇ ταῦτα δρῶσιν, οἱ δὲ διὰ συν-ήθειαν ἀπὸ ἕξεως. ἐπεὶ δ᾽ ἀμφοτέρως ἐνδέχεται, δῆλον ὅτι εἴη ἂν αὐτὰ καὶ ὁδοποιεῖν· δι᾽ ὃ γὰρ ἐπιτυγχάνουσιν οἵ τε διὰ συνήθειαν καὶ οἱ ἀπὸ ταὐ-τομάτου, τὴν αἰτίαν θεωρεῖν ἐνδέχεται, τὸ δὲ τοιοῦτον ἤδη πάντες ἂν ὁμολογήσαιεν τέχνης ἔργον εἶναι.
3   Νῦν μὲν οὖν οἱ τὰς τέχνας τῶν λόγων συντιθέντες ὀλίγον πεπορίκασιν αὐτῆς μόριον· αἱ γὰρ πίστεις

[1] These figures refer to the pages of Bekker's Berlin edition (1831).

[a] Not an exact copy, but making a kind of pair with it, and corresponding to it as the antistrophe to the strophe in a choral ode.

2

ARISTOTLE'S
"ART" OF RHETORIC

BOOK I

1. RHETORIC is a counterpart[a] of Dialectic; for
both have to do with matters that are in a manner
within the cognizance of all men and not confined[b]
to any special science. Hence all men in a manner
have a share of both; for all, up to a certain point,
endeavour to criticize or uphold an argument, to
defend themselves or to accuse. Now, the majority
of people do this either at random or with a familiarity arising from habit. But since both these
ways are possible, it is clear that matters can be
reduced to a system, for it is possible to examine
the reason why some attain their end by familiarity
and others by chance; and such an examination all
would at once admit to be the function of an art.[c]

Now, previous compilers of "Arts"[d] of Rhetoric
have provided us with only a small portion of this
art, for proofs are the only things in it that come

---

[b] Or "and they (Rhetoric and Dialectic) are not confined."

[c] The special characteristic of an art is the discovery of a
system or method, as distinguished from mere knack
(ἐμπειρία).

[d] Manuals or handbooks treating of the rules of any art
or science.

ARISTOTLE

ἔντεχνόν ἐστι μόνον, τὰ δ' ἄλλα προσθῆκαι, οἱ δὲ
περὶ μὲν ἐνθυμημάτων οὐδὲν λέγουσιν, ὅπερ ἐστὶ
σῶμα τῆς πίστεως, περὶ δὲ τῶν ἔξω τοῦ πράγ-
4 ματος τὰ πλεῖστα πραγματεύονται· διαβολὴ γὰρ καὶ
ἔλεος καὶ ὀργὴ καὶ τὰ τοιαῦτα πάθη τῆς ψυχῆς οὐ
περὶ τοῦ πράγματός ἐστιν ἀλλὰ πρὸς τὸν δικαστήν.
ὥστ' εἰ περὶ πάσας ἦν τὰς κρίσεις καθάπερ ἐν
ἐνίαις τε νῦν ἐστι τῶν πόλεων καὶ μάλιστα ταῖς
5 εὐνομουμέναις, οὐδὲν ἂν εἶχον ὅ τι λέγωσιν· ἅπαντες
γὰρ οἱ μὲν οἴονται δεῖν οὕτω τοὺς νόμους ἀγορεύειν,
οἱ δὲ καὶ χρῶνται καὶ κωλύουσιν ἔξω τοῦ πράγματος λέγειν, καθάπερ καὶ ἐν Ἀρείῳ πάγῳ, ὀρθῶς
τοῦτο νομίζοντες· οὐ γὰρ δεῖ τὸν δικαστὴν δια-
στρέφειν εἰς ὀργὴν προάγοντας ἢ φθόνον ἢ ἔλεον·
ὅμοιον γὰρ κἂν εἴ τις, ᾧ μέλλει χρῆσθαι κανόνι,
6 τοῦτον ποιήσειε στρεβλόν. ἔτι δὲ φανερὸν ὅτι τοῦ
μὲν ἀμφισβητοῦντος οὐδέν ἐστιν ἔξω τοῦ δεῖξαι τὸ
πρᾶγμα ὅτι ἔστιν ἢ οὐκ ἔστιν ἢ γέγονεν ἢ οὐ
γέγονεν· εἰ δὲ μέγα ἢ μικρὸν ἢ δίκαιον ἢ ἄδικον,
ὅσα μὴ ὁ νομοθέτης διώρικεν, αὐτὸν δή που τὸν
δικαστὴν δεῖ γιγνώσκειν καὶ οὐ μανθάνειν παρὰ
τῶν ἀμφισβητούντων.
7 Μάλιστα μὲν οὖν προσήκει τοὺς ὀρθῶς κειμένους
νόμους, ὅσα ἐνδέχεται, πάντα διορίζειν αὐτούς, καὶ
ὅτι ἐλάχιστα καταλείπειν ἐπὶ τοῖς κρίνουσι, πρῶτον
μὲν ὅτι ἕνα λαβεῖν καὶ ὀλίγους ῥᾷον ἢ πολλοὺς εὖ
1354 b φρονοῦντας καὶ δυναμένους νομοθετεῖν καὶ δικάζειν·
ἔπειθ' αἱ μὲν νομοθεσίαι ἐκ πολλοῦ χρόνου σκε-

---

[a] His functions were a combination of those of the modern
judge and juryman.
[b] That is, forbid speaking of matters that have nothing
to do with the case.

4

within the province of art ; everything else is merely an accessory. And yet they say nothing about enthymemes which are the body of proof, but chiefly devote their attention to matters outside the subject ; for the arousing of prejudice, compassion, anger, and similar emotions has no connexion with the matter in hand, but is directed only to the dicast.[a] The result would be that, if all trials were now carried on as they are in some States, especially those that are well administered, there would be nothing left for the rhetorician to say. For all men either think that all the laws ought so to prescribe,[b] or in fact carry out the principle and forbid speaking outside the subject, as in the court of Areopagus, and in this they are right. For it is wrong to warp the dicast's feelings, to arouse him to anger, jealousy, or compassion, which would be like making the rule crooked which one intended to use. Further, it is evident that the only business of the litigant is to prove that the fact in question is or is not so, that it has happened or not ; whether it is important or unimportant, just or unjust, in all cases in which the legislator has not laid down a ruling, is a matter for the dicast himself to decide ; it is not the business of the litigants to instruct him.

First of all, therefore, it is proper that laws, properly enacted, should themselves define the issue of all cases as far as possible, and leave as little as possible to the discretion of the judges ; in the first place, because it is easier to find one or a few men of good sense, capable of framing laws and pronouncing judgements, than a large number ; secondly, legislation is the result of long consideration, whereas

ψαμένων γίνονται, αἱ δὲ κρίσεις ἐξ ὑπογυίου, ὥστε
χαλεπὸν ἀποδιδόναι τὸ δίκαιον καὶ τὸ συμφέρον
καλῶς τοὺς κρίνοντας. τὸ δὲ πάντων μέγιστον,
ὅτι ἡ μὲν τοῦ νομοθέτου κρίσις οὐ κατὰ μέρος,
ἀλλὰ περὶ μελλόντων τε καὶ καθόλου ἐστίν, ὁ δ᾽
ἐκκλησιαστὴς καὶ δικαστὴς ἤδη περὶ παρόντων
καὶ ἀφωρισμένων κρίνουσιν· πρὸς οὓς καὶ τὸ φιλεῖν
ἤδη καὶ τὸ μισεῖν καὶ τὸ ἴδιον συμφέρον συνήρτηται
πολλάκις, ὥστε μηκέτι δύνασθαι θεωρεῖν ἱκανῶς
τὸ ἀληθές, ἀλλ᾽ ἐπισκοτεῖν τῇ κρίσει τὸ ἴδιον ἡδὺ
ἢ λυπηρόν.

8   Περὶ μὲν οὖν τῶν ἄλλων, ὥσπερ λέγομεν, δεῖ ὡς
ἐλαχίστων ποιεῖν κύριον τὸν κριτήν· περὶ δὲ τοῦ
γεγονέναι ἢ μὴ γεγονέναι, ἢ ἔσεσθαι ἢ μὴ ἔσεσθαι,
ἢ εἶναι ἢ μὴ εἶναι, ἀνάγκη ἐπὶ τοῖς κριταῖς κατα-
λείπειν· οὐ γὰρ δυνατὸν ταῦτα τὸν νομοθέτην προ-
9 ϊδεῖν. εἰ δὴ ταῦθ᾽ οὕτως ἔχει, φανερὸν ὅτι τὰ ἔξω
τοῦ πράγματος τεχνολογοῦσιν ὅσοι τἆλλα διορί-
ζουσιν, οἷον τί δεῖ τὸ προοίμιον ἢ τὴν διήγησιν
ἔχειν, καὶ τῶν ἄλλων ἕκαστον μορίων· οὐδὲν γὰρ ἐν
αὐτοῖς ἄλλο πραγματεύονται πλὴν ὅπως τὸν κριτὴν
ποιόν τινα ποιήσωσιν. περὶ δὲ τῶν ἐντέχνων
πίστεων οὐδὲν δεικνύουσιν· τοῦτο δ᾽ ἐστίν, ὅθεν ἄν
τις γένοιτο ἐνθυμηματικός.

10   Διὰ γὰρ τοῦτο τῆς αὐτῆς οὔσης μεθόδου περὶ τὰ
δημηγορικὰ καὶ δικανικά, καὶ καλλίονος καὶ πολι-
τικωτέρας τῆς δημηγορικῆς πραγματείας οὔσης ἢ

---

[a] Systematic logical proofs (enthymeme, example), including testimony as to character and appeals to the emotions
(2. 3), which the rhetorician has to invent (εὑρεῖν, *inventio*)
for use in particular cases. They are contrasted with " inartificial " proofs, which have nothing to do with the rules of
the art, but are already in existence, and only need to be

judgements are delivered on the spur of the moment,
so that it is difficult for the judges properly to decide
questions of justice or expediency. But what is
most important of all is that the judgement of the
legislator does not apply to a particular case, but is
universal and applies to the future, whereas the
member of the public assembly and the dicast have
to decide present and definite issues, and in their
case love, hate, or personal interest is often involved,
so that they are no longer capable of discerning the
truth adequately, their judgement being obscured
by their own pleasure or pain.

All other cases, as we have just said, should be
left to the authority of the judge as seldom as
possible, except where it is a question of a thing
having happened or not, of its going to happen or
not, of being or not being so ; this must be left to
the discretion of the judges, for it is impossible for
the legislator to foresee such questions. If this is
so, it is obvious that all those who definitely lay
down, for instance, what should be the contents of
the exordium or the narrative, or of the other parts
of the discourse, are bringing under the rules of art
what is outside the subject ; for the only thing to
which their attention is devoted is how to put the
judge into a certain frame of mind. They give no
account of the artificial proofs,[a] which make a man
a master of rhetorical argument.

Hence, although the method of deliberative and
forensic Rhetoric is the same, and although the
pursuit of the former is nobler and more worthy of
a statesman than that of the latter, which is limited

made use of. The former are dealt with in chs. iv.-xiv., the
latter in ch. xv. of this book.

7

τῆς περὶ τὰ συναλλάγματα, περὶ μὲν ἐκείνης οὐδὲν λέγουσι, περὶ δὲ τοῦ δικάζεσθαι πάντες πειρῶνται τεχνολογεῖν, ὅτι ἧττόν ἐστι πρὸ ἔργου τὰ ἔξω τοῦ πράγματος λέγειν ἐν τοῖς δημηγορικοῖς καὶ ἧττόν ἐστι κακοῦργον ἡ δημηγορία δικολογίας, ὅτι κοινό- τερον.[a] ἐνταῦθα μὲν γὰρ ὁ κριτὴς περὶ οἰκείων κρίνει, ὥστ' οὐδὲν ἄλλο δεῖ πλὴν ἀποδεῖξαι ὅτι οὕτως ἔχει ὥς φησιν ὁ συμβουλεύων· ἐν δὲ τοῖς δικανικοῖς οὐχ ἱκανὸν τοῦτο, ἀλλὰ πρὸ ἔργου ἐστὶν ἀναλαβεῖν τὸν ἀκροατήν· περὶ ἀλλοτρίων γὰρ ἡ κρίσις, ὥστε πρὸς τὸ αὐτῶν σκοπούμενοι καὶ πρὸς χάριν ἀκροώμενοι διδόασι τοῖς ἀμφισβητοῦσιν, 1355 a ἀλλ' οὐ κρίνουσιν.[b] διὸ καὶ πολλαχοῦ, ὥσπερ καὶ πρότερον εἶπον, ὁ νόμος κωλύει λέγειν ἔξω τοῦ πράγματος· ἐκεῖ δ' αὐτοὶ οἱ κριταὶ τοῦτο τηροῦσιν ἱκανῶς.

11 Ἐπεὶ δὲ φανερόν ἐστιν ὅτι ἡ μὲν ἔντεχνος μέθοδος περὶ τὰς πίστεις ἐστίν, ἡ δὲ πίστις ἀπό- δειξίς τις (τότε γὰρ πιστεύομεν μάλιστα ὅταν ἀπο- δεδεῖχθαι ὑπολάβωμεν), ἔστι δ' ἀπόδειξις ῥητορικὴ[c] ἐνθύμημα, καὶ ἔστι τοῦτο ὡς εἰπεῖν ἁπλῶς κυριώ- τατον τῶν πίστεων, τὸ δ' ἐνθύμημα συλλογισμός τις, περὶ δὲ συλλογισμοῦ ὁμοίως ἅπαντος τῆς διαλεκτικῆς[d] ἐστιν ἰδεῖν, ἢ αὐτῆς ὅλης ἢ μέρους τινός, δῆλον δ' ὅτι ὁ μάλιστα τοῦτο δυνάμενος

---

[a] κοινότερον: or, "more intelligible to the ordinary man."
[b] The case as a rule being a matter of personal indifference, the judges are likely to be led away by the arguments which seem most plausible.
[c] Exact scientific proof (ἀπόδειξις), which probable proof (πίστις) only to a certain extent resembles.
[d] Dialectic here apparently includes logic generally, the

8

to transactions between private citizens, they say nothing about the former, but without exception endeavour to bring forensic speaking under the rules of art. The reason of this is that in public speaking it is less worth while to talk of what is outside the subject, and that deliberative oratory lends itself to trickery less than forensic, because it is of more general interest.[a] For in the assembly the judges decide upon their own affairs, so that the only thing necessary is to prove the truth of the statement of one who recommends a measure, but in the law courts this is not sufficient; there it is useful to win over the hearers, for the decision concerns other interests than those of the judges, who, having only themselves to consider and listening merely for their own pleasure, surrender to the pleaders but do not give a real decision.[b] That is why, as I have said before, in many places the law prohibits speaking outside the subject in the law courts, whereas in the assembly the judges themselves take adequate precautions against this.

It is obvious, therefore, that a system arranged according to the rules of art is only concerned with proofs; that proof is a sort of demonstration,[c] since we are most strongly convinced when we suppose anything to have been demonstrated; that rhetorical demonstration is an enthymeme, which, generally speaking, is the strongest of rhetorical proofs; and lastly, that the enthymeme is a kind of syllogism. Now, as it is the function of Dialectic as a whole, or of one of its parts,[d] to consider every kind of syllogism in a similar manner, it is clear that he who is most

"part" being either the *Analytica Priora*, which deals with the syllogism, or the *Sophistici Elenchi*, on Fallacies.

θεωρεῖν, ἐκ τίνων καὶ πῶς γίνεται συλλογισμός,
οὗτος καὶ ἐνθυμηματικὸς ἂν εἴη μάλιστα, προσ-
λαβὼν περὶ ποῖά τ' ἐστὶ τὰ ἐνθυμήματα καὶ τίνας
ἔχει διαφορὰς πρὸς τοὺς λογικοὺς συλλογισμούς·
τό τε γὰρ ἀληθὲς καὶ τὸ ὅμοιον τῷ ἀληθεῖ τῆς
αὐτῆς ἐστι δυνάμεως ἰδεῖν, ἅμα δὲ καὶ οἱ ἄνθρωποι
πρὸς τὸ ἀληθὲς πεφύκασιν ἱκανῶς καὶ τὰ πλείω
τυγχάνουσι τῆς ἀληθείας· διὸ πρὸς τὰ ἔνδοξα στο-
χαστικῶς ἔχειν τοῦ ὁμοίως ἔχοντος καὶ πρὸς τὴν
ἀλήθειάν ἐστιν.

Ὅτι μὲν οὖν τὰ ἔξω τοῦ πράγματος οἱ ἄλλοι
τεχνολογοῦσι, καὶ διότι μᾶλλον ἀπονενεύκασι πρὸς
12 τὸ δικολογεῖν, φανερόν· χρήσιμος δ' ἐστὶν ἡ ῥητορικὴ διά τε τὸ φύσει εἶναι κρείττω τἀληθῆ καὶ
τὰ δίκαια τῶν ἐναντίων, ὥστε ἐὰν μὴ κατὰ τὸ
προσῆκον αἱ κρίσεις γίγνωνται, ἀνάγκη δι' αὑτῶν
ἡττᾶσθαι· τοῦτο δ' ἐστὶν ἄξιον ἐπιτιμήσεως. ἔτι
δὲ πρὸς ἐνίους οὐδ' εἰ τὴν ἀκριβεστάτην ἔχοιμεν
ἐπιστήμην, ῥᾴδιον ἀπ' ἐκείνης πεῖσαι λέγοντας·
διδασκαλίας γάρ ἐστιν ὁ κατὰ τὴν ἐπιστήμην λόγος,
τοῦτο δὲ ἀδύνατον, ἀλλ' ἀνάγκη διὰ τῶν κοινῶν
ποιεῖσθαι τὰς πίστεις καὶ τοὺς λόγους, ὥσπερ καὶ
ἐν τοῖς τοπικοῖς ἐλέγομεν περὶ τῆς πρὸς τοὺς πολλοὺς ἐντεύξεως. ἔτι δὲ τἀναντία δεῖ δύνασθαι
πείθειν, καθάπερ καὶ ἐν τοῖς συλλογισμοῖς, οὐχ
ὅπως ἀμφότερα πράττωμεν (οὐ γὰρ δεῖ τὰ φαῦλα

---

[a] ἔνδοξα, "resting on opinion"; defined in the *Topics*
(i. 1) as "things generally admitted by all, or by most
men, or by the wise, and by all or most of these, or by the
most notable and esteemed."

[b] διότι either = ὅτι, "that"; or, (it is clear) "why."

[c] Almost equivalent to demonstration or strictly logical
proof.

capable of examining the matter and forms of a syllogism will be in the highest degree a master of rhetorical argument, if to this he adds a knowledge of the subjects with which enthymemes deal and the differences between them and logical syllogisms. For, in fact, the true and that which resembles it come under the purview of the same faculty, and at the same time men have a sufficient natural capacity for the truth and indeed in most cases attain to it ; wherefore one who divines well in regard to the truth will also be able to divine well in regard to probabilities.[a]

It is clear, then, that all other rhetoricians bring under the rules of art what is outside the subject, and [b] have rather inclined to the forensic branch of oratory. Nevertheless, Rhetoric is useful, because the true and the just are naturally superior to their opposites, so that, if decisions are improperly made, they must owe their defeat to their own advocates ; which is reprehensible. Further, in dealing with certain persons, even if we possessed the most accurate scientific knowledge, we should not find it easy to persuade them by the employment of such knowledge. For scientific discourse is concerned with instruction,[c] but in the case of such persons instruction is impossible ; our proofs and arguments must rest on generally accepted principles, as we said in the *Topics*,[d] when speaking of converse with the multitude. Further, the orator should be able to prove opposites, as in logical arguments ; not that we should do both (for one ought not to persuade people to do what is wrong), but that the real state

[d] i. 2. The *Topics* is a treatise in eight books on Dialectic and drawing conclusions from probabilities.

πείθειν) ἀλλ᾽ ἵνα μήτε λανθάνῃ πῶς ἔχει, καὶ ὅπως ἄλλου χρωμένου τοῖς λόγοις μὴ δικαίως αὐτοὶ λύειν ἔχωμεν. τῶν μὲν οὖν ἄλλων τεχνῶν οὐδεμία τὰναντία συλλογίζεται, ἡ δὲ διαλεκτικὴ καὶ ἡ ῥητορικὴ μόναι τοῦτο ποιοῦσιν· ὁμοίως γάρ εἰσιν ἀμφότεραι τῶν ἐναντίων. τὰ μέντοι ὑποκείμενα πράγματα οὐχ ὁμοίως ἔχει, ἀλλ᾽ ἀεὶ τἀληθῆ καὶ τὰ βελτίω τῇ φύσει εὐσυλλογιστότερα καὶ πιθανώτερα ὡς ἁπλῶς εἰπεῖν. πρὸς δὲ τούτοις ἄτοπον, εἰ τῷ σώματι μὲν αἰσχρὸν μὴ δύνασθαι βοηθεῖν ἑαυτῷ, λόγῳ δ᾽ οὐκ αἰσχρόν· ὃ μᾶλλον ἴδιόν ἐστιν ἀνθρώπου τῆς τοῦ σώματος χρείας. εἰ δ᾽ ὅτι μεγάλα βλάψειεν ἂν ὁ χρώμενος ἀδίκως τῇ τοιαύτῃ δυνάμει τῶν λόγων, τοῦτό γε κοινόν ἐστι κατὰ πάντων τῶν ἀγαθῶν πλὴν ἀρετῆς, καὶ μάλιστα κατὰ τῶν χρησιμωτάτων, οἷον ἰσχύος ὑγιείας πλούτου στρατηγίας· τούτοις γὰρ ἄν τις ὠφελήσειε τὰ μέγιστα χρώμενος δικαίως καὶ βλάψειεν ἀδίκως.

14 Ὅτι μὲν οὖν οὐκ ἔστιν οὔτε ἑνός τινος γένους ἀφωρισμένου ἡ ῥητορική, ἀλλὰ καθάπερ ἡ διαλεκτική, καὶ ὅτι χρήσιμος, φανερόν, καὶ ὅτι οὐ τὸ πεῖσαι ἔργον αὐτῆς, ἀλλὰ τὸ ἰδεῖν τὰ ὑπάρχοντα πιθανὰ περὶ ἕκαστον, καθάπερ καὶ ἐν ταῖς ἄλλαις τέχναις πάσαις· οὐδὲ γὰρ ἰατρικῆς τὸ ὑγιᾶ ποιῆσαι, ἀλλὰ μέχρι οὗ ἐνδέχεται, μέχρι τούτου προαγαγεῖν· ἔστι γὰρ καὶ τοὺς ἀδυνάτους μεταλαβεῖν ὑγιείας ὅμως θεραπεῦσαι καλῶς. πρὸς δὲ τούτοις ὅτι τῆς αὐτῆς τό τε πιθανὸν καὶ τὸ φαινόμενον ἰδεῖν πιθανόν, ὥσπερ καὶ ἐπὶ τῆς διαλεκτικῆς συλλογισμόν τε καὶ φαινόμενον συλλογισμόν. ὁ γὰρ σοφιστικὸς οὐκ

---

[a] The early sophistic definition was " the art of persuasion."

of the case may not escape us, and that we ourselves may be able to counteract false arguments, if another makes an unfair use of them. Rhetoric and Dialectic alone of all the arts prove opposites; for both are equally concerned with them. However, it is not the same with the subject matter, but, generally speaking, that which is true and better is naturally always easier to prove and more likely to persuade. Besides, it would be absurd if it were considered disgraceful not to be able to defend oneself with the help of the body, but not disgraceful as far as speech is concerned, whose use is more characteristic of man than that of the body. If it is argued that one who makes an unfair use of such faculty of speech may do a great deal of harm, this objection applies equally to all good things except virtue, and above all to those things which are most useful, such as strength, health, wealth, generalship; for as these, rightly used, may be of the greatest benefit, so, wrongly used, they may do an equal amount of harm.

It is thus evident that Rhetoric does not deal with any one definite class of subjects, but, like Dialectic, [is of general application]; also, that it is useful; and further, that its function is not so much to persuade, as to find out in each case the existing means of persuasion.[a] The same holds good in respect to all the other arts. For instance, it is not the function of medicine to restore a patient to health, but only to promote this end as far as possible; for even those whose recovery is impossible may be properly treated. It is further evident that it belongs to Rhetoric to discover the real and apparent means of persuasion, just as it belongs to Dialectic to discover the real and apparent syllogism. For what

ARISTOTLE

ἐν τῇ δυνάμει ἀλλ' ἐν τῇ προαιρέσει· πλὴν ἐνταῦθα μὲν ἔσται ὁ μὲν κατὰ τὴν ἐπιστήμην ὁ δὲ κατὰ τὴν προαίρεσιν ῥήτωρ, ἐκεῖ δὲ σοφιστὴς μὲν κατὰ τὴν προαίρεσιν, διαλεκτικὸς δὲ οὐ κατὰ τὴν προαίρεσιν ἀλλὰ κατὰ τὴν δύναμιν.

Περὶ δὲ αὐτῆς ἤδη τῆς μεθόδου πειρώμεθα λέγειν, πῶς τε καὶ ἐκ τίνων δυνησόμεθα τυγχάνειν τῶν προκειμένων. πάλιν οὖν οἷον ἐξ ὑπαρχῆς ὁρισάμενοι αὐτὴν τίς ἐστι, λέγωμεν τὰ λοιπά.

2. Ἔστω δὴ ῥητορικὴ δύναμις περὶ ἕκαστον τοῦ θεωρῆσαι τὸ ἐνδεχόμενον πιθανόν. τοῦτο γὰρ οὐδεμιᾶς ἑτέρας ἐστὶ τέχνης ἔργον· τῶν γὰρ ἄλλων ἑκάστη περὶ τὸ αὐτῇ ὑποκείμενόν ἐστι διδασκαλικὴ καὶ πειστική, οἷον ἰατρικὴ περὶ ὑγιεινὸν καὶ νοσερὸν καὶ γεωμετρία περὶ τὰ συμβεβηκότα πάθη τοῖς μεγέθεσι καὶ ἀριθμητικὴ περὶ ἀριθμόν, ὁμοίως δὲ καὶ αἱ λοιπαὶ τῶν τεχνῶν καὶ ἐπιστημῶν· ἡ δὲ ῥητορικὴ περὶ τοῦ δοθέντος ὡς εἰπεῖν δοκεῖ δύνασθαι θεωρεῖν τὸ πιθανόν. διὸ καί φαμεν αὐτὴν οὐ περί τι γένος ἴδιον ἀφωρισμένον ἔχειν τὸ τεχνικόν.

2 Τῶν δὲ πίστεων αἱ μὲν ἄτεχνοί εἰσιν αἱ δ' ἔντεχνοι. ἄτεχνα δὲ λέγω ὅσα μὴ δι' ἡμῶν πεπόρισται ἀλλὰ προϋπῆρχεν, οἷον μάρτυρες βάσανοι συγγραφαὶ καὶ ὅσα τοιαῦτα, ἔντεχνα δὲ ὅσα διὰ τῆς μεθόδου καὶ δι' ἡμῶν κατασκευασθῆναι δυνατόν. ὥστε δεῖ τούτων τοῖς μὲν χρήσασθαι τὰ δὲ εὑρεῖν.

---

[a] The essence of sophistry consists in the moral purpose, the deliberate use of fallacious arguments. In Dialectic, the dialectician has the power or faculty of making use of them when he pleases ; when he does so deliberately, he is called a sophist. In Rhetoric, this distinction does not exist ; he who uses sound arguments as well as he who uses false ones, are both known as rhetoricians.

makes the sophist is not the faculty but the moral purpose. But there is a difference : in Rhetoric, one who acts in accordance with sound argument, and one who acts in accordance with moral purpose, are both called rhetoricians ; but in Dialectic it is the moral purpose that makes the sophist, the dialectician being one whose arguments rest, not on moral purpose but on the faculty.[a]

Let us now endeavour to treat of the method itself, to see how and by what means we shall be able to attain our objects. And so let us as it were start again, and having defined Rhetoric anew, pass on to the remainder of the subject.

2. Rhetoric then may be defined as the faculty of discovering the possible means of persuasion in reference to any subject whatever. This is the function of no other of the arts, each of which is able to instruct and persuade in its own special subject ; thus, medicine deals with health and sickness, geometry with the properties of magnitudes, arithmetic with number, and similarly with all the other arts and sciences. But Rhetoric, so to say, appears to be able to discover the means of persuasion in reference to any given subject. That is why we say that as an art its rules are not applied to any particular definite class of things.

As for proofs, some are inartificial, others artificial. By the former I understand all those which have not been furnished by ourselves but were already in existence, such as witnesses, tortures, contracts, and the like ; by the latter, all that can be constructed by system and by our own efforts. Thus we have only to make use of the former, whereas we must invent the latter.

ARISTOTLE

3 Τῶν δὲ διὰ τοῦ λόγου ποριζομένων πίστεων τρία
1856 a εἴδη ἐστίν· αἱ μὲν γάρ εἰσιν ἐν τῷ ἤθει τοῦ λέγοντος,
αἱ δὲ ἐν τῷ τὸν ἀκροατὴν διαθεῖναί πως, αἱ δὲ ἐν
αὐτῷ τῷ λόγῳ, διὰ τοῦ δεικνύναι ἢ φαίνεσθαι
δεικνύναι.

4 Διὰ μὲν οὖν τοῦ ἤθους, ὅταν οὕτω λεχθῇ ὁ λόγος
ὥστε ἀξιόπιστον ποιῆσαι τὸν λέγοντα· τοῖς γὰρ
ἐπιεικέσι πιστεύομεν μᾶλλον καὶ θᾶττον, περὶ
πάντων μὲν ἁπλῶς, ἐν οἷς δὲ τὸ ἀκριβὲς μή ἐστιν
ἀλλὰ τὸ ἀμφιδοξεῖν, καὶ παντελῶς. δεῖ δὲ καὶ
τοῦτο συμβαίνειν διὰ τὸν λόγον, ἀλλὰ μὴ διὰ τὸ
προδεδοξάσθαι ποιόν τινα εἶναι τὸν λέγοντα· οὐ
γὰρ ὥσπερ ἔνιοι τῶν τεχνολογούντων τιθέασιν ἐν
τῇ τέχνῃ καὶ τὴν ἐπιείκειαν τοῦ λέγοντος ὡς οὐδὲν
συμβαλλομένην πρὸς τὸ πιθανόν, ἀλλὰ σχεδὸν ὡς
5 εἰπεῖν κυριωτάτην ἔχει πίστιν τὸ ἦθος. διὰ δὲ
τῶν ἀκροατῶν, ὅταν εἰς πάθος ὑπὸ τοῦ λόγου προ-
αχθῶσιν· οὐ γὰρ ὁμοίως ἀποδίδομεν τὰς κρίσεις λυ-
πούμενοι καὶ χαίροντες ἢ φιλοῦντες καὶ μισοῦντες·
πρὸς ὃ καὶ μόνον πειρᾶσθαί φαμεν πραγματεύεσθαι
τοὺς νῦν τεχνολογοῦντας. (περὶ μὲν οὖν τούτων
δηλωθήσεται καθ᾽ ἕκαστον, ὅταν περὶ τῶν παθῶν
6 λέγωμεν·) διὰ δὲ τῶν λόγων πιστεύουσιν, ὅταν
ἀληθὲς ἢ φαινόμενον δείξωμεν ἐκ τῶν περὶ ἕκαστα
πιθανῶν.

7 Ἐπεὶ δ᾽ αἱ πίστεις διὰ τούτων εἰσί, φανερὸν ὅτι
ταύτας ἐστὶ λαβεῖν τοῦ συλλογίσασθαι δυναμένου
καὶ τοῦ θεωρῆσαι περὶ τὰ ἤθη καὶ τὰς ἀρετὰς καὶ

16

Now the proofs furnished by the speech are of three kinds. The first depends upon the moral character of the speaker, the second upon putting the hearer into a certain frame of mind, the third upon the speech itself, in so far as it proves or seems to prove.

The orator persuades by moral character when his speech is delivered in such a manner as to render him worthy of confidence ; for we feel confidence in a greater degree and more readily in persons of worth in regard to everything in general, but where there is no certainty and there is room for doubt, our confidence is absolute. But this confidence must be due to the speech itself, not to any preconceived idea of the speaker's character ; for it is not the case, as some writers of rhetorical treatises lay down in their " Art," that the worth of the orator in no way contributes to his powers of persuasion ; on the contrary, moral character, so to say, constitutes the most effective means of proof. The orator persuades by means of his hearers, when they are roused to emotion by his speech ; for the judgements we deliver are not the same when we are influenced by joy or sorrow, love or hate ; and it is to this alone that, as we have said, the present-day writers of treatises endeavour to devote their attention. (We will discuss these matters in detail when we come to speak of the emotions.) Lastly, persuasion is produced by the speech itself, when we establish the true or apparently true from the means of persuasion applicable to each individual subject.

Now, since proofs are effected by these means, it is evident that, to be able to grasp them, a man must be capable of logical reasoning, of studying characters and the virtues, and thirdly the emotions

τρίτον τοῦ περὶ τὰ πάθη, τί τε ἕκαστόν ἐστι τῶν
παθῶν καὶ ποῖόν τι, καὶ ἐκ τίνων ἐγγίνεται καὶ πῶς.
ὥστε συμβαίνει τὴν ῥητορικὴν οἷον παραφυές τι
τῆς διαλεκτικῆς εἶναι καὶ τῆς περὶ τὰ ἤθη πραγματείας, ἣν δίκαιόν ἐστι προσαγορεύειν πολιτικήν.
διὸ καὶ ὑποδύεται ὑπὸ τὸ σχῆμα τὸ τῆς πολιτικῆς ἡ
ῥητορικὴ καὶ οἱ ἀντιποιούμενοι ταύτης τὰ μὲν δι᾽
ἀπαιδευσίαν τὰ δὲ δι᾽ ἀλαζονείαν τὰ δὲ καὶ δι᾽ ἄλλας
αἰτίας ἀνθρωπικάς· ἔστι γὰρ μόριόν τι τῆς διαλεκτικῆς καὶ ὁμοίωμα, καθάπερ καὶ ἀρχόμενοι εἴπομεν·
περὶ οὐδενὸς γὰρ ὡρισμένου οὐδετέρα αὐτῶν ἐστιν
ἐπιστήμη, πῶς ἔχει, ἀλλὰ δυνάμεις τινὲς τοῦ
πορίσαι λόγους. περὶ μὲν οὖν τῆς δυνάμεως αὐτῶν,
καὶ πῶς ἔχουσι πρὸς ἀλλήλας, εἴρηται σχεδὸν
ἱκανῶς.

8   Τῶν δὲ διὰ τοῦ δεικνύναι ἢ φαίνεσθαι δεικνύναι,
καθάπερ καὶ ἐν τοῖς διαλεκτικοῖς τὸ μὲν ἐπαγωγή
1356 b ἐστι τὸ δὲ συλλογισμὸς τὸ δὲ φαινόμενος συλλογισμός, καὶ ἐνταῦθα ὁμοίως ἔχει· ἔστι γὰρ τὸ μὲν
παράδειγμα ἐπαγωγή, τὸ δ᾽ ἐνθύμημα συλλογισμός,
[τὸ δὲ φαινόμενον ἐνθύμημα φαινόμενος συλλογι-
σμός].[1]   καλῶ δ᾽ ἐνθύμημα μὲν ῥητορικὸν συλλογισμόν, παράδειγμα δὲ ἐπαγωγὴν ῥητορικήν.
πάντες δὲ τὰς πίστεις ποιοῦνται διὰ τοῦ δεικνύναι
ἢ παραδείγματα λέγοντες ἢ ἐνθυμήματα, καὶ παρὰ
ταῦτα οὐδέν πως· ὥστ᾽ εἴπερ καὶ ὅλως ἀνάγκη ἢ

____

[1] Inserted by Spengel from Dionysius of Halicarnassus
(first letter to Ammaeus, vi.).

____

[a] Rhetoric, as dealing with human actions, characters,
virtues, and emotions, is closely connected with Politics,
which includes Ethics.   The two latter treat of the same
subject from a different point of view.   Both deal with
happiness and virtue, but the object of Politics is, by com-

—the nature and character of each, its origin, and the manner in which it is produced. Thus it appears that Rhetoric is as it were an offshoot of Dialectic and of the science of Ethics, which may be reasonably called Politics.[a] That is why Rhetoric assumes[b] the character of Politics, and those who claim to possess it, partly from ignorance, partly from boastfulness, and partly from other human weaknesses, do the same. For, as we said at the outset, Rhetoric is a sort of division or likeness of Dialectic, since neither of them is a science that deals with the nature of any definite subject, but they are merely faculties of furnishing arguments. We have now said nearly enough about the faculties of these arts and their mutual relations.

But for purposes of demonstration, real or apparent, just as Dialectic possesses two modes of argument, induction and the syllogism, real or apparent, the same is the case in Rhetoric; for the example is induction, and the enthymeme a syllogism, and the apparent enthymeme an apparent syllogism. Accordingly I call an enthymeme a rhetorical syllogism, and an example rhetorical induction. Now all orators produce belief by employing as proofs either examples or enthymemes and nothing else; so that if, generally speaking, it is necessary to prove any

parison of the different forms of States to find the one in which man will be most virtuous. Lastly, Rhetoric, as an important factor in the training and education of the individual citizen and of the members of the State as a whole, may be described as an offshoot of Politics, with which the sophistical rhetoricians *identified* it. For the relation of Rhetoric to Dialectic see Glossary.

[b] Or, "slips into the garb of" (Jebb). Probably a stage metaphor.

ARISTOTLE

συλλογιζόμενον ἢ ἐπάγοντα δεικνύναι ὁτιοῦν (δῆλον
δ' ἡμῖν τοῦτο ἐκ τῶν ἀναλυτικῶν), ἀναγκαῖον
ἑκάτερον αὐτῶν ἑκατέρῳ τούτων τὸ αὐτὸ εἶναι.
9 τίς δ' ἐστὶ διαφορὰ παραδείγματος καὶ ἐνθυμήματος, φανερὸν ἐκ τῶν τοπικῶν· ἐκεῖ γὰρ περὶ
συλλογισμοῦ καὶ ἐπαγωγῆς εἴρηται πρότερον, ὅτι
τὸ μὲν τὸ ἐπὶ πολλῶν καὶ ὁμοίων δείκνυσθαι ὅτι
οὕτως ἔχει ἐκεῖ μὲν ἐπαγωγή ἐστιν ἐνταῦθα δὲ
παράδειγμα, τὸ δὲ τινῶν ὄντων ἕτερόν τι διὰ ταῦτα
συμβαίνειν παρὰ ταῦτα τῷ ταῦτα εἶναι, ἢ καθόλου ἢ
ὡς ἐπὶ τὸ πολύ, ἐκεῖ μὲν συλλογισμὸς ἐνταῦθα δὲ
ἐνθύμημα καλεῖται.

10   Φανερὸν δ' ὅτι καὶ ἑκάτερον ἔχει ἀγαθὸν τὸ εἶδος
τῆς ῥητορικῆς· καθάπερ γὰρ καὶ ἐν τοῖς μεθοδικοῖς
εἴρηται, καὶ ἐν τούτοις ὁμοίως ἔχει· εἰσὶ γὰρ αἱ μὲν
παραδειγματώδεις ῥητορεῖαι αἱ δὲ ἐνθυμηματικαί,
καὶ ῥήτορες ὁμοίως οἱ μὲν παραδειγματώδεις οἱ δὲ
ἐνθυμηματικοί. πιθανοὶ μὲν οὖν οὐχ ἧττον οἱ
λόγοι οἱ διὰ τῶν παραδειγμάτων, θορυβοῦνται δὲ
11 μᾶλλον οἱ ἐνθυμηματικοί. τὴν δ' αἰτίαν αὐτῶν, καὶ
πῶς ἑκατέρῳ χρηστέον, ἐροῦμεν ὕστερον· νῦν δὲ
περὶ αὐτῶν τούτων μᾶλλον διορίσωμεν καθαρῶς.

    Ἐπεὶ γὰρ τὸ πιθανὸν τινὶ πιθανόν ἐστι, καὶ τὸ

---

[a] *Anal. Priora*, ii. 23 ; *Anal. Posteriora*, i. 1.
[b] That is, enthymeme and example must be the same as
syllogism and induction.
[c] From the definitions of syllogism (i. 1) and induction
(i. 12).   No particular passage, however, explains the
difference here mentioned.
[d] The employment of syllogism and induction, τὸ εἶδος
τῆς ῥητορικῆς being taken as simply = ἡ ῥητορική.   Another
rendering is : " that each kind of Rhetoric (that which de-

fact whatever either by syllogism or by induction—
and that this is so is clear from the *Analytics* [a]—each
of the two former must be identical with each of the
two latter.[b] The difference between example and
enthymeme is evident from the *Topics*,[c] where, in
discussing syllogism and induction, it has previously
been said that the proof from a number of particular
cases that such is the rule, is called in Dialectic
induction, in Rhetoric example ; but when, certain
things being posited, something different results by
reason of them, alongside of them, from their being
true, either universally or in most cases, such a
conclusion in Dialectic is called a syllogism, in
Rhetoric an enthymeme.

It is evident that Rhetoric enjoys both these advantages [d]—for what has been said in the *Methodica* [e]
holds good also in this case—for rhetorical speeches
are sometimes characterized by examples and sometimes by enthymemes, and orators themselves may
be similarly distinguished by their fondness for one
or the other. Now arguments that depend on examples are not less calculated to persuade, but those
which depend upon enthymemes meet with greater
approval. Their origin and the way in which each
should be used will be discussed later [f] ; for the
moment let us define more clearly these proofs
themselves.

Now, that which is persuasive is persuasive in

pends upon example or upon enthymeme) enjoys some
special advantage."

[e] A lost treatise, mentioned by Diogenes Laërtius in his
Life of Aristotle, xxiv., and by Dionysius of Halicarnassus
in the first letter to Ammaeus, vi. It is supposed to have
dealt with some branch of Logic.

[f] ii. 20-24.

μὲν εὐθὺς ὑπάρχει δι' αὑτὸ πιθανὸν καὶ πιστὸν τὸ
δὲ τῷ δείκνυσθαι δοκεῖν διὰ τοιούτων, οὐδεμία δὲ
τέχνη σκοπεῖ τὸ καθ' ἕκαστον, οἷον ἡ ἰατρικὴ τί
Σωκράτει τὸ ὑγιεινόν ἐστιν ἢ Καλλίᾳ, ἀλλὰ τί τῷ
τοιῷδε ἢ τοῖς τοιοῖσδε (τοῦτο μὲν γὰρ ἔντεχνον, τὸ
δὲ καθ' ἕκαστον ἄπειρον καὶ οὐκ ἐπιστητόν), οὐδὲ
ἡ ῥητορικὴ τὸ καθ' ἕκαστον ἔνδοξον θεωρήσει,
οἷον Σωκράτει ἢ Ἱππίᾳ, ἀλλὰ τὸ τοιοῖσδε, καθάπερ καὶ ἡ διαλεκτική. καὶ γὰρ ἐκείνη συλλογίζεται οὐκ ἐξ ὧν ἔτυχεν (φαίνεται γὰρ ἄττα καὶ τοῖς
1357 a παραληροῦσιν), ἀλλ' ἐκείνη μὲν ἐκ τῶν λόγου
δεομένων, ἡ δὲ ῥητορικὴ ἐκ τῶν ἤδη βουλεύεσθαι
εἰωθότων.

12 Ἔστι δὲ τὸ ἔργον αὐτῆς περί τε τοιούτων περὶ
ὧν βουλευόμεθα καὶ τέχνας μὴ ἔχομεν, καὶ ἐν τοῖς
τοιούτοις ἀκροαταῖς οἳ οὐ δύνανται διὰ πολλῶν
συνορᾶν οὐδὲ λογίζεσθαι πόρρωθεν. βουλευόμεθα
δὲ περὶ τῶν φαινομένων ἐνδέχεσθαι ἀμφοτέρως
ἔχειν· περὶ γὰρ τῶν ἀδυνάτων ἄλλως ἢ γενέσθαι ἢ
ἔσεσθαι ἢ ἔχειν οὐδεὶς βουλεύεται οὕτως ὑπολαμ-
13 βάνων· οὐδὲν γὰρ πλέον. ἐνδέχεται δὲ συλλογίζεσθαι καὶ συνάγειν τὰ μὲν ἐκ συλλελογισμένων
πρότερον, τὰ δ' ἐξ ἀσυλλογίστων μὲν δεομένων δὲ
συλλογισμοῦ διὰ τὸ μὴ εἶναι ἔνδοξα. ἀνάγκη δὲ
τούτων τὸ μὲν μὴ εἶναι εὐεπακολούθητον διὰ τὸ

---

* Or, " by persons who are so " (Jebb).
b Certain propositions, which seem paradoxical and improbable to a popular audience, must be proved before it is
able to understand them.

reference to some one, and is persuasive and convincing either at once and in and by itself, or because it appears to be proved by propositions that are convincing [a] ; further, no art has the particular in view, medicine for instance what is good for Socrates or Callias, but what is good for this or that class of persons (for this is a matter that comes within the province of an art, whereas the particular is infinite and cannot be the subject of a true science) ; similarly, therefore, Rhetoric will not consider what seems probable in each individual case, for instance to Socrates or Hippias, but that which seems probable to this or that class of persons. It is the same with Dialectic, which does not draw conclusions from any random premises—for even madmen have some fancies—but it takes its material from subjects which demand reasoned discussion, as Rhetoric does from those which are common subjects of deliberation.

The function of Rhetoric, then, is to deal with things about which we deliberate, but for which we have no systematic rules ; and in the presence of such hearers as are unable to take a general view of many stages, or to follow a lengthy chain of argument. But we only deliberate about things which seem to admit of issuing in two ways ; as for those things which cannot in the past, present, or future be otherwise, no one deliberates about them, if he supposes that they are such ; for nothing would be gained by it. Now, it is possible to draw conclusions and inferences partly from what has been previously demonstrated syllogistically, partly from what has not, which however needs demonstration, because it is not probable.[b] The first of these methods is necessarily difficult to follow owing to its length, for

μῆκος (ὁ γὰρ κριτὴς ὑπόκειται εἶναι ἁπλοῦς), τὰ
δὲ μὴ πιθανὰ διὰ τὸ μὴ ἐξ ὁμολογουμένων εἶναι
μηδ' ἐνδόξων· ὥστ' ἀναγκαῖον τό τε ἐνθύμημα
εἶναι καὶ τὸ παράδειγμα περὶ τῶν ἐνδεχομένων ὡς
τὰ πολλὰ ἔχειν καὶ ἄλλως, τὸ μὲν παράδειγμα
ἐπαγωγὴν τὸ δ' ἐνθύμημα συλλογισμόν, καὶ ἐξ
ὀλίγων τε καὶ πολλάκις ἐλαττόνων ἢ ἐξ ὧν ὁ
πρῶτος συλλογισμός· ἐὰν γὰρ ᾖ τι τούτων γνώρι-
μον, οὐδὲ δεῖ λέγειν· αὐτὸς γὰρ τοῦτο προστίθησιν
ὁ ἀκροατής. οἷον ὅτι Δωριεὺς στεφανίτην ἀγῶνα
νενίκηκεν, ἱκανὸν εἰπεῖν ὅτι Ὀλύμπια νενίκηκεν·
τὸ δ' ὅτι στεφανίτης τὰ Ὀλύμπια, οὐδὲ δεῖ προσ-
θεῖναι· γιγνώσκουσι γὰρ πάντες.

14   Ἐπεὶ δ' ἐστὶν ὀλίγα μὲν τῶν ἀναγκαίων ἐξ ὧν οἱ
ῥητορικοὶ συλλογισμοί εἰσι (τὰ γὰρ πολλὰ περὶ ὧν
αἱ κρίσεις καὶ αἱ σκέψεις, ἐνδέχεται καὶ ἄλλως
ἔχειν· περὶ ὧν μὲν γὰρ πράττουσι, βουλεύονται
καὶ σκοποῦσι, τὰ δὲ πραττόμενα πάντα τοιούτου
γένους ἐστί, καὶ οὐδὲν ὡς ἔπος εἰπεῖν ἐξ ἀνάγκης
τούτων), τὰ δ' ὡς ἐπὶ τὸ πολὺ συμβαίνοντα καὶ
ἐνδεχόμενα ἐκ τοιούτων ἀνάγκη ἑτέρων συλλογίζεσθαι, τὰ δ' ἀναγκαῖα ἐξ ἀναγκαίων (δῆλον δ'
ἡμῖν καὶ τοῦτο ἐκ τῶν ἀναλυτικῶν), φανερὸν ὅτι
ἐξ ὧν τὰ ἐνθυμήματα λέγεται, τὰ μὲν ἀναγκαῖα
ἔσται, τὰ δὲ πλεῖστα ὡς ἐπὶ τὸ πολύ. λέγεται
γὰρ ἐνθυμήματα ἐξ εἰκότων καὶ σημείων, ὥστε

---

[a] πρῶτος : the primary, typical syllogism of the first figure.

[b] Son of Diagoras of Rhodes, and like his father celebrated
for his victories in the Greek athletic contests. He played
a considerable part in political and naval affairs in support
of the Spartans (412-407 B.C.), whom he afterwards offended,
and by whom he is said to have been put to death.

[c] *Anal. Priora*, i. 8, 13-14.

the judge is supposed to be a simple person; the second will obtain little credence, because it does not depend upon what is either admitted or probable. The necessary result then is that the enthymeme and the example are concerned with things which may, generally speaking, be other than they are, the example being a kind of induction and the enthymeme a kind of syllogism, and deduced from few premises, often from fewer than the regular [a] syllogism; for if any one of these is well known, there is no need to mention it, for the hearer can add it himself. For instance, to prove that Dorieus [b] was the victor in a contest at which the prize was a crown, it is enough to say that he won a victory at the Olympic games; there is no need to add that the prize at the Olympic games is a crown, for everybody knows it.

But since few of the propositions of the rhetorical syllogism are necessary, for most of the things which we judge and examine can be other than they are, human actions, which are the subject of our deliberation and examination, being all of such a character and, generally speaking, none of them necessary; since, further, facts which only generally happen or are merely possible can only be demonstrated by other facts of the same kind, and necessary facts by necessary propositions (and that this is so is clear from the *Analytics* [c]), it is evident that the materials from which enthymemes are derived will be sometimes necessary, but for the most part only generally true; and these materials being probabilities and signs, it follows that these two elements must corre-

ἀνάγκη τούτων ἑκάτερον ἑκατέρῳ ταὐτὸ εἶναι.
15 τὸ μὲν γὰρ εἰκός ἐστιν ὡς ἐπὶ τὸ πολὺ γινόμενον,
οὐχ ἁπλῶς δέ, καθάπερ ὁρίζονταί τινες, ἀλλὰ τὸ
περὶ τὰ ἐνδεχόμενα ἄλλως ἔχειν, οὕτως ἔχον πρὸς
1357 b ἐκεῖνο πρὸς ὃ εἰκός, ὡς τὸ καθόλου πρὸς τὸ κατὰ
16 μέρος· τῶν δὲ σημείων τὸ μὲν οὕτως ἔχει ὡς τῶν
καθ᾽ ἕκαστόν τι πρὸς τὸ καθόλου, τὸ δὲ ὡς τῶν
καθόλου τι πρὸς τὸ κατὰ μέρος. τούτων δὲ τὸ
μὲν ἀναγκαῖον τεκμήριον, τὸ δὲ μὴ ἀναγκαῖον
17 ἀνώνυμόν ἐστι κατὰ τὴν διαφοράν. ἀναγκαῖα μὲν
οὖν λέγω ἐξ ὧν γίνεται συλλογισμός, διὸ καὶ
τεκμήριον τὸ τοιοῦτον τῶν σημείων ἐστίν· ὅταν
γὰρ μὴ ἐνδέχεσθαι οἴωνται λῦσαι τὸ λεχθέν, τότε
φέρειν οἴονται τεκμήριον ὡς δεδειγμένον καὶ πεπε-
ρασμένον· τὸ γὰρ τέκμαρ καὶ πέρας ταὐτόν ἐστι
κατὰ τὴν ἀρχαίαν γλῶτταν.
18 Ἔστι δὲ τῶν σημείων τὸ μὲν ὡς τὸ καθ᾽ ἕκαστον πρὸς τὸ καθόλου ὧδε, οἷον εἴ τις εἴπειεν
σημεῖον εἶναι ὅτι οἱ σοφοὶ δίκαιοι, Σωκράτης γὰρ
σοφὸς ἦν καὶ δίκαιος. τοῦτο μὲν οὖν σημεῖόν
ἐστι, λυτὸν δέ, κἂν ἀληθὲς ᾖ τὸ εἰρημένον· ἀσυλλόγιστον γάρ. τὸ δέ, οἷον εἴ τις εἴπειεν σημεῖον
ὅτι νοσεῖ, πυρέττει γάρ, ἢ τέτοκεν ὅτι γάλα ἔχει,
ἀναγκαῖον. ὅπερ τῶν σημείων τεκμήριον μόνον
ἐστίν· μόνον γάρ, ἂν ἀληθὲς ᾖ, ἄλυτόν ἐστιν. τὸ
δὲ ὡς τὸ καθόλου πρὸς τὸ κατὰ μέρος ἔχον, οἷον
εἴ τις εἴπειεν, ὅτι πυρέττει, σημεῖον εἶναι, πυκνὸν
γὰρ ἀναπνεῖ. λυτὸν δὲ καὶ τοῦτο, κἂν ἀληθὲς ᾖ·

---

[a] That is, probabilities and signs correspond to general
and necessary propositions. This is not strictly correct;
only the τεκμήρια correspond to the necessary propositions,
the other signs and the probabilities to the general or contingent propositions.

26

spond to these two kinds of propositions, each to each.[a] For that which is probable is that which generally happens, not however unreservedly, as some define it, but that which is concerned with things that may be other than they are, being so related to that in regard to which it is probable as the universal to the particular. As to signs, some are related as the particular to the universal, others as the universal to the particular. Necessary signs are called *tekmēria*; those which are not necessary have no distinguishing name. I call those necessary signs from which a logical syllogism can be constructed, wherefore such a sign is called *tekmērion*; for when people think that their arguments are irrefutable, they think that they are bringing forward a *tekmērion*, something as it were proved and concluded; for in the old language *tekmar* and *peras* have the same meaning (limit, conclusion).

Among signs, some are related as the particular to the universal; for instance, if one were to say that all wise men are just, because Socrates was both wise and just. Now this is a sign, but even though the particular statement is true, it can be refuted, because it cannot be reduced to syllogistic form. But if one were to say that it is a sign that a man is ill, because he has a fever, or that a woman has had a child because she has milk, this is a necessary sign. This alone among signs is a *tekmērion*; for only in this case, if the fact is true, is the argument irrefutable. Other signs are related as the universal to the particular, for instance, if one were to say that it is a sign that this man has a fever, because he breathes hard; but even if the fact be true, this argument also can be refuted, for it is possible for

ἐνδέχεται γὰρ καὶ μὴ πυρέττοντα πνευστιᾶν. τί
μὲν οὖν εἰκός ἐστι καὶ τί σημεῖον καὶ τεκμήριον,
καὶ τί διαφέρουσιν, εἴρηται μὲν καὶ νῦν· μᾶλλον δὲ
φανερῶς καὶ περὶ τούτων, καὶ διὰ τίν᾽ αἰτίαν τὰ
μὲν ἀσυλλόγιστά ἐστι τὰ δὲ συλλελογισμένα, ἐν
τοῖς ἀναλυτικοῖς διώρισται περὶ αὐτῶν.

19 Παράδειγμα δὲ ὅτι μέν ἐστιν ἐπαγωγὴ καὶ περὶ
ποῖα ἐπαγωγή, εἴρηται. ἔστι δὲ οὔτε ὡς μέρος
πρὸς ὅλον οὔθ᾽ ὡς ὅλον πρὸς μέρος οὔθ᾽ ὡς ὅλον
πρὸς ὅλον, ἀλλ᾽ ὡς μέρος πρὸς μέρος, ὅμοιον πρὸς
ὅμοιον, ὅταν ἄμφω μὲν ᾖ ὑπὸ τὸ αὐτὸ γένος, γνω-
ριμώτερον δὲ θάτερον ᾖ θατέρου, παράδειγμά
ἐστιν. οἷον ὅτι ἐπιβουλεύει τυραννίδι Διονύσιος
αἰτῶν τὴν φυλακήν· καὶ γὰρ Πεισίστρατος πρότερον
ἐπιβουλεύων ᾔτει φυλακὴν καὶ λαβὼν ἐτυράν-
νευσε, καὶ Θεαγένης ἐν Μεγάροις· καὶ ἄλλοι ὅσους
ἴσασι, παράδειγμα πάντες γίγνονται τοῦ Διονυσίου,
ὃν οὐκ ἴσασί πω εἰ διὰ τοῦτο αἰτεῖ. πάντα δὲ
ταῦτα ὑπὸ τὸ αὐτὸ καθόλου, ὅτι ὁ ἐπιβουλεύων
τυραννίδι φυλακὴν αἰτεῖ.

358 a ᾽Εξ ὧν μὲν οὖν λέγονται αἱ δοκοῦσαι εἶναι πίστεις
20 ἀποδεικτικαί, εἴρηται. τῶν δὲ ἐνθυμημάτων μεγί-
στη διαφορὰ καὶ μάλιστα λεληθυῖα σχεδὸν πάντας
ἐστὶν ἥπερ καὶ περὶ τὴν διαλεκτικὴν μέθοδον τῶν
συλλογισμῶν· τὰ μὲν γὰρ αὐτῶν ἐστι κατὰ τὴν
ῥητορικὴν ὥσπερ καὶ κατὰ τὴν διαλεκτικὴν μέθοδον
τῶν συλλογισμῶν, τὰ δὲ κατ᾽ ἄλλας τέχνας καὶ
δυνάμεις, τὰς μὲν οὔσας τὰς δ᾽ οὔπω κατ-
ειλημμένας· διὸ καὶ λανθάνουσί τε, καὶ μᾶλλον
ἁπτόμενοι κατὰ τρόπον μεταβαίνουσιν ἐξ αὐτῶν.

ᵃ Anal. Priora, ii. 27.

a man to breathe hard without having a fever. We have now explained the meaning of probable, sign, and necessary sign, and the difference between them; in the *Analytics* [a] we have defined them more clearly and stated why some of them can be converted into logical syllogisms, while others cannot.

We have said that example is a kind of induction and with what kind of material it deals by way of induction. It is neither the relation of part to whole, nor of whole to part, nor of one whole to another whole, but of part to part, of like to like, when both come under the same genus, but one of them is better known than the other. For example, to prove that Dionysius is aiming at a tyranny, because he asks for a bodyguard, one might say that Pisistratus before him and Theagenes of Megara did the same, and when they obtained what they asked for made themselves tyrants. All the other tyrants known may serve as an example of Dionysius, whose reason, however, for asking for a bodyguard we do not yet know. All these examples are contained under the same universal proposition, that one who is aiming at a tyranny asks for a bodyguard.

We have now stated the materials of proofs which are thought to be demonstrative. But a very great difference between enthymemes has escaped the notice of nearly every one, although it also exists in the dialectical method of syllogisms. For some of them belong to Rhetoric, some syllogisms only to Dialectic, and others to other arts and faculties, some already existing and others not yet established. Hence it is that this escapes the notice of the speakers, and the more they specialize in a subject, the more they transgress the limits of Rhetoric and

μᾶλλον δὲ σαφὲς ἔσται τὸ λεγόμενον διὰ πλειόνων
ῥηθέν.

21 Λέγω γὰρ διαλεκτικούς τε καὶ ῥητορικοὺς συλ-
λογισμοὺς εἶναι περὶ ὧν τοὺς τόπους λέγομεν·
οὗτοι δ' εἰσὶν οἱ κοινῇ περὶ δικαίων καὶ φυσικῶν
καὶ περὶ πολιτικῶν καὶ περὶ πολλῶν διαφερόντων
εἴδει, οἷον ὁ τοῦ μᾶλλον καὶ ἧττον τόπος· οὐδὲν
γὰρ μᾶλλον ἔσται ἐκ τούτου συλλογίσασθαι ἢ
ἐνθύμημα εἰπεῖν περὶ δικαίων ἢ φυσικῶν ἢ περὶ
ὁτουοῦν· καίτοι ταῦτα εἴδει διαφέρει. ἴδια δὲ
ὅσα ἐκ τῶν περὶ ἕκαστον εἶδος καὶ γένος προτά-
σεών ἐστιν, οἷον περὶ φυσικῶν εἰσὶ προτάσεις ἐξ
ὧν οὔτε ἐνθύμημα οὔτε συλλογισμός ἐστι περὶ τῶν
ἠθικῶν, καὶ περὶ τούτων ἄλλαι ἐξ ὧν οὐκ ἔσται
περὶ τῶν φυσικῶν· ὁμοίως δὲ τοῦτ' ἔχει ἐπὶ πάντων.
κἀκεῖνα μὲν οὐ ποιήσει περὶ οὐδὲν γένος ἔμφρονα·
περὶ οὐδὲν γὰρ ὑποκείμενόν ἐστιν· ταῦτα δέ, ὅσῳ
τις ἂν βέλτιον ἐκλέγηται τὰς προτάσεις, λήσει
ποιήσας ἄλλην ἐπιστήμην τῆς διαλεκτικῆς καὶ
ῥητορικῆς· ἂν γὰρ ἐντύχῃ ἀρχαῖς, οὐκέτι διαλεκτικὴ οὐδὲ ῥητορικὴ ἀλλ' ἐκείνη ἔσται ἧς ἔχει τὰς
22 ἀρχάς. ἔστι δὲ τὰ πλεῖστα τῶν ἐνθυμημάτων ἐκ
τούτων τῶν εἰδῶν λεγόμενα τῶν κατὰ μέρος καὶ
ἰδίων, ἐκ δὲ τῶν κοινῶν ἐλάττω. καθάπερ οὖν
καὶ ἐν τοῖς τοπικοῖς, καὶ ἐνταῦθα διαιρετέον τῶν
ἐνθυμημάτων τά τε εἴδη καὶ τοὺς τόπους ἐξ ὧν

---

a The common topics do not deal with particular subject
matter, as the specific topics do. In making use of the latter,
the "better" (that is, in regard to a special science) the
propositions chosen by a man, the more he will without
knowing it quit the domain of Rhetoric and Dialectic, and
become a professor of that special science whose first principles
he has hit upon.

Dialectic. But this will be clearer if stated at greater length.

I mean by dialectical and rhetorical syllogisms those which are concerned with what we call "topics," which may be applied alike to Law, Physics, Politics, and many other sciences that differ in kind, such as the topic of the more or less, which will furnish syllogisms and enthymemes equally well for Law, Physics, or any other science whatever, although these subjects differ in kind. Specific topics on the other hand are derived from propositions which are peculiar to each species or genus of things ; there are, for example, propositions about Physics which can furnish neither enthymemes nor syllogisms about Ethics, and there are propositions concerned with Ethics which will be useless for furnishing conclusions about Physics ; and the same holds good in all cases. The first kind of topics will not make a man practically wise about any particular class of things, because they do not deal with any particular subject matter ; but as to the specific topics, the happier a man is in his choice of propositions, the more he will unconsciously produce a science quite different from Dialectic and Rhetoric. .For if once he hits upon first principles, it will no longer be Dialectic or Rhetoric, but that science whose principles he has arrived at.[a] Most enthymemes are constructed from these specific topics, which are called particular and special, fewer from those that are common or universal. As then we have done in the *Topics*,[b] so here we must distinguish the specific and universal topics, from which enthymemes may be constructed.

[b] *Sophistici Elenchi* (*Fallacies*), 9. This treatise is really the ninth and concluding part of the *Topics*.

ληπτέον. λέγω δ' εἴδη μὲν τὰς καθ' ἕκαστον γένος
ἰδίας προτάσεις, τόπους δὲ τοὺς κοινοὺς ὁμοίως
πάντων. πρότερον οὖν εἴπωμεν περὶ τῶν εἰδῶν·
πρῶτον δὲ λάβωμεν τὰ γένη τῆς ῥητορικῆς, ὅπως
διελόμενοι πόσα ἐστί, περὶ τούτων χωρὶς λαμ-
βάνωμεν τὰ στοιχεῖα καὶ τὰς προτάσεις.

3. Ἔστι δὲ τῆς ῥητορικῆς εἴδη τρία τὸν ἀριθμόν·
τοσοῦτοι γὰρ καὶ οἱ ἀκροαταὶ τῶν λόγων ὑπάρχουσιν ὄντες. σύγκειται μὲν γὰρ ἐκ τριῶν ὁ
λόγος, ἔκ τε τοῦ λέγοντος καὶ περὶ οὗ λέγει καὶ
1358 b πρὸς ὅν, καὶ τὸ τέλος πρὸς τοῦτόν ἐστι, λέγω δὲ
2 τὸν ἀκροατήν. ἀνάγκη δὲ τὸν ἀκροατὴν ἢ θεωρὸν
εἶναι ἢ κριτήν, κριτὴν δὲ ἢ τῶν γεγενημένων ἢ τῶν
μελλόντων. ἔστι δ' ὁ μὲν περὶ τῶν μελλόντων
κρίνων οἷον ἐκκλησιαστής, ὁ δὲ περὶ τῶν γεγενημένων οἷον ὁ δικαστής, ὁ δὲ περὶ τῆς δυνάμεως ὁ
3 θεωρός· ὥστ' ἐξ ἀνάγκης ἂν εἴη τρία γένη τῶν
λόγων τῶν ῥητορικῶν, συμβουλευτικόν, δικανικόν,
ἐπιδεικτικόν.

Συμβουλῆς δὲ τὸ μὲν προτροπὴ τὸ δὲ ἀποτροπή·
ἀεὶ γὰρ καὶ οἱ ἰδίᾳ συμβουλεύοντες καὶ οἱ κοινῇ δη-
μηγοροῦντες τούτων θάτερον ποιοῦσιν. δίκης δὲ
τὸ μὲν κατηγορία τὸ δ' ἀπολογία· τούτων γὰρ
ὁποτερονοῦν ποιεῖν ἀνάγκη τοὺς ἀμφισβητοῦντας.
ἐπιδεικτικοῦ δὲ τὸ μὲν ἔπαινος τὸ δὲ ψόγος.

4 Χρόνοι δὲ ἑκάστου τούτων εἰσὶ τῷ μὲν συμβουλεύοντι ὁ μέλλων (περὶ γὰρ τῶν ἐσομένων συμβου-

---

[a] Propositions (or premises), the name given to the two first
statements in a syllogism from which the conclusion is drawn:
All men are mortal (major premise); Socrates is a man
(minor premise); therefore Socrates is mortal.
[b] All three kinds of hearers are regarded as judges (the

By specific topics I mean the propositions peculiar to each class of things, by universal those common to all alike. Let us then first speak of the specific topics, but before doing so let us ascertain the different kinds of Rhetoric, so that, having determined their number, we may separately ascertain their elements and propositions.[a]

3. The kinds of Rhetoric are three in number, corresponding to the three kinds of hearers. For every speech is composed of three parts : the speaker, the subject of which he treats, and the person to whom it is addressed, I mean the hearer, to whom the end or object of the speech refers. Now the hearer must necessarily be either a mere spectator or a judge, and a judge either of things past or of things to come.[b] For instance, a member of the general assembly is a judge of things to come ; the dicast, of things past ; the mere spectator, of the ability of the speaker. Therefore there are necessarily three kinds of rhetorical speeches, deliberative, forensic, and epideictic.

The deliberative kind is either hortatory or dissuasive ; for both those who give advice in private and those who speak in the assembly invariably either exhort or dissuade. The forensic kind is either accusatory or defensive ; for litigants must necessarily either accuse or defend. The epideictic kind has for its subject praise or blame.

Further, to each of these a special time is appropriate : to the deliberative the future,[c] for the

mere spectator as a " critic "), although strictly κριτής should be limited to the law courts.

[c] In i. 6. 1 and 8. 7 the present is also mentioned as a time appropriate to deliberative Rhetoric.

λεύει ἢ προτρέπων ἢ ἀποτρέπων), τῷ δὲ δικαζομένῳ ὁ γενόμενος (περὶ γὰρ τῶν πεπραγμένων
ἀεὶ ὁ μὲν κατηγορεῖ ὁ δὲ ἀπολογεῖται), τῷ δ᾽
ἐπιδεικτικῷ κυριώτατος μὲν ὁ παρών· κατὰ γὰρ
τὰ ὑπάρχοντα ἐπαινοῦσιν ἢ ψέγουσι πάντες, προσ-
χρῶνται δὲ πολλάκις καὶ τὰ γενόμενα ἀναμιμνῄσ-
κοντες καὶ τὰ μέλλοντα προεικάζοντες.

5 Τέλος δὲ ἑκάστοις τούτων ἕτερόν ἐστι, καὶ
τρισὶν οὖσι τρία, τῷ μὲν συμβουλεύοντι τὸ συμφέρον καὶ βλαβερόν· ὁ μὲν γὰρ προτρέπων ὡς
βέλτιον συμβουλεύει, ὁ δὲ ἀποτρέπων ὡς χεῖρον
ἀποτρέπει, τὰ δ᾽ ἄλλα πρὸς τοῦτο συμπαραλαμβάνει, ἢ δίκαιον ἢ ἄδικον, ἢ καλὸν ἢ αἰσχρόν· τοῖς
δὲ δικαζομένοις τὸ δίκαιον καὶ τὸ ἄδικον, τὰ δ᾽
ἄλλα καὶ οὗτοι συμπαραλαμβάνουσι πρὸς ταῦτα· τοῖς
δ᾽ ἐπαινοῦσι καὶ ψέγουσι τὸ καλὸν καὶ τὸ αἰσχρόν,
τὰ δ᾽ ἄλλα καὶ οὗτοι πρὸς ταῦτα ἐπαναφέρουσιν.
6 σημεῖον δ᾽ ὅτι τὸ εἰρημένον ἑκάστοις τέλος· περὶ
μὲν γὰρ τῶν ἄλλων ἐνίοτε οὐκ ἂν ἀμφισβητήσαιεν,
οἷον ὁ δικαζόμενος ὡς οὐ γέγονεν ἢ ὡς οὐκ ἔβλα-
ψεν· ὅτι δ᾽ ἀδικεῖ, οὐδέ ποτ᾽ ἂν ὁμολογήσειεν·
οὐδὲν γὰρ ἂν ἔδει δίκης. ὁμοίως δὲ καὶ οἱ συμβουλεύοντες τὰ μὲν ἄλλα πολλάκις προΐενται, ὡς
δὲ ἀσύμφορα συμβουλεύουσιν ἢ ἀπ᾽ ὠφελίμων
ἀποτρέπουσιν οὐκ ἂν ὁμολογήσαιεν· ὡς δ᾽ οὐκ
34

speaker, whether he exhorts or dissuades, always advises about things to come; to the forensic the past, for it is always in reference to things done that one party accuses and the other defends; to the epideictic most appropriately the present, for it is the existing condition of things that all those who praise or blame have in view. It is not uncommon, however, for epideictic speakers to avail themselves of other times, of the past by way of recalling it, or of the future by way of anticipating it.

Each of the three kinds has a different special end, and as there are three kinds of Rhetoric, so there are three special ends. The end of the deliberative speaker is the expedient or harmful; for he who exhorts recommends a course of action as better, and he who dissuades advises against it as worse; all other considerations, such as justice and injustice, honour and disgrace, are included as accessory in reference to this. The end of the forensic speaker is the just or the unjust; in this case also all other considerations are included as accessory. The end of those who praise or blame is the honourable and disgraceful; and they also refer all other considerations to these. A sign that what I have stated is the end which each has in view is the fact that sometimes the speakers will not dispute about the other points. For example, a man on trial does not always deny that an act has been committed or damage inflicted by him, but he will never admit that the act is unjust; for otherwise a trial would be unnecessary. Similarly, the deliberative orator, although he often sacrifices everything else, will never admit that he is recommending what is inexpedient or is dissuading from what is useful; but

ARISTOTLE

ἄδικον τοὺς ἀστυγείτονας καταδουλοῦσθαι καὶ
τοὺς μηδὲν ἀδικοῦντας, πολλάκις οὐδὲν φροντί-
1359a ζουσιν. ὁμοίως δὲ καὶ οἱ ἐπαινοῦντες καὶ οἱ
ψέγοντες οὐ σκοποῦσιν εἰ συμφέροντα ἔπραξεν ἢ
βλαβερά, ἀλλὰ καὶ ἐν ἐπαίνῳ πολλάκις τιθέασιν
ὅτι ὀλιγωρήσας τοῦ αὑτῷ λυσιτελοῦντος ἔπραξέ τι
καλόν, οἷον Ἀχιλλέα ἐπαινοῦσιν ὅτι ἐβοήθησε τῷ
ἑταίρῳ Πατρόκλῳ εἰδὼς ὅτι δεῖ αὐτὸν ἀποθανεῖν,
ἐξὸν ζῆν. τούτῳ δὲ ὁ μὲν τοιοῦτος θάνατος κάλλιον, τὸ δὲ ζῆν συμφέρον.

7 Φανερὸν δὲ ἐκ τῶν εἰρημένων ὅτι ἀνάγκη περὶ
τούτων ἔχειν πρῶτον τὰς προτάσεις· τὰ γὰρ τεκμήρια καὶ τὰ εἰκότα καὶ τὰ σημεῖα προτάσεις εἰσὶ
ῥητορικαί· ὅλως μὲν γὰρ συλλογισμὸς ἐκ προ-
τάσεών ἐστι, τὸ δ' ἐνθύμημα συλλογισμός ἐστι
8 συνεστηκὼς ἐκ τῶν εἰρημένων προτάσεων. ἐπεὶ
δὲ οὔτε πραχθῆναι οἷόν τε οὔτε πραχθήσεσθαι τὰ
ἀδύνατα ἀλλὰ τὰ δυνατά, οὐδὲ τὰ μὴ γενόμενα ἢ
μὴ ἐσόμενα οὐχ οἷόν τε τὰ μὲν πεπρᾶχθαι τὰ δὲ
πραχθήσεσθαι, ἀναγκαῖον καὶ τῷ συμβουλεύοντι
καὶ τῷ δικαζομένῳ καὶ τῷ ἐπιδεικτικῷ ἔχειν προτάσεις περὶ δυνατοῦ καὶ ἀδυνάτου, καὶ εἰ γέγονεν ἢ
9 μή, καὶ εἰ ἔσται ἢ μή. ἔτι δ' ἐπεὶ ἅπαντες καὶ

ᵃ The omission of οὐκ before ἄδικον has been suggested.
The sense would then be : " As to the injustice of enslaving
. . . he is quite indifferent." There is no doubt a reference
to the cruel treatment by Athens of the inhabitants of the
island of Melos (416 B.C.) for its loyalty to the Spartans
during the Peloponnesian war (Thuc. v. 84-116). The
Athenian envoys declined to discuss the question of right or
wrong, which they said was only possible between equal
powers, and asserted that *expediency* was the only thing that
had to be considered. The question of justice or injustice
36

often he is quite indifferent about showing that the enslavement of neighbouring peoples, even if they have done no harm, is not an act of injustice.[a] Similarly, those who praise or blame do not consider whether a man has done what is expedient or harmful, but frequently make it a matter for praise that, disregarding his own interest, he performed some deed of honour. For example, they praise Achilles because he went to the aid of his comrade Patroclus,[b] knowing that he was fated to die, although he might have lived. To him such a death was more honourable, although life was more expedient.

From what has been said it is evident that the orator must first have in readiness the propositions on these three subjects.[c] Now, necessary signs, probabilities, and signs are the propositions of the rhetorician; for the syllogism universally[d] consists of propositions, and the enthymeme is a syllogism composed of the propositions above mentioned. Again, since what is impossible can neither have been done nor will be done, but only what is possible, and since what has not taken place nor will take place can neither have been done nor will be done, it is necessary for each of the three kinds of orators to have in readiness propositions dealing with the possible and the impossible, and as to whether anything has taken place or will take place, or not. Further, since all, whether they praise or blame,

---

(in the Melian case entirely disregarded), even when taken into account, was merely accessory and intended to serve as a specious justification for the policy of might.

[b] To protect his body and avenge his death (*Iliad*, xviii.).

[c] The expedient, the just, the honourable, and their contraries.

[d] ὅλως : or, reading ὅλος, " the syllogism as a whole."

ARISTOTLE

ἐπαινοῦντες καὶ ψέγοντες καὶ προτρέποντες καὶ
ἀποτρέποντες καὶ κατηγοροῦντες καὶ ἀπολογούμενοι οὐ μόνον τὰ εἰρημένα δεικνύναι πειρῶνται
ἀλλὰ καὶ ὅτι μέγα ἢ μικρὸν τὸ ἀγαθὸν ἢ τὸ κακὸν
ἢ τὸ καλὸν ἢ τὸ αἰσχρὸν ἢ τὸ δίκαιον ἢ τὸ ἄδικον,
ἢ καθ' αὑτὰ λέγοντες ἢ πρὸς ἄλληλα ἀντιπαραβάλ-
λοντες, δῆλον ὅτι δέοι ἂν καὶ περὶ μεγέθους καὶ
μικρότητος καὶ τοῦ μείζονος καὶ τοῦ ἐλάττονος
προτάσεις ἔχειν, καὶ καθόλου καὶ περὶ ἑκάστου,
οἷον τί μεῖζον ἀγαθὸν ἢ ἔλαττον ἢ ἀδίκημα ἢ
δικαίωμα· ὁμοίως δὲ καὶ περὶ τῶν ἄλλων. περὶ
ὧν μὲν οὖν ἐξ ἀνάγκης δεῖ λαβεῖν τὰς προτάσεις,
εἴρηται· μετὰ δὲ ταῦτα διαιρετέον ἰδίᾳ περὶ ἑκάστου
τούτων, οἷον περὶ ὧν συμβουλὴ καὶ περὶ ὧν οἱ ἐπι-
δεικτικοὶ λόγοι, τρίτον δὲ περὶ ὧν αἱ δίκαι.

4. Πρῶτον μὲν οὖν ληπτέον περὶ ποῖα ἀγαθὰ ἢ
κακὰ ὁ συμβουλεύων συμβουλεύει, ἐπειδὴ οὐ περὶ
ἄπαντα ἀλλ' ὅσα ἐνδέχεται καὶ γενέσθαι καὶ μή.
2 ὅσα δὲ ἐξ ἀνάγκης ἢ ἐστὶν ἢ ἔσται ἢ ἀδύνατον εἶναι
ἢ γενέσθαι, περὶ δὲ τούτων οὐκ ἔστι συμβουλή.
3 οὐδὲ δὴ περὶ τῶν ἐνδεχομένων ἁπάντων· ἔστι γὰρ
καὶ φύσει ἔνια καὶ ἀπὸ τύχης γινόμενα ἀγαθὰ τῶν
ἐνδεχομένων καὶ γίγνεσθαι καὶ μή, περὶ ὧν οὐδὲν
πρὸ ἔργου τὸ συμβουλεύειν· ἀλλὰ δῆλον ὅτι περὶ
ὅσων ἐστὶ τὸ βουλεύεσθαι. τοιαῦτα δ' ἐστὶν ὅσα
πέφυκεν ἀνάγεσθαι εἰς ἡμᾶς, καὶ ὧν ἡ ἀρχὴ τῆς
γενέσεως ἐφ' ἡμῖν ἐστίν· μέχρι γὰρ τούτου σκοποῦ-
μεν, ἕως ἂν εὕρωμεν εἰ ἡμῖν δυνατὰ ἢ ἀδύνατα
πρᾶξαι.

1359 b

38

exhort or dissuade, accuse or defend, not only endeavour to prove what we have stated, but also that the same things, whether good or bad, honourable or disgraceful, just or unjust, are great or small, either in themselves or when compared with each other, it is clear that it will be necessary for the orator to be ready with propositions dealing with greatness and smallness and the greater and the less, both universally and in particular; for instance, which is the greater or less good, or act of injustice or justice; and similarly with regard to all other subjects. We have now stated the topics concerning which the orator must provide himself with propositions; after this, we must distinguish between each of them individually, that is, what the three kinds of Rhetoric, deliberative, epideictic, and forensic, are concerned with.

4. We must first ascertain about what kind of good or bad things the deliberative orator advises, since he cannot do so about everything, but only about things which may possibly happen or not. Everything which of necessity either is or will be, or which cannot possibly be or come to pass, is outside the scope of deliberation. Indeed, even in the case of things that are possible advice is not universally appropriate; for they include certain advantages, natural and accidental, about which it is not worth while to offer advice. But it is clear that advice is limited to those subjects about which we take counsel; and such are all those which can naturally be referred to ourselves and the first cause of whose origination is in our own power; for our examination is limited to finding out whether such things are possible or impossible for us to perform.

4 Καθ' ἕκαστον μὲν οὖν ἀκριβῶς διαριθμήσασθαι
καὶ διαλαβεῖν εἰς εἴδη περὶ ὧν εἰώθασι χρηματίζειν,
ἔτι δ' ὅσον ἐνδέχεται περὶ αὐτῶν διορίσαι κατὰ τὴν
ἀλήθειαν, οὐ δεῖ κατὰ τὸν παρόντα καιρὸν ζητεῖν
διὰ τὸ μήτε τῆς ῥητορικῆς εἶναι τέχνης ἀλλ' ἐμ-
φρονεστέρας καὶ μᾶλλον ἀληθινῆς, πολλῷ δὲ πλείω
δεδόσθαι καὶ νῦν αὐτῇ τῶν οἰκείων θεωρημάτων·
5 ὅπερ γὰρ καὶ πρότερον εἰρηκότες τυγχάνομεν,
ἀληθές ἐστιν, ὅτι ἡ ῥητορικὴ σύγκειται μὲν ἔκ τε
τῆς ἀναλυτικῆς ἐπιστήμης καὶ τῆς περὶ τὰ ἤθη
πολιτικῆς, ὁμοία δ' ἐστὶ τὰ μὲν τῇ διαλεκτικῇ τὰ
6 δὲ τοῖς σοφιστικοῖς λόγοις. ὅσῳ δ' ἄν τις ἢ τὴν
διαλεκτικὴν ἢ ταύτην μὴ καθάπερ ἂν δυνάμεις ἀλλ'
ἐπιστήμας πειρᾶται κατασκευάζειν, λήσεται τὴν
φύσιν αὐτῶν ἀφανίσας τῷ μεταβαίνειν ἐπισκευάζων εἰς ἐπιστήμας ὑποκειμένων τινῶν πραγμάτων,
7 ἀλλὰ μὴ μόνον λόγων. ὅμως δ' ὅσα πρὸ ἔργου
μέν ἐστι διελεῖν, ἔτι δ' ὑπολείπει σκέψιν τῇ πολιτικῇ
ἐπιστήμῃ, εἴπωμεν καὶ νῦν.

Σχεδὸν γάρ, περὶ ὧν βουλεύονται πάντες καὶ
περὶ ἃ ἀγορεύουσιν οἱ συμβουλεύοντες, τὰ μέγιστα
τυγχάνει πέντε τὸν ἀριθμὸν ὄντα· ταῦτα δ' ἐστὶ
περί τε πόρων, καὶ πολέμου καὶ εἰρήνης, ἔτι δὲ
περὶ φυλακῆς τῆς χώρας, καὶ τῶν εἰσαγομένων
καὶ ἐξαγομένων, καὶ περὶ νομοθεσίας.

8 Ὥστε περὶ μὲν πόρων τὸν μέλλοντα συμβου-
λεύσειν δέοι ἂν τὰς προσόδους τῆς πόλεως εἰδέναι
τίνες καὶ πόσαι, ὅπως εἴτε τις παραλείπεται προστεθῇ καὶ εἴ τις ἐλάττων αὐξηθῇ, ἔτι δὲ τὰς δα-

---

ᵃ The analytical science is Dialectic, incorrectly regarded
as a branch of Analytics, which properly implies scientific
demonstration.

However, there is no need at present to endeavour
to enumerate with scrupulous exactness or to classify
those subjects which men are wont to discuss, or to
define them as far as possible with strict accuracy,
since this is not the function of the rhetorical art
but of one that is more intelligent and exact, and
further, more than its legitimate subjects of inquiry
have already been assigned to it. For what we have
said before is true *a* : that Rhetoric is composed of
analytical science and of that branch of political
science which is concerned with Ethics, and that it
resembles partly Dialectic and partly sophistical
arguments. But in proportion as anyone endeavours
to make of Dialectic or Rhetoric, not what they are,
faculties, but sciences, to that extent he will, without
knowing it, destroy their real nature, in thus altering
their character, by crossing over into the domain of
sciences,*b* whose subjects are certain definite things,
not merely words. Nevertheless, even at present
we may mention such matters as it is worth while
to analyse, while still leaving much for political
science to investigate.

Now, we may say that the most important subjects
about which all men deliberate and deliberative
orators harangue, are five in number, to wit : ways
and means, war and peace, the defence of the
country, imports and exports, legislation.

Accordingly, the orator who is going to give advice
on ways and means should be acquainted with the
nature and extent of the State resources, so that if
any is omitted it may be added, and if any is in-

b Taking εἰς ἐπιστήμας with μεταβαίνειν. If taken with
ἐπισκευάζων, the sense will be : " by changing his ground
(μεταβαίνειν being used absolutely) while altering their characters from faculties to sciences."

πάνας τῆς πόλεως ἁπάσας, ὅπως εἴ τις περίεργος
ἀφαιρεθῇ καὶ εἴ τις μείζων ἐλάττων γένηται· οὐ
γὰρ μόνον πρὸς τὰ ὑπάρχοντα προστιθέντες πλου-
σιώτεροι γίνονται, ἀλλὰ καὶ ἀφαιροῦντες τῶν δα-
πανημάτων. ταῦτα δ᾽ οὐ μόνον ἐκ τῆς περὶ τὰ
ἴδια ἐμπειρίας ἐνδέχεται συνορᾶν, ἀλλ᾽ ἀναγκαῖον
καὶ τῶν παρὰ τοῖς ἄλλοις εὑρημένων ἱστορικὸν εἶναι
πρὸς τὴν περὶ τούτων συμβουλήν.

9 Περὶ δὲ πολέμου καὶ εἰρήνης τὴν δύναμιν εἰδέναι
τῆς πόλεως, ὁπόση τε ὑπάρχει ἤδη καὶ πόσην ἐνδέχεται ὑπάρξαι, καὶ ποία τις ἥ τε ὑπάρχουσά ἐστι
καὶ ἥτις ἐνδέχεται προσγενέσθαι, ἔτι δὲ πολέμους
τίνας καὶ πῶς πεπολέμηκεν. οὐ μόνον δὲ τῆς
οἰκείας πόλεως ἀλλὰ καὶ τῶν ὁμόρων ταῦτα ἀναγκαῖον εἰδέναι, καὶ πρὸς οὓς ἐπίδοξον πολεμεῖν, ὅπως
πρὸς μὲν τοὺς κρείττους εἰρηνεύηται, πρὸς δὲ τοὺς
1360 a ἥττους ἐπ᾽ αὐτοῖς ᾖ τὸ πολεμεῖν. καὶ τὰς δυνάμεις,
πότερον ὅμοιαι ἢ ἀνόμοιαι· ἔστι γὰρ καὶ ταύτῃ
πλεονεκτεῖν ἢ ἐλαττοῦσθαι. ἀναγκαῖον δὲ καὶ
πρὸς ταῦτα μὴ μόνον τοὺς οἰκείους πολέμους τεθεωρηκέναι ἀλλὰ καὶ τοὺς τῶν ἄλλων, πῶς ἀποβαί-
νουσιν· ἀπὸ γὰρ τῶν ὁμοίων τὰ ὅμοια γίγνεσθαι
πέφυκεν.

10 Ἔτι δὲ περὶ φυλακῆς τῆς χώρας μὴ λανθάνειν
πῶς φυλάττεται, ἀλλὰ καὶ τὸ πλῆθος εἰδέναι τῆς
φυλακῆς καὶ τὸ εἶδος καὶ τοὺς τόπους τῶν φυλακ-

sufficient, it may be increased. Further, he should know all the expenses of the State, that if any is superfluous, it may be removed, or, if too great, may be curtailed. For men become wealthier, not only by adding to what they already possess, but also by cutting down expenses. Of these things it is not only possible to acquire a general view from individual experience, but in view of advising concerning them it is further necessary to be well informed about what has been discovered among others.

In regard to war and peace, the orator should be acquainted with the power of the State, how great it is already and how great it may possibly become; of what kind it is already and what additions may possibly be made to it; further, what wars it has waged and its conduct of them. These things he should be acquainted with, not only as far as his own State is concerned, but also in reference to neighbouring States, and particularly those with whom there is a likelihood of war, so that towards the stronger a pacific attitude may be maintained, and in regard to the weaker, the decision as to making war on them may be left to his own State. Again, he should know whether their forces are like or unlike his own, for herein also advantage or disadvantage may lie. With reference to these matters he must also have examined the results, not only of the wars carried on by his own State, but also of those carried on by others; for similar results naturally arise from similar causes.

Again, in regard to the defence of the country, he should not be ignorant how it is carried on; he should know both the strength of the guard, its character, and the positions of the guard-houses

τηρίων (τοῦτο δ᾽ ἀδύνατον μὴ ἔμπειρον ὄντα τῆς χώρας), ἵν᾽ εἴτ᾽ ἐλάττων ἡ φυλακὴ προστεθῇ καὶ εἴ τις περίεργος ἀφαιρεθῇ καὶ τοὺς ἐπιτηδείους τόπους τηρῶσι μᾶλλον.

11 Ἔτι δὲ περὶ τροφῆς, πόση δαπάνη ἱκανὴ τῇ πόλει καὶ ποία ἥ αὑτοῦ τε γιγνομένη καὶ εἰσαγώγιμος, καὶ τίνων τ᾽ ἐξαγωγῆς δέονται καὶ τίνων εἰσαγωγῆς, ἵνα πρὸς τούτους καὶ συνθῆκαι καὶ συμβολαὶ γίγνωνται· πρὸς δύο γὰρ διαφυλάττειν ἀναγκαῖον ἀνεγκλήτους τοὺς πολίτας, πρός τε τοὺς κρείττους καὶ πρὸς τοὺς εἰς ταῦτα χρησίμους.

12 Εἰς δ᾽ ἀσφάλειαν ἅπαντα μὲν ταῦτα ἀναγκαῖον δύνασθαι θεωρεῖν, οὐκ ἐλάχιστον δὲ περὶ νομοθεσίας ἐπαΐειν· ἐν γὰρ τοῖς νόμοις ἐστὶν ἡ σωτηρία τῆς πόλεως, ὥστ᾽ ἀναγκαῖον εἰδέναι πόσα τ᾽ ἐστὶ πολιτειῶν εἴδη, καὶ ποῖα συμφέρει ἑκάστῃ, καὶ ὑπὸ τίνων φθείρεσθαι πέφυκε καὶ οἰκείων τῆς πολιτείας καὶ ἐναντίων. λέγω δὲ τὸ ὑπὸ οἰκείων φθείρεσθαι, ὅτι ἔξω τῆς βελτίστης πολιτείας αἱ ἄλλαι πᾶσαι καὶ ἀνιέμεναι καὶ ἐπιτεινόμεναι φθείρονται, οἷον δημοκρατία οὐ μόνον ἀνιεμένη ἀσθενεστέρα γίνεται ὥστε τέλος ἥξει εἰς ὀλιγαρχίαν, ἀλλὰ καὶ ἐπιτεινομένη σφόδρα, ὥσπερ καὶ ἡ γρυπότης καὶ ἡ σιμότης οὐ μόνον ἀνιέμενα ἔρχεται εἰς τὸ μέσον, ἀλλὰ καὶ σφόδρα γρυπὰ γινόμενα ἢ σιμὰ οὕτω διατίθεται ὥστε

ᵃ τούτους : those who will receive exports and send imports.

(which is impossible for one who is unacquainted with the country), so that if any guard is insufficient it may be increased, or if any is superfluous it may be disbanded, and greater attention devoted to suitable positions.

Again, in regard to food, he should know what amount of expenditure is sufficient to support the State; what kind of food is produced at home or can be imported; and what exports and imports are necessary, in order that contracts and agreements may be made with those *a* who can furnish them; for it is necessary to keep the citizens free from reproach in their relations with two classes of people —those who are stronger and those who are useful for commercial purposes.

With a view to the safety of the State, it is necessary that the orator should be able to judge of all these questions, but an understanding of legislation is of special importance, for it is on the laws that the safety of the State is based. Wherefore he must know how many forms of government there are; what is expedient for each; and the natural causes of its downfall, whether they are peculiar to the particular form of government or opposed to it. By being ruined by causes peculiar to itself, I mean that, with the exception of the perfect form of government, all the rest are ruined by being relaxed or strained to excess. Thus democracy, not only when relaxed, but also when strained to excess, becomes weaker and will end in an oligarchy; similarly, not only does an aquiline or snub nose reach the mean, when one of these defects is relaxed, but when it becomes aquiline or snub to excess, it is altered to such an extent that even the likeness

13 μηδὲ μυκτῆρα δοκεῖν εἶναι. χρήσιμον δὲ πρὸς τὰς
νομοθεσίας τὸ μὴ μόνον ἐπαΐειν τίς πολιτεία συμφέρει ἐκ τῶν παρεληλυθότων θεωροῦντι, ἀλλὰ καὶ
τὰς παρὰ τοῖς ἄλλοις εἰδέναι, αἱ ποῖαι τοῖς ποίοις
ἁρμόττουσιν. ὥστε δῆλον ὅτι πρὸς μὲν τὴν νομο-
θεσίαν αἱ τῆς γῆς περίοδοι χρήσιμοι (ἐντεῦθεν γὰρ
λαβεῖν ἔστι τοὺς τῶν ἐθνῶν νόμους), πρὸς δὲ τὰς
πολιτικὰς συμβουλὰς αἱ τῶν περὶ τὰς πράξεις
γραφόντων ἱστορίαι· ἅπαντα δὲ ταῦτα πολιτικῆς
ἀλλ' οὐ ῥητορικῆς ἔργον ἐστίν.

1360 b   Περὶ ὧν μὲν οὖν ἔχειν δεῖ τὸν μέλλοντα συμβουλεύειν, τὰ μέγιστα τοσαῦτά ἐστιν· ἐξ ὧν δὲ δεῖ καὶ
περὶ τούτων καὶ περὶ τῶν ἄλλων προτρέπειν ἢ
ἀποτρέπειν, λέγωμεν πάλιν.

5. Σχεδὸν δὲ καὶ ἰδίᾳ ἑκάστῳ καὶ κοινῇ πᾶσι
σκοπός τις ἐστιν, οὗ στοχαζόμενοι καὶ αἱροῦνται
καὶ φεύγουσιν· καὶ τοῦτ' ἐστὶν ἐν κεφαλαίῳ εἰπεῖν
2 ἥ τ' εὐδαιμονία καὶ τὰ μόρια αὐτῆς. ὥστε παραδείγματος χάριν λάβωμεν τί ἐστιν ὡς ἁπλῶς εἰπεῖν
ἡ εὐδαιμονία, καὶ ἐκ τίνων τὰ μόρια ταύτης· περὶ
γὰρ ταύτης καὶ τῶν εἰς ταύτην συντεινόντων καὶ
τῶν ἐναντίων ταύτῃ αἵ τε προτροπαὶ καὶ αἱ ἀπο-
τροπαὶ πᾶσαί εἰσιν· τὰ μὲν γὰρ παρασκευάζοντα
ταύτην ἢ τῶν μορίων τι, ἢ μεῖζον ἀντ' ἐλάττονος
ποιοῦντα, δεῖ πράττειν, τὰ δὲ φθείροντα ἢ ἐμ-
ποδίζοντα ἢ τὰ ἐναντία ποιοῦντα μὴ πράττειν.

3   Ἔστω δὴ εὐδαιμονία εὐπραξία μετ' ἀρετῆς, ἢ
αὐτάρκεια ζωῆς, ἢ ὁ βίος ὁ μετ' ἀσφαλείας ἥδιστος,

---

a This rendering, although convenient, hardly represents

46

of a nose is lost. Moreover, with reference to acts
of legislation, it is useful not only to understand
what form of government is expedient by judging
in the light of the past, but also to become acquainted
with those in existence in other nations, and to
learn what kinds of government are suitable to what
kinds of people. It is clear, therefore, that for
legislation books of travel are useful, since they help
us to understand the laws of other nations, and for
political debates historical works.*a* All these things,
however, belong to Politics and not to Rhetoric.

Such, then, are the most important questions upon
which the would-be deliberative orator must be well
informed. Now let us again state the sources whence
we must derive our arguments for exhortation or
discussion on these and other questions.

5. Men, individually and in common, nearly all
have some aim, in the attainment of which they
choose or avoid certain things. This aim, briefly
stated, is happiness and its component parts. Therefore, for the sake of illustration, let us ascertain
what happiness, generally speaking, is, and what its
parts consist in ; for all who exhort or dissuade discuss happiness and the things which conduce or are
detrimental to it. For one should do the things
which procure happiness or one of its parts, or increase instead of diminishing it, and avoid doing
those things which destroy or hinder it or bring
about what is contrary to it.

Let us then define happiness as well-being combined with virtue, or independence of life, or the
life that is most agreeable combined with security, or

the Greek, which, literally translated, is " the *investigations*
of those who write about human actions " (*cf. ἱστορικός,* § 8).

ARISTOTLE

ἢ εὐθηνία κτημάτων καὶ σωμάτων μετὰ δυνάμεως
φυλακτικῆς τε καὶ πρακτικῆς τούτων· σχεδὸν γὰρ
τούτων ἓν ἢ πλείω τὴν εὐδαιμονίαν ὁμολογοῦσιν
4 εἶναι ἅπαντες. εἰ δή ἐστιν ἡ εὐδαιμονία τοιοῦτον,
ἀνάγκη αὐτῆς εἶναι μέρη εὐγένειαν, πολυφιλίαν,
χρηστοφιλίαν, πλοῦτον, εὐτεκνίαν, πολυτεκνίαν,
εὐγηρίαν, ἔτι τὰς τοῦ σώματος ἀρετάς, οἷον ὑγίειαν,
κάλλος, ἰσχύν, μέγεθος, δύναμιν ἀγωνιστικήν, δόξαν,
τιμήν, εὐτυχίαν, ἀρετήν· οὕτω γὰρ ἂν αὐταρκέσ-
τατος εἴη, εἰ ὑπάρχοι αὐτῷ τά τ᾽ ἐν αὐτῷ καὶ τὰ
ἐκτὸς ἀγαθά· οὐ γάρ ἐστιν ἄλλα παρὰ ταῦτα.
ἔστι δ᾽ ἐν αὐτῷ μὲν τὰ περὶ ψυχὴν καὶ τὰ ἐν
σώματι, ἔξω δὲ εὐγένεια καὶ φίλοι καὶ χρήματα
καὶ τιμή. ἔτι δὲ προσήκειν οἰόμεθα δυνάμεις
ὑπάρχειν καὶ τύχην· οὕτω γὰρ ἂν ἀσφαλέστατος
ὁ βίος εἴη. λάβωμεν τοίνυν ὁμοίως καὶ τούτων
ἕκαστον τί ἐστιν.

5 Εὐγένεια μὲν οὖν ἐστιν ἔθνει μὲν καὶ πόλει τὸ
αὐτόχθονας ἢ ἀρχαίους εἶναι, καὶ ἡγεμόνας τοὺς
πρώτους ἐπιφανεῖς, καὶ πολλοὺς ἐπιφανεῖς γεγονέναι ἐξ αὐτῶν ἐπὶ τοῖς ζηλουμένοις· ἰδίᾳ δὲ εὐγένεια ἢ ἀπ᾽ ἀνδρῶν ἢ ἀπὸ γυναικῶν, καὶ γνησιότης
ἀπ᾽ ἀμφοῖν, καὶ ὥσπερ ἐπὶ πόλεως τούς τε πρώτους
γνωρίμους ἢ ἐπ᾽ ἀρετῇ ἢ πλούτῳ ἢ ἄλλῳ τῳ τῶν
τιμωμένων, καὶ πολλοὺς ἐπιφανεῖς ἐκ τοῦ γένους
καὶ ἄνδρας καὶ γυναῖκας καὶ νέους καὶ πρεσ-
βυτέρους.

---

[a] This is the usual rendering, although it is hardly satisfactory. Jebb translates " a flourishing state . . . of body."
[b] Or, "bring about," "effect them."
[c] *i.e.* of mind and body ; or δυνάμεις may mean " positions
of authority and influence."
[d] This was a favourite boast of the Athenians.

abundance of possessions and slaves,[a] combined with power to protect and make use of them [b] ; for nearly all men admit that one or more of these things constitutes happiness. If, then, such is the nature of happiness, its component parts must necessarily be : noble birth, numerous friends, good friends, wealth, good children, numerous children, a good old age ; further, bodily excellences, such as health, beauty, strength, stature, fitness for athletic contests, a good reputation, honour, good luck, virtue. For a man would be entirely independent, provided he possessed all internal and external goods ; for there are no others. Internal goods are those of mind and body ; external goods are noble birth, friends, wealth, honour. To these we think should be added certain capacities [c] and good luck ; for on these conditions life will be perfectly secure. Let us now in the same way define each of these in detail.

Noble birth, in the case of a nation or State, means that its members or inhabitants are sprung from the soil,[d] or of long standing ; that its first members were famous as leaders, and that many of their descendants have been famous for qualities that are highly esteemed. In the case of private individuals, noble birth is derived from either the father's or the mother's side, and on both sides there must be legitimacy ; and, as in the case of a State, it means that its founders were distinguished for virtue, or wealth, or any other of the things that men honour, and that a number of famous persons, both men and women, young and old, belong to the family.

6 Εὐτεκνία δὲ καὶ πολυτεκνία οὐκ ἄδηλα· ἔστι δὲ
1361 a τῷ κοινῷ μέν, νεότης ἂν ᾖ πολλὴ καὶ ἀγαθή, ἀγαθὴ
δὲ κατ' ἀρετὴν σώματος, οἶον μέγεθος κάλλος ἰσχὺν
δύναμιν ἀγωνιστικήν· ψυχῆς δὲ σωφροσύνη καὶ
ἀνδρία νέου ἀρεταί. ἰδίᾳ δὲ εὐτεκνία καὶ πολυτεκνία τὸ τὰ ἴδια τέκνα πολλὰ καὶ τοιαῦτα εἶναι,
καὶ θήλεα καὶ ἄρρενα· θηλειῶν δὲ ἀρετὴ σώματος
μὲν κάλλος καὶ μέγεθος, ψυχῆς δὲ σωφροσύνη καὶ
φιλεργία ἄνευ ἀνελευθερίας.[a] ὁμοίως δὲ καὶ ἰδίᾳ
καὶ κοινῇ καὶ κατ' ἄνδρας καὶ κατὰ γυναῖκας δεῖ
ζητεῖν ἕκαστον ὑπάρχειν τῶν τοιούτων· ὅσοις γὰρ
τὰ κατὰ γυναῖκας φαῦλα ὥσπερ Λακεδαιμονίοις,[b]
σχεδὸν κατὰ τὸ ἥμισυ οὐκ εὐδαιμονοῦσιν.

7 Πλούτου δὲ μέρη νομίσματος πλῆθος, γῆς,
χωρίων κτῆσις, ἔτι δὲ ἐπίπλων κτῆσις καὶ βοσκη-
μάτων καὶ ἀνδραπόδων πλήθει καὶ μεγέθει καὶ
κάλλει διαφερόντων, ταῦτα δὲ πάντα καὶ ἀσφαλῆ
καὶ ἐλευθέρια καὶ χρήσιμα. ἔστι δὲ χρήσιμα μὲν
μᾶλλον τὰ κάρπιμα, ἐλευθέρια δὲ τὰ πρὸς ἀπό-
λαυσιν· κάρπιμα δὲ λέγω ἀφ' ὧν αἱ πρόσοδοι, ἀπο-
λαυστικὰ δὲ ἀφ' ὧν μηδὲν παρὰ τὴν χρῆσιν γίγνεται,
ὅ τι καὶ ἄξιον. ὅρος δὲ ἀσφαλείας μὲν τὸ ἐνταῦθα
καὶ οὕτω κεκτῆσθαι ὥστ' ἐφ' αὑτῷ εἶναι τὴν χρῆσιν
αὐτῶν· τοῦ δὲ οἰκεῖα εἶναι ὅταν ἐφ' αὑτῷ ᾖ ἀπαλ-
λοτριῶσαι ἢ μή, λέγω δὲ ἀπαλλοτρίωσιν δόσιν καὶ

---

[a] ἀνελευθερία : literally, qualities unbecoming to a free
man or woman, ungentlemanly, unladylike ; hence, mean,
servile, sordid.

[b] A similar charge against the Spartan women is made in
the *Politics* (ii. 9. 5): " Further, the looseness (ἄνεσις) of the
Spartan women is injurious both to the purpose of the constitution and the well-being of the State . . . their life is one
of absolute luxury and intemperance " (compare Euripides,
Andromache, 595-6 "even if she wished it, a Spartan girl

The blessing of good children and numerous children needs little explanation. For the commonwealth it consists in a large number of good young men, good in bodily excellences, such as stature, beauty, strength, fitness for athletic contests ; the moral excellences of a young man are self-control and courage. For the individual it consists in a number of good children of his own, both male and female, and such as we have described. Female bodily excellences are beauty and stature, their moral excellences self-control and industrious habits, free from servility.[a] The object of both the individual and of the community should be to secure the existence of each of these qualities in both men and women ; for all those States in which the character of women is unsatisfactory, as in Lacedaemon,[b] may be considered only half-happy.

Wealth consists in abundance of money, ownership of land and properties, and further of movables, cattle, and slaves, remarkable for number, size, and beauty, if they are all secure, liberal, and useful. Property that is productive is more useful, but that which has enjoyment for its object is more liberal. By productive I mean that which is a source of income, by enjoyable that which offers no advantage beyond the use of it — at least, none worth mentioning. Security may be defined as possession of property in such places and on such conditions that the use of it is in our own hands ; and ownership as the right of alienation or not,[c] by which I mean giving

could not be chaste "). The opinion of Xenophon and Plutarch is much more favourable.

[c] $\mathring{\eta}$ μή : in the MS. readings these words follow τοῦ οἰκεῖα εἶναι : " ownership or non-ownership." The alteration is Spengel's.

πρᾶσιν. ὅλως δὲ τὸ πλουτεῖν ἐστὶν ἐν τῷ χρῆσθαι
μᾶλλον ἢ ἐν τῷ κεκτῆσθαι· καὶ γὰρ ἡ ἐνέργειά
ἐστι τῶν τοιούτων καὶ ἡ χρῆσις πλοῦτος.

8 Εὐδοξία δ' ἐστὶ τὸ ὑπὸ πάντων σπουδαῖον ὑπο-
λαμβάνεσθαι, ἢ τοιοῦτόν τι ἔχειν οὗ πάντες ἐφίενται
ἢ οἱ πολλοὶ ἢ οἱ ἀγαθοὶ ἢ οἱ φρόνιμοι.

9 Τιμὴ δ' ἐστὶ μὲν σημεῖον εὐεργετικῆς δόξης,
τιμῶνται δὲ δικαίως μὲν καὶ μάλιστα οἱ εὐεργετη-
κότες, οὐ μὴν ἀλλὰ τιμᾶται καὶ ὁ δυνάμενος εὐεργε-
τεῖν· εὐεργεσία δὲ ἢ εἰς σωτηρίαν καὶ ὅσα αἴτια τοῦ
εἶναι, ἢ εἰς πλοῦτον, ἢ εἴς τι τῶν ἄλλων ἀγαθῶν,
ὧν μὴ ῥᾳδία ἡ κτῆσις ἢ ὅλως ἢ ἐνταῦθα ἢ ποτέ·
πολλοὶ γὰρ διὰ μικρὰ δοκοῦντα τιμῆς τυγχάνουσιν,
ἀλλ' οἱ τόποι καὶ οἱ καιροὶ αἴτιοι. μέρη δὲ τιμῆς
θυσίαι, μνῆμαι ἐν μέτροις καὶ ἄνευ μέτρων, γέρα,
τεμένη, προεδρίαι, τάφοι, εἰκόνες, τροφαὶ δη-
μόσιαι, τὰ βαρβαρικά, οἷον προσκυνήσεις καὶ
ἐκστάσεις, δῶρα τὰ παρ' ἑκάστοις τίμια. καὶ γὰρ
τὸ δῶρόν ἐστι κτήματος δόσις καὶ τιμῆς σημεῖον,
διὸ καὶ οἱ φιλοχρήματοι καὶ οἱ φιλότιμοι ἐφίενται
1361 b αὐτῶν· ἀμφοτέροις γὰρ ἔχει ὧν δέονται· καὶ γὰρ
κτῆμά ἐστιν, οὗ ἐφίενται οἱ φιλοχρήματοι, καὶ
τιμὴν ἔχει, οὗ οἱ φιλότιμοι.

10 Σώματος δὲ ἀρετὴ ὑγίεια, αὕτη δὲ οὕτως ὥστε
ἀνόσους εἶναι χρωμένους τοῖς σώμασιν· πολλοὶ γὰρ
ὑγιαίνουσιν ὥσπερ Ἡρόδικος λέγεται, οὓς οὐδεὶς

---

^a ἐνέργεια : realization in action or fact.
^b Of Selymbria, physician and teacher of hygienic gym-
nastics (c. 420 b.c.). He is said to have made his patients
walk from Athens to Megara and back, about 70 miles.
He was satirized by Plato and by his old pupil Hippo-

the property away or selling it. In a word, being wealthy consists rather in use than in possession; for the actualization[a] and use of such things is wealth.

A good reputation consists in being considered a man of worth by all, or in possessing something of such a nature that all or most men, or the good, or the men of practical wisdom desire it.

Honour is a token of a reputation for doing good; and those who have already done good are justly and above all honoured, not but that he who is capable of doing good is also honoured. Doing good relates either to personal security and all the causes of existence; or to wealth; or to any other good things which are not easy to acquire, either in any conditions, or at such a place, or at such a time; for many obtain honour for things that appear trifling, but this depends upon place and time. The components of honour are sacrifices, memorials in verse and prose, privileges, grants of land, front seats, public burial, State maintenance, and among the barbarians, prostration and giving place, and all gifts which are highly prized in each country. For a gift is at once a giving of a possession and a token of honour; wherefore gifts are desired by the ambitious and by those who are fond of money, since they are an acquisition for the latter and an honour for the former; so that they furnish both with what they want.

Bodily excellence is health, and of such a kind that when exercising the body we are free from sickness; for many are healthy in the way Herodicus[b] is said to have been, whom no one would consider

crates as one who killed those for whom he prescribed (*cf.* ii. 23. 29).

ἂν εὐδαιμονίσειε τῆς ὑγιείας διὰ τὸ πάντων ἀπέχεσθαι τῶν ἀνθρωπίνων ἢ τῶν πλείστων.

11 Κάλλος δὲ ἕτερον καθ᾽ ἑκάστην ἡλικίαν ἐστίν. νέου μὲν οὖν κάλλος τὸ πρὸς τοὺς πόνους χρήσιμον ἔχειν τὸ σῶμα τούς τε πρὸς δρόμον καὶ πρὸς βίαν, ἡδὺν ὄντα ἰδεῖν πρὸς ἀπόλαυσιν, διὸ οἱ πένταθλοι κάλλιστοι, ὅτι πρὸς βίαν καὶ πρὸς τάχος ἅμα πεφύκασιν· ἀκμάζοντος δὲ πρὸς μὲν πόνους τοὺς πολεμικούς, ἡδὺν δὲ εἶναι δοκεῖν μετὰ φοβερότητος· γέροντος δὲ πρὸς μὲν πόνους τοὺς ἀναγκαίους ἱκανόν, ἄλυπον δὲ διὰ τὸ μηδὲν ἔχειν ὧν τὸ γῆρας λωβᾶται.

12 Ἰσχὺς δ᾽ ἐστὶ μὲν δύναμις τοῦ κινεῖν ἕτερον ὡς βούλεται, ἀνάγκη δὲ κινεῖν ἕτερον ἢ ἕλκοντα ἢ ὠθοῦντα ἢ αἴροντα ἢ πιέζοντα ἢ συνθλίβοντα, ὥστε ὁ ἰσχυρὸς ἢ πᾶσιν ἢ τούτων τισίν ἐστιν ἰσχυρός.

13 Μεγέθους δὲ ἀρετὴ τὸ ὑπερέχειν κατὰ μῆκος καὶ βάθος καὶ πλάτος τῶν πολλῶν τοσούτῳ μείζονι ὥστε μὴ βραδυτέρας ποιεῖν τὰς κινήσεις διὰ τὴν ὑπερβολήν.

14 Ἀγωνιστικὴ δὲ σώματος ἀρετὴ σύγκειται ἐκ μεγέθους καὶ ἰσχύος καὶ τάχους· καὶ γὰρ ὁ ταχὺς ἰσχυρός ἐστιν· ὁ γὰρ δυνάμενος τὰ σκέλη ῥιπτεῖν πως καὶ κινεῖν ταχὺ καὶ πόρρω δρομικός, ὁ δὲ θλίβειν καὶ κατέχειν παλαιστικός, ὁ δὲ ὦσαι τῇ

ᵃ Five contests : jumping, running, discus-throwing, javelin-throwing, wrestling.

ᵇ Or simply, " freedom from pain " (§ 15).

happy in the matter of health, because they are obliged to abstain from all or nearly all human enjoyments.

Beauty varies with each age. In a young man, it consists in possessing a body capable of enduring all efforts, either of the racecourse or of bodily strength, while he himself is pleasant to look upon and a sheer delight. This is why the athletes in the pentathlum [a] are most beautiful, because they are naturally adapted for bodily exertion and for swiftness of foot. In a man who has reached his prime, beauty consists in being naturally adapted for the toils of war, in being pleasant to look upon and at the same time awe-inspiring. In an old man, beauty consists in being naturally adapted to contend with unavoidable labours and in not causing annoyance [b] to others, thanks to the absence of the disagreeable accompaniments of old age.

Strength consists in the power of moving another as one wills, for which purpose it is necessary to pull or push, to lift, to squeeze or crush, so that the strong man is strong by virtue of being able to do all or some of these things.

Excellence of stature consists in being superior to most men in height, depth, and breadth, but in such proportion as not to render the movements of the body slower as the result of excess.

Bodily excellence in athletics consists in size, strength, and swiftness of foot ; for to be swift is to be strong. For one who is able to throw his legs about in a certain way, to move them rapidly and with long strides, makes a good runner ; one who can hug and grapple, a good wrestler ; one who can thrust away by a blow of the fist, a good boxer ;

πληγῇ πυκτικός, ὁ δ' ἀμφοτέροις τούτοις παγ-
κρατιαστικός, ὁ δὲ πᾶσι πένταθλος.

15 Εὐγηρία δ' ἐστὶ βραδυτὴς γήρως μετ' ἀλυπίας·
οὔτε γὰρ εἰ ταχὺ γηράσκει, εὐγηρως, οὔτ' εἰ μόγις
μὲν λυπηρῶς δέ. ἔστι δὲ καὶ ἐκ τῶν τοῦ σώματος
ἀρετῶν καὶ τύχης· μὴ ἄνοσος γὰρ ὢν μηδὲ ἰσχυρὸς
οὐκ ἔσται ἀπαθὴς οὐδ' ἄλυπος καὶ πολυχρόνιος
ἄνευ τύχης διαμείνειεν ἄν. ἔστι δέ τις καὶ χωρὶς
ἰσχύος καὶ ὑγιείας ἄλλη δύναμις μακροβιότητος·
πολλοὶ γὰρ ἄνευ τῶν τοῦ σώματος ἀρετῶν μακρό-
βιοί εἰσιν· ἀλλ' οὐδὲν ἡ ἀκριβολογία χρήσιμος ἡ
περὶ τούτων εἰς τὰ νῦν.

16 Πολυφιλία δὲ καὶ χρηστοφιλία οὐκ ἄδηλα τοῦ
φίλου ὡρισμένου, ὅτι ἐστὶν ὁ τοιοῦτος φίλος ὅστις
ἃ οἴεται ἀγαθὰ εἶναι ἐκείνῳ, πρακτικός ἐστιν
αὐτῶν δι' ἐκεῖνον. ᾧ δὴ πολλοὶ τοιοῦτοι, πολύ-
φιλος, ᾧ δὲ καὶ ἐπιεικεῖς ἄνδρες, χρηστόφιλος.

17 Εὐτυχία δ' ἐστίν, ὧν ἡ τύχη ἀγαθῶν αἰτία, ταῦτα
1362a γίγνεσθαι καὶ ὑπάρχειν ἢ πάντα ἢ τὰ πλεῖστα ἢ τὰ
μέγιστα. αἰτία δ' ἐστὶν ἡ τύχη ἐνίων μὲν ὧν καὶ
αἱ τέχναι, πολλῶν δὲ καὶ ἀτέχνων, οἷον ὅσων
φύσις (ἐνδέχεται δὲ καὶ παρὰ φύσιν εἶναι)· ὑγιείας
μὲν γὰρ τέχνη αἰτία, κάλλους δὲ καὶ μεγέθους

---

[a] A combination of wrestling and boxing.

[b] The results of art and the results due to nature are often
assisted (or hindered) by the interference of the irregular
operations of fortune or chance. Health may be the result
of fortune, as well as of art (a sick man may be cured by a
drug taken by chance, one not prescribed by the physician);
beauty and strength, of fortune as well as nature. It is
parenthetically remarked that fortune may also produce
unnatural monstrosities. The removal of the brackets and
the substitution of a comma for the colon after φύσις have

56

one who excels in boxing and wrestling is fit for the pancratium,[a] he who excels in all for the pentathlum.

A happy old age is one that comes slowly with freedom from pain ; for neither one who rapidly grows old nor one who grows old insensibly but with pain enjoys a happy old age. This also depends upon bodily excellences and good fortune ; for unless a man is free from illness and is strong, he will never be free from suffering, nor will he live long and painlessly without good fortune. Apart from health and strength, however, there is a power of vitality in certain cases ; for many live long who are not endowed with bodily excellences. But a minute examination of such questions is needless for the present purpose.

The meaning of numerous and worthy friends is easy to understand from the definition of a friend. A friend is one who exerts himself to do for the sake of another what he thinks is advantageous to him. A man to whom many persons are so disposed, has many friends ; if they are virtuous, he has worthy friends.

Good fortune consists in the acquisition or possession of either all, or the most, or the most important of those goods of which fortune is the cause. Now fortune is the cause of some things with which the arts also are concerned, and also of many which have nothing to do with art, for instance, such as are due to nature (though it is possible that the results of fortune may be contrary to nature) ; for art is a cause of health, but nature of beauty and stature.[b]

been suggested. The meaning would then be : " for instance, such as are due to nature, but possibly may be also contrary to nature."

φύσις. ὅλως δὲ τὰ τοιαῦτα τῶν ἀγαθῶν ἐστὶν
ἀπὸ τύχης, ἐφ' οἷς ἐστὶν ὁ φθόνος. ἔστι δὲ καὶ
τῶν παρὰ λόγον ἀγαθῶν αἰτία τύχη, οἷον εἰ οἱ
ἄλλοι αἰσχροὶ ἀδελφοί, ὁ δὲ καλός, ἢ οἱ ἄλλοι μὴ
εἶδον τὸν θησαυρόν, ὁ δ' εὗρεν, ἢ εἰ τοῦ πλησίον
ἔτυχε τὸ βέλος, τούτου δὲ μή, ἢ εἰ μὴ ἦλθε μόνος
ἀεὶ φοιτῶν, οἱ δὲ ἅπαξ ἐλθόντες διεφθάρησαν·
πάντα γὰρ τὰ τοιαῦτα εὐτυχήματα δοκεῖ εἶναι.

18 Περὶ δὲ ἀρετῆς, ἐπείπερ οἰκειότατος ὁ περὶ τοὺς
ἐπαίνους τόπος, ὅταν περὶ ἐπαίνου ποιώμεθα τὸν
λόγον, τότε διοριστέον.

6. Ὧν μὲν οὖν δεῖ στοχάζεσθαι προτρέποντα ὡς
ἐσομένων ἢ ὑπαρχόντων, καὶ ὧν ἀποτρέποντα,
φανερόν· τὰ γὰρ ἐναντία τούτων ἐστίν. ἐπεὶ δὲ
πρόκειται τῷ συμβουλεύοντι σκοπὸς τὸ συμφέρον,
βουλεύονται δὲ οὐ περὶ τοῦ τέλους ἀλλὰ περὶ τῶν
πρὸς τὸ τέλος, ταῦτα δ' ἐστὶ τὰ συμφέροντα κατὰ
τὰς πράξεις, τὸ δὲ συμφέρον ἀγαθόν, ληπτέον ἂν
εἴη στοιχεῖα περὶ ἀγαθοῦ καὶ συμφέροντος ἁπλῶς.

2 Ἔστω δὴ ἀγαθὸν ὃ ἂν αὐτὸ ἑαυτοῦ ἕνεκα ᾖ
αἱρετόν, καὶ οὗ ἕνεκα ἄλλο αἱρούμεθα, καὶ οὗ
ἐφίεται πάντα ἢ πάντα τὰ αἴσθησιν ἔχοντα ἢ νοῦν,
ἢ εἰ λάβοι νοῦν. καὶ ὅσα ὁ νοῦς ἂν ἑκάστῳ ἀποδοίη,
καὶ ὅσα ὁ περὶ ἕκαστον νοῦς ἀποδίδωσιν ἑκάστῳ,
τοῦτό ἐστιν ἑκάστῳ ἀγαθόν, καὶ οὗ παρόντος εὖ
διάκειται καὶ αὐτάρκως ἔχει, καὶ τὸ αὔταρκες, καὶ

Speaking generally, the goods which come from fortune are such as excite envy. Fortune is also a cause of those goods which are beyond calculation; for instance, a man's brothers are all ugly, while he is handsome; they did not see the treasure, while he found it; the arrow hit one who stood by and not the man aimed at; or, one who frequented a certain place was the only one who did not go there on a certain occasion, while those who went there then for the first time met their death. All such instances appear to be examples of good fortune.

The definition of virtue, with which the topic of praise is most closely connected, must be left until we come to treat of the latter.

6. It is evident, then, what things, likely to happen or already existing, the orator should aim at, when exhorting, and what when dissuading; for they are opposites. But since the aim before the deliberative orator is that which is expedient, and men deliberate, not about the end, but about the means to the end, which are the things which are expedient in regard to our actions; and since, further, the expedient is good, we must first grasp the elementary notions of good and expedient in general.

Let us assume good to be whatever is desirable for its own sake, or for the sake of which we choose something else; that which is the aim of all things, or of all things that possess sensation or reason; or would be, if they could acquire the latter. Whatever reason might assign to each and whatever reason does assign to each in individual cases, that is good for each; and that whose presence makes a man fit and also independent; and independence in

59

τὸ ποιητικὸν ἢ φυλακτικὸν τῶν τοιούτων, καὶ ᾧ ἀκολουθεῖ τὰ τοιαῦτα, καὶ τὰ κωλυτικὰ τῶν ἐναντίων καὶ τὰ φθαρτικά.

3 Ἀκολουθεῖ δὲ διχῶς· ἢ γὰρ ἅμα ἢ ὕστερον, οἷον τῷ μὲν μανθάνειν τὸ ἐπίστασθαι ὕστερον, τῷ δὲ ὑγιαίνειν τὸ ζῆν ἅμα. καὶ τὰ ποιητικὰ τριχῶς, τὰ μὲν ὡς τὸ ὑγιαίνειν ὑγιείας, τὰ δὲ ὡς σιτία ὑγιείας, τὰ δὲ ὡς τὸ γυμνάζεσθαι, ὅτι ὡς ἐπὶ τὸ 4 πολὺ ποιεῖ ὑγίειαν. τούτων δὲ κειμένων ἀνάγκη τάς τε λήψεις τῶν ἀγαθῶν ἀγαθὰς εἶναι καὶ τὰς τῶν κακῶν ἀποβολάς· ἀκολουθεῖ γὰρ τῷ μὲν τὸ μὴ ἔχειν τὸ κακὸν ἅμα, τῷ δὲ τὸ ἔχειν τὸ ἀγαθὸν 5 ὕστερον. καὶ ἡ ἀντ᾽ ἐλάττονος ἀγαθοῦ μείζονος λῆψις καὶ ἀντὶ μείζονος κακοῦ ἐλάττονος· ᾧ γὰρ 362 b ὑπερέχει τὸ μεῖζον τοῦ ἐλάττονος, τούτῳ γίνεται 6 τοῦ μὲν λῆψις τοῦ δ᾽ ἀποβολή. καὶ τὰς ἀρετὰς δὲ ἀνάγκη ἀγαθὸν εἶναι· κατὰ γὰρ ταύτας εὖ τε διάκεινται οἱ ἔχοντες, καὶ ποιητικαὶ τῶν ἀγαθῶν εἰσὶ καὶ πρακτικαί. περὶ ἑκάστης δέ, καὶ τίς καὶ ποία, 7 χωρὶς ῥητέον. καὶ τὴν ἡδονὴν ἀγαθὸν εἶναι· πάντα γὰρ ἐφίεται τὰ ζῷα αὐτῆς τῇ φύσει. ὥστε καὶ τὰ ἡδέα καὶ τὰ καλὰ ἀνάγκη ἀγαθὰ εἶναι· τὰ μὲν γὰρ ἡδονῆς ποιητικά, τῶν δὲ καλῶν τὰ μὲν ἡδέα τὰ δὲ αὐτὰ καθ᾽ ἑαυτὰ αἱρετά ἐστιν.

8 Ὡς δὲ καθ᾽ ἓν εἰπεῖν, ἀνάγκη ἀγαθὰ εἶναι τάδε. εὐδαιμονία· καὶ γὰρ καθ᾽ αὑτὸ αἱρετὸν καὶ αὔτ9 αρκες, καὶ ἕνεκα αὐτοῦ πολλὰ αἱρούμεθα. δικαιοσύνη, ἀνδρία, σωφροσύνη, μεγαλοψυχία, μεγαλοπρέπεια καὶ αἱ ἄλλαι αἱ τοιαῦται ἕξεις· ἀρεταὶ γὰρ

60

general; and that which produces or preserves such
things, or on which such things follow, or all that is
likely to prevent or destroy their opposites.

Now things follow in two ways—simultaneously or
subsequently; for instance, knowledge is subsequent
to learning, but life is simultaneous with health.
Things which produce act in three ways; thus, healthi-
ness produces health; and so does food; and exercise
as a rule. This being laid down, it necessarily follows
that the acquisition of good things and the loss of
evil things are both good; for it follows simultaneously on the latter that we are rid of that which is
bad, and subsequently on the former that we obtain
possession of that which is good. The same applies
to the acquisition of a greater in place of a less good,
and a less in place of a greater evil; for in proportion
as the greater exceeds the less, there is an acquisition of the one and a loss of the other. The virtues
also must be a good thing; for those who possess
them are in a sound condition, and they are also
productive of good things and practical. However,
we must speak separately concerning each—what it
is, and of what kind. Pleasure also must be a good;
for all living creatures naturally desire it. Hence it
follows that both agreeable and beautiful things must
be good; for the former produce pleasure, while
among beautiful things some are pleasant and others
are desirable in themselves.

To enumerate them one by one, the following
things must necessarily be good. Happiness, since
it is desirable in itself and self-sufficient, and to
obtain it we choose a number of things. Justice,
courage, self-control, magnanimity, magnificence, and
all other similar states of mind, for they are virtues

10 ψυχῆς. καὶ ὑγίεια καὶ κάλλος καὶ τὰ τοιαῦτα·
ἀρεταὶ γὰρ σώματος καὶ ποιητικαὶ πολλῶν, οἷον ἡ
ὑγίεια καὶ ἡδονῆς καὶ τοῦ ζῆν, διὸ καὶ ἄριστον
δοκεῖ εἶναι, ὅτι δύο τῶν τοῖς πολλοῖς τιμιωτάτων
11 αἴτιόν ἐστιν, ἡδονῆς καὶ τοῦ ζῆν. πλοῦτος· ἀρετὴ
12 γὰρ κτήσεως καὶ ποιητικὸν πολλῶν. φίλος καὶ
φιλία· καὶ γὰρ καθ' αὑτὸν αἱρετὸς ὁ φίλος καὶ
13 ποιητικὸς πολλῶν. τιμή, δόξα· καὶ γὰρ ἡδέα καὶ
ποιητικὰ πολλῶν, καὶ ἀκολουθεῖ αὐτοῖς ὡς ἐπὶ τὸ
14 πολὺ τὸ ὑπάρχειν ἐφ' οἷς τιμῶνται. δύναμις τοῦ
λέγειν, τοῦ πράττειν· ποιητικὰ γὰρ πάντα τὰ
15 τοιαῦτα ἀγαθῶν. ἔτι εὐφυΐα, μνήμη, εὐμάθεια,
ἀγχίνοια, πάντα τὰ τοιαῦτα· ποιητικαὶ γὰρ αὗται
ἀγαθῶν αἱ δυνάμεις εἰσίν. ὁμοίως δὲ καὶ αἱ ἐπιστῆμαι πᾶσαι καὶ αἱ τέχναι καὶ τὸ ζῆν· εἰ γὰρ
16 μηδὲν ἄλλο ἔποιτο ἀγαθόν, καθ' αὑτὸ αἱρετόν
ἐστιν. καὶ τὸ δίκαιον· συμφέρον γάρ τι κοινῇ ἐστιν.
17 Ταῦτα μὲν οὖν σχεδὸν τὰ ὁμολογούμενα ἀγαθά
18 ἐστιν· ἐν δὲ τοῖς ἀμφισβητησίμοις ἐκ τῶνδε οἱ
συλλογισμοί. ᾧ τὸ ἐναντίον κακόν, τοῦτ' ἀγαθόν.
19 καὶ οὗ τὸ ἐναντίον τοῖς ἐχθροῖς συμφέρει· οἷον εἰ
τὸ δειλοὺς εἶναι μάλιστα συμφέρει τοῖς ἐχθροῖς,
δῆλον ὅτι ἀνδρία μάλιστα ὠφέλιμον τοῖς πολίταις.
20 καὶ ὅλως ὃ οἱ ἐχθροὶ βούλονται ἢ ἐφ' ᾧ χαίρουσι,
τοὐναντίον τούτῳ ὠφέλιμον φαίνεται· διὸ εὖ εἴρηται

---

^a The excellence of anything is proportionate to its success
in the performance of its proper function. The function of
acquisition is to get something valuable, such as money, and
its " excellence " may be judged by the amount of wealth
obtained.

of the soul. Health, beauty, and the like, for they are virtues of the body and produce many advantages ; for instance, health is productive of pleasure and of life, wherefore it is thought to be best of all, because it is the cause of two things which the majority of men prize most highly. Wealth, since it is the excellence of acquisition *a* and productive of many things. A friend and friendship, since a friend is desirable in himself and produces many advantages. Honour and good repute, since they are agreeable and produce many advantages, and are generally accompanied by the possession of those things for which men are honoured. Eloquence and capacity for action ; for all such faculties are productive of many advantages. Further, natural cleverness, good memory, readiness to learn, quick-wittedness, and all similar qualities ; for these faculties are productive of advantages. The same applies to all the sciences, arts, and even life, for even though no other good should result from it, it is desirable in itself. Lastly, justice, since it is expedient in general for the common weal.

These are nearly all the things generally recognized as good ; in the case of doubtful goods, the arguments in their favour are drawn from the following. That is good the opposite of which is evil, or the opposite of which is advantageous to our enemies ; for instance, if it is specially advantageous to our enemies that we should be cowards, it is clear that courage is specially advantageous to the citizens. And, speaking generally, the opposite of what our enemies desire or of that in which they rejoice, appears to be advantageous ; wherefore it was well said :

ἦ κεν γηθήσαι Πρίαμος.

ἔστι δ' οὐκ ἀεὶ τοῦτο, ἀλλ' ὡς ἐπὶ τὸ πολύ· οὐδὲν
γὰρ κωλύει ἐνίοτε ταὐτὸ συμφέρειν τοῖς ἐναντίοις·
ὅθεν λέγεται ὡς τὰ κακὰ συνάγει τοὺς ἀνθρώπους,
1363 a ὅταν ἦ ταὐτὸ βλαβερὸν ἀμφοῖν.

21 Καὶ ὃ μή ἐστιν ὑπερβολή, τοῦτο ἀγαθόν, ὃ δ' ἂν
22 ἦ μεῖζον ἢ δεῖ, κακόν. καὶ οὗ ἕνεκα πολλὰ πεπόνη-
ται ἢ δεδαπάνηται· φαινόμενον γὰρ ἀγαθὸν ἤδη,
καὶ ὡς τέλος τὸ τοιοῦτον ὑπολαμβάνεται, καὶ
τέλος πολλῶν· τὸ δὲ τέλος ἀγαθόν. ὅθεν ταῦτ'
εἴρηται,

κὰδ δέ κεν εὐχωλὴν Πριάμῳ [καὶ Τρωσὶ λίποιεν
Ἀργείην Ἑλένην]

καὶ

αἰσχρόν τοι δηρόν τε μένειν [κενεόν τε νέεσθαι],

καὶ ἡ παροιμία δέ, τὸ ἐπὶ θύραις τὴν ὑδρίαν.

23 Καὶ οὗ πολλοὶ ἐφίενται, καὶ τὸ περιμάχητον
φαινόμενον· οὗ γὰρ πάντες ἐφίενται, τοῦτ' ἀγαθὸν
24 ἦν, οἱ δὲ πολλοὶ ὥσπερ πάντες φαίνονται. καὶ τὸ
ἐπαινετόν· οὐδεὶς γὰρ τὸ μὴ ἀγαθὸν ἐπαινεῖ. καὶ
ὃ οἱ ἐχθροὶ ἐπαινοῦσιν· ὥσπερ γὰρ πάντες ἤδη

---

[a] *Iliad*, i. 255. The words are those of Nestor to Achilles
and Agamemnon, in which he points out how their enemies
would rejoice if they heard all the story of their quarrel.

[b] Reading ὅ. The ordinary reading οὗ is taken to mean
"that which does not permit of excess," that which is midway between two extremes, the mean. Another suggested
rendering is, "that of which one cannot have too much."

[c] *Iliad*, ii. 160. Addressed by Hera to Athene, begging
her to prevent the Greeks departing from Troy and leaving
Helen behind.

Of a truth Priam would exult.[a]

This is not always the case, but only as a general rule, for there is nothing to prevent one and the same thing being sometimes advantageous to two opposite parties; hence it is said that misfortune brings men together, when a common danger threatens them.

That which is not in excess[b] is good, whereas that which is greater than it should be, is bad. And that which has cost much labour and expense, for it at once is seen to be an apparent good, and such a thing is regarded as an end, and an end of many efforts; now, an end is a good. Wherefore it was said:

And they would [leave Argive Helen for Priam and the Trojans] to boast of,[c]

and,

It is disgraceful to tarry long,[d]

and the proverb, "[to break] the pitcher at the door."[e]

And that which many aim at and which is seen to be competed for by many; for that which all aim at was recognized as a good, and the majority may almost stand for "all." And that which is the object of praise, for no one praises that which is not good. And that which is praised by enemies; for if even

[a] *Iliad*, ii. 298. Spoken by Odysseus. While sympathizing with the desire of the army to leave, he points out that it would be "disgraceful after waiting so long" to return unsuccessful, and exhorts them to hold out.

[e] Proverbial for "lost labour." *Cf.* French "*faire naufrage au port*," and the English "there's many a slip 'twixt cup and lip."

ARISTOTLE

ὁμολογοῦσιν, εἰ καὶ οἱ κακῶς πεπονθότες· διὰ γὰρ
τὸ φανερὸν ὁμολογοῖεν ἄν, ὥσπερ καὶ φαῦλοι οὓς
οἱ ἐχθροὶ ἐπαινοῦσιν. διὸ λελοιδορῆσθαι ὑπέλαβον
Κορίνθιοι ὑπὸ Σιμωνίδου ποιήσαντος

Κορινθίοις δ' οὐ μέμφεται τὸ Ἴλιον.

25 καὶ ὃ τῶν φρονίμων τις ἢ τῶν ἀγαθῶν ἀνδρῶν ἢ
γυναικῶν προέκρινεν, οἷον Ὀδυσσέα Ἀθηνᾶ καὶ
Ἑλένην Θησεὺς καὶ Ἀλέξανδρον αἱ θεαὶ καὶ
Ἀχιλλέα Ὅμηρος.

26 Καὶ ὅλως τὰ προαιρετά· προαιροῦνται δὲ πράττειν τά τε εἰρημένα καὶ τὰ τοῖς ἐχθροῖς κακὰ καὶ
27 τὰ τοῖς φίλοις ἀγαθὰ καὶ τὰ δυνατά. ταῦτα δὲ
διχῶς ἐστί, τά τε γενόμενα ἂν καὶ τὰ ῥᾳδίως γιγνόμενα. ῥᾴδια δὲ ὅσα ἢ ἄνευ λύπης ἢ ἐν ὀλίγῳ χρόνῳ·
τὸ γὰρ χαλεπὸν ὁρίζεται ἢ λύπῃ ἢ πλήθει χρόνου.
καὶ ἐὰν ὡς βούλονται· βούλονται δὲ ἢ μηδὲν κακὸν
ἢ ἔλαττον τοῦ ἀγαθοῦ· τοῦτο δ' ἔσται, ἐὰν ἢ λαν-
28 θάνῃ ἡ τιμωρία ἢ μικρὰ ᾖ. καὶ τὰ ἴδια, καὶ ἃ
μηδείς, καὶ τὰ περιττά· τιμὴ γὰρ οὕτω μᾶλλον.
καὶ τὰ ἁρμόττοντα αὐτοῖς· τοιαῦτα δὲ τά τε προσ-
ήκοντα κατὰ γένος καὶ δύναμιν, καὶ ὧν ἐλλείπειν

---

[a] Meaning that they cannot have done their duty against
their enemies, who would then have blamed them. Another
suggested reading is οὓς οἱ φίλοι ψέγουσι καὶ οὓς οἱ ἐχθροὶ μὴ
ψέγουσι ("those whom their friends blame and whom their
enemies do not blame").

[b] In the *Iliad* Glaucus, a Corinthian, is described as an
ally of the Trojans. Simonides meant to praise, but the
Corinthians were suspicious and thought his words were
meant satirically, in accordance with the view just expressed
by Aristotle. The Simonides referred to is Simonides of
Ceos (Frag. 50, *P.L.G.* iii., where the line is differently
given). Aristotle is evidently quoting from memory, as he
often does, although not always accurately.

those who are injured by it acknowledge its goodness, this amounts to a universal recognition of it ; for it is because of its goodness being evident that they acknowledge it, just as those whom their enemies praise are worthless.[a] Wherefore the Corinthians imagined themselves insulted by Simonides, when he wrote,

> Ilium does not blame the Corinthians.[b]

And that which one of the practically wise or good, man or woman, has chosen before others, as Athene chose Odysseus, Theseus Helen, the goddesses Alexander (Paris), and Homer Achilles.

And, generally speaking, all that is deliberately chosen is good. Now, men deliberately choose to do the things just mentioned, and those which are harmful to their enemies, and advantageous to their friends, and things which are possible. The last are of two kinds : things which might happen,[c] and things which easily happen ; by the latter are meant things that happen without labour or in a short time, for difficulty is defined by labour or length of time. And anything that happens as men wish is good ; and what they wish is either what is not evil at all or is less an evil than a good, which will be the case for instance, whenever the penalty attached to it is unnoticed or light. And things that are peculiar to them, or which no one else possesses,[d] or which are out of the common ; for thus the honour is greater. And things which are appropriate to them ; such are all things befitting them in respect of birth and power. And things which they think they lack,

[c] γενόμενα ἄν: Spengel omits ἄν: i.e. "things which *have* happened."
[d] "Or which no one else has done" (Jebb).

οἴονται, κἂν μικρὰ ᾖ· οὐδὲν γὰρ ἧττον προαιροῦνται
29 ταῦτα πράττειν. καὶ τὰ εὐκατέργαστα· δυνατὰ
γὰρ ὡς ῥᾴδια· εὐκατέργαστα δέ, ἃ πάντες ἢ οἱ
πολλοὶ ἢ οἱ ὅμοιοι ἢ οἱ ἥττους κατώρθωσαν. καὶ
ἃ χαριοῦνται τοῖς φίλοις, ἢ ἃ ἀπεχθήσονται τοῖς
ἐχθροῖς. καὶ ὅσα οὓς θαυμάζουσι προαιροῦνται
πράττειν. καὶ πρὸς ἃ εὐφυεῖς εἰσι καὶ ἔμπειροι·
ῥᾷον γὰρ κατορθώσειν οἴονται. καὶ ἃ μηδεὶς
φαῦλος· ἐπαινετὰ γὰρ μᾶλλον. καὶ ὧν ἐπιθυμοῦντες τυγχάνουσιν· οὐ γὰρ μόνον ἡδὺ ἀλλὰ καὶ
30 βέλτιον φαίνεται. καὶ μάλιστα ἕκαστοι πρὸς ἃ
1363 b τοιοῦτοι, οἷον οἱ φιλόνικοι εἰ νίκη ἔσται, οἱ φιλότιμοι εἰ τιμή, οἱ φιλοχρήματοι εἰ χρήματα, καὶ οἱ
ἄλλοι ὡσαύτως. περὶ μὲν οὖν ἀγαθοῦ καὶ τοῦ
συμφέροντος ἐκ τούτων ληπτέον τὰς πίστεις.

7. Ἐπεὶ δὲ πολλάκις ὁμολογοῦντες ἄμφω συμφέρειν περὶ τοῦ μᾶλλον ἀμφισβητοῦσιν, ἐφεξῆς ἂν
εἴη λεκτέον περὶ τοῦ μείζονος ἀγαθοῦ καὶ τοῦ
2 μᾶλλον συμφέροντος. ἔστω δὴ ὑπερέχον μὲν τοσοῦτον καὶ ἔτι, ὑπερεχόμενον δὲ τὸ ἐνυπάρχον.
καὶ μεῖζον μὲν ἀεὶ καὶ πλεῖον πρὸς ἔλαττον, μέγα
δὲ καὶ μικρὸν καὶ πολὺ καὶ ὀλίγον πρὸς τὸ τῶν
πολλῶν μέγεθος, καὶ ὑπερέχον μὲν τὸ μέγα, τὸ δὲ
ἐλλεῖπον μικρόν, καὶ πολὺ καὶ ὀλίγον ὡσαύτως.
3 ἐπεὶ οὖν ἀγαθὸν λέγομεν τό τε αὐτὸ αὑτοῦ ἕνεκα

however unimportant ; for none the less they deliberately choose to acquire them. And things which are easy of accomplishment, for being easy they are possible ; such things are those in which all, or most men, or those who are equals or inferiors have been successful. And things whereby they will gratify friends or incur the hatred of enemies. And all things that those whom they admire deliberately choose to do. And those things in regard to which they are clever naturally or by experience ; for they hope to be more easily successful in them. And things which no worthless man would approve, for that makes them the more commendable. And things which they happen to desire, for such things seem not only agreeable, but also better. Lastly, and above all, each man thinks those things good which are the object of his special desire, as victory of the man who desires victory, honour of the ambitious man, money of the avaricious, and so in other instances. These then are the materials from which we must draw our arguments in reference to good and the expedient.

7. But since men often agree that both of two things are useful, but dispute which is the more so, we must next speak of the greater good and the more expedient. Let one thing, then, be said to exceed another, when it is as great and something more—and to be exceeded when it is contained in the other. " Greater " and " more " always imply a relation with less ; " great " and " small," " much " and " little " with the general size of things ; the " great " is that which exceeds, and that which falls short of it is " small " ; and similarly " much " and " little." Since, besides, we call good that which is

καὶ μὴ ἄλλου αἱρετόν, καὶ οὗ πάντ' ἐφίεται, καὶ ὃ
νοῦν ἂν καὶ φρόνησιν λαβόντα ἕλοιτο, καὶ τὸ ποιητικὸν καὶ τὸ φυλακτικόν, ἢ ᾧ ἕπεται τὰ τοιαῦτα,
τὸ δ' οὗ ἕνεκα τὸ τέλος ἐστί, τέλος δ' ἐστὶν οὗ
ἕνεκα τὰ ἄλλα, αὐτῷ δὲ ἀγαθὸν τὸ πρὸς αὐτὸν
ταῦτα πεπονθός, ἀνάγκη τά τε πλείω τοῦ ἑνὸς καὶ
τῶν ἐλαττόνων, συναριθμουμένου τοῦ ἑνὸς ἢ τῶν
ἐλαττόνων, μεῖζον ἀγαθὸν εἶναι· ὑπερέχει γάρ, τὸ
δὲ ἐνυπάρχον ὑπερέχεται.

4 Καὶ ἐὰν τὸ μέγιστον τοῦ μεγίστου ὑπερέχῃ, καὶ
αὐτὰ αὐτῶν· καὶ ὅσα αὐτὰ αὐτῶν, καὶ τὸ μέγιστον
τοῦ μεγίστου· οἷον εἰ ὁ μέγιστος ἀνὴρ γυναικὸς
τῆς μεγίστης μείζων, καὶ ὅλως οἱ ἄνδρες τῶν
γυναικῶν μείζους· καὶ εἰ οἱ ἄνδρες ὅλως τῶν γυναικῶν μείζους, καὶ ἀνὴρ ὁ μέγιστος τῆς μεγίστης
γυναικὸς μείζων· ἀνάλογον γὰρ ἔχουσιν αἱ ὑπερ-
οχαὶ τῶν γενῶν καὶ τῶν μεγίστων ἐν αὐτοῖς. καὶ
5 ὅταν τόδε μὲν τῷδε ἕπηται, ἐκεῖνο δὲ τούτῳ μή·
ἕπεται δὲ ἢ τῷ ἅμα ἢ τῷ ἐφεξῆς ἢ τῇ δυνάμει·
ἐνυπάρχει γὰρ ἡ χρῆσις ἡ τοῦ ἑπομένου ἐν τῇ
θατέρου. ἕπεται δὲ ἅμα μὲν τῷ ὑγιαίνειν τὸ ζῆν,
τούτῳ δὲ ἐκεῖνο οὔ, ὕστερον δὲ τῷ μανθάνειν τὸ
ἐπίστασθαι, δυνάμει δὲ τῷ ἱεροσυλεῖν τὸ ἀπο-
στερεῖν· ὁ γὰρ ἱεροσυλήσας κἂν ἀποστερήσειεν. καὶ

---

[a] The one, the smaller number, and the greater number
must be of the same species. Thus, 5 pounds is a greater
good than 2 pounds; but 5 farthings is not a greater good
than 2 pounds, since the smaller number is not reckoned in
with the greater (Buckley).

[b] If B (life) follows on, is the consequent of A (health),
but A is not the consequent of B, then A is a greater good
than B.

desirable for its own sake and not for anything else,
and that which all things aim at and which they
would choose if they possessed reason and practical
wisdom ; and that which is productive or protective
of good, or on which such things follow ; and since that
for the sake of which anything is done is the end,
and the end is that for the sake of which everything
else is done, and that is good for each man which
relatively to him presents all these conditions, it
necessarily follows that a larger number of good
things is a greater good than one or a smaller
number, if the one or the smaller number is reckoned
as one of them ;[a] for it exceeds them and that
which is contained is exceeded.

And if that which is greatest in one class surpass
that which is greatest in another class, the first class
will surpass the second ; and whenever one class
surpasses another, the greatest of that class will
surpass the greatest of the other. For instance, if
the biggest man is greater than the biggest woman,
men in general will be bigger than women ; and if
men in general are bigger than women, the biggest
man will be bigger than the biggest woman ; for the
superiority of classes and of the greatest things contained in them are proportionate. And when this
follows on that, but not that on this [then " that "
is the greater good] ;[b] for the enjoyment of that
which follows is contained in that of the other.
Now, things follow simultaneously, or successively,
or potentially ; thus, life follows simultaneously on
health, but not health on life ; knowledge follows
subsequently on learning [but not learning on
knowledge] ; and simple theft potentially on sacrilege, for one who commits sacrilege will also steal.

6 τὰ ὑπερέχοντα τοῦ αὐτοῦ μείζονι μείζω· ἀνάγκη
7 γὰρ ὑπερέχειν καὶ τοῦ μείζονος. καὶ τὰ μείζονος
ἀγαθοῦ ποιητικὰ μείζω· τοῦτο γὰρ ἦν τὸ μείζονος
ποιητικῷ εἶναι. καὶ οὗ τὸ ποιητικὸν μείζον, ὡσ-
αύτως· εἰ γὰρ τὸ ὑγιεινὸν αἱρετώτερον τοῦ ἡδέος
καὶ μεῖζον ἀγαθόν, καὶ ἡ ὑγίεια τῆς ἡδονῆς μείζων.
8 καὶ τὸ αἱρετώτερον καθ᾽ αὑτὸ τοῦ μὴ καθ᾽ αὑτό,
1364a οἷον ἰσχὺς ὑγιεινοῦ· τὸ μὲν γὰρ οὐχ αὑτοῦ ἕνεκα,
9 τὸ δὲ αὑτοῦ, ὅπερ ἦν τὸ ἀγαθόν. κἂν ᾖ τὸ μὲν
τέλος, τὸ δὲ μὴ τέλος· τὸ μὲν γὰρ ἄλλου ἕνεκα, τὸ
δὲ αὑτοῦ, οἷον τὸ γυμνάζεσθαι τοῦ εὖ ἔχειν τὸ
10 σῶμα. καὶ τὸ ἧττον προσδεόμενον θατέρου ἢ
ἑτέρων· αὐταρκέστερον γάρ· ἧττον δὲ προσδεῖται
11 τὸ ἐλαττόνων ἢ ῥαόνων προσδεόμενον. καὶ ὅταν
τόδε μὲν ἄνευ τοῦδε μὴ ᾖ ἢ μὴ δυνατὸν ᾖ γενέσθαι,
θάτερον δὲ ἄνευ τούτου· αὐταρκέστερον δὲ τὸ μὴ
δεόμενον, ὥστε φαίνεται μεῖζον ἀγαθόν.
12. Κἂν ᾖ ἀρχή, τὸ δὲ μὴ ἀρχή. κἂν ᾖ αἴτιον, τὸ δ᾽
οὐκ αἴτιον, διὰ τὸ αὐτό· ἄνευ γὰρ αἰτίου καὶ ἀρχῆς
ἀδύνατον εἶναι ἢ γενέσθαι. καὶ δυοῖν ἀρχαῖν τὸ
ἀπὸ τῆς μείζονος μεῖζον, καὶ δυοῖν αἰτίοιν τὸ ἀπὸ
τοῦ μείζονος αἰτίου μεῖζον. καὶ ἀνάπαλιν δὴ δυοῖν
ἀρχαῖν ἡ τοῦ μείζονος ἀρχὴ μείζων καὶ δυοῖν αἰτίοιν

• Eight is greater than 2 by 6, which itself is greater than 2.

And things which exceed the same thing by a greater amount [than something else] are greater, for they must also exceed the greater.[a] And things which produce a greater good are greater ; for this we agreed was the meaning of productive of greater. And similarly, that which is produced by a greater cause ; for if that which produces health is more desirable than that which produces pleasure and a greater good, then health is a greater good than pleasure. And that which is more desirable in itself is superior to that which is not ; for example, strength is a greater good than the wholesome, which is not desirable for its own sake, while strength is ; and this we agreed was the meaning of a good. And the end is a greater good than the means ; for the latter is desirable for the sake of something else, the former for its own sake ; for instance, exercise is only a means for the acquirement of a good constitution. And that which has less need of one or several other things in addition is a greater good, for it is more independent (and " having less need " means needing fewer or easier additions). And when one thing does not exist or cannot be brought into existence without the aid of another, but that other can, then that which needs no aid is more independent, and accordingly is seen to be a greater good.

And if one thing is a first principle, and another not ; if one thing is a cause and another not, for the same reason ; for without cause or first principle nothing can exist or come into existence. And if there are two first principles or two causes, that which results from the greater is greater ; and conversely, when there are two first principles or two causes, that which is the first cause or principle

13 τὸ τοῦ μείζονος αἴτιον μεῖζον. δῆλον οὖν ἐκ τῶν εἰρημένων ὅτι ἀμφοτέρως μεῖζόν ἐστιν· καὶ γὰρ εἰ ἀρχή, τὸ δὲ μὴ ἀρχή, δόξει μεῖζον εἶναι, καὶ εἰ μὴ ἀρχή, τὸ δὲ ἀρχή, τὸ γὰρ τέλος μεῖζον καὶ οὐκ ἀρχή, ὥσπερ ὁ Λεωδάμας κατηγορῶν ἔφη Καλλιστράτου τὸν βουλεύσαντα τοῦ πράξαντος μᾶλλον ἀδικεῖν· οὐ γὰρ ἂν πραχθῆναι μὴ βουλευσαμένου· πάλιν δὲ καὶ Χαβρίου, τὸν πράξαντα τοῦ βουλεύσαντος· οὐ γὰρ ἂν γενέσθαι, εἰ μὴ ἦν ὁ πράξων· τούτου γὰρ ἕνεκα ἐπιβουλεύειν, ὅπως πράξωσιν.

14 Καὶ τὸ σπανιώτερον τοῦ ἀφθόνου, οἷον χρυσὸς σιδήρου ἀχρηστότερος ὤν· μεῖζον γὰρ ἡ κτῆσις διὰ τὸ χαλεπωτέραν εἶναι. ἄλλον δὲ τρόπον τὸ ἄφθονον τοῦ σπανίου, ὅτι ἡ χρῆσις ὑπερέχει· τὸ γὰρ πολλάκις τοῦ ὀλιγάκις ὑπερέχει· ὅθεν λέγεται

ἄριστον μὲν ὕδωρ.

15 καὶ ὅλως τὸ χαλεπώτερον τοῦ ῥᾴονος· σπανιώτερον γάρ. ἄλλον δὲ τρόπον τὸ ῥᾷον τοῦ χαλεπω-

---

[a] A thing may be of greater importance in two ways: (*a*) that which is a first principle is superior to that which is not; (*b*) that which is not a first principle, but an end, is superior to that which is a first principle; for the end is superior to the means. In the illustration that follows: (*a*) the first principle (suggesting the plot) is said to be of more importance (worse) than the end or result (carrying out the plot); (*b*) on the other hand, this end is said to be worse than the first principle, since the end is superior to the means. Thus the question of the amount of guilt can be argued both ways.

[b] Oropus, a frontier-town of Boeotia and Attica, had been occupied by the Thebans (366 B.C.). Callistratus suggested an arrangement which was agreed to and carried out by Chabrias—that the town should remain in Theban possession for the time being. Negotiations proved unsuccessful and

of the greater is greater. It is clear then, from what has been said, that a thing may be greater in two ways ; for if it is a first principle but another is not, it will appear to be greater, and if it is not a first principle [but an end], while another is ; for the end is greater and not a first principle.[a] Thus, Leodamas, when accusing Callistratus,[b] declared that the man who had given the advice was more guilty than the one who carried it out ; for if he had not suggested it, it could not have been carried out. And conversely, when accusing Chabrias, he declared that the man who had carried out the advice was more guilty than the one who had given it ; for it could not have been carried out, had there not been some one to do so, and the reason why people devised plots was that others might carry them out.

And that which is scarcer is a greater good than that which is abundant, as gold than iron, although it is less useful, but the possession of it is more valuable, since it is more difficult of acquisition. From another point of view, that which is abundant is to be preferred to that which is scarce, because the use of it is greater, for " often " exceeds " seldom "; whence the saying :

Water is best.[c]

And, speaking generally, that which is more difficult is preferable to that which is easier of attainment, for it is scarcer ; but from another point of view that which is easier is preferable to that which is more

the Thebans refused to leave, whereupon Chabrias and Callistratus were brought to trial. Leodamas was an Athenian orator, pupil of Isocrates, and pro-Theban in his political views.

[c] Pindar, *Olympia*, i. 1.

ARISTOTLE

16 τέρου· ἔχει γὰρ ὡς βουλόμεθα. καὶ ᾧ τὸ ἐναντίον
μεῖζον, καὶ οὗ ἡ στέρησις μείζων. καὶ ἀρετὴ μὴ
ἀρετῆς καὶ κακία μὴ κακίας μείζων· τὰ μὲν γὰρ
17 τέλη, τὰ δ᾽ οὐ τέλη. καὶ ὧν τὰ ἔργα καλλίω ἢ
αἰσχίω, μείζω αὐτά. καὶ ὧν αἱ κακίαι καὶ αἱ
ἀρεταὶ μείζους, καὶ τὰ ἔργα μείζω, ἐπείπερ ὡς τὰ
αἴτια καὶ αἱ ἀρχαί, καὶ τὰ ἀποβαίνοντα, καὶ ὡς τὰ
18 ἀποβαίνοντα, καὶ τὰ αἴτια καὶ αἱ ἀρχαί. καὶ ὧν
ἡ ὑπεροχὴ αἱρετωτέρα ἢ καλλίων, οἷον τὸ ἀκριβῶς
ὁρᾶν αἱρετώτερον τοῦ ὀσφραίνεσθαι· καὶ γὰρ ὄψις
1364 b ὀσφρήσεως· καὶ τὸ φιλεταῖρον εἶναι τοῦ φιλοχρή-
ματον μᾶλλον κάλλιον, ὥστε καὶ φιλεταιρία φιλο-
χρηματίας. καὶ ἀντικειμένως δὲ τῶν βελτιόνων
αἱ ὑπερβολαὶ βελτίους καὶ καλλιόνων καλλίους.
19 καὶ ὧν αἱ ἐπιθυμίαι καλλίους ἢ βελτίους· αἱ γὰρ
μείζους ὀρέξεις μειζόνων εἰσίν. καὶ τῶν καλλιόνων δὲ ἢ καὶ βελτιόνων αἱ ἐπιθυμίαι βελτίους καὶ
καλλίους διὰ τὸ αὐτό.

20 Καὶ ὧν αἱ ἐπιστῆμαι καλλίους ἢ σπουδαιότεραι,
καὶ τὰ πράγματα καλλίω καὶ σπουδαιότερα· ὡς
γὰρ ἔχει ἡ ἐπιστήμη, καὶ τὸ ἀληθές· κελεύει δὲ τὸ
αὑτῆς ἑκάστη. καὶ τῶν σπουδαιοτέρων δὲ καὶ
21 καλλιόνων αἱ ἐπιστῆμαι ἀνάλογον διὰ ταῦτα. καὶ
ὃ κρίνειαν ἂν ἢ κεκρίκασιν οἱ φρόνιμοι ἢ πάντες ἢ
οἱ πολλοὶ ἢ οἱ πλείους ἢ οἱ κράτιστοι ἀγαθὸν ἢ

---

a e.g. it is worse to be blind than deaf; therefore sight is
better than hearing (Schrader).

difficult; for its nature is as we wish. And that, the contrary or the deprivation of which is greater, is the greater good.[a] And virtue is greater than non-virtue, and vice than non-vice; for virtues and vices are ends, the others not. And those things whose works are nobler or more disgraceful are themselves greater; and the works of those things, the vices and virtues of which are greater, will also be greater, since between causes and first principles compared with results there is the same relation as between results compared with causes and first principles. Things, superiority in which is more desirable or nobler, are to be preferred; for instance, sharpness of sight is preferable to keenness of smell; for sight is better than smell. And loving one's friends more than money is nobler, whence it follows that love of friends is nobler than love of money. And, on the other hand, the better and nobler things are, the better and nobler will be their superiority; and similarly, those things, the desire for which is nobler and better, are themselves nobler and better, for greater longings are directed towards greater objects. For the same reason, the better and nobler the object, the better and nobler are the desires.

And when the sciences are nobler and more dignified, the nobler and more dignified are their subjects; for as is the science, so is the truth which is its object, and each science prescribes that which properly belongs to it; and, by analogy, the nobler and more dignified the objects of a science, the nobler and more dignified is the science itself, for the same reasons. And that which men of practical wisdom, either all, or more, or the best of them, would judge, or have judged, to be a greater good, must necessarily

77

ARISTOTLE

μεῖζον, ἀνάγκη οὕτως ἔχειν, ἢ ἁπλῶς ἢ ᾗ κατὰ τὴν
φρόνησιν ἔκριναν. ἔστι δὲ τοῦτο κοινὸν καὶ κατὰ
τῶν ἄλλων· καὶ γὰρ τὶ καὶ ποσὸν καὶ ποιὸν οὕτως
ἔχει ὡς ἂν ἡ ἐπιστήμη καὶ ἡ φρόνησις εἴποι. ἀλλ'
ἐπ' ἀγαθῶν εἰρήκαμεν· ὥρισται γὰρ ἀγαθὸν εἶναι,
ὃ λαβόντα τὰ πράγματα φρόνησιν ἕλοιτ' ἂν ἕκα-
στον· δῆλον οὖν ὅτι καὶ μεῖζον, ὃ μᾶλλον ἡ φρόνησις
22 λέγει. καὶ τὸ τοῖς βελτίοσιν ὑπάρχον, ἢ ἁπλῶς ἢ
ᾗ βελτίους, οἷον ἀνδρία ἰσχύος. καὶ ὃ ἕλοιτ' ἂν ὁ
βελτίων, ἢ ἁπλῶς ἢ ᾗ βελτίων, οἷον τὸ ἀδικεῖσθαι
μᾶλλον ἢ ἀδικεῖν· τοῦτο γὰρ ὁ δικαιότερος ἂν
23 ἕλοιτο. καὶ τὸ ἥδιον τοῦ ἧττον ἡδέος· τὴν γὰρ
ἡδονὴν πάντα διώκει, καὶ αὐτοῦ ἕνεκα τοῦ ἥδεσθαι
ὀρέγονται, ὥρισται δὲ τούτοις τὸ ἀγαθὸν καὶ τὸ
τέλος. ἥδιον δὲ τό τε ἀλυπότερον καὶ τὸ πολυ-
24 χρονιώτερον ἡδύ. καὶ τὸ κάλλιον τοῦ ἧττον καλοῦ·
τὸ γὰρ καλόν ἐστιν ἤτοι τὸ ἡδὺ ἢ τὸ καθ' αὑτὸ
25 αἱρετόν. καὶ ὅσων αὐτοὶ αὑτοῖς ἢ φίλοις βούλονται αἴτιοι εἶναι μᾶλλον, ταῦτα μείζω ἀγαθά,
26 ὅσων δὲ ἥκιστα, μείζω κακά. καὶ τὰ πολυχρο-
νιώτερα τῶν ὀλιγοχρονιωτέρων καὶ τὰ βεβαιότερα
τῶν μὴ βεβαιοτέρων· ὑπερέχει γὰρ ἡ χρῆσις τῶν
μὲν τῷ χρόνῳ τῶν δὲ τῇ βουλήσει· ὅταν γὰρ βού-
λωνται, ὑπάρχει μᾶλλον ἡ τοῦ βεβαίου.
27 Καὶ ὡς ἂν ἐκ τῶν συστοίχων καὶ τῶν ὁμοίων

78

be such, either absolutely or in so far as they have judged as men of practical wisdom. The same may be said in regard to everything else ; for the nature, quantity, and quality of things are such as would be defined by science and practical wisdom. But our statement only applies to goods ; for we defined that as good which everything, if possessed of practical wisdom, would choose ; hence it is evident that that is a greater good to which practical wisdom assigns the superiority. So also are those things which better men possess, either absolutely, or in so far as they are better ; for instance courage is better than strength. And what the better man would choose, either absolutely or in so far as he is better ; thus, it is better to suffer wrong than to commit it, for that is what the juster man would choose. And that which is more agreeable rather than that which is less so ; for all things pursue pleasure and desire it for its own sake ; and it is by these conditions that the good and the end have been defined. And that is more agreeable which is less subject to pain and is agreeable for a longer time. And that which is nobler than that which is less noble ; for the noble is that which is either agreeable or desirable in itself. And all things which we have a greater desire to be instrumental in procuring for ourselves or for our friends are greater goods, and those as to which our desire is least are greater evils. And things that last longer are preferable to those that are of shorter duration, and those that are safer to those that are less so ; for time increases the use of the first and the wish that of the second ; for whenever we wish, we can make greater use of things that are safe.

And things in all cases follow the relations between

πτώσεων, καὶ τἆλλ' ἀκολουθεῖ· οἷον εἰ τὸ ἀνδρείως
κάλλιον καὶ αἱρετώτερον τοῦ σωφρόνος, καὶ ἀνδρία
σωφροσύνης αἱρετωτέρα καὶ τὸ ἀνδρεῖον εἶναι τοῦ
28 σωφρονεῖν. καὶ ὃ πάντες αἱροῦνται τοῦ μὴ ὃ
πάντες. καὶ ὃ οἱ πλείους ἢ [ὃ]¹ οἱ ἐλάττους· ἀγαθὸν
1365a γὰρ ἦν οὗ πάντες ἐφίενται, ὥστε καὶ μεῖζον οὗ
μᾶλλον. καὶ ὃ οἱ ἀμφισβητοῦντες ἢ οἱ ἐχθροὶ ἢ οἱ
κρίνοντες ἢ οὓς οὗτοι κρίνουσιν· τὸ μὲν γὰρ ὡς ἂν
εἰ πάντες φαῖεν ἐστί, τὸ δὲ οἱ κύριοι καὶ οἱ εἰδότες.
29 καὶ ὁτὲ μὲν οὗ πάντες μετέχουσι μεῖζον· ἀτιμία
γὰρ τὸ μὴ μετέχειν· ὁτὲ δὲ οὗ μηδεὶς ἢ οὗ ὀλίγοι·
30 σπανιώτερον γάρ. καὶ τὰ ἐπαινετώτερα· καλλίω
γάρ. καὶ ὧν αἱ τιμαὶ μείζους, ὡσαύτως· ἡ γὰρ
τιμὴ ὥσπερ ἀξία τις ἐστίν. καὶ ὧν αἱ ζημίαι
31 μείζους. καὶ τὰ τῶν ὁμολογουμένων ἢ φαινομένων
μεγάλων μείζω. καὶ διαιρούμενα δὲ εἰς τὰ μέρη
τὰ αὐτὰ μείζω φαίνεται· πλειόνων γὰρ ὑπερέχειν
φαίνεται. ὅθεν καὶ ὁ ποιητής φησι πεῖσαι τὸν
Μελέαγρον ἀναστῆναι

ὅσσα κάκ' ἀνθρώποισι πέλει τῶν ἄστυ ἁλώῃ·
λαοὶ μὲν φθινύθουσι, πόλιν δέ τε πῦρ ἀμαθύνει,
τέκνα δέ τ' ἄλλοι ἄγουσιν.

Καὶ τὸ συντιθέναι καὶ ἐποικοδομεῖν, ὥσπερ

¹ Inserted by Spengel.

a "Things of which the prices are greater, price being a sort of worth" (Jebb).

b Or, "superiority over a greater number of things."

c After πεῖσαι all the mss. except Aᶜ (Paris) have λέγουσαν. If this is retained, it must refer to Meleager's wife Cleopatra, who "persuaded him . . . by quoting." As the text stands, the literal rendering is: "the poet says that (the recital of the three verses) persuaded." The passage is from *Iliad*, ix. 592-594 (slightly different). d See Glossary.

co-ordinates and similar inflexions; for instance, if "courageously" is nobler than and preferable to "temperately," then "courage" is preferable to "temperance," and it is better to be "courageous" than "temperate." And that which is chosen by all is better than that which is not; and that which the majority choose than that which the minority choose; for, as we have said, the good is that which all desire, and consequently a good is greater, the more it is desired. The same applies to goods which are recognized as greater by opponents or enemies, by judges, or by those whom they select; for in the one case it would be, so to say, the verdict of all mankind, in the other that of those who are acknowledged authorities and experts. And sometimes a good is greater in which all participate, for it is a disgrace not to participate in it; sometimes when none or only a few participate in it, for it is scarcer. And things which are more praiseworthy, since they are nobler. And in the same way things which are more highly honoured,[a] for honour is a sort of measure of worth; and conversely those things are greater evils, the punishment for which is greater. And those things which are greater than what is acknowledged, or appears, to be great, are greater. And the same whole when divided into parts appears greater, for there appears to be superiority in a greater number of things.[b] Whence the poet says that Meleager was persuaded to rise up and fight by the recital of[c]

All the ills that befall those whose city is taken; the people perish, and fire utterly destroys the city, and strangers carry off the children.

Combination and building up,[d] as employed by

Ἐπίχαρμος, διά τε τὸ αὐτὸ τῇ διαιρέσει (ἡ γὰρ
σύνθεσις ὑπεροχὴν δείκνυσι πολλήν) καὶ ὅτι ἀρχὴ
32 φαίνεται μεγάλων καὶ αἴτιον. ἐπεὶ δὲ τὸ χαλεπώτερον καὶ σπανιώτερον μεῖζον, καὶ οἱ καιροὶ
καὶ αἱ ἡλικίαι καὶ οἱ τόποι καὶ οἱ χρόνοι καὶ αἱ
δυνάμεις ποιοῦσι μεγάλα· εἰ γὰρ παρὰ δύναμιν καὶ
παρ' ἡλικίαν καὶ παρὰ τοὺς ὁμοίους, καὶ εἰ οὕτως
ἢ ἐνταῦθα ἢ τόθ', ἕξει μέγεθος καὶ καλῶν καὶ
ἀγαθῶν καὶ δικαίων καὶ τῶν ἐναντίων. ὅθεν καὶ
τὸ ἐπίγραμμα τῷ ὀλυμπιονίκῃ·

πρόσθε μὲν ἀμφ' ὤμοισιν ἔχων τραχεῖαν ἄσιλλαν
ἰχθῦς ἐξ Ἄργους εἰς Τέγεαν ἔφερον.

καὶ ὁ Ἰφικράτης αὐτὸν ἐνεκωμίαζε λέγων ἐξ ὧν
33 ὑπῆρξε ταῦτα. καὶ τὸ αὐτοφυὲς τοῦ ἐπικτήτου·
χαλεπώτερον γάρ. ὅθεν καὶ ὁ ποιητής φησιν

αὐτοδίδακτος δ' εἰμί.

34 καὶ τὸ μεγάλου μέγιστον μέρος· οἷον Περικλῆς τὸν
ἐπιτάφιον λέγων, τὴν νεότητα ἐκ τῆς πόλεως ἀν-
ῃρῆσθαι ὥσπερ τὸ ἔαρ ἐκ τοῦ ἐνιαυτοῦ εἰ ἐξαιρεθείη.
35 καὶ τὰ ἐν χρείᾳ μείζονι χρήσιμα, οἷον τὰ ἐν γήρᾳ
καὶ νόσοις. καὶ δυοῖν τὸ ἐγγύτερον τοῦ τέλους.
καὶ τὸ αὐτῷ τοῦ ἁπλῶς. καὶ τὸ δυνατὸν τοῦ

---

[a] Epicharmus (c. 550-460 B.C.), writer of comedies and
Pythagorean philosopher, was born at Megara in Sicily
(according to others, in the island of Cos). His comedies,
written in the Doric dialect, and without a chorus, were
either mythological or comedies of manners, as extant titles
show. Plato speaks of him as "the prince of comedy" and
Horace states definitely that he was imitated by Plautus.

[b] Simonides, Frag. 163 (*P.L.G.* iii.).

[c] Or, the yoke to which the basket, like our milk-pails
long ago, was attached.

Epicharmus,[a] produce the same effect as division, and for the same reason ; for combination is an exhibition of great superiority and appears to be the origin and cause of great things. And since that which is harder to obtain and scarcer is greater, it follows that special occasions, ages, places, times, and powers, produce great effects ; for if a man does things beyond his powers, beyond his age, and beyond what his equals could do, if they are done in such a manner, in such a place, and at such a time, they will possess importance in actions that are noble, good, or just, or the opposite. Hence the epigram [b] on the Olympian victor :

> Formerly, with a rough basket [c] on my shoulders, I used to carry fish from Argos to Tegea.

And Iphicrates lauded himself, saying, " Look what I started from ! " And that which is natural is a greater good than that which is acquired, because it is harder. Whence the poet says :

> Self-taught am I.[d]

And that which is the greatest part of that which is great is more to be desired ; as Pericles said in his Funeral Oration, that the removal of the youth from the city was like the year being robbed of its spring.[e] And those things which are available in greater need, as in old age and illness, are greater goods. And of two things that which is nearer the end proposed is preferable. And that which is useful for the individual is preferable to that which is useful ab-

---

[d] *Odyssey*, xxii. 347. The words are those of the minstrel Phemius, who was forced to sing to the suitors of Penelope.

[e] Not in the oration in Thucydides (ii. 35).

ἀδυνάτου· τὸ μὲν γὰρ αὐτῷ, τὸ δ' οὔ. καὶ τὰ ἐν
τέλει τοῦ βίου· τέλη γὰρ μᾶλλον τὰ πρὸς τῷ τέλει.

36 Καὶ τὰ πρὸς ἀλήθειαν τῶν πρὸς δόξαν. ὅρος δὲ
1365 b τοῦ πρὸς δόξαν, ὃ λανθάνειν μέλλων οὐκ ἂν ἕλοιτο.
διὸ καὶ τὸ εὖ πάσχειν τοῦ εὖ ποιεῖν δόξειεν ἂν
αἱρετώτερον εἶναι· τὸ μὲν γὰρ κἂν λανθάνῃ αἱρή-
σεται, ποιεῖν δ' εὖ λανθάνων οὐ δοκεῖ ἂν ἑλέσθαι.

37 καὶ ὅσα εἶναι μᾶλλον ἢ δοκεῖν βούλονται· πρὸς
ἀλήθειαν γὰρ μᾶλλον. διὸ καὶ τὴν δικαιοσύνην
φασὶ μικρὸν εἶναι, ὅτι δοκεῖν ἢ εἶναι αἱρετώτερον·

38 τὸ δὲ ὑγιαίνειν οὔ. καὶ τὸ πρὸς πολλὰ χρησιμώτερον, οἷον τὸ πρὸς τὸ ζῆν καὶ εὖ ζῆν καὶ τὴν
ἡδονὴν καὶ τὸ πράττειν τὰ καλά. διὸ καὶ ὁ πλοῦτος
καὶ ἡ ὑγίεια μέγιστα δοκεῖ εἶναι· ἅπαντα γὰρ ἔχει

39 ταῦτα. καὶ τὸ ἀλυπότερον καὶ τὸ μεθ' ἡδονῆς·
πλείω γὰρ ἑνός, ὥστε ὑπάρχει καὶ ἡ ἡδονὴ ἀγαθὸν
καὶ ἡ ἀλυπία. καὶ δυοῖν ὃ τῷ αὐτῷ προστιθέ-

40 μενον μεῖζον τὸ ὅλον ποιεῖ. καὶ ἃ μὴ λανθάνει
παρόντα ἢ [ἃ] λανθάνει· πρὸς ἀλήθειαν γὰρ τείνει
ταῦτα. διὸ τὸ πλουτεῖν φανείη ἂν μεῖζον ἀγαθὸν

---

^a Or, reading καὶ ἁπλῶς : " that which is useful both to
the individual and absolutely is a greater good " (than that
which is only useful in one way), but this necessitates a
considerable ellipse.

solutely ;[a] that which is possible to that which is impossible ; for it is the possible that is useful to us, not the impossible. And those things which are at the end of life ; for things near the end are more like ends.

And real things are preferable to those that have reference to public opinion, the latter being defined as those which a man would not choose if they were likely to remain unnoticed by others. It would seem then that it is better to receive than to confer a benefit ; for one would choose the former even if it should pass unnoticed, whereas one would not choose to confer a benefit, if it were likely to remain unknown. Those things also are to be preferred, which men would rather possess in reality than in appearance, because they are nearer the truth ; wherefore it is commonly said that justice is a thing of little importance, because people prefer to appear just than to be just ; and this is not the case, for instance, in regard to health. The same may be said of things that serve several ends ; for instance, those that assist us to live, to live well, to enjoy life, and to do noble actions ; wherefore health and wealth seem to be the greatest goods, for they include all these advantages. And that which is more free from pain and accompanied by pleasure is a greater good ; for there is more than one good, since pleasure and freedom from pain combined are both goods. And of two goods the greater is that which, added to one and the same, makes the whole greater. And those things, the presence of which does not escape notice, are preferable to those which pass unnoticed, because they appear more real ; whence being wealthy would appear to be a greater good than the appearance of

41 τοῦ δοκεῖν καὶ τὸ ἀγαπητόν, καὶ τοῖς μὲν μόνον
τοῖς δὲ μετ᾽ ἄλλων. διὸ καὶ οὐκ ἴση ζημία, ἄν τις
τὸν ἑτερόφθαλμον τυφλώσῃ καὶ τὸν δύ᾽ ἔχοντα·
ἀγαπητὸν γὰρ ἀφῄρηται.

8. Ἐκ τίνων μὲν οὖν δεῖ τὰς πίστεις φέρειν ἐν
τῷ προτρέπειν καὶ ἀποτρέπειν, σχεδὸν εἴρηται.
μέγιστον δὲ καὶ κυριώτατον ἁπάντων πρὸς τὸ
δύνασθαι πείθειν καὶ καλῶς συμβουλεύειν, τὰς
πολιτείας ἁπάσας λαβεῖν καὶ τὰ ἑκάστης ἔθη καὶ

2 νόμιμα καὶ συμφέροντα διελεῖν. πείθονται γὰρ
ἅπαντες τῷ συμφέροντι, συμφέρει δὲ τὸ σῶζον τὴν
πολιτείαν. ἔτι δὲ κυρία μέν ἐστιν ἡ τοῦ κυρίου
ἀπόφανσις,[1] τὰ δὲ κύρια διῄρηται κατὰ τὰς πολι-
τείας· ὅσαι γὰρ αἱ πολιτεῖαι, τοσαῦτα καὶ τὰ κύριά
ἐστιν.

3 Εἰσὶ δὲ πολιτεῖαι τέτταρες, δημοκρατία ὀλιγαρχία ἀριστοκρατία μοναρχία· ὥστε τὸ μὲν κύριον
καὶ τὸ κρῖνον τούτων τί ἐστιν ἀεὶ μόριον, ἢ ὅλον

4 τούτων. ἔστι δὲ δημοκρατία μὲν πολιτεία ἐν ᾗ
κλήρῳ διανέμονται τὰς ἀρχάς, ὀλιγαρχία δὲ ἐν ᾗ
οἱ ἀπὸ τιμημάτων, ἀριστοκρατία δὲ ἐν ᾗ οἱ κατὰ
παιδείαν. παιδείαν δὲ λέγω τὴν ὑπὸ τοῦ νόμου
κειμένην· οἱ γὰρ ἐμμεμενηκότες ἐν τοῖς νομίμοις
ἐν τῇ ἀριστοκρατίᾳ ἄρχουσιν. ἀνάγκη δὲ τούτους

---

[1] The ordinary ms. reading is ἀπόφασις, but this word
appears most commonly to mean "negation" (from ἀπόφημι)
in Aristotle, as opposed to "affirmation" (from κατάφημι).
ἀπόφανσις is from ἀποφαίνω.

---

[a] It is difficult to see the connexion here. Munro's suggestion, τῷ δοκεῖν for τοῦ δοκεῖν, adopted by Roemer, would
mean "by the show of it," that is, by its attracting notice.

[b] Or, "is not punished equally."

[c] The pronouncements of the supreme authority are them-

it.[a] And that which is held most dear, sometimes alone, sometimes accompanied by other things, is a greater good. Wherefore he who puts out the eye of a one-eyed man and he who puts out one eye of another who has two, does not do equal injury[b]; for in the former case, a man has been deprived of that which he held most dear.

8. These are nearly all the topics from which arguments may be drawn in persuading and dissuading; but the most important and effective of all the means of persuasion and good counsel is to know all the forms of government and to distinguish the manners and customs, institutions, and interests of each; for all men are guided by considerations of expediency, and that which preserves the State is expedient. Further, the declaration of the authority is authoritative,[c] and the different kinds of authority are distinguished according to forms of government; in fact, there are as many authorities as there are forms of government.

Now, there are four kinds of government, democracy, oligarchy, aristocracy, monarchy, so that the supreme and deciding authority is always a part or the whole of these. Democracy is a form of government in which the offices are distributed by the people among themselves by lot; in an oligarchy, by those who possess a certain property-qualification; in an aristocracy, by those who possess an educational qualification, meaning an education that is laid down by the law. In fact, in an aristocracy, power and office are in the hands of those who have remained faithful to what the law prescribes, and

selves authoritative as laying down laws and regulations for the citizens.

ARISTOTLE

φαίνεσθαι ἀρίστους· ὅθεν καὶ τοὔνομα εἴληφε τοῦτο.
1366 a μοναρχία δ' ἐστὶ κατὰ τοὔνομα ἐν ᾗ εἷς ἁπάντων
κύριός ἐστιν· τούτων δὲ ἡ μὲν κατὰ τάξιν τινὰ
βασιλεία, ἡ δ' ἀόριστος τυραννίς.

5 Τὸ δὴ τέλος ἑκάστης πολιτείας οὐ δεῖ λανθάνειν·
αἱροῦνται γὰρ τὰ πρὸς τὸ τέλος. ἔστι δὲ δημο-
κρατίας μὲν τέλος ἐλευθερία, ὀλιγαρχίας δὲ πλοῦτος,
ἀριστοκρατίας δὲ τὰ πρὸς παιδείαν καὶ τὰ νόμιμα,
τυραννίδος δὲ φυλακή. δῆλον οὖν ὅτι τὰ πρὸς τὸ
τέλος ἑκάστης ἔθη καὶ νόμιμα καὶ συμφέροντα
διαιρετέον, εἴπερ αἱροῦνται πρὸς τοῦτο ἐπανα-
6 φέροντες. ἐπεὶ δὲ οὐ μόνον αἱ πίστεις γίνονται δι'
ἀποδεικτικοῦ λόγου ἀλλὰ καὶ δι' ἠθικοῦ (τῷ γὰρ
ποιόν τινα φαίνεσθαι τὸν λέγοντα πιστεύομεν, τοῦτο
δ' ἐστὶν ἂν ἀγαθὸς φαίνηται ἢ εὔνους ἢ ἄμφω),
δέοι ἂν τὰ ἤθη τῶν πολιτειῶν ἑκάστης ἔχειν ἡμᾶς·
τὸ μὲν γὰρ ἑκάστης ἦθος πιθανώτατον ἀνάγκη
πρὸς ἑκάστην εἶναι. ταῦτα δὲ ληφθήσεται διὰ
τῶν αὐτῶν· τὰ μὲν γὰρ ἤθη φανερὰ κατὰ τὴν
προαίρεσιν, ἡ δὲ προαίρεσις ἀναφέρεται πρὸς τὸ
τέλος.

7 Ὧν μὲν οὖν δεῖ ὀρέγεσθαι προτρέποντας ὡς ἐσομένων ἢ ὄντων, καὶ ἐκ τίνων δεῖ τὰς περὶ τοῦ
συμφέροντος πίστεις λαμβάνειν, ἔτι δὲ περὶ τῶν
περὶ τὰς πολιτείας ἠθῶν καὶ νομίμων διὰ τίνων τε
καὶ πῶς εὐπορήσομεν, ἐφ' ὅσον ἦν τῷ παρόντι
καιρῷ σύμμετρον, εἴρηται· διηκρίβωται γὰρ ἐν τοῖς
πολιτικοῖς περὶ τούτων.

---

[a] The "end" of monarchy is wanting here.
[b] iii. 7-18, iv.

88

who must of necessity appear best, whence this form
of government has taken its name. In a monarchy,
as its name indicates, one man alone is supreme over
all ; if it is subject to certain regulations, it is called
a kingdom ; if it is unlimited, a tyranny.

Nor should the end of each form of government
be neglected, for men choose the things which have
reference to the end. Now, the end of democracy
is liberty, of oligarchy wealth, of aristocracy things
relating to education and what the law prescribes,
. . . ,[a] of tyranny self-protection. It is clear then
that we must distinguish the manners and customs,
institutions, and interests of each form of government, since it is in reference to this that men make
their choice. But as proofs are established not only
by demonstrative, but also by ethical argument—
since we have confidence in an orator who exhibits
certain qualities, such as goodness, goodwill, or both
—it follows that we ought to be acquainted with the
characters of each form of government ; for, in
reference to each, the character most likely to persuade must be that which is characteristic of it. These
characters will be understood by the same means ; for
characters reveal themselves in accordance with moral
purpose, and moral purpose has reference to the end.

We have now stated what things, whether future
or present, should be the aim of those who recommend a certain course ; from what topics they should
derive their proofs of expediency ; further, the ways
and means of being well equipped for dealing with
the characters and institutions of each form of government, so far as was within the scope of the present
occasion ; for the subject has been discussed in detail
in the *Politics*.[b]

9. Μετὰ δὲ ταῦτα λέγωμεν περὶ ἀρετῆς καὶ κακίας καὶ καλοῦ καὶ αἰσχροῦ· οὗτοι γὰρ σκοποὶ τῷ ἐπαινοῦντι καὶ ψέγοντι· συμβήσεται γὰρ ἅμα περὶ τούτων λέγοντας κἀκεῖνα δηλοῦν ἐξ ὧν ποιοί τινες ὑποληφθησόμεθα κατὰ τὸ ἦθος, ἥπερ ἦν δευτέρα πίστις· ἐκ τῶν αὐτῶν γὰρ ἡμᾶς τε καὶ ἄλλον ἀξιόπιστον δυνησόμεθα ποιεῖν πρὸς ἀρετήν. 2 ἐπεὶ δὲ συμβαίνει καὶ χωρὶς σπουδῆς καὶ μετὰ σπουδῆς ἐπαινεῖν πολλάκις οὐ μόνον ἄνθρωπον ἢ θεὸν ἀλλὰ καὶ ἄψυχα καὶ τῶν ἄλλων ζῴων τὸ τυχόν, τὸν αὐτὸν τρόπον καὶ περὶ τούτων ληπτέον τὰς προτάσεις· ὥστε ὅσον παραδείγματος χάριν εἴπωμεν καὶ περὶ τούτων.

3 Καλὸν μὲν οὖν ἐστίν, ὃ ἂν δι᾿ αὑτὸ αἱρετὸν ὂν ἐπαινετὸν ᾖ, ἢ ὃ ἂν ἀγαθὸν ὂν ἡδὺ ᾖ, ὅτι ἀγαθόν. εἰ δὲ τοῦτό ἐστι τὸ καλόν, ἀνάγκη τὴν ἀρετὴν 4 καλὸν εἶναι· ἀγαθὸν γὰρ ὂν ἐπαινετόν ἐστιν. ἀρετὴ δ᾿ ἐστὶ μὲν δύναμις, ὡς δοκεῖ, ποριστικὴ ἀγαθῶν 1366 b καὶ φυλακτική, καὶ δύναμις εὐεργετικὴ πολλῶν 5 καὶ μεγάλων, καὶ πάντων περὶ πάντα. μέρη δὲ ἀρετῆς δικαιοσύνη, ἀνδρία, σωφροσύνη, μεγαλο- πρέπεια, μεγαλοψυχία, ἐλευθεριότης, πρᾳότης, φρό- 6 νησις, σοφία. ἀνάγκη δὲ μεγίστας εἶναι ἀρετὰς τὰς τοῖς ἄλλοις χρησιμωτάτας, εἴπερ ἐστὶν ἡ ἀρετὴ δύναμις εὐεργετική. διὰ τοῦτο τοὺς δικαίους καὶ ἀνδρείους μάλιστα τιμῶσιν· ἡ μὲν γὰρ ἐν πολέμῳ ἡ δὲ καὶ ἐν εἰρήνῃ χρήσιμος ἄλλοις. εἶτα ἡ ἐλευ- θεριότης· προΐενται γὰρ καὶ οὐκ ἀνταγωνίζονται περὶ τῶν χρημάτων, ὧν μάλιστα ἐφίενται ἄλλοι. 7 ἔστι δὲ δικαιοσύνη μὲν ἀρετὴ δι᾿ ἣν τὰ αὑτῶν

---

a Or, "a faculty of doing many and great benefits to all men in all cases " (Jebb).

9. We will next speak of virtue and vice, of the noble and the disgraceful, since they constitute the aim of one who praises and of one who blames ; for, when speaking of these, we shall incidentally bring to light the means of making us appear of such and such a character, which, as we have said, is a second method of proof ; for it is by the same means that we shall be able to inspire confidence in ourselves or others in regard to virtue. But since it happens that men, seriously or not, often praise not only a man or a god but even inanimate things or any ordinary animal, we ought in the same way to make ourselves familiar with the propositions relating to these subjects. Let us, then, discuss these matters also, so far as may serve for illustration.

The noble, then, is that which, being desirable in itself, is at the same time worthy of praise, or which, being good, is pleasant because it is good. If this is the noble, then virtue must of necessity be noble, for, being good, it is worthy of praise. Virtue, it would seem, is a faculty of providing and preserving good things, a faculty productive of many and great benefits, in fact, of all things in all cases.[a] The components of virtue are justice, courage, self-control, magnificence, magnanimity, liberality, gentleness, practical and speculative wisdom. The greatest virtues are necessarily those which are most useful to others, if virtue is the faculty of conferring benefits. For this reason justice and courage are the most esteemed, the latter being useful to others in war, the former in peace as well. Next is liberality, for the liberal spend freely and do not dispute the possession of wealth, which is the chief object of other men's desire. Justice is a virtue which assigns

ἕκαστοι ἔχουσι, καὶ ὡς ὁ νόμος, ἀδικία δὲ δι᾽ ἣν
8 τὰ ἀλλότρια, οὐχ ὡς ὁ νόμος. ἀνδρία δὲ δι᾽ ἣν
πρακτικοί εἰσι τῶν καλῶν ἔργων ἐν τοῖς κινδύνοις,
καὶ ὡς ὁ νόμος κελεύει, καὶ ὑπηρετικοὶ τῷ νόμῳ·
9 δειλία δὲ τοὐναντίον. σωφροσύνη δὲ ἀρετὴ δι᾽ ἣν
πρὸς τὰς ἡδονὰς τὰς τοῦ σώματος οὕτως ἔχουσιν
ὡς ὁ νόμος κελεύει· ἀκολασία δὲ τοὐναντίον.
10 ἐλευθεριότης δὲ περὶ χρήματα εὖ ποιητική, ἀν-
11 ελευθερία δὲ τοὐναντίον. μεγαλοψυχία δὲ ἀρετὴ
μεγάλων ποιητικὴ εὐεργετημάτων, μικροψυχία δὲ
12 τοὐναντίον. μεγαλοπρέπεια δὲ ἀρετὴ ἐν δαπανή-
μασι μεγέθους ποιητική· μικροψυχία δὲ καὶ μικρο-
13 πρέπεια τἀναντία. φρόνησις δ᾽ ἐστὶν ἀρετὴ διανοίας,
καθ᾽ ἣν εὖ βουλεύεσθαι δύνανται περὶ ἀγαθῶν καὶ
κακῶν τῶν εἰρημένων εἰς εὐδαιμονίαν.[a]

14 Περὶ μὲν οὖν ἀρετῆς καὶ κακίας καθόλου καὶ
περὶ τῶν μορίων εἴρηται κατὰ τὸν ἐνεστῶτα καιρὸν ἱκανῶς, περὶ δὲ τῶν ἄλλων οὐ χαλεπὸν ἰδεῖν·
φανερὸν γὰρ ὅτι ἀνάγκη τά τε ποιητικὰ τῆς ἀρετῆς
εἶναι καλά (πρὸς ἀρετὴν γάρ) καὶ τὰ ἀπ᾽ ἀρετῆς
γινόμενα, τοιαῦτα δὲ τά τε σημεῖα τῆς ἀρετῆς καὶ
15 τὰ ἔργα. ἐπεὶ δὲ τὰ σημεῖα καὶ τὰ τοιαῦτα ἃ
ἐστιν ἀγαθοῦ ἔργα ἢ πάθη καλά, ἀνάγκη ὅσα τε
ἀνδρίας ἔργα ἢ σημεῖα ἀνδρίας ἢ ἀνδρείως πέπρακται καλὰ εἶναι, καὶ τὰ δίκαια καὶ τὰ δικαίως ἔργα
(πάθη δὲ οὔ· ἐν μόνῃ γὰρ ταύτῃ τῶν ἀρετῶν οὐκ
ἀεὶ τὸ δικαίως καλόν, ἀλλ᾽ ἐπὶ τοῦ ζημιοῦσθαι
αἰσχρὸν τὸ δικαίως μᾶλλον ἢ τὸ ἀδίκως), καὶ κατὰ

---

[a] Or, taking εἰς εὐδαιμονίαν with βουλεύεσθαι, " come to a wise decision conducive to their happiness."

to each man his due in conformity with the law;
injustice claims what belongs to others, in opposition
to the law.   Courage makes men perform noble acts
in the midst of dangers according to the dictates of
the law and in submission to it;   the contrary is
cowardice.   Self-control is a virtue which disposes
men in regard to the pleasures of the body as the
law prescribes;   the contrary is licentiousness.
Liberality does good in many matters;   the contrary
is avarice.   Magnanimity is a virtue productive of
great benefits;   the contrary is little-mindedness.
Magnificence is a virtue which produces greatness in
matters of expenditure;   the contraries are little-
mindedness and meanness.   Practical wisdom is a
virtue of reason, which enables men to come to a
wise decision in regard to good and evil things, which
have been mentioned as connected with happiness.[a]

Concerning virtue and vice in general and their
separate parts, enough has been said for the moment.
To discern the rest [b] presents no difficulty;   for it is
evident that whatever produces virtue, as it tends to
it, must be noble, and so also must be what comes
from virtue;   for such are its signs and works.   But
since the signs of virtue and such things as are the
works and sufferings of a good man are noble, it necessarily follows that all the works and signs of courage
and all courageous acts are also noble.   The same
may be said of just things and of just actions; (but not
of what one suffers justly;   for in this alone amongst
the virtues that which is justly done is not always
noble, and a just punishment is more disgraceful
than an unjust punishment).   The same applies

[b]   *i.e.* the causes and results of virtue (Cope);   or, the noble
and the disgraceful (Jebb).

ARISTOTLE

16 τὰς ἄλλας δὲ ἀρετὰς ὡσαύτως. καὶ ἐφ' ὅσοις τὰ ἆθλα τιμή, καλά. καὶ ἐφ' ὅσοις τιμὴ μᾶλλον ἢ χρήματα. καὶ ὅσα μὴ αὑτοῦ ἕνεκα πράττει τις

17 τῶν αἱρετῶν. καὶ τὰ ἁπλῶς ἀγαθά, ὅσα ὑπὲρ τῆς πατρίδος τις ἐποίησε, παριδὼν τὸ αὑτοῦ. καὶ τὰ τῇ φύσει ἀγαθά· καὶ ἃ μὴ αὑτῷ ἀγαθά· αὑτοῦ

1367 a γὰρ ἕνεκα τὰ τοιαῦτα.

18 Καὶ ὅσα τεθνεῶτι ἐνδέχεται ὑπάρχειν μᾶλλον ἢ ζῶντι· τὸ γὰρ αὑτοῦ ἕνεκα μᾶλλον ἔχει τὰ ζῶντι.

19 καὶ ὅσα ἔργα τῶν ἄλλων ἕνεκα· ἧττον γὰρ αὑτοῦ. καὶ ὅσαι εὐπραγίαι περὶ ἄλλους, ἀλλὰ μὴ περὶ αὑτόν. καὶ περὶ τοὺς εὖ ποιήσαντας· δίκαιον γάρ.

20 καὶ τὰ εὐεργετήματα· οὐ γὰρ εἰς αὑτόν. καὶ τὰ ἐναντία ἢ ἐφ' οἷς αἰσχύνονται· τὰ γὰρ αἰσχρὰ αἰσχύνονται καὶ λέγοντες καὶ ποιοῦντες καὶ μέλλοντες ὥσπερ καὶ Σαπφὼ πεποίηκεν, εἰπόντος τοῦ Ἀλκαίου

> θέλω τι ϝείπην, ἀλλά με κωλύει
> αἰδώς,
> αἰ δ' εἶχες ἐσθλῶν ἵμερον ἢ καλῶν
> καὶ μή τι ϝείπην γλῶσσ' ἐκύκα κακόν,
> αἰδώς κεν οὐκί σ' εἶχεν ὄμματ',
> ἀλλ' ἔλεγες περὶ τῶ δικαίω.

21 Καὶ περὶ ὧν ἀγωνιῶσι μὴ φοβούμενοι· περὶ γὰρ τῶν πρὸς δόξαν φερόντων ἀγαθῶν τοῦτο πάσχου-

22 σιν. καὶ αἱ τῶν φύσει σπουδαιοτέρων ἀρεταὶ καλ-

23 λίους καὶ τὰ ἔργα, οἷον ἀνδρὸς ἢ γυναικός. καὶ αἱ ἀπολαυστικαὶ ἄλλοις μᾶλλον ἢ αὑτοῖς· διὸ τὸ

---

^a Frag. 55 (*P.L.G.* iii.).   ^b Frag. 28 (*P.L.G.* iii.).

94

equally to the other virtues. Those things of which the reward is honour are noble ; also those which are done for honour rather than money. Also, those desirable things which a man does not do for his own sake ; things which are absolutely good, which a man has done for the sake of his country, while neglecting his own interests ; things which are naturally good; and not such as are good for the individual, since such things are inspired by selfish motives.

And those things are noble which it is possible for a man to possess after death rather than during his lifetime, for the latter involve more selfishness ; all acts done for the sake of others, for they are more disinterested ; the successes gained, not for oneself, but for others, and for one's benefactors, for that is justice ; in a word, all acts of kindness, for they are disinterested. And the contrary of those things of which we are ashamed ; for we are ashamed of what is disgraceful, in words, acts, or intention ; as, for instance, when Alcaeus said :

I would fain say something, but shame holds me back,[a]

Sappho rejoined :

Hadst thou desired what was good or noble, and had not thy tongue stirred up some evil to utter it, shame would not have filled thine eyes, but thou would'st have spoken of what is right.[b]

Those things also are noble for which men anxiously strive, but without fear ; for men are thus affected about goods which lead to good repute. Virtues and actions are nobler, when they proceed from those who are naturally worthier, for instance, from a man rather than from a woman. It is the same with those which are the cause of enjoyment to others

24 δίκαιον καὶ ἡ δικαιοσύνη καλόν. καὶ τὸ τοὺς ἐχθροὺς τιμωρεῖσθαι μᾶλλον καὶ μὴ καταλλάττεσθαι.
τό τε γὰρ ἀνταποδιδόναι δίκαιον, τὸ δὲ δίκαιον
25 καλόν, καὶ ἀνδρείου τὸ μὴ ἡττᾶσθαι. καὶ νίκη καὶ
τιμὴ τῶν καλῶν· αἱρετά τε γὰρ ἄκαρπα ὄντα, καὶ
ὑπεροχὴν ἀρετῆς δηλοῖ. καὶ τὰ μνημονευτά, καὶ
τὰ μᾶλλον μᾶλλον. καὶ ἃ μὴ ζῶντι ἕπεται. καὶ οἷς
τιμὴ ἀκολουθεῖ. καὶ τὰ περιττά. καὶ τὰ μόνῳ
26 ὑπάρχοντα καλλίω· εὐμνημονευτότερα γάρ. καὶ
κτήματα ἄκαρπα· ἐλευθεριώτερα γάρ. καὶ τὰ παρ'
ἑκάστοις δὲ ἴδια καλά. καὶ ὅσα σημεῖά ἐστι τῶν
παρ' ἑκάστοις ἐπαινουμένων, οἷον ἐν Λακεδαίμονι
κομᾶν καλόν· ἐλευθέρου γὰρ σημεῖον· οὐ γάρ ἐστι
27 κομῶντα ῥάδιον οὐδὲν ποιεῖν ἔργον θητικόν. καὶ
τὸ μηδεμίαν ἐργάζεσθαι βάναυσον τέχνην· ἐλευθέρου γὰρ τὸ μὴ πρὸς ἄλλον ζῆν.

28 Ληπτέον δὲ καὶ τὰ σύνεγγυς τοῖς ὑπάρχουσιν ὡς
ταὐτὰ ὄντα καὶ πρὸς ἔπαινον καὶ πρὸς ψόγον, οἷον
τὸν εὐλαβῆ ψυχρὸν καὶ ἐπίβουλον καὶ τὸν ἠλίθιον
29 χρηστὸν καὶ τὸν ἀνάλγητον πρᾶον. καὶ ἕκαστον δ'
ἐκ τῶν παρακολουθούντων ἀεὶ κατὰ τὸ βέλτιστον,
οἷον τὸν ὀργίλον καὶ τὸν μανικὸν ἁπλοῦν καὶ τὸν
1367 b αὐθάδη μεγαλοπρεπῆ καὶ σεμνόν. καὶ τοὺς ἐν ταῖς
ὑπερβολαῖς ὡς ἐν ταῖς ἀρεταῖς ὄντας, οἷον τὸν

96

rather than to ourselves; this is why justice and that which is just are noble. To take vengeance on one's enemies is nobler than to come to terms with them; for to retaliate is just, and that which is just is noble; and further, a courageous man ought not to allow himself to be beaten. Victory and honour also are noble; for both are desirable even when they are fruitless, and are manifestations of superior virtue. And things worthy of remembrance, which are the more honourable the longer their memory lasts; those which follow us after death; those which are accompanied by honour; and those which are out of the common. Those which are only possessed by a single individual, because they are more worthy of remembrance. And possessions which bring no profit; for they are more gentlemanly. Customs that are peculiar to individual peoples and all the tokens of what is esteemed among them are noble; for instance, in Lacedaemon it is noble to wear one's hair long, for it is the mark of a gentleman, the performance of any servile task being difficult for one whose hair is long. And not carrying on any vulgar profession is noble, for a gentleman does not live in dependence on others.

We must also assume, for the purpose of praise or blame, that qualities which closely resemble the real qualities are identical with them; for instance, that the cautious man is cold and designing, the simpleton good-natured, and the emotionless gentle. And in each case we must adopt a term from qualities closely connected, always in the more favourable sense; for instance, the choleric and passionate man may be spoken of as frank and open, the arrogant as magnificent and dignified; those in excess as

ARISTOTLE

θρασὺν ἀνδρεῖον καὶ τὸν ἄσωτον ἐλευθέριον· δόξει
τε γὰρ τοῖς πολλοῖς, καὶ ἅμα παραλογιστικὸν ἐκ
τῆς αἰτίας· εἰ γὰρ οὗ μὴ ἀνάγκη κινδυνευτικός,
πολλῷ μᾶλλον ἂν δόξειεν ὅπου καλόν, καὶ εἰ προ-
ετικὸς τοῖς τυχοῦσι, καὶ τοῖς φίλοις· ὑπερβολὴ γὰρ
30 ἀρετῆς τὸ πάντας εὖ ποιεῖν. σκοπεῖν δὲ καὶ παρ᾽
οἷς ὁ ἔπαινος· ὥσπερ γὰρ ὁ Σωκράτης ἔλεγεν, οὐ
χαλεπὸν Ἀθηναίους ἐν Ἀθηναίοις ἐπαινεῖν. δεῖ δὲ
τὸ παρ᾽ ἑκάστοις τίμιον λέγειν ὡς ὑπάρχει, οἷον
ἐν Σκύθαις ἢ Λάκωσιν ἢ φιλοσόφοις. καὶ ὅλως δὲ
τὸ τίμιον ἄγειν εἰς τὸ καλόν, ἐπείπερ δοκεῖ γειτνιᾶν.
31 καὶ ὅσα κατὰ τὸ προσῆκον, οἷον εἰ ἄξια τῶν προγόνων καὶ τῶν προϋπηργμένων· εὐδαιμονικὸν γὰρ
καὶ καλὸν τὸ προσεπικτᾶσθαι τιμήν. καὶ εἰ παρὰ
τὸ προσῆκον δὲ ἐπὶ τὸ βέλτιον καὶ τὸ κάλλιον, οἷον
εἰ εὐτυχῶν μὲν μέτριος ἀτυχῶν δὲ μεγαλόψυχος,
ἢ μείζων γιγνόμενος βελτίων καὶ καταλλακτικώ-
τερος. τοιοῦτον δὲ τὸ τοῦ Ἰφικράτους, ἐξ οἵων
εἰς οἷα, καὶ τὸ τοῦ ὀλυμπιονίκου

πρόσθε μὲν ἀμφ᾽ ὤμοισιν ἔχων τραχεῖαν,

καὶ τὸ τοῦ Σιμωνίδου·

---

[a] Those whose qualities are extreme may be described as
possessing the virtues of which these are the excess.
[b] Plato, *Menexenus*, 235 D.
[c] Thus, the Scythians may be assumed to be brave and
great hunters; the Spartans hardy, courageous, and brief
in speech; the Athenians fond of literature—and they should
be praised accordingly.
[d] That is, τὸ τίμιον looks as if it were really καλόν, and
should be spoken of as if it were so.
[e] Cp. 7. 32 above.
[f] Frag. 111 (*P.L.G.* iii.).

98

possessing the corresponding virtue,[a] the fool-
hardy as courageous, the recklessly extravagant as
liberal. For most people will think so, and at the
same time a fallacious argument may be drawn from
the motive ; for if a man risks his life when there is
no necessity, much more will he be thought likely
to do so when it is honourable; and if he is lavish
to all comers, the more so will he be to his friends ;
for the height of virtue is to do good to all. We
ought also to consider in whose presence we praise,
for, as Socrates said, it is not difficult to praise
Athenians among Athenians.[b] We ought also to
speak of what is esteemed among the particular
audience, Scythians, Lacedaemonians, or philosophers,[c] as actually existing there. And, generally
speaking, that which is esteemed should be classed
as noble, since there seems to be a close resemblance
between the two.[d] Again, all such actions as are in
accord with what is fitting are noble ; if, for instance,
they are worthy of a man's ancestors or of his own
previous achievements ; for to obtain additional
honour is noble and conduces to happiness. Also,
if the tendency of what is done is better and
nobler, and goes beyond what is to be expected;
for instance, if a man is moderate in good
fortune and stout-hearted in adversity, or if, when
he becomes greater, he is better and more for-
giving. Such was the phrase of Iphicrates, " Look
what I started from ! "[e] and of the Olympian
victor :

Formerly, with a rough basket on my shoulders, I used
to carry fish from Argos to Tegea.[f]

and of Simonides :

99

ἢ πατρός τε καὶ ἀνδρὸς ἀδελφῶν τ' οὖσα τυράννων.

32 Ἐπεὶ δ' ἐκ τῶν πράξεων ὁ ἔπαινος, ἴδιον δὲ τοῦ σπουδαίου τὸ κατὰ προαίρεσιν, πειρατέον δεικνύναι πράττοντα κατὰ προαίρεσιν. χρήσιμον δὲ τὸ πολλάκις φαίνεσθαι πεπραχότα. διὸ καὶ τὰ συμπτώματα καὶ τὰ ἀπὸ τύχης ὡς ἐν προαιρέσει ληπτέον· ἂν γὰρ πολλὰ καὶ ὅμοια προφέρηται, σημεῖον ἀρετῆς εἶναι δόξει καὶ προαιρέσεως.

33 Ἔστι δ' ἔπαινος λόγος ἐμφανίζων μέγεθος ἀρετῆς. δεῖ οὖν τὰς πράξεις ἐπιδεικνύναι ὡς τοιαῦται. τὸ δ' ἐγκώμιον τῶν ἔργων ἐστίν, τὰ δὲ κύκλῳ εἰς πίστιν, οἷον εὐγένεια καὶ παιδεία· εἰκὸς γὰρ ἐξ ἀγαθῶν ἀγαθοὺς καὶ τὸν οὕτω τραφέντα τοιοῦτον εἶναι. διὸ καὶ ἐγκωμιάζομεν πράξαντας. τὰ δ' ἔργα σημεῖα τῆς ἕξεώς ἐστιν, ἐπεὶ ἐπαινοῖμεν ἂν καὶ μὴ πεπραγότα, εἰ πιστεύοιμεν εἶναι τοιοῦτον.

34 μακαρισμὸς δὲ καὶ εὐδαιμονισμὸς αὑτοῖς μὲν ταὐτά, τούτοις δ' οὐ ταὐτά, ἀλλ' ὥσπερ ἡ εὐδαιμονία τὴν ἀρετήν, καὶ ὁ εὐδαιμονισμὸς περιέχει ταῦτα.

35 Ἔχει δὲ κοινὸν εἶδος ὁ ἔπαινος καὶ αἱ συμβουλαί· ἃ γὰρ ἐν τῷ συμβουλεύειν ὑπόθειο ἄν, ταῦτα

36 μετατεθέντα τῇ λέξει ἐγκώμια γίγνεται. ἐπεὶ
1368 a οὖν ἔχομεν ἃ δεῖ πράττειν καὶ ποῖόν τινα εἶναι, δεῖ ταῦτα ὡς ὑποθήκας λέγοντας τῇ λέξει μετατιθέναι καὶ στρέφειν, οἷον ὅτι οὐ δεῖ μέγα φρονεῖν ἐπὶ τοῖς διὰ τύχην ἀλλὰ τοῖς δι' αὑτόν. οὕτω μὲν

---

a Archedice, daughter of Hippias, tyrant of Athens, and wife of Aeantides, son of Hippocles, tyrant of Lampsacus.

Daughter, wife, and sister of tyrants.[a]

Since praise is founded on actions, and acting according to moral purpose is characteristic of the worthy man, we must endeavour to show that a man is acting in that manner, and it is useful that it should appear that he has done so on several occasions. For this reason also one must assume that accidents and strokes of good fortune are due to moral purpose; for if a number of similar examples can be adduced, they will be thought to be signs of virtue and moral purpose.

Now praise is language that sets forth greatness of virtue; hence it is necessary to show that a man's actions are virtuous. But encomium deals with achievements—all attendant circumstances, such as noble birth and education, merely conduce to persuasion; for it is probable that virtuous parents will have virtuous offspring and that a man will turn out as he has been brought up. Hence we pronounce an encomium upon those who have achieved something. Achievements, in fact, are signs of moral habit; for we should praise even a man who had not achieved anything, if we felt confident that he was likely to do so. Blessing and felicitation are identical with each other, but are not the same as praise and encomium, which, as virtue is contained in happiness, are contained in felicitation.

Praise and counsels have a common aspect; for what you might suggest in counselling becomes encomium by a change in the phrase. Accordingly, when we know what we ought to do and the qualities we ought to possess, we ought to make a change in the phrase and turn it, employing this knowledge as a suggestion. For instance, the statement that " one ought not to pride oneself on goods which are

101

ARISTOTLE

οὖν λεχθὲν ὑποθήκην δύναται, ὡδὶ δ' ἔπαινον
" μέγα φρονῶν οὐ τοῖς διὰ τύχην ὑπάρχουσιν ἀλλὰ
τοῖς δι' αὐτόν." ὥστε ὅταν ἐπαινεῖν βούλῃ, ὅρα τί
ἂν ὑπόθοιο, καὶ ὅταν ὑποθέσθαι, ὅρα τί ἂν ἐπαι-
37 νέσειας. ἡ δὲ λέξις ἔσται ἀντικειμένη ἐξ ἀνάγκης,
ὅταν τὸ μὲν κωλῦον τὸ δὲ μὴ κωλῦον μετατεθῇ.

38 Χρηστέον δὲ καὶ τῶν αὐξητικῶν πολλοῖς, οἷον εἰ
μόνος ἢ πρῶτος ἢ μετ' ὀλίγων ἢ καὶ [ὁ] μάλιστα
πεποίηκεν. ἅπαντα γὰρ ταῦτα καλά. καὶ τὰ ἐκ
τῶν χρόνων καὶ τῶν καιρῶν· ταῦτα δὲ παρὰ τὸ
προσῆκον. καὶ εἰ πολλάκις τὸ αὐτὸ κατώρθωκεν·
μέγα γάρ, καὶ οὐκ ἀπὸ τύχης ἀλλὰ δι' αὐτὸν ἂν
δόξειεν. καὶ εἰ τὰ προτρέποντα καὶ τιμῶντα διὰ
τοῦτον εὕρηται καὶ κατεσκευάσθη. καὶ εἰς ὃν
πρῶτον ἐγκώμιον ἐποιήθη, οἷον εἰς Ἱππόλοχον, καὶ
Ἁρμόδιον καὶ Ἀριστογείτονα τὸ ἐν ἀγορᾷ σταθῆναι. ὁμοίως δὲ καὶ ἐπὶ τῶν ἐναντίων. κἂν μὴ
καθ' αὑτὸν εὐπορῇς, πρὸς ἄλλους ἀντιπαραβάλλειν·
ὅπερ Ἰσοκράτης ἐποίει διὰ τὴν ἀσυνήθειαν τοῦ
δικολογεῖν. δεῖ δὲ πρὸς ἐνδόξους συγκρίνειν· αὐξη-
39 τικὸν γὰρ καὶ καλόν, εἰ σπουδαίων βελτίων. πίπτει
δ' εὐλόγως ἡ αὔξησις εἰς τοὺς ἐπαίνους· ἐν ὑπερ-

---

[a] In the first sentence, the statement is imperative, there
is a prohibition; in the second, it is a simple affirmative,
implying praise. In the one case there is forbidding, in the
other not-forbidding, which are opposites.

[b] Nothing more is known of him.

[c] Who slew Hipparchus, tyrant of Athens.

[d] Reading ἀσυνήθειαν. He had no legal practice, which
would have shown the irrelevancy of comparisons in a
law court, whereas in epideictic speeches they are useful.
συνήθειαν gives exactly the opposite sense, and must refer
to his having written speeches for others to deliver in the
courts.

due to fortune, but on those which are due to oneself alone," when expressed in this way, has the force of a suggestion ; but expressed thus, " he was proud, not of goods which were due to fortune, but of those which were due to himself alone," it becomes praise. Accordingly, if you desire to praise, look what you would suggest ; if you desire to suggest, look what you would praise. The form of the expression will necessarily be opposite, when the prohibitive has been changed into the non-prohibitive.[a]

We must also employ many of the means of amplification ; for instance, if a man has done anything alone, or first, or with a few, or has been chiefly responsible for it ; all these circumstances render an action noble. Similarly, topics derived from times and seasons, that is to say, if our expectation is surpassed. Also, if a man has often been successful in the same thing ; for this is of importance and would appear to be due to the man himself, and not to be the result of chance. And if it is for his sake that distinctions which are an encouragement or honour have been invented and established ; and if he was the first on whom an encomium was pronounced, as Hippolochus,[b] or to whom a statue was set up in the market-place, as to Harmodius and Aristogiton.[c] And similarly in opposite cases. If he does not furnish you with enough material in himself, you must compare him with others, as Isocrates used to do, because of his inexperience [d] of forensic speaking. And you must compare him with illustrious personages, for it affords ground for amplification and is noble, if he can be proved better than men of worth. Amplification is with good reason ranked as one of the forms of praise, since it

οχῇ γάρ ἐστιν, ἡ δ' ὑπεροχὴ τῶν καλῶν. διὸ κἂν
μὴ πρὸς τοὺς ἐνδόξους, ἀλλὰ πρὸς τοὺς ἄλλους δεῖ
παραβάλλειν, ἐπείπερ ἡ ὑπεροχὴ δοκεῖ μηνύειν
40 ἀρετήν. ὅλως δὲ τῶν κοινῶν εἰδῶν ἅπασι τοῖς
λόγοις ἡ μὲν αὔξησις ἐπιτηδειοτάτη τοῖς ἐπιδεικτι-
κοῖς· τὰς γὰρ πράξεις ὁμολογουμένας λαμβάνουσιν,
ὥστε λοιπὸν μέγεθος περιθεῖναι καὶ κάλλος· τὰ δὲ
παραδείγματα τοῖς συμβουλευτικοῖς· ἐκ γὰρ τῶν
προγεγονότων τὰ μέλλοντα καταμαντευόμενοι κρί-
νομεν· τὰ δ' ἐνθυμήματα τοῖς δικανικοῖς· αἰτίαν γὰρ
καὶ ἀπόδειξιν μάλιστα δέχεται τὸ γεγονὸς διὰ τὸ
41 ἀσαφές. ἐκ τίνων μὲν οὖν οἱ ἔπαινοι καὶ οἱ ψόγοι
λέγονται σχεδὸν πάντες, καὶ πρὸς ποῖα δεῖ βλέπον-
τας ἐπαινεῖν καὶ ψέγειν, καὶ ἐκ τίνων τὰ ἐγκώμια
γίγνεται καὶ τὰ ὀνείδη, ταῦτ' ἐστίν· ἐχομένων γὰρ
τούτων τὰ ἐναντία τούτοις φανερά· ὁ γὰρ ψόγος ἐκ
τῶν ἐναντίων ἐστίν.

1368 b 10. Περὶ δὲ κατηγορίας καὶ ἀπολογίας, ἐκ
πόσων καὶ ποίων ποιεῖσθαι δεῖ τοὺς συλλογισμούς,
2 ἐχόμενον ἂν εἴη λέγειν. δεῖ δὴ λαβεῖν τρία, ἓν
μὲν τίνων καὶ πόσων ἕνεκα ἀδικοῦσι, δεύτερον δὲ
πῶς αὐτοὶ διακείμενοι, τρίτον δὲ τοὺς ποίους καὶ
3 πῶς ἔχοντας. διορισάμενοι οὖν τὸ ἀδικεῖν λέγωμεν
ἑξῆς.

Ἔστω δὴ τὸ ἀδικεῖν τὸ βλάπτειν ἑκόντα παρὰ
τὸν νόμον. νόμος δ' ἐστὶν ὁ μὲν ἴδιος ὁ δὲ κοινός.
λέγω δὲ ἴδιον μὲν καθ' ὃν γεγραμμένον πολιτεύονται,

consists in superiority, and superiority is one of the things that are noble. That is why, if you cannot compare him with illustrious personages, you must compare him with ordinary persons, since superiority is thought to indicate virtue. Speaking generally, of the topics common to all rhetorical arguments, amplification is most suitable for epideictic speakers, whose subject is actions which are not disputed, so that all that remains to be done is to attribute beauty and importance to them. Examples are most suitable for deliberative speakers, for it is by examination of the past that we divine and judge the future. Enthymemes are most suitable for forensic speakers, because the past, by reason of its obscurity, above all lends itself to the investigation of causes and to demonstrative proof. Such are nearly all the materials of praise or blame, the things which those who praise or blame should keep in view, and the sources of encomia and invective; for when these are known their contraries are obvious, since blame is derived from the contrary things.

10. We have next to speak of the number and quality of the propositions of which those syllogisms are constructed which have for their object accusation and defence. Three things have to be considered; first, the nature and the number of the motives which lead men to act unjustly; secondly, what is the state of mind of those who so act; thirdly, the character and dispositions of those who are exposed to injustice. We will discuss these questions in order, after we have first defined acting unjustly.

Let injustice, then, be defined as voluntarily causing injury contrary to the law. Now, the law is particular or general. By particular, I mean the

κοινὸν δὲ ὅσα ἄγραφα παρὰ πᾶσιν ὁμολογεῖσθαι
δοκεῖ. ἑκόντες δὲ ποιοῦσιν ὅσα εἰδότες καὶ μὴ
ἀναγκαζόμενοι. ὅσα μὲν οὖν ἑκόντες, οὐ πάντα
προαιρούμενοι, ὅσα δὲ προαιρούμενοι, εἰδότες
4 ἅπαντα· οὐδεὶς γὰρ ὃ προαιρεῖται ἀγνοεῖ. δι’ ἃ
δὲ προαιροῦνται βλάπτειν καὶ φαῦλα ποιεῖν παρὰ
τὸν νόμον, κακία ἐστὶ καὶ ἀκρασία· ἐὰν γάρ τινες
ἔχωσι μοχθηρίαν ἢ μίαν ἢ πλείους, περὶ δὲ τοῦτο
ὃ μοχθηροὶ τυγχάνουσιν ὄντες, καὶ ἄδικοί εἰσιν,
οἷον ὁ μὲν ἀνελεύθερος περὶ χρήματα, ὁ δ’ ἀκόλα-
στος περὶ τὰς τοῦ σώματος ἡδονάς, ὁ δὲ μαλακὸς
περὶ τὰ ῥάθυμα, ὁ δὲ δειλὸς περὶ τοὺς κινδύνους
(τοὺς γὰρ συγκινδυνεύοντας ἐγκαταλιμπάνουσι διὰ
τὸν φόβον), ὁ δὲ φιλότιμος διὰ τιμήν, ὁ δ’ ὀξύθυμος
δι’ ὀργήν, ὁ δὲ φιλόνικος διὰ νίκην, ὁ δὲ πικρὸς διὰ
τιμωρίαν, ὁ δ’ ἄφρων διὰ τὸ ἀπατᾶσθαι περὶ τὸ
δίκαιον καὶ ἄδικον, ὁ δ’ ἀναίσχυντος δι’ ὀλιγωρίαν
δόξης. ὁμοίως δὲ καὶ τῶν ἄλλων ἕκαστος περὶ
ἕκαστον τῶν ὑποκειμένων.

5 Ἀλλὰ περὶ μὲν τούτων δῆλον, τὰ μὲν ἐκ τῶν
περὶ τὰς ἀρετὰς εἰρημένων, τὰ δ’ ἐκ τῶν περὶ τὰ
πάθη ῥηθησομένων· λοιπὸν δ’ εἰπεῖν τίνος ἕνεκα
6 καὶ πῶς ἔχοντες ἀδικοῦσι, καὶ τίνας. πρῶτον μὲν
οὖν διελώμεθα τίνων ὀρεγόμενοι καὶ ποῖα φεύγοντες ἐγχειροῦσιν ἀδικεῖν· δῆλον γὰρ ὡς τῷ μὲν

ᵃ προαίρεσις (premeditation, deliberate or moral choice)
is always voluntary, but all voluntary action is not premeditated; we sometimes act on the spur of the moment.
Choice is a voluntary act, the result of deliberate counsel,
including the use of reason and knowledge. In the *Ethics*
(iii. 3. 19) Aristotle defines προαίρεσις as " a deliberate appeti-

written law in accordance with which a state is administered ; by general, the unwritten regulations which appear to be universally recognized.   Men act voluntarily when they know what they do, and do not act under compulsion.   What is done voluntarily is not always done with premeditation ; but what is done with premeditation is always known to the agent, for no one is ignorant of what he does with a purpose.[a]   The motives which lead men to do injury and commit wrong actions are depravity and incontinence.   For if men have one or more vices, it is in that which makes him vicious that he shows himself unjust ; for example, the illiberal in regard to money, the licentious in regard to bodily pleasures, the effeminate in regard to what makes for ease,[b] the coward in regard to dangers, for fright makes him desert his comrades in peril ; the ambitious in his desire for honour, the irascible owing to anger, one who is eager to conquer in his desire for victory, the rancorous in his desire for vengeance ; the foolish man from having mistaken ideas of right and wrong, the shameless from his contempt for the opinion of others.   Similarly, each of the rest of mankind is unjust in regard to his special weakness.

This will be perfectly clear, partly from what has already been said about the virtues, and partly from what will be said about the emotions.   It remains to state the motives and character of those who do wrong and of those who suffer from it.   First, then, let us decide what those who set about doing wrong long for or avoid ; for it is evident that the accuser

tion of (longing for, ὄρεξις) things in our power," as to which we should necessarily be well-informed.

[b] Or, "in the matter of ease," taking τὰ ῥάθυμα as = ῥαθυμία.

κατηγοροῦντι πόσα καὶ ποῖα τούτων ὑπάρχει τῷ
ἀντιδίκῳ σκεπτέον, τῷ δ' ἀπολογουμένῳ ποῖα καὶ
7 πόσα τούτων οὐχ ὑπάρχει. πάντες δὴ πράττουσι
πάντα τὰ μὲν οὐ δι' αὑτοὺς τὰ δὲ δι' αὑτούς. τῶν
μὲν οὖν μὴ δι' αὑτοὺς τὰ μὲν διὰ τύχην πράττουσι
τὰ δ' ἐξ ἀνάγκης, τῶν δ' ἐξ ἀνάγκης τὰ μὲν βίᾳ
τὰ δὲ φύσει. ὥστε πάντα ὅσα μὴ δι' αὑτοὺς
πράττουσι, τὰ μὲν ἀπὸ τύχης τὰ δὲ φύσει τὰ δὲ
βίᾳ. ὅσα δὲ δι' αὑτούς, καὶ ὧν αὐτοὶ αἴτιοι, τὰ
1369 a μὲν δι' ἔθος τὰ δὲ δι' ὄρεξιν, καὶ τὰ μὲν διὰ λογι-
8 στικὴν ὄρεξιν τὰ δὲ δι' ἀλόγιστον· ἔστι δ' ἡ μὲν
βούλησις ἀγαθοῦ ὄρεξις (οὐδεὶς γὰρ βούλεται ἀλλ'
ἢ ὅταν οἰηθῇ εἶναι ἀγαθόν), ἄλογοι δ' ὀρέξεις ὀργὴ
καὶ ἐπιθυμία, ὥστε πάντα ὅσα πράττουσιν ἀνάγκη
πράττειν δι' αἰτίας ἑπτά, διὰ τύχην, διὰ φύσιν, διὰ
βίαν, δι' ἔθος, διὰ λογισμόν, διὰ θυμόν, δι' ἐπιθυμίαν.
9 Τὸ δὲ προσδιαιρεῖσθαι καθ' ἡλικίας ἢ ἕξεις ἢ
ἄλλ' ἄττα τὰ πραττόμενα περίεργον· εἰ γὰρ συμβέβηκε τοῖς νέοις ὀργίλοις εἶναι ἢ ἐπιθυμητικοῖς,
οὐ διὰ τὴν νεότητα πράττουσι τὰ τοιαῦτα ἀλλὰ
δι' ὀργὴν καὶ ἐπιθυμίαν. οὐδὲ διὰ πλοῦτον καὶ
πενίαν, ἀλλὰ συμβέβηκε τοῖς μὲν πένησι διὰ τὴν
ἔνδειαν ἐπιθυμεῖν χρημάτων, τοῖς δὲ πλουσίοις
διὰ τὴν ἐξουσίαν ἐπιθυμεῖν τῶν μὴ ἀναγκαίων
ἡδονῶν. ἀλλὰ πράξουσι καὶ οὗτοι οὐ διὰ πλοῦτον
καὶ πενίαν ἀλλὰ διὰ τὴν ἐπιθυμίαν. ὁμοίως δὲ
καὶ οἱ δίκαιοι καὶ οἱ ἄδικοι, καὶ οἱ ἄλλοι οἱ λεγό-

---

[a] In the cases of the young, the poor, and the rich, their
youth etc. are only "accidents," accidental not real causes.
Aristotle defines τὸ συμβεβηκός (*Metaphysica*, iv. 30) as "that
which is inherent in something, and may be predicated of it
as true, but neither necessarily, nor in most cases; for
instance, if a man, when digging a hole for a plant, finds a

must examine the number and nature of the motives which are to be found in his opponent; the defendant, which of them are not to be found in him. Now, all human actions are either the result of man's efforts or not. Of the latter some are due to chance, others to necessity. Of those due to necessity, some are to be attributed to compulsion, others to nature, so that the things which men do not do of themselves are all the result of chance, nature, or compulsion. As for those which they do of themselves and of which they are the cause, some are the result of habit, others of longing, and of the latter some are due to rational, others to irrational longing. Now wish is a [rational] longing for good, for no one wishes for anything unless he thinks it is good; irrational longings are anger and desire. Thus all the actions of men must necessarily be referred to seven causes: chance, nature, compulsion, habit, reason, anger, and desire.

But it is superfluous to establish further distinctions of men's acts based upon age, moral habits, or anything else. For if the young happen to be [a] irascible, or passionately desire anything, it is not because of their youth that they act accordingly, but because of anger and desire. Nor is it because of wealth or poverty; but the poor happen to desire wealth because of their lack of it, and the rich desire unnecessary pleasures because they are able to procure them. Yet in their case too it will not be wealth or poverty, but desire, that will be the mainspring of their action. Similarly, the just and the unjust, and all the others who are said to act in accordance with

treasure." The colour of a man's eyes is an "inseparable" accident, the fact that a man is a lawyer is a "separable" accident.

109

μενοι κατὰ τὰς ἕξεις πράττειν, διὰ ταῦτα πράξουσιν·
ἢ γὰρ διὰ λογισμὸν ἢ διὰ πάθος· ἀλλ' οἱ μὲν δι'
10 ἤθη καὶ πάθη χρηστά, οἱ δὲ διὰ τἀναντία. συμβαίνει μέντοι ταῖς μὲν τοιαύταις ἕξεσι τὰ τοιαῦτα
ἀκολουθεῖν, ταῖς δὲ τοιαῖσδε τὰ τοιάδε· εὐθὺς γὰρ
ἴσως τῷ μὲν σώφρονι διὰ τὸ σώφρονα εἶναι δόξαι
τε καὶ ἐπιθυμίαι χρησταὶ ἐπακολουθοῦσι περὶ τῶν
ἡδέων, τῷ δ' ἀκολάστῳ αἱ ἐναντίαι περὶ τῶν
11 αὐτῶν τούτων. διὸ τὰς μὲν τοιαύτας διαιρέσεις
ἐατέον, σκεπτέον δὲ ποῖα ποίοις εἴωθεν ἕπεσθαι·
εἰ μὲν γὰρ λευκὸς ἢ μέλας ἢ μέγας ἢ μικρός,
οὐδὲν τέτακται τῶν τοιούτων ἀκολουθεῖν, εἰ δὲ
νέος ἢ πρεσβύτης ἢ δίκαιος ἢ ἄδικος, ἤδη διαφέρει.
καὶ ὅλως ὅσα τῶν συμβαινόντων ποιεῖ διαφέρειν
τὰ ἤθη τῶν ἀνθρώπων, οἷον πλουτεῖν δοκῶν
ἑαυτῷ ἢ πένεσθαι διοίσει τι, καὶ εὐτυχεῖν ἢ ἀτυχεῖν.
ταῦτα μὲν οὖν ὕστερον ἐροῦμεν, νῦν δὲ περὶ τῶν
λοιπῶν εἴπωμεν πρῶτον.

12 Ἔστι δ' ἀπὸ τύχης μὲν τὰ τοιαῦτα γιγνόμενα,
ὅσων ἥ τε αἰτία ἀόριστος καὶ μὴ ἕνεκά του γίγνεται
καὶ μήτε ἀεὶ μήτε ὡς ἐπὶ τὸ πολὺ μήτε τεταγ-
μένως· δῆλον δ' ἐκ τοῦ ὁρισμοῦ τῆς τύχης περὶ
13 τούτων. φύσει δέ, ὅσων ἥ τ' αἰτία ἐν αὐτοῖς καὶ
1369 b τεταγμένη· ἢ γὰρ ἀεὶ ἢ ὡς ἐπὶ τὸ πολὺ ὡσαύτως
ἀποβαίνει. τὰ γὰρ παρὰ φύσιν οὐδὲν δεῖ ἀκριβο-
λογεῖσθαι, πότερα κατὰ φύσιν τινὰ ἢ ἄλλην αἰτίαν
γίγνεται· δόξειε δ' ἂν καὶ ἡ τύχη αἰτία εἶναι τῶν
14 τοιούτων. βίᾳ δέ, ὅσα παρ' ἐπιθυμίαν ἢ τοὺς λογι-

---

[a] ii. 12-18.

their moral habits, will act from the same causes, either from reason or emotion, but some from good characters and emotions, and others from the opposite. Not but that it does happen that such and such moral habits are followed by such and such consequences; for it may be that from the outset the fact of being temperate produces in the temperate man good opinions and desires in the matter of pleasant things, in the intemperate man the contrary. Therefore we must leave these distinctions on one side, but we must examine what are the usual consequences of certain conditions. For, if a man is fair or dark, tall or short, there is no rule that any such consequences should follow, but if he is young or old, just or unjust, it does make a difference. In a word, it will be necessary to take account of all the circumstances that make men's characters different; for instance, if a man fancies himself rich or poor, fortunate or unfortunate, it will make a difference. We will, however, discuss this later [a]; let us now speak of what remains to be said here.

Things which are the result of chance are all those of which the cause is indefinite, those which happen without any end in view, and that neither always, nor generally, nor regularly. The definition of chance will make this clear. Things which are the result of nature are all those of which the cause is in themselves and regular; for they turn out always, or generally, in the same way. As for those which happen contrary to nature there is no need to investigate minutely whether their occurrence is due to a certain force of nature or some other cause (it would seem, however, that such cases also are due to chance). Those things are the result of com-

ARISTOTLE

σμοὺς γίγνεται δι' αὐτῶν τῶν πραττόντων. ἔθει
15 δέ, ὅσα διὰ τὸ πολλάκις πεποιηκέναι ποιοῦσιν.
16 διὰ λογισμὸν δὲ τὰ δοκοῦντα συμφέρειν ἐκ τῶν
εἰρημένων ἀγαθῶν ἢ ὡς τέλος ἢ ὡς πρὸς τὸ
τέλος, ὅταν διὰ τὸ συμφέρειν πράττηται· ἔνια
γὰρ καὶ οἱ ἀκόλαστοι συμφέροντα πράττουσιν, ἀλλ'
οὐ διὰ τὸ συμφέρειν ἀλλὰ δι' ἡδονήν. διὰ θυμὸν
17 δὲ καὶ ὀργὴν τὰ τιμωρητικά. διαφέρει δὲ τιμωρία
καὶ κόλασις· ἡ μὲν γὰρ κόλασις τοῦ πάσχοντος
ἕνεκά ἐστιν, ἡ δὲ τιμωρία τοῦ ποιοῦντος, ἵνα
18 ἀποπληρωθῇ. τί μὲν οὖν ἐστιν ἡ ὀργή, δῆλον
ἔσται ἐν τοῖς περὶ παθῶν, δι' ἐπιθυμίαν δὲ πράτ-
τεται ὅσα φαίνεται ἡδέα. ἔστι δὲ καὶ τὸ σύνηθες
καὶ τὸ ἐθιστὸν ἐν τοῖς ἡδέσιν· πολλὰ γὰρ καὶ τῶν
φύσει μὴ ἡδέων, ὅταν ἐθισθῶσιν, ἡδέως ποιοῦσιν.

Ὥστε συλλαβόντι εἰπεῖν, ὅσα δι' αὑτοὺς πράττουσιν, ἅπαντ' ἐστὶν ἢ ἀγαθὰ ἢ φαινόμενα ἀγαθὰ
ἢ ἡδέα ἢ φαινόμενα ἡδέα. ἐπεὶ δ' ὅσα δι' αὑτούς,
ἑκόντες πράττουσιν, οὐχ ἑκόντες δὲ ὅσα μὴ δι'
αὑτούς, πάντ' ἂν εἴη, ὅσα ἑκόντες πράττουσιν, ἢ
ἀγαθὰ ἢ φαινόμενα ἀγαθὰ ἢ ἡδέα ἢ φαινόμενα
ἡδέα· τίθημι γὰρ καὶ τὴν τῶν κακῶν ἢ φαινομένων
κακῶν ἢ ἀπαλλαγὴν ἢ ἀντὶ μείζονος ἐλάττονος μετάληψιν ἐν τοῖς ἀγαθοῖς (αἱρετὰ γάρ πως), καὶ τὴν τῶν
λυπηρῶν ἢ φαινομένων ἢ ἀπαλλαγὴν ἢ μετάληψιν
ἀντὶ μειζόνων ἐλαττόνων ἐν τοῖς ἡδέσιν ὡσαύτως.

* ii. 2.

pulsion which are done by the agents themselves in opposition to their desire or calculation. Things are the result of habit, when they are done because they have often been done. Things are the result of calculation which are done because, of the goods already mentioned, they appear to be expedient either as an end or means to an end, provided they are done by reason of their being expedient; for even the intemperate do certain things that are expedient, for the sake, not of expediency, but of pleasure. Passion and anger are the causes of acts of revenge. But there is a difference between revenge and punishment; the latter is inflicted in the interest of the sufferer, the former in the interest of him who inflicts it, that he may obtain satisfaction. We will define anger when we come to speak of the emotions.[a] Desire is the cause of things being done that are apparently pleasant. The things which are familiar and to which we have become accustomed are among pleasant things; for men do with pleasure many things which are not naturally pleasant, when they have become accustomed to them.

In short, all things that men do of themselves either are, or seem, good or pleasant; and since men do voluntarily what they do of themselves, and involuntarily what they do not, it follows that all that men do voluntarily will be either that which is or seems good, or that which is or seems pleasant. For I reckon among good things the removal of that which is evil or seems evil, or the exchange of a greater evil for a less, because these two things are in a way desirable; in like manner, I reckon among pleasant things the removal of that which is or appears painful, and the exchange of a greater pain

113

ληπτέον ἄρα τὰ συμφέροντα καὶ τὰ ἡδέα, πόσα
19 καὶ ποῖα. περὶ μὲν οὖν τοῦ συμφέροντος ἐν τοῖς
συμβουλευτικοῖς εἴρηται πρότερον, περὶ δὲ τοῦ ἡδέος
εἴπωμεν νῦν. δεῖ δὲ νομίζειν ἱκανοὺς εἶναι τοὺς ὅρους,
ἐὰν ὦσι περὶ ἑκάστου μήτε ἀσαφεῖς μήτε ἀκριβεῖς.
11. Ὑποκείσθω δ᾽ ἡμῖν εἶναι τὴν ἡδονὴν κίνησίν
τινα τῆς ψυχῆς καὶ κατάστασιν ἀθρόαν καὶ αἰσθητὴν
εἰς τὴν ὑπάρχουσαν φύσιν, λύπην δὲ τοὐναντίον.
2 εἰ δ᾽ ἐστὶν ἡδονὴ τὸ τοιοῦτον, δῆλον ὅτι καὶ ἡδύ
1370 a ἐστι τὸ ποιητικὸν τῆς εἰρημένης διαθέσεως, τὸ δὲ
φθαρτικὸν ἢ τῆς ἐναντίας καταστάσεως ποιητικὸν
3 λυπηρόν. ἀνάγκη οὖν ἡδὺ εἶναι τό τε εἰς τὸ κατὰ
φύσιν ἰέναι ὡς ἐπὶ τὸ πολύ, καὶ μάλιστα ὅταν
ἀπειληφότα ᾖ τὴν ἑαυτῶν φύσιν τὰ κατ᾽ αὐτὴν
γιγνόμενα, καὶ τὰ ἔθη· καὶ γὰρ τὸ εἰθισμένον
ὥσπερ πεφυκὸς ἤδη γίγνεται· ὅμοιον γάρ τι τὸ
ἔθος τῇ φύσει· ἐγγὺς γὰρ καὶ τὸ πολλάκις τῷ ἀεί,
ἔστι δ᾽ ἡ μὲν φύσις τοῦ ἀεί, τὸ δὲ ἔθος τοῦ πολλά-
4 κις. καὶ τὸ μὴ βίαιον· παρὰ φύσιν γὰρ ἡ βία.
διὸ τὸ ἀναγκαῖον λυπηρόν, καὶ ὀρθῶς εἴρηται

πᾶν γὰρ ἀναγκαῖον πρᾶγμ᾽ ἀνιαρὸν ἔφυ.

τὰς δ᾽ ἐπιμελείας καὶ τὰς σπουδὰς καὶ τὰς συν-
τονίας λυπηράς· ἀναγκαῖα γὰρ καὶ βίαια ταῦτα,
ἐὰν μὴ ἐθισθῶσιν· οὕτω δὲ τὸ ἔθος ποιεῖ ἡδύ. τὰ
δ᾽ ἐναντία ἡδέα· διὸ αἱ ῥαθυμίαι καὶ αἱ ἀπονίαι
καὶ αἱ ἀμέλειαι καὶ αἱ παιδιαὶ καὶ αἱ ἀναπαύσεις
καὶ ὁ ὕπνος τῶν ἡδέων· οὐδὲν γὰρ πρὸς ἀνάγκην

---

[a] Cf. i. 6 above.
[b] The true nature of the "normal state" was lost during
the period of disturbance and unsettlement.
[c] From Evenus of Paros (Frag. 8, *P.L.G.* ii.): see Introd.
[d] Or, "rest" (bodily).

114

for a less. We must therefore make ourselves acquainted with the number and quality of expedient and pleasant things. We have already spoken of the expedient when discussing deliberative rhetoric; [a] let us now speak of the pleasant. And we must regard our definitions as sufficient in each case, provided they are neither obscure nor too precise.

11. Let it be assumed by us that pleasure is a certain movement of the soul, a sudden and perceptible settling down into its natural state, and pain the opposite. If such is the nature of pleasure, it is evident that that which produces the disposition we have just mentioned is pleasant, and that that which destroys it or produces the contrary settling down is painful. Necessarily, therefore, it must be generally pleasant to enter into a normal state (especially when what is done in accordance with that state has come into its own again); [b] and the same with habits. For that which has become habitual becomes as it were natural; in fact, habit is something like nature, for the distance between " often " and " always " is not great, and nature belongs to the idea of " always," habit to that of " often." That which is not compulsory is also pleasant, for compulsion is contrary to nature. That is why what is necessary is painful, and it was rightly said,

> For every act of necessity is disagreeable.[c]

Application, study, and intense effort are also painful, for these involve necessity and compulsion, if they have not become habitual; for then habit makes them pleasant. Things contrary to these are pleasant; wherefore states of ease, idleness, carelessness, amusement, recreation,[d] and sleep are among pleasant things, because none of these is in any way compulsory.

ARISTOTLE

5 τούτων. καὶ οὗ ἂν ἡ ἐπιθυμία ἐνῇ, ἅπαν ἡδύ· ἡ
γὰρ ἐπιθυμία τοῦ ἡδέος ἐστὶν ὄρεξις.

Τῶν δὲ ἐπιθυμιῶν αἱ μὲν ἄλογοί εἰσιν αἱ δὲ
μετὰ λόγου. λέγω δὲ ἀλόγους μέν, ὅσας μὴ ἐκ
τοῦ ὑπολαμβάνειν τι ἐπιθυμοῦσιν· εἰσὶ δὲ τοιαῦται
ὅσαι εἶναι λέγονται φύσει, ὥσπερ αἱ διὰ τοῦ
σώματος ὑπάρχουσαι, οἷον ἡ τροφῆς, δίψα καὶ
πεῖνα, καὶ καθ᾽ ἕκαστον τροφῆς εἶδος ἐπιθυμία,
καὶ αἱ περὶ τὰ γευστὰ καὶ περὶ τὰ ἀφροδίσια καὶ
ὅλως τὰ ἁπτά, καὶ περὶ ὀσμὴν καὶ ἀκοὴν καὶ
ὄψιν. μετὰ λόγου δὲ ὅσα ἐκ τοῦ πεισθῆναι ἐπι-
θυμοῦσιν· πολλὰ γὰρ καὶ θεάσασθαι καὶ κτήσασθαι
ἐπιθυμοῦσιν ἀκούσαντες καὶ πεισθέντες.

6 Ἐπεὶ δ᾽ ἐστὶ τὸ ἥδεσθαι ἐν τῷ αἰσθάνεσθαί τινος
πάθους, ἡ δὲ φαντασία ἐστὶν αἴσθησίς τις ἀσθενής,
κἂν¹ τῷ μεμνημένῳ καὶ τῷ ἐλπίζοντι ἀκολουθοῖ
ἂν φαντασία τις οὗ μέμνηται ἢ ἐλπίζει. εἰ δὲ

---

¹ Keeping Bekker's κἂν = καὶ ἐν. Roemer reads κἀεὶ = καὶ
ἀεί, Spengel ἀεὶ ἐν.

ᵃ There is no consideration or "definite theory" (Jebb,
Welldon) of the results that may follow. The desires arise
without anything of the kind; they simply come.

ᵇ The passage ἐπεὶ δ᾽ ἐστὶ ... αἴσθησις has been punctuated
in two ways. (1) With a full stop at ἐλπίζει (Roemer, Jebb).
The conclusion then drawn is that memory and hope are
accompanied by imagination of what is remembered or
hoped. To this it is objected that what Aristotle really
wants to prove is that memory and hope are a cause of
pleasure. (2) With a comma at ἐλπίζει (Cope, Victorius).
The steps in the argument will then be: if pleasure is the
sensation of a certain emotion; if imagination is a weakened
(faded) sensation; if one who remembers or hopes is attended
by an imagination of what he remembers or hopes; then,
this being so, pleasure will attend one who remembers or

Everything of which we have in us the desire is pleasant, for desire is a longing for the pleasant.

Now, of desires some are irrational, others rational. I call irrational all those that are not the result of any assumption.[a] Such are all those which are called natural; for instance, those which come into existence through the body—such as the desire of food, thirst, hunger, the desire of such and such food in particular; the desires connected with taste, sexual pleasures, in a word, with touch, smell, hearing, and sight. I call those desires rational which are due to our being convinced; for there are many things which we desire to see or acquire when we have heard them spoken of and are convinced that they are pleasant.

And if pleasure consists in the sensation of a certain emotion, and imagination is a weakened sensation, then both the man who remembers and the man who hopes will be attended by an imagination of what he remembers or hopes.[b] This being so, it is evident

hopes, since there is sensation, and pleasure is sensation and a kind of movement (§ 1).

φαντασία, the faculty of forming mental images (variously translated "imagination," "mental impression," "fantasy") is defined by Aristotle (*De Anima*, iii. 3. 11) as a *kind of movement*, which cannot arise apart from sensation, and the movement produced must resemble the sensation which produced it. But φαντασία is more than this; it is not merely a faculty of sense, but occupies a place midway between sense and intellect; while imagination has need of the senses, the intellect has need of imagination.

If φαντασία is referred to an earlier perception of which the sense image is a copy, this is memory. Imagination carries the sense images (φαντάσματα) to the seat of memory. They are then transformed into memory (of something past) or hope (of something future) and are handed on to the intellect. (See Cope here, and R. D. Hicks in his edition of the *De Anima*.)

τοῦτο, δῆλον ὅτι καὶ ἡδοναὶ ἅμα μεμνημένοις καὶ
7 ἐλπίζουσιν, ἐπείπερ καὶ αἴσθησις. ὥστ᾽ ἀνάγκη
πάντα τὰ ἡδέα ἢ ἐν τῷ αἰσθάνεσθαι εἶναι παρόντα
ἢ ἐν τῷ μεμνῆσθαι γεγενημένα ἢ ἐν τῷ ἐλπίζειν
μέλλοντα· αἰσθάνονται μὲν γὰρ τὰ παρόντα, μέ-
1370 b μνηνται δὲ τὰ γεγενημένα, ἐλπίζουσι δὲ τὰ μέλ-
8 λοντα. τὰ μὲν οὖν μνημονευτὰ ἡδέα ἐστίν, οὐ
μόνον ὅσα ἐν τῷ παρόντι, ὅτε παρῆν, ἡδέα ἦν,
ἀλλ᾽ ἔνια καὶ οὐχ ἡδέα, ἂν ᾖ ὕστερον καλὸν καὶ
ἀγαθὸν τὸ μετὰ τοῦτο· ὅθεν καὶ τοῦτ᾽ εἴρηται,

> ἀλλ᾽ ἡδύ τοι σωθέντα μεμνῆσθαι πόνων,

καὶ

> μετὰ γάρ τε καὶ ἄλγεσι τέρπεται ἀνὴρ
> μνήμενος, ὅς τις πολλὰ πάθῃ καὶ πολλὰ ἐόργῃ.

9 τούτου δ᾽ αἴτιον ὅτι ἡδὺ καὶ τὸ μὴ ἔχειν κακόν.
τὰ δ᾽ ἐν ἐλπίδι, ὅσα παρόντα ἢ εὐφραίνειν ἢ ὠφελεῖν
φαίνεται μεγάλα, καὶ ἄνευ λύπης ὠφελεῖν. ὅλως
δ᾽ ὅσα παρόντα εὐφραίνει, καὶ ἐλπίζοντας καὶ
μεμνημένους ὡς ἐπὶ τὸ πολύ. διὸ καὶ τὸ ὀργίζεσθαι ἡδύ, ὥσπερ καὶ Ὅμηρος ἐποίησε περὶ τοῦ
θυμοῦ

> ὅς τε πολὺ γλυκίων μέλιτος καταλειβομένοιο·

οὐθεὶς γὰρ ὀργίζεται τῷ ἀδυνάτῳ φαινομένῳ
τιμωρίας τυχεῖν, οὐδὲ τοῖς πολὺ ὑπὲρ αὑτοὺς τῇ
δυνάμει· ἢ οὐκ ὀργίζονται ἢ ἧττον.

10 Καὶ ἐν ταῖς πλείσταις ἐπιθυμίαις ἀκολουθεῖ τις
ἡδονή· ἢ γὰρ μεμνημένοι ὡς ἔτυχον ἢ ἐλπίζοντες

---

[a] Euripides, *Andromeda* (Frag. 133, *T.G.F.*).
[b] *Odyssey*, xv. 400, 401, but misquoted in the second line,
which runs: ὅς τις δὴ μάλα πολλὰ πάθῃ καὶ πόλλ᾽ ἐπαληθῇ.

that there is pleasure both for those who remember
and for those who hope, since there is sensation.
Therefore all pleasant things must either be present
in sensation, or past in recollection, or future in
hope ; for one senses the present, recollects the past,
and hopes for the future.   Therefore our recollections
are pleasant, not only when they recall things which
when present were agreeable, but also some things
which were not, if their consequence subsequently
proves honourable or good ; whence the saying :

Truly it is pleasant to remember toil after one has escaped it,[a]

and,

When a man has suffered much and accomplished much,
he afterwards takes pleasure even in his sorrows when he
recalls them.[b]

The reason of this is that even to be free from evil
is pleasant.   Things which we hope for are pleasant,
when their presence seems likely to afford us great
pleasure or advantage, without the accompaniment
of pain.   In a word, all things that afford pleasure
by their presence *as* a rule also afford pleasure when
we hope for or remember them.   Wherefore even
resentment is pleasant, as Homer said of anger that
it is

Far sweeter than dripping honey ;[c]

for no one feels resentment against those whom
vengeance clearly cannot overtake, or those who are
far more powerful than he is ; against such, men feel
either no resentment or at any rate less.
    Most of our desires are accompanied by a feeling
of pleasure, for the recollection of a past or the hope

[c] *Iliad*, xviii. 108.

ὡς τεύξονται χαίρουσί τινα ἡδονήν, οἷον οἵ τ' ἐν
τοῖς πυρετοῖς ἐχόμενοι ταῖς δίψαις καὶ μεμνημένοι
ὡς ἔπιον καὶ ἐλπίζοντες πιεῖσθαι χαίρουσιν, καὶ
11 οἱ ἐρῶντες καὶ διαλεγόμενοι καὶ γράφοντες, καὶ
ποιοῦντές τι ἀεὶ περὶ τοῦ ἐρωμένου χαίρουσιν· ἐν
ἅπασι γὰρ τοῖς τοιούτοις μεμνημένοι οἷον αἰσθάνεσθαι οἴονται τοῦ ἐρωμένου. καὶ ἀρχὴ δὲ τοῦ
ἔρωτος αὕτη γίγνεται πᾶσιν, ὅταν μὴ μόνον παρόντος χαίρωσιν ἀλλὰ καὶ ἀπόντος μεμνημένοι
12 ἐρῶσιν. διὸ καὶ ὅταν λυπηρὸς γένηται τῷ μὴ παρ-
εῖναι, καὶ ἐν τοῖς πένθεσι καὶ θρήνοις ἐγγίνεταί
τις ἡδονή· ἡ μὲν γὰρ λύπη ἐπὶ τῷ μὴ ὑπάρχειν,
ἡδονὴ δ' ἐν τῷ μεμνῆσθαι καὶ ὁρᾶν πως ἐκεῖνον,
καὶ ἃ ἔπραττε, καὶ οἷος ἦν. διὸ καὶ τοῦτ' εἰκότως
εἴρηται,

ὡς φάτο, τοῖσι δὲ πᾶσιν ὑφ' ἵμερον ὦρσε γόοιο.

13 Καὶ τὸ τιμωρεῖσθαι ἡδύ· οὗ γὰρ τὸ μὴ τυγχάνειν
λυπηρόν, τὸ τυγχάνειν ἡδύ· οἱ δ' ὀργιζόμενοι
λυποῦνται ἀνυπερβλήτως μὴ τιμωρούμενοι, ἐλπί-
14 ζοντες δὲ χαίρουσιν. καὶ τὸ νικᾶν ἡδύ, οὐ μόνον
τοῖς φιλονίκοις ἀλλὰ πᾶσιν· φαντασία γὰρ ὑπεροχῆς
γίγνεται, οὗ πάντες ἔχουσιν ἐπιθυμίαν ἢ ἠρέμα ἢ
15 μᾶλλον. ἐπεὶ δὲ τὸ νικᾶν ἡδύ, ἀνάγκη καὶ τὰς
1371 a παιδιὰς ἡδείας εἶναι τὰς μαχητικὰς καὶ τὰς ἐριστικάς (πολλάκις γὰρ ἐν ταύταις γίγνεται τὸ νικᾶν)

---

[a] Or " doing something that has to do with the beloved."
[b] Iliad, xxiii. 108, on the occasion of the mourning for
120

of a future pleasure creates a certain pleasurable enjoyment ; thus, those suffering from fever and tormented by thirst enjoy the remembrance of having drunk and the hope that they will drink again. The lovesick always take pleasure in talking, writing, or composing verses [a] about the beloved ; for it seems to them that in all this recollection makes the object of their affection perceptible. Love always begins in this manner, when men are happy not only in the presence of the beloved, but also in his absence when they recall him to mind. This is why, even when his absence is painful, there is a certain amount of pleasure even in mourning and lamentation ; for the pain is due to his absence, but there is pleasure in remembering and, as it were, seeing him and recalling his actions and personality. Wherefore it was rightly said by the poet :

Thus he spake, and excited in all a desire of weeping.[b]

And revenge is pleasant ; for if it is painful to be unsuccessful, it is pleasant to succeed. Now, those who are resentful are pained beyond measure when they fail to secure revenge, while the hope of it delights them. Victory is pleasant, not only to those who love to conquer, but to all ; for there is produced an idea of superiority, which all with more or less eagerness desire. And since victory is pleasant, competitive and disputatious [c] amusements must be so too, for victories are often gained in them ; among

Patroclus ; *Odyssey*, iv. 183, referring to the mourning for the absence of Odysseus.

[c] *Controversiae* or school rhetorical exercises, as well as arguing in the law courts; unless ἐριστικάς means simply " in which there is rivalry."

121

καὶ ἀστραγαλίσεις καὶ σφαιρίσεις καὶ κυβείας καὶ
πεττείας. καὶ περὶ τὰς ἐσπουδασμένας δὲ παιδιὰς
ὁμοίως· αἱ μὲν γὰρ ἡδεῖαι γίγνονται, ἄν τις ᾖ
συνήθης, αἱ δ' εὐθὺς ἡδεῖαι, οἷον κυνηγία καὶ
πᾶσα θηρευτική· ὅπου γὰρ ἅμιλλα, ἐνταῦθα καὶ
νίκη ἐστίν. διὸ καὶ ἡ δικανικὴ καὶ ἡ ἐριστικὴ
16 ἡδεῖα τοῖς εἰθισμένοις καὶ δυναμένοις. καὶ τιμὴ
καὶ εὐδοξία τῶν ἡδίστων διὰ τὸ γίγνεσθαι φαν-
τασίαν ἑκάστῳ ὅτι τοιοῦτος οἷος ὁ σπουδαῖος, καὶ
μᾶλλον ὅταν φῶσιν οὓς οἴεται ἀληθεύειν. τοιοῦτοι
δ' οἱ ἐγγὺς μᾶλλον τῶν πόρρω, καὶ οἱ συνήθεις καὶ
οἱ πολῖται τῶν ἄπωθεν, καὶ οἱ ὄντες τῶν μελλόντων,
καὶ οἱ φρόνιμοι ἀφρόνων, καὶ πολλοὶ ὀλίγων·
μᾶλλον γὰρ εἰκὸς ἀληθεύειν τοὺς εἰρημένους τῶν
ἐναντίων· ἐπεὶ ὧν τις πολὺ καταφρονεῖ, ὥσπερ
παιδίων ἢ θηρίων, οὐδὲν μέλει τῆς τούτων τιμῆς
ἢ τῆς δόξης αὐτῆς γε τῆς δόξης χάριν, ἀλλ' εἴπερ,
δι' ἄλλο τι.

17 Καὶ ὁ φίλος τῶν ἡδέων· τό τε γὰρ φιλεῖν ἡδύ
(οὐδεὶς γὰρ φίλοινος μὴ χαίρων οἴνῳ) καὶ τὸ
φιλεῖσθαι ἡδύ· φαντασία γὰρ καὶ ἐνταῦθα τοῦ
ὑπάρχειν αὐτῷ ἀγαθὸν εἶναι, οὗ πάντες ἐπιθυμοῦσιν οἱ αἰσθανόμενοι· τὸ δὲ φιλεῖσθαι ἀγαπᾶσθαί
18 ἐστιν αὐτὸν δι' αὐτόν. καὶ τὸ θαυμάζεσθαι ἡδὺ
δι' αὐτὸ τὸ τιμᾶσθαι. καὶ τὸ κολακεύεσθαι καὶ
ὁ κόλαξ ἡδύ· φαινόμενος γὰρ θαυμαστὴς καὶ
19 φαινόμενος φίλος ὁ κόλαξ ἐστίν. καὶ τὸ ταὐτὰ

---

[a] For the meaning of φιλία, φιλεῖν cf. ii. 4.

these we may include games with knuckle-bones, ball-games, dicing, and draughts. It is the same with serious sports ; for some become pleasant when one is familiar with them, while others are so from the outset, such as the chase and every description of outdoor sport ; for rivalry implies victory. It follows from this that practice in the law courts and disputation are pleasant to those who are familiar with them and well qualified. Honour and good repute are among the most pleasant things, because every one imagines that he possesses the qualities of a worthy man, and still more when those whom he believes to be trustworthy say that he does. Such are neighbours rather than those who live at a distance ; intimate friends and fellow-citizens rather than those who are unknown ; contemporaries rather than those who come later ; the sensible rather than the senseless ; the many rather than the few ; for such persons are more likely to be trustworthy than their opposites. As for those for whom men feel great contempt, such as children and animals, they pay no heed to their respect or esteem, or, if they do, it is not for the sake of their esteem, but for some other reason.

A friend also is among pleasant things, for it is pleasant to love [a]—for no one loves wine unless he finds pleasure in it—just as it is pleasant to be loved ; for in this case also a man has an impression that he is really endowed with good qualities, a thing desired by all who perceive it ; and to be loved is to be cherished for one's own sake. And it is pleasant to be admired, because of the mere honour. Flattery and the flatterer are pleasant, the latter being a sham admirer and friend. It is pleasant to do the

πράττειν πολλάκις ἡδύ· τὸ γὰρ σύνηθες ἡδὺ ἦν.
20 καὶ τὸ μεταβάλλειν ἡδύ· εἰς φύσιν γὰρ γίγνεται
μεταβάλλειν· τὸ γὰρ αὐτὸ ἀεὶ ὑπερβολὴν ποιεῖ
τῆς καθεστώσης ἕξεως· ὅθεν εἴρηται

μεταβολὴ πάντων γλυκύ.

διὰ τοῦτο καὶ τὰ διὰ χρόνου ἡδέα ἐστί, καὶ ἄνθρωποι
καὶ πράγματα· μεταβολὴ γὰρ ἐκ τοῦ παρόντος
21 ἐστίν, ἅμα δὲ καὶ σπάνιον τὸ διὰ χρόνου. καὶ τὸ
μανθάνειν καὶ τὸ θαυμάζειν ἡδὺ ὡς ἐπὶ τὸ πολύ·
ἐν μὲν γὰρ τῷ θαυμάζειν τὸ ἐπιθυμεῖν μαθεῖν
ἐστίν, ὥστε τὸ θαυμαστὸν ἐπιθυμητόν, ἐν δὲ τῷ
22 μανθάνειν εἰς τὸ κατὰ φύσιν καθίστασθαι. καὶ
τὸ εὖ ποιεῖν καὶ τὸ εὖ πάσχειν τῶν ἡδέων· τὸ μὲν
γὰρ εὖ πάσχειν τυγχάνειν ἐστὶν ὧν ἐπιθυμοῦσι,
τὸ δὲ εὖ ποιεῖν ἔχειν καὶ ὑπερέχειν, ὧν ἀμφοτέρων
1371 b ἐφίενται. διὰ δὲ τὸ ἡδὺ εἶναι τὸ εὐποιητικόν,
καὶ τὸ ἐπανορθοῦν ἡδὺ τοῖς ἀνθρώποις ἐστὶ τοὺς
23 πλησίον, καὶ τὸ τὰ ἐλλιπῆ ἐπιτελεῖν. ἐπεὶ δὲ τὸ
μανθάνειν τε ἡδὺ καὶ τὸ θαυμάζειν, καὶ τὰ τοιάδε
ἀνάγκη ἡδέα εἶναι οἷον τό τε μιμούμενον,[1] ὥσπερ
γραφικὴ καὶ ἀνδριαντοποιία καὶ ποιητική, καὶ
πᾶν ὃ ἂν εὖ μεμιμημένον ᾖ, κἂν ᾖ μὴ ἡδὺ αὐτὸ
τὸ μεμιμημένον· οὐ γὰρ ἐπὶ τούτῳ χαίρει, ἀλλὰ
συλλογισμός ἐστιν ὅτι τοῦτο ἐκεῖνο, ὥστε μαν-
24 θάνειν τι συμβαίνει. καὶ αἱ περιπέτειαι καὶ τὸ
παρὰ μικρὸν σώζεσθαι ἐκ τῶν κινδύνων· πάντα
25 γὰρ θαυμαστὰ ταῦτα. καὶ ἐπεὶ τὸ κατὰ φύσιν

---

[1] Roemer reads τό τε μιμητικόν. The meaning is much the same, only μιμούμενον is passive.

[a] Euripides, *Orestes*, 234.
[b] True knowledge or philosophy, which is the result of learning, is the highest condition of the intellect, its normal

same things often; for that which is familiar is, as we said, pleasant. Change also is pleasant, since change is in the order of nature; for perpetual sameness creates an excess of the normal condition; whence it was said:

Change in all things is sweet.[a]

This is why what we only see at intervals, whether men or things, is pleasant; for there is a change from the present, and at the same time it is rare. And learning and admiring are as a rule pleasant; for admiring implies the desire to learn, so that what causes admiration is to be desired, and learning implies a return to the normal.[b] It is pleasant to bestow and to receive benefits; the latter is the attainment of what we desire, the former the possession of more than sufficient means,[c] both of them things that men desire. Since it is pleasant to do good, it must also be pleasant for men to set their neighbours on their feet, and to supply their deficiencies. And since learning and admiring are pleasant, all things connected with them must also be pleasant; for instance, a work of imitation, such as painting, sculpture, poetry, and all that is well imitated, even if the object of imitation is not pleasant; for it is not this that causes pleasure or the reverse, but the inference that the imitation and the object imitated are identical, so that the result is that we learn something. The same may be said of sudden changes and narrow escapes from danger; for all these things excite wonder. And since that

or settled state. Consequently, a return to this is pleasure, which is defined (§ 1) as a settling down of the soul into its natural state after a period of disturbance.

[c] Or, " larger means than the person benefited."

ἡδύ, τὰ συγγενῆ δὲ κατὰ φύσιν ἀλλήλοις ἐστίν,
πάντα τὰ συγγενῆ καὶ ὅμοια ἡδέα ὡς ἐπὶ τὸ πολύ,
οἷον ἄνθρωπος ἀνθρώπῳ καὶ ἵππος ἵππῳ καὶ
νέος νέῳ. ὅθεν καὶ αἱ παροιμίαι εἴρηνται, ὡς

ἧλιξ ἥλικα τέρπει,

καὶ

ὡς αἰεὶ τὸν ὁμοῖον,

καὶ

ἔγνω δὲ θὴρ θῆρα,

καὶ

ἀεὶ κολοιὸς παρὰ κολοιόν,

καὶ ὅσα ἄλλα τοιαῦτα.

26 Ἐπεὶ δὲ τὸ ὅμοιον καὶ τὸ συγγενὲς ἡδὺ ἑαυτῷ
ἅπαν, μάλιστα δ᾽ αὐτὸς πρὸς ἑαυτὸν ἕκαστος
τοῦτο πέπονθεν, ἀνάγκη πάντας φιλαύτους εἶναι
ἢ μᾶλλον ἢ ἧττον· πάντα γὰρ τὰ τοιαῦτα ὑπάρχει
πρὸς αὐτὸν μάλιστα. ἐπεὶ δὲ φίλαυτοι πάντες,
καὶ τὰ αὑτῶν ἀνάγκη ἡδέα εἶναι πᾶσιν, οἷον ἔργα
καὶ λόγους. διὸ καὶ φιλοκόλακες ὡς ἐπὶ τὸ πολὺ
καὶ φιλερασταί καὶ φιλότιμοι καὶ φιλότεκνοι·
αὑτῶν γὰρ ἔργα τὰ τέκνα. καὶ τὰ ἐλλιπῆ ἐπι-
27 τελεῖν ἡδύ· αὑτῶν γὰρ ἔργον ἤδη γίγνεται. καὶ
ἐπεὶ τὸ ἄρχειν ἥδιστον, καὶ τὸ σοφὸν δοκεῖν εἶναι
ἡδύ· ἀρχικὸν γὰρ τὸ φρονεῖν, ἔστι δ᾽ ἡ σοφία
πολλῶν καὶ θαυμαστῶν ἐπιστήμη. ἔτι ἐπεὶ φιλότιμοι ὡς ἐπὶ τὸ πολύ, ἀνάγκη καὶ τὸ ἐπιτιμᾶν τοῖς
28 πέλας ἡδὺ εἶναι. καὶ τὸ ἐν ᾧ βέλτιστος δοκεῖ
εἶναι αὐτὸς αὑτοῦ, ἐνταῦθα διατρίβειν, ὥσπερ καὶ
Εὐριπίδης φησὶ

---

[a] *Odyssey*, xvii. 218 ὡς αἰεὶ τὸν ὁμοῖον ἄγει θεὸς ὡς τὸν
ὁμοῖον.

which is in accordance with nature is pleasant, and things which are akin are akin in accordance with nature, all things akin and like are for the most part pleasant to each other, as man to man, horse to horse, youth to youth. This is the origin of the proverbs :

> The old have charms for the old, the young for the young,
> Like to like,[a]
> Beast knows beast,
> Birds of a feather flock together,[b]

and all similar sayings.

And since things which are akin and like are always pleasant to one another, and every man in the highest degree feels this in regard to himself, it must needs be that all men are more or less selfish ; for it is in himself above all that such conditions[c] are to be found. Since, then, all men are selfish, it follows that all find pleasure in what is their own, such as their works and words. That is why men as a rule are fond of those who flatter and love them, of honour, and of children ; for the last are their own work. It is also pleasant to supply what is wanting,[d] for then it becomes our work. And since it is most pleasant to command, it is also pleasant to be regarded as wise ;[e] for practical wisdom is commanding, and philosophy consists in the knowledge of many things that excite wonder. Further, since men are generally ambitious, it follows that it is also agreeable to find fault with our neighbours. And if a man thinks he excels in anything, he likes to devote his time to it ; as Euripides says :

---

[b] Literally, "ever jackdaw to jackdaw."
[c] Of likeness and kinship.   [d] § 22.
[e] Both practically and speculatively or philosophically.

κἀπὶ τοῦτ' ἐπείγεται,
νέμων ἑκάστης ἡμέρας πλεῖστον μέρος,
ἵν' αὐτὸς αὐτοῦ τυγχάνει βέλτιστος ὤν.

29 ὁμοίως δὲ καὶ ἐπεὶ ἡ παιδιὰ τῶν ἡδέων καὶ πᾶσα
ἄνεσις, καὶ ὁ γέλως τῶν ἡδέων, ἀνάγκη καὶ τὰ
1372 a γελοῖα ἡδέα εἶναι, καὶ ἀνθρώπους καὶ λόγους καὶ
ἔργα· διώρισται δὲ περὶ γελοίων χωρὶς ἐν τοῖς περὶ
ποιητικῆς. περὶ μὲν οὖν ἡδέων εἰρήσθω ταῦτα,
τὰ δὲ λυπηρὰ ἐκ τῶν ἐναντίων τούτοις φανερά.

12. Ὧν μὲν οὖν ἕνεκα ἀδικοῦσι, ταῦτ' ἐστίν·
πῶς δ' ἔχοντες καὶ τίνας, λέγωμεν νῦν. αὐτοὶ
μὲν οὖν ὅταν οἴωνται δυνατὸν εἶναι τὸ πρᾶγμα
πραχθῆναι καὶ ἑαυτοῖς δυνατόν, εἴτε ἂν λαθεῖν
πράξαντες, ἢ μὴ λαθόντες μὴ δοῦναι δίκην, ἢ
δοῦναι μὲν ἀλλ' ἐλάττω τὴν ζημίαν εἶναι τοῦ
2 κέρδους ἑαυτοῖς ἢ ὧν κήδονται. ποῖα μὲν οὖν
δυνατὰ φαίνεται καὶ ποῖα ἀδύνατα ἐν τοῖς ὕστερον
ῥηθήσεται (κοινὰ γὰρ ταῦτα πάντων τῶν λόγων),
αὐτοὶ δ' οἴονται δυνατοὶ εἶναι μάλιστα ἀζήμιοι
ἀδικεῖν οἱ εἰπεῖν δυνάμενοι καὶ οἱ πρακτικοὶ καὶ
οἱ ἔμπειροι πολλῶν ἀγώνων, κἂν πολύφιλοι ὦσιν,
3 κἂν πλούσιοι. καὶ μάλιστα μέν, ἂν αὐτοὶ ὦσιν
ἐν τοῖς εἰρημένοις, οἴονται δύνασθαι, εἰ δὲ μή,
κἂν ὑπάρχωσιν αὐτοῖς τοιοῦτοι φίλοι ἢ ὑπηρέται
ἢ κοινωνοί· διὰ γὰρ ταῦτα δύνανται καὶ πράττει
4 καὶ λανθάνειν καὶ μὴ δοῦναι δίκην. καὶ ἐὰν φίλοι
ὦσι τοῖς ἀδικουμένοις ἢ τοῖς κριταῖς· οἱ μὲν γὰρ
φίλοι ἀφύλακτοί τε πρὸς τὸ ἀδικεῖσθαι καὶ προσ-

---

[a] *Antiope* (Frag. 183, *T.G.F.*).
[b] Only the definition appears in the existing text:
"The ridiculous is an error, painless and non-destructive
ugliness (5)."

And allotting the best part of each day to that in which he happens to surpass himself, he presses eagerly towards it.[c]

Similarly, since amusement, every kind of relaxation, and laughter are pleasant, ridiculous things—men, words, or deeds—must also be pleasant. The ridiculous has been discussed separately in the *Poetics*.[b] Let this suffice for things that are pleasant; those that are painful will be obvious from the contraries of these.

12. Such are the motives of injustice; let us now state the frame of mind of those who commit it, and who are the sufferers from it. Men do wrong when they think that it can be done and that it can be done by them; when they think that their action will either be undiscovered, or if discovered will remain unpunished; or if it is punished, that the punishment will be less than the profit to themselves or to those for whom they care. As for the kind of things which seem possible or impossible, we will discuss them later,[c] for these topics are common to all kinds of rhetoric. Now men who commit wrong think they are most likely to be able to do so with impunity, if they are eloquent, business-like, experienced in judicial trials, if they have many friends, and if they are wealthy. They think there is the greatest chance of their being able to do so, if they themselves belong to the above classes; if not, if they have friends, servants, or accomplices who do; for thanks to these qualities they are able to commit wrong and to escape discovery and punishment. Similarly, if they are friends of those who are being wronged, or of the judges; for friends are not on their guard against being wronged and, besides, they

[c] ii. 19.

καταλλάττονται πρὶν ἐπεξελθεῖν, οἱ δὲ κριταὶ
χαρίζονται οἷς ἂν φίλοι ὦσι, καὶ ἢ ὅλως ἀφιᾶσιν
ἢ μικροῖς ζημιοῦσιν.

5 Λαθητικοὶ δ' εἰσὶν οἵ τ' ἐναντίοι τοῖς ἐγκλή-
μασιν, οἷον ἀσθενὴς περὶ αἰκίας καὶ ὁ πένης καὶ
ὁ αἰσχρὸς περὶ μοιχείας. καὶ τὰ λίαν ἐν φανερῷ
καὶ ἐν ὀφθαλμοῖς· ἀφύλακτα γὰρ διὰ τὸ μηδένα
6 ἂν οἴεσθαι. καὶ τὰ τηλικαῦτα καὶ τὰ τοιαῦτα οἷα
μηδ' ἂν εἷς· ἀφύλακτα γὰρ καὶ ταῦτα· πάντες γὰρ
τὰ εἰωθότα ὥσπερ ἀρρωστήματα φυλάττονται καὶ
τἀδικήματα, ὃ δὲ μηδείς πω ἠρρώστηκεν, οὐδεὶς
7 εὐλαβεῖται. καὶ οἷς μηδεὶς ἐχθρὸς ἢ πολλοί· οἱ
μὲν γὰρ οἴονται λήσειν διὰ τὸ μὴ φυλάττεσθαι,
οἱ δὲ λανθάνουσι διὰ τὸ μὴ δοκεῖν ἂν ἐπιχειρῆσαι
φυλαττομένοις, καὶ διὰ τὸ ἀπολογίαν ἔχειν ὅτι
8 οὐκ ἂν ἐνεχείρησαν. καὶ οἷς ὑπάρχει κρύψις ἢ
τρόπος ἢ τόπος ἢ διάθεσις εὔπορος. καὶ ὅσοις
μὴ λαθοῦσίν ἐστι δίωσις δίκης ἢ ἀναβολὴ χρόνου
ἢ διαφθοραὶ κριτῶν. καὶ οἷς, ἐὰν γένηται ζημία,
ἐστὶ δίωσις τῆς ἐκτίσεως ἢ ἀναβολὴ χρόνιος, ἢ
9 δι' ἀπορίαν μηδὲν ἕξει ὅ τι ἀπολέσῃ. καὶ οἷς τὰ
μὲν κέρδη φανερὰ ἢ μεγάλα ἢ ἐγγύς, αἱ δὲ ζημίαι
1372 b μικραὶ ἢ ἀφανεῖς ἢ πόρρω. καὶ ὧν μή ἐστι τιμωρία
10 ἴση τῇ ὠφελείᾳ, οἷον δοκεῖ ἡ τυραννίς. καὶ ὅσοις

---

[a] Two different persons. If the second ὁ be omitted, the reference is to one.
[b] Or, a " resourceful mind."

prefer reconciliation to taking proceedings; and judges favour those whom they are fond of, and either let them off altogether or inflict a small penalty.

Those are likely to remain undetected whose qualities are out of keeping with the charges, for instance, if a man wanting in physical strength were accused of assault and battery, or a poor and an ugly man [a] of adultery. Also, if the acts are done quite openly and in sight of all; for they are not guarded against, because no one would think them possible. Also, if they are so great and of such a nature that no one would even be likely to attempt them, for these also are not guarded against; for all guard against ordinary ailments and wrongs, but no one takes precautions against those ailments from which no one has ever yet suffered. And those who have either no enemy at all or many; the former hope to escape notice because they are not watched, the latter do escape because they would not be thought likely to attack those who are on their guard and because they can defend themselves by the plea that they would never have attempted it. And those who have ways or places of concealment for stolen property, or abundant opportunities of disposing of it. [b] And those who, even if they do not remain undetected, can get the trial set aside or put off, or corrupt the judges. And those who, if a fine be imposed, can get payment in full set aside or put off for a long time, or those who, owing to poverty, have nothing to lose. And in cases where the profit is certain, large, or immediate, while the punishment is small, uncertain, or remote. And where there can be no punishment equal to the advantages, as seems to be the case in a tyranny. And when the unjust

τὰ μὲν ἀδικήματα λήμματα, αἱ δὲ ζημίαι ὀνείδη
μόνον. καὶ οἷς τοὐναντίον τὰ μὲν ἀδικήματα εἰς
ἔπαινόν τινα, οἷον εἰ συνέβη ἅμα τιμωρήσασθαι
ὑπὲρ πατρὸς ἢ μητρός, ὥσπερ Ζήνωνι, αἱ δὲ
ζημίαι εἰς χρήματα ἢ φυγὴν ἢ τοιοῦτόν τι· δι'
ἀμφότερα γὰρ ἀδικοῦσι καὶ ἀμφοτέρως ἔχοντες,
πλὴν οὐχ οἱ αὐτοὶ ἀλλ' οἱ ἐναντίοι τοῖς ἤθεσιν.
11 καὶ οἱ πολλάκις ἢ λεληθότες ἢ μὴ ἐζημιωμένοι.
καὶ οἱ πολλάκις ἀποτετυχηκότες· εἰσὶ γάρ τινες
καὶ ἐν τοῖς τοιούτοις, ὥσπερ ἐν τοῖς πολεμικοῖς,
12 οἷοι ἀναμάχεσθαι. καὶ οἷς ἂν παραχρῆμα ᾖ τὸ
ἡδύ, τὸ δὲ λυπηρὸν ὕστερον, ἢ τὸ κέρδος, ἡ δὲ
ζημία ὕστερον· οἱ γὰρ ἀκρατεῖς τοιοῦτοι, ἔστι δ'
13 ἀκρασία περὶ πάντα ὅσων ὀρέγονται. καὶ οἷς ἂν
τοὐναντίον τὸ μὲν λυπηρὸν ἤδη ᾖ ἢ ἡ ζημία, τὸ δὲ
ἡδὺ καὶ ὠφέλιμον ὕστερα καὶ χρονιώτερα· οἱ γὰρ
ἐγκρατεῖς καὶ φρονιμώτεροι τὰ τοιαῦτα διώκουσιν.
14 καὶ οἷς ἂν ἐνδέχηται διὰ τύχην δόξαι πρᾶξαι ἢ δι'
ἀνάγκην ἢ διὰ φύσιν ἢ δι' ἔθος, καὶ ὅλως ἁμαρ-
15 τεῖν ἀλλὰ μὴ ἀδικεῖν. καὶ οἷς ἂν ᾖ τοῦ ἐπιεικοῦς
τυχεῖν. καὶ ὅσοι ἂν ἐνδεεῖς ὦσιν. διχῶς δ' εἰσὶν
ἐνδεεῖς· ἢ γὰρ ὡς ἀναγκαίου, ὥσπερ οἱ πένητες, ἢ
16 ὡς ὑπερβολῆς, ὥσπερ οἱ πλούσιοι. καὶ οἱ σφόδρα
εὐδοκιμοῦντες καὶ οἱ σφόδρα ἀδοξοῦντες, οἱ μὲν
ὡς οὐ δόξοντες, οἱ δ' ὡς οὐδὲν μᾶλλον δόξοντες.
17 Αὐτοὶ μὲν οὖν οὕτως ἔχοντες ἐπιχειροῦσιν,
ἀδικοῦσι δὲ τοὺς τοιούτους καὶ τὰ τοιαῦτα, τοὺς

---

a Who Zeno was, and what the story, is unknown.

b Some do wrong for the sake of gain, others for the sake
of praise ; but the former sacrifice honour for self-interest,
the latter self-interest for honour.

c " More distant " (Jebb).

acts are real gains and the only punishment is disgrace ; and when, on the contrary, the unjust acts tend to our credit, for instance, if one avenges father or mother, as was the case with Zeno,[a] while the punishment only involves loss of money, exile, or something of the kind. For men do wrong from both these motives and in both these conditions of mind ; but the persons are not the same, and their characters are exactly opposite.[b] And those who have often been undetected or have escaped punishment ; and those who have often been unsuccessful ; for in such cases, as in actual warfare, there are always men ready to return to the fight. And all who hope for pleasure and profit at once, while the pain and the loss come later ; such are the intemperate, intemperance being concerned with all things that men long for. And when, on the contrary, the pain or the loss is immediate, while the pleasure and the profit are later and more lasting[c] ; for temperate and wiser men pursue such aims. And those who may possibly be thought to have acted by chance or from necessity, from some natural impulse or from habit, in a word, to have committed an error rather than a crime. And those who hope to obtain indulgence ; and all those who are in need, which is of two kinds ; for men either need what is necessary, as the poor, or what is superfluous, as the wealthy. And those who are highly esteemed or held in great contempt ; the former will not be suspected, the latter no more than they are already.

In such a frame of mind men attempt to do wrong, and the objects of their wrongdoing are men and circumstances of the following kind.[d] Those who

[d] With a comma or colon after τὰ τοιαῦτα ; without these render : " those who possess such things as they . . ."

ἔχοντας ὧν αὐτοὶ ἐνδεεῖς ἢ εἰς τἀναγκαῖα ἢ εἰς
18 ὑπεροχὴν ἢ εἰς ἀπόλαυσιν, καὶ τοὺς πόρρω καὶ
τοὺς ἐγγύς· τῶν μὲν γὰρ ἡ λῆψις ταχεῖα, τῶν δ'
ἡ τιμωρία βραδεῖα, οἷον οἱ συλῶντες τοὺς Καρχη-
19 δονίους. καὶ τοὺς μὴ εὐλαβεῖς μηδὲ φυλακτικοὺς
ἀλλὰ πιστευτικούς· ῥᾴδιον γὰρ πάντας λαθεῖν.
καὶ τοὺς ῥαθύμους· ἐπιμελοῦς γὰρ τὸ ἐπεξελθεῖν.
καὶ τοὺς αἰσχυντηλούς· οὐ γὰρ μαχητικοὶ περὶ
20 κέρδους. καὶ τοὺς ὑπὸ πολλῶν ἀδικηθέντας καὶ
μὴ ἐπεξελθόντας ὡς ὄντας κατὰ τὴν παροιμίαν
21 τούτους Μυσῶν λείαν. καὶ οὓς μηδεπώποτε καὶ
οὓς πολλάκις· ἀμφότεροι γὰρ ἀφύλακτοι, οἱ μὲν
22 ὡς οὐδέποτε, οἱ δ' ὡς οὐκ ἂν ἔτι. καὶ τοὺς δια-
βεβλημένους ἢ εὐδιαβόλους· οἱ τοιοῦτοι γὰρ οὔτε
προαιροῦνται, φοβούμενοι τοὺς κριτάς, οὔτε δύνανται πείθειν· ὧν οἱ μισούμενοι καὶ φθονούμενοί
23 εἰσιν. καὶ πρὸς οὓς ἔχουσι πρόφασιν ἢ προγόνων
1373a ἢ αὑτῶν ἢ φίλων ἢ ποιησάντων κακῶς ἢ μελ-
λησάντων ἢ αὐτοὺς ἢ προγόνους ἢ ὧν κήδονται·
ὥσπερ γὰρ ἡ παροιμία, προφάσεως δεῖται μό-
24 νον ἡ πονηρία. καὶ τοὺς ἐχθροὺς καὶ τοὺς φίλους·
τοὺς μὲν γὰρ ῥᾴδιον, τοὺς δ' ἡδύ. καὶ τοὺς
ἀφίλους. καὶ τοὺς μὴ δεινοὺς εἰπεῖν ἢ πρᾶξαι· ἢ
γὰρ οὐκ ἐγχειροῦσιν ἐπεξιέναι, ἢ καταλλάττονται,
25 ἢ οὐδὲν περαίνουσιν. καὶ οἷς μὴ λυσιτελεῖ δια-

ᵃ Who were too far off to retaliate.
ᵇ A proverb meaning " an easy prey." The Mysians
were regarded as cowardly and unwarlike.
134

possess what they themselves lack, things either
necessary, or superfluous, or enjoyable ; both those
who are far off and those who are near, for in the
one case the gain is speedy, in the other reprisals
are slow, as if, for instance, Greeks were to plunder
Carthaginians.[a] And those who never take precautions and are never on their guard, but are
confiding ; for all these are easily taken unawares.
And those who are indolent ; for it requires a man
who takes pains to prosecute. And those who are
bashful ; for they are not likely to fight about
money. And those who have often been wronged
but have not prosecuted, being, as the proverb says,
" Mysian booty." [b] And those who have never, or
those who have often, suffered wrong ; for both are
off their guard, the one because they have never yet
been attacked, the others because they do not expect
to be attacked again. And those who have been
slandered, or are easy to slander ; for such men
neither care to go to law, for fear of the judges,
nor, if they do, can they convince them ; to this
class belong those who are exposed to hatred or
envy. And those against whom the wrongdoer can
pretend that either their ancestors, or themselves,
or their friends, have either committed, or intended
to commit, wrong either against himself, or his
ancestors, or those for whom he has great regard ;
for, as the proverb says, " evil-doing only needs an
excuse." And both enemies and friends ; for it is
easy to injure the latter, and pleasant to injure the
former. And those who are friendless. And those
who are unskilled in speech or action ; for either
they make no attempt to prosecute, or come to terms,
or accomplish nothing. And those to whom it is no

τρίβειν ἐπιτηροῦσιν ἢ δίκην ἢ ἔκτισιν, οἷον οἱ ξένοι
καὶ αὐτουργοί· ἐπὶ μικρῷ τε γὰρ διαλύονται καὶ
26 ῥᾳδίως καταπαύονται. καὶ τοὺς πολλὰ ἠδικηκό-
τας, ἢ τοιαῦτα οἷα ἀδικοῦνται· ἐγγὺς γάρ τι δοκεῖ
τοῦ μὴ ἀδικεῖν εἶναι, ὅταν τι τοιοῦτον ἀδικηθῇ
τις οἷον εἰώθει καὶ αὐτὸς ἀδικεῖν· λέγω δ' οἷον
27 εἴ τις τὸν εἰωθότα ὑβρίζειν αἰκίσαιτο. καὶ τοὺς
ἢ πεποιηκότας κακῶς ἢ βουληθέντας ἢ βουλο-
μένους ἢ ποιήσοντας· ἔχει γὰρ καὶ τὸ ἡδὺ καὶ τὸ
28 καλόν, καὶ ἐγγὺς τοῦ μὴ ἀδικεῖν φαίνεται. καὶ
οἷς χαριοῦνται ἢ φίλοις ἢ θαυμαζομένοις ἢ ἐρω-
μένοις ἢ κυρίοις ἢ ὅλως πρὸς οὓς ζῶσιν αὐτοί·
29 καὶ πρὸς οὓς ἐστιν ἐπιεικείας τυχεῖν. καὶ οἷς ἂν
ἐγκεκληκότες ὦσι καὶ προδιακεχωρηκότες, οἷον
Κάλλιππος ἐποίει τὰ περὶ Δίωνα· καὶ γὰρ τὰ
30 τοιαῦτα ἐγγὺς τοῦ μὴ ἀδικεῖν φαίνεται. καὶ τοὺς
ὑπ' ἄλλων μέλλοντας, ἂν μὴ αὐτοί, ὡς οὐκέτι
ἐνδεχόμενον βουλεύσασθαι, ὥσπερ λέγεται Αἰνεσί-
δημος Γέλωνι πέμψαι κοττάβια ἀνδραποδισαμένῳ,
31 ὅτι ἔφθασεν, ὡς καὶ αὐτὸς μέλλων. καὶ οὓς ἀδι-
κήσαντες δυνήσονται πολλὰ δίκαια πράττειν, ὡς

---

[a] αἰκία (assault) was a less serious offence than ὕβρις
(wanton outrage).

[b] οἷς, i.e. supplying ἀδικουμένοις, "by whose being
wronged." οὓς has been suggested, i.e. supplying ἀδικοῦντες,
"wronging whom."

[c] In our relations with whom, almost=from whom.
Another interpretation is: "In reference to whom there is a
chance . . . consideration *from others*, meaning the judges"
(Welldon).

[d] Callippus was a friend of Dion, who freed Syracuse
from Dionysius the Younger. He afterwards accused Dion
and contrived his murder. His excuse was that Dion knew
what he intended to do, and would be likely to strike first,
if he did not anticipate him.

advantage to waste time waiting for the verdict or damages, such as strangers or husbandmen ; for they are ready to compromise on easy terms and to drop proceedings. And those who have committed numerous wrongs, or such as those from which they themselves are suffering ; for it seems almost an act of justice that a man should suffer a wrong such as he had been accustomed to make others suffer ; if, for instance, one were to assault a man who was in the habit of outraging others.[a] And those who have already injured us, or intended, or intend, or are about to do so ; for in such a case vengeance is both pleasant and honourable, and seems to be almost an act of justice. And those whom we wrong [b] in order to ingratiate ourselves with our friends, or persons whom we admire or love, or our masters, in a word, those by whom our life is ruled. And those in reference to whom there is a chance of obtaining merciful consideration.[c] And those against whom we have a complaint, or with whom we have had a previous difference, as Callippus acted in the matter of Dion ; [d] for in such cases it seems almost an act of justice. And those who are going to be attacked by others, if we do not attack first, since it is no longer possible to deliberate ; thus, Aenesidemus is said to have sent the prize in the game of cottabus to Gelon,[e] who, having reduced a town to slavery, had anticipated him by doing what he had intended to do himself. And those to whom, after having injured them, we shall be enabled to do many acts of justice, in the

[e] Aenesidemus, tyrant of Leontini, being anticipated by Gelon, tyrant of Syracuse, in the enslavement of a neighbouring state, sent him the cottabus prize, as a compliment for having " played the game " so skilfully. The cottabus was originally a Sicilian game.

137

ῥᾳδίως ἰασόμενοι, ὥσπερ ἔφη Ἰάσων ὁ Θετταλὸς
δεῖν ἀδικεῖν ἔνια, ὅπως δύνηται καὶ δίκαια πολλὰ
ποιεῖν.

32 Καὶ ἃ πάντες ἢ πολλοὶ ἀδικεῖν εἰώθασιν· συγ-
33 γνώμης γὰρ οἴονται τεύξεσθαι. καὶ τὰ ῥᾴδια
κρύψαι· τοιαῦτα δ' ὅσα ταχὺ ἀναλίσκεται, οἷον
τὰ ἐδώδιμα, ἢ τὰ εὐμετάβλητα σχήμασιν ἢ χρώ-
34 μασιν ἢ κράσεσιν. ἢ ἃ πολλαχοῦ ἀφανίσαι εὔπορον·
τοιαῦτα δὲ τὰ εὐβάστακτα καὶ ἐν μικροῖς τόποις
35 ἀφανιζόμενα. καὶ οἷς ἀδιάφορα καὶ ὅμοια πολλὰ
προϋπῆρχε τῷ ἀδικοῦντι. καὶ ὅσα αἰσχύνονται οἱ
ἀδικηθέντες λέγειν, οἷον γυναικῶν οἰκείων ὕβρεις
ἢ εἰς αὑτοὺς ἢ εἰς υἱεῖς: καὶ ὅσα φιλοδικεῖν
δόξειεν ἂν ὁ ἐπεξιών· τοιαῦτα δὲ τά τε μικρὰ καὶ
ἐφ' οἷς συγγνώμη. ὡς μὲν οὖν ἔχοντες ἀδικοῦσι,
καὶ ποῖα καὶ ποίους καὶ διὰ τί, σχεδὸν ταῦτ' ἐστίν.

1373 b 13. Τὰ δ' ἀδικήματα πάντα καὶ τὰ δικαιώματα
διέλωμεν, ἀρξάμενοι πρῶτον ἐντεῦθεν. ὥρισται
δὴ τὰ δίκαια καὶ τὰ ἄδικα πρός τε νόμους [δύο],[1]
2 καὶ πρὸς οὕς ἐστι, διχῶς. λέγω δὲ νόμον τὸν μὲν
ἴδιον τὸν δὲ κοινόν, ἴδιον μὲν τὸν ἑκάστοις ὡρισμένον πρὸς αὑτούς, καὶ τοῦτον τὸν μὲν ἄγραφον
τὸν δὲ γεγραμμένον, κοινὸν δὲ τὸν κατὰ φύσιν.
ἔστι γάρ, ὃ μαντεύονταί τι πάντες, φύσει κοινὸν
δίκαιον καὶ ἄδικον, κἂν μηδεμία κοινωνία πρὸς

---

[1] Bracketed by Spengel, but retained by Roemer.

[a] Tyrant of Pherae.

idea that it will be easy to repair the wrong ; as Jason the Thessalian[a] said one should sometimes commit injustice, in order to be able also to do justice often.

Men are ready to commit wrongs which all or many are in the habit of committing, for they hope to be pardoned for their offences. They steal objects that are easy to conceal ; such are things that are quickly consumed, as eatables ; things which can easily be changed in form or colour or composition ; things for which there are many convenient hiding-places, such as those that are easy to carry or stow away in a corner ; those of which a thief already possesses a considerable number exactly similar or hard to distinguish. Or they commit wrongs which the victims are ashamed to disclose, such as outrages upon the women of their family, upon themselves, or upon their children. And all those wrongs in regard to which appeal to the law would create the appearance of litigiousness ; such are wrongs which are unimportant or venial. These are nearly all the dispositions which induce men to commit wrong, the nature and motive of the wrongs, and the kind of persons who are the victims of wrong.

13. Let us now classify just and unjust actions generally, starting from what follows. Justice and injustice have been defined in reference to laws and persons in two ways. Now there are two kinds of laws, particular and general. By particular laws I mean those established by each people in reference to themselves, which again are divided into written and unwritten ; by general laws I mean those based upon nature. In fact, there is a general idea of just and unjust in accordance with nature, as all men in a manner divine, even if there is neither communica-

ἀλλήλους ᾖ μηδὲ συνθήκη, οἷον καὶ ἡ Σοφοκλέους
Ἀντιγόνη φαίνεται λέγουσα, ὅτι δίκαιον ἀπειρη-
μένον θάψαι τὸν Πολυνείκη, ὡς φύσει ὂν τοῦτο
δίκαιον·

> οὐ γάρ τι νῦν γε κἀχθές, ἀλλ' ἀεί ποτε
> ζῇ τοῦτο, κοὐδεὶς οἶδεν ἐξ ὅτου φάνη.

καὶ ὡς Ἐμπεδοκλῆς λέγει περὶ τοῦ μὴ κτείνειν
τὸ ἔμψυχον· τοῦτο γὰρ οὐ τισὶ μὲν δίκαιον τισὶ δ'
οὐ δίκαιον,

> ἀλλὰ τὸ μὲν πάντων νόμιμον διά τ' εὐρυμέδοντος
> αἰθέρος ἠνεκέως τέταται διά τ' ἀπλέτου αὖ γῆς.

καὶ ὡς ἐν τῷ Μεσσηνιακῷ λέγει Ἀλκιδάμας.
3 πρὸς οὓς δὲ διώρισται, διχῶς διώρισται· ἢ γὰρ
πρὸς τὸ κοινὸν ἢ πρὸς ἕνα τῶν κοινωνούντων, ἃ
δεῖ πράττειν καὶ μὴ πράττειν.

Διὸ καὶ τἀδικήματα καὶ τὰ δικαιώματα διχῶς
ἔστιν ἀδικεῖν καὶ δικαιοπραγεῖν· ἢ γὰρ πρὸς ἕνα
καὶ ὡρισμένον ἢ πρὸς τὸ κοινόν· ὁ γὰρ μοιχεύων
καὶ τύπτων ἀδικεῖ τινὰ τῶν ὡρισμένων, ὁ δὲ μὴ
4 στρατευόμενος τὸ κοινόν. ἁπάντων δὴ τῶν ἀδικημάτων διῃρημένων, καὶ τῶν μὲν ὄντων πρὸς τὸ
κοινὸν τῶν δὲ πρὸς ἄλλον καὶ πρὸς ἄλλους, ἀνα-
λαβόντες τί ἐστι τὸ ἀδικεῖσθαι, λέγομεν τὰ λοιπά.
5 ἔστι δὴ τὸ ἀδικεῖσθαι τὸ ὑπὸ ἑκόντος τὰ ἄδικα
πάσχειν· τὸ γὰρ ἀδικεῖν ὥρισται πρότερον ἑκούσιον

---

tion nor agreement between them. This is what Antigone in Sophocles [a] evidently means, when she declares that it is just, though forbidden, to bury Polynices, as being naturally just :

For neither to-day nor yesterday, but from all eternity, these statutes live and no man knoweth whence they came.

And as Empedocles says in regard to not killing that which has life, for this is not right for some and wrong for others,

But a universal precept, which extends without a break throughout the wide-ruling sky and the boundless earth.

Alcidamas [b] also speaks of this precept in his *Messeniacus*. . . . And in relation to persons, there is a twofold division of law ; for what one ought to do or ought not to do is concerned with the community generally, or one of its members.

Therefore there are two kinds of just and unjust acts, since they can be committed against a definite individual or against the community ; he who commits adultery or an assault is guilty of wrong against a definite individual, he who refuses to serve in the army of wrong against the State. All kinds of wrong acts having been thus distinguished, some of which affect the State, others one or several individuals, let us repeat the definition of being wronged,[c] and then go on to the rest. Being wronged is to suffer injustice at the hands of one who voluntarily inflicts it, for it has been established

the scholiast supplies his words : ἐλευθέρους ἀφῆκε πάντας θεός · οὐδένα δοῦλον ἡ φύσις πεποίηκεν ("God has left all men free ; Nature has made none a slave "). The Messenians had revolted from Sparta.

  [c] i. 10. 3.

ARISTOTLE

6 εἶναι. ἐπεὶ δ᾽ ἀνάγκη τὸν ἀδικούμενον βλάπτεσθαι καὶ ἀκουσίως βλάπτεσθαι, αἱ μὲν βλάβαι ἐκ τῶν πρότερον φανεραί εἰσιν· τὰ γὰρ ἀγαθὰ καὶ τὰ κακὰ διῄρηται καθ᾽ αὑτὰ πρότερον, καὶ τὰ ἑκούσια,

7 ὅτι ἐστὶν ὅσα εἰδότες. ὥστ᾽ ἀνάγκη πάντα τὰ ἐγκλήματα ἢ πρὸς τὸ κοινὸν ἢ πρὸς τὸ ἴδιον εἶναι, καὶ ἢ ἀγνοοῦντος ἢ ἄκοντος, ἢ ἑκόντος καὶ εἰδότος, καὶ τούτων τὰ μὲν προελομένου τὰ δὲ διὰ πάθος.

8 περὶ μὲν οὖν θυμοῦ ῥηθήσεται ἐν τοῖς περὶ τὰ πάθη, ποῖα δὲ προαιροῦνται καὶ πῶς ἔχοντες, εἴρηται πρότερον.

9 Ἐπεὶ δ᾽ ὁμολογοῦντες πολλάκις πεπραχέναι ἢ
1374a τὸ ἐπίγραμμα οὐχ ὁμολογοῦσιν ἢ περὶ ὃ τὸ ἐπίγραμμα, οἷον λαβεῖν μὲν ἀλλ᾽ οὐ κλέψαι, καὶ πατάξαι πρότερον ἀλλ᾽ οὐχ ὑβρίσαι, καὶ συγγενέσθαι ἀλλ᾽ οὐ μοιχεῦσαι, ἢ κλέψαι ἀλλ᾽ οὐχ ἱεροσυλῆσαι ῾ου γὰρ θεοῦ τι), ἢ ἐπεργάσασθαι μὲν ἀλλ᾽ οὐ δημοσίαν, ἢ διειλέχθαι μὲν τοῖς πολεμίοις ἀλλ᾽ οὐ προδοῦναι, διὰ ταῦτα δέοι ἂν καὶ περὶ τούτων διωρίσθαι, τί κλοπή, τί ὕβρις, τί μοιχεία, ὅπως ἐάν τε ὑπάρχειν ἐάν τε μὴ ὑπάρχειν βουλώμεθα

10 δεικνύναι, ἔχωμεν ἐμφανίζειν τὸ δίκαιον. ἔστι δὲ πάντα τὰ τοιαῦτα περὶ τοῦ ἄδικον εἶναι καὶ φαῦλον ἢ μὴ ἄδικον ἡ ἀμφισβήτησις· ἐν γὰρ τῇ προαιρέσει

^a i. 6.　　^b i. 10. 3.　　^c ii. 2.　　^d i. 11, 12.

that injustice is a voluntary act. And since the man
who suffers injustice necessarily sustains injury and
that against his will, it is evident from what has been
said in what the injuries consist; for things good
and bad have already been distinguished in themselves,[a] and it has been said that voluntary acts are
all such as are committed with knowledge of the
case.[b] Hence it necessarily follows that all accusations concern the State or the individual, the accused
having acted either ignorantly and against his will,
or voluntarily and with knowledge, and in the latter
case with malice aforethought or from passion. We
will speak of anger when we come to treat of the
passions,[c] and we have already stated[d] in what
circumstances and with what dispositions men act
with deliberate purpose.

But since a man, while admitting the fact, often
denies the description of the charge or the point on
which it turns—for instance, admits that he took
something, but did not steal it; that he was the
first to strike, but committed no outrage; that he
had relations, but did not commit adultery, with a
woman; or that he stole something but was not
guilty of sacrilege, since the object in question was
not consecrated; or that he trespassed, but not on
public land; or that he held converse with the
enemy, but was not guilty of treason—for this reason
it will be necessary that a definition should be given
of theft, outrage, or adultery, in order that, if we
desire to prove that an offence has or has not been
committed, we may be able to put the case in a true
light. In all such instances the question at issue is
to know whether the supposed offender is a wrongdoer and a worthless person, or not; for vice and

ἢ μοχθηρία καὶ τὸ ἀδικεῖν, τὰ δὲ τοιαῦτα τῶν
ὀνομάτων προσσημαίνει τὴν προαίρεσιν, οἷον ὕβρις
καὶ κλοπή· οὐ γὰρ εἰ ἐπάταξε, πάντως ὕβρισεν,
ἀλλ' εἰ ἕνεκά του, οἷον τοῦ ἀτιμάσαι ἐκεῖνον ἢ
αὐτὸς ἡσθῆναι. οὐδὲ πάντως, εἰ λάθρα ἔλαβεν,
ἔκλεψεν, ἀλλ' εἰ ἐπὶ βλάβῃ καὶ σφετερισμῷ ἑαυτοῦ.[a]
ὁμοίως δὲ καὶ περὶ τῶν ἄλλων ἔχει, ὥσπερ καὶ
περὶ τούτων.

11 Ἐπεὶ δὲ τῶν δικαίων καὶ τῶν ἀδίκων ἦν δύο
εἴδη (τὰ μὲν γὰρ γεγραμμένα τὰ δ' ἄγραφα), περὶ
ὧν μὲν οἱ νόμοι ἀγορεύουσιν εἴρηται, τῶν δ' ἀγρά-
12 φων δύο ἐστὶν εἴδη· ταῦτα δ' ἐστὶ τὰ μὲν καθ'
ὑπερβολὴν ἀρετῆς καὶ κακίας, ἐφ' οἷς ὀνείδη καὶ
ἔπαινοι καὶ ἀτιμίαι· καὶ τιμαὶ καὶ δωρεαί, οἷον
τὸ χάριν ἔχειν τῷ ποιήσαντι εὖ καὶ ἀντευποιεῖν
τὸν εὖ ποιήσαντα καὶ βοηθητικὸν εἶναι τοῖς φίλοις
καὶ ὅσα ἄλλα τοιαῦτα, τὰ δὲ τοῦ ἰδίου νόμου καὶ
13 γεγραμμένου ἔλλειμμα. τὸ γὰρ ἐπιεικὲς δοκεῖ
δίκαιον εἶναι, ἔστι δὲ ἐπιεικὲς τὸ παρὰ τὸν γεγραμμένον νόμον δίκαιον. συμβαίνει δὲ τοῦτο τὰ
μὲν ἀκόντων τὰ δὲ ἑκόντων τῶν νομοθετῶν,
ἀκόντων μὲν ὅταν λάθῃ, ἑκόντων δ' ὅταν μὴ
δύνωνται διορίσαι, ἀλλ' ἀναγκαῖον μὲν ᾖ καθόλου
εἰπεῖν, μὴ ᾖ δέ, ἀλλ' ὡς ἐπὶ τὸ πολύ. καὶ ὅσα

---

[a] Roemer reads, after Dittmeyer, εἰ ἐπὶ βλάβῃ [τούτου ἀφ'
οὗ ἔλαβε] καὶ . . . from the old Latin translation.
[b] Laws are special and general, the former being written
or unwritten. The unwritten law, again, is of two kinds:
(1) general; (2) supplementary to the special written law.
This general law (not the same as the general law "based
upon nature" § 2) refers to acts which go beyond the legal
standard of virtuous or vicious acts and are characterized by

wrongdoing consist in the moral purpose, and such terms as outrage and theft further indicate purpose; for if a man has struck, it does not in all cases follow that he has committed an outrage, but only if he has struck with a certain object, for instance, to bring disrepute upon the other or to please himself. Again, if a man has taken something by stealth, it is by no means certain that he has committed theft, but only if he has taken it to injure another [a] or to get something for himself. It is the same in all other cases as in these.

We have said that there are two kinds of just and unjust actions (for some are written, but others are unwritten), and have spoken of those concerning which the laws are explicit; of those that are unwritten there are two kinds. One kind arises from an excess of virtue or vice, which is followed by praise or blame, honour or dishonour, and rewards; for instance, to be grateful to a benefactor, to render good for good, to help one's friends, and the like; [b] the other kind contains what is omitted in the special written law. For that which is equitable seems to be just, and equity is justice that goes beyond the written law. These omissions are sometimes involuntary, sometimes voluntary, on the part of the legislators; involuntary when it may have escaped their notice, voluntary when, being unable to define for all cases, they are obliged to make a universal statement, which is not applicable to all, but only to most, cases; and whenever it is difficult to give

a remarkable degree (καθ' ὑπερβολήν) of virtue or the opposite. For these laws do not prescribe any special reward or punishment, but acts are praised or blamed, honoured or dishonoured, rewarded or punished, in accordance with the general feeling of mankind.

145

μὴ ῥᾴδιον διορίσαι δι᾽ ἀπειρίαν, οἷον τὸ τρῶσαι
σιδήρῳ πηλίκῳ καὶ ποίῳ τινί· ὑπολείποι γὰρ ἂν
14 ὁ αἰὼν διαριθμοῦντα. ἂν οὖν ᾖ ἀδιόριστον, δέῃ
δὲ νομοθετῆσαι, ἀνάγκη ἁπλῶς εἰπεῖν, ὥστε κἂν
δακτύλιον ἔχων ἐπάρηται τὴν χεῖρα ἢ πατάξῃ,
κατὰ μὲν τὸν γεγραμμένον νόμον ἔνοχός ἐστι καὶ
ἀδικεῖ, κατὰ δὲ τὸ ἀληθὲς οὐκ ἀδικεῖ, καὶ τὸ
1374 b ἐπιεικὲς τοῦτο ἐστίν.
15 Εἰ δ᾽ ἐστὶ τὸ εἰρημένον τὸ ἐπιεικές, φανερὸν
ποῖά ἐστι τὰ ἐπιεικῆ καὶ οὐκ ἐπιεικῆ, καὶ ποῖοι
16 οὐκ ἐπιεικεῖς ἄνθρωποι· ἐφ᾽ οἷς τε γὰρ δεῖ συγγνώμην ἔχειν, ἐπιεικῆ ταῦτα, καὶ τὸ τὰ ἁμαρτήματα καὶ τὰ ἀδικήματα μὴ τοῦ ἴσου ἀξιοῦν, μηδὲ
τὰ ἀτυχήματα· ἔστι δ᾽ ἀτυχήματα μὲν ὅσα παράλογα καὶ μὴ ἀπὸ μοχθηρίας, ἁμαρτήματα δὲ ὅσα
μὴ παράλογα καὶ μὴ ἀπὸ πονηρίας, ἀδικήματα
δὲ ὅσα μήτε παράλογα ἀπὸ πονηρίας τ᾽ ἐστίν·
17 τὰ γὰρ δι᾽ ἐπιθυμίαν ἀπὸ πονηρίας. καὶ τὸ τοῖς
ἀνθρωπίνοις συγγινώσκειν ἐπιεικές. καὶ τὸ μὴ
πρὸς τὸν νόμον ἀλλὰ πρὸς τὸν νομοθέτην σκοπεῖν,
καὶ μὴ πρὸς τὸν λόγον ἀλλὰ πρὸς τὴν διάνοιαν
τοῦ νομοθέτου, καὶ μὴ πρὸς τὴν πρᾶξιν ἀλλὰ πρὸς
18 τὴν προαίρεσιν, καὶ μὴ πρὸς τὸ μέρος ἀλλὰ πρὸς
τὸ ὅλον, μηδὲ ποῖός τις νῦν, ἀλλὰ ποῖός τις ἦν
ἀεὶ ἢ ὡς ἐπὶ τὸ πολύ. καὶ τὸ μνημονεύειν μᾶλλον
ὧν ἔπαθεν ἀγαθῶν ἢ κακῶν, καὶ ἀγαθῶν ὧν
ἔπαθε μᾶλλον ἢ ἐποίησεν. καὶ τὸ ἀνέχεσθαι
ἀδικούμενον. καὶ τὸ μᾶλλον λόγῳ ἐθέλειν κρί-
19 νεσθαι ἢ ἔργῳ. καὶ τὸ εἰς δίαιταν μᾶλλον ἢ εἰς
δίκην βούλεσθαι ἰέναι· ὁ γὰρ διαιτητὴς τὸ ἐπιεικὲς

---

a definition owing to the infinite number of cases,[a] as, for instance, the size and kind of an iron instrument used in wounding ; for life would not be long enough to reckon all the possibilities. If then no exact definition is possible, but legislation is necessary, one must have recourse to general terms ; so that, if a man wearing a ring lifts up his hand to strike or actually strikes, according to the written law he is guilty of wrongdoing, but in reality he is not ; and this is a case for equity.

If then our definition of equity is correct, it is easy to see what things and persons are equitable or not. Actions which should be leniently treated are cases for equity ; errors, wrong acts, and misfortunes, must not be thought deserving of the same penalty. Misfortunes are all such things as are unexpected and not vicious ; errors are not unexpected, but are not vicious ; wrong acts are such as might be expected and vicious, for acts committed through desire arise from vice. And it is equitable to pardon human weaknesses, and to look, not to the law but to the legislator ; not to the letter of the law but to the intention of the legislator ; not to the action itself, but to the moral purpose ; not to the part, but to the whole ; not to what a man is now, but to what he has been, always or generally ; to remember good rather than ill treatment, and benefits received rather than those conferred ; to bear injury with patience ; to be willing to appeal to the judgement of reason rather than to violence ;[b] to prefer arbitration to the law court, for the arbitrator keeps equity in view, whereas the dicast looks

---

[b] " To be willing that a judicial sentence should be nominal rather than real " (Jebb).

ὁρᾷ, ὁ δὲ δικαστὴς τὸν νόμον· καὶ τούτου ἕνεκα
διαιτητὴς εὑρέθη, ὅπως τὸ ἐπιεικὲς ἰσχύῃ. περὶ
μὲν οὖν τῶν ἐπιεικῶν διωρίσθω τὸν τρόπον τοῦτον.

14. ᾿Αδίκημα δὲ μεῖζον, ὅσῳ ἂν ἀπὸ μείζονος
ᾖ ἀδικίας· διὸ καὶ τὰ ἐλάχιστα μέγιστα, οἷον ὁ
Μελανώπου Καλλίστρατος κατηγόρει, ὅτι παρ-
ελογίσατο τρία ἡμιωβέλια ἱερὰ τοὺς ναοποιούς·
ἐπὶ δικαιοσύνης δὲ τοὐναντίον. ἔστι δὲ ταῦτα ἐκ
τοῦ ἐνυπάρχειν τῇ δυνάμει· ὁ γὰρ τρία ἡμιωβέλια
ἱερὰ κλέψας κἂν ὁτιοῦν ἀδικήσειεν. ὁτὲ μὲν δὴ
οὕτω τὸ μεῖζον, ὁτὲ δ᾿ ἐκ τοῦ βλάβους κρίνεται.
2 καὶ οὗ μή ἐστιν ἴση τιμωρία, ἀλλὰ πᾶσα ἐλάττων.
καὶ οὗ μή ἐστιν ἴασις· χαλεπὸν γὰρ καὶ ἀδύνατον.
καὶ οὗ μή ἔστι δίκην λαβεῖν τὸν παθόντα· ἀνίατον
3 γάρ· ἡ γὰρ δίκη καὶ κόλασις ἴασις. καὶ εἰ ὁ
παθὼν καὶ ἀδικηθεὶς αὐτὸς αὑτὸν μεγάλως ἐκό-
λασεν· ἔτι γὰρ μείζονι ὁ ποιήσας δίκαιος κολα-
σθῆναι, οἷον Σοφοκλῆς ὑπὲρ Εὐκτήμονος συνηγορῶν, ἐπεὶ ἀπέσφαξεν ἑαυτὸν ὑβρισθείς, οὐ
1375 a τιμήσειν ἔφη ἐλάττονος ἢ οὗ ὁ παθὼν ἑαυτῷ
4 ἐτίμησεν. καὶ ὃ μόνος ἢ πρῶτος ἢ μετ᾿ ὀλίγων
πεποίηκεν. καὶ τὸ πολλάκις τὸ αὐτὸ ἁμαρτάνειν
μέγα. καὶ δι᾿ ὃ ἂν ζητηθῇ καὶ εὑρεθῇ τὰ κωλύοντα
καὶ ζημιοῦντα, οἷον ἐν ῎Αργει ζημιοῦται δι᾿ ὃν ἂν

---

[a] i. 7. 13. Callistratus and Melanopus were rival orators.
Nothing is known of this particular charge.
[b] The magistrates who superintended the building and
repairing operations.
[c] Understanding ἰᾶσθαι. Or " to punish adequately,"
supplying οὗ μὴ ἴση τιμωρία.
[d] An orator, not the tragic poet.
[e] " Or has been seldom paralleled " (Cope, but cp. i. 9. 38).

only to the law, and the reason why arbitrators were appointed was that equity might prevail. Let this manner of defining equity suffice.

14. Wrong acts are greater in proportion to the injustice from which they spring. For this reason the most trifling are sometimes the greatest, as in the charge brought by Callistratus [a] against Melanopus that he had fraudulently kept back three consecrated half-obols from the temple-builders [b]; whereas, in the case of just actions, it is quite the contrary. The reason is that the greater potentially inheres in the less; for he who has stolen three consecrated half-obols will commit any wrong whatever. Wrong acts are judged greater sometimes in this way, sometimes by the extent of the injury done. A wrong act is greater when there is no adequate punishment for it, but all are insufficient; when there is no remedy, because it is difficult if not impossible to repair it; [c] and when the person injured cannot obtain legal satisfaction, since it is irremediable; for justice and punishment are kinds of remedies. And if the sufferer, having been wronged, has inflicted some terrible injury upon himself, the guilty person deserves greater punishment; wherefore Sophocles,[d] when pleading on behalf of Euctemon, who had committed suicide after the outrage he had suffered, declared that he would not assess the punishment at less than the victim had assessed it for himself. A wrong act is also greater when it is unprecedented, or the first of its kind, or when committed with the aid of few accomplices [e]; and when it has been frequently committed; or when because of it new prohibitions and penalties have been sought and found: thus, at Argos the citizen owing to whom a new

νόμος τεθῇ καὶ δι' οὓς τὸ δεσμωτήριον ᾠκοδο-
5 μήθη. καὶ τὸ θηριωδέστερον ἀδίκημα μεῖζον.
καὶ ὃ ἐκ προνοίας μᾶλλον. καὶ ὃ οἱ ἀκούοντες
φοβοῦνται μᾶλλον ἢ ἐλεοῦσιν. καὶ τὰ μὲν ῥητορικά
ἐστι τοιαῦτα, ὅτι πολλὰ ἀνῄρηκε δίκαια ἢ ὑπερ-
βέβηκεν, οἷον ὅρκους δεξιὰς πίστεις ἐπιγαμίας·
6 πολλῶν γὰρ ἀδικημάτων ὑπεροχή. καὶ τὸ ἐνταῦθα
οὗ κολάζονται οἱ ἀδικοῦντες, ὅπερ ποιοῦσιν οἱ
ψευδομαρτυροῦντες· ποῦ γὰρ οὐκ ἂν ἀδικήσειεν,
εἴ γε καὶ ἐν τῷ δικαστηρίῳ; καὶ ἐφ' οἷς αἰσχύνη
μάλιστα. καὶ εἰ τοῦτον ὑφ' οὗ εὖ πέπονθεν·
πλείω γὰρ ἀδικεῖ, ὅτι τε κακῶς ποιεῖ καὶ ὅτι οὐκ
7 εὖ. καὶ ὃ παρὰ τὰ ἄγραφα δίκαια· ἀμείνονος γὰρ
μὴ δι' ἀνάγκην δίκαιον εἶναι. τὰ μὲν οὖν γεγραμμένα ἐξ ἀνάγκης, τὰ δ' ἄγραφα οὔ. ἄλλον δὲ
τρόπον, εἰ παρὰ τὰ γεγραμμένα· ὁ γὰρ τὰ φοβερὰ
ἀδικῶν καὶ τὰ ἐπιζήμια καὶ τὰ μὴ ἐπιζήμια
ἀδικήσειεν ἄν. περὶ μὲν οὖν ἀδικήματος μείζονος
καὶ ἐλάττονος εἴρηται.

15. Περὶ δὲ τῶν ἀτέχνων καλουμένων πίστεων
ἐχόμενόν ἐστι τῶν εἰρημένων ἐπιδραμεῖν· ἴδιαι γὰρ
2 αὗται τῶν δικανικῶν. εἰσὶ δὲ πέντε τὸν ἀριθμόν,

---

a And therefore the violation of them is more discreditable.
b When he thinks of the punishment they may entail.

law has been passed, is punished, as well as those on whose account a new prison had to be built. The crime is greater, the more brutal it is ; or when it has been for a long time premeditated ; when the recital of it inspires terror rather than pity. Rhetorical tricks of the following kind may be used :—the statement that the accused person has swept away or violated several principles of justice, for example, oaths, pledges of friendship, plighted word, the sanctity of marriage ; for this amounts to heaping crime upon crime. Wrong acts are greater when committed in the very place where wrongdoers themselves are sentenced, as is done by false witnesses ; for where would a man not commit wrong, if he does so in a court of justice ? They are also greater when accompanied by the greatest disgrace ; when committed against one who has been the guilty person's benefactor, for in that case, the wrongdoer is guilty of wrong twice over, in that he not only does wrong, but does not return good for good. So too, again, when a man offends against the unwritten laws of right, for there is greater merit in doing right without being compelled[a]; now the written laws involve compulsion, the unwritten do not. Looked at in another way, wrongdoing is greater, if it violates the written laws ; for a man who commits wrongs that alarm him [b] and involve punishment, will be ready to commit wrong for which he will not be punished. Let this suffice for the treatment of the greater or less degree of wrongdoing.

15. Following on what we have just spoken of, we have now briefly to run over what are called the inartificial proofs, for these properly belong to forensic oratory. These proofs are five in number : laws,

3 νόμοι μάρτυρες συνθῆκαι βάσανοι ὅρκος. πρῶτον
μὲν οὖν περὶ νόμων εἴπωμεν, πῶς χρηστέον καὶ
προτρέποντα καὶ ἀποτρέποντα καὶ κατηγοροῦντα
4 καὶ ἀπολογούμενον. φανερὸν γὰρ ὅτι, ἐὰν μὲν
ἐναντίος ᾖ ὁ γεγραμμένος τῷ πράγματι, τῷ κοινῷ
νόμῳ χρηστέον καὶ τοῖς ἐπιεικέσιν ὡς δικαιο-
5 τέροις. καὶ ὅτι τὸ γνώμῃ τῇ ἀρίστῃ τοῦτ' ἐστί,
6 τὸ μὴ παντελῶς χρῆσθαι τοῖς γεγραμμένοις. καὶ
ὅτι τὸ μὲν ἐπιεικὲς ἀεὶ μένει καὶ οὐδέποτε μετα-
βάλλει, οὐδ' ὁ κοινός (κατὰ φύσιν γάρ ἐστιν), οἱ
δὲ γεγραμμένοι πολλάκις· ὅθεν εἴρηται τὰ ἐν τῇ
Σοφοκλέους Ἀντιγόνῃ· ἀπολογεῖται γὰρ ὅτι ἔθαψε
παρὰ τὸν τοῦ Κρέοντος νόμον, ἀλλ' οὐ παρὰ τὸν
ἄγραφον·

1375 b   οὐ γάρ τι νῦν γε κἀχθές, ἀλλ' ἀεί ποτε . . .
          ταῦτ' οὖν ἐγὼ οὐκ ἔμελλον ἀνδρὸς οὐδενός.

7 καὶ ὅτι τὸ δίκαιόν ἐστιν ἀληθές τι καὶ συμφέρον,
ἀλλ' οὐ τὸ δοκοῦν· ὥστ' οὐ νόμος ὁ γεγραμμένος·
οὐ γὰρ ποιεῖ τὸ ἔργον τὸ τοῦ νόμου· καὶ ὅτι
ὥσπερ ἀργυρογνώμων ὁ κριτής ἐστιν, ὅπως
8 διακρίνῃ τὸ κίβδηλον δίκαιον καὶ τὸ ἀληθές. καὶ
ὅτι βελτίονος ἀνδρὸς τὸ τοῖς ἀγράφοις ἢ τοῖς
9 γεγραμμένοις χρῆσθαι καὶ ἐμμένειν. καὶ εἴ που
ἐναντίος νόμῳ εὐδοκιμοῦντι ἢ καὶ αὐτὸς αὑτῷ·
οἷον ἐνίοτε ὁ μὲν κελεύει κύρια εἶναι ἅττ' ἂν

---

a Although the use of inartificial proofs is almost entirely
confined to forensic oratory, they *may* be used in deliberative
oratory.

b The first line is quoted i. 13. 2. The second differs
somewhat from Sophocles (*Antigone*, 458), where the passage
runs, τούτων ἐγὼ οὐκ ἔμελλον, ἀνδρὸς οὐδενὸς | φρόνημα δείσασ', ἐν
θεοῖσι τὴν δίκην | δώσειν (" I was not likely, through fear of the

witnesses, contracts, torture, oaths.   Let us first then
speak of the laws, and state what use should be made
of them when exhorting or dissuading,[a] accusing or
defending.   For it is evident that, if the written law
is counter to our case, we must have recourse to
the general law and equity, as more in accordance
with justice; and we must argue that, when the dicast
takes an oath to decide to the best of his judgement,
he means that he will not abide rigorously by the
written laws ; that equity is ever constant and never
changes, even as the general law, which is based on
nature, whereas the written laws often vary (this
is why Antigone in Sophocles justifies herself for
having buried Polynices contrary to the law of
Creon, but not contrary to the unwritten law :

> For this law is not of now or yesterday, but is eternal . . .
> this I was not likely [to infringe through fear of the pride]
> of any man);[b]

and further, that justice is real and expedient, but
not that which only appears just; nor the written
law either, because it does not do the work of the
law[c]; that the judge is like an assayer of silver,
whose duty is to distinguish spurious from genuine
justice ; that it is the part of a better man to make
use of and abide by the unwritten rather than the
written law.[d]   Again, it is necessary to see whether
the law is contradictory to another approved law or
to itself ; for instance, one law enacts that all con-

pride of any man, to incur the penalty for violating these
statutes at the bar of heaven ").
   [c] Which is the administration of real justice, not that
which appears to the legislator to be such and is embodied
in legal enactments.
   [d] Cp. 14. 7 above.

ARISTOTLE

συνθῶνται, ὁ δ' ἀπαγορεύει μὴ συντίθεσθαι παρὰ
10 τὸν νόμον. καὶ εἰ ἀμφίβολος, ὥστε στρέφειν καὶ
ὁρᾶν ἐφ' ὁποτέραν τὴν ἀγωγὴν ἢ τὸ δίκαιον ἐφ-
11 αρμόσει ἢ τὸ συμφέρον, εἶτα τούτῳ χρῆσθαι. καὶ
εἰ τὰ μὲν πράγματα ἐφ' οἷς ἐτέθη ὁ νόμος μηκέτι
μένει, ὁ δὲ νόμος, πειρατέον τοῦτο δηλοῦν καὶ
12 μάχεσθαι ταύτῃ πρὸς τὸν νόμον. ἐὰν δὲ ὁ γεγραμμένος ᾖ πρὸς τὸ πρᾶγμα, τό τε γνώμῃ τῇ
ἀρίστῃ λεκτέον ὅτι οὐ τοῦ παρὰ τὸν νόμον ἕνεκα
δικάζειν ἐστίν, ἀλλ' ἵνα, ἐὰν ἀγνοήσῃ τί λέγει ὁ
νόμος, μὴ ἐπιορκῇ. καὶ ὅτι οὐ τὸ ἁπλῶς ἀγαθὸν
αἱρεῖται οὐδείς, ἀλλὰ τὸ αὑτῷ. καὶ ὅτι οὐδὲν
διαφέρει ἢ μὴ κεῖσθαι ἢ μὴ χρῆσθαι. καὶ ὅτι ἐν
ταῖς ἄλλαις τέχναις οὐ λυσιτελεῖ παρασοφίζεσθαι
τὸν ἰατρόν· οὐ γὰρ τοσοῦτο βλάπτει ἡ ἁμαρτία
τοῦ ἰατροῦ ὅσον τὸ ἐθίζεσθαι ἀπειθεῖν τῷ ἄρχοντι.
καὶ ὅτι τὸ τῶν νόμων σοφώτερον ζητεῖν εἶναι,
τοῦτ' ἐστὶν ὃ ἐν τοῖς ἐπαινουμένοις νόμοις ἀπαγο-
ρεύεται. καὶ περὶ μὲν τῶν νόμων οὕτω διωρίσθω.
13 Περὶ δὲ μαρτύρων, μάρτυρές εἰσι διττοί, οἱ
μὲν παλαιοὶ οἱ δὲ πρόσφατοι, καὶ τούτων οἱ μὲν
μετέχοντες τοῦ κινδύνου οἱ δ' ἐκτός. λέγω δὲ
παλαιοὺς μὲν τούς τε ποιητὰς καὶ ὅσων ἄλλων
γνωρίμων εἰσὶ κρίσεις φανεραί, οἷον Ἀθηναῖοι
Ὁμήρῳ μάρτυρι ἐχρήσαντο περὶ Σαλαμῖνος καὶ
Τενέδιοι ἔναγχος Περιάνδρῳ τῷ Κορινθίῳ πρὸς

---

[a] Αἴας δ' ἐκ Σαλαμῖνος ἄγεν δυοκαίδεκα νῆας, | στῆσε δ' ἄγων ἵν'
Ἀθηναίων ἵσταντο φάλαγγες, Iliad, ii. 557-8. The Lacedaemonians, acting as arbitrators between Athens and Megara,
who were fighting for the possession of Salamis, decided in
favour of Athens on the strength of the two lines in the Iliad,
which were taken to show that Salamis belonged to Athens.
154

tracts should be binding, while another forbids making contracts contrary to the law. If the meaning of the law is equivocal, we must turn it about, and see in which way it is to be interpreted so as to suit the application of justice or expediency, and have recourse to that. If the conditions which led to the enactment of the law are now obsolete, while the law itself remains, one must endeavour to make this clear and to combat the law by this argument. But if the written law favours our case, we must say that the oath of the dicast " to decide to the best of his judgement " does not justify him in deciding contrary to the law, but is only intended to relieve him from the charge of perjury, if he is ignorant of the meaning of the law; that no one chooses that which is good absolutely, but that which is good for himself; that there is no difference between not using the laws and their not being enacted; that in the other arts there is no advantage in trying to be wiser than the physician, for an error on his part does not do so much harm as the habit of disobeying the authority; that to seek to be wiser than the laws is just what is forbidden in the most approved laws. Thus much for the laws.

Witnesses are of two kinds, ancient and recent; of the latter some share the risk of the trial, others are outside it. By ancient I mean the poets and men of repute whose judgements are known to all; for instance, the Athenians, in the matter of Salamis, appealed to Homer [a] as a witness, and recently the inhabitants of Tenedos to Periander of Corinth [b]

It was reported that the second line was the invention of Solon.
[b] It is not known to what this refers.

Σιγειεῖς. καὶ Κλεοφῶν κατὰ Κριτίου τοῖς Σόλωνος ἐλεγείοις ἐχρήσατο, λέγων ὅτι πάλαι ἀσελγὴς ἡ οἰκία· οὐ γὰρ ἂν ποτε ἐποίησε Σόλων

εἰπεῖν μοι Κριτίᾳ πυρρότριχι πατρὸς ἀκούειν.

14 περὶ μὲν οὖν τῶν γενομένων οἱ τοιοῦτοι μάρτυρες,
1376 a περὶ δὲ τῶν ἐσομένων καὶ οἱ χρησμολόγοι, οἷον Θεμιστοκλῆς, ὅτι ναυμαχητέον, τὸ ξύλινον τεῖχος λέγων. ἔτι καὶ αἱ παροιμίαι, ὥσπερ εἴρηται, μαρτύρια ἐστίν· οἷον εἴ τις συμβουλεύει μὴ ποιεῖσθαι φίλον γέροντα, τούτῳ μαρτυρεῖ ἡ παροιμία,

μήποτ' εὖ ἔρδειν γέροντα.

καὶ τὸ τοὺς υἱοὺς ἀναιρεῖν ὧν καὶ τοὺς πατέρας,

νήπιος ὃς πατέρα κτείνας παῖδας καταλείπει.

15 Πρόσφατοι δ' ὅσοι γνώριμοί τι κεκρίκασιν· χρήσιμοι γὰρ αἱ τούτων κρίσεις τοῖς περὶ τῶν αὐτῶν ἀμφισβητοῦσιν· οἷον Εὔβουλος ἐν τοῖς δικαστηρίοις ἐχρήσατο κατὰ Χάρητος ὃ Πλάτων εἶπε πρὸς Ἀρχίβιον, ὅτι ἐπιδέδωκεν ἐν τῇ πόλει
16 τὸ ὁμολογεῖν πονηροὺς εἶναι. καὶ οἱ μετέχοντες τοῦ κινδύνου, ἂν δόξωσι ψεύδεσθαι. οἱ μὲν οὖν τοιοῦτοι τῶν τοιούτων μόνον μάρτυρές εἰσιν, εἰ

---

[a] (Frag. 22, *P.L.G.* ii., where the line runs, εἰπέμεναι Κριτίᾳ ξανθότριχι πατρὸς ἀκούειν). The Critias attacked by Cleophon is the well-known oligarch and grandson of the first. Cleophon argued from the phrase "bid him listen to his father" that his ancestor was a disobedient son and a degenerate. In reality, Solon had a high opinion of the family, and probably meant to praise the father.

[b] Herodotus, vii. 141.

[c] They have not been mentioned before. Spengel would therefore omit εἴρηται, and remove the commas: "proverbs are, as it were, evidence."

against the Sigeans. Cleophon also made use of the elegiacs of Solon against Critias, to prove that his family had long been notorious for licentiousness, otherwise Solon would never have written :

Bid me the fair-haired Critias listen to his father.[a]

One should appeal to such witnesses for the past, but also to interpreters of oracles for the future ; thus, for instance, Themistocles interpreted the wooden wall to mean that they must fight at sea.[b] Further, proverbs, as stated,[c] are evidence ; for instance, if one man advises another not to make a friend of an old man, he can appeal to the proverb,

Never do good to an old man.

And if he advises another to kill the children, after having killed the fathers, he can say,

Foolish is he who, having killed the father, suffers the children to live.[d]

By recent witnesses I mean all well-known persons who have given a decision on any point, for their decisions are useful to those who are arguing about similar cases. Thus, for instance, Eubulus,[e] when attacking Chares in the law courts, made use of what Plato said against Archibius, namely, " that the open confession of wickedness had increased in the city." And those who share the risk of the trial, if they are thought to be perjurers. Such witnesses only serve to establish whether an act has taken place or

[d] From the *Cypria* of Stasinus, of the " epic cycle."
[e] Opponent of Demosthenes. Chares was an Athenian commander, both naval and military. Nothing is known of Archibius. Plato is probably the comic poet.

γέγονεν ἢ μή, εἰ ἔστιν ἢ μή, περὶ δὲ τοῦ ποῖον οὐ
μάρτυρες, οἷον εἰ δίκαιον ἢ ἄδικον, εἰ συμφέρον
17 ἢ ἀσύμφορον· οἱ δ' ἄπωθεν καὶ περὶ τούτων
πιστότατοι. πιστότατοι δ' οἱ παλαιοί· ἀδιάφθοροι
γάρ. πιστώματα δὲ περὶ μαρτυριῶν μάρτυρας
μὲν μὴ ἔχοντι, ὅτι ἐκ τῶν εἰκότων δεῖ κρίνειν καὶ
τοῦτ' ἐστὶ τὸ γνώμῃ τῇ ἀρίστῃ, καὶ ὅτι οὐκ ἔστιν
ἐξαπατῆσαι τὰ εἰκότα ἐπὶ ἀργυρίῳ, καὶ ὅτι οὐχ
ἁλίσκεται τὰ εἰκότα ψευδομαρτυριῶν. ἔχοντι δὲ
πρὸς μὴ ἔχοντα, ὅτι οὐχ ὑπόδικα τὰ εἰκότα, καὶ
ὅτι οὐδὲν ἂν ἔδει μαρτυριῶν, εἰ ἐκ τῶν λόγων
18 ἱκανὸν ἦν θεωρῆσαι. εἰσὶ δὲ αἱ μαρτυρίαι αἱ
μὲν περὶ αὑτοῦ αἱ δὲ περὶ τοῦ ἀμφισβητοῦντος,
καὶ αἱ μὲν περὶ τοῦ πράγματος αἱ δὲ περὶ τοῦ
ἤθους, ὥστε φανερὸν ὅτι οὐδέποτ' ἔστιν ἀπορῆσαι
μαρτυρίας χρησίμης· εἰ μὴ γὰρ κατὰ τοῦ πράγματος ἢ αὑτῷ ὁμολογουμένης ἢ τῷ ἀμφισβητοῦντι ἐναντίας, ἀλλὰ περὶ τοῦ ἤθους ἢ αὑτοῦ εἰς
ἐπιείκειαν ἢ τοῦ ἀμφισβητοῦντος εἰς φαυλότητα.
19 τὰ δ' ἄλλα περὶ μάρτυρος ἢ φίλου ἢ ἐχθροῦ ἢ
μεταξύ, ἢ εὐδοκιμοῦντος ἢ ἀδοξοῦντος ἢ μεταξύ,
καὶ ὅσαι ἄλλαι τοιαῦται διαφοραί, ἐκ τῶν αὐτῶν
τόπων λεκτέον ἐξ οἷωνπερ καὶ τὰ ἐνθυμήματα
λέγομεν.
20   Περὶ δὲ τῶν συνθηκῶν τοσαύτη τοῦ λόγου χρῆ-
1376 b σίς ἐστιν ὅσον αὔξειν ἢ καθαιρεῖν ἢ πιστὰς ποιεῖν

---

^a Or, "witnesses wholly unconnected with the case."

not, whether it is or is not the case ; but if it is a
question of the quality of the act, for instance,
whether it is just or unjust, expedient or inexpedient,
they are not competent witnesses ; but witnesses
from a distance [a] are very trustworthy even in regard
to this. But ancient witnesses are the most trustworthy of all, for they cannot be corrupted. In
regard to the confirmation of evidence, when a man
has no witnesses, he can say that the decision should
be given in accordance with probabilities, and that
this is the meaning of the oath " according to the
best of one's judgement " ; that probabilities cannot
be bribed to deceive, and that they cannot be convicted of bearing false witness. But if a man has
witnesses and his adversary has none, he can say that
probabilities incur no responsibility, and that there
would have been no need of evidence, if an investigation according to the arguments were sufficient.
Evidence partly concerns ourselves, partly our adversary, as to the fact itself or moral character ; so
that it is evident that one never need lack useful
evidence. For, if we have no evidence as to the fact
itself, neither in confirmation of our own case nor
against our opponent, it will always be possible to
obtain some evidence as to character that will
establish either our own respectability or the worth-
lessness of our opponent. As for all the other
questions relative to a witness, whether he is a friend,
an enemy, or neutral, of good or bad or middling
reputation, and for all other differences of this kind,
we must have recourse to the same topics as those
from which we derive our enthymemes.

As for contracts, argument may be used to the
extent of magnifying or minimizing their importance,

ἢ ἀπίστους, ἐὰν μὲν αὐτῷ ὑπάρχωσι, πιστὰς καὶ
κυρίας, ἐπὶ δὲ τοῦ ἀμφισβητοῦντος τοὐναντίον.
21 πρὸς μὲν οὖν τὸ πιστὰς ἢ ἀπίστους κατασκευάζειν
οὐδὲν διαφέρει τῆς περὶ τοὺς μάρτυρας πραγ-
ματείας· ὁποῖοι γὰρ ἄν τινες ὦσιν οἱ ἐπιγεγραμ-
μένοι ἢ φυλάττοντες, τούτοις αἱ συνθῆκαι πισταί
εἰσιν. ὁμολογουμένης δ' εἶναι τῆς συνθήκης,
οἰκείας μὲν οὔσης αὐξητέον· ἡ γὰρ συνθήκη νόμος
ἐστὶν ἴδιος καὶ κατὰ μέρος, καὶ αἱ μὲν συνθῆκαι
οὐ ποιοῦσι τὸν νόμον κύριον, οἱ δὲ νόμοι τὰς κατὰ
τὸν νόμον συνθήκας. καὶ ὅλως αὐτὸς ὁ νόμος
συνθήκη τις ἐστίν, ὥστε ὅστις ἀπιστεῖ ἢ ἀναιρεῖ
22 συνθήκην, τοὺς νόμους ἀναιρεῖ. ἔτι δὲ πράττε-
ται τὰ πολλὰ τῶν συναλλαγμάτων καὶ τὰ ἑκούσια
κατὰ συνθήκας, ὥστε ἀκύρων γιγνομένων ἀναι-
ρεῖται ἡ πρὸς ἀλλήλους χρεία τῶν ἀνθρώπων.
καὶ τἆλλα δὲ ὅσα ἁρμόττει, ἐπιπολῆς ἰδεῖν ἔστιν.
23 ἂν δ' ἐναντία ᾖ καὶ μετὰ τῶν ἀμφισβητούντων,
πρῶτον μέν, ἅπερ ἄν τις πρὸς νόμον ἐναντίον μα-
χέσαιτο, ταῦθ' ἁρμόττει· ἄτοπον γὰρ εἰ τοῖς μὲν
νόμοις, ἂν μὴ ὀρθῶς κείμενοι ὦσιν ἀλλ' ἐξαμάρ-
τωσιν οἱ τιθέμενοι, οὐκ οἰόμεθα δεῖν πείθεσθαι,
24 ταῖς δὲ συνθήκαις ἀναγκαῖον. εἶθ' ὅτι τοῦ δικαίου
ἐστὶ βραβευτὴς ὁ δικαστής· οὔκουν τοῦτο σκεπτέον,
25 ἀλλ' ὡς δικαιότερον. καὶ τὸ μὲν δίκαιον οὐκ ἔστι
μεταστρέψαι οὔτ' ἀπάτῃ οὔτ' ἀνάγκῃ (πεφυκὸς
γάρ ἐστιν), συνθῆκαι δὲ γίγνονται καὶ ἐξαπατη-
θέντων καὶ ἀναγκασθέντων. πρὸς δὲ τούτοις

of proving that they do or do not deserve credit.
If we have them on our side, we must try to prove
them worthy of credit and authoritative ; but if they
are on the side of our opponent, we must do the
opposite. In view of rendering them worthy or
unworthy of credit, the method of procedure is
exactly the same as in the case of witnesses ; for
contracts are trustworthy according to the character
of their signatories or depositaries. When the existence of the contract is admitted, if it is in our favour,
we must strengthen it by asserting that the contract
is a law, special and partial ; and it is not the contracts that make the law authoritative, but it is the
laws that give force to legal contracts. And in a
general sense the law itself is a kind of contract, so
that whoever disobeys or subverts a contract, subverts the laws. Further, most ordinary and all
voluntary transactions are carried out according to
contract ; so that if you destroy the authority of
contracts, the mutual intercourse of men is destroyed.
All other arguments suitable to the occasion are easy
to see. But if the contract is against us and in
favour of our opponents, in the first place those
arguments are suitable which we should oppose to
the law if it were against us ; that it would be strange
if, while we consider ourselves entitled to refuse to
obey ill-made laws, whose authors have erred, we
should be obliged to consider ourselves always bound
by contracts. Or, that the judge is the dispenser of
justice ; so that it is not the contents of the contract
that he has to consider, but what is juster. Further,
that one cannot alter justice either by fraud or
compulsion, for it is based upon nature, whereas
contracts may be entered into under both conditions.

ARISTOTLE

σκοπεῖν εἰ ἐναντία ἐστί τινι ἢ τῶν γεγραμμένων
νόμων ἢ τῶν κοινῶν, καὶ τῶν γεγραμμένων ἢ
τοῖς οἰκείοις ἢ τοῖς ἀλλοτρίοις, ἔπειτα εἰ ἄλλαις
συνθήκαις ὑστέραις ἢ προτέραις· ἢ γὰρ αἱ ὕστεραι
κύριαι, ἄκυροι δ' αἱ πρότεραι, ἢ αἱ πρότεραι ὀρθαί,
αἱ δ' ὕστεραι ἠπατήκασιν, ὁποτέρως ἂν ᾖ χρήσιμον. ἔτι δὲ τὸ συμφέρον ὁρᾶν, εἴ πῃ ἐναντιοῦται
τοῖς κριταῖς, καὶ ὅσα ἄλλα τοιαῦτα· καὶ γὰρ ταῦτα
εὐθεώρητα ὁμοίως.

26 Αἱ δὲ βάσανοι μαρτυρίαι τινές εἰσιν, ἔχειν δὲ
δοκοῦσι τὸ πιστόν, ὅτι ἀνάγκη τις πρόσεστιν.
οὔκουν χαλεπὸν οὐδὲ περὶ τούτων εἰπεῖν τὰ ἐνδεχόμενα, ἐξ ὧν ἐάν τε ὑπάρχωσιν οἰκεῖαι αὔξειν
ἔστιν, ὅτι ἀληθεῖς μόναι τῶν μαρτυριῶν εἰσιν
1377 a αὗται· ἐάν τε ὑπεναντίαι ὦσι καὶ μετὰ τοῦ ἀμφισβητοῦντος, διαλύοι ἄν τις τἀληθῆ λέγων καθ'
ὅλου τοῦ γένους τῶν βασάνων· οὐδὲν γὰρ ἧττον
ἀναγκαζόμενοι τὰ ψευδῆ λέγουσιν ἢ τἀληθῆ, καὶ
διακαρτεροῦντες μὴ λέγειν τἀληθῆ, καὶ ῥᾳδίως
καταψευδόμενοι ὡς παυσόμενοι θᾶττον. δεῖ δ'
ἔχειν ἐπαναφέρειν ἐπὶ τοιαῦτα γεγενημένα παραδείγματα ἃ ἴσασιν οἱ κρίνοντες. δεῖ δὲ λέγειν ὡς
οὐκ εἰσὶν ἀληθεῖς αἱ βάσανοι· πολλοὶ μὲν γὰρ
παχύφρονες, καὶ λιθόδερμοι καὶ ταῖς ψυχαῖς ὄντες
δυνατοὶ γενναίως ἐγκαρτεροῦσι ταῖς ἀνάγκαις, οἱ
δὲ δειλοὶ καὶ εὐλαβεῖς πρὸ τοῦ τὰς ἀνάγκας ἰδεῖν
αὐτῶν καταθαρροῦσιν, ὥστε οὐδέν ἐστι πιστὸν ἐν
βασάνοις.[1]

[1] This passage [δεῖ δ' ἔχειν . . . βασάνοις], which is found
in the best (Paris. A^c) ms., is now generally rejected, mainly
as being linguistically un-Aristotelian.

In addition to this, we must examine whether the contract is contrary to any written law of our own or foreign countries, or to any general law, or to other previous or subsequent contracts. For either the latter are valid and the former not, or the former are right and the latter fraudulent; we may put it in whichever way it seems fit. We must also consider the question of expediency—whether the contract is in any way opposed to the interest of the judges. There are a number of other arguments of the same kind, which are equally easy to discern.

Torture is a kind of evidence, which appears trustworthy, because a sort of compulsion is attached to it. Nor is it difficult to see what may be said concerning it, and by what arguments, if it is in our favour, we can exaggerate its importance by asserting that it is the only true kind of evidence; but if it is against us and in favour of our opponent, we can destroy its value by telling the truth about all kinds of torture generally; for those under compulsion are as likely to give false evidence as true, some being ready to endure everything rather than tell the truth, while others are equally ready to make false charges against others, in the hope of being sooner released from torture. It is also necessary to be able to quote actual examples of the kind with which the judges are acquainted. It may also be said that evidence given under torture is not true; for many thick-witted and thick-skinned persons, and those who are stout-hearted heroically hold out under sufferings, while the cowardly and cautious, before they see the sufferings before them, are bold enough; wherefore evidence from torture may be considered utterly untrustworthy.

ARISTOTLE

27 Περὶ δ' ὅρκων τετραχῶς ἔστι διελεῖν· ἢ γὰρ
δίδωσι καὶ λαμβάνει, ἢ οὐδέτερον, ἢ τὸ μὲν τὸ
δ' οὔ, καὶ τούτων ἢ δίδωσι μὲν οὐ λαμβάνει δέ,
ἢ λαμβάνει μὲν δίδωσι δ' οὔ. ἔτι ἄλλως παρὰ
ταῦτα, εἰ ὀμώμοσται οὗτος ἢ ὑπ' αὐτοῦ ἢ ὑπ'

28 ἐκείνου. οὐ δίδωσι μὲν οὖν, ὅτι ῥᾳδίως ἐπιορ-
κοῦσιν, καὶ διότι ὁ μὲν ὀμόσας οὐκ ἀποδίδωσι,
τοὺς δὲ μὴ ὀμόσαντος οἴεται καταδικάσειν. καὶ
ὡς οὗτος ὁ κίνδυνος κρείττων ὁ ἐν τοῖς δικασταῖς·

29 τοῖς μὲν γὰρ πιστεύει τῷ δ' οὔ. οὐ λαμβάνει δ',
ὅτι ἀντὶ χρημάτων ὅρκος. καὶ ὅτι εἰ ἦν φαῦλος,
κατωμόσατο ἄν· κρεῖττον γὰρ ἕνεκά του φαῦλον
εἶναι ἢ μηδενός· ὀμόσας μὲν οὖν ἕξει, μὴ ὀμόσας
δ' οὔ. οὕτω δὲ δι' ἀρετὴν ἂν εἴη, ἀλλ' οὐ δι'
ἐπιορκίαν τὸ μή. καὶ τὸ τοῦ Ξενοφάνους ἁρμόττει, ὅτι οὐκ ἴση πρόκλησις αὕτη ἀσεβεῖ πρὸς
εὐσεβῆ, ἀλλ' ὁμοία καὶ εἰ ἰσχυρὸς ἀσθενῆ πατάξαι

30 ἢ πληγῆναι προκαλέσαιτο. εἰ δὲ λαμβάνει, ὅτι
πιστεύει αὑτῷ, ἐκείνῳ δ' οὔ. καὶ τὸ τοῦ Ξενοφάνους μεταστρέψαντα φατέον οὕτως ἴσον εἶναι
ἂν ὁ μὲν ἀσεβὴς διδῷ, ὁ δ' εὐσεβὴς ὀμνύῃ· δεινὸν

---

^a In Attic legal procedure, the challenge (πρόκλησις) to take
an oath on the question at issue was one method of deciding it.
One party offered the other something to swear by (δίδωσι
ὅρκον), this being the real meaning of ὅρκος, and the other
party either accepted (λαμβάνει, δέχεται) it or refused it.
Both parties, of their own accord, might propose to take
the oath.

^b There are three reasons for not tendering the oath : (1)
men are always ready to perjure themselves, if they are
likely to benefit by doing so ; (2) if your adversary takes the
oath, he will decline to pay, trusting that he will be acquitted,
whereas, if he is not on his oath, he will probably be condemned ; (3) there is less risk in leaving the decision to the
dicasts, who can be trusted.

164

As to oaths [a] four divisions may be made; for either we tender an oath and accept it, or we do neither, or one without the other, and in the last case we either tender but do not accept, or accept but do not tender. Besides this, one may consider whether the oath has already been taken by us or by the other party. If you do not tender the oath to the adversary, it is because men readily perjure themselves, and because, after he has taken the oath, he will refuse to repay the money, while, if he does not take the oath, you think that the dicasts will condemn him; and also because the risk incurred in leaving the decision to the dicasts is preferable, for you have confidence in them, but not in your adversary.[b] If you refuse to take the oath yourself, you may argue that the oath is only taken with a view to money; that, if you had been a scoundrel, you would have taken it at once, for it is better to be a scoundrel for something than for nothing; that, if you take it, you will win your case, if not, you will probably lose it; consequently, your refusal to take it is due to moral excellence, not to fear of committing perjury. And the apophthegm of Xenophanes [c] is apposite—that "it is unfair for an impious man to challenge a pious one," for it is the same as a strong man challenging a weak one to hit or be hit. If you accept the oath, you may say that you have confidence in yourself, but not in your opponent, and, reversing the apophthegm of Xenophanes, that the only fair way is that the impious man should tender the oath and the pious man take it; and that it

[c] Born at Colophon in Asia Minor, he migrated to Elea in Italy, where he founded the Eleatic school of philosophy.

τε τὸ μὴ θέλειν αὐτόν, ὑπὲρ ὧν ἐκείνους ἀξιοῖ
31 ὀμόσαντας δικάζειν. εἰ δὲ δίδωσιν, ὅτι εὐσεβὲς
τὸ θέλειν τοῖς θεοῖς ἐπιτρέπειν, καὶ ὅτι οὐδὲν δεῖ
αὐτὸν ἄλλων κριτῶν δεῖσθαι· αὐτῷ γὰρ δίδωσι
32 κρίνειν. καὶ ὅτι ἄτοπον τὸ μὴ θέλειν ὀμνύναι
περὶ ὧν ἄλλους ἀξιοῖ ὀμνύναι.

Ἐπεὶ δὲ καθ' ἕκαστον δῆλον πῶς λεκτέον, καὶ
συνδυαζόμενον πῶς λεκτέον δῆλον· οἷον εἰ αὐτὸς
μὲν θέλει λαμβάνειν διδόναι δὲ μή, καὶ εἰ δίδωσι
μὲν λαμβάνειν δὲ μὴ θέλει, καὶ εἰ λαμβάνειν καὶ
1377 b διδόναι θέλει εἴτε μηδέτερον· ἐκ γὰρ τῶν εἰρημένων
ἀνάγκη συγκεῖσθαι, ὥστε καὶ τοὺς λόγους ἀνάγκη
συγκεῖσθαι ἐκ τῶν εἰρημένων. ἐὰν δὲ ᾖ γεγενη-
μένος ὑπ' αὐτοῦ καὶ ἐναντίος, ὅτι οὐκ ἐπιορκία·
ἑκούσιον γὰρ τὸ ἀδικεῖν, τὸ δ' ἐπιορκεῖν ἀδικεῖν
33 ἐστί, τὰ δὲ βίᾳ καὶ ἀπάτῃ ἀκούσια. ἐνταῦθα οὖν
συνακτέον καὶ τὸ ἐπιορκεῖν, ὅτι ἔστι τὸ τῇ διανοίᾳ,
ἀλλ' οὐ τῷ στόματι. ἐὰν δὲ τῷ ἀντιδίκῳ ᾖ ὀμω-
μοσμένος, ὅτι πάντα ἀναιρεῖ ὁ μὴ ἐμμένων οἷς
ὤμοσεν· διὰ γὰρ τοῦτο καὶ τοῖς νόμοις χρῶνται
ὀμόσαντες. καὶ "ὑμᾶς μὲν ἀξιοῦσιν ἐμμένειν
οἷς ὀμόσαντες δικάζετε, αὐτοὶ δ' οὐκ ἐμμένουσιν."
καὶ ὅσα ἂν ἄλλα αὔξων τις εἴπειεν. περὶ μὲν οὖν
τῶν ἀτέχνων πίστεων εἰρήσθω τοσαῦτα.

---

[a] The defence in such cases is: (1) that the previous oath
was taken as the result of fraud or compulsion; (2) that you
did not mean what you said.

would be monstrous to refuse to take the oath
yourself, while demanding that the judges should
take it before giving their verdict. But if you tender
the oath, you may say that it is an act of piety to
be willing to leave the matter to the gods ; that
your opponent has no need to look for other judges,
for you allow him to make the decision himself ; and
that it would be ridiculous that he should be un-
willing to take an oath in cases where he demands
that the dicasts should take one.

Now, since we have shown how we must deal with
each case individually, it is clear how we must deal
with them when taken two and two ; for instance,
if we wish to take the oath but not to tender it,
to tender it but not to take it, to accept and tender it,
or to do neither the one nor the other. For such
cases, and similarly the arguments, must be a com·
bination of those already mentioned. And if we
have already taken an oath which contradicts the
present one, we may argue that it is not perjury ;
for whereas wrongdoing is voluntary, and perjury is
wrongdoing, what is done in error or under compulsion is involuntary. Here we must draw the
conclusion that perjury consists in the intention, not
in what is said.[a] But if the opponent has taken such
an oath, we may say that one who does not abide
by what he has sworn subverts everything, for this
is the reason why the dicasts take an oath before
applying the laws ; and [we may make this appeal] :
"They demand that you abide by your oath as judges,
while they themselves do not abide by theirs."
Further, we should employ all means of amplification.
Let this suffice for the inartificial proofs.

B

1. Ἐκ τίνων μὲν οὖν δεῖ καὶ προτρέπειν καὶ
ἀποτρέπειν καὶ ἐπαινεῖν καὶ ψέγειν καὶ κατηγορεῖν
καὶ ἀπολογεῖσθαι, καὶ ποῖαι δόξαι καὶ προτάσεις
χρήσιμοι πρὸς τὰς τούτων πίστεις, ταῦτ' ἐστίν·
περὶ γὰρ τούτων καὶ ἐκ τούτων τὰ ἐνθυμήματα,
ὡς περὶ ἕκαστον εἰπεῖν ἰδίᾳ τὸ γένος τῶν λόγων.
2 ἐπεὶ δ' ἕνεκα κρίσεώς ἐστιν ἡ ῥητορική (καὶ γὰρ
τὰς συμβουλὰς κρίνουσι καὶ ἡ δίκη κρίσις ἐστίν),
ἀνάγκη μὴ μόνον πρὸς τὸν λόγον ὁρᾶν, ὅπως
ἀποδεικτικὸς ἔσται καὶ πιστός, ἀλλὰ καὶ αὐτὸν
3 ποιόν τινα καὶ τὸν κριτὴν κατασκευάζειν· πολὺ
γὰρ διαφέρει πρὸς πίστιν, μάλιστα μὲν ἐν ταῖς
συμβουλαῖς, εἶτα καὶ ἐν ταῖς δίκαις, τὸ ποιόν τινα
φαίνεσθαι τὸν λέγοντα καὶ τὸ πρὸς αὐτοὺς ὑπολαμβάνειν ἔχειν πως αὐτόν, πρὸς δὲ τούτοις ἐὰν καὶ
4 αὐτοὶ διακείμενοί πως τυγχάνωσιν. τὸ μὲν οὖν
ποιόν τινα φαίνεσθαι τὸν λέγοντα χρησιμώτερον

ᵃ This is Cope's interpretation. Jebb renders : " If we
take each branch of Rhetoric by itself." The classes are of
course the deliberative, forensic, and epideictic.

ᵇ The instructions given for enthymematic or logical proof
should suffice ; but since the function of Rhetoric is to find
the available means of persuasion and its end is a judgement ;
and since an appeal to the speaker's own character and to
the passions of those who are to give the judgement is bound
to carry great weight, the speaker must be provided with
rules for ethical and " pathetic " (emotional) proofs. In i. 5

BOOK II

1. Such then are the materials which we must employ in exhorting and dissuading, praising and blaming, accusing and defending, and such are the opinions and propositions that are useful to produce conviction in these circumstances; for they are the subject and source of enthymemes, which are specially suitable to each class (so to say) of speeches.[a] But since the object of Rhetoric is judgement—for judgements are pronounced in deliberative rhetoric and judicial proceedings are a judgement—it is not only necessary to consider how to make the speech itself demonstrative and convincing, but also that the speaker should show himself to be of a certain character and should know how to put the judge into a certain frame of mind. For it makes a great difference with regard to producing conviction—especially in demonstrative, and, next to this, in forensic oratory—that the speaker should show himself to be possessed of certain qualities and that his hearers should think that he is disposed in a certain way towards them; and further, that they themselves should be disposed in a certain way towards him.[b] In deliberative oratory, it is more useful that the orator

Aristotle mentions appeals to the emotions with disapproval, but this does not apply to all such appeals, but only to those which are likely to bias the judges unfairly (*e.g.* stirring up envy, hatred, a desire for revenge).

εἰς τὰς συμβουλάς ἐστιν, τὸ δὲ διακεῖσθαι πως
τὸν ἀκροατὴν εἰς τὰς δίκας· οὐ γὰρ ταὐτὰ φαίνεται
φιλοῦσι καὶ μισοῦσιν, οὐδ᾽ ὀργιζομένοις καὶ πράως
ἔχουσιν, ἀλλ᾽ ἢ τὸ παράπαν ἕτερα ἢ κατὰ τὸ
1378 a μέγεθος ἕτερα· τῷ μὲν γὰρ φιλοῦντι, περὶ οὗ
ποιεῖται τὴν κρίσιν, ἢ οὐκ ἀδικεῖν ἢ μικρὰ δοκεῖ
ἀδικεῖν, τῷ δὲ μισοῦντι τοὐναντίον· καὶ τῷ μὲν
ἐπιθυμοῦντι καὶ εὐέλπιδι ὄντι, ἐὰν ᾖ τὸ ἐσόμενον
ἡδύ, καὶ ἔσεσθαι καὶ ἀγαθὸν ἔσεσθαι φαίνεται,
τῷ δ᾽ ἀπαθεῖ καὶ δυσχεραίνοντι τοὐναντίον.

5 Τοῦ μὲν οὖν αὐτοὺς εἶναι πιστοὺς τοὺς λέγοντας
τρία ἐστὶ τὰ αἴτια· τοσαῦτα γάρ ἐστι δι᾽ ἃ πιστεύομεν ἔξω τῶν ἀποδείξεων. ἔστι δὲ ταῦτα
φρόνησις καὶ ἀρετὴ καὶ εὔνοια· διαψεύδονται γὰρ
περὶ ὧν λέγουσιν ἢ συμβουλεύουσιν ἢ διὰ πάντα
6 ταῦτα ἢ διὰ τούτων τι· ἢ γὰρ δι᾽ ἀφροσύνην οὐκ
ὀρθῶς δοξάζουσιν, ἢ δοξάζοντες ὀρθῶς διὰ μοχθηρίαν οὐ τὰ δοκοῦντα λέγουσιν, ἢ φρόνιμοι μὲν
καὶ ἐπιεικεῖς εἰσὶν ἀλλ᾽ οὐκ εὖνοι· διόπερ ἐνδέχεται μὴ τὰ βέλτιστα συμβουλεύειν γιγνώσκοντας.
καὶ παρὰ ταῦτα οὐδέν. ἀνάγκη ἄρα τὸν ἅπαντα
δοκοῦντα ταῦτ᾽ ἔχειν εἶναι τοῖς ἀκρωμένοις
7 πιστόν. ὅθεν μὲν τοίνυν φρόνιμοι καὶ σπουδαῖοι
φανεῖεν ἄν, ἐκ τῶν περὶ τὰς ἀρετὰς διῃρημένων
ληπτέον· ἐκ τῶν αὐτῶν γὰρ κἂν ἕτερόν τις κἂν
ἑαυτὸν κατασκευάσειε τοιοῦτον· περὶ δ᾽ εὐνοίας
καὶ φιλίας ἐν τοῖς περὶ τὰ πάθη λεκτέον.

ᵃ Opposed to εὐέλπιδι. Others render " in a bad humour."
ᵇ ἐπιεικής and σπουδαῖος both = ἀγαθός. In a restricted
sense ἐπιεικής is " respectable," σπουδαῖος " serious."
ᶜ i. 9.

should appear to be of a certain character, in forensic, that the hearer should be disposed in a certain way; for opinions vary, according as men love or hate, are wrathful or mild, and things appear either altogether different, or different in degree; for when a man is favourably disposed towards one on whom he is passing judgement, he either thinks that the accused has committed no wrong at all or that his offence is trifling; but if he hates him, the reverse is the case. And if a man desires anything and has good hopes of getting it, if what is to come is pleasant, he thinks that it is sure to come to pass and will be good; but if a man is unemotional or not hopeful[a] it is quite the reverse.

For the orator to produce conviction three qualities are necessary; for, independently of demonstrations, the things which induce belief are three in number. These qualities are good sense, virtue, and goodwill; for speakers are wrong both in what they say and in the advice they give, because they lack either all three or one of them. For either through want of sense they form incorrect opinions, or, if their opinions are correct, through viciousness they do not say what they think, or, if they are sensible and good,[b] they lack goodwill; wherefore it may happen that they do not give the best advice, although they know what it is. These qualities are all that are necessary, so that the speaker who appears to possess all three will necessarily convince his hearers. The means whereby he may appear sensible and good[b] must be inferred from the classification of the virtues;[c] for to make himself appear such he would employ the same means as he would in the case of others. We must now speak of goodwill and friendship in our discussion of the emotions.

ARISTOTLE

8 Ἔστι δὲ τὰ πάθη, δι' ὅσα μεταβάλλοντες δια-
φέρουσι πρὸς τὰς κρίσεις, οἷς ἕπεται λύπη καὶ
ἡδονή, οἷον ὀργὴ ἔλεος φόβος καὶ ὅσα ἄλλα τοιαῦτα,
9 καὶ τὰ τούτοις ἐναντία. δεῖ δὲ διαιρεῖν τὰ περὶ
ἕκαστον εἰς τρία· λέγω δ' οἷον περὶ ὀργῆς, πῶς
τε διακείμενοι ὀργίλοι εἰσί, καὶ τίσιν εἰώθασιν
ὀργίζεσθαι, καὶ ἐπὶ ποίοις· εἰ γὰρ τὸ μὲν ἓν ἢ τὰ
δύο ἔχοιμεν τούτων, ἅπαντα δὲ μή, ἀδύνατον ἂν
εἴη τὴν ὀργὴν ἐμποιεῖν· ὁμοίως δὲ καὶ ἐπὶ τῶν
ἄλλων. ὥσπερ οὖν καὶ ἐπὶ τῶν προειρημένων
διεγράψαμεν τὰς προτάσεις, οὕτω καὶ ἐπὶ τούτων
ποιήσωμεν καὶ διέλωμεν τὸν εἰρημένον τρόπον.

2. Ἔστω δὴ ὀργὴ ὄρεξις μετὰ λύπης τιμωρίας
φαινομένης διὰ φαινομένην ὀλιγωρίαν τῶν εἰς
αὑτὸν ἢ τῶν αὑτοῦ, τοῦ ὀλιγωρεῖν μὴ προσήκοντος.
2 εἰ δὴ τοῦτ' ἐστὶν ἡ ὀργή, ἀνάγκη τὸν ὀργιζόμενον
ὀργίζεσθαι ἀεὶ τῶν καθ' ἕκαστόν τινι, οἷον Κλέωνι
1378 b ἀλλ' οὐκ ἀνθρώπῳ, καὶ ὅτι αὐτὸν ἢ τῶν αὑτοῦ
τι πεποίηκεν ἢ ἤμελλεν, καὶ πάσῃ ὀργῇ ἕπεσθαί
τινα ἡδονὴν τὴν ἀπὸ τῆς ἐλπίδος τοῦ τιμωρήσασθαι·
ἡδὺ μὲν γὰρ τὸ οἴεσθαι τεύξεσθαι ὧν ἐφίεται,
οὐδεὶς δὲ τῶν φαινομένων ἀδυνάτων ἐφίεται
αὑτῷ, ὁ δ' ὀργιζόμενος ἐφίεται δυνατῶν αὑτῷ.
διὸ καλῶς εἴρηται περὶ θυμοῦ

> ὅς τε πολὺ γλυκίων μέλιτος καταλειβομένοιο
> ἀνδρῶν ἐν στήθεσσιν ἀέξεται·

---

[a] In i. generally (cp. i. 2. 22).
[b] Gomperz translates φαινομένης "real or apparent"; Jebb
omits φαινομένης and translates φαινομένην "apparent";
Cope confines both to the meaning "manifest."
[c] *Iliad*, xviii. 109 (cp. i. 11. 9).

172

The emotions are all those affections which cause men to change their opinion in regard to their judgements, and are accompanied by pleasure and pain ; such are anger, pity, fear, and all similar emotions and their contraries. And each of them must be divided under three heads ; for instance, in regard to anger, the disposition of mind which makes men angry, the persons with whom they are usually angry, and the occasions which give rise to anger. For if we knew one or even two of these heads, but not all three, it would be impossible to arouse that emotion. The same applies to the rest. Just as, then, we have given a list of propositions [a] in what we have previously said, we will do the same here and divide the emotions in the same manner.

2. Let us then define anger as a longing, accompanied by pain, for a real or apparent revenge for a real or apparent slight,[b] affecting a man himself or one of his friends, when such a slight is undeserved. If this definition is correct, the angry man must always be angry with a particular individual (for instance, with Cleon, but not with men generally), and because this individual has done, or was on the point of doing, something against him or one of his friends ; and lastly, anger is always accompanied by a certain pleasure, due to the hope of revenge to come. For it is pleasant to think that one will obtain what one aims at ; now, no one aims at what is obviously impossible of attainment by him, and the angry man aims at what is possible for himself. Wherefore it has been well said of anger, that

Far sweeter than dripping honey down the throat it spreads in men's hearts.[c]

ἀκολουθεῖ γὰρ καὶ ἡδονή τις διά τε τοῦτο καὶ
διότι διατρίβουσιν ἐν τῷ τιμωρεῖσθαι τῇ διανοίᾳ·
ἡ οὖν τότε γινομένη φαντασία ἡδονὴν ἐμποιεῖ,
ὥσπερ ἡ τῶν ἐνυπνίων.

3 Ἐπεὶ δ' ἡ ὀλιγωρία ἐστὶν ἐνέργεια δόξης περὶ
τὸ μηδενὸς ἄξιον φαινόμενον· καὶ γὰρ τὰ κακὰ
καὶ τἀγαθὰ ἄξια οἰόμεθα σπουδῆς εἶναι, καὶ τὰ
συντείνοντα πρὸς αὐτά· ὅσα δὲ μηδέν τι ἢ μικρόν,
οὐδενὸς ἄξια ὑπολαμβάνομεν. τρία δ' ἐστὶν εἴδη
ὀλιγωρίας, καταφρόνησίς τε καὶ ἐπηρεασμὸς καὶ
4 ὕβρις· ὅ τε γὰρ καταφρονῶν ὀλιγωρεῖ· ὅσα γὰρ
οἴονται μηδενὸς ἄξια, τούτων καταφρονοῦσιν, τῶν
δὲ μηδενὸς ἀξίων ὀλιγωροῦσιν· καὶ ὁ ἐπηρεάζων
φαίνεται καταφρονεῖν. ἔστι γὰρ ὁ ἐπηρεασμὸς
ἐμποδισμὸς ταῖς βουλήσεσιν οὐχ ἵνα τι αὑτῷ ἀλλ'
ἵνα μὴ ἐκείνῳ. ἐπεὶ οὖν οὐχ ἵνα αὑτῷ τι, ὀλι-
γωρεῖ· δῆλον γὰρ ὅτι οὔτε βλάψειν ὑπολαμβάνει·
ἐφοβεῖτο γὰρ ἂν καὶ οὐκ ὠλιγώρει· οὔτ' ὠφελῆσαι
ἂν οὐδὲν ἄξιον λόγου· ἐφρόντιζε γὰρ ἂν ὥστε
φίλος εἶναι.

5 Καὶ ὁ ὑβρίζων δ' ὀλιγωρεῖ· ἔστι γὰρ ὕβρις τὸ
βλάπτειν καὶ λυπεῖν[1] ἐφ' οἷς αἰσχύνη ἐστὶ τῷ

---

[1] Aᶜ reads πράττειν καὶ λέγειν, adopted by Roemer.

---

[a] The thought of revenge in the future, as distinguished from dwelling upon it in the present.

[b] Or, "those in which this tendency does not exist, or is trifling."

[c] Or, "how to make him his friend," φίλος being for φίλον by attraction.

[d] In Attic law ὕβρις (insulting, degrading treatment) was

for it is accompanied by a certain pleasure, for this reason first,[a] and also because men dwell upon the thought of revenge, and the vision that rises before us produces the same pleasure as one seen in dreams.

Slighting is an actualization of opinion in regard to something which appears valueless; for things which are really bad or good, or tend to become so, we consider worthy of attention, but those which are of no importance or trifling[b] we ignore. Now there are three kinds of slight : disdain, spitefulness, and insult. For he who disdains, slights, since men disdain those things which they consider valueless and slight what is of no account. And the spiteful man appears to show disdain ; for spitefulness consists in placing obstacles in the way of another's wishes, not in order that any advantage may accrue to him who spites, but to prevent any accruing to the other. Since then he does not act in this manner from self-interest, it is a slight ; for it is evident that he has no idea that the other is likely to hurt him, for in that case he would be afraid of him instead of slighting him ; nor that he will be of any use to him worth speaking of, for in that case his thought would be how to become his friend.[c]

Similarly, he who insults another also slights him ; for insult[d] consists in causing injury or annoyance

a more serious offence than αἰκία (bodily ill-treatment). It was the subject of a State criminal prosecution (γραφή), αἰκία of a private action (δίκη) for damages. The penalty was assessed in court, and might even be death. It had to be proved that the defendant struck the first blow (ii. 24. 9). One of the best known instances is the action brought by Demosthenes against Midias for a personal outrage on himself, when *choregus* of his tribe and responsible for the equipment of a chorus for musical competitions at public festivals.

πάσχοντι, μὴ ἵνα τι γένηται αὐτῷ ἄλλο ἢ ὅτι
ἐγένετο, ἀλλ᾽ ὅπως ἡσθῇ· οἱ γὰρ ἀντιποιοῦντες
6 οὐχ ὑβρίζουσιν ἀλλὰ τιμωροῦνται. αἴτιον δὲ τῆς
ἡδονῆς τοῖς ὑβρίζουσιν, ὅτι οἴονται κακῶς δρῶντες
αὐτοὺς ὑπερέχειν μᾶλλον. διὸ οἱ νέοι καὶ οἱ
πλούσιοι ὑβρισταί· ὑπερέχειν γὰρ οἴονται ὑβρί-
ζοντες. ὕβρεως δὲ ἀτιμία, ὁ δ᾽ ἀτιμάζων ὀλιγωρεῖ·
τὸ γὰρ μηδενὸς ἄξιον οὐδεμίαν ἔχει τιμήν, οὔτ᾽
ἀγαθοῦ οὔτε κακοῦ. διὸ λέγει ὀργιζόμενος ὁ
Ἀχιλλεύς

> ἠτίμησεν· ἑλὼν γὰρ ἔχει γέρας αὐτὸς

καὶ

> ὡσεί τιν᾽ ἀτίμητον μετανάστην,

7 ὡς διὰ ταῦτα ὀργιζόμενος. προσήκειν δ᾽ οἴονται
πολυωρεῖσθαι ὑπὸ τῶν ἡττόνων κατὰ γένος, κατὰ
1379 a δύναμιν, κατ᾽ ἀρετήν, καὶ ὅλως ἐν ᾧ ἂν ταὐτῷ
ὑπερέχῃ πολύ, οἷον ἐν χρήμασιν ὁ πλούσιος πένητος
καὶ ἐν τῷ λέγειν ῥητορικὸς ἀδυνάτου εἰπεῖν καὶ
ἄρχων ἀρχομένου καὶ ἄρχειν ἄξιος οἰόμενος τοῦ
ἄρχεσθαι ἀξίου. διὸ εἴρηται

> θυμὸς δὲ μέγας ἐστι διοτρεφέων βασιλήων

καὶ

> ἀλλά τε καὶ μετόπισθεν ἔχει κότον·

---

[a] *Iliad*, i. 356.
[b] *Iliad*, ix. 648. μετανάστης, lit. "one who changes his
home," used as a term of reproach (see also Glossary).
[c] ταὐτῷ. Other readings are ταῦτα, or τις.
[d] *Iliad*, ii. 196.
[e] *Iliad*, i. 82. The words are those of the soothsayer
Calchas to Achilles, and the reference is to Agamemnon.

whereby the sufferer is disgraced, not to obtain any other advantage for oneself besides the performance of the act, but for one's own pleasure ; for retaliation is not insult, but punishment. The cause of the pleasure felt by those who insult is the idea that, in ill-treating others, they are more fully showing superiority. That is why the young and the wealthy are given to insults ; for they think that, in committing them, they are showing their superiority. Dishonour is characteristic of insult ; and one who dishonours another slights him ; for that which is worthless has no value, either as good or evil. Hence Achilles in his wrath exclaims :

He has dishonoured me, since he keeps the prize he has taken for himself,[a]

and

[has treated me] like a dishonoured vagrant,[b]

as if being wrath for these reasons. Now men think that they have a right to be highly esteemed by those who are inferior to them in birth, power, and virtue, and generally, in whatever similar respect [c] a man is far superior to another ; for example, the rich man to the poor man in the matter of money, the eloquent to the incompetent speaker in the matter of oratory, the governor to the governed, and the man who thinks himself worthy to rule to one who is only fit to be ruled. Wherefore it has been said :

Great is the wrath of kings cherished by Zeus,[d]

and

Yet it may be that even afterwards he cherishes his resentment,[e]

177

8 ἀγανακτοῦσι γὰρ διὰ τὴν ὑπεροχήν. ἔτι ὑφ' ὧν τις οἴεται εὖ πάσχειν δεῖν· οὗτοι δ' εἰσὶν οὓς εὖ πεποίηκεν ἢ ποιεῖ, ἢ αὐτὸς ἢ δι' αὐτόν τις ἢ τῶν αὑτοῦ τις, ἢ βούλεται ἢ ἐβουλήθη.

9 Φανερὸν οὖν ἐκ τούτων ἤδη πῶς τ' ἔχοντες ὀργίζονται αὐτοὶ καὶ τίσι καὶ διὰ ποῖα. αὐτοὶ μὲν γάρ, ὅταν λυπῶνται· ἐφίεται γάρ τινος ὁ λυπούμενος· ἐάν τε οὖν κατ' εὐθυωρίαν ὁτιοῦν ἀντικρούσῃ τις, οἷον τῷ διψῶντι πρὸς τὸ πιεῖν, ἐάν τε μή, ὁμοίως ταὐτὸ φαίνεται ποιεῖν· καὶ ἐάν τε ἀντιπράττῃ τις ἐάν τε μὴ συμπράττῃ ἐάν τε ἄλλο τι ἐνοχλῇ οὕτως ἔχοντα, τοῖς πᾶσιν

10 ὀργίζεται. διὸ κάμνοντες, πενόμενοι, [πολεμοῦν-τες], ἐρῶντες, διψῶντες, ὅλως ἐπιθυμοῦντες καὶ μὴ κατορθοῦντες ὀργίλοι εἰσὶ καὶ εὐπαρόρμητοι, μάλιστα μὲν πρὸς τοὺς τοῦ παρόντος ὀλιγωροῦντας, οἷον κάμνων μὲν τοῖς πρὸς τὴν νόσον,ᵃ πενόμενος δὲ τοῖς πρὸς τὴν πενίαν, πολεμῶν δὲ τοῖς πρὸς τὸν πόλεμον, ἐρῶν δὲ τοῖς πρὸς τὸν ἔρωτα· ὁμοίως δὲ καὶ τοῖς ἄλλοις· προωδοποίηται γὰρ ἕκαστος πρὸς τὴν ἑκάστου ὀργὴν ὑπὸ τοῦ ὑπάρχοντος

11 πάθους.ᵇ ἔτι δ' ἐὰν τἀναντία τύχῃ προσδεχόμενος· λυπεῖ γὰρ μᾶλλον τὸ πολὺ παρὰ δόξαν, ὥσπερ καὶ τέρπει τὸ πολὺ παρὰ δόξαν, ἐὰν γένηται ὃ βούλεται.

ᵃ τοῖς πρὸς τὴν νόσον : lit. "the sick man [is angry with those who slight him] in regard to his illness," that is, by making light of it.

ᵇ Or, "his suffering at the moment."

for kings are resentful in consideration of their superior rank. Further, men are angry at slights from those by whom they think they have a right to expect to be well treated ; such are those on whom they have conferred or are conferring benefits, either themselves, or some one else for them, or one of their friends ; and all those whom they desire, or did desire, to benefit.

It is now evident from these considerations what is the disposition of those who are angry, with whom they are angry, and for what reasons. Men are angry when they are pained, because one who is pained aims at something ; if then anyone directly opposes him in anything, as, for instance, prevents him from drinking when thirsty, or not directly, but seems to be doing just the same ; and if anyone goes against him or refuses to assist him, or troubles him in any other way when he is in this frame of mind, he is angry with all such persons. Wherefore the sick, the necessitous, [those at war], the lovesick, the thirsty, in a word, all who desire something and cannot obtain it, are prone to anger and easily excited, especially against those who make light of their present condition ; for instance, the sick man is easily provoked in regard to his illness,[a] the necessitous in regard to his poverty, the warrior in regard to warlike affairs, the lover in regard to love-affairs, and so with all the rest ; for the passion[b] present in his mind in each case paves the way for his anger. Again, men are angry when the event is contrary to their expectation, for the more unexpected a thing is, the more it pains ; just as they are overjoyed if, contrary to expectation, what they desire comes to pass. From this it is obvious what

διὸ καὶ ὧραι καὶ χρόνοι καὶ διαθέσεις καὶ ἡλικίαι
ἐκ τούτων φανεραί, ποῖαι εὐκίνητοι πρὸς ὀργὴν
καὶ ποῦ καὶ πότε, καὶ ὅτι ὅτε μᾶλλον ἐν τούτοις
εἰσί, μᾶλλον καὶ εὐκίνητοι.

12 Αὐτοὶ μὲν οὖν οὕτως ἔχοντες εὐκίνητοι πρὸς
ὀργήν, ὀργίζονται δὲ τοῖς τε καταγελῶσι καὶ
χλευάζουσι καὶ σκώπτουσιν· ὑβρίζουσι γάρ. καὶ
τοῖς τὰ τοιαῦτα βλάπτουσιν ὅσα ὕβρεως σημεῖα.
ἀνάγκη δὲ τοιαῦτα εἶναι ἃ μήτε ἀντί τινος μήτ᾽
ὠφέλιμα τοῖς ποιοῦσιν· ἤδη γὰρ δοκεῖ δι᾽ ὕβριν.

13 καὶ τοῖς κακῶς λέγουσι καὶ καταφρονοῦσι περὶ
ἃ αὐτοὶ μάλιστα σπουδάζουσιν, οἷον οἱ ἐπὶ φιλο-
σοφίᾳ φιλοτιμούμενοι ἐάν τις εἰς τὴν φιλοσοφίαν,
οἱ δ᾽ ἐπὶ τῇ ἰδέᾳ ἐάν τις εἰς τὴν ἰδέαν, ὁμοίως δὲ

14 καὶ ἐπὶ τῶν ἄλλων. ταῦτα δὲ πολλῷ μᾶλλον, ἐὰν
ὑποπτεύσωσι μὴ ὑπάρχειν αὐτοῖς, ἢ ὅλως ἢ μὴ

1379 b ἰσχυρῶς, ἢ μὴ δοκεῖν· ἐπειδὰν γὰρ σφόδρα οἴωνται
ὑπάρχειν ἐν τούτοις[1] ἐν οἷς σκώπτονται, οὐ φροντί-

15 ζουσιν. καὶ τοῖς φίλοις μᾶλλον ἢ τοῖς μὴ φίλοις·
οἴονται γὰρ προσήκειν μᾶλλον πάσχειν εὖ ὑπ᾽

16 αὐτῶν ἢ μή. καὶ τοῖς εἰθισμένοις τιμᾶν ἢ φροντίζειν, ἐὰν πάλιν μὴ οὕτως ὁμιλῶσιν· καὶ γὰρ ὑπὸ
τούτων οἴονται καταφρονεῖσθαι· ταὐτὰ γὰρ ἂν

---

[1] ἐν τούτοις is bracketed by Spengel: Cope explains it as
" in those particular things " (philosophy, personal beauty,
and the like).

---

[a] εὐκίνητοι refers grammatically to διαθέσεις and ἡλικίαι.

are the seasons, times, states of mind, and conditions of age in which we are easily moved [a] to anger; and what are the various times, places, and reasons, which make us more prone to anger in proportion as we are subject to their influence.

Such then are the dispositions of those who are easily roused to anger. As to the objects of their anger, men are angry with those who ridicule, mock, and scoff at them, for this is an insult. And with those who injure them in ways that are indications of insult. But these acts must be of such a kind that they are neither retaliatory nor advantageous to those who commit them; for if they are, they then appear due to gratuitous insult. And men are angry with those who speak ill of or despise things which they themselves consider of the greatest importance; for instance, if a man speaks contemptuously of philosophy or of personal beauty in the presence of those who pride themselves upon them; and so in all other cases. But they are far more angry if they suspect that they do not possess these qualities, either not at all, or not to any great extent, or when others do not think they possess them. For when they feel strongly that they do possess those qualities which are the subject of mockery, they pay no heed to it. And they are more angry with those who are their friends than with those who are not, for they think that they have a right to be treated well by them rather than ill. And they are angry with those who have been in the habit of honouring and treating them with respect, if they no longer behave so towards them; for they think that they are being treated with contempt by them, otherwise they would treat them as

ARISTOTLE

17 ποιεῖν. καὶ τοῖς μὴ ἀντιποιοῦσιν εὖ, μηδὲ τὴν
ἴσην ἀνταποδιδοῦσιν. καὶ τοῖς τἀναντία ποιοῦσιν
αὐτοῖς, ἐὰν ἥττους ὦσιν· καταφρονεῖν γὰρ πάντες
οἱ τοιοῦτοι φαίνονται, καὶ οἱ μὲν ὡς ἡττόνων οἱ
δ' ὡς παρ' ἡττόνων.

18 Καὶ τοῖς ἐν μηδενὶ λόγῳ οὖσιν, ἄν τι ὀλιγωρῶσι,
μᾶλλον· ὑπόκειται γὰρ ἡ ὀργὴ τῆς ὀλιγωρίας πρὸς
τοὺς μὴ προσήκοντας, προσήκει δὲ τοῖς ἥττοσι

19 μὴ ὀλιγωρεῖν. τοῖς δὲ φίλοις, ἐάν τε μὴ εὖ λέγωσιν
ἢ ποιῶσιν, καὶ ἔτι μᾶλλον ἐὰν τἀναντία, καὶ ἐὰν
μὴ αἰσθάνωνται δεομένων, ὥσπερ ὁ Ἀντιφῶντος
Πλήξιππος τῷ Μελεάγρῳ· ὀλιγωρίας γὰρ τὸ μὴ
αἰσθάνεσθαι σημεῖον· ὧν γὰρ φροντίζομεν, οὐ

20 λανθάνει. καὶ τοῖς ἐπιχαίρουσι ταῖς ἀτυχίαις καὶ
ὅλως εὐθυμουμένοις ἐν ταῖς αὐτῶν ἀτυχίαις· ἢ
γὰρ ἐχθροῦ ἢ ὀλιγωροῦντος σημεῖον. καὶ τοῖς
μὴ φροντίζουσιν, ἐὰν λυπήσωσιν· διὸ καὶ τοῖς

21 κακὰ ἀγγέλλουσιν ὀργίζονται. καὶ τοῖς ἢ ἀκούουσι
περὶ αὐτῶν ἢ θεωμένοις τὰ αὐτῶν φαῦλα· ὅμοιοι
γάρ εἰσιν ἢ ὀλιγωροῦσιν ἢ ἐχθροῖς· οἱ γὰρ φίλοι

22 συναλγοῦσι, θεώμενοι δὲ τὰ οἰκεῖα φαῦλα πάντες
ἀλγοῦσιν. ἔτι τοῖς ὀλιγωροῦσι πρὸς πέντε, πρὸς
οὓς φιλοτιμοῦνται, πρὸς οὓς θαυμάζουσιν, ὑφ' ὧν
βούλονται θαυμάζεσθαι, ἢ οὓς αἰσχύνονται, ἢ ἐν
τοῖς αἰσχυνομένοις αὐτούς· ἐν τούτοις ἐάν τις

---

^a Plexippus was the uncle of Meleager. The allusion is
obscure. It may refer to Meleager giving the skin of the
Calydonian boar to Atalanta, which his uncle wanted. One
of Antiphon's tragedies was named *Meleager* (*T.G.F.* p. 792).
 ^b Literally, "for the things which (= the persons whom)
one respects, do not escape notice."

before. And with those who do not return their
kindnesses nor requite them in full; and with those
who oppose them, if they are inferiors; for all such
appear to treat them with contempt, the latter as if
they regarded them as inferiors, the former as if
they had received kindnesses from inferiors.

And they are more angry with those who are of
no account, if they slight them; for anger at a slight
was assumed to be felt at those who ought not to
behave in such a manner; for inferiors ought not
to slight their superiors. And they are angry with
friends, if they neither speak well of nor treat them
well, and in an even greater degree, if they do the
opposite. And if they fail to perceive that they
want something from them, as Plexippus [a] in Antiphon's tragedy reproached Meleager; for failure to
perceive this is a sign of slight; since, when we care
for people, these things are noticed.[b] And they are
angry with those who rejoice, or in a general way
are cheerful when they are unfortunate; for this is
an indication of enmity or slight. And with those
who do not care if they pain them; whence they are
angry with those who bring bad news. And with
those who listen to the tale of their faults, or look
on them with indifference, for they resemble slighters
or enemies; for friends sympathize and all men are
pained to see their own faults exposed.[c] And further,
with those who slight them before five classes of
persons: namely, their rivals, those whom they admire,
those by whom they would like to be admired, those
whom they respect, or those who respect them;
when anyone slights them before these, their anger is

---

[c] The real friend, therefore, would feel as much pain as
the other whose faults are exposed.

23 ὀλιγωρῇ, ὀργίζονται μᾶλλον. καὶ τοῖς εἰς τὰ
τοιαῦτα ὀλιγωροῦσιν ὑπὲρ ὧν αὐτοῖς αἰσχρὸν μὴ
βοηθεῖν, οἷον γονεῖς, τέκνα, γυναῖκας, ἀρχομένους.[a]
καὶ τοῖς χάριν μὴ ἀποδιδοῦσιν· παρὰ τὸ προσῆκον
24 γὰρ ἡ ὀλιγωρία. καὶ τοῖς εἰρωνευομένοις πρὸς
25 σπουδάζοντας· καταφρονητικὸν γὰρ ἡ εἰρωνεία.
καὶ τοῖς τῶν ἄλλων εὐποιητικοῖς, ἐὰν μὴ καὶ
αὐτῶν· καὶ γὰρ τοῦτο καταφρονητικόν, τὸ μὴ
26 ἀξιοῦν ὧν πάντας καὶ αὐτόν. ποιητικὸν δ᾽ ὀργῆς
καὶ ἡ λήθη, οἷον καὶ ἡ τῶν ὀνομάτων οὕτως οὖσα
περὶ μικρόν· ὀλιγωρίας γὰρ δοκεῖ καὶ ἡ λήθη
σημεῖον εἶναι· δι᾽ ἀμέλειαν μὲν γὰρ ἡ λήθη γίγ-
27 νεται, ἡ δ᾽ ἀμέλεια ὀλιγωρία ἐστίν. οἷς μὲν οὖν
ὀργίζονται καὶ ὡς ἔχοντες καὶ διὰ ποῖα, ἅμα
1380 a εἴρηται· δῆλον δ᾽ ὅτι δέοι ἂν αὐτὸν κατασκευάζειν
τῷ λόγῳ τοιούτους οἷοι ὄντες ὀργίλως ἔχουσιν,
καὶ τοὺς ἐναντίους τούτοις ἐνόχους ὄντας ἐφ᾽ οἷς
ὀργίζονται, καὶ τοιούτους οἵοις ὀργίζονται.

3. Ἐπεὶ δὲ τὸ ὀργίζεσθαι ἐναντίον τῷ πραΰ-
νεσθαι καὶ ὀργὴ πραότητι, ληπτέον πῶς ἔχοντες
πρᾶοί εἰσι καὶ πρὸς τίνας πράως ἔχουσι καὶ διὰ
2 τίνων πραΰνονται. ἔστω δὴ πράϋνσις κατάστασις
3 καὶ ἠρέμησις ὀργῆς. εἰ οὖν ὀργίζονται τοῖς
ὀλιγωροῦσιν, ὀλιγωρία δ᾽ ἐστὶν ἑκούσιον, φανερὸν
ὅτι καὶ τοῖς μηδὲν τούτων ποιοῦσιν ἢ ἀκουσίως[b]
4 ποιοῦσιν ἢ φαινομένοις τοιούτοις πρᾶοί εἰσιν. καὶ
τοῖς τἀναντία ὧν ἐποίησαν βουλομένοις. καὶ ὅσοι

---

[a] Cope translates "rulers and governors"; but can
ἄρχεσθαι be used in a middle sense?

[b] To avoid the apparent tautology (§ 17), Roemer (*Rhein. Mus.* xxxix. p. 503) boldly conjectures χαίρειν : "not to return another's greeting."

greater. They are also angry with those who slight such persons as it would be disgraceful for them not to defend, for instance, parents, children, wives, and dependents.[a] And with those who are ungrateful,[b] for the slight is contrary to all sense of obligation. And with those who employ irony, when they themselves are in earnest; for irony shows contempt. And with those who do good to others, but not to them; for not to think them worthy of what they bestow upon all others also shows contempt. Forgetfulness also is a cause of anger, such as forgetting names, although it is a mere trifle, since even forgetfulness seems a sign of slight; for it is caused by indifference, and indifference is a slight. We have thus stated at one and the same time the frame of mind and the reasons which make men angry, and the objects of their anger. It is evident then that it will be necessary for the speaker, by his eloquence, to put the hearers into the frame of mind of those who are inclined to anger, and to show that his opponents are responsible for things which rouse men to anger and are people of the kind with whom men are angry.

3. And since becoming angry is the opposite of becoming mild, and anger of mildness, we must determine the state of mind which makes men mild, towards whom they become mild, and the reasons which make them so. Let us then define making mild as the quieting and appeasing of anger. If then men are angry with those who slight them, and slight is voluntary, it is evident that they are mild towards those who do none of these things, or do them involuntarily, or at least appear to be such; and towards those who intended the opposite of what

ARISTOTLE

καὶ αὐτοὶ εἰς αὑτοὺς τοιοῦτοι· οὐδεὶς γὰρ αὐτὸς
5 αὑτοῦ δοκεῖ ὀλιγωρεῖν. καὶ τοῖς ὁμολογοῦσι καὶ
μεταμελομένοις· ὡς γὰρ ἔχοντες δίκην τὸ λυπεῖσθαι ἐπὶ τοῖς πεποιημένοις παύονται τῆς ὀργῆς.
σημεῖον δὲ ἐπὶ τῆς τῶν οἰκετῶν κολάσεως· τοὺς
μὲν γὰρ ἀντιλέγοντας καὶ ἀρνουμένους μᾶλλον
κολάζομεν, πρὸς δὲ τοὺς ὁμολογοῦντας δικαίως
κολάζεσθαι παυόμεθα θυμούμενοι. αἴτιον δ' ὅτι
ἀναισχυντία τὸ τὰ φανερὰ ἀρνεῖσθαι, ἡ δ' ἀναισχυντία ὀλιγωρία καὶ καταφρόνησις· ὧν γοῦν
6 πολὺ καταφρονοῦμεν, οὐκ αἰσχυνόμεθα. καὶ τοῖς
ταπεινουμένοις πρὸς αὐτοὺς καὶ μὴ ἀντιλέγουσιν·
φαίνονται γὰρ ὁμολογεῖν ἥττους εἶναι, οἱ δ' ἥττους
φοβοῦνται, φοβούμενος δὲ οὐδεὶς ὀλιγωρεῖ. ὅτι
δὲ πρὸς τοὺς ταπεινουμένους παύεται ἡ ὀργή, καὶ
οἱ κύνες δηλοῦσιν οὐ δάκνοντες τοὺς καθίζοντας.
7 καὶ τοῖς σπουδάζουσι πρὸς τοὺς σπουδάζοντας·
δοκεῖ γὰρ σπουδάζεσθαι ἀλλ' οὐ καταφρονεῖσθαι.
8 καὶ τοῖς μείζω κεχαρισμένοις. καὶ τοῖς δεομένοις
9 καὶ παραιτουμένοις· ταπεινότεροι γάρ. καὶ τοῖς
μὴ ὑβρισταῖς μηδὲ χλευασταῖς μηδ' ὀλιγώροις, ἢ
εἰς μηδένα ἢ μὴ εἰς χρηστοὺς μηδ' εἰς τοιούτους
10 οἷοί περ αὐτοί. ὅλως δ' ἐκ τῶν ἐναντίων δεῖ
σκοπεῖν τὰ πραϋντικά. καὶ οὓς φοβοῦνται ἢ αἰ-
σχύνονται· ἕως γὰρ ἂν οὕτως ἔχωσιν, οὐκ ὀρ-
γίζονται· ἀδύνατον γὰρ ἅμα φοβεῖσθαι καὶ ὀρ-

---

[a] ἐξαπίνης δ' Ὀδυσῆα ἴδον κύνες ὑλακόμωροι | οἱ μὲν κεκλή-
γοντες ἐπέδραμον· αὐτὰρ Ὀδυσσεὺς | ἕζετο κερδοσύνῃ (*Odyssey*,
xiv. 29-31).
[b] That is, greater than their present disservices.
186

they have done, and all who behave in the same way
to themselves, for no one is likely to slight himself.
And towards those who admit and are sorry for a
slight ; for finding as it were satisfaction in the pain
the offenders feel at what they have done, men
cease to be angry. Evidence of this may be seen in
the punishment of slaves ; for we punish more
severely those who contradict us and deny their
offence, but cease to be angry with those who admit
that they are justly punished. The reason is that
to deny what is evident is disrespect, and disrespect
is slight and contempt ; anyhow, we show no
respect for those for whom we entertain a profound
contempt. Men also are mild towards those who
humble themselves before them and do not contradict
them, for they seem to recognize that they are
inferior ; now, those who are inferior are afraid, and
no one who is afraid slights another. Even the be-
haviour of dogs proves that anger ceases towards
those who humble themselves, for they do not bite
those who sit down.[a] And men are mild towards
those who are serious with them when they are
serious, for they think they are being treated
seriously, not with contempt. And towards those
who have rendered them greater services.[b] And
towards those who want something and deprecate
their anger, for they are humbler. And towards
those who refrain from insulting, mocking, or slighting anyone, or any virtuous man, or those who
resemble themselves. And generally speaking, one
can determine the reasons that make for mildness
by their opposites. Thus, men are mild towards
those whom they fear or respect, as long as they feel
so towards them, for it is impossible to be afraid and

11 γίζεσθαι. καὶ τοῖς δι᾽ ὀργὴν ποιήσασιν ἢ οὐκ
ὀργίζονται ἢ ἧττον ὀργίζονται· οὐ γὰρ δι᾽ ὀλιγωρίαν
φαίνονται πρᾶξαι· οὐδεὶς γὰρ ὀργιζόμενος ὀλιγωρεῖ·
1380 b ἡ μὲν γὰρ ὀλιγωρία ἄλυπον, ἡ δ᾽ ὀργὴ μετὰ λύπης.
12 καὶ τοῖς αἰσχυνομένοις αὐτούς.

Καὶ ἔχοντες δὲ ἐναντίως τῷ ὀργίζεσθαι δῆλον
ὅτι πρᾶοι εἰσίν, οἷον ἐν παιδιᾷ, ἐν γέλωτι, ἐν
ἑορτῇ, ἐν εὐημερίᾳ, ἐν κατορθώσει, ἐν πληρώσει,
ὅλως ἐν ἀλυπίᾳ καὶ ἡδονῇ μὴ ὑβριστικῇ καὶ ἐν
ἐλπίδι ἐπιεικεῖ. ἔτι κεχρονικότες καὶ μὴ ὑπόγυιοι
13 τῇ ὀργῇ ὄντες· παύει γὰρ ὀργὴν ὁ χρόνος. παύει
δὲ καὶ ἑτέρου ὀργὴν μείζω ἢ παρ᾽ ἄλλου ληφθεῖσα
τιμωρία πρότερον· διὸ εὖ Φιλοκράτης, εἰπόντος
τινὸς ὀργιζομένου τοῦ δήμου " τί οὐκ ἀπολογεῖ; "
" οὔπω γε " ἔφη. " ἀλλὰ πότε; " " ὅταν ἄλλον ἴδω διαβεβλημένον·" πρᾶοι γὰρ γίγνονται,
ὅταν εἰς ἄλλον τὴν ὀργὴν ἀναλώσωσιν, οἷον συνέβη
ἐπὶ Ἐργοφίλου· μᾶλλον γὰρ χαλεπαίνοντες ἢ
Καλλισθένει ἀφεῖσαν διὰ τὸ Καλλισθένους τῇ
14 προτεραίᾳ καταγνῶναι θάνατον. καὶ ἐὰν ἐλεῶσιν·
καὶ ἐὰν. μεῖζον κακὸν πεπονθότες ὦσιν ἢ οἱ ὀργι-

---

[a] They regard the disrespectful treatment as merely a
temporary lapse.

[b] πλήρωσις: lit. "filling up." The reference may be to the
"fulfilment" of one's desires, or to "repletion" in the
matter of food (L. and S.), which seems less likely; "in
fulness of content" (Jebb).

[c] Opponent of Demosthenes, and one of the pro-Mace-
donian party. Impeached for his share in the disastrous
"Peace of Philocrates," he went into exile and was condemned to death during his absence.

[d] Ergophilus failed in an attack on Cotys, king of Thrace,
while Callisthenes concluded a premature peace with
Perdiccas, king of Macedonia.

angry at the same time. And against those who have acted in anger they either feel no anger or in a less degree, for they do not seem to have acted from a desire to slight. For no one slights another when angry, since slight is free from pain, but anger is accompanied by it. And men are not angry with those who usually show respect for them.[a]

It is also evident that those are mild whose condition is contrary to that which excites anger, as when laughing, in sport, at a feast, in prosperity, in success, in abundance,[b] and, in general, in freedom from pain, in pleasure which does not imply insult, or in virtuous hope. Further, those whose anger is of long standing and not in its full flush, for time appeases anger. Again, vengeance previously taken upon one person appeases anger against another, even though it be greater. Wherefore Philocrates,[c] when someone asked him why he did not justify himself when the people were angry with him, made the judicious reply, " Not yet." " When then ? " " When I see someone accused of the same offence " ; for men grow mild when they have exhausted their anger upon another, as happened in the case of Ergophilus.[d] For although the Athenians were more indignant with him than with Callisthenes, they acquitted him, because they had condemned Callicrates to death on the previous day. Men also grow mild towards those whom they pity[e]; and if an offender has suffered greater evil than those

---

[e] Another reading is ἐὰν ἕλωσι, " if they have convicted him." This is adopted by Roemer, who refers to Plato, *Republic*, 558 A, where, in speaking of the freedom allowed to all who live under a democracy, it is remarked that, even if a man is convicted by a court of justice, he takes no heed of the sentence, which is very often not enforced.

189

ζόμενοι ἂν ἔδρασαν· ὥσπερ εἰληφέναι γὰρ οἴονται
15 τιμωρίαν. καὶ ἐὰν ἀδικεῖν οἴωνται αὐτοὶ καὶ
δικαίως πάσχειν· οὐ γίγνεται γὰρ ἡ ὀργὴ πρὸς
τὸ δίκαιον· οὐ γὰρ ἔτι παρὰ τὸ προσῆκον οἴονται
πάσχειν, ἡ δ' ὀργὴ τοῦτο ἦν. διὸ δεῖ τῷ λόγῳ
προκολάζειν· ἀγανακτοῦσι γὰρ ἧττον κολαζόμενοι
16 καὶ οἱ δοῦλοι. καὶ ἐὰν μὴ αἰσθήσεσθαι οἴωνται
ὅτι δι' αὐτοὺς καὶ ἀνθ' ὧν ἔπαθον· ἡ γὰρ ὀργὴ
τῶν καθ' ἕκαστόν ἐστιν· δῆλον δ' ἐκ τοῦ ὁρισμοῦ.
διὸ ὀρθῶς πεποίηται

φάσθαι 'Οδυσσῆα πτολιπόρθιον,

ὡς οὐ τετιμωρημένος, εἰ μὴ ᾔσθετο καὶ ὑφ' οὗ
καὶ ἀνθ' ὅτου. ὥστε οὔτε τοῖς ἄλλοις ὅσοι μὴ
αἰσθάνονται ὀργίζονται, οὔτε τοῖς τεθνεῶσιν ἔτι,
ὡς πεπονθόσι τε τὸ ἔσχατον καὶ οὐκ ἀλγήσουσιν
οὐδ' αἰσθησομένοις, οὗ οἱ ὀργιζόμενοι ἐφίενται.
διὸ εὖ περὶ τοῦ Ἕκτορος ὁ ποιητής, παῦσαι βουλόμενος τὸν Ἀχιλλέα τῆς ὀργῆς τεθνεῶτος,

κωφὴν γὰρ δὴ γαῖαν ἀεικίζει μενεαίνων.

17 δῆλον οὖν ὅτι τοῖς καταπραΰνειν βουλομένοις ἐκ
τούτων τῶν τόπων λεκτέον, αὐτοὺς μὲν παρα-

---

a Therefore, if you think that a man will never learn *who* took vengeance on him, you will be less cruel; for anger is personal, and so Odysseus, because he was angry, inflicted a savage punishment, and wished Polyphemus to know it.

b *Odyssey*, ix. 504.

c Or, "as if Odysseus would not have considered himself avenged, had P. remained ignorant . . . "

d Or, "with any who can no longer feel their anger." Cope translates : "with all the rest (besides those actually within reach) who are out of sight."

who are angry would have inflicted, for they have an idea that they have as it were obtained reparation. And if they think that they themselves are wrong and deserve what they suffer, for anger is not aroused against what is just ; they no longer think that they are being treated otherwise than they should be, which, as we have said, is the essence of anger. Wherefore we should inflict a preliminary verbal chastisement, for even slaves are less indignant at punishment of this kind. And men are milder if they think that those punished will never know that the punishment comes from *them* in requital for their own wrongs ; for anger has to do with the individual, as is clear from our definition.^a Wherefore it is justly said by the poet :

> Tell him that it is Odysseus, sacker of cities,^b

as if Polyphemus would not have been punished,^c had he remained ignorant who had blinded him and for what. So that men are not angry either with any others who cannot know who punishes them,^d or with the dead, since they have paid the last penalty and can feel neither pain nor anything else, which is the aim of those who are angry.^e So then, in regard to Hector, Homer, when desirous of restraining the anger of Achilles against a dead man, well says :

> For it is senseless clay that he outrages in his wrath.

It is evident, then, that men must have recourse to these topics when they desire to appease their audience, putting them into the frame of mind

---

^e To make the offender *feel* pain as part of the punishment.

^f *Iliad*, xxiv. 54.

σκευάζουσι τοιούτους, οἷς δ' ὀργίζονται, ἢ φοβερούς ἢ αἰσχύνης ἀξίους ἢ κεχαρισμένους ἢ
ἄκοντας ἢ ὑπεραλγοῦντας τοῖς πεποιημένοις.

4. Τίνας δὲ φιλοῦσι καὶ μισοῦσι, καὶ διὰ τί,
τὴν φιλίαν καὶ τὸ φιλεῖν ὁρισάμενοι λέγωμεν.
2 ἔστω δὴ τὸ φιλεῖν τὸ βούλεσθαί τινι ἃ οἴεται
ἀγαθά, ἐκείνου ἕνεκα ἀλλὰ μὴ αὑτοῦ, καὶ τὸ κατὰ
1381 a δύναμιν πρακτικὸν εἶναι τούτων. φίλος δ' ἐστὶν
ὁ φιλῶν καὶ ἀντιφιλούμενος. οἴονται δὲ φίλοι
εἶναι οἱ οὕτως ἔχειν οἰόμενοι πρὸς ἀλλήλους.
3 τούτων δὲ ὑποκειμένων ἀνάγκη φίλον εἶναι τὸν
συνηδόμενον τοῖς ἀγαθοῖς καὶ συναλγοῦντα τοῖς
λυπηροῖς μὴ διά τι ἕτερον ἀλλὰ δι' ἐκεῖνον. γιγνομένων γὰρ ὧν βούλονται χαίρουσι πάντες, τῶν
ἐναντίων δὲ λυποῦνται, ὥστε τῆς βουλήσεως
4 σημεῖον αἱ λῦπαι καὶ αἱ ἡδοναί. καὶ οἷς δὴ ταὐτὰ
ἀγαθὰ καὶ κακά, καὶ οἱ τοῖς αὐτοῖς φίλοι, καὶ οἱ
τοῖς αὐτοῖς ἐχθροί· ταὐτὰ γὰρ τούτοις βούλεσθαι
ἀνάγκη, ὥστε ἅ περ αὑτῷ καὶ ἄλλῳ βουλόμενος,
τούτῳ φαίνεται φίλος εἶναι.
5 Καὶ τοὺς πεποιηκότας εὖ φιλοῦσιν, ἢ αὐτοὺς ἢ
ὧν κήδονται· ἢ εἰ μεγάλα, ἢ εἰ προθύμως, ἢ εἰ
ἐν τοιούτοις καιροῖς, καὶ αὐτῶν ἕνεκα· ἢ οὓς ἂν
6 οἴωνται βούλεσθαι ποιεῖν εὖ. καὶ τοὺς τῶν φίλων
φίλους καὶ φιλοῦντας οὓς αὐτοὶ φιλοῦσιν. καὶ
7 τοὺς φιλουμένους ὑπὸ τῶν φιλουμένων αὐτοῖς. καὶ
τοὺς τοῖς αὐτοῖς ἐχθροὺς καὶ μισοῦντας οὓς αὐτοὶ

---

[a] φιλεῖν may be translated " to love " or "to like "; φιλία
by " love," " liking," or " friendship " ; for φίλος "friend"
alone is suitable.   For the two meanings cp. the use of *aimer*
in French, and *lieben* in German.

required and representing those with whom they are angry as either formidable or deserving of respect, or as having rendered them great services, or acted involuntarily, or as exceedingly grieved at what they have done.

4. Let us now state who are the persons that men love *a* or hate, and why, after we have defined love and loving. Let loving, then, be defined as wishing for anyone the things which we believe to be good, for his sake but not for our own, and procuring them for him as far as lies in our power. A friend is one who loves and is loved in return, and those who think their relationship is of this character consider themselves friends. This being granted, it necessarily follows that he is a friend who shares our joy in good fortune and our sorrow in affliction, for our own sake and not for any other reason. For all men rejoice when what they desire comes to pass and are pained when the contrary happens, so that pain and pleasure are indications of their wish. And those are friends who have the same ideas of good and bad, and love and hate the same persons, since they necessarily wish the same things ; wherefore one who wishes for another what he wishes for himself seems to be the other's friend.

We also like those who have done good either to us or to those whom we hold dear, if the services are important, or are cordially rendered, or under certain circumstances, and for our sake only ; and all those whom we think desirous of doing us good. And those who are friends of our friends and who like those whom we like, and those who are liked by those who are liked by us ; and those whose enemies are ours, those who hate those whom we ourselves

μισοῦσιν, καὶ τοὺς μισουμένους ὑπὸ τῶν αὐτοῖς
μισουμένων· πᾶσι γὰρ τούτοις ταὐτὰ ἀγαθὰ φαίνεται εἶναι καὶ αὐτοῖς, ὥστε βούλεσθαι τὰ αὐτοῖς
8 ἀγαθά, ὅ περ ἦν τοῦ φίλου. ἔτι τοὺς εὐποιητικοὺς
εἰς χρήματα καὶ εἰς σωτηρίαν· διὸ τοὺς ἐλευ-
θερίους καὶ τοὺς ἀνδρείους τιμῶσι καὶ τοὺς δικαίους.
9 τοιούτους δ' ὑπολαμβάνουσι τοὺς μὴ ἀφ' ἑτέρων
ζῶντας· τοιοῦτοι δ' οἱ ἀπὸ τοῦ ἐργάζεσθαι, καὶ
τούτων οἱ ἀπὸ γεωργίας καὶ τῶν ἄλλων οἱ αὐτ-
10 ουργοὶ μάλιστα. καὶ τοὺς σώφρονας, ὅτι οὐκ
11 ἄδικοι. καὶ τοὺς ἀπράγμονας διὰ τὸ αὐτό. καὶ
οἷς βουλόμεθα φίλοι εἶναι, ἐὰν φαίνωνται βου-
λόμενοι· εἰσὶ δὲ τοιοῦτοι οἵ τ' ἀγαθοὶ κατ' ἀρετὴν
καὶ οἱ εὐδόκιμοι ἢ ἐν ἅπασιν ἢ ἐν τοῖς βελτίστοις
ἢ ἐν τοῖς θαυμαζομένοις ὑφ' αὐτῶν ἢ ἐν τοῖς θαυ-
12 μάζουσιν αὐτούς. ἔτι τοὺς ἡδεῖς συνδιαγαγεῖν καὶ
συνδιημερεῦσαι· τοιοῦτοι δ' οἱ εὔκολοι καὶ μὴ
ἐλεγκτικοὶ τῶν ἁμαρτανομένων καὶ μὴ φιλόνεικοι
μηδὲ δυσέριδες· πάντες γὰρ οἱ τοιοῦτοι μαχητικοί,
οἱ δὲ μαχόμενοι τἀναντία φαίνονται βούλεσθαι.

ᵃ Aristotle's opinion of husbandry, in which tillage and
planting, keeping of bees, fish, and fowl were included, was
not nearly so favourable as that of Xenophon in his
Oeconomicus. In two lists of the elements of a State given
in the *Politics*, it comes first at the head of the lower
occupations. In its favour it is said that it forms the best
material of a rural democracy, furnishes good sailors, a
healthy body of men, not money-grabbers like merchants
and tradesmen, and does not make men unfit to bear arms.
On the other hand, it claims so much of a man's time that

hate, and those who are hated by those who are hated by us ; for all such persons have the same idea as ourselves of what is good, so that they wish what is good for us, which, as we said, is the characteristic of a friend. Further, we like those who are ready to help others in the matter of money or personal safety ; wherefore men honour those who are liberal and courageous and just. And such we consider those who do not live upon others ; the sort of men who live by their exertions, and among them agriculturists, and, beyond all others, those who work with their own hands.[a] And the self-controlled, because they are not likely to commit injustice ; and those who are not busybodies, for the same reason. And those with whom we wish to be friends, if they also seem to wish it ; such are those who excel in virtue and enjoy a good reputation, either generally, or amongst the best, or amongst those who are admired by us or by whom we are admired.[b] Further, those who are agreeable to live or spend the time with ; such are those who are good-tempered and not given to carping at our errors, neither quarrelsome nor contentious, for all such persons are pugnacious, and the wishes of the pugnacious appear to be opposed to ours.

he is unable to devote proper attention to political duties, and should be excluded from holding office. He further says that husbandmen, if possible, should be slaves (neither of the same race nor hot-tempered, for they will work better and are less likely to revolt); or, as the next best alternative, barbarians or serfs. The favourable view taken by Aristotle here and in the *Oeconomics* (probably not his) does not agree with that put forward in the *Politics*.

[b] Spengel reads ἢ ἐν οἷς θαυμάζουσιν αὐτοί and brackets [ἢ ἐν τοῖς θαυμαζομένοις ὑφ' αὐτῶν]. ἅπασιν, βελτίστοις, and οἷς will then all be neuter.

13 Καὶ οἱ ἐπιδέξιοι καὶ τωθάσαι[1] καὶ ὑπομεῖναι·
ἐπὶ ταὐτὸ γὰρ ἀμφότεροι σπεύδουσι τῷ πλησίον,
δυνάμενοί τε σκώπτεσθαι καὶ ἐμμελῶς σκώπ-
14 τοντες. καὶ τοὺς ἐπαινοῦντας τὰ ὑπάρχοντα ἀγαθά,
καὶ τούτων μάλιστα ἃ φοβοῦνται μὴ ὑπάρχειν
15 αὐτοῖς. καὶ τοὺς καθαρίους περὶ ὄψιν, περὶ ἀμπ-
16 εχόνην, περὶ ὅλον τὸν βίον. καὶ τοὺς μὴ ὀνειδι-
1381 b στὰς μήτε τῶν ἁμαρτημάτων μήτε τῶν εὐεργε-
17 τημάτων· ἀμφότεροι γὰρ ἐλεγκτικοί. καὶ τοὺς μὴ
μνησικάκους, μηδὲ φυλακτικοὺς τῶν ἐγκλημάτων,
ἀλλ' εὐκαταλλάκτους· οἵους γὰρ ἂν ὑπολαμβάνωσιν
εἶναι πρὸς τοὺς ἄλλους, καὶ πρὸς αὑτοὺς οἴονται.
18 καὶ τοὺς μὴ κακολόγους μηδὲ εἰδότας μήτε τὰ
τῶν πλησίον κακὰ μήτε τὰ αὑτῶν, ἀλλὰ τἀγαθά·
19 ὁ γὰρ ἀγαθὸς τοῦτο δρᾷ. καὶ τοὺς μὴ ἀντιτείνον-
τας τοῖς ὀργιζομένοις ἢ σπουδάζουσιν· μαχητικοὶ
γὰρ οἱ τοιοῦτοι. καὶ τοὺς πρὸς αὐτοὺς σπουδαίως
πως ἔχοντας, οἷον θαυμάζοντας αὐτοὺς καὶ σπου-
20 δαίους ὑπολαμβάνοντας καὶ χαίροντας αὐτοῖς, καὶ
ταῦτα μάλιστα πεπονθότας περὶ ἃ μάλιστα βούλονται αὐτοὶ ἢ θαυμάζεσθαι ἢ σπουδαῖοι δοκεῖν
21 εἶναι ἢ ἡδεῖς. καὶ τοὺς ὁμοίους καὶ ταὐτὰ ἐπι-
τηδεύοντας, ἐὰν μὴ παρενοχλῶσι μηδ' ἀπὸ ταὐτοῦ
ᾖ ὁ βίος· γίγνεται γὰρ οὕτω τὸ

κεραμεὺς κεραμεῖ.

22 καὶ τοὺς τῶν αὐτῶν ἐπιθυμοῦντας, ὧν ἐνδέχεται
ἅμα μετέχειν αὐτούς· εἰ δὲ μή, ταὐτὸ καὶ οὕτω

---

[1] Spengel reads τῷ παῖσαι καὶ τῷ ὑπομεῖναι (from A^c).
Roemer (*Rhein. Mus.* xxxix. p. 504) supports this, on the
ground that τωθάζειν implies gross abuse, and would hardly
be spoken of as ἐμμελῶς σκώπτειν.

196

And those are liked who are clever at making or taking a joke, for each has the same end in view as his neighbour, being able to take a joke and return it in good taste. And those who praise our good qualities, especially those which we ourselves are afraid we do not possess ; those who are neat in their personal appearance and dress, and clean-living ; those who do not make our errors or the benefits they have conferred a matter of reproach, for both these are inclined to be censorious ; those who bear no malice and do not cherish the memory of their wrongs, but are easily appeased ; for we think that they will be to ourselves such as we suppose them to be to others ; and those who are neither given to slander, or eager to know the faults of their neighbours nor our own, but only the good qualities ; for this is the way in which the good man acts. And those who do not oppose us when we are angry or occupied, for such persons are pugnacious ; and those who show any good feeling towards us ; for instance, if they admire us, think us good men, and take pleasure in our company, especially those who are so disposed towards us in regard to things for which we particularly desire to be either admired or to be thought worthy or agreeable. And we like those who resemble us and have the same tastes, provided their interests do not clash with ours and that they do not gain their living in the same way ; for then it becomes a case of

> Potter [being jealous] of potter.[a]

And those who desire the same things, provided it is possible for us to share them ; otherwise the same

[a] Two of a trade never agree (Hesiod, *Works and Days*, 25).

23 συμβαίνει. καὶ πρὸς οὓς οὕτως ἔχουσιν ὥστε μὴ
αἰσχύνεσθαι τὰ πρὸς δόξαν, μὴ καταφρονοῦντες.
24 καὶ πρὸς οὓς αἰσχύνονται τὰ πρὸς ἀλήθειαν. καὶ
πρὸς οὓς φιλοτιμοῦνται, ἢ ὑφ' ὧν ζηλοῦσθαι βούλονται καὶ μὴ φθονεῖσθαι, τούτους ἢ φιλοῦσιν ἢ
25 βούλονται φίλοι εἶναι. καὶ οἷς ἂν τἀγαθὰ συμ-
πράττωσιν, ἐὰν μὴ μέλλῃ αὐτοῖς ἔσεσθαι μείζω
26 κακά. καὶ τοῖς ὁμοίως καὶ τοὺς ἀπόντας καὶ τοὺς
παρόντας φιλοῦσιν· διὸ καὶ τοὺς περὶ τοὺς τεθνεῶτας τοιούτους πάντες φιλοῦσιν.

Καὶ ὅλως τοὺς σφόδρα φιλοφίλους καὶ μὴ
ἐγκαταλείποντας· μάλιστα γὰρ φιλοῦσι τῶν ἀγαθῶν
27 τοὺς φιλεῖν ἀγαθούς. καὶ τοὺς μὴ πλαττομένους
πρὸς αὐτούς· τοιοῦτοι δὲ καὶ οἱ τὰ φαῦλα τὰ
ἑαυτῶν λέγοντες. εἴρηται γὰρ ὅτι πρὸς τοὺς
φίλους τὰ πρὸς δόξαν οὐκ αἰσχυνόμεθα· εἰ οὖν ὁ
αἰσχυνόμενος μὴ φιλεῖ, ὁ μὴ αἰσχυνόμενος φιλοῦντι
ἔοικεν. καὶ τοὺς μὴ φοβερούς, καὶ οὓς θαρροῦμεν·
28 οὐδεὶς γὰρ ὃν φοβεῖται φιλεῖ. εἴδη δὲ φιλίας
ἑταιρεία οἰκειότης συγγένεια καὶ ὅσα τοιαῦτα.
29 ποιητικὰ δὲ φιλίας χάρις, καὶ τὸ μὴ δεηθέντος
ποιῆσαι, καὶ τὸ ποιήσαντα μὴ δηλῶσαι· αὐτοῦ
30 γὰρ οὕτως ἕνεκα φαίνεται καὶ οὐ διά τι ἕτερον.
1382 a   Περὶ δ' ἔχθρας καὶ τοῦ μισεῖν φανερὸν ὡς ἐκ
τῶν ἐναντίων δεῖ θεωρεῖν. ποιητικὰ δ' ἔχθρας
31 ὀργή, ἐπηρεασμός, διαβολή. ὀργὴ μὲν οὖν ἐστιν

---

[a] Those with whom we are ambitious of entering into
competition " in the race for distinction " (Cope). There is
no unfriendliness, whereas envy produces it.

[b] A parenthetical remark. Aristotle explains that he is
not thinking of merely conventional faults; if, then, one
who *is* ashamed of these is no friend, then one who is *not* . . .

thing would happen again. And those with whom we are on such terms that we do not blush before them for faults merely condemned by public opinion, provided that this is not due to contempt; and those before whom we do blush for faults that are really bad. And those whose rivals we are,[a] or by whom we wish to be emulated, but not envied,—these we either like or wish to be friends with them. And those whom we are ready to assist in obtaining what is good, provided greater evil does not result for ourselves. And those who show equal fondness for friends, whether absent or present; wherefore all men like those who show such feeling for the dead.

In a word, men like those who are strongly attached to their friends and do not leave them in the lurch; for among good men they chiefly like those who are good friends. And those who do not dissemble with them; such are those who do not fear to mention even their faults. (For, as we have said, before friends we do not blush for faults merely condemned by public opinion; if then he who blushes for such faults is not a friend, he who does not is likely to be one).[b] And men like those who are not formidable, and in whom they have confidence; for no one likes one whom he fears. Companionship, intimacy, kinship, and similar relations are species of friendship. Things that create friendship are doing a favour, and doing it unasked, and not making it public after doing it; for then it seems to have been rendered for the sake of the friend, and not for any other reason.

As for enmity and hatred, it is evident that they must be examined in the light of their contraries. The causes which produce enmity are anger, spitefulness, slander. Anger arises from acts committed

ἐκ τῶν πρὸς ἑαυτόν, ἔχθρα δὲ καὶ ἄνευ τῶν πρὸς
ἑαυτόν· ἐὰν γὰρ ὑπολαμβάνωμεν εἶναι τοιόνδε, μι-
σοῦμεν. καὶ ἡ μὲν ὀργὴ ἀεὶ περὶ τὰ καθ' ἕκαστα,
οἷον Καλλίᾳ ἢ Σωκράτει, τὸ δὲ μῖσος καὶ πρὸς
τὰ γένη· τὸν γὰρ κλέπτην μισεῖ καὶ τὸν συκοφάντην
ἅπας. καὶ τὸ μὲν ἰατὸν χρόνῳ, τὸ δ' ἀνίατον.
καὶ τὸ μὲν λύπης ἔφεσις, τὸ δὲ κακοῦ· αἰσθέσθαι
γὰρ βούλεται ὁ ὀργιζόμενος, τῷ δ' οὐδὲν διαφέρει.
ἔστι δὲ τὰ μὲν λυπηρὰ αἰσθητὰ πάντα, τὰ δὲ
μάλιστα κακὰ ἥκιστα αἰσθητά, ἀδικία καὶ ἀ-
φροσύνη· οὐδὲν γὰρ λυπεῖ ἡ παρουσία τῆς κακίας.
καὶ τὸ μὲν μετὰ λύπης, τὸ δ' οὐ μετὰ λύπης· ὁ μὲν
γὰρ ὀργιζόμενος λυπεῖται, ὁ δὲ μισῶν οὔ. καὶ
ὁ μὲν πολλῶν ἂν γενομένων ἐλεήσειεν, ὁ δ' οὐδενός·
ὁ μὲν γὰρ ἀντιπαθεῖν βούλεται ᾧ ὀργίζεται, ὁ
32 δὲ μὴ εἶναι. φανερὸν οὖν ἐκ τούτων ὅτι ἐνδέχεται
ἐχθροὺς καὶ φίλους καὶ ὄντας ἀποδεικνύναι καὶ
μὴ ὄντας ποιεῖν καὶ φάσκοντας διαλύειν, καὶ δι'
ὀργὴν ἢ δι' ἔχθραν ἀμφισβητοῦντας ἐφ' ὁπότερ'
ἂν προαιρῆταί τις ἄγειν.[a] ποῖα δὲ φοβοῦνται καὶ
τίνας καὶ πῶς ἔχοντες, ὧδ' ἔσται φανερόν.

5. Ἔστω δὴ φόβος λύπη τις ἢ ταραχὴ ἐκ
φαντασίας μέλλοντος κακοῦ φθαρτικοῦ ἢ λυπηροῦ·
οὐ γὰρ πάντα τὰ κακὰ φοβοῦνται, οἷον εἰ ἔσται
ἄδικος ἢ βραδύς, ἀλλ' ὅσα λύπας μεγάλας ἢ
φθορὰς δύναται, καὶ ταῦτ' ἐὰν μὴ πόρρω ἀλλὰ
σύνεγγυς φαίνηται ὥστε μέλλειν. τὰ γὰρ πόρρω
σφόδρα οὐ φοβοῦνται· ἴσασι γὰρ πάντες ὅτι ἀπο-

---

[a] He wishes to see and know the result of the measures
taken against those with whom he is angry. Or, it may
mean that he wishes the object of his anger to feel his wrath,
and to know by whom, and for what, he is punished.

against us, enmity even from those that are not ; for if we imagine a man to be of such and such a character, we hate him. Anger has always an individual as its object, for instance Callias or Socrates, whereas hatred applies to classes ; for instance, every one hates a thief or informer. Anger is curable by time, hatred not ; the aim of anger is pain, of hatred evil ; for the angry man wishes to see what happens ;[a] to one who hates it does not matter. Now, the things which cause pain are all perceptible, while things which are especially bad, such as injustice or folly, are least perceptible ; for the presence of vice causes no pain. Anger is accompanied by pain, but hatred not ; for he who is angry suffers pain, but he who hates does not. One who is angry might feel compassion in many cases, but one who hates, never ; for the former wishes that the object of his anger should suffer in his turn, the latter, that he should perish. It is evident, then, from what we have just said, that it is possible to prove that men are enemies or friends, or to make them such if they are not ; to refute those who pretend that they are, and when they oppose us through anger or enmity, to bring them over to whichever side may be preferred. The things and persons that men fear and in what frame of mind, will be evident from the following considerations.

5. Let fear be defined as a painful or troubled feeling caused by the impression of an imminent evil that causes destruction or pain ; for men do not fear all evils, for instance, becoming unjust or slow-witted, but only such as involve great pain or destruction, and only if they appear to be not far off but near at hand and threatening, for men do not fear things that are very remote ; all know that they

θανοῦνται, ἀλλ' ὅτι οὐκ ἐγγύς, οὐδὲν φροντίζουσιν.
2 εἰ δὴ ὁ φόβος τοῦτ' ἐστίν, ἀνάγκη τὰ τοιαῦτα
φοβερὰ εἶναι ὅσα φαίνεται δύναμιν ἔχειν μεγάλην
τοῦ φθείρειν ἢ βλάπτειν βλάβας εἰς λύπην μεγάλην
συντεινούσας. διὸ καὶ τὰ σημεῖα τῶν τοιούτων
φοβερά· ἐγγὺς γὰρ φαίνεται τὸ φοβερόν· τοῦτο
3 γάρ ἐστι κίνδυνος, φοβεροῦ πλησιασμός. τοιαῦτα δὲ
ἔχθρα τε καὶ ὀργὴ δυναμένων ποιεῖν τι· δῆλον
γὰρ ὅτι βούλονται, ὥστε ἐγγύς εἰσι τοῦ ποιεῖν.
4 καὶ ἀδικία δύναμιν ἔχουσα· τῷ προαιρεῖσθαι γὰρ
5 ὁ ἄδικος ἄδικος. καὶ ἀρετὴ ὑβριζομένη δύναμιν
1382 b ἔχουσα· δῆλον γὰρ ὅτι προαιρεῖται μέν, ὅταν
6 ὑβρίζηται, ἀεί, δύναται δὲ νῦν. καὶ φόβος τῶν
δυναμένων τι ποιῆσαι· ἐν παρασκευῇ γὰρ ἀνάγκη
7 εἶναι καὶ τὸν τοιοῦτον. ἐπεὶ δ' οἱ πολλοὶ χείρους
καὶ ἥττους τοῦ κερδαίνειν καὶ δειλοὶ ἐν τοῖς
κινδύνοις, φοβερὸν ὡς ἐπὶ τὸ πολὺ τὸ ἐπ' ἄλλῳ
αὐτὸν εἶναι, ὥστε οἱ συνειδότες πεποιηκότι τι
8 δεινὸν φοβεροὶ ἢ κατειπεῖν ἢ ἐγκαταλιπεῖν. καὶ
οἱ δυνάμενοι ἀδικεῖν τοῖς δυναμένοις ἀδικεῖσθαι·
ὡς γὰρ ἐπὶ τὸ πολὺ ἀδικοῦσιν οἱ ἄνθρωποι, ὅταν
δύνωνται. καὶ οἱ ἠδικημένοι ἢ νομίζοντες ἀδικεῖ-
σθαι· ἀεὶ γὰρ τηροῦσι καιρόν. καὶ οἱ ἠδικηκότες, ἐὰν
δύναμιν ἔχωσι, φοβεροί, δεδιότες τὸ ἀντιπαθεῖν.
9 ὑπέκειτο γὰρ τὸ τοιοῦτο φοβερόν. καὶ οἱ τῶν
αὐτῶν ἀνταγωνισταί, ὅσα μὴ ἐνδέχεται ἅμα
ὑπάρχειν ἀμφοῖν· ἀεὶ γὰρ πολεμοῦσι πρὸς τοὺς

---

[a] By the definitions of anger and hatred.
[b] And therefore, having the inclination to be unjust, if he
has the power, he will be so.

have to die, but as death is not near at hand, they are indifferent. If then this is fear, all things must be fearful that appear to have great power of destroying or inflicting injuries that tend to produce great pain. That is why even the signs of such misfortunes are fearful, for the fearful thing itself appears to be near at hand, and danger is the approach of anything fearful. Such signs are the enmity and anger of those able to injure us in any way; for it is evident that they have the wish,[a] so that they are not far from doing so. And injustice possessed of power is fearful, for the unjust man is unjust through deliberate inclination.[b] And outraged virtue when it has power, for it is evident that it always desires satisfaction, whenever it is outraged, and now it has the power. And fear felt by those able to injure us in any way, for such as these also must be ready to act. And since most men are rather bad than good and the slaves of gain and cowardly in time of danger, being at the mercy of another is generally fearful, so that one who has committed a crime has reason to fear his accomplices as likely to denounce or leave him in the lurch. And those who are able to ill-treat others are to be feared by those who can be so treated; for as a rule men do wrong whenever they can. Those who have been, or think they are being, wronged, are also to be feared, for they are ever on the look out for an opportunity. And those who have committed some wrong, when they have the power, since they are afraid of retaliation, which was assumed to be something to be feared. And those who are our rivals for the same things, whenever it is impossible to share them, for men are always contending with

10 τοιούτους. καὶ οἱ τοῖς κρείττοσιν αὐτῶν φοβεροί·
μᾶλλον γὰρ ἂν δύναιντο βλάπτειν αὐτούς, εἰ καὶ
τοὺς κρείττους. καὶ οὓς φοβοῦνται οἱ κρείττους
11 αὐτῶν, διὰ ταὐτό. καὶ οἱ τοὺς κρείττους αὐτῶν
ἀνῃρηκότες. καὶ οἱ τοῖς ἥττοσιν αὐτῶν ἐπι-
τιθέμενοι· ἢ γὰρ ἤδη φοβεροὶ ἢ αὐξηθέντες.

Καὶ τῶν ἠδικημένων καὶ ἐχθρῶν ἢ ἀντιπάλων
οὐχ οἱ ὀξύθυμοι καὶ παρρησιαστικοί, ἀλλ᾿ οἱ πρᾶοι
καὶ εἴρωνες καὶ πανοῦργοι· ἄδηλοι γὰρ εἰ ἐγγύς,
12 ὥστ᾿ οὐδέποτε φανεροὶ ὅτι πόρρω. πάντα δὲ τὰ
φοβερὰ φοβερώτερα, ὅσα, ἂν ἁμάρτωσιν, ἐπανορ-
θώσασθαι μὴ ἐνδέχεται, ἀλλ᾿ ἢ ὅλως ἀδύνατα, ἢ
μὴ ἐφ᾿ ἑαυτοῖς ἀλλ᾿ ἐπὶ τοῖς ἐναντίοις. καὶ ὧν
βοήθειαι μή εἰσιν ἢ μὴ ῥᾴδιαι. ὡς δ᾿ ἁπλῶς
εἰπεῖν, φοβερά ἐστιν ὅσα ἐφ᾿ ἑτέρων γιγνόμενα ἢ
μέλλοντα ἐλεεινά ἐστιν. τὰ μὲν οὖν φοβερά, καὶ
ἃ φοβοῦνται, σχεδὸν ὡς εἰπεῖν τὰ μέγιστα ταῦτ᾿
ἐστίν· ὡς δὲ διακείμενοι αὐτοὶ φοβοῦνται, νῦν
λέγωμεν.

13 Εἰ δή ἐστιν ὁ φόβος μετὰ προσδοκίας τοῦ
πείσεσθαί τι φθαρτικὸν πάθος, φανερὸν ὅτι οὐδεὶς
φοβεῖται τῶν οἰομένων μηδὲν ἂν παθεῖν, οὐδὲ
ταῦτα ἃ μὴ οἴονται παθεῖν, οὐδὲ τούτους ὑφ᾿ ὧν
μὴ οἴονται, οὐδὲ τότε ὅτε μὴ οἴονται. ἀνάγκη

ᵃ Or simply, " near . . . far from us."

such persons. And those who are feared by those
who are stronger than we are, for they would be
better able to injure us, if they could injure those
stronger than ourselves ; and those whom those who
are stronger than ourselves are afraid of, for the
same reason. And those who have overthrown those
who are stronger than us and those who attack those
who are weaker, for they are either already to be
feared, or will be, when they have grown stronger.

And among those whom we have wronged, or are
our enemies or rivals, we should fear not the hot-
tempered or outspoken, but those who are mild,
dissemblers, and thorough rascals ; for it is uncertain
whether they are on the point of acting, so that one
never knows whether they are far from it.[a] All
things that are to be feared are more so when, after
an error has once been committed, it is impossible
to repair it, either because it is absolutely impossible,
or no longer in our power, but in that of our opponents ; also when there is no possibility of help or
it is not easy to obtain. In a word, all things are to be
feared which, when they happen, or are on the point
of happening, to others, excite compassion. These
are, so to say, nearly all the most important things
which are to be feared and which men fear. Let us
now state the frame of mind which leads men to fear.

If then fear is accompanied by the expectation
that we are going to suffer some fatal misfortune, it
is evident that none of those who think that they
will suffer nothing at all is afraid either of those
things which he does not think will happen to him,
or of those from whom he does not expect them, or
at a time when he does not think them likely to
happen. It therefore needs be that those who think

τοίνυν φοβεῖσθαι τοὺς οἰομένους τι παθεῖν ἄν, καὶ
14 τοὺς ὑπὸ τούτων καὶ ταῦτα καὶ τότε. οὐκ οἴονται
1383 a δὲ παθεῖν ἂν οὔτε οἱ ἐν εὐτυχίαις μεγάλαις ὄντες
καὶ δοκοῦντες, διὸ ὑβρισταὶ καὶ ὀλίγωροι καὶ
θρασεῖς (ποιεῖ δὲ τοιούτους πλοῦτος ἰσχὺς πολυφιλία δύναμις), οὔτε οἱ ἤδη πεπονθέναι πάντα
νομίζοντες τὰ δεινὰ καὶ ἀπεψυγμένοι πρὸς τὸ
μέλλον, ὥσπερ οἱ ἀποτυμπανιζόμενοι ἤδη· ἀλλὰ
δεῖ τινὰ ἐλπίδα ὑπεῖναι σωτηρίας, περὶ οὗ ἀγω-
νιῶσιν. σημεῖον δέ· ὁ γὰρ φόβος βουλευτικοὺς
ποιεῖ, καίτοι οὐδεὶς βουλεύεται περὶ τῶν ἀν-
15 ελπίστων. ὥστε δεῖ τοιούτους παρασκευάζειν, ὅταν
ᾖ βέλτιον τὸ φοβεῖσθαι αὐτούς, ὅτι τοιοῦτοί εἰσιν
οἷοι παθεῖν· καὶ γὰρ ἄλλοι μείζους ἔπαθον· καὶ
τοὺς ὁμοίους δεικνύναι πάσχοντας ἢ πεπονθότας,
καὶ ὑπὸ τοιούτων ὑφ' ὧν οὐκ ᾤοντο, καὶ ταῦτα
καὶ τότε ὅτε οὐκ ᾤοντο.
16 Ἐπεὶ δὲ περὶ φόβου φανερὸν τί ἐστι, καὶ τῶν
φοβερῶν, καὶ ὡς ἕκαστοι ἔχοντες δεδίασι, φανερὸν
ἐκ τούτων καὶ τὸ θαρρεῖν τί ἐστι, καὶ περὶ ποῖα
θαρραλέοι καὶ πῶς διακείμενοι θαρραλέοι εἰσίν·
τό τε γὰρ θάρσος ἐναντίον τῷ φόβῳ καὶ τὸ θαρραλέον τῷ φοβερῷ· ὥστε μετὰ φαντασίας ἡ ἐλπὶς
τῶν σωτηρίων ὡς ἐγγὺς ὄντων, τῶν δὲ φοβερῶν
17 ἢ μὴ ὄντων ἢ πόρρω ὄντων. ἔστι δὲ θαρραλέα

they are likely to suffer anything should be afraid, either of the persons at whose hands they expect it, or of certain things, and at certain times. Those who either are, or seem to be, highly prosperous do not think they are likely to suffer anything; wherefore they are insolent, contemptuous, and rash, and what makes them such is wealth, strength, a number of friends, power. It is the same with those who think that they have already suffered all possible ills and are coldly indifferent to the future, like those who are being beaten to death; for it is a necessary incentive to fear that there should remain some hope of being saved from the cause of their distress. A sign of this is that fear makes men deliberate, whereas no one deliberates about things that are hopeless. So that whenever it is preferable that the audience should feel afraid, it is necessary to make them think they are likely to suffer, by reminding them that others greater than they have suffered, and showing that their equals are suffering or have suffered, and that at the hands of those from whom they did not expect it, in such a manner and at times when they did not think it likely.

Now, since we have made clear what fear and fearful things are, and the frame of mind in each case which makes men fear, one can see from this what confidence is, what are the things that give it, and the frame of mind of those who possess it; for confidence is the contrary of fear and that which gives confidence of that which causes fear, so that the hope of what is salutary is accompanied by an impression that it is quite near at hand, while the things to be feared are either non-existent or far off. Confidence is inspired by the remoteness of fearful

τά τε δεινὰ πόρρω ὄντα καὶ τὰ θαρραλέα ἐγγύς.
καὶ ἐπανορθώσεις ἐὰν ὦσι καὶ βοήθειαι, ἢ πολλαὶ
ἢ μεγάλαι ἢ ἄμφω, καὶ μήτε ἠδικημένοι μήτε
ἠδικηκότες ὦσιν, ἀνταγωνισταί τε ἢ μὴ ὦσιν
ὅλως, ἢ μὴ ἔχωσι δύναμιν, ἢ δύναμιν ἔχοντες ὦσι
φίλοι ἢ πεποιηκότες εὖ ἢ πεπονθότες. ἢ ἐὰν
πλείους ὦσιν οἷς ταὐτὰ συμφέρει, ἢ κρείττους, ἢ
18 ἄμφω. αὐτοὶ δὲ οὕτως ἔχοντες θαρραλέοι εἰσίν,
ἐὰν πολλὰ κατωρθωκέναι οἴωνται καὶ μὴ πεπονθέναι, ἢ ἐὰν πολλάκις ἐληλυθότες εἰς τὰ δεινὰ
καὶ διαπεφευγότες ὦσιν· διχῶς γὰρ ἀπαθεῖς
γίγνονται οἱ ἄνθρωποι, ἢ τῷ μὴ πεπειρᾶσθαι ἢ
τῷ βοηθείας ἔχειν, ὥσπερ ἐν τοῖς κατὰ θάλατταν
κινδύνοις οἵ τε ἄπειροι χειμῶνος θαρροῦσι τὰ μέλλοντα καὶ οἱ βοηθείας ἔχοντες διὰ τὴν ἐμπειρίαν.
19 καὶ ὅταν τοῖς ὁμοίοις ᾖ μὴ φοβερόν, μηδὲ τοῖς
ἥττοσι καὶ ὧν κρείττους οἴονται εἶναι· οἴονται δέ,
20 ὧν κεκρατήκασιν ἢ αὐτῶν ἢ τῶν κρειττόνων ἢ
τῶν ὁμοίων. καὶ ἐὰν ὑπάρχειν αὐτοῖς οἴωνται
πλείω καὶ μείζω, οἷς ὑπερέχοντες φοβεροί εἰσιν·
1383 b ταῦτα δ᾽ ἐστὶ πλῆθος χρημάτων καὶ ἰσχὺς σωμάτων
καὶ φίλων καὶ χώρας καὶ τῶν πρὸς πόλεμον παρα-
σκευῶν, ἢ πασῶν ἢ τῶν μεγίστων. καὶ ἐὰν μὴ
ἠδικηκότες ὦσιν ἢ μηδένα ἢ μὴ πολλοὺς ἢ μὴ
21 τοιούτους περὶ ὧν φοβοῦνται. καὶ ὅλως ἂν τὰ
πρὸς θεοὺς αὐτοῖς καλῶς ἔχῃ, τά τε ἄλλα καὶ τὰ
ἀπὸ σημείων καὶ λογίων· θαρραλέον γὰρ ἡ ὀργή,
τὸ δὲ μὴ ἀδικεῖν ἀλλ᾽ ἀδικεῖσθαι ὀργῆς ποιητικόν,

ᵃ τὰ σωτήρια or some other word instead of τὰ θαρραλέα
would be expected, to avoid the tautology. The fact of
remoteness inspires confidence, because we do not expect
fearful things to happen ; while salutary things inspire it if
near at hand, because we expect them to happen.

things, or by the nearness of things that justify it.[a] If remedies are possible, if there are means of help, either great or numerous, or both ; if we have neither committed nor suffered wrong ; if we have no rivals at all, or only such as are powerless, or, if they have power, are our friends, or have either done us good or have received it from us ; if those whose interests are the same as ours are more numerous, or stronger, or both. We feel confidence in the following states of mind : if we believe that we have often succeeded and have not suffered, or if we have often been in danger and escaped it ; for men are unaffected by fear in two ways, either because they have never been tested or have means of help ; thus, in dangers at sea, those who have never experienced a storm and those who have means of help as the result of experience have confidence as to the future. We are also reassured, when a thing does not inspire fear in our equals, our inferiors, or those to whom we think ourselves superior ; and we think ourselves superior to those whom we have conquered, either themselves or their superiors or equals. And if we think we possess more or more considerable advantages, such as make their possessors formidable ; such are abundance of money, strength of body, friends, territory, military equipments, either all or the most important. And if we have never done wrong to anyone, or only to a few, or not to such as are to be feared ; and, generally, if it is well with us in regard to the gods, especially as to intimations from signs and oracles, and everything else of the kind ; for anger inspires confidence, and it is the wrong that we suffer and not that which we inflict upon others that

τὸ δὲ θεῖον ὑπολαμβάνεται βοηθεῖν τοῖς ἀδικου-
22 μένοις. καὶ ὅταν ἐπιχειροῦντες ἢ μηδὲν ἂν παθεῖν
μηδὲ πείσεσθαι ἢ κατορθώσειν οἴωνται. καὶ περὶ
μὲν τῶν φοβερῶν καὶ θαρραλέων εἴρηται.

6. Ποῖα δ' αἰσχύνονται καὶ ἀναισχυντοῦσιν, καὶ
πρὸς τίνας καὶ πῶς ἔχοντες, ἐκ τῶνδε δῆλον.
2 ἔστω δὴ αἰσχύνη λύπη τις ἢ ταραχὴ περὶ τὰ εἰς
ἀδοξίαν φαινόμενα φέρειν τῶν κακῶν, ἢ παρόντων
ἢ γεγονότων ἢ μελλόντων, ἡ δ' ἀναισχυντία ὀλι-
3 γωρία τις καὶ ἀπάθεια περὶ τὰ αὐτὰ ταῦτα. εἰ
δή ἐστιν αἰσχύνη ἡ ὁρισθεῖσα, ἀνάγκη αἰσχύνεσθαι
ἐπὶ τοῖς τοιούτοις τῶν κακῶν ὅσα αἰσχρὰ δοκεῖ
εἶναι ἢ αὐτῷ ἢ ὧν φροντίζει· τοιαῦτα δ' ἐστὶν
ὅσα ἀπὸ κακίας ἔργα ἐστίν, οἷον τὸ ἀποβαλεῖν
ἀσπίδα ἢ φυγεῖν· ἀπὸ δειλίας γάρ. καὶ τὸ ἀπο-
4 στερῆσαι παρακαταθήκην· ἀπ' ἀδικίας γάρ. καὶ τὸ
συγγενέσθαι οἷς οὐ δεῖ ἢ ὅπου οὐ δεῖ ἢ ὅτε μὴ
5 δεῖ· ἀπ' ἀκολασίας γάρ. καὶ τὸ κερδαίνειν ἀπὸ
μικρῶν ἢ ἀπ' αἰσχρῶν ἢ ἀπ' ἀδυνάτων, οἷον πενή-
των ἢ τεθνεώτων· ὅθεν καὶ ἡ παροιμία, τὸ κἂν
ἀπὸ νεκροῦ φέρειν· ἀπὸ αἰσχροκερδείας γὰρ καὶ
6 ἀνελευθερίας. καὶ τὸ μὴ βοηθεῖν δυνάμενον εἰς
χρήματα, ἢ ἧττον βοηθεῖν. καὶ τὸ βοηθεῖσθαι
7 παρὰ τῶν ἧττον εὐπόρων. καὶ δανείζεσθαι ὅτε
δόξει αἰτεῖν, καὶ αἰτεῖν ὅτε ἀπαιτεῖν, καὶ ἀπαιτεῖν
ὅτε αἰτεῖν, καὶ ἐπαινεῖν ἵνα δόξῃ αἰτεῖν, καὶ τὸ

ᵃ It is assumed that the gods will be on our side if we have
suffered wrong ; suffering wrong rouses anger and at the same
time inspires confidence, if our relations with the gods are
such that we feel we can rely upon them for assistance.
210

causes anger, and the gods are supposed to assist those who are wronged.[a] Lastly, we feel confidence when, at the beginning of any undertaking, we do not expect disaster either in the present or future, or hope for success. Such are the things that inspire fear or confidence.

6. What are the things of which men are ashamed or the contrary, and before whom, and in what frame of mind, will be clear from the following considerations. Let shame then be defined as a kind of pain or uneasiness in respect of misdeeds, past, present, or future, which seem to tend to bring dishonour ; and shamelessness as contempt and indifference in regard to these same things. If this definition of shame is correct, it follows that we are ashamed of all such misdeeds as seem to be disgraceful, either for ourselves or for those whom we care for. Such are all those that are due to vice, such as throwing away one's shield or taking to flight, for this is due to cowardice ; or withholding a deposit, for this is due to injustice. And illicit relations with any persons, at forbidden places or times, for this is due to licentiousness. And making profit out of what is petty or disgraceful, or out of the weak, such as the indigent or dead ; whence the proverb, " to rob even a corpse," for this is due to base love of gain and stinginess. And to refuse assistance in money matters when we are able to render it, or to give less than we can ; to accept assistance from those less able to afford it than ourselves ; to borrow when anyone seems likely to ask for a loan, to ask for a loan from one who wants his money back, and asking for repayment from one who wants to borrow ; to praise in order to seem to be asking for a loan, and

ARISTOTLE

ἀποτετυχηκότα μηδὲν ἧττον· πάντα γὰρ ἀνελευ-
8 θερίας ταῦτα σημεῖα. τὸ δ᾽ ἐπαινεῖν παρόντας,
καὶ τὸ τἀγαθὰ μὲν ὑπερεπαινεῖν τὰ δὲ φαῦλα
συναλείφειν, καὶ τὸ ὑπεραλγεῖν ἀλγοῦντι παρόντα,
καὶ τἆλλα πάντα ὅσα τοιαῦτα· κολακείας γὰρ
σημεῖα.

9 Καὶ τὸ μὴ ὑπομένειν πόνους οὓς οἱ πρεσβύτεροι
1384 a ἢ οἱ τρυφῶντες ἢ οἱ ἐν ἐξουσίᾳ μᾶλλον ὄντες ἢ
ὅλως οἱ ἀδυνατώτεροι· πάντα γὰρ μαλακίας σημεῖα.
10 καὶ τὸ ὑφ᾽ ἑτέρου εὖ πάσχειν, καὶ τὸ πολλάκις, καὶ
ἃ εὖ ἐποίησεν ὀνειδίζειν· μικροψυχίας γὰρ πάντα
11 καὶ ταπεινότητος σημεῖα. καὶ τὸ περὶ αὑτοῦ
πάντα λέγειν καὶ ἐπαγγέλλεσθαι, καὶ τὸ τἀλλότρια
αὑτοῦ φάσκειν· ἀλαζονείας γάρ. ὁμοίως δὲ καὶ
ἀπὸ τῶν ἄλλων ἑκάστης τῶν τοῦ ἤθους κακιῶν
τὰ ἔργα καὶ τὰ σημεῖα καὶ τὰ ὅμοια· αἰσχρὰ γὰρ
12 καὶ αἰσχυντικά. καὶ ἐπὶ τούτοις τὸ τῶν καλῶν
ὧν πάντες μετέχουσιν ἢ οἱ ὅμοιοι πάντες ἢ οἱ
πλεῖστοι, μὴ μετέχειν. ὁμοίους δὲ λέγω ὁμοεθνεῖς,
πολίτας, ἥλικας, συγγενεῖς, ὅλως τοὺς ἐξ ἴσου·
αἰσχρὸν γὰρ ἤδη τὸ μὴ μετέχειν, οἷον παιδεύσεως
ἐπὶ τοσοῦτον καὶ τῶν ἄλλων ὁμοίως. πάντα δὲ
ταῦτα μᾶλλον, ἂν δι᾽ ἑαυτὸν φαίνηται· οὕτω γὰρ
ἤδη ἀπὸ κακίας μᾶλλον, ἂν αὐτὸς ᾖ αἴτιος τῶν
13 ὑπαρξάντων ἢ ὑπαρχόντων ἢ μελλόντων. πάσχον-
τες δὲ ἢ πεπονθότες ἢ πεισόμενοι τὰ τοιαῦτα

212

when you have failed to obtain it to keep on asking ; for all these are signs of stinginess. And to praise people when they are present, to overpraise their good qualities and to palliate the bad, to show excessive grief at another's grief when present, and all similar actions ; for they are signs of flattery.

And not to submit to toils, which those put up with who are older or live luxuriously or hold higher positions, or, generally speaking, are less fitted to do so ; for all these are signs of effeminacy. To accept favours from another and often, and then to throw them in his teeth ; for all these things are signs of littleness and abasement of soul. And to speak at great length about oneself and to make all kinds of professions, and to take the credit for what another has done ; for this is a sign of boastfulness. Similarly, in regard to each of all the other vices of character, the acts resulting from them, their signs, and the things which resemble them, all these are disgraceful, and should make us ashamed. It is also shameful not to have a share in the honourable things which all men, or all who resemble us, or the majority of them, have a share in. By those who resemble us I mean those of the same race, of the same city, of the same age, of the same family, and, generally speaking, those who are on an equality ; for then it is disgraceful not to have a share, for instance, in education and other things, to the same extent. All these things are the more disgraceful, if the fault appears to be our own ; for they are at once seen to be due rather to natural depravity if we ourselves are the cause of past, present, or future defects. And we are ashamed when we suffer or have suffered or are likely to suffer things which tend

αἰσχύνονται ὅσα εἰς ἀτιμίαν φέρει καὶ ὀνείδη·
ταῦτα δ' ἐστὶ τὰ εἰς ὑπηρετήσεις ἢ σώματος ἢ
ἔργων αἰσχρῶν, ὧν ἐστὶ τὸ ὑβρίζεσθαι. καὶ τὰ
μὲν εἰς ἀκολασίαν καὶ ἑκόντα καὶ ἄκοντα (τὰ δ'
εἰς βίαν ἄκοντα)· ἀπὸ ἀνανδρίας γὰρ ἢ δειλίας ἡ
ὑπομονὴ καὶ τὸ μὴ ἀμύνεσθαι.

Ἃ μὲν οὖν αἰσχύνονται, ταῦτ' ἐστὶ καὶ τὰ
14 τοιαῦτα· ἐπεὶ δὲ περὶ ἀδοξίας φαντασία ἐστὶν ἡ
αἰσχύνη, καὶ ταύτης αὐτῆς χάριν ἀλλὰ μὴ τῶν
ἀποβαινόντων, οὐδεὶς δὲ τῆς δόξης φροντίζει ἀλλ'
ἢ διὰ τοὺς δοξάζοντας, ἀνάγκη τούτους αἰσχύ-
15 νεσθαι ὧν λόγον ἔχει. λόγον δ' ἔχει τῶν θαυμα-
ζόντων, καὶ οὓς θαυμάζει, καὶ ὑφ' ὧν βούλεται
θαυμάζεσθαι, καὶ πρὸς οὓς φιλοτιμεῖται, καὶ ὧν
16 μὴ καταφρονεῖ τῆς δόξης. θαυμάζεσθαι μὲν οὖν
βούλονται ὑπὸ τούτων καὶ θαυμάζουσι τούτους
ὅσοι τι ἔχουσιν ἀγαθὸν τῶν τιμίων, ἢ παρ' ὧν
τυγχάνουσι δεόμενοι σφόδρα τινὸς ὧν ἐκεῖνοι κύριοι,
17 οἷον οἱ ἐρῶντες· φιλοτιμοῦνται δὲ πρὸς τοὺς ὁμοίους,
φροντίζουσι δ' ὡς ἀληθευόντων τῶν φρονίμων·
τοιοῦτοι δ' οἵ τε πρεσβύτεροι καὶ οἱ πεπαιδευμένοι.
18 καὶ τὰ ἐν ὀφθαλμοῖς καὶ τὰ ἐν φανερῷ μᾶλλον·
ὅθεν καὶ ἡ παροιμία, τὸ ἐν ὀφθαλμοῖς εἶναι αἰδῶ.
διὰ τοῦτο τοὺς ἀεὶ παρεσομένους μᾶλλον αἰσχύνονται καὶ τοὺς προσέχοντας αὐτοῖς, διὰ τὸ ἐν
1384 b ὀφθαλμοῖς ἀμφότερα.
19 Καὶ τοὺς μὴ περὶ ταῦτα ἐνόχους· δῆλον γὰρ ὅτι

ᵃ Euripides, *Cresphontes*: αἰδὼς ἐν ὀφθαλμοῖσι γίγνεται,
τέκνον (*T.G.F.* frag. 457).

214

to ignominy and reproach; such are prostituting one's person or performing disgraceful actions, including unnatural lust. And of these actions those that promote licentiousness are disgraceful, whether voluntary or involuntary (the latter being those that are done under compulsion), since meek endurance and the absence of resistance are the result of unmanliness or cowardice.

These and similar things are those of which men are ashamed. And since shame is an impression about dishonour, and that for its own sake and not for its results; and since no one heeds the opinion of others except on account of those who hold it, it follows that men feel shame before those whom they esteem. Now men esteem those who admire them and those whom they admire, those by whom they wish to be admired, those whose rivals they are, and whose opinion they do not despise. They desire to be admired by those, and admire those who possess anything good that is greatly esteemed, or from whom they urgently require something which it is in their power to give, as is the case with lovers. And they are rivals of those who are like them; and they give heed to the men of practical wisdom as likely to be truthful; such are the older and well educated. They are also more ashamed of things that are done before their eyes and in broad daylight; whence the proverb, The eyes are the abode of shame.[a] That is why they feel more ashamed before those who are likely to be always with them or who keep watch upon them, because in both cases they are under the eyes of others.

Men are also ashamed before those who are not open to the same accusations, for it is evident that

τἀναντία δοκεῖ τούτοις. καὶ τοὺς μὴ συγγνω-
μονικοὺς τοῖς φαινομένοις ἁμαρτάνειν· ἃ γάρ τις
αὐτὸς ποιεῖ, ταῦτα λέγεται τοῖς πέλας οὐ νεμεσᾶν,
20 ὥστε ἃ μὴ ποιεῖ, δῆλον ὅτι νεμεσᾷ. καὶ τοὺς
ἐξαγγελτικοὺς πολλοῖς· οὐδὲν γὰρ διαφέρει μὴ
δοκεῖν ἢ μὴ ἐξαγγέλλειν. ἐξαγγελτικοὶ δὲ οἵ τε
ἠδικημένοι διὰ τὸ παρατηρεῖν καὶ οἱ κακόλογοι·
εἴπερ γὰρ καὶ τοὺς μὴ ἁμαρτάνοντας, ἔτι μᾶλλον
τοὺς ἁμαρτάνοντας. καὶ οἷς ἡ διατριβὴ ἐπὶ ταῖς
τῶν πέλας ἁμαρτίαις, οἷον χλευασταῖς καὶ κωμῳδο-
ποιοῖς· κακόλογοι γάρ πως οὗτοι καὶ ἐξαγγελτι-
κοί. καὶ ἐν οἷς μηδὲν ἀποτετυχήκασιν· ὥσπερ
γὰρ θαυμαζόμενοι διάκεινται· διὸ καὶ τοὺς πρῶτον
δεηθέντας τι αἰσχύνονται ὡς οὐδέν πω ἠδοξηκότες
ἐν αὐτοῖς. τοιοῦτοι δ' οἵ τε ἄρτι βουλόμενοι φίλοι
εἶναι (τὰ γὰρ βέλτιστα τεθέανται, διὸ εὖ ἔχει ἡ
τοῦ Εὐριπίδου ἀπόκρισις πρὸς τοὺς Συρακοσίους)
καὶ τῶν πάλαι γνωρίμων οἱ μηδὲν συνειδότες.
21 αἰσχύνονται δ' οὐ μόνον αὐτὰ τὰ ῥηθέντα αἰσχυν-
τηλὰ ἀλλὰ καὶ τὰ σημεῖα, οἷον οὐ μόνον ἀφροδι-
σιάζοντες ἀλλὰ καὶ τὰ σημεῖα αὐτοῦ. καὶ οὐ
22 μόνον ποιοῦντες τὰ αἰσχρά, ἀλλὰ καὶ λέγοντες.
ὁμοίως δὲ οὐ τοὺς εἰρημένους μόνον αἰσχύνονται,
ἀλλὰ καὶ τοὺς δηλώσοντας αὐτοῖς, οἷον θεράποντας
23 καὶ φίλους τούτων. ὅλως δ' οὐκ αἰσχύνονται οὔθ'

ᵃ Jebb translates, " who have never seen us break down."
ᵇ The Greek scholiast says : "Euripides, having been sent
as ambassador to the Syracusans, to ask for peace and
friendship, when they refused said : O Syracusans, if for no
other reason than that we are just feeling the need of your
friendship, you ought to respect our admiration." Nothing
is known of this embassy. Hyperides has been suggested
instead of Euripides.

their feelings are contrary. And before those who are not indulgent towards those who appear to err; for a man is supposed not to reproach others with what he does himself, so it is clear that what he reproaches them with is what he does not do himself. And before those who are fond of gossiping generally; for not to gossip about the fault of another amounts to not regarding it as a fault at all. Now those who are inclined to gossip are those who have suffered wrong, because they always have their eyes upon us; and slanderers, because, if they traduce the innocent, still more will they traduce the guilty. And before those who spend their time in looking for their neighbours' faults, for instance, mockers and comic poets; for they are also in a manner slanderers and gossips. And before those from whom they have never asked anything in vain,[a] for they feel as if they were greatly esteemed. For this reason they feel ashamed before those who ask them for something for the first time, as never yet having lost their good opinion. Such are those who have recently sought their friendship (for they have only seen what is best in them, which is the point of the answer of Euripides to the Syracusans),[b] or old acquaintances who know nothing against us. And men are ashamed not only of the disgraceful things we have spoken of, but also of indications of them, for instance, not only of sensual pleasures, but also of the indications of them; and not only of doing, but also of saying disgraceful things. Similarly, men are ashamed not only before those who have been mentioned, but also before those who will reveal their faults to them, such as their servants or friends. In a word, they are not ashamed either before those

ὧν πολὺ καταφρονοῦσι τῆς δόξης τοῦ ἀληθεύειν
(οὐδεὶς γὰρ παιδία καὶ θηρία αἰσχύνεται) οὔτε
ταὐτὰ τοὺς γνωρίμους καὶ τοὺς ἀγνῶτας, ἀλλὰ
τοὺς μὲν γνωρίμους τὰ πρὸς ἀλήθειαν δοκοῦντα
τοὺς δὲ ἄπωθεν τὰ πρὸς τὸν νόμον.

24 Αὐτοὶ δὲ ὧδε διακείμενοι αἰσχυνθεῖεν ἄν, πρῶτον
μὲν εἰ ὑπάρχοιεν πρὸς αὐτοὺς ἔχοντες οὕτω τινὲς
οἵους ἔφαμεν εἶναι οὓς αἰσχύνονται. ἦσαν δ' οὗτοι
ἢ θαυμαζόμενοι ἢ θαυμάζοντες ἢ ὑφ' ὧν βούλονται
θαυμάζεσθαι, ἢ ὧν δέονταί τινα χρείαν ὧν μὴ
τεύξονται ἄδοξοι ὄντες, καὶ οὗτοι ἢ ὁρῶντες
(ὥσπερ Κυδίας περὶ τῆς Σάμου κληρουχίας ἐδη-
μηγόρησεν· ἠξίου γὰρ ὑπολαβεῖν τοὺς Ἀθηναίους
περιεστάναι κύκλῳ τοὺς Ἕλληνας, ὡς ὁρῶντας
καὶ μὴ μόνον ἀκουσομένους ἃ ἂν ψηφίσωνται), ἢ
ἂν πλησίον ὦσιν οἱ τοιοῦτοι, ἢ μέλλωσιν αἰσθήσεσθαι. διὸ καὶ ὁρᾶσθαι ἀτυχοῦντες ὑπὸ τῶν
1385 a ζηλούντων ποτὲ οὐ βούλονται· θαυμασταὶ γὰρ οἱ
25 ζηλωταί. καὶ ὅταν ἔχωσιν ἃ καταισχύνουσιν ἔργα
καὶ πράγματα ἢ αὐτῶν ἢ προγόνων ἢ ἄλλων τινῶν
πρὸς οὓς ὑπάρχει αὐτοῖς ἀγχιστεία τις. καὶ ὅλως
ὑπὲρ ὧν αἰσχύνονται αὐτοί· εἰσὶ δ' οὗτοι οἱ εἰρημένοι καὶ οἱ εἰς αὐτοὺς ἀναφερόμενοι, ὧν διδά-
σκαλοι ἢ σύμβουλοι γεγόνασι, ἢ ἐὰν ὦσιν ἕτεροι

---

[a] This rendering involves a plural neuter with a plural
verb. Others take the actions or things in a good sense,
" deeds and fortunes, their own or their ancestors, which
they are likely to disgrace."

whose opinion in regard to the truth they greatly despise—for instance, no one feels shame before children or animals—or of the same things before those who are known to them and those who are not; before the former, they are ashamed of things that appear really disgraceful, before strangers, of those which are only condemned by convention.

Men are likely to feel shame in the following situations; first, if there are any who are so related to them as those before whom we said that they feel shame. These, as we pointed out, are those who are admired by them or who admire them, or by whom they wish to be admired, or from whom they need some service, which they will not obtain if they lose their reputation. These, again, are either persons who directly see what is going on (just as Cydias, when haranguing the people about the allotment of the territory of Samos, begged the Athenians to picture to themselves that the Greeks were standing round them and would not only hear, but also see what they were going to decree); or neighbours; or those likely to be aware of what they say or do. That is why men do not like, when unfortunate, to be seen by those who were once their rivals, for rivalry presumes admiration. Men also feel shame when they are connected with actions or things which entail disgrace,[a] for which either they themselves, or their ancestors, or any others with whom they are closely connected are responsible. In a word, men feel shame for those whom they themselves respect;[b] such are those mentioned and those who have any relation to them, for instance, whose teachers or advisers they have been; similarly, when they are

[b] *i.e.* when they have done anything disgraceful.

26 ὅμοιοι, πρὸς οὓς φιλοτιμοῦνται· πολλὰ γὰρ αἰ-
σχυνόμενοι διὰ τοὺς τοιούτους καὶ ποιοῦσι καὶ οὐ
27 ποιοῦσιν. καὶ μέλλοντες ὁρᾶσθαι καὶ ἐν φανερῷ
ἀναστρέφεσθαι τοῖς συνειδόσιν αἰσχυντηλοὶ μᾶλλον εἰσίν. ὅθεν καὶ Ἀντιφῶν ὁ ποιητὴς μέλλων
ἀποτυμπανίζεσθαι ὑπὸ Διονυσίου εἶπεν, ἰδὼν τοὺς
συναποθνήσκειν μέλλοντας ἐγκαλυπτομένους ὡς
ᾔεσαν διὰ τῶν πυλῶν, " τί ἐγκαλύπτεσθε " ἔφη·
" ἢ μὴ αὔριόν τις ὑμᾶς ἴδῃ τούτων; " περὶ μὲν
οὖν αἰσχύνης ταῦτα· περὶ δὲ ἀναισχυντίας δῆλον
ὡς ἐκ τῶν ἐναντίων εὐπορήσομεν.

7. Τίσι δὲ χάριν ἔχουσι καὶ ἐπὶ τίσιν ἢ πῶς
αὐτοὶ ἔχοντες, ὁρισαμένοις τὴν χάριν δῆλον ἔσται.
2 ἔστω δὴ χάρις, καθ' ἣν ὁ ἔχων λέγεται χάριν
ὑπουργεῖν[1] δεομένῳ μὴ ἀντί τινος, μηδ' ἵνα τι
αὐτῷ τῷ ὑπουργοῦντι, ἀλλ' ἵνα ἐκείνῳ τι· μεγάλη
δ' ἂν ᾖ σφόδρα δεομένῳ, ἢ μεγάλων καὶ χαλεπῶν,
ἢ ἐν καιροῖς τοιούτοις, ἢ μόνος, ἢ πρῶτος, ἢ
3 μάλιστα. δεήσεις δ' εἰσὶν αἱ ὀρέξεις, καὶ τούτων
μάλιστα αἱ μετὰ λύπης τοῦ μὴ γιγνομένου· τοιαῦται
δὲ αἱ ἐπιθυμίαι, οἷον ὁ ἔρως. καὶ αἱ ἐν ταῖς τοῦ

---

[1] Spengel reads καθ' ἣν ὁ ἔχων λέγεται χάριν ἔχειν, ὑπουργία
"favour, in accordance with which he who has it is said to
feel benevolence, is rendering a service to one who needs
it."

---

[a] When on an embassy to Syracuse, he was asked by
Dionysius which was the best kind of brass. On his replying,

in rivalry with others who are like them ; for there
are many things which they either do or do not do
owing to the feeling of shame which these men
inspire. And they are more likely to be ashamed
when they have to be seen and to associate openly
with those who are aware of their disgrace. Wherefore the tragic poet Antiphon,[a] when he was about
to be flogged to death by order of Dionysius, seeing
that those who were to die with him covered their
faces as they passed through the gates, said, " Why
cover your faces ? Is it because you are afraid that
one of the crowd should see you to-morrow ? " Let
this account of shame suffice ; as for shamelessness,
it is evident that we shall be able to obtain ample
knowledge of it from the contrary arguments.

7. The persons towards whom men feel benevolent,[b]
and for what reasons, and in what frame of mind,
will be clear when we have defined what favour is.
Let it then be taken to be the feeling in accordance
with which one who has it is said to render a service
to one who needs it, not in return for something nor
in the interest of him who renders it, but in that of
the recipient. And the favour will be great if the
recipient is in pressing need, or if the service or the
times and circumstances are important or difficult, or
if the benefactor is the only one, or the first who has
rendered it, or has done so in the highest degree.
By needs I mean longings, especially for things
the failure to obtain which is accompanied by pain ;
such are the desires, for instance, love ; also those

" that from which the Athenians made their statues of
Harmodius and Aristogiton," Dionysius ordered him to be
put to death.

   [b] χάρις may mean (1) benevolence, the feeling which prompts
a favour ; (2) an actual favour conferred ; (3) gratitude.

ARISTOTLE

σώματος κακώσεσι καὶ ἐν κινδύνοις· καὶ γὰρ ὁ
κινδυνεύων ἐπιθυμεῖ καὶ ὁ λυπούμενος. διὸ οἱ ἐν
πενίᾳ παριστάμενοι καὶ φυγαῖς, κἂν μικρὰ ὑπη-
ρετήσωσιν, διὰ τὸ μέγεθος τῆς δεήσεως καὶ τὸν
καιρὸν κεχαρισμένοι, οἷον ὁ ἐν Λυκείῳ τὸν φορμὸν
4 δούς. ἀνάγκη οὖν μάλιστα μὲν εἰς ταὐτὰ ἔχειν
τὴν ὑπουργίαν, εἰ δὲ μή, εἰς ἴσα ἢ μείζω.

"Ωστ' ἐπεὶ φανερὸν καὶ ὅτε καὶ ἐφ' οἷς γίγνεται
χάρις καὶ πῶς ἔχουσι, δῆλον ὅτι ἐκ τούτων παρα-
σκευαστέον, τοὺς μὲν δεικνύντας ἢ ὄντας ἢ γε-
γενημένους ἐν τοιαύτῃ δεήσει καὶ λύπῃ, τοὺς δὲ
5 ὑπηρετηκότας ἐν τοιαύτῃ χρείᾳ τοιοῦτόν τι ἢ
ὑπηρετοῦντας. φανερὸν δὲ καὶ ὅθεν ἀφαιρεῖσθαι
ἐνδέχεται τὴν χάριν καὶ ποιεῖν ἀχαρίστους· ἢ γὰρ
1385 b ὅτι αὐτῶν ἕνεκα ὑπηρετοῦσιν ἢ ὑπηρέτησαν (τοῦτο
δ' οὐκ ἦν χάρις), ἢ ὅτι ἀπὸ τύχης συνέπεσεν ἢ
συνηναγκάσθησαν, ἢ ὅτι ἀπέδωκαν ἀλλ' οὐκ
ἔδωκαν, εἴτ' εἰδότες εἴτε μή· ἀμφοτέρως γὰρ τὶ
6 ἀντί τινος, ὥστ' οὐδ' οὕτως ἂν εἴη χάρις. καὶ
περὶ ἁπάσας τὰς κατηγορίας σκεπτέον· ἢ γὰρ
χάρις ἐστὶν ἢ ὅτι τοδὶ ἢ τοσονδὶ ἢ τοιονδὶ ἢ ποτὲ
ἢ πού. σημεῖον δέ, εἰ ἔλαττον μὴ ὑπηρέτησαν,
καὶ εἰ τοῖς ἐχθροῖς ἢ ταὐτὰ ἢ ἴσα ἢ μείζω· δῆλον

---

^a Probably given to a beggar or vagrant who had nothing to sleep on.

^b That is, should have in view the satisfaction of urgent wants and desires (Cope).

^c Reading ὅτε ; others read οἶς, " by whom."

^d ἀχαρίστους : the word generally means " ungrateful," and so Jebb takes it here: "and to make men ungrateful."

^e The other five categories in Aristotle's list are : relation, position, possession, activity, passivity.

^f Because in that case their motives in rendering the greater service cannot be disinterested.

222

which arise in bodily sufferings and dangers, for
when a man is in pain or danger he desires
something. That is why those who help a man
who is poor or an exile, even if the service be
ever so small, are regarded with favour owing to
the urgency and occasion of the need; for instance, the man who gave the mat [a] to another
in the Lyceum. It is necessary then, if possible,
that the service should be in the same direction [b];
if not, that it should apply to cases of similar or
greater need.

Since then it is evident on what occasions, [c] for
what reasons, and in what frame of mind a feeling
of benevolence arises, it is clear that we must derive
our arguments from this—to show that the one side
either has been, or still is, in such pain or need, and
that the other has rendered, or is rendering, such a
service in such a time of need. It is evident also by
what means it is possible to make out that there is
no favour at all, or that those who render it are not
actuated by benevolence [d]; for it can either be said
that they do, or have done so, for their own sake,
in which case there is no favour; or that it was mere
chance; or that they acted under compulsion; or that
they were making a return, not a gift, whether they
knew it or not; for in both cases it is an equivalent
return, so that in this case also there is no favour.
And the action must be considered in reference to
all the categories; for if there is a favour it is
so because of substance, quantity, quality, time, or
place. [e] And it denotes lack of goodwill, if persons
have not rendered a smaller service, [f] or if they have
rendered similar, equal, or greater services to our
enemies; for it is evident that they do not act for

γὰρ ὅτι οὐδὲ ταῦτα ἡμῶν ἕνεκα. ἢ εἰ φαῦλα
εἰδώς· οὐδεὶς γὰρ ὁμολογεῖ δεῖσθαι φαύλων.

8. Καὶ περὶ μὲν τοῦ χαρίζεσθαι καὶ ἀχαριστεῖν
εἴρηται· ποῖα δ' ἐλεεινὰ καὶ τίνας ἐλεοῦσι, καὶ
2 πῶς αὐτοὶ ἔχοντες, λέγωμεν. ἔστω δὴ ἔλεος λύπη
τις ἐπὶ φαινομένῳ κακῷ φθαρτικῷ ἢ λυπηρῷ
τοῦ ἀναξίου τυγχάνειν, ὃ κἂν αὐτὸς προσδοκή-
σειεν ἂν παθεῖν ἢ τῶν αὑτοῦ τινα, καὶ τοῦτο, ὅταν
πλησίον φαίνηται· δῆλον γὰρ ὅτι ἀνάγκη τὸν μέλλοντα ἐλεήσειν ὑπάρχειν τοιοῦτον οἷον οἴεσθαι
παθεῖν ἄν τι κακὸν ἢ αὐτὸν ἢ τῶν αὑτοῦ τινα, καὶ
τοιοῦτο κακὸν οἷον εἴρηται ἐν τῷ ὅρῳ ἢ ὅμοιον ἢ
3 παραπλήσιον. διὸ οὔτε οἱ παντελῶς ἀπολωλότες
ἐλεοῦσιν (οὐδὲν γὰρ ἂν ἔτι παθεῖν οἴονται· πεπόν-
θασι γάρ) οὔτε οἱ ὑπερευδαιμονεῖν οἰόμενοι, ἀλλ'
ὑβρίζουσιν· εἰ γὰρ ἅπαντα οἴονται ὑπάρχειν τὰ-
γαθά, δῆλον ὅτι καὶ τὸ μὴ ἐνδέχεσθαι παθεῖν
4 μηδὲν κακόν· καὶ γὰρ τοῦτο τῶν ἀγαθῶν. εἰσὶ
δὲ τοιοῦτοι οἷοι νομίζειν παθεῖν ἂν οἵ τε πεπονθότες ἤδη καὶ διαπεφευγότες, καὶ οἱ πρεσβύτεροι
καὶ διὰ τὸ φρονεῖν καὶ δι' ἐμπειρίαν, καὶ οἱ ἀσθενεῖς,
καὶ οἱ δειλότεροι μᾶλλον, καὶ οἱ πεπαιδευμένοι·
5 εὐλόγιστοι γάρ. καὶ οἷς ὑπάρχουσι γονεῖς ἢ τέκνα
ἢ γυναῖκες· αὑτοῦ τε γὰρ ταῦτα, καὶ οἷα παθεῖν
6 τὰ εἰρημένα. καὶ οἱ μήτε ἐν ἀνδρίας πάθει ὄντες,
οἷον ἐν ὀργῇ ἢ θάρρει (ἀλόγιστα γὰρ τοῦ ἐσομένου
ταῦτα) μήτ' ἐν ὑβριστικῇ διαθέσει (καὶ γὰρ οὗτοι

our sake in this case either. Or if the service was insignificant, and rendered by one who knew it; for no one admits that he has need of what is insignificant.

8. Let this suffice for benevolence and the opposite. We will now state what things and persons excite pity, and the state of mind of those who feel it. Let pity then be a kind of pain excited by the sight of evil, deadly or painful, which befalls one who does not deserve it; an evil which one might expect to come upon himself or one of his friends, and when it seems near. For it is evident that one who is likely to feel pity must be such as to think that he, or one of his friends, is liable to suffer some evil, and such an evil as has been stated in the definition, or one similar, or nearly similar. Wherefore neither those who are utterly ruined, are capable of pity, for they think they have nothing more to suffer, since they have exhausted suffering; nor those who think themselves supremely fortunate, who rather are insolent. For if they think that all good things are theirs, it is clear that they think that they cannot possibly suffer evil, and this is one of the good things. Now those persons who think they are likely to suffer are those who have already suffered and escaped; the advanced in age, by reason of their wisdom and experience; and the weak, and those who are rather more timid; and the educated, for they reckon rightly; and those who have parents, children, or wives, for these are part of them and likely to suffer the evils of which we have spoken; and those who are not influenced by any courageous emotion, such as anger or confidence, for these emotions do not take thought of the future; and those who are not in a wantonly insolent frame of

ARISTOTLE

ἀλόγιστοι τοῦ πείσεσθαί τι), ἀλλ' οἱ μεταξὺ
τούτων. μήτ' αὖ φοβούμενοι σφόδρα· οὐ γὰρ
ἐλεοῦσιν οἱ ἐκπεπληγμένοι διὰ τὸ εἶναι πρὸς τῷ
7 οἰκείῳ πάθει. κἂν οἴωνταί τινας εἶναι ἐπιεικεῖς·
ὁ γὰρ μηδένα οἰόμενος πάντας οἰήσεται ἀξίους
1386 a εἶναι κακοῦ. καὶ ὅλως δὴ ὅταν ἔχῃ οὕτως ὥστ'
ἀναμνησθῆναι τοιαῦτα συμβεβηκότα ἢ αὑτῷ ἢ τῶν
αὑτοῦ, ἢ ἐλπίσαι γενέσθαι ἢ αὑτῷ ἢ τῶν αὑτοῦ.

8 Ὡς μὲν οὖν ἔχοντες ἐλεοῦσιν, εἴρηται, ἃ δ'
ἐλεοῦσιν, ἐκ τοῦ ὁρισμοῦ δῆλον· ὅσα τε γὰρ τῶν
λυπηρῶν καὶ ὀδυνηρῶν φθαρτικά, πάντα ἐλεεινά,
καὶ ὅσα ἀναιρετικά, καὶ ὅσων ἡ τύχη αἰτία κακῶν
9 μέγεθος ἐχόντων. ἔστι δ' ὀδυνηρὰ μὲν καὶ φθαρ-
τικὰ θάνατοι καὶ αἰκίαι σωμάτων καὶ κακώσεις
10 καὶ γῆρας καὶ νόσοι καὶ τροφῆς ἔνδεια, ὧν δ' ἡ
τύχη αἰτία κακῶν, ἀφιλία, ὀλιγοφιλία (διὸ καὶ τὸ
διεσπάσθαι ἀπὸ τῶν φίλων καὶ συνήθων ἐλεεινόν),
αἶσχος, ἀσθένεια, ἀναπηρία. καὶ τὸ ὅθεν προσῆκεν
11 ἀγαθόν τι πρᾶξαι, κακόν τι συμβῆναι. καὶ τὸ
πολλάκις τοιοῦτον. καὶ τὸ πεπονθότος γενέσθαι
τι ἀγαθόν, οἷον Διοπείθει τὰ παρὰ βασιλέως
τεθνεῶτι κατεπέμφθη. καὶ τὸ ἢ μηδὲν γεγενῆσθαι ἀγαθόν, ἢ γενομένων μὴ εἶναι ἀπόλαυσιν.

Ἐφ' οἷς μὲν οὖν ἐλεοῦσι, ταῦτα καὶ τὰ τοιαῦτά
12 ἐστιν· ἐλεοῦσι δὲ τούς τε γνωρίμους, ἐὰν μὴ σφό-

mind, for they also take no thought of future suffering ; but it is those who are between the two extremes that feel pity. Those who are not in great fear ; for those who are panic-stricken are incapable of pity, because they are preoccupied with their own emotion. And men feel pity if they think that some persons are virtuous ; for he who thinks that no one is will think that all deserve misfortune. And, generally speaking, a man is moved to pity when he is so affected that he remembers that such evils have happened, or expects that they may happen, either to himself or to one of his friends.

We have stated the frame of mind which leads men to pity ; and the things which arouse this feeling are clearly shown by the definition. They are all painful and distressing things that are also destructive, and all that are ruinous ; and all evils of which fortune is the cause, if they are great. Things distressing and destructive are various kinds of death, personal ill-treatment and injuries, old age, disease, and lack of food. The evils for which fortune is responsible are lack of friends, or few friends (wherefore it is pitiable to be torn away from friends and intimates), ugliness, weakness, mutilation ; if some misfortune comes to pass from a quarter whence one might have reasonably expected something good ; and if this happens often ; and if good fortune does not come until a man has already suffered, as when the presents from the Great King were not dispatched to Diopithes until he was dead. Those also are to be pitied to whom no good has ever accrued, or who are unable to enjoy it when it has.

These and the like things, then, excite pity. The persons men pity are those whom they know, pro-

δρα ἐγγὺς ὦσιν οἰκειότητι· περὶ δὲ τούτους ὥσπερ
περὶ αὑτοὺς μέλλοντας ἔχουσιν. διὸ καὶ Ἄμασις
ἐπὶ μὲν τῷ υἱεῖ ἀγομένῳ ἐπὶ τὸ ἀποθανεῖν οὐκ
ἐδάκρυσεν, ὡς φασίν, ἐπὶ δὲ τῷ φίλῳ προσαιτοῦντι·
τοῦτο μὲν γὰρ ἐλεεινόν, ἐκεῖνο δὲ δεινόν· τὸ γὰρ
δεινὸν ἕτερον τοῦ ἐλεεινοῦ καὶ ἐκκρουστικὸν τοῦ
13 ἐλέου καὶ πολλάκις τῷ ἐναντίῳ χρήσιμον. ἔτι
ἐλεοῦσιν ἐγγὺς αὐτοῖς τοῦ δεινοῦ ὄντος. καὶ τοὺς
ὁμοίους ἐλεοῦσι κατὰ ἡλικίας, κατὰ ἤθη, κατὰ
ἕξεις, κατὰ ἀξιώματα, κατὰ γένη· ἐν πᾶσι γὰρ
τούτοις μᾶλλον φαίνεται καὶ αὐτῷ ἂν ὑπάρξαι·
ὅλως γὰρ καὶ ἐνταῦθα δεῖ λαβεῖν ὅτι, ὅσα ἐφ'
αὑτῶν φοβοῦνται, ταῦτα ἐπ' ἄλλων γιγνόμενα
14 ἐλεοῦσιν. ἐπεὶ δ' ἐγγὺς φαινόμενα τὰ πάθη
ἐλεεινά ἐστι, τὰ δὲ μυριοστὸν ἔτος γενόμενα ἢ
ἐσόμενα οὔτ' ἐλπίζοντες οὔτε μεμνημένοι ἢ ὅλως
οὐκ ἐλεοῦσιν ἢ οὐχ ὁμοίως, ἀνάγκη τοὺς συν-
απεργαζομένους σχήμασι καὶ φωναῖς καὶ ἐσθῆτι
καὶ ὅλως τῇ ὑποκρίσει ἐλεεινοτέρους εἶναι· ἐγγὺς
γὰρ ποιοῦσι φαίνεσθαι τὸ κακὸν πρὸ ὀμμάτων
15 ποιοῦντες, ἢ ὡς μέλλον ἢ ὡς γεγονός. καὶ τὰ
1386 b γεγονότα ἄρτι ἢ μέλλοντα διὰ ταχέων ἐλεεινότερα
16 διὰ τὸ αὐτό. καὶ τὰ σημεῖα καὶ τὰς πράξεις,
οἷον ἐσθῆτάς τε τῶν πεπονθότων καὶ ὅσα τοιαῦτα,
καὶ λόγους καὶ ὅσα ἄλλα τῶν ἐν τῷ πάθει ὄντων,
οἷον ἤδη τελευτώντων. καὶ μάλιστα τὸ σπου-

---

[a] Herodotus, iii. 14, where the story is told, not of Amasis,
but of his son Psammenitus.

[b] Jebb renders: "Again men pity when the danger is
near themselves," which may mean when they see something
terrible happening to others and likely soon to befall them-

vided they are not too closely connected with them ;
for if they are, they feel the same as if they themselves were likely to suffer. This is why Amasis [a] is
said not to have wept when his son was led to execu-
tion, but did weep at the sight of a friend reduced
to beggary, for the latter excited pity, the former
terror. The terrible is different from the pitiable,
for it drives out pity, and often serves to produce
the opposite feeling. Further, the nearness of the
terrible makes men pity.[b] Men also pity those who
resemble them in age, character, habits, position, or
family ; for all such relations make a man more likely
to think that their misfortune may befall him as
well. For, in general, here also we may conclude
that all that men fear in regard to themselves excites
their pity when others are the victims. And since
sufferings are pitiable when they appear close at
hand, while those that are past or future, ten thousand years backwards or forwards, either do not
excite pity at all or only in a less degree, because
men neither expect the one nor remember the other,
it follows that those who contribute to the effect by
gestures, voice, dress, and dramatic action generally,
are more pitiable ; for they make the evil appear
close at hand, setting it before our eyes as either
future or past. And disasters that have just happened or are soon about to happen excite more pity
for the same reason. Pity is also aroused by signs
and actions, such as the dress of those who have
suffered, and all such objects, and the words and
everything else that concerns those who are actually
suffering, for instance, at the point of death. And

selves. Vahlen inserts οὐ γὰρ before ἔτι : "For men cease
to pity when the terrible comes close to themselves."

ARISTOTLE

δαίους εἶναι ἐν τοῖς τοιούτοις καιροῖς ὄντας ἐλεει-
νόν· ἅπαντα γὰρ ταῦτα διὰ τὸ ἐγγὺς φαίνεσθαι
μᾶλλον ποιεῖ τὸν ἔλεον, καὶ ὡς ἀναξίου ὄντος, καὶ
ἐν ὀφθαλμοῖς φαινομένου τοῦ πάθους.

9. Ἀντίκειται δὲ τῷ ἐλεεῖν μάλιστα μὲν ὃ
καλοῦσι νεμεσᾶν· τῷ γὰρ λυπεῖσθαι ἐπὶ ταῖς ἀναξίαις κακοπραγίαις ἀντικείμενόν ἐστι τρόπον τινὰ
καὶ ἀπὸ τοῦ αὐτοῦ ἤθους τὸ λυπεῖσθαι ἐπὶ ταῖς
ἀναξίαις εὐπραγίαις. καὶ ἄμφω τὰ πάθη ἤθους
2 χρηστοῦ· δεῖ γὰρ ἐπὶ μὲν τοῖς ἀναξίως πράττουσι
κακῶς συνάχθεσθαι καὶ ἐλεεῖν, τοῖς δὲ εὖ νεμεσᾶν·
ἄδικον γὰρ τὸ παρὰ τὴν ἀξίαν γιγνόμενον, διὸ
3 καὶ τοῖς θεοῖς ἀποδίδομεν τὸ νεμεσᾶν. δόξειε δ᾽
ἂν καὶ ὁ φθόνος τῷ ἐλεεῖν τὸν αὐτὸν ἀντικεῖσθαι
τρόπον ὡς σύνεγγυς ὢν καὶ ταὐτὸν τῷ νεμεσᾶν,
ἔστι δ᾽ ἕτερον· λύπη μὲν γὰρ ταραχώδης καὶ ὁ
φθόνος ἐστὶ καὶ εἰς εὐπραγίαν, ἀλλ᾽ οὐ τοῦ ἀναξίου
ἀλλὰ τοῦ ἴσου καὶ ὁμοίου. τὸ δὲ μὴ ὅτι αὐτῷ τι
συμβήσεται ἕτερον, ἀλλὰ δι᾽ αὐτὸν τὸν πλησίον,
ἅπασιν ὁμοίως δεῖ ὑπάρχειν. οὐ γὰρ ἔτι ἔσται τὸ
μὲν νέμεσις τὸ δὲ φθόνος, ἀλλὰ φόβος, ἐὰν διὰ
τοῦτο ἡ λύπη ὑπάρχῃ καὶ ἡ ταραχή, ὅτι αὐτῷ τι
4 ἔσται φαῦλον ἀπὸ τῆς ἐκείνου εὐπραξίας. φανερὸν δ᾽ ὅτι ἀκολουθήσει καὶ τὰ ἐναντία πάθη τού-
τοις· ὁ μὲν γὰρ λυπούμενος ἐπὶ τοῖς ἀναξίως κακο-
πραγοῦσιν ἡσθήσεται ἢ ἄλυπος ἔσται ἐπὶ τοῖς

---

[a] " When the men, who are in such crises, are good men "
(Jebb). If they were not, their misfortune would appear
deserved.

[b] The signs and actions, and the demeanour of the
sufferer.

when men show themselves undaunted [a] at such critical times it is specially pitiable ; for all these things,[b] because they come immediately under our observation, increase the feeling of pity, both because the sufferer does not seem to deserve his fate, and because the suffering is before our eyes.

9. Now what is called indignation [c] is the antithesis to pity ; for the being pained at undeserved good fortune is in a manner contrary to being pained at undeserved bad fortune and arises from the same character. And both emotions show good character, for if we sympathize with and pity those who suffer undeservedly, we ought to be indignant with those who prosper undeservedly ; for that which happens beyond a man's deserts is unjust, wherefore we attribute this feeling even to gods. It would seem that envy also is similarly opposed to pity, as being akin to or identical with indignation, although it is really different ; envy also is indeed a disturbing pain and directed against good fortune, but not that of one who does not deserve it, but of one who is our equal and like. Now, all who feel envy and indignation must have this in common, that they are disturbed, not because they think that any harm will happen to themselves, but on account of their neighbour ; for it will cease to be indignation and envy, but will be fear, if the pain and disturbance arise from the idea that harm may come to themselves from another's good fortune. And it is evident that these feelings will be accompanied by opposite feelings ; for he who is pained at the sight of those who are undeservedly unfortunate will rejoice or will at least not be pained at the sight of those who are

---

[c] νεμεσᾶν : " the nobler brother of envy " (Nietzsche).

ARISTOTLE

ἐναντίως κακοπραγοῦσιν· οἷον τοὺς πατραλοίας
καὶ μιαιφόνους, ὅταν τύχωσι τιμωρίας, οὐδεὶς ἂν
λυπηθείη χρηστός· δεῖ γὰρ χαίρειν ἐπὶ τοῖς τοιούτοις, ὡς δ' αὔτως καὶ ἐπὶ τοῖς εὖ πράττουσι κατ'
ἀξίαν· ἄμφω γὰρ δίκαια, καὶ ποιεῖ χαίρειν τὸν
ἐπιεικῆ· ἀνάγκη γὰρ ἐλπίζειν ὑπάρξαι ἄν, ἅπερ
5 τῷ ὁμοίῳ, καὶ αὐτῷ. καὶ ἔστι τοῦ αὐτοῦ ἤθους
ἅπαντα ταῦτα, τὰ δ' ἐναντία τοῦ ἐναντίου· ὁ γὰρ
αὐτός ἐστιν ἐπιχαιρέκακος καὶ φθονερός· ἐφ' ᾧ
1387 a γάρ τις λυπεῖται γιγνομένῳ καὶ ὑπάρχοντι, ἀναγκαῖον τοῦτον ἐπὶ τῇ στερήσει καὶ τῇ φθορᾷ τῇ
τούτου χαίρειν. διὸ κωλυτικὰ μὲν ἐλέου πάντα
ταῦτα ἐστί, διαφέρει δὲ διὰ τὰς εἰρημένας αἰτίας·
ὥστε πρὸς τὸ μὴ ἐλεεινὰ ποιεῖν ἅπαντα ὁμοίως
χρήσιμα.

6 Πρῶτον μὲν οὖν περὶ τοῦ νεμεσᾶν λέγωμεν,
τίσι τε νεμεσῶσι καὶ ἐπὶ τίσι καὶ πῶς ἔχοντες
7 αὐτοί, εἶτα μετὰ ταῦτα περὶ τῶν ἄλλων. φανερὸν
δ' ἐκ τῶν εἰρημένων· εἰ γάρ ἐστι τὸ νεμεσᾶν
λυπεῖσθαι ἐπὶ τῷ φαινομένῳ ἀναξίως εὐπραγεῖν,
πρῶτον μὲν δῆλον ὅτι οὐχ οἷόν τ' ἐπὶ πᾶσι τοῖς
8 ἀγαθοῖς νεμεσᾶν· οὐ γὰρ εἰ δίκαιος ἢ ἀνδρεῖος, ἢ
εἰ ἀρετὴν λήψεται, νεμεσήσει τούτῳ (οὐδὲ γὰρ
ἔλεοι ἐπὶ τοῖς ἐναντίοις τούτων εἰσίν), ἀλλ' ἐπὶ
πλούτῳ καὶ δυνάμει καὶ τοῖς τοιούτοις, ὅσων ὡς
ἁπλῶς εἰπεῖν ἄξιοί εἰσιν οἱ ἀγαθοί [καὶ οἱ τὰ φύσει
ἔχοντες ἀγαθά, οἷον εὐγένειαν καὶ κάλλος καὶ ὅσα

---

a There is justice both in the punishment of the parricide
and in the deserved good fortune of others.   The conclusion

232

deservedly so ; for instance, no good man would be
pained at seeing parricides or assassins punished ;
we should rather rejoice at their lot, and at that of
men who are deservedly fortunate ; for both these [a]
are just and cause the worthy man to rejoice, because
he cannot help hoping that what has happened to his
like may also happen to himself. And all these
feelings arise from the same character and their
contraries from the contrary ; for he who is malicious
is also envious, since, if the envious man is pained
at another's possession or acquisition of good fortune,
he is bound to rejoice at the destruction or non-
acquisition of the same. Wherefore all these
emotions are a hindrance to pity, although they
differ for the reasons stated ; so that they are all
equally useful for preventing any feeling of pity.

Let us then first speak of indignation, the persons
with whom men feel indignant, for what reasons,
and in what frame of mind ; and then proceed to
the rest of the emotions. What we have just said
will make matters clear. For if indignation is being
pained at the sight of good fortune that is apparently
undeserved, in the first place it is clear that it is
not possible to feel indignation at all good things ;
for no one will be indignant with a man who is just
or courageous, or may acquire any virtue (for one
does not feel pity in the case of opposites of
those qualities),[b] but men are indignant at wealth,
power, in a word, at all the advantages of which
good men are worthy. [And those who possess natural
advantages, such as noble birth, beauty, and all such

must refer to the latter ; if his like is fortunate, he hopes he
may be.

[b] Because it is a man's own fault, and pity is only felt for
what is undeserved.

9 τοιαῦτα]. ἐπειδὴ δὲ τὸ ἀρχαῖον ἐγγύς τι φαίνεται
τοῦ φύσει, ἀνάγκη τοῖς ταὐτὸ ἔχουσιν ἀγαθόν,
ἐὰν νεωστὶ ἔχοντες τυγχάνωσι καὶ διὰ τοῦτο
εὐπραγῶσι, μᾶλλον νεμεσᾶν· μᾶλλον γὰρ λυποῦσιν
οἱ νεωστὶ πλουτοῦντες τῶν πάλαι καὶ διὰ γένος·
ὁμοίως δὲ καὶ ἄρχοντες καὶ δυνάμενοι καὶ πολύφιλοι καὶ εὔτεκνοι καὶ ὁτιοῦν τῶν τοιούτων. κἂν
διὰ ταῦτ’ ἄλλο τι ἀγαθὸν γίγνηται αὐτοῖς, ὡσαύτως·
καὶ γὰρ ἐνταῦθα μᾶλλον λυποῦσιν οἱ νεόπλουτοι
ἄρχοντες διὰ τὸν πλοῦτον ἢ οἱ ἀρχαιόπλουτοι.
10 ὁμοίως δὲ καὶ ἐπὶ τῶν ἄλλων. αἴτιον δ’ ὅτι οἱ
μὲν δοκοῦσι τὰ αὑτῶν ἔχειν οἱ δ’ οὔ· τὸ γὰρ ἀεὶ
οὕτω φαινόμενον ἔχειν ἀληθὲς δοκεῖ, ὥστε οἱ
11 ἕτεροι οὐ τὰ αὑτῶν ἔχειν. καὶ ἐπεὶ ἕκαστον τῶν
ἀγαθῶν οὐ τοῦ τυχόντος ἄξιον, ἀλλά τις ἐστὶν
ἀναλογία καὶ τὸ ἁρμόττον, οἷον ὅπλων κάλλος
οὐ τῷ δικαίῳ ἁρμόττει ἀλλὰ τῷ ἀνδρείῳ, καὶ
γάμοι διαφέροντες οὐ τοῖς νεωστὶ πλουτοῦσιν
ἀλλὰ τοῖς εὐγενέσιν,—ἐὰν οὖν ἀγαθὸς ὢν μὴ τοῦ
ἁρμόττοντος τυγχάνῃ, νεμεσητόν. καὶ τὸν ἥττω
τῷ κρείττονι ἀμφισβητεῖν, μάλιστα μὲν οὖν τοὺς
ἐν τῷ αὐτῷ· ὅθεν καὶ τοῦτ’ εἴρηται,

---

[a] The first part of the sentence is clear: men are indignant
when what good men deserve is possessed by those who are
not good. The literal translation of the text as it stands is:
" Men are indignant . . . at all the advantages of which
good men and those who possess natural advantages are
worthy "; but this cannot be right, since there is nothing in
natural advantages to arouse moral indignation, there is no
question of their being deserved or undeserved. Something
may have fallen out like "but they will not be indignant
with those who possess natural advantages." Roemer (*Rhein.
Mus.* xxxix. p. 504) suggests: οὐδ’ εἰ τὰ φύσει ἔχουσιν ἀγαθά
(understanding νεμεσήσει τούτοις).

things.]ᵃ And since that which is old seems closely
to resemble that which is natural, it follows that, if
two parties have the same good, men are more
indignant with the one who has recently acquired it
and owes his prosperity to it; for the newly rich
cause more annoyance than those who have long
possessed or inherited wealth. The same applies to
offices of state, power, numerous friends, virtuous
children, and any other advantages of the kind. And
if these advantages bring them some other advantage, men are equally indignant; for in this case
also the newly rich who attain to office owing to
their wealth cause more annoyance than those who
have long been wealthy; and similarly in all other
cases of the same kind. The reason is that the
latter seem to possess what belongs to them, the
former not; for that which all along shows itself
in the same light suggests a reality, so that the
former seem to possess what is not theirs.ᵇ And since
every kind of good is not suitable to the first comer,
but a certain proportion and suitability are necessary
(as for instance beautiful weapons are not suitable
to the just but to the courageous man, and distinguished marriages not to the newly rich but to
the nobly born), if a virtuous man does not obtain
what is suitable to him, we feel indignant. Similarly,
if the inferior contends with the superior, especially
among those engaged in the same pursuit,—whence
the saying of the poet,

ᵇ δοκεῖν is a stronger word than φαίνεσθαι, indicating an
intellectual operation as opposed to an impression received
through the senses. The idea is that where anything has
been so long in a person's possession, it has come to be
regarded as his by right.

Αἴαντος δ' ἀλέεινε μάχην Τελαμωνιάδαο·
Ζεὺς γάρ οἱ νεμέσασχ', ὅτ' ἀμείνονι φωτὶ μάχοιτο.

1887 b εἰ δὲ μή, κἂν ὁπωσοῦν ὁ ἥττων τῷ κρείττονι, οἷον
εἰ ὁ μουσικὸς τῷ δικαίῳ· βέλτιον γὰρ ἡ δικαιοσύνη
τῆς μουσικῆς.

Οἷς μὲν οὖν νεμεσῶσι καὶ δι' ἅ, ἐκ τούτων δῆλον·
12 ταῦτα γὰρ καὶ τὰ τοιαῦτά ἐστιν. αὐτοὶ δὲ νε-
μεσητικοί εἰσιν, ἐὰν ἄξιοι τυγχάνωσιν ὄντες τῶν
μεγίστων ἀγαθῶν καὶ ταῦτα κεκτημένοι· τὸ γὰρ
τῶν ὁμοίων ἠξιῶσθαι τοὺς μὴ ὁμοίους οὐ δίκαιον·
13 δεύτερον δ', ἂν ὄντες ἀγαθοὶ καὶ σπουδαῖοι τυγ-
χάνωσιν· κρίνουσί τε γὰρ εὖ, καὶ τὰ ἄδικα μισοῦσιν.
14 καὶ ἐὰν φιλότιμοι καὶ ὀρεγόμενοι τινῶν πράξεων,
καὶ μάλιστα περὶ ταῦτα φιλότιμοι ὦσιν ὧν ἕτεροι
15 ἀνάξιοι ὄντες τυγχάνουσιν. καὶ ὅλως οἱ ἀξιοῦντες
αὐτοὶ αὑτούς, ὧν ἑτέρους μὴ ἀξιοῦσι, νεμεσητικοὶ
τούτοις καὶ τούτων. διὸ καὶ οἱ ἀνδραποδώδεις
καὶ φαῦλοι καὶ ἀφιλότιμοι οὐ νεμεσητικοί· οὐδὲν
16 γάρ ἐστιν οὗ ἑαυτοὺς οἴονται ἀξίους εἶναι. φανερὸν
δ' ἐκ τούτων ἐπὶ ποίοις ἀτυχοῦσι καὶ κακο-
πραγοῦσιν ἢ μὴ τυγχάνουσι χαίρειν ἢ ἀλύπως
ἔχειν δεῖ· ἐκ γὰρ τῶν εἰρημένων τὰ ἀντικείμενά
ἐστι δῆλα, ὥστ' ἐὰν τούς τε κριτὰς τοιούτους
παρασκευάσῃ ὁ λόγος, καὶ τοὺς ἀξιοῦντας ἐλεεῖσθαι, καὶ ἐφ' οἷς ἐλεεῖσθαι, δείξῃ ἀναξίους μὲν

---

a *Iliad*, xi. 542. Only the first verse is given in the
received text of Homer; the second is not found in any of
the mss. The reference is to Cebriones, a son of Priam slain
by Patroclus.

b It has been suggested to insert μὴ before τυγχάνωσι: " if,
although virtuous and worthy, they do not happen to possess
such advantages."

He avoided battle with Ajax, son of Telamon,[a] for Zeus was indignant with him, when he would fight with a better man;

or, if the pursuit is not the same, wherever the inferior contends with the superior in anything whatever, as for instance, the musician with the just man; for justice is better than music.

From this it is clear, then, with whom men are indignant and for what reasons; they are these or of such a kind. Men are prone to indignation, first, if they happen to deserve or possess the greatest advantages, for it is not just that those who do not resemble them should be deemed worthy of the same advantages; secondly, if they happen to be virtuous and worthy,[b] for they both judge correctly and hate what is unjust. And those who are ambitious and long for certain positions, especially if they are those which others, although unworthy, have obtained.[c] And, in general, those who think themselves worthy of advantages of which they consider others unworthy, are inclined to be indignant with the latter and because of these advantages. This is why the servile and worthless and unambitious are not inclined to indignation; for there is nothing of which they think themselves worthy. It is evident from this what kind of men they are whose ill fortunes, calamities, and lack of success must make us rejoice or at least feel no pain; for the opposites are clear from what has been said. If then the speaker puts the judges into such a frame of mind and proves that those who claim our pity (and the reasons why they do so) are unworthy to obtain it and deserve

---

[c] Or, " of which others happen to be unworthy."

ὄντας τυγχάνειν ἀξίους δὲ μὴ τυγχάνειν, ἀδύνατον
ἐλεεῖν.

10. Δῆλον δὲ καὶ ἐπὶ τίσι φθονοῦσι καὶ τίσι
καὶ πῶς ἔχοντες, εἴπερ ἐστὶν ὁ φθόνος λύπη τις
ἐπὶ εὐπραγίᾳ φαινομένῃ τῶν εἰρημένων ἀγαθῶν
περὶ τοὺς ὁμοίους, μὴ ἵνα τι αὑτῷ, ἀλλὰ δι᾽
ἐκείνους· φθονήσουσι μὲν γὰρ οἱ τοιοῦτοι οἷς εἰσί
2 τινες ὅμοιοι ἢ φαίνονται. ὁμοίους δὲ λέγω κατὰ
γένος, κατὰ συγγένειαν, καθ᾽ ἡλικίαν, καθ᾽ ἕξιν,
κατὰ δόξαν, κατὰ τὰ ὑπάρχοντα. καὶ οἷς μικροῦ
ἐλλείπει τὸ μὴ πάντα ὑπάρχειν. διὸ οἱ μεγάλα
πράττοντες καὶ οἱ εὐτυχοῦντες φθονεροί εἰσιν·
3 πάντας γὰρ οἴονται τὰ αὑτῶν φέρειν. καὶ οἱ
τιμώμενοι ἐπί τινι διαφερόντως, καὶ μάλιστα ἐπὶ
σοφίᾳ ἢ εὐδαιμονίᾳ. καὶ οἱ φιλότιμοι φθονερώ-
τεροι τῶν ἀφιλοτίμων. καὶ οἱ δοξόσοφοι· φιλότιμοι γὰρ ἐπὶ σοφίᾳ. καὶ ὅλως οἱ φιλόδοξοι περί
τι φθονεροὶ περὶ τοῦτο. καὶ οἱ μικρόψυχοι·
πάντα γὰρ μεγάλα δοκεῖ αὐτοῖς εἶναι.

4 Ἐφ᾽ οἷς δὲ φθονοῦσιν, τὰ μὲν ἀγαθὰ εἴρηται· ἐφ᾽
1388 a ὅσοις γὰρ φιλοδοξοῦσι καὶ φιλοτιμοῦνται ἔργοις ἢ
κτήμασι καὶ ὀρέγονται δόξης, καὶ ὅσα εὐτυχήματά
ἐστι, σχεδὸν περὶ πάντα φθόνος ἐστί, καὶ μάλιστα
ὧν αὐτοὶ ἢ ὀρέγονται ἢ οἴονται δεῖν αὑτοὺς ἔχειν,
ἢ ὧν τῇ κτήσει μικρῷ ὑπερέχουσιν ἢ μικρῷ ἐλ-
λείπουσιν.[a]

5 Φανερὸν δὲ καὶ οἷς φθονοῦσιν· ἅμα γὰρ εἴρηται·

---

[a] If some one else possesses the one thing which they think
necessary to complete their happiness, they are envious of
him, because they consider it ought to be theirs.

that it should be refused them, then pity will be impossible.

10. It is equally clear for what reason, and of whom, and in what frame of mind, men are envious, if envy is a kind of pain at the sight of good fortune in regard to the goods mentioned; in the case of those like themselves; and not for the sake of a man getting anything, but because of others possessing it. For those men will be envious who have, or seem to have, others " like " them. I mean like in birth, relationship, age, moral habit, reputation, and possessions. And those will be envious who possess all but one of these advantages *a*; that is why those who attempt great things and succeed are envious, because they think that every one is trying to deprive them of their own. And those who are honoured for some special reason, especially for wisdom or happiness. And the ambitious are more envious than the unambitious. And those who are wise in their own conceit, for they are ambitious of a reputation for wisdom; and, in general, those who wish to be distinguished in anything are envious in regard to it. And the little-minded, because everything appears to them to be great.

The advantages which excite envy have already been stated. Nearly all the actions or possessions which make men desire glory or honour and long for fame, and the favours of fortune, create envy, especially when men long for them themselves, or think that they have a right to them, or the possession of which makes them slightly superior or slightly inferior.

And it is evident whom men envy, for it has just been stated by implication. They envy those who

τοῖς γὰρ ἐγγὺς καὶ χρόνῳ καὶ τόπῳ καὶ ἡλικίᾳ
καὶ δόξῃ φθονοῦσιν. ὅθεν εἴρηται

τὸ συγγενὲς γὰρ καὶ φθονεῖν ἐπίσταται.

καὶ πρὸς οὓς φιλοτιμοῦνται· φιλοτιμοῦνται μὲν γὰρ
πρὸς τοὺς εἰρημένους, πρὸς δὲ τοὺς μυριοστὸν ἔτος
ὄντας ἢ πρὸς τοὺς ἐσομένους ἢ τεθνεῶτας οὐδείς,
οὐδὲ πρὸς τοὺς ἐφ' Ἡρακλείαις στήλαις. οὐδ' ὧν
πολὺ οἴονται παρ' αὐτοῖς ἢ παρὰ τοῖς ἄλλοις λεί-
πεσθαι, οὐδ' ὧν πολὺ ὑπερέχειν, ὡσαύτως καὶ πρὸς
6 τούτους καὶ περὶ τὰ τοιαῦτα. ἐπεὶ δὲ πρὸς τοὺς
ἀνταγωνιστὰς καὶ ἀντεραστὰς καὶ ὅλως τοὺς τῶν
αὐτῶν ἐφιεμένους φιλοτιμοῦνται, ἀνάγκη μάλιστα
τούτοις φθονεῖν· ὅθεν εἴρηται

καὶ κεραμεὺς κεραμεῖ.

7 καὶ τοῖς ταχὺ οἱ ἢ μόλις τυχόντες ἢ μὴ τυχόντες
8 φθονοῦσιν. καὶ ὧν ἢ κεκτημένων ἢ κατορθούντων
ὄνειδος αὐτοῖς· εἰσὶ δὲ καὶ οὗτοι ἐγγὺς καὶ ὅμοιοι·
δῆλον γὰρ ὅτι παρ' αὐτοὺς οὐ τυγχάνουσι τοῦ
ἀγαθοῦ, ὥστε τοῦτο λυποῦν ποιεῖ τὸν φθόνον.
9 καὶ τοῖς ἢ ἔχουσι ταῦτα ἢ κεκτημένοις ὅσα αὐτοῖς
προσῆκεν ἢ κέκτηντό ποτε· διὸ πρεσβύτεροι νεω-
10 τέροις. καὶ οἱ πολλὰ δαπανήσαντες εἰς ταὐτὸ τοῖς
11 ὀλίγα φθονοῦσιν. δῆλον δὲ καὶ ἐφ' οἷς χαίρουσιν
οἱ τοιοῦτοι καὶ ἐπὶ τίσι καὶ πῶς ἔχοντες· ὡς γὰρ

---

[a] According to the scholiast, from Aeschylus.
[b] Two rocks at the east end of the Straits of Gibraltar,
supposed to be the limit westwards of the ancient world.
[c] That is, no one will attempt to compete with them in
their special branch of study. Roemer reads καὶ πρὸς τοὺς
περὶ τὰ τοιαῦτα, translated by Jebb as if there were a full

are near them in time, place, age, and reputation, whence it was said,

Kinship knows how to envy also ; [a]

and those with whom they are in rivalry, who are those just spoken of ; for no man tries to rival those who lived ten thousand years ago, or are about to be born, or are already dead : nor those who live near the Pillars of Hercules ; [b] nor those who, in his own opinion or in that of others, are either far inferior or superior to him ; and the people and things which one envies are on the same footing. [c] And since men strive for honour with those who are competitors, or rivals in love, in short, with those who aim at the same things, they are bound to feel most envious of these ; whence the saying,

Potter [being jealous] of potter. [d]

And those who have succeeded with difficulty or have failed envy those whose success has been rapid. And those whose possessions or successes are a reproach to themselves, and these, too, are those near or like them ; for it is clear that it is their own fault that they do not obtain the same advantage, so that this pains and causes envy. And those who either have or have acquired what was naturally theirs or what they had once acquired ; this is why an older man is envious of a younger one. Those who have spent much envy those who have only spent little to obtain the same thing. And it is clear at what things and persons the envious rejoice, and in what frame of mind ; for, as when they do

stop at ὑπερέχειν. " In like manner we vie with those engaged in such or such pursuits."

[d] ii. 4. 21.

οὐκ ἔχοντες λυποῦνται, οὕτως ἔχοντες ἐπὶ τοῖς ἐναντίοις ἡσθήσονται. ὥστε ἂν αὐτοὶ μὲν παρασκευα-
σθῶσιν οὕτως ἔχειν, οἱ δ' ἐλεεῖσθαι ἢ τυγχάνειν
τινὸς ἀγαθοῦ ἀξιούμενοι ὦσιν οἷοι οἱ εἰρημένοι,
δῆλον ὡς οὐ τεύξονται ἐλέου παρὰ τῶν κυρίων.

11. Πῶς δ' ἔχοντες ζηλοῦσι καὶ τὰ ποῖα καὶ
ἐπὶ τίσιν, ἐντεῦθέν ἐστι δῆλον. εἰ γάρ ἐστι ζῆλος
λύπη τις ἐπὶ φαινομένῃ παρουσίᾳ ἀγαθῶν ἐντίμων
καὶ ἐνδεχομένων αὐτῷ λαβεῖν περὶ τοὺς ὁμοίους τῇ
φύσει, οὐχ ὅτι ἄλλῳ ἀλλ' ὅτι οὐχὶ καὶ αὐτῷ ἐστίν·
διὸ καὶ ἐπιεικές ἐστιν ὁ ζῆλος καὶ ἐπιεικῶν, τὸ
δὲ φθονεῖν φαῦλον καὶ φαύλων· ὁ μὲν γὰρ αὑτὸν
παρασκευάζει διὰ τὸν ζῆλον τυγχάνειν τῶν ἀγαθῶν,
ὁ δὲ τὸν πλησίον μὴ ἔχειν διὰ τὸν φθόνον· ἀνάγκη
δὴ ζηλωτικοὺς μὲν εἶναι τοὺς ἀξιοῦντας αὑτοὺς
1388 b ἀγαθῶν ὧν μὴ ἔχουσιν· οὐδεὶς γὰρ ἀξιοῖ τὰ φαινό-
2 μενα ἀδύνατα. διὸ οἱ νέοι καὶ οἱ μεγαλόψυχοι
τοιοῦτοι. καὶ οἷς ὑπάρχει τοιαῦτα ἀγαθὰ ἃ τῶν
ἐντίμων ἄξιά ἐστιν ἀνδρῶν· ἔστι γὰρ ταῦτα πλοῦτος
καὶ πολυφιλία καὶ ἀρχαὶ καὶ ὅσα τοιαῦτα· ὡς γὰρ
προσῆκον αὐτοῖς ἀγαθοῖς εἶναι, ὅτι προσῆκε τοῖς
ἀγαθῶς ἔχουσι, ζηλοῦσι τὰ τοιαῦτα τῶν ἀγαθῶν.
3 καὶ οὓς οἱ ἄλλοι ἀξιοῦσιν. καὶ ὧν πρόγονοι ἢ
συγγενεῖς ἢ οἰκεῖοι ἢ τὸ ἔθνος ἢ ἡ πόλις ἔντιμοι,

─────────────

[a] " The same state of mind which is absent in the painful
feeling will be present in the joy excited by the opposite
occasions," meaning that, if one set of circumstances produces pain, the opposite will produce pleasure (Cope). Or,
omitting οὐκ before ἔχοντες, " For in the same frame of
mind as they are pained (at another's good fortune) they
will rejoice in the contrary state of things " (at another's bad
fortune).

[b] Something like " although they are within their grasp "
is needed to complete the sense.

not possess certain things, they are pained, so when they do possess them, they will rejoice in the opposite circumstances.[a] So that if the judges are brought into that frame of mind, and those who claim their pity or any other boon are such as we have stated, it is plain that they will not obtain pity from those with whom the decision rests.

11. The frame of mind in which men feel emulation, what things and persons give rise to it, will be clear from the following considerations. Let us assume that emulation is a feeling of pain at the evident presence of highly valued goods, which are possible for us to obtain, in the possession of those who naturally resemble us—pain not due to the fact that another possesses them, but to the fact that we ourselves do not. Emulation therefore is virtuous and characteristic of virtuous men, whereas envy is base and characteristic of base men; for the one, owing to emulation, fits himself to obtain such goods, while the object of the other, owing to envy, is to prevent his neighbour possessing them. Necessarily, then, those are emulous who hold that they have a claim to goods that they do not possess;[b] for no one claims what seems impossible. Hence the young and high-minded are emulous. And so are those who possess such advantages as are worthy of honourable men, which include wealth, a number of friends, positions of office, and all similar things. For, believing it their duty to be good, because such goods naturally belong to those who are good, they strive to preserve them. And those are emulous, whom others think worthy of them. Honours obtained by ancestors, kinsfolk, intimates, nation, or

ζηλωτικοὶ περὶ ταῦτα· οἰκεῖα γὰρ οἴονται αὑτοῖς
4 εἶναι, καὶ ἄξιοι τούτων. εἰ δ' ἐστὶ ζηλωτὰ τὰ
ἔντιμα ἀγαθά, ἀνάγκη τάς τε ἀρετὰς εἶναι τοιαύτας,
καὶ ὅσα τοῖς ἄλλοις ὠφέλιμα καὶ εὐεργετικά·
τιμῶσι γὰρ τοὺς εὐεργετοῦντας καὶ τοὺς ἀγαθούς.
καὶ ὅσων ἀγαθῶν ἀπόλαυσις τοῖς πλησίον ἐστίν,
οἷον πλοῦτος καὶ κάλλος μᾶλλον ὑγιείας.
5 Φανερὸν δὲ καὶ οἱ ζηλωτοὶ τίνες· οἱ γὰρ ταῦτα
καὶ τὰ τοιαῦτα κεκτημένοι ζηλωτοί. ἔστι δὲ
ταῦτα τὰ εἰρημένα, οἷον ἀνδρία σοφία ἀρχή· οἱ γὰρ
ἄρχοντες πολλοὺς δύνανται εὖ ποιεῖν, στρατηγοί,
6 ῥήτορες, πάντες οἱ τὰ τοιαῦτα δυνάμενοι. καὶ
οἷς πολλοὶ ὅμοιοι βούλονται εἶναι, ἢ πολλοὶ γνώ-
ριμοι, ἢ φίλοι πολλοί. ἢ οὓς πολλοὶ θαυμάζουσιν,
7 ἢ οὓς αὐτοὶ θαυμάζουσιν. καὶ ὧν ἔπαινοι καὶ
ἐγκώμια λέγονται ἢ ὑπὸ ποιητῶν ἢ λογογράφων.
καταφρονοῦσι δὲ τῶν ἐναντίων· ἐναντίον γὰρ
ζήλῳ καταφρόνησίς ἐστι, καὶ τὸ ζηλοῦν τῷ καταφρονεῖν. ἀνάγκη δὲ τοὺς οὕτως ἔχοντας ὥστε ζη-
λῶσαί τινας ἢ ζηλοῦσθαι, καταφρονητικοὺς εἶναι
τούτων τε καὶ ἐπὶ τούτοις ὅσοι τὰ ἐναντία κακὰ
ἔχουσι τῶν ἀγαθῶν τῶν ζηλωτῶν. διὸ πολλάκις
καταφρονοῦσι τῶν εὐτυχούντων, ὅταν ἄνευ τῶν ἐντίμων ἀγαθῶν ὑπάρχῃ αὐτοῖς ἡ τύχη. δι' ὧν μὲν

---

[a] Spending one's money benefits one's neighbour to a
certain extent, and beauty is always pleasant to look upon.
One does not admire anyone because he is in good health,
so much as because he is handsome.

[b] " Who have many acquaintances or friends " (Jebb).

[c] λογογράφοι means either the oldest Greek historians
(or rather " chroniclers "), or the writers of speeches for use
in the law courts, or of panegyrics.

[d] καὶ ἐπὶ τούτοις. According to Cope, an unnecessary

city make men emulous in regard to such honours; for
they think that these honours really belong to them
and that they are worthy of them. And if highly
valued goods are the object of emulation, it necessarily follows that the virtues must be such and all
things that are useful and beneficial to the rest of
mankind, for benefactors and virtuous men are
honoured; to these we may add all the goods which
our neighbours can enjoy with us, such as wealth
and beauty, rather than health.[a]

It is also evident who are the objects of emulation;
for they are those who possess these or similar
goods, such as have already been spoken of, for
instance, courage, wisdom, authority; for those in
authority, such as generals, orators, and all who have
similar powers, can do good to many. And those
whom many desire to be like, or to be their acquaintances or friends;[b] those whom many or ourselves
admire; those who are praised or eulogized either
by poets or by prose writers.[c] The opposite characters we despise; for contempt is the opposite of
emulation, and the idea of emulation of the idea of
contempt. And those who are in a condition which
makes them emulate, or be emulated by, others, must
be inclined to despise those persons[d] (and for that
reason) who suffer from defects contrary to the
good things which excite emulation. That is why
we often despise those who are fortunate, whenever
their good fortune is not accompanied by highly
valued goods. The means of producing and destroy-

parenthetical note ("and on such occasions"). Jebb refers
both τούτων and τούτοις to persons: "tend to show contempt
to or about those who." The "reason" in the translation
above is that they suffer from the want of "the highly
valued goods."

οὖν τὰ πάθη ἐγγίγνεται καὶ διαλύεται, ἐξ ὧν αἱ
πίστεις γίγνονται περὶ αὐτῶν, εἴρηται.

12. Τὰ δὲ ἤθη ποῖοί τινες κατὰ τὰ πάθη καὶ
τὰς ἕξεις καὶ τὰς ἡλικίας καὶ τὰς τύχας, διέλθωμεν
2 μετὰ ταῦτα. λέγω δὲ πάθη μὲν ὀργὴν ἐπιθυμίαν
καὶ τὰ τοιαῦτα, περὶ ὧν εἰρήκαμεν πρότερον,
ἕξεις δὲ ἀρετὰς καὶ κακίας· εἴρηται δὲ περὶ τούτων
πρότερον, καὶ ποῖα προαιροῦνται ἕκαστοι, καὶ ποίων
1389 a πρακτικοί. ἡλικίαι δ' εἰσὶ νεότης καὶ ἀκμὴ καὶ
γῆρας. τύχην δὲ λέγω εὐγένειαν καὶ πλοῦτον καὶ
δυνάμεις καὶ τἀναντία τούτοις καὶ ὅλως εὐτυχίαν καὶ
δυστυχίαν.

3 Οἱ μὲν οὖν νέοι τὰ ἤθη εἰσὶν ἐπιθυμητικοί, καὶ
οἷοι ποιεῖν ὧν ἂν ἐπιθυμήσωσιν. καὶ τῶν περὶ
τὸ σῶμα ἐπιθυμιῶν μάλιστα ἀκολουθητικοί εἰσι
ταῖς περὶ τὰ ἀφροδίσια, καὶ ἀκρατεῖς ταύτης.
4 εὐμετάβολοι δὲ καὶ ἁψίκοροι πρὸς τὰς ἐπιθυμίας,
καὶ σφόδρα μὲν ἐπιθυμοῦσι, ταχέως δὲ παύονται·
ὀξεῖαι γὰρ αἱ βουλήσεις καὶ οὐ μεγάλαι, ὥσπερ
5 αἱ τῶν καμνόντων δίψαι καὶ πεῖναι. καὶ θυμικοὶ
καὶ ὀξύθυμοι καὶ οἷοι ἀκολουθεῖν τῇ ὁρμῇ, καὶ
ἥττους εἰσὶ τοῦ θυμοῦ· διὰ γὰρ φιλοτιμίαν οὐκ
ἀνέχονται ὀλιγωρούμενοι, ἀλλ' ἀγανακτοῦσιν, ἂν
6 οἴωνται ἀδικεῖσθαι. καὶ φιλότιμοι μέν εἰσι, μᾶλλον δὲ φιλόνικοι· ὑπεροχῆς γὰρ ἐπιθυμεῖ ἡ νεότης,
ἡ δὲ νίκη ὑπεροχή τις. καὶ ἄμφω ταῦτα μᾶλλον
ἢ φιλοχρήματοι· φιλοχρήματοι δὲ ἥκιστα διὰ τὸ
μήπω ἐνδείας πεπειρᾶσθαι, ὥσπερ τὸ Πιττακοῦ
7 ἔχει ἀπόφθεγμα εἰς Ἀμφιάραον. καὶ οὐ κακοήθεις

ᵃ The πίστις ἠθική is resumed from ii. 1. 8. As the πάθη
and ἕξεις have been discussed already, only the ages and
their character remain.

ing the various emotions in men, from which the
methods of persuasion that concern them are derived,
have now been stated.

12. Let us now describe the nature of the characters of men according to their emotions, habits,
ages, and fortunes. By the emotions I mean anger,
desire, and the like, of which we have already spoken;
by habits virtues and vices, of which also we have
previously spoken, as well as the kind of things men
individually and deliberately choose and practise.
The ages are youth, the prime of life, and old age.
By fortune I mean noble birth, wealth, power, and
their contraries, and, in general, good or bad fortune.[a]

The young, as to character, are ready to desire
and to carry out what they desire. Of the bodily
desires they chiefly obey those of sensual pleasure
and these they are unable to control. Changeable
in their desires and soon tiring of them, they desire
with extreme ardour, but soon cool; for their will,
like the hunger and thirst of the sick, is keen rather
than strong. They are passionate, hot-tempered,
and carried away by impulse, and unable to control
their passion; for owing to their ambition they
cannot endure to be slighted, and become indignant
when they think they are being wronged. They are
ambitious of honour, but more so of victory; for
youth desires superiority, and victory is a kind of
superiority. And their desire for both these is
greater than their desire for money, to which they
attach only the slightest value, because they have
never yet experienced want, as Pittacus[b] said in
his pithy remark on Amphiaraus. They are not ill-

[b] One of the Seven Wise Men of Greece.

ἀλλ' εὐήθεις διὰ τὸ μήπω τεθεωρηκέναι πολλὰς
πονηρίας. καὶ εὔπιστοι διὰ τὸ μήπω πολλὰ
8 ἐξηπατῆσθαι. καὶ εὐέλπιδες· ὥσπερ γὰρ οἱ οἰνω-
μένοι, οὕτω διάθερμοί εἰσιν οἱ νέοι ὑπὸ τῆς φύσεως·
ἅμα δὲ καὶ διὰ τὸ μήπω πολλὰ ἀποτετυχηκέναι.
καὶ ζῶσι τὰ πλεῖστα ἐλπίδι· ἡ μὲν γὰρ ἐλπὶς τοῦ
μέλλοντός ἐστιν ἡ δὲ μνήμη τοῦ παροιχομένου,
τοῖς δὲ νέοις τὸ μὲν μέλλον πολὺ τὸ δὲ παρεληλυθὸς βραχύ· τῇ γὰρ πρώτῃ ἡμέρᾳ μεμνῆσθαι
μὲν οὐδὲν οἷόν τε, ἐλπίζειν δὲ πάντα. καὶ εὐ-
εξαπάτητοί εἰσι διὰ τὸ εἰρημένον· ἐλπίζουσι γὰρ
9 ῥᾳδίως. καὶ ἀνδρειότεροι· θυμώδεις γὰρ καὶ εὐέλ-
πιδες, ὧν τὸ μὲν μὴ φοβεῖσθαι τὸ δὲ θαρρεῖν ποιεῖ·
οὔτε γὰρ ὀργιζόμενος οὐδεὶς φοβεῖται, τό τε
10 ἐλπίζειν ἀγαθόν τι θαρραλέον ἐστίν. καὶ αἰσχυν-
τηλοί· οὐ γάρ πω καλὰ ἕτερα ὑπολαμβάνουσιν, ἀλλὰ
11 πεπαίδευνται ὑπὸ τοῦ νόμου μόνον. καὶ μεγαλό-
ψυχοι· οὔτε γὰρ ὑπὸ τοῦ βίου πω τεταπείνωνται,
ἀλλὰ τῶν ἀναγκαίων ἄπειροί εἰσιν, καὶ τὸ ἀξιοῦν
αὑτὸν μεγάλων μεγαλοψυχία· τοῦτο δ' εὐέλπιδος.
12 Καὶ μᾶλλον αἱροῦνται πράττειν τὰ καλὰ τῶν
συμφερόντων· τῷ γὰρ ἤθει ζῶσι μᾶλλον ἢ τῷ
λογισμῷ, ἔστι δ' ὁ μὲν λογισμὸς τοῦ συμφέροντος
13 ἡ δὲ ἀρετὴ τοῦ καλοῦ. καὶ φιλόφιλοι καὶ φιλ-
1389 b ἑταιροι μᾶλλον τῶν ἄλλων ἡλικιῶν διὰ τὸ χαίρειν
τῷ συζῆν καὶ μήπω πρὸς τὸ συμφέρον κρίνειν

---

[a] Or, "they do not look at things in a bad light, but in a
good," *i.e.* they are not always ready to suspect.

[b] Social convention is the only law that they know, and
they are ashamed if they violate it, because as yet they have
no idea of higher laws which may command them to do so.

[c] ἦθος "in the widest sense, includes all that is habitual

248

natured but simple-natured,[a] because they have never yet witnessed much depravity ; confiding, because they have as yet not been often deceived ; full of hope, for they are naturally as hot-blooded as those who are drunken with wine, and besides they have not yet experienced many failures. For the most part they live in hope, for hope is concerned with the future as memory is with the past. For the young the future is long, the past short ; for in the morning of life it is not possible for them to re-member anything, but they have everything to hope ; which makes them easy to deceive, for they readily hope. And they are more courageous, for they are full of passion and hope, and the former of these prevents them fearing, while the latter inspires them with confidence, for no one fears when angry, and hope of some advantage inspires confidence. And they are bashful, for as yet they fail to conceive of other things that are noble, but have been educated solely by convention.[b] They are high-minded, for they have not yet been humbled by life nor have they experienced the force of necessity ; further, there is high-mindedness in thinking oneself worthy of great things, a feeling which belongs to one who is full of hope.

In their actions, they prefer the noble to the useful ; their life is guided by their character[c] rather than by calculation, for the latter aims at the useful, virtue at the noble. At this age more than any other they are fond of their friends and companions, because they take pleasure in living in company and as yet judge nothing by expediency, not even their

and characteristic ; in a limited sense, it expresses the habitual temper or disposition " (Twining).

ARISTOTLE

14 μηδέν, ὥστε μηδὲ τοὺς φίλους. καὶ ἄπαντα ἐπὶ
τὸ μᾶλλον καὶ σφοδρότερον ἁμαρτάνουσι παρὰ
τὸ Χιλώνειον· πάντα γὰρ ἄγαν πράττουσιν· φιλοῦσί
τε γὰρ ἄγαν καὶ μισοῦσιν ἄγαν καὶ τἆλλα πάντα
ὁμοίως. καὶ εἰδέναι πάντα οἴονται καὶ διισχυρί-
ζονται· τοῦτο γὰρ αἴτιόν ἐστι καὶ τοῦ πάντα ἄγαν.
15 καὶ τὰ ἀδικήματα ἀδικοῦσιν εἰς ὕβριν καὶ οὐ
κακουργίαν. καὶ ἐλεητικοὶ διὰ τὸ πάντας χρηστοὺς καὶ βελτίους ὑπολαμβάνειν· τῇ γὰρ αὑτῶν
ἀκακίᾳ τοὺς πέλας μετροῦσιν, ὥστ' ἀνάξια πάσχειν
16 ὑπολαμβάνουσιν αὐτούς. καὶ φιλογέλωτες, διὸ καὶ
εὐτράπελοι· ἡ γὰρ εὐτραπελία πεπαιδευμένη ὕβρις
ἐστίν. τὸ μὲν οὖν τῶν νέων τοιοῦτόν ἐστιν ἦθος.

13. Οἱ δὲ πρεσβύτεροι καὶ παρηκμακότες σχεδὸν
ἐκ τῶν ἐναντίων τούτοις τὰ πλεῖστα ἔχουσιν ἤθη·
διὰ γὰρ τὸ πολλὰ ἔτη βεβιωκέναι καὶ πλείω ἐξηπατῆσθαι καὶ ἡμαρτηκέναι, καὶ τὰ πλείω φαῦλα
εἶναι τῶν πραγμάτων, οὔτε διαβεβαιοῦνται οὐδέν,
2 ἧττόν τε ἄγαν ἄπαντα ἢ δεῖ. καὶ οἴονται, ἴσασι
δ' οὐδέν. καὶ ἀμφισβητοῦντες προστιθέασιν ἀεὶ
τὸ ἴσως καὶ τάχα, καὶ πάντα λέγουσιν οὕτω,
3 παγίως δ' οὐδέν. καὶ κακοήθεις εἰσίν· ἔστι γὰρ
κακοήθεια τὸ ἐπὶ τὸ χεῖρον ὑπολαμβάνειν πάντα.
ἔτι δὲ καχύποπτοί εἰσι διὰ τὴν ἀπιστίαν, ἄπιστοι
4 δὲ δι' ἐμπειρίαν. καὶ οὔτε φιλοῦσι σφόδρα οὔτε
μισοῦσι διὰ ταῦτα, ἀλλὰ κατὰ τὴν Βίαντος ὑποθήκην
καὶ φιλοῦσιν ὡς μισήσοντες καὶ μισοῦσιν ὡς
5 φιλήσοντες. καὶ μικρόψυχοι διὰ τὸ τεταπεινῶσθαι

---

[a] One of the Seven Wise Men of Greece. The maxim was
Μηδὲν ἄγαν, *Ne quid nimis,* Never go to extremes.
[b] Or, " better than they really are."
[c] One of the Seven Wise Men of Greece.

250

friends. All their errors are due to excess and vehemence and their neglect of the maxim of Chilon,[a] for they do everything to excess, love, hate, and everything else. And they think they know everything, and confidently affirm it, and this is the cause of their excess in everything. If they do wrong, it is due to insolence, not to wickedness. And they are inclined to pity, because they think all men are virtuous and better than themselves [b]; for they measure their neighbours by their own inoffensiveness, so that they think that they suffer undeservedly. And they are fond of laughter, and therefore witty; for wit is cultured insolence. Such then is the character of the young.

13. Older men and those who have passed their prime have in most cases characters opposite to those of the young. For, owing to their having lived many years and having been more often deceived by others or made more mistakes themselves, and since most human things turn out badly, they are positive about nothing, and in everything they show an excessive lack of energy. They always " think," but " know " nothing; and in their hesitation they always add " perhaps," or " maybe "; all their statements are of this kind, never unqualified. They are malicious; for malice consists in looking upon the worse side of everything. Further, they are always suspicious owing to mistrust, and mistrustful owing to experience. And neither their love nor their hatred is strong for the same reasons; but, according to the precept of Bias,[c] they love as if they would one day hate, and hate as if they would one day love. And they are little-minded, because they

ὑπὸ τοῦ βίου· οὐδενὸς γὰρ μεγάλου οὐδὲ περιττοῦ,
6 ἀλλὰ τῶν πρὸς τὸν βίον ἐπιθυμοῦσιν. καὶ ἀν-
ελεύθεροι· ἓν γάρ τι τῶν ἀναγκαίων ἡ οὐσία, ἅμα
δὲ καὶ διὰ τὴν ἐμπειρίαν ἴσασιν ὡς χαλεπὸν τὸ
7 κτήσασθαι καὶ ῥᾴδιον τὸ ἀποβαλεῖν. καὶ δειλοὶ
καὶ πάντα προφοβητικοί· ἐναντίως γὰρ διάκεινται
τοῖς νέοις· κατεψυγμένοι γάρ εἰσιν, οἱ δὲ θερμοί.
ὥστε προωδοποίηκε τὸ γῆρας τῇ δειλίᾳ· καὶ γὰρ
8 ὁ φόβος κατάψυξίς τις ἐστίν. καὶ φιλόζωοι, καὶ
μάλιστα ἐπὶ τῇ τελευταίᾳ ἡμέρᾳ διὰ τὸ τοῦ ἀπόντος
εἶναι τὴν ἐπιθυμίαν, καὶ οὗ δὲ ἐνδεεῖς, τούτου
9 μάλιστα ἐπιθυμεῖν. καὶ φίλαυτοι μᾶλλον ἢ δεῖ·
μικροψυχία γάρ τις καὶ αὕτη. καὶ πρὸς τὸ συμφέρον ζῶσιν, ἀλλ' οὐ πρὸς τὸ καλόν, μᾶλλον ἢ
δεῖ, διὰ τὸ φίλαυτοι εἶναι· τὸ μὲν γὰρ συμφέρον
1390 a αὐτῷ ἀγαθόν ἐστι, τὸ δὲ καλὸν ἁπλῶς.
10 Καὶ ἀναίσχυντοι μᾶλλον ἢ αἰσχυντηλοί· διὰ γὰρ
τὸ μὴ φροντίζειν ὁμοίως τοῦ καλοῦ καὶ τοῦ συμ-
11 φέροντος ὀλιγωροῦσι τοῦ δοκεῖν. καὶ δυσέλπιδες
διὰ τὴν ἐμπειρίαν· τὰ γὰρ πλείω τῶν γιγνομένων
φαῦλά ἐστιν· ἀποβαίνει γοῦν τὰ πολλὰ ἐπὶ τὸ
12 χεῖρον· καὶ ἔτι διὰ τὴν δειλίαν. καὶ ζῶσι τῇ μνήμῃ
μᾶλλον ἢ τῇ ἐλπίδι· τοῦ γὰρ βίου τὸ μὲν λοιπὸν
ὀλίγον τὸ δὲ παρεληλυθὸς πολύ, ἔστι δὲ ἡ μὲν
ἐλπὶς τοῦ μέλλοντος ἡ δὲ μνήμη τῶν παροιχομένων.
ὅπερ αἴτιον καὶ τῆς ἀδολεσχίας αὐτοῖς· διατελοῦσι
γὰρ τὰ γενόμενα λέγοντες· ἀναμιμνησκόμενοι γὰρ
13 ἥδονται. καὶ οἱ θυμοὶ ὀξεῖς μὲν ἀσθενεῖς δέ
εἰσιν, καὶ αἱ ἐπιθυμίαι αἱ μὲν ἐκλελοίπασιν αἱ
δὲ ἀσθενεῖς εἰσιν, ὥστε οὔτ' ἐπιθυμητικοὶ οὔτε
πρακτικοὶ κατὰ τὰς ἐπιθυμίας, ἀλλὰ κατὰ τὸ

have been humbled by life ; for they desire nothing great or uncommon, but only the necessaries of life. They are not generous, for property is one of these necessaries, and at the same time, they know from experience how hard it is to get and how easy to lose. And they are cowardly and inclined to anticipate evil, for their state of mind is the opposite of that of the young ; they are chilled, whereas the young are hot, so that old age paves the way for cowardice, for fear is a kind of chill. And they are fond of life, especially in their last days, because desire is directed towards that which is absent and men especially desire what they lack. And they are unduly selfish, for this also is littleness of mind. And they live not for the noble, but for the useful, more than they ought, because they are selfish ; for the useful is a good for the individual, whereas the noble is good absolutely.

And they are rather shameless than modest ; for since they do not care for the noble so much as for the useful, they pay little attention to what people think. And they are little given to hope owing to their experience, for things that happen are mostly bad and at all events generally turn out for the worse, and also owing to their cowardice. They live in memory rather than in hope ; for the life that remains to them is short, but that which is past is long, and hope belongs to the future, memory to the past. This is the reason of their loquacity ; for they are incessantly talking of the past, because they take pleasure in recollection. Their outbursts of anger are violent, but feeble ; of their desires some have ceased, while others are weak, so that they neither feel them nor act in accordance with them, but only

253

κέρδος. διὸ καὶ σωφρονικοὶ φαίνονται οἱ τηλικοῦτοι·
αἵ τε γὰρ ἐπιθυμίαι ἀνείκασι, καὶ δουλεύουσι τῷ
14 κέρδει. καὶ μᾶλλον ζῶσι κατὰ λογισμὸν ἢ κατὰ
τὸ ἦθος· ὁ μὲν γὰρ λογισμὸς τοῦ συμφέροντος τὸ
δ' ἦθος τῆς ἀρετῆς ἐστιν. καὶ τἀδικήματα ἀδι-
15 κοῦσιν εἰς κακουργίαν, οὐκ εἰς ὕβριν. ἐλεητικοὶ δὲ
καὶ οἱ γέροντές εἰσιν, ἀλλ' οὐ διὰ ταὐτὸ τοῖς νέοις·
οἱ μὲν γὰρ διὰ φιλανθρωπίαν, οἱ δὲ δι' ἀσθένειαν·
πάντα γὰρ οἴονται ἐγγὺς εἶναι αὑτοῖς παθεῖν,
τοῦτο δ' ἦν ἐλεητικόν. ὅθεν ὀδυρτικοί εἰσι, καὶ
οὐκ εὐτράπελοι οὐδὲ φιλογέλοιοι· ἐναντίον γὰρ τὸ
16 ὀδυρτικὸν τῷ φιλογέλωτι. τῶν μὲν οὖν νέων καὶ
τῶν πρεσβυτέρων τὰ ἤθη τοιαῦτα· ὥστ' ἐπεὶ
ἀποδέχονται πάντες τοὺς τῷ σφετέρῳ ἤθει λεγο-
μένους λόγους καὶ τοὺς ὁμοίους, οὐκ ἄδηλον πῶς
χρώμενοι τοῖς λόγοις τοιοῦτοι φανοῦνται καὶ αὐτοὶ
καὶ οἱ λόγοι.

14. Οἱ δὲ ἀκμάζοντες φανερὸν ὅτι μεταξὺ
τούτων τὸ ἦθος ἔσονται, ἑκατέρων ἀφαιροῦντες
τὴν ὑπερβολήν, καὶ οὔτε σφόδρα θαρροῦντες
(θρασύτης γὰρ τὸ τοιοῦτον) οὔτε λίαν φοβούμενοι,
2 καλῶς δὲ πρὸς ἄμφω ἔχοντες, οὔτε πᾶσι πιστεύοντες
οὔτε πᾶσιν ἀπιστοῦντες, ἀλλὰ κατὰ τὸ ἀληθὲς
1390 b κρίνοντες μᾶλλον. καὶ οὔτε πρὸς τὸ καλὸν ζῶντες
μόνον οὔτε πρὸς τὸ συμφέρον, ἀλλὰ πρὸς ἄμφω.
καὶ οὔτε πρὸς φειδὼ οὔτε πρὸς ἀσωτίαν, ἀλλὰ πρὸς
3 τὸ ἁρμόττον. ὁμοίως δὲ καὶ πρὸς θυμὸν καὶ
πρὸς ἐπιθυμίαν. καὶ σώφρονες μετ' ἀνδρίας καὶ

ᵃ Or, " speeches which resemble (or reflect) it " (their
character).

from motives of gain. Hence men of this age are regarded as self-controlled, for their desires have slackened, and they are slaves to gain. In their manner of life there is more calculation than moral character, for calculation is concerned with that which is useful, moral character with virtue. If they commit acts of injustice it is due to vice rather than to insolence. The old, like the young, are inclined to pity, but not for the same reason ; the latter show pity from humanity, the former from weakness, because they think that they are on the point of suffering all kinds of misfortunes, and this is one of the reasons that incline men to pity. That is why the old are querulous, and neither witty nor fond of laughter ; for a querulous disposition is the opposite of a love of laughter. Such are the characters of the young and older men. Wherefore, since all men are willing to listen to speeches which harmonize with their own character and to speakers who resemble them,[a] it is easy to see what language we must employ so that both ourselves and our speeches may appear to be of such and such a character.

14. It is evident that the character of those in the prime of life will be the mean between that of the other two, if the excess in each case be removed. At this age, men are neither over-confident, which would show rashness, nor too fearful, but preserving a right attitude in regard to both, neither trusting nor distrusting all, but judging rather in accordance with actual facts. Their rule of conduct is neither the noble nor the useful alone, but both at once. They are neither parsimonious nor prodigal, but preserve the due mean. It is the same in regard to passion and desire. Their self-control is combined

ἀνδρεῖοι μετὰ σωφροσύνης. ἐν γὰρ τοῖς νέοις καὶ
τοῖς γέρουσι διήρηται ταῦτα· εἰσὶ γὰρ οἱ μὲν νέοι
ἀνδρεῖοι καὶ ἀκόλαστοι, οἱ δὲ πρεσβύτεροι σώφρονες
καὶ δειλοί. ὡς δὲ καθόλου εἰπεῖν, ὅσα μὲν διήρηται
ἡ νεότης καὶ τὸ γῆρας τῶν ὠφελίμων, ταῦτα ἄμφω
ἔχουσιν, ὅσα δ' ὑπερβάλλουσιν ἢ ἐλλείπουσι,
4 τούτων τὸ μέτριον καὶ τὸ ἁρμόττον. ἀκμάζει δὲ
τὸ μὲν σῶμα ἀπὸ τῶν τριάκοντα ἐτῶν μέχρι τῶν
πέντε καὶ τριάκοντα, ἡ δὲ ψυχὴ περὶ τὰ ἑνὸς δεῖν
πεντήκοντα. περὶ μὲν οὖν νεότητος καὶ γήρως
καὶ ἀκμῆς, ποίων ἠθῶν ἔκαστόν ἐστιν, εἰρήσθω
τοσαῦτα.

15. Περὶ δὲ τῶν ἀπὸ τύχης γιγνομένων ἀγαθῶν,
δι' ὅσα αὐτῶν καὶ τὰ ἤθη ποιά ἄττα συμβαίνει
2 τοῖς ἀνθρώποις, λέγωμεν ἐφεξῆς. εὐγενείας μὲν
οὖν ἦθός ἐστι τὸ φιλοτιμότερον εἶναι τὸν κεκτη-
μένον αὐτήν· ἅπαντες γάρ, ὅταν ὑπάρχῃ τι, πρὸς
τοῦτο σωρεύειν εἰώθασιν, ἡ δ' εὐγένεια ἐντιμότης
τις προγόνων ἐστίν. καὶ καταφρονητικὸν καὶ
τῶν ὁμοίων ἐστὶ τοῖς προγόνοις τοῖς αὑτῶν, διότι
πόρρω ταῦτα μᾶλλον ἢ ἐγγὺς γιγνόμενα ἐντιμότερα
3 καὶ εὐαλαζόνευτα. ἔστι δὲ εὐγενὲς μὲν κατὰ τὴν
τοῦ γένους ἀρετήν, γενναῖον δὲ κατὰ τὸ μὴ ἐξ-
ίστασθαι τῆς φύσεως· ὅπερ ὡς ἐπὶ τὸ πολὺ οὐ
συμβαίνει τοῖς εὐγενέσιν, ἀλλ' εἰσὶν οἱ πολλοὶ
εὐτελεῖς· φορὰ γάρ τίς ἐστιν ἐν τοῖς γένεσιν ἀνδρῶν
ὥσπερ ἐν τοῖς κατὰ τὰς χώρας γιγνομένοις, καὶ
ἐνίοτε ἂν ᾖ ἀγαθὸν τὸ γένος, ἐγγίνονται διά τινος
χρόνου ἄνδρες περιττοί, κἄπειτα πάλιν ἀναδιδωσιν.
ἐξίσταται δὲ τὰ μὲν εὐφυᾶ γένη εἰς μανικώτερα

---

* i.e. the advantages and distinctions the family possessed

with courage and their courage with self-control, whereas in the young and old these qualities are found separately; for the young are courageous but without self-control, the old are self-controlled but cowardly. Speaking generally, all the advantages that youth and old age possess separately, those in the prime of life possess combined; and all cases of excess or defect in the other two are replaced by due moderation and fitness. The body is most fully developed from thirty to thirty-five years of age, the mind at about forty-nine. Let this suffice for youth, old age, and the prime of life, and the characters which belong to each.

15. Let us next speak of the goods that are due to fortune, all those, at least, which produce certain characters in men. A characteristic of noble birth is that he who possesses it is more ambitious; for all men, when they start with any good, are accustomed to heap it up, and noble birth is a heritage of honour from one's ancestors. Such men are prone to look down even upon·those who are as important as their ancestors, because the same things [a] are more honourable and inspire greater vanity when remote than when they are recent. The idea of noble birth refers to excellence of race, that of noble character to not degenerating from the family type, a quality not as a rule found in those of noble birth, most of whom are good for nothing. For in the generations of men there is a kind of crop as in the fruits of the field; sometimes, if the race is good, for a certain period men out of the common are born in it, and then it deteriorates. Highly gifted families often

of old; such distinctions, when possessed by those of later date, are less thought of.

ἤθη, οἷον οἱ ἀπ᾽ Ἀλκιβιάδου καὶ οἱ ἀπὸ Διονυσίου
τοῦ προτέρου, τὰ δὲ στάσιμα εἰς ἀβελτερίαν καὶ
νωθρότητα, οἷον οἱ ἀπὸ Κίμωνος καὶ Περικλέους
καὶ Σωκράτους.

16. Τῷ δὲ πλούτῳ ἃ ἕπεται ἤθη, ἐπιπολῆς
ἐστιν ἰδεῖν ἅπασιν· ὑβρισταὶ γὰρ καὶ ὑπερήφανοι,
πάσχοντές τι ὑπὸ τῆς κτήσεως τοῦ πλούτου· ὥσ-
1391 a περ γὰρ ἔχοντες ἅπαντα τἀγαθὰ οὕτω διάκεινται·
ὁ γὰρ πλοῦτος οἷον τιμή τις τῆς ἀξίας τῶν ἄλλων,
2 διὸ φαίνεται ὤνια ἅπαντα εἶναι αὐτοῦ. καὶ τρυφεροὶ καὶ σαλάκωνες, τρυφεροὶ μὲν διὰ τὴν τρυφὴν
καὶ τὴν ἔνδειξιν τῆς εὐδαιμονίας, σαλάκωνες δὲ
καὶ σόλοικοι διὰ τὸ πάντας εἰωθέναι διατρίβειν
περὶ τὸ ἐρώμενον καὶ θαυμαζόμενον ὑπ᾽ αὐτῶν,
καὶ τῷ οἴεσθαι ζηλοῦν τοὺς ἄλλους ἃ καὶ αὐτοί.
ἅμα δὲ καὶ εἰκότως τοῦτο πάσχουσιν· πολλοὶ γάρ
εἰσιν οἱ δεόμενοι τῶν ἐχόντων. ὅθεν καὶ τὸ
Σιμωνίδου εἴρηται περὶ τῶν σοφῶν καὶ πλουσίων
πρὸς τὴν γυναῖκα τὴν Ἱέρωνος ἐρομένην πότερον
γενέσθαι κρεῖττον πλούσιον ἢ σοφόν· πλούσιον
εἰπεῖν· τοὺς σοφοὺς γὰρ ἔφη ὁρᾶν ἐπὶ ταῖς τῶν
3 πλουσίων θύραις διατρίβοντας. καὶ τὸ οἴεσθαι
ἀξίους εἶναι ἄρχειν· ἔχειν γὰρ οἴονται ὧν ἕνεκεν
ἄρχειν ἄξιον. καὶ ὡς ἐν κεφαλαίῳ, ἀνοήτου εὐ-
4 δαίμονος ἦθος πλούτου ἐστίν. διαφέρει δὲ τοῖς
νεωστὶ κεκτημένοις καὶ τοῖς πάλαι τὰ ἤθη τῷ
ἅπαντα μᾶλλον καὶ φαυλότερα τὰ κακὰ ἔχειν τοὺς
νεοπλούτους· ὥσπερ γὰρ ἀπαιδευσία πλούτου ἐστὶ
τὸ νεόπλουτον εἶναι. καὶ ἀδικήματα ἀδικοῦσιν

degenerate into maniacs, as, for example, the descendants of Alcibiades and the elder Dionysius; those that are stable into fools and dullards, like the descendants of Cimon, Pericles, and Socrates.

16. The characters which accompany wealth are plain for all to see. The wealthy are insolent and arrogant, being mentally affected by the acquisition of wealth, for they seem to think that they possess all good things; for wealth is a kind of standard of value of everything else, so that everything seems purchasable by it. They are luxurious and swaggerers, luxurious because of their luxury and the display of their prosperity, swaggerers and ill-mannered because all men are accustomed to devote their attention to what they like and admire, and the rich suppose that what they themselves are emulous of is the object of all other men's emulation. At the same time this feeling is not unreasonable; for those who have need of the wealthy are many in number. Hence the answer of Simonides to the wife of Hiero concerning the wise and the rich, when she asked which was preferable, to be wise or to be rich. "Rich," he answered, "for we see the wise spending their time at the doors of the rich." And the rich think they are worthy to rule, because they believe they possess that which makes them so.[a] In a word, the character of the rich man is that of a fool favoured by fortune. At the same time there is a difference between the character of the newly rich and of those whose wealth is of long standing, because the former have the vices of wealth in a greater degree and more; for, so to say, they have not been educated to the use of wealth. Their unjust acts are not due to malice,

<hr>

[a] " What makes power worth having " (Cope).

ARISTOTLE

οὐ κακουργικά, ἀλλὰ τὰ μὲν ὑβριστικὰ τὰ δὲ ἀκρατευτικά, οἷον εἰς αἰκίαν καὶ μοιχείαν.

17. Ὁμοίως δὲ καὶ περὶ δυνάμεως σχεδὸν τὰ πλεῖστα φανερά ἐστιν ἤθη· τὰ μὲν γὰρ τὰ αὐτὰ ἔχει
2 ἡ δύναμις τῷ πλούτῳ τὰ δὲ βελτίω· φιλοτιμότεροι γὰρ καὶ ἀνδρωδέστεροί εἰσι τὰ ἤθη οἱ δυνάμενοι τῶν πλουσίων διὰ τὸ ἐφίεσθαι ἔργων ὅσα ἐξουσία
3 αὐτοῖς πράττειν διὰ τὴν δύναμιν. καὶ σπουδαστικώτεροι διὰ τὸ ἐν ἐπιμελείᾳ εἶναι, ἀναγκαζό-
4 μενοι σκοπεῖν τὰ περὶ τὴν δύναμιν. καὶ σεμνότεροι ἢ βαρύτεροι· ποιεῖ γὰρ ἐμφανεστέρους τὸ ἀξίωμα, διὸ μετριάζουσιν· ἔστι δὲ ἡ σεμνότης μαλακὴ καὶ εὐσχήμων βαρύτης. κἂν ἀδικῶσιν, οὐ μικραδικηταί εἰσιν ἀλλὰ μεγαλάδικοι.

5 Ἡ δ᾽ εὐτυχία κατὰ τὰ μόρια τῶν εἰρημένων ἔχει τὰ ἤθη· εἰς γὰρ ταῦτα συντείνουσιν αἱ μέγισται δοκοῦσαι εἶναι εὐτυχίαι, καὶ ἔτι εἰς εὐτεκνίαν καὶ
1391 b τὰ κατὰ τὸ σῶμα ἀγαθὰ παρασκευάζει ἡ εὐτυχία
6 πλεονεκτεῖν. ὑπερηφανώτεροι μὲν οὖν καὶ ἀλογιστότεροι διὰ τὴν εὐτυχίαν εἰσίν, ἓν δ᾽ ἀκολουθεῖ βέλτιστον ἦθος τῇ εὐτυχίᾳ, ὅτι φιλόθεοί εἰσι καὶ ἔχουσι πρὸς τὸ θεῖόν πως, πιστεύοντες διὰ τὰ γιγνόμενα ἀγαθὰ ἀπὸ τῆς τύχης. περὶ μὲν οὖν τῶν καθ᾽ ἡλικίαν καὶ τύχην ἠθῶν εἴρηται· τὰ γὰρ ἐναντία τῶν εἰρημένων ἐκ τῶν ἐναντίων

---

[a] ἐν ἐπιμελείᾳ: " because they are administrators " (Jebb).
[b] The three divisions are noble birth, wealth, and power. The meaning is that the highest kinds of good fortune tend or converge to these (*i.e.* to noble birth, wealth, and power). κατὰ τὰ μόρια might also mean "in part." Hobbes, in his *Brief of the Art of Rhetorick*, paraphrases: "the manners

260

but partly to insolence, partly to incontinence, which
tends to make them commit assault and battery and
adultery.

17. In regard to power, nearly all the characters
to which it gives rise are equally clear ; for power,
compared with wealth, exhibits partly identical, and
partly superior characteristics. Thus, the powerful
are more ambitious and more manly in character
than the rich, since they aim at the performance of
deeds which their power gives them the opportunity
of carrying out. And they are more energetic ; for
being obliged to look after their power, they are
always on the watch.[a] And they are dignified rather
than heavily pompous ; for their rank renders them
more conspicuous, so that they avoid excess ; and
this dignity is a mild and decent pomposity. And
their wrongdoings are never petty, but great.

Good fortune in its divisions [b] exhibits characters
corresponding to those which have just been mentioned ; for those which appear to be the most
important kinds of good fortune tend in their direction ; further, good fortune furnishes advantages
over others in the blessing of children and bodily
goods. Now, although men are more arrogant and
thoughtless owing to good fortune, it is accompanied
by a most precious quality. Fortunate men stand
in a certain relation to the divinity and love the
gods, having confidence in them owing to the benefits
they have received from fortune. We have spoken [c]
of the characters associated with different ages and
fortunes ; the opposite characters to those described,
of men that prosper, are compounded of the manners of the
nobility, the rich, and those that are in power, for to some of
these all prosperity appertains."

[c] ii. 12-14 ; ii. 15-17.

φανερά ἐστιν, οἷον πένητος καὶ ἀτυχοῦς ἦθος καὶ
ἀδυνάτου.

18. Ἐπεὶ δ' ἡ τῶν πιθανῶν λόγων χρῆσις πρὸς
κρίσιν ἐστί (περὶ ὧν γὰρ ἴσμεν καὶ κεκρίκαμεν,
οὐδὲν ἔτι δεῖ λόγου), ἔστι δέ, ἄν τε πρὸς ἕνα τις
τῷ λόγῳ χρώμενος προτρέπῃ ἢ ἀποτρέπῃ, οἷον
οἱ νουθετοῦντες ποιοῦσιν ἢ πείθοντες (οὐδὲν γὰρ
ἧττον κριτὴς ὁ εἷς· ὃν γὰρ δεῖ πεῖσαι, οὗτός ἐστιν
ὡς ἁπλῶς εἰπεῖν κριτής), ἐάν τε πρὸς ἀμφισβητοῦντα
ἐάν τε πρὸς ὑπόθεσιν λέγῃ τις, ὁμοίως· τῷ γὰρ
λόγῳ ἀνάγκη χρῆσθαι καὶ ἀναιρεῖν τἀναντία,
πρὸς ἃ ὥσπερ ἀμφισβητοῦντα τὸν λόγον ποιεῖται.
ὡσαύτως δὲ καὶ ἐν τοῖς ἐπιδεικτικοῖς· ὥσπερ γὰρ
πρὸς κριτὴν τὸν θεωρὸν ὁ λόγος συνέστηκεν.
ὅλως δὲ μόνος ἐστὶν ἁπλῶς κριτὴς ἐν τοῖς πολιτικοῖς ἀγῶσιν ὁ τὰ ζητούμενα κρίνων· τά τε γὰρ
ἀμφισβητούμενα ζητεῖται πῶς ἔχει, καὶ περὶ ὧν
βουλεύονται. περὶ δὲ τῶν κατὰ τὰς πολιτείας
ἠθῶν ἐν τοῖς συμβουλευτικοῖς εἴρηται πρότερον.
ὥστε διωρισμένον ἂν εἴη πῶς τε καὶ διὰ τίνων
τοὺς λόγους ἠθικοὺς ποιητέον.

ᵃ Having dealt with ethical and pathetic proofs, Aristotle
proceeds to the discussion of topics of enthymemes common
to all three kinds of Rhetoric. The difficulty *in the Greek*
lies in the absence of a suitable apodosis to the long sentence
beginning ἐπεὶ δὲ ἡ τῶν πιθανῶν. Grammatically, it might be
ὥστε διωρισμένον ἂν εἴη, but it by no means follows that "since
the employment of persuasive speeches is directed towards a
judgement . . . *therefore* it has been determined how . . .
we must make our speeches ethical." Spengel, regarding
ἐπεὶ δὲ . . . βουλεύονται merely as an enlargement of ii. 1, 2,
brackets the passage. Cope suggests that something has
fallen out after βουλεύονται: "Since in all the three kinds of
Rhetoric the object is to secure a judgement, [I have shown
how to put the judges into a certain frame of mind in the

for instance, of the poor, of the unfortunate, and of the weak, are obvious from their opposites.

18.[a] Now the employment of persuasive speeches is directed towards a judgement; for when a thing is known and judged, there is no longer any need of argument. And there is judgement, whether a speaker addresses himself to a single individual and makes use of his speech to exhort or dissuade, as those do who give advice or try to persuade, for this single individual is equally a judge, since, speaking generally, he who has to be persuaded is a judge; if the speaker is arguing against an opponent or against some theory, it is just the same, for it is necessary to make use of speech to destroy the opposing arguments, against which he speaks as if they were the actual opponent; and similarly in epideictic speeches, for the speech is put together with reference to the spectator as if he were a judge. Generally speaking, however, only he who decides questions at issue in civil controversies [b] is a judge in the proper sense of the word, for in judicial cases the point at issue is the state of the case, in deliberative the subjects of deliberation.[c] We have already spoken of the characters of forms of government in treating of deliberative rhetoric,[d] so that it has been determined how and by what means we must make our speeches conform to those characters.

discussion of the characters and emotions]. I have also spoken of the characters of the forms of government; so that this part of the subject need no longer detain us." It is generally agreed that we have not the chapter as originally arranged, although it is not supposed that any part of it is non-Aristotelian (see Cope and note in Jebb's translation).

[b] Both forensic and deliberative.

[c] Or, "for in both forensic and deliberative arguments the issue is the state of the case."   [d] i. 8.

2 Ἐπεὶ δὲ περὶ ἕκαστον μὲν γένος τῶν λόγων
ἕτερον ἦν τὸ τέλος, περὶ ἁπάντων δ' αὐτῶν εἰλημμέ-
ναι δόξαι καὶ προτάσεις εἰσίν, ἐξ ὧν τὰς πίστεις
φέρουσι καὶ συμβουλεύοντες καὶ ἐπιδεικνύμενοι
καὶ ἀμφισβητοῦντες, ἔτι δ' ἐξ ὧν ἠθικοὺς τοὺς
λόγους ἐνδέχεται ποιεῖν, καὶ περὶ τούτων διώρισται,
3 λοιπὸν ἡμῖν διελθεῖν περὶ τῶν κοινῶν· πᾶσι γὰρ
ἀναγκαῖον τὰ περὶ τοῦ δυνατοῦ καὶ ἀδυνάτου
προσχρῆσθαι ἐν τοῖς λόγοις, καὶ τοὺς μὲν ὡς
ἔσται τοὺς δὲ ὡς γέγονε πειρᾶσθαι δεικνύναι.
4 ἔτι δὲ περὶ μεγέθους κοινὸν ἁπάντων ἐστὶ τῶν
λόγων· χρῶνται γὰρ πάντες τῷ μειοῦν καὶ αὔξειν
καὶ συμβουλεύοντες καὶ ἐπαινοῦντες ἢ ψέγοντες
5 καὶ κατηγοροῦντες ἢ ἀπολογούμενοι. τούτων δὲ
1392a διορισθέντων περί τε ἐνθυμημάτων κοινῇ πειραθῶμεν
εἰπεῖν, εἴ τι ἔχομεν, καὶ περὶ παραδειγμάτων, ὅπως
τὰ λοιπὰ προσθέντες ἀποδῶμεν τὴν ἐξ ἀρχῆς πρό-
θεσιν. ἔστι δὲ τῶν κοινῶν τὸ μὲν αὔξειν οἰκειότατον
τοῖς ἐπιδεικτικοῖς, ὥσπερ εἴρηται, τὸ δὲ γεγονὸς
τοῖς δικανικοῖς (περὶ τούτων γὰρ ἡ κρίσις), τὸ δὲ
δυνατὸν καὶ ἐσόμενον τοῖς συμβουλευτικοῖς.

19. Πρῶτον μὲν οὖν περὶ δυνατοῦ καὶ ἀδυνάτου
λέγωμεν. ἂν δὴ τοὐναντίον ᾖ δυνατὸν ἢ εἶναι ἢ
γενέσθαι, καὶ τὸ ἐναντίον δόξειεν ἂν εἶναι δυνατόν·
οἷον εἰ δυνατὸν ἄνθρωπον ὑγιασθῆναι, καὶ νοσῆσαι·
ἡ γὰρ αὐτὴ δύναμις τῶν ἐναντίων, ᾗ ἐναντία. καὶ

---

[a] i. 3.   [b] i. 4-8.   [c] i. 9 ; 10-15.
[d] i. 9. 40. Amplication is to be understood of the
exaggeration of both great and small things. It is most

264

Now, since each kind of Rhetoric, as was said,[a] has its own special end, and in regard to all of them we have gathered popular opinions and premises whence men derive their proofs in deliberative, epideictic, and judicial speeches,[b] and, further, we have determined[c] the special rules according to which it is possible to make our speeches ethical, it only remains to discuss the topics common to the three kinds of rhetoric. For all orators are obliged, in their speeches, also to make use of the topic of the possible and impossible, and to endeavour to show, some of them that a thing will happen, others that it has happened. Further, the topic of magnitude is common to all kinds of Rhetoric, for all men employ extenuation or amplification whether deliberating, praising or blaming, accusing or defending. When these topics have been determined, we will endeavour to say what we can in general about enthymemes and examples, in order that, when we have added what remains, we may carry out what we proposed at the outset. Now, of the commonplaces amplification is most appropriate to epideictic rhetoric, as has been stated;[d] the past to forensic, since things past are the subject of judgement; and the possible and future to deliberative.

19. Let us first speak of the possible and the impossible. If of two contrary things it is possible that one should exist or come into existence, then it would seem that the other is equally possible; for instance, if a man can be cured, he can also be ill; for the potentiality of contraries, *qua* contraries, is

suited to epideictic oratory, in which there is no doubt as to the facts; so that it is only necessary to accentuate their importance or non-importance.

ARISTOTLE

2 εἰ τὸ ὅμοιον δυνατόν, καὶ τὸ ὅμοιον. καὶ εἰ τὸ
3 χαλεπώτερον δυνατόν, καὶ τὸ ῥᾷον. καὶ εἰ τὸ
4 σπουδαῖον καὶ καλὸν γενέσθαι δυνατόν, καὶ ὅλως
δυνατὸν γενέσθαι· χαλεπώτερον γὰρ καλὴν οἰκίαν
5 ἢ οἰκίαν εἶναι. καὶ οὗ ἡ ἀρχὴ δύναται γενέσθαι,
καὶ τὸ τέλος· οὐδὲν γὰρ γίγνεται οὐδ' ἄρχεται
γίγνεσθαι τῶν ἀδυνάτων, οἷον τὸ σύμμετρον τὴν
διάμετρον εἶναι οὔτ' ἂν ἄρξαιτο γίγνεσθαι οὔτε
γίγνεται. καὶ οὗ τὸ τέλος, καὶ ἡ ἀρχὴ δυνατή·
6 ἅπαντα γὰρ ἐξ ἀρχῆς γίγνεται. καὶ εἰ τὸ ὕστερον
τῇ οὐσίᾳ ἢ τῇ γενέσει δυνατὸν γενέσθαι, καὶ τὸ
πρότερον, οἷον εἰ ἄνδρα γενέσθαι δυνατόν, καὶ παῖδα·
πρότερον γὰρ ἐκεῖνο γίγνεται· καὶ εἰ παῖδα, καὶ
7 ἄνδρα· ἀρχὴ γὰρ ἐκείνη. καὶ ὧν ἔρως ἢ ἐπιθυμία
φύσει ἐστίν· οὐδεὶς γὰρ τῶν ἀδυνάτων ἐρᾷ οὐδ'
8 ἐπιθυμεῖ ὡς ἐπὶ τὸ πολύ. καὶ ὧν ἐπιστῆμαί εἰσι
καὶ τέχναι, δυνατὰ ταῦτα καὶ εἶναι καὶ γενέσθαι.
9 καὶ ὅσων ἡ ἀρχὴ τῆς γενέσεως ἐν τούτοις ἐστὶν ἃ
ἡμεῖς ἀναγκάσαιμεν ἂν ἢ πείσαιμεν· ταῦτα δ'
10 ἐστὶν ὧν κρείττους ἢ κύριοι ἢ φίλοι. καὶ ὧν τὰ
μέρη δυνατά, καὶ τὸ ὅλον. καὶ ὧν τὸ ὅλον δυνατόν,
καὶ τὰ μέρη ὡς ἐπὶ τὸ πολύ· εἰ γὰρ πρόσχισμα
καὶ κεφαλὶς καὶ χιτὼν δύναται γενέσθαι, καὶ
ὑποδήματα δυνατὸν γενέσθαι, καὶ εἰ ὑποδήματα,
11 καὶ πρόσχισμα καὶ κεφαλὶς καὶ χιτών. καὶ εἰ τὸ

---

* As a general rule, from their nature as contraries, although it may not be true in particular cases. If a man is ill, he may also be well, although in particular cases certain qualities may make him more liable to one or the other, *e.g.* he may suffer from an incurable disease (Schrader).

the same.[a] Similarly, if of two like things the one is possible, so also is the other. And if the harder of two things is possible, so also is the easier. And if it is possible for a thing to be made excellent or beautiful, it is possible for it to be made in general ; for it is harder for a beautiful house to be made than a mere house.[b] Again, if the beginning is possible, so also is the end ; for no impossible thing comes, or begins to come, into existence ; for instance, that the diameter of a square should be commensurable with the side of a square is neither possible nor could be possible. And when the end is possible, so also is the beginning ; for all things arise from a beginning. And if that which is subsequent in being or generation can come into being, so then can that which is antecedent ; for instance, if a man can come into being, so can a child, for the child is antecedent ; and similarly, if a child can come into being, so can a man, for the child is a beginning. And things which we love or desire naturally are possible ; for as a rule no one loves the impossible or desires it. And those things which form the subject of sciences or arts can also exist and come into existence. And so with all those things, the productive principles of which reside in those things which we can control by force or persuasion, when they depend upon those whose superiors, masters, or friends we are. And if the parts are possible, so also is the whole ; and if the whole is possible, so also are the parts, speaking generally ; for instance, if the front, toe-cap, and upper leather,[c] can be made, then shoes can be made, and if shoes, then the above parts. And if

[b] An argument *a fortiori*. If a beautiful house can be built, so can a house of any kind ; for this is easier.

[c] The meaning of the Greek words is quite uncertain.

1392 b γένος ὅλον τῶν δυνατῶν γενέσθαι, καὶ τὸ εἶδος,
καὶ εἰ τὸ εἶδος, καὶ τὸ γένος, οἷον εἰ πλοῖον γενέσθαι
δυνατόν, καὶ τριήρη, καὶ εἰ τριήρη, καὶ πλοῖον.
12 καὶ εἰ θάτερον τῶν πρὸς ἄλληλα πεφυκότων, καὶ
θάτερον, οἷον εἰ διπλάσιον, καὶ ἥμισυ, καὶ εἰ ἥμισυ,
13 καὶ διπλάσιον. καὶ εἰ ἄνευ τέχνης καὶ παρασκευῆς
δυνατὸν γενέσθαι, μᾶλλον διὰ τέχνης καὶ ἐπιμελείας
δυνατόν· ὅθεν καὶ Ἀγάθωνι εἴρηται

> καὶ μὴν τὰ μέν γε χρὴ τέχνῃ πράσσειν, τὰ δὲ
> ἡμῖν ἀνάγκῃ καὶ τύχῃ προσγίγνεται.

14 καὶ εἰ τοῖς χείροσι καὶ ἥττοσι καὶ ἀφρονεστέροις
δυνατόν, καὶ τοῖς ἐναντίοις μᾶλλον, ὥσπερ καὶ
Ἰσοκράτης ἔφη δεινὸν εἶναι εἰ ὁ μὲν Εὔθυνος
15 ἔμαθεν, αὐτὸς δὲ μὴ δυνήσεται εὑρεῖν. περὶ δὲ
ἀδυνάτου δῆλον ὅτι ἐκ τῶν ἐναντίων τοῖς εἰρημένοις
ὑπάρχει.

16 Εἰ δὲ γέγονεν ἢ μὴ γέγονεν, ἐκ τῶνδε σκεπτέον.
πρῶτον μὲν γάρ, εἰ τὸ ἧττον γίγνεσθαι πεφυκὸς
17 γέγονεν, γεγονὸς ἂν εἴη καὶ τὸ μᾶλλον. καὶ εἰ τὸ
ὕστερον εἰωθὸς γίγνεσθαι γέγονεν, καὶ τὸ πρότερον
γέγονεν, οἷον εἰ ἐπιλέληται, καὶ ἔμαθέ ποτε
18 τοῦτο. καὶ εἰ ἐδύνατο καὶ ἐβούλετο, πέπραχεν·
πάντες γάρ, ὅταν δυνάμενοι βουληθῶσι, πράτ-
19 τουσιν· ἐμποδὼν γὰρ οὐδέν. ἔτι εἰ ἐβούλετο καὶ

ᵃ T.G.F. p. 765.

the whole genus is among things possible to be made, so is the species, and if the species, so the genus; for example, if a vessel can be built, so can a trireme, if a trireme can, so can a vessel. If of two naturally corresponding things one is possible, so also is the other; for instance, if the double is possible, so is the half, if the half, so the double. If a thing can be made without art or preparation, much the more can it be made with the help of art and carefulness. Whence it was said by Agathon [a]:

And moreover we have to do some things by art, while others fall to our lot by compulsion or chance.

And if a thing is possible for those who are inferior, or weaker, or less intelligent, it will be still more so for those whose qualities are the opposite; as Isocrates said, it would be very strange if he were unable by himself to find out what Euthynus had learnt [with the help of others]. As for the impossible, it is clear that there is a supply of arguments to be derived from the opposite of what has been said about the possible.

The question whether a thing has or has not happened must be considered from the following points of view. In the first place, if that which is naturally less likely has happened, then that which is more likely will most probably have happened. If that which usually happens afterwards has happened, then that which precedes must also have happened; for instance, if a man has forgotten a thing, he must once have learnt it. If a man was able and wished to do a thing, he has done it; for all men do a thing, when they are able and resolve to do it, for nothing hinders them. Further, if a man wished to do it

μηδὲν τῶν ἔξω ἐκώλυεν, καὶ εἰ ἐδύνατο καὶ ὠργί-
ζετο, καὶ εἰ ἐδύνατο καὶ ἐπεθύμει· ὡς γὰρ ἐπὶ τὸ
πολύ, ὧν ὀρέγονται, ἂν δύνωνται, καὶ ποιοῦσιν,
οἱ μὲν φαῦλοι δι᾽ ἀκρασίαν, οἱ δ᾽ ἐπιεικεῖς ὅτι τῶν
20 ἐπιεικῶν ἐπιθυμοῦσιν. καὶ εἰ ἔμελλε γίγνεσθαι,
καὶ ποιεῖν· εἰκὸς γὰρ τὸν μέλλοντα καὶ ποιῆσαι.
21 καὶ εἰ γέγονεν ὅσα πεφύκει πρὸ ἐκείνου ἢ ἕνεκα
ἐκείνου, οἷον εἰ ἤστραψε, καὶ ἐβρόντησεν, καὶ εἰ
ἐπείρασε, καὶ ἔπραξεν. καὶ εἰ ὅσα ὕστερον πεφύκει γίγνεσθαι ἢ οὗ ἕνεκα γίγνεται γέγονεν, καὶ
τὸ πρότερον καὶ τὸ τούτου ἕνεκα γέγονεν, οἷον εἰ
ἐβρόντησε, καὶ ἤστραψεν, καὶ εἰ ἔπραξε, καὶ
22 ἐπείρασεν. ἔστι δὲ τούτων ἁπάντων τὰ μὲν ἐξ
ἀνάγκης τὰ δ᾽ ὡς ἐπὶ τὸ πολὺ οὕτως ἔχοντα. περὶ
δὲ τοῦ μὴ γεγονέναι φανερὸν ὅτι ἐκ τῶν ἐναντίων
τοῖς εἰρημένοις.

1393 a Καὶ περὶ τοῦ ἐσομένου ἐκ τῶν αὐτῶν δῆλον· τό
23 τε γὰρ ἐν δυνάμει καὶ βουλήσει ὂν ἔσται, καὶ τὰ
ἐν ἐπιθυμίᾳ καὶ ὀργῇ καὶ λογισμῷ μετὰ δυνάμεως
ὄντα. διὰ ταῦτα καὶ εἰ ἐν ὁρμῇ τοῦ ποιεῖν ἢ
μελλήσει, ἔσται· ὡς γὰρ ἐπὶ τὸ πολὺ γίγνεται
24 μᾶλλον τὰ μέλλοντα ἢ τὰ μὴ μέλλοντα. καὶ εἰ
προγέγονεν ὅσα πρότερον πεφύκει γίγνεσθαι, οἷον
25 εἰ συννεφεῖ, εἰκὸς ὗσαι. καὶ εἰ τὸ ἕνεκα τούτου

and there was no external obstacle ; if he was able to do it and was in a state of anger ; if he was able and desired to do it ; for men as a rule, whenever they can, do those things which they long for, the vicious owing to want of self-control, the virtuous because they desire what is good. And if anything was on the point of being done, it most probably was done ; for it is likely that one who was on the point of doing something has carried it out. And if all the natural antecedents or causes of a thing have happened ; for instance, if it has lightened, it has also thundered ; and if a man has already attempted a crime, he has also committed it. And if all the natural consequences or motives of actions have happened, then the antecedent or the cause has happened ; for instance, if it has thundered, it has also lightened, and if a man has committed a crime, he has also attempted it. Of all these things some are so related necessarily, others only as a general rule. To establish that a thing has not happened, it is evident that our argument must be derived from the opposite of what has been said.

In regard to the future, it is clear that one can argue in the same way; for if we are able and wish to do a thing, it will be done ; and so too will those things which desire, anger, and reasoning urge us to do, if we have the power. For this reason also, if a man has an eager desire, or intention, of doing a thing, it will probably be done ; since, as a rule, things that are about to happen are more likely to happen than those which are not. And if all the natural antecedents have happened ; for instance, if the sky is cloudy, it will probably rain. And if one thing has been done with a view to another, it is probable that the latter

γέγονεν, καὶ τοῦτο εἰκὸς γενέσθαι, οἷον εἰ θεμέλιος, καὶ οἰκία.

26 Περὶ δὲ μεγέθους καὶ μικρότητος τῶν πραγμάτων καὶ μείζονός τε καὶ ἐλάττονος καὶ ὅλως μεγάλων καὶ μικρῶν ἐκ τῶν προειρημένων ἡμῖν ἐστι φανερόν· εἴρηται γὰρ ἐν τοῖς συμβουλευτικοῖς περί τε μεγέθους ἀγαθῶν καὶ περὶ τοῦ μείζονος ἁπλῶς καὶ ἐλάττονος. ὥστ᾽ ἐπεὶ καθ᾽ ἕκαστον τῶν λόγων τὸ προκείμενον τέλος ἀγαθόν ἐστιν, οἷον τὸ συμφέρον καὶ τὸ καλὸν καὶ τὸ δίκαιον, φανερὸν ὅτι δι᾽ 27 ἐκείνων ληπτέον τὰς αὐξήσεις πᾶσιν. τὸ δὲ παρὰ ταῦτά τι ζητεῖν περὶ μεγέθους ἁπλῶς καὶ ὑπεροχῆς κενολογεῖν ἐστίν· κυριώτερα γάρ ἐστι πρὸς τὴν χρείαν τῶν καθόλου τὰ καθ᾽ ἕκαστα τῶν πραγμάτων. περὶ μὲν οὖν δυνατοῦ καὶ ἀδυνάτου, καὶ πότερον γέγονεν ἢ οὐ γέγονεν καὶ ἔσται ἢ οὐκ ἔσται, ἔτι δὲ περὶ μεγέθους καὶ μικρότητος τῶν πραγμάτων εἰρήσθω ταῦτα.

20. Λοιπὸν δὲ περὶ τῶν κοινῶν πίστεων ἅπασιν εἰπεῖν, ἐπείπερ εἴρηται περὶ τῶν ἰδίων. εἰσὶ δ᾽ αἱ κοιναὶ πίστεις δύο τῷ γένει, παράδειγμα καὶ ἐνθύμημα· ἡ γὰρ γνώμη μέρος ἐνθυμήματός ἐστιν.
2 πρῶτον μὲν οὖν περὶ παραδείγματος λέγωμεν· ὅμοιον γὰρ ἐπαγωγῇ τὸ παράδειγμα, ἡ δ᾽ ἐπαγωγὴ ἀρχή.

Παραδειγμάτων δ᾽ εἴδη δύο· ἓν μὲν γάρ ἐστι παραδείγματος εἶδος τὸ λέγειν πράγματα προγεγενημένα, ἓν δὲ τὸ αὐτὸν ποιεῖν. τούτου δ᾽ ἓν 3 μὲν παραβολὴ ἓν δὲ λόγοι, οἷον οἱ Αἰσώπειοι καὶ Λιβυκοί. ἔστι δὲ τὸ μὲν πράγματα λέγειν[1] τοιόνδε

---

[1] Spengel's alteration of the Paris ms. (A^c) reading παραδείγματα λέγειν.

will also be done; for instance, if a foundation
has been laid, a house will probably be built.

What we have previously said clearly shows the
nature of the greatness and smallness of things, of
the greater and less, and of things great and small
generally. For, when treating of deliberative
rhetoric,[a] we spoke of greatness of goods, and of the
greater and less generally. Therefore, since in each
branch of Rhetoric the end set before it is a good,
such as the expedient, the noble, or the just, it is
evident that all must take the materials of amplification from these. To make any further inquiry as to
magnitude and superiority absolutely would be waste
of words; for the particular has more authority than
the general for practical purposes. Let this suffice
for the possible and impossible; for the question
whether a thing has happened, or will happen, or
not; and for the greatness or smallness of things.

20. It remains to speak of the proofs common to
all branches of Rhetoric, since the particular proofs
have been discussed. These common proofs are of
two kinds, example and enthymeme (for the maxim
is part of an enthymeme). Let us then first speak of
the example; for the example resembles induction,
and induction is a beginning.[b]

There are two kinds of examples; namely, one
which consists in relating things that have happened
before, and another in inventing them oneself. The
latter are subdivided into comparisons or fables, such
as those of Aesop and the Libyan.[c] It would be an

---

[a] i. 7.
[b] As a starting-point and first principle of knowledge.
[c] The Libyan fables were of African origin. They are
mentioned by Quintilian (*Inst. Orat.* v. 11. 20) and belonged
to the class of animal fables.

τι, ὥσπερ εἴ τις λέγοι ὅτι δεῖ πρὸς βασιλέα παρα-
1393 b σκευάζεσθαι καὶ μὴ ἐᾶν Αἴγυπτον χειρώσασθαι·
καὶ γὰρ Δαρεῖος οὐ πρότερον διέβη πρὶν Αἴγυπτον
λαβεῖν, λαβὼν δὲ διέβη, καὶ πάλιν Ξέρξης οἳ
πρότερον ἐπεχείρησε πρὶν ἔλαβεν, λαβὼν δὲ διέβη·
ὥστε καὶ οὗτος ἐὰν λάβῃ, διαβήσεται· διὸ οὐκ
4 ἐπιτρεπτέον. παραβολὴ δὲ τὰ Σωκρατικά, οἷον
εἴ τις λέγοι ὅτι οὐ δεῖ κληρωτοὺς ἄρχειν· ὅμοιοι
γὰρ ὥσπερ ἂν εἴ τις τοὺς ἀθλητὰς κληροίη μὴ οἳ
ἂν δύνωνται ἀγωνίζεσθαι ἀλλ' οἳ ἂν λάχωσιν, ἢ
τῶν πλωτήρων ὅν τινα δεῖ κυβερνᾶν κληρώσειεν,
ὡς δέον τὸν λαχόντα ἀλλὰ μὴ τὸν ἐπιστάμενον.
5 Λόγος δέ, οἷος ὁ Στησιχόρου περὶ Φαλάριδος
καὶ Αἰσώπου ὑπὲρ τοῦ δημαγωγοῦ. Στησίχορος
μὲν γάρ, ἑλομένων στρατηγὸν αὐτοκράτορα τῶν
Ἱμεραίων Φάλαριν καὶ μελλόντων φυλακὴν διδόναι
τοῦ σώματος, τἆλλα διαλεχθεὶς εἶπεν αὐτοῖς λόγον
ὡς ἵππος κατεῖχε λειμῶνα μόνος, ἐλθόντος δ'
ἐλάφου καὶ διαφθείροντος τὴν νομὴν βουλόμενος
τιμωρήσασθαι τὸν ἔλαφον ἠρώτα τινὰ ἄνθρωπον
εἰ δύναιτ' ἂν μετ' αὐτοῦ κολάσαι τὸν ἔλαφον, ὁ δ'
ἔφησεν, ἐὰν λάβῃ χαλινὸν καὶ αὐτὸς ἀναβῇ ἐπ'
αὐτὸν ἔχων ἀκόντια· συνομολογήσαντος δὲ καὶ
ἀναβάντος, ἀντὶ τοῦ τιμωρήσασθαι αὐτὸς ἐδού-

ᵃ The παραβολή as understood by Aristotle is a comparison
and application of cases easily supposable and such as occur
in real life, for the purpose of illustrating the point in question; the fable, on the other hand, is pure fiction.

274

instance of the historical kind of example, if one
were to say that it is necessary to make preparations
against the Great King and not to allow him to
subdue Egypt ; for Darius did not cross over to
Greece until he had obtained possession of Egypt ;
but as soon as he had done so, he did. Again,
Xerxes did not attack us until he had obtained
possession of that country, but when he had, he
crossed over ; consequently, if the present Great
King shall do the same, he will cross over, wherefore
it must not be allowed. Comparison is illustrated
by the sayings of Socrates ; for instance, if one were
to say that magistrates should not be chosen by lot,
for this would be the same as choosing as representative athletes not those competent to contend, but
those on whom the lot falls ; or as choosing any of
the sailors as the man who should take the helm, as
if it were right that the choice should be decided by
lot, not by a man's knowledge.[a]

A fable, to give an example, is that of Stesichorus
concerning Phalaris, or that of Aesop on behalf of
the demagogue. For Stesichorus, when the people
of Himera had chosen Phalaris dictator and were on
the point of giving him a body-guard, after many
arguments related a fable to them : " A horse was
in sole occupation of a meadow. A stag having
come and done much damage to the pasture, the
horse, wishing to avenge himself on the stag, asked
a man whether he could help him to punish the stag.
The man consented, on condition that the horse
submitted to the bit and allowed him to mount him
javelins in hand. The horse agreed to the terms
and the man mounted him, but instead of obtaining
vengeance on the stag, the horse from that time

λευσεν ἤδη τῷ ἀνθρώπῳ. "οὕτω δὲ καὶ ὑμεῖς,"
ἔφη, "ὁρᾶτε μὴ βουλόμενοι τοὺς πολεμίους
τιμωρήσασθαι ταὐτὸ πάθητε τῷ ἵππῳ· τὸν μὲν
γὰρ χαλινὸν ἔχετε ἤδη, ἑλόμενοι στρατηγὸν αὐτο-
κράτορα· ἐὰν δὲ φυλακὴν δῶτε καὶ ἀναβῆναι
6 ἐάσητε, δουλεύσετε ἤδη Φαλάριδι." Αἴσωπος δὲ
ἐν Σάμῳ συνηγορῶν δημαγωγῷ κρινομένῳ περὶ
θανάτου ἔφη ἀλώπεκα διαβαίνουσαν ποταμὸν ἀπ-
ωσθῆναι εἰς φάραγγα, οὐ δυναμένην δ' ἐκβῆναι πολὺν
χρόνον κακοπαθεῖν, καὶ κυνοραϊστὰς πολλοὺς
ἔχεσθαι αὐτῆς· ἐχῖνον δὲ πλανώμενον, ὡς εἶδεν
αὐτήν, κατοικτείραντα ἐρωτᾶν εἰ ἀφέλοι αὐτῆς
τοὺς κυνοραϊστάς· τὴν δὲ οὐκ ἐᾶν· ἐρομένου δὲ
διὰ τί, ὅτι οὗτοι μὲν φάναι ἤδη μου πλήρεις εἰσὶ
καὶ ὀλίγον ἕλκουσιν αἷμα· ἐὰν δὲ τούτους ἀφέλῃ,
ἕτεροι ἐλθόντες πεινῶντες ἐκπιοῦνταί μου τὸ
λοιπὸν αἷμα. "ἀτὰρ καὶ ὑμᾶς," ἔφη, "ὦ
1394 a ἄνδρες Σάμιοι, οὗτος μὲν οὐδὲν ἔτι βλάψει (πλούσιος γάρ ἐστιν)· ἐὰν δὲ τοῦτον ἀποκτείνητε, ἕτεροι
ἥξουσι πένητες, οἳ ὑμῖν ἀναλώσουσι τὰ κοινὰ
7 κλέπτοντες." εἰσὶ δ' οἱ λόγοι δημηγορικοί, καὶ
ἔχουσιν ἀγαθὸν τοῦτο, ὅτι πράγματα μὲν εὑρεῖν
ὅμοια γεγενημένα χαλεπόν, λόγους δὲ ῥᾷον·
ποιῆσαι γὰρ δεῖ ὥσπερ καὶ παραβολάς, ἄν τις
δύνηται τὸ ὅμοιον ὁρᾶν, ὅπερ ῥᾷόν ἐστιν ἐκ φιλο-
8 σοφίας. ῥᾷω μὲν οὖν πορίσασθαι τὰ διὰ τῶν
λόγων, χρησιμώτερα δὲ πρὸς τὸ βουλεύσασθαι
τὰ διὰ τῶν πραγμάτων· ὅμοια γὰρ ὡς ἐπὶ τὸ πολὺ
τὰ μέλλοντα τοῖς γεγονόσιν.

ᵃ " Literary knowledge " (Jebb) ; " literature " (Cope.
276

became the man's slave. So then," said he, " do you take care lest, in your desire to avenge yourselves on the enemy, you be treated like the horse. You already have the bit, since you have chosen a dictator ; if you give him a body-guard and allow him to mount you, you will at once be the slaves of Phalaris." Aesop, when defending at Samos a demagogue who was being tried for his life, related the following anecdote. " A fox, while crossing a river, was driven into a ravine. Being unable to get out, she was for a long time in sore distress, and a number of dog-fleas clung to her skin. A hedgehog, wandering about, saw her and, moved with compassion, asked her if he should remove the fleas. The fox refused and when the hedgehog asked the reason, she answered : ' They are already full of me and draw little blood ; but if you take them away, others will come that are hungry and will drain what remains to me.' You in like manner, O Samians, will suffer no more harm from this man, for he is wealthy ; but if you put him to death, others will come who are poor, who will steal and squander your public funds." Fables are suitable for public speaking, and they have this advantage that, while it is difficult to find similar things that have really happened in the past, it is easier to invent fables ; for they must be invented, like comparisons, if a man is capable of seizing the analogy ; and this is easy if one studies philosophy.[a] Thus, while the lessons conveyed by fables are easier to provide, those derived from facts are more useful for deliberative oratory, because as a rule the future resembles the past.

Introd. p. 256, who, however, in his annotated ed. explains : " intellectual study and mental exercises in general ").

ARISTOTLE

9 Δεῖ δὲ χρῆσθαι τοῖς παραδείγμασι μὴ ἔχοντα
μὲν ἐνθυμήματα ὡς ἀποδείξεσιν (ἡ γὰρ πίστις
διὰ τούτων), ἔχοντα δὲ ὡς μαρτυρίοις, ἐπιλόγῳ
χρώμενον τοῖς ἐνθυμήμασιν· προτιθέμενα μὲν γὰρ
ἔοικεν ἐπαγωγῇ, τοῖς δὲ ῥητορικοῖς οὐκ οἰκεῖον
ἐπαγωγὴ πλὴν ἐν ὀλίγοις, ἐπιλεγόμενα δὲ μαρτυρίοις, ὁ δὲ μάρτυς πανταχοῦ πιθανός. διὸ καὶ
προτιθέντι μὲν ἀνάγκη πολλὰ λέγειν, ἐπιλέγοντι
δὲ καὶ ἓν ἱκανόν· μάρτυς γὰρ πιστὸς καὶ εἷς
χρήσιμος. πόσα μὲν οὖν εἴδη παραδειγμάτων,
καὶ πῶς αὐτοῖς καὶ πότε χρηστέον, εἴρηται.

21. Περὶ δὲ γνωμολογίας, ῥηθέντος τί ἐστι
γνώμη, μάλιστ' ἂν γένοιτο φανερὸν περὶ ποίων
τε καὶ πότε καὶ τίσιν ἁρμόττει χρῆσθαι τῷ γνωμο-
2 λογεῖν ἐν τοῖς λόγοις. ἔστι δὲ γνώμη ἀπόφανσις,
οὐ μέντοι περὶ τῶν καθ' ἕκαστον, οἷον ποῖός τις
Ἰφικράτης, ἀλλὰ καθόλου· καὶ οὐ περὶ πάντων
καθόλου, οἷον ὅτι τὸ εὐθὺ τῷ καμπύλῳ ἐναντίον,
ἀλλὰ περὶ ὅσων αἱ πράξεις εἰσί, καὶ αἱρετὰ ἢ
φευκτά ἐστι πρὸς τὸ πράττειν. ὥστ' ἐπεὶ τὰ ἐνθυμήματα ὁ περὶ τούτων συλλογισμός ἐστι σχεδόν,
τά τε συμπεράσματα τῶν ἐνθυμημάτων καὶ αἱ ἀρχαὶ
ἀφαιρεθέντος τοῦ συλλογισμοῦ γνῶμαί εἰσι, οἷον

χρὴ δ' οὔ ποθ', ὅς τις ἀρτίφρων πέφυκ' ἀνήρ,
παῖδας περισσῶς ἐκδιδάσκεσθαι σοφούς.

τοῦτο μὲν οὖν γνώμη· προστεθείσης δὲ τῆς αἰτίας
καὶ τοῦ διὰ τί, ἐνθύμημά ἐστι τὸ ἅπαν, οἷον

---

[a] If we have no enthymemes, we must use examples
instead of them; for they are useful for persuasion,
although they do not really demonstrate anything. If we
have enthymemes, we must use examples in corroboration
of them (see 21. 3 note).

If we have no enthymemes, we must employ examples as demonstrative proofs, for conviction is produced by these; but if we have them, examples must be used as evidence and as a kind of epilogue to the enthymemes.[a] For if they stand first, they resemble induction, and induction is not suitable to rhetorical speeches except in very few cases; if they stand last they resemble evidence, and a witness is in every case likely to induce belief. Wherefore also it is necessary to quote a number of examples if they are put first, but one alone is sufficient if they are put last; for even a single trustworthy witness is of use. We have thus stated how many kinds of examples there are, and how and when they should be made use of.

21. In regard to the use of maxims, it will most readily be evident on what subjects, and on what occasions, and by whom it is appropriate that maxims should be employed in speeches, after a maxim has been defined. Now, a maxim is a statement, not however concerning particulars, as, for instance, what sort of a man Iphicrates was, but general; it does not even deal with all general things, as for instance that the straight is the opposite of the crooked, but with the objects of human actions, and with what should be chosen or avoided with reference to them. And as the enthymeme is, we may say,[b] the syllogism dealing with such things, maxims are the premises or conclusions of enthymemes without the syllogism. For example:

No man who is sensible ought to have his children taught to be excessively clever,[c]

is a maxim; but when the why and the wherefore are added, the whole makes an enthymeme; for instance,

[b] Putting the comma after σχεδόν.   [c] Eur. *Medea*, 296.

ARISTOTLE

χωρὶς γὰρ ἄλλης ἧς ἔχουσιν ἀργίας,
φθόνον παρ' ἀστῶν ἀλφάνουσι δυσμενῆ.

1394 b καὶ τὸ

οὐκ ἔστιν ὅς τις πάντ' ἀνὴρ εὐδαιμονεῖ.

καὶ τὸ

οὐκ ἔστι ἀνδρῶν ὅς τις ἔστ' ἐλεύθερος
γνώμη, πρὸς δὲ τῷ ἐχομένῳ ἐνθύμημα·

ἢ χρημάτων γὰρ δοῦλός ἐστιν ἢ τύχης.

3 εἰ δή ἐστι γνώμη τὸ εἰρημένον, ἀνάγκη τέτταρα
εἴδη εἶναι γνώμης· ἢ γὰρ μετ' ἐπιλόγου ἔσται ἢ
4 ἄνευ ἐπιλόγου. ἀποδείξεως μὲν οὖν δεόμεναί
εἰσιν ὅσαι παράδοξόν τι λέγουσιν ἢ ἀμφισβητού-
μενον· ὅσαι δὲ μηδὲν παράδοξον, ἄνευ ἐπιλόγου.
5 τούτων δ' ἀνάγκη τὰς μὲν διὰ τὸ προεγνῶσθαι
μηδὲν δεῖσθαι ἐπιλόγου, οἷον

ἀνδρὶ δ' ὑγιαίνειν ἄριστόν ἐστιν, ὥς γ' ἡμῖν δοκεῖ·

φαίνεται γὰρ τοῖς πολλοῖς οὕτω· τὰς δ' ἅμα λεγο-
μένας δήλας εἶναι ἐπιβλέψασιν, οἷον

οὐδεὶς ἐραστὴς ὅς τις οὐκ ἀεὶ φιλεῖ.

6 τῶν δὲ μετ' ἐπιλόγου αἱ μὲν ἐνθυμήματος μέρος
εἰσίν, ὥσπερ

---

[a] "The idle habits which they contract" (Cope).
[b] Euripides, Stheneboea (frag. 661, T.G.F.).
[c] Euripides, Hecuba, 858.
[d] Maxims with an epilogue are (1) imperfect enthymemes, or (2) enthymematic in character, but not in form; those without an epilogue are (1) such as are well known, or (2) such as are clear as soon as they are uttered.

280

for, not to speak of the charge of idleness brought against them,[a] they earn jealous hostility from the citizens.

Another example :

There is no man who is happy in everything ; [b]

or,

There is no man who is really free.

The latter is a maxim, but taken with the next verse it is an enthymeme :

for he is the slave of either wealth or fortune.[c]

Now, if a maxim is what we have stated, it follows that maxims are of four kinds ; for they are either accompanied by an epilogue or not.[d] Now all those that state anything that is contrary to the general opinion or is a matter of dispute, need demonstrative proof ; but those that do not, need no epilogue,[e] either because they are already known, as, for instance,

Health is a most excellent thing for a man, at least in our opinion,[f]

for this is generally agreed ; or because, no sooner are they uttered than they are clear to those who consider them, for instance,

He is no lover who does not love always.[g]

As for the maxims that are accompanied by an epilogue, some form part of an enthymeme, as

[e] Something added as a supplementary proof, the why and the wherefore ; in iii. 19 it is used for the peroration of a speech.
[f] From Simonides or Epicharmus.
[g] Euripides, *Troades*, 1051.

χρὴ δ' οὔ ποθ' ὅστις ἀρτίφρων,

αἱ δ' ἐνθυμηματικαὶ μέν, οὐκ ἐνθυμήματος δὲ μέρος· αἵπερ καὶ μάλιστ' εὐδοκιμοῦσιν. εἰσὶ δ' αὗται ἐν ὅσαις ἐμφαίνεται τοῦ λεγομένου τὸ αἴτιον, οἷον ἐν τῷ

ἀθάνατον ὀργὴν μὴ φύλασσε θνητὸς ὤν·

τὸ μὲν γὰρ φάναι μὴ δεῖν ἀεὶ φυλάττειν τὴν ὀργὴν γνώμη, τὸ δὲ προσκείμενον " θνητὸν ὄντα " τὸ διὰ τί λέγει. ὅμοιον δὲ καὶ τὸ

θνατὰ χρὴ τὸν θνατόν, οὐκ ἀθάνατα τὸν θνατὸν φρονεῖν.

7 Φανερὸν οὖν ἐκ τῶν εἰρημένων πόσα τε εἴδη γνώμης, καὶ περὶ ποῖον ἕκαστον ἁρμόττει· περὶ μὲν γὰρ τῶν ἀμφισβητουμένων ἢ παραδόξων μὴ ἄνευ ἐπιλόγου, ἀλλ' ἢ προθέντα τὸν ἐπίλογον γνώμῃ χρῆσθαι τῷ συμπεράσματι, οἷον εἴ τις εἴποι " ἐγὼ μὲν οὖν, ἐπειδὴ οὔτε φθονεῖσθαι δεῖ οὔτ' ἀργὸν εἶναι, οὔ φημι χρῆναι παιδεύεσθαι," ἢ τοῦτο προειπόντα ἐπειπεῖν τὰ ἔμπροσθεν. περὶ δὲ τῶν μὴ παραδόξων ἀδήλων δέ, προστιθέντα τὸ 8 διότι στρογγυλώτατα. ἁρμόττει δ' ἐν τοῖς τοιούτοις καὶ τὰ Λακωνικὰ ἀποφθέγματα καὶ τὰ αἰνιγματώδη, οἷον εἴ τις λέγει ὅπερ Στησίχορος 1395 a ἐν Λοκροῖς εἶπεν, ὅτι οὐ δεῖ ὑβριστὰς εἶναι, ὅπως 9 μὴ οἱ τέττιγες χαμόθεν ᾄδωσιν. ἁρμόττει δὲ γνωμολογεῖν ἡλικίᾳ μὲν πρεσβυτέροις, περὶ δὲ

---

[a] See § 2.
[b] They partake of the nature of, but not of the form of, enthymemes.
[c] Author unknown (*T.G.F.* p. 854).

No one who is sensible, etc.,[a]

while others are enthymematic, but are not part of an enthymeme;[b] and these are most highly esteemed. Such are those maxims in which the reason of what is said is apparent: for instance,

Being a mortal, do not nourish immortal wrath;[c]

to say that one should not always nourish immortal wrath is a maxim, but the addition " being a mortal " states the reason. It is the same with

A mortal should have mortal, not immortal thoughts.[d]

It is evident, therefore, from what has been said, how many kinds of maxims there are, and to what it is appropriate to apply them in each case. For in the case of matters of dispute or what is contrary to the general opinion, the epilogue is necessary; but either the epilogue may be put first and the conclusion used as a maxim, as, for example, if one were to say, " As for me, since one ought neither to be the object of jealousy nor to be idle, I say that children ought not to be educated "; or put the maxim first and append the epilogue. In all cases where the statements made, although not para-doxical, are obscure, the reason should be added as concisely as possible. In such cases Laconic apo-phthegms and riddling sayings are suitable; as, for instance, to say what Stesichorus said to the Locrians, that they ought not to be insolent, lest their cicadas should be forced to chirp from the ground.[e] The use of maxims is suitable for one who is advanced

[d] According to Bentley, from Epicharmus.
[e] Meaning that the land would be devastated and the trees cut down.

ARISTOTLE

τούτων ὧν ἔμπειρός τις ἐστίν, ὡς τὸ μὲν μὴ
τηλικοῦτον ὄντα γνωμολογεῖν ἀπρεπὲς ὥσπερ καὶ
τὸ μυθολογεῖν, περὶ δ' ὧν ἄπειρος, ἠλίθιον καὶ
ἀπαίδευτον. σημεῖον δ' ἱκανόν· οἱ γὰρ ἀγροῖκοι
μάλιστα γνωμοτύποι εἰσὶ καὶ ῥᾳδίως ἀποφαίνονται.
10 Καθόλου δὲ μὴ ὄντος καθόλου εἰπεῖν μάλιστα
ἁρμόττει ἐν σχετλιασμῷ καὶ δεινώσει, καὶ ἐν
11 τούτοις ἢ ἀρχόμενον ἢ ἀποδείξαντα. χρῆσθαι δὲ
δεῖ καὶ ταῖς τεθρυλημέναις καὶ κοιναῖς γνώμαις,
ἐὰν ὦσι χρήσιμοι· διὰ γὰρ τὸ εἶναι κοιναί, ὡς ὁμο-
λογούντων ἁπάντων, ὀρθῶς ἔχειν δοκοῦσιν, οἷον
παρακαλοῦντι ἐπὶ τὸ κινδυνεύειν μὴ θυσαμένους

εἷς οἰωνὸς ἄριστος ἀμύνεσθαι περὶ πάτρης,

καὶ ἐπὶ τὸ ἥττους ὄντας

ξυνὸς Ἐννάλιος,

καὶ ἐπὶ τὸ ἀναιρεῖν τῶν ἐχθρῶν τὰ τέκνα καὶ μηδὲν
ἀδικοῦντα

νήπιος ὃς πατέρα κτείνας παῖδας καταλείπει.

12 Ἔτι ἔνιαι τῶν παροιμιῶν καὶ γνῶμαί εἰσιν,
13 οἷον παροιμία " Ἀττικὸς πάροικος." δεῖ δὲ τὰς
γνώμας λέγειν καὶ παρὰ τὰ δεδημοσιευμένα (λέγω
δὲ δεδημοσιευμένα οἷον τὸ Γνῶθι σαυτόν καὶ τὸ
Μηδὲν ἄγαν), ὅταν ἢ τὸ ἦθος φαίνεσθαι μέλλῃ
βέλτιον, ἢ παθητικῶς εἰρημένη ᾖ. ἔστι δὲ παθητικὴ μέν, οἷον εἴ τις ὀργιζόμενος φαίη ψεῦδος

---

[a] *Iliad*, xii. 243. [b] *Iliad*, xviii. 309. [c] i. 15. 14.
[d] *Cf.* Thucydides, i. 70, where the Corinthians complain
of the lack of energy shown by the Spartans, as compared
with their own restless and troublesome neighbours, the
Athenians.

284

in years, and in regard to things in which one has experience ; since the use of maxims before such an age is unseemly, as also is story-telling ; and to speak about things of which one has no experience shows foolishness and lack of education. A sufficient proof of this is that rustics especially are fond of coining maxims and ready to make display of them.

To express in general terms what is not general is especially suitable in complaint or exaggeration, and then either at the beginning or after the demonstration. One should even make use of common and frequently quoted maxims, if they are useful ; for because they are common, they seem to be true, since all as it were acknowledge them as such ; for instance, one who is exhorting his soldiers to brave danger before having sacrificed may say,

> The best of omens is to defend one's country,[a]

and if they are inferior in numbers,

> The chances of war are the same for both,[b]

and if advising them to destroy the children of the enemy even though they are innocent of wrong,

> Foolish is he who, having slain the father, suffers the children to live.[c]

Further, some proverbs are also maxims ; for example, " An Attic neighbour." [d] Maxims should also be used even when contrary to the most popular sayings, such as " Know thyself " and " Nothing in excess," either when one's character is thereby likely to appear better, or if they are expressed in the language of passion. It would be an instance of the latter if a man in a rage were to say, " It is not

ARISTOTLE

εἶναι ὡς δεῖ γιγνώσκειν αὐτόν· οὗτος γοῦν εἰ
ἐγίγνωσκεν ἑαυτόν, οὐκ ἄν ποτε στρατηγεῖν
ἠξίωσεν. τὸ δὲ ἦθος βέλτιον, ὅτι οὐ δεῖ, ὥσπερ
φασί, φιλεῖν ὡς μισήσοντας ἀλλὰ μᾶλλον μισεῖν
14 ὡς φιλήσοντας. δεῖ δὲ τῇ λέξει τὴν προαίρεσιν
συνδηλοῦν, εἰ δὲ μή, τὴν αἰτίαν ἐπιλέγειν, οἷον ἢ
οὕτως εἰπόντα, ὅτι " δεῖ φιλεῖν οὐχ ὥσπερ φασίν,
ἀλλ' ὡς ἀεὶ φιλήσοντα· ἐπιβούλου γὰρ θάτερον,"
ἢ ὧδε " οὐκ ἀρέσκει δέ μοι τὸ λεγόμενον· δεῖ γὰρ
τόν γ' ἀληθινὸν φίλον ὡς φιλήσοντα ἀεὶ φιλεῖν."
καὶ " οὐδὲ τὸ μηδὲν ἄγαν· δεῖ γὰρ τούς γε κακοὺς
1395 b ἄγαν μισεῖν."
15 Ἔχουσι δ' εἰς τοὺς λόγους βοήθειαν μεγάλην
μίαν μὲν δὴ διὰ τὴν φορτικότητα τῶν ἀκροατῶν·
χαίρουσι γάρ, ἐάν τις καθόλου λέγων ἐπιτύχῃ τῶν
δοξῶν ἃς ἐκεῖνοι κατὰ μέρος ἔχουσιν. ὃ δὲ λέγω,
δῆλον ἔσται ὧδε, ἅμα δὲ καὶ πῶς δεῖ αὐτὰς θηρεύειν.
ἡ μὲν γὰρ γνώμη, ὥσπερ εἴρηται, ἀπόφανσις καθόλου ἐστίν, χαίρουσι δὲ καθόλου λεγομένου ὃ κατὰ
μέρος προϋπολαμβάνοντες τυγχάνουσιν· οἷον εἴ τις
γείτοσι τύχοι κεχρημένος ἢ τέκνοις φαύλοις, ἀπο-
δέξαιτ' ἂν τοῦ εἰπόντος ὅτι

οὐδὲν γειτονίας χαλεπώτερον,

ἢ ὅτι οὐδὲν ἠλιθιώτερον τεκνοποιίας. ὥστε δεῖ
στοχάζεσθαι πῶς τυγχάνουσι ποῖα προϋπολαμβάνοντες, εἶθ' οὕτω περὶ τούτων καθόλου λέγειν.
16 ταύτην τε δὴ ἔχει μίαν χρῆσιν τὸ γνωμολογεῖν,

---

a "Want of cultivation and intelligence" (Cope). "*Amour-propre*" (St. Hilaire).
b In reference to their own particular case.

286

true that a man should know himself ; at any rate,
such a man as this, if he had known himself, would
never have claimed the chief command." And one's
character would appear better, if one were to say
that it is not right, as men say, to love as if one
were bound to hate, but rather to hate as if one were
bound to love. The moral purpose also should be
made clear by the language, or else one should add
the reason ; for example, either by saying " that it
is right to love, not as men say, but as if one were
going to love for ever, for the other kind of love
would imply treachery " ; or thus, " The maxim does
not please me, for the true friend should love as if
he were going to love for ever. Nor do I approve
the maxim ' Nothing in excess,' for one cannot hate
the wicked too much."

Further, maxims are of great assistance to speakers,
first, because of the vulgarity[a] of the hearers, who are
pleased if an orator, speaking generally, hits upon
the opinions which they specially hold.[b] What I
mean will be clear from the following, and also how
one should hunt for maxims. The maxim, as we
have said, is a statement of the general ; accordingly,
the hearers are pleased to hear stated in general
terms the opinion which they have already specially
formed. For instance, a man who happened to have
bad neighbours or children would welcome any one's
statement that nothing is more troublesome than
neighbours or more stupid than to beget children.
Wherefore the speaker should endeavour to guess
how his hearers formed their preconceived opinions
and what they are, and then express himself in
general terms in regard to them. This is one of
the advantages of the use of maxims, but another

καὶ ἑτέραν κρείττω· ἠθικοὺς γὰρ ποιεῖ τοὺς λόγους.
ἦθος δ᾽ ἔχουσιν οἱ λόγοι, ἐν ὅσοις δήλη ἡ προαίρεσις.
αἱ δὲ γνῶμαι πᾶσαι τοῦτο ποιοῦσι διὰ τὸ ἀπο-
φαίνεσθαι τὸν τὴν γνώμην λέγοντα καθόλου περὶ
τῶν προαιρετῶν, ὥστ᾽ ἂν χρησταὶ ὦσιν αἱ γνῶμαι,
καὶ χρηστοήθη φαίνεσθαι ποιοῦσι τὸν λέγοντα.
περὶ μὲν οὖν γνώμης, καὶ τί ἐστι καὶ πόσα εἴδη
αὐτῆς καὶ πῶς χρηστέον αὐτῇ καὶ τίνα ὠφέλειαν
ἔχει, εἰρήσθω τοσαῦτα.

22. Περὶ δ᾽ ἐνθυμημάτων καθόλου τε εἴπωμεν,
τίνα τρόπον δεῖ ζητεῖν, καὶ μετὰ ταῦτα τοὺς
τόπους· ἄλλο γὰρ εἶδος ἑκατέρου τούτων ἐστίν.
2 ὅτι μὲν οὖν τὸ ἐνθύμημα συλλογισμός τίς ἐστιν,
εἴρηται πρότερον, καὶ πῶς συλλογισμός, καὶ τί
3 διαφέρει τῶν διαλεκτικῶν· οὔτε γὰρ πόρρωθεν
οὔτε πάντα δεῖ λαμβάνοντας συνάγειν· τὸ μὲν γὰρ
ἀσαφὲς διὰ τὸ μῆκος, τὸ δὲ ἀδολεσχία διὰ τὸ
φανερὰ λέγειν. τοῦτο γὰρ αἴτιον καὶ τοῦ πιθανω-
τέρους εἶναι τοὺς ἀπαιδεύτους τῶν πεπαιδευμένων
ἐν τοῖς ὄχλοις, ὥσπερ φασὶν οἱ ποιηταὶ τοὺς
ἀπαιδεύτους παρ᾽ ὄχλῳ μουσικωτέρως λέγειν· οἱ
μὲν γὰρ τὰ κοινὰ καὶ καθόλου λέγουσιν, οἱ δ᾽ ἐξ
ὧν ἴσασι, καὶ τὰ ἐγγύς. ὥστ᾽ οὐκ ἐξ ἁπάντων
τῶν δοκούντων ἀλλ᾽ ἐκ τῶν ὡρισμένων λεκτέον
1396 a οἷον ἢ τοῖς κρίνουσιν ἢ οὓς ἀποδέχονται. καὶ
τοῦτο δ᾽, ὅτι οὕτω φαίνεται, δῆλον εἶναι ἢ πᾶσιν

ᵃ The conclusion must not be reached by means of a long
series of arguments, as it were strung together in a chain:
cp. i. 2. 12, where the hearers are spoken of as unable to
take in at a glance a long series of arguments or " to follow a
long chain of reasoning " (οὐδὲ λογίζεσθαι πόρρωθεν).

is greater ; for it makes speeches ethical. Speeches have this character, in which the moral purpose is clear. And this is the effect of all maxims, because he who employs them in a general manner declares his moral preferences ; if then the maxims are good, they show the speaker also to be a man of good character. Let this suffice for what we had to say concerning maxims, their nature, how many kinds of them there are, the way they should be used, and what their advantages are.

22. Let us now speak of enthymemes in general and the manner of looking for them, and next of their topics ; for each of these things is different in kind. We have already said that the enthymeme is a kind of syllogism, what makes it so, and in what it differs from the dialectic syllogisms ; for the conclusion must neither be drawn from too far back [a] nor should it include all the steps of the argument. In the first case its length causes obscurity, in the second, it is simply a waste of words, because it states much that is obvious. It is this that makes the ignorant more persuasive than the educated in the presence of crowds ; as the poets say, " the ignorant are more skilled at speaking before a mob." [b] For the educated use commonplaces and generalities, whereas the ignorant speak of what they know and of what more nearly concerns the audience. Wherefore one must not argue from all possible opinions, but only from such as are definite and admitted, for instance, either by the judges themselves or by those of whose judgement they approve. Further, it should be clear that this is the opinion

[b] Euripides, *Hippolytus*, 989.

ἢ τοῖς πλείστοις. καὶ μὴ μόνον συνάγειν ἐκ τῶν
ἀναγκαίων, ἀλλὰ καὶ ἐκ τῶν ὡς ἐπὶ τὸ πολύ.

4 Πρῶτον μὲν οὖν δεῖ λαβεῖν ὅτι περὶ οὗ δεῖ
λέγειν καὶ συλλογίζεσθαι εἴτε πολιτικῷ συλλογισμῷ
εἴθ᾽ ὁποιῳοῦν, ἀναγκαῖον καὶ τὰ τούτῳ ἔχειν
ὑπάρχοντα, ἢ πάντα ἢ ἔνια· μηδὲν γὰρ ἔχων ἐξ
5 οὐδενὸς ἂν ἔχοις συνάγειν. λέγω δ᾽ οἷον πῶς ἂν
δυναίμεθα συμβουλεύειν Ἀθηναίοις εἰ πολεμητέον
ἢ μὴ πολεμητέον, μὴ ἔχοντες τίς ἡ δύναμις αὐτῶν,
πότερον ναυτικὴ ἢ πεζικὴ ἢ ἄμφω, καὶ αὕτη πόση,
καὶ πρόσοδοι τίνες ἢ φίλοι καὶ ἐχθροί, ἔτι δὲ τίνας
πολέμους πεπολεμήκασι καὶ πῶς, καὶ τἆλλα τὰ
6 τοιαῦτα; ἢ ἐπαινεῖν, εἰ μὴ ἔχοιμεν τὴν ἐν Σαλαμῖνι
ναυμαχίαν ἢ τὴν ἐν Μαραθῶνι μάχην ἢ τὰ ὑπὲρ
Ἡρακλειδῶν πραχθέντα ἢ ἄλλο τι τῶν τοιούτων;
ἐκ γὰρ τῶν ὑπαρχόντων ἢ δοκούντων ὑπάρχειν
7 καλῶν ἐπαινοῦσι πάντες. ὁμοίως δὲ καὶ ψέγουσιν
ἐκ τῶν ἐναντίων, σκοποῦντες τί ὑπάρχει τοιοῦτον
αὐτοῖς ἢ δοκεῖ ὑπάρχειν, οἷον ὅτι τοὺς Ἕλληνας
κατεδουλώσαντο, καὶ τοὺς πρὸς τὸν βάρβαρον
συμμαχεσαμένους καὶ ἀριστεύσαντας ἠνδραπο-
δίσαντο Αἰγινήτας καὶ Ποτιδαιάτας, καὶ ὅσα
ἄλλα τοιαῦτα, καὶ εἴ τι ἄλλο τοιοῦτον ἁμάρτημα
ὑπάρχει αὐτοῖς. ὡς δ᾽ αὕτως καὶ οἱ κατηγοροῦντες
καὶ οἱ ἀπολογούμενοι ἐκ τῶν ὑπαρχόντων σκοπού-
8 μενοι κατηγοροῦσι καὶ ἀπολογοῦνται. οὐδὲν δὲ

290

of all or most of the hearers; and again, conclusions
should not be drawn from necessary premises alone,
but also from those which are only true as a rule.

First of all, then, it must be understood that, in
regard to the subject of our speech or reasoning,
whether it be political or of any other kind, it is
necessary to be also acquainted with the elements
of the question, either entirely or in part; for if you
know none of these things, you will have nothing
from which to draw a conclusion. I should like to
know, for instance, how we are to give advice to the
Athenians as to making war or not, if we do not
know in what their strength consists, whether it is
naval, military, or both, how great it is, their sources
of revenue, their friends and enemies, and further,
what wars they have already waged, with what
success, and all similar things? Again, how could
we praise them, if we did not know of the naval
engagement at Salamis or the battle of Marathon,
or what they did for the Heraclidae, and other
similar things? for men always base their praise
upon what really are, or are thought to be, glorious
deeds. Similarly, they base their censure upon
actions that are contrary to these, examining whether
those censured have really, or seem to have, committed them; for example, that the Athenians sub-
jugated the Greeks, and reduced to slavery the
Aeginetans and Potidaeans who had fought with
distinction on their side against the barbarians, and
all such acts, and whatever other similar offences
may have been committed by them. Similarly, in
accusation and defence, speakers argue from an
examination of the circumstances of the case. It
makes no difference in doing this, whether it is a

διαφέρει περὶ Ἀθηναίων ἢ Λακεδαιμονίων ἢ
ἀνθρώπου ἢ θεοῦ ταὐτὸ τοῦτο δρᾶν· καὶ γὰρ
συμβουλεύοντα τῷ Ἀχιλλεῖ καὶ ἐπαινοῦντα καὶ
ψέγοντα καὶ κατηγοροῦντα καὶ ἀπολογούμενον
ὑπὲρ αὐτοῦ τὰ ὑπάρχοντα ἢ δοκοῦντα ὑπάρχειν
ληπτέον, ἵν' ἐκ τούτων λέγωμεν ἐπαινοῦντες ἢ
ψέγοντες εἴ τι καλὸν ἢ αἰσχρὸν ὑπάρχει, κατηγοροῦντες δ' ἢ ἀπολογούμενοι εἴ τι δίκαιον ἢ ἄδικον,
συμβουλεύοντες δ' εἴ τι συμφέρον ἢ βλαβερόν.
9 ὁμοίως δὲ τούτοις καὶ περὶ πράγματος ὁτουοῦν,
οἷον περὶ δικαιοσύνης, εἰ ἀγαθὸν ἢ μὴ ἀγαθόν,
ἐκ τῶν ὑπαρχόντων τῇ δικαιοσύνῃ καὶ τῷ ἀγαθῷ.
10 Ὥστ' ἐπειδὴ καὶ πάντες οὕτω φαίνονται ἀπο-
δεικνύντες, ἐάν τε ἀκριβέστερον ἐάν τε μαλακώτερον
1396 b συλλογίζωνται (οὐ γὰρ ἐξ ἁπάντων λαμβάνουσιν
ἀλλ' ἐκ τῶν περὶ ἕκαστον ὑπαρχόντων, καὶ διὰ
τοῦ λόγου δῆλον ὅτι ἀδύνατον ἄλλως δεικνύναι),
φανερὸν ὅτι ἀναγκαῖον, ὥσπερ ἐν τοῖς τοπικοῖς,
πρῶτον περὶ ἕκαστον ἔχειν ἐξειλεγμένα περὶ τῶν
11 ἐνδεχομένων καὶ τῶν ἐπικαιροτάτων, περὶ δὲ τῶν
ἐξ ὑπογυίου γιγνομένων ζητεῖν τὸν αὐτὸν τρόπον,
ἀποβλέποντα μὴ εἰς ἀόριστα ἀλλ' εἰς τὰ ὑπάρχοντα,
περὶ ὧν ὁ λόγος, καὶ περιγράφοντας ὅτι πλεῖστα
καὶ ἐγγύτατα τοῦ πράγματος· ὅσῳ μὲν γὰρ ἂν
πλείω ἔχηται τῶν ὑπαρχόντων, τοσούτῳ ῥᾶον
δεικνύναι, ὅσῳ δ' ἐγγύτερον, τοσούτῳ οἰκειότερα
12 καὶ ἧττον κοινά. λέγω δὲ κοινὰ μὲν τὸ ἐπαινεῖν
τὸν Ἀχιλλέα ὅτι ἄνθρωπος καὶ ὅτι τῶν ἡμιθέων

---

[a] Or, " by means of the *speech* it is impossible to prove
anything otherwise " (Cope).
[b] i. 14. πρῶτον : *i.e.* " the speaker's chief care should be . . ."

question of Athenians or Lacedaemonians, of a man or a god. For, when advising Achilles, praising or censuring, accusing or defending him, we must grasp all that really belongs, or appears to belong to him, in order that we may praise or censure in accordance with this, if there is anything noble or disgraceful; defend or accuse, if there is anything just or unjust; advise, if there is anything expedient or harmful. And similarly in regard to any subject whatever. For instance, in regard to justice, whether it is good or not, we must consider the question in the light of what is inherent in justice or the good.

Therefore, since it is evident that all men follow this procedure in demonstration, whether they reason strictly or loosely—since they do not derive their arguments from all things indiscriminately, but from what is inherent in each particular subject, and reason makes it clear that it is impossible to prove anything in any other way [a]—it is evidently necessary, as has been stated in the *Topics*,[b] to have first on each subject a selection of premises about probabilities and what is most suitable. As for those to be used in sudden emergencies, the same method of inquiry must be adopted; we must look, not at what is indefinite but at what is inherent in the subject treated of in the speech, marking off as many facts as possible, particularly those intimately connected with the subject; for the more facts one has, the easier it is to demonstrate, and the more closely connected they are with the subject, the more suitable are they and less common.[c] By common I mean, for instance, praising Achilles because he is a man,

[c] The more suitable they will be, and the less they will resemble ordinary, trivial generalities.

ARISTOTLE

καὶ ὅτι ἐπὶ τὸ Ἴλιον ἐστρατεύσατο· ταῦτα γὰρ
καὶ ἄλλοις ὑπάρχει πολλοῖς, ὥστ' οὐδὲν μᾶλλον ὁ
τοιοῦτος Ἀχιλλέα ἐπαινεῖ ἢ Διομήδην. ἴδια δὲ ἃ
μηδενὶ ἄλλῳ συμβέβηκεν ἢ τῷ Ἀχιλλεῖ, οἷον τὸ
ἀποκτεῖναι τὸν Ἕκτορα τὸν ἄριστον τῶν Τρώων
καὶ τὸν Κύκνον, ὃς ἐκώλυσεν ἅπαντας ἀποβαίνειν
ἄτρωτος ὤν, καὶ ὅτι νεώτατος καὶ οὐκ ἔνορκος
ὢν ἐστράτευσεν, καὶ ὅσα ἄλλα τοιαῦτα.

13   Εἷς μὲν οὖν τρόπος τῆς ἐκλογῆς καὶ πρῶτος
οὗτος ὁ τοπικός, τὰ δὲ στοιχεῖα τῶν ἐνθυμημάτων
λέγωμεν (στοιχεῖον δὲ λέγω καὶ τόπον ἐνθυμήματος
τὸ αὐτό). πρῶτον δ' εἴπωμεν περὶ ὧν ἀναγκαῖον
14 εἰπεῖν πρῶτον. ἔστι γὰρ τῶν ἐνθυμημάτων εἴδη
δύο· τὰ μὲν γὰρ δεικτικά ἐστιν ὅτι ἔστιν ἢ οὐκ
ἔστιν, τὰ δ' ἐλεγκτικά· καὶ διαφέρει ὥσπερ ἐν
15 τοῖς διαλεκτικοῖς ἔλεγχος καὶ συλλογισμός. ἔστι
δὲ τὸ μὲν δεικτικὸν ἐνθύμημα τὸ ἐξ ὁμολογουμένων συνάγειν, τὸ δὲ ἐλεγκτικὸν τὸ τὰ ἀνομο-
16 λογούμενα συνάγειν. σχεδὸν μὲν οὖν ἡμῖν περὶ
ἑκάστων τῶν εἰδῶν τῶν χρησίμων καὶ ἀναγκαίων
ἔχονται οἱ τόποι· ἐξειλεγμέναι γὰρ αἱ προτάσεις
περὶ ἕκαστόν εἰσιν, ὥστ' ἐξ ὧν δεῖ φέρειν τὰ
ἐνθυμήματα τόπων περὶ ἀγαθοῦ ἢ κακοῦ ἢ καλοῦ
ἢ αἰσχροῦ ἢ δικαίου ἢ ἀδίκου, καὶ περὶ τῶν ἠθῶν
καὶ παθημάτων καὶ ἕξεων ὡσαύτως εἰλημμένοι
17 ἡμῖν ὑπάρχουσι πρότερον οἱ τόποι. ἔτι δ' ἄλλον
1397 a τρόπον καθόλου περὶ ἁπάντων λάβωμεν, καὶ

---

^a The demonstrative enthymeme draws its conclusion

or one of the demigods, or because he went on the
expedition against Troy; for this is applicable to
many others as well, so that such praise is no more
suited to Achilles than to Diomedes. By particular
I mean what belongs to Achilles, but to no one else;
for instance, to have slain Hector, the bravest of the
Trojans, and Cycnus, who prevented all the Greeks
from disembarking, being invulnerable; to have
gone to the war when very young, and without
having taken the oath; and all such things.

One method of selection then, and this the first,
is the topical. Let us now speak of the elements of
enthymemes (by element and topic of enthymeme I
mean the same thing). But let us first make some
necessary remarks. There are two kinds of enthymemes, the one demonstrative, which proves that a
thing is or is not, and the other refutative, the two
differing like refutation and syllogism in Dialectic.
The demonstrative enthymeme draws conclusions
from admitted premises, the refutative draws conclusions disputed by the adversary.[a] We know
nearly all the general heads of each of the special
topics that are useful or necessary; for the propositions relating to each have been selected, so that
we have in like manner already established all the
topics from which enthymemes may be derived on
the subject of good or bad, fair or foul, just or
unjust, characters, emotions, and habits. Let us
now endeavour to find topics about enthymemes in
general in another way, noting in passing [b] those

from facts admitted by the opponent; the refutative draws
its conclusion from the same, but the conclusion is one
which is disputed by the opponent.

[b] Or, " noting in addition " (Victorius); or, " pointing
out, side by side " (Jebb).

λέγωμεν παρασημαινόμενοι τοὺς ἐλεγκτικοὺς καὶ
τοὺς ἀποδεικτικοὺς καὶ τοὺς τῶν φαινομένων
ἐνθυμημάτων, οὐκ ὄντων δὲ ἐνθυμημάτων, ἐπείπερ
οὐδὲ συλλογισμῶν. δηλωθέντων δὲ τούτων, περὶ
τῶν λύσεων καὶ ἐνστάσεων διορίσωμεν, πόθεν
δεῖ πρὸς τὰ ἐνθυμήματα φέρειν.

23. Ἔστι δ' εἷς μὲν τόπος τῶν δεικτικῶν ἐκ
τῶν ἐναντίων· δεῖ γὰρ σκοπεῖν εἰ τῷ ἐναντίῳ τὸ
ἐναντίον ὑπάρχει, ἀναιροῦντα μὲν εἰ μὴ ὑπάρχει,
κατασκευάζοντα δὲ εἰ ὑπάρχει, οἷον ὅτι τὸ σωφρονεῖν ἀγαθόν· τὸ γὰρ ἀκολασταίνειν βλαβερόν. ἢ
ὡς ἐν τῷ Μεσσηνιακῷ· εἰ γὰρ ὁ πόλεμος αἴτιος
τῶν παρόντων κακῶν, μετὰ τῆς εἰρήνης δεῖ ἐπαν-
ορθώσασθαι.

> εἴπερ γὰρ οὐδὲ τοῖς κακῶς δεδρακόσιν
> ἀκουσίως δίκαιον εἰς ὀργὴν πεσεῖν,
> οὐδ' ἂν ἀναγκασθείς τις εὖ δράσῃ τινά,
> προσῆκόν ἐστι τῷδ' ὀφείλεσθαι χάριν.

> ἀλλ' εἴπερ ἐστὶν ἐν βροτοῖς ψευδηγορεῖν
> πιθανά, νομίζειν χρή σε καὶ τοὐναντίον,
> ἄπιστ' ἀληθῆ πολλὰ συμβαίνειν βροτοῖς.

2 Ἄλλος ἐκ τῶν ὁμοίων πτώσεων· ὁμοίως γὰρ
δεῖ ὑπάρχειν ἢ μὴ ὑπάρχειν, οἷον ὅτι τὸ δίκαιον
οὐ πᾶν ἀγαθόν· καὶ γὰρ ἂν τὸ δικαίως· νῦν δ' οὐχ
αἱρετὸν τὸ δικαίως ἀποθανεῖν.

3 Ἄλλος ἐκ τῶν πρὸς ἄλληλα· εἰ γὰρ θατέρῳ
ὑπάρχει τὸ καλῶς ἢ δικαίως ποιῆσαι, θατέρῳ τὸ

ᵃ Assuming that self-control is good, then if the opposite
of good (that is, bad) can be predicated of lack of self-
control, this proves the truth of the first proposition; otherwise, it may be refuted.

which are refutative and those which are demonstrative, and those of apparent enthymemes, which are not really enthymemes, since they are not syllogisms. After this has been made clear, we will settle the question of solutions and objections, and whence they must be derived to refute enthymemes.

23. One topic of demonstrative enthymemes is derived from opposites ; for it is necessary to consider whether one opposite is predicable of the other, as a means of destroying an argument, if it is not, as a means of constructing one, if it is ;[a] for instance, self-control is good, for lack of self-control is harmful ; or as in the *Messeniacus*,[b]

If the war is responsible for the present evils, one must repair them with the aid of peace.

And,

For if it is unfair to be angry with those who have done wrong unintentionally, it is not fitting to feel beholden to one who is forced to do us good.[c]

Or,

If men are in the habit of gaining credit for false statements, you must also admit the contrary, that men often disbelieve what is true.[d]

Another topic is derived from similar inflexions, for in like manner the derivatives must either be predicable of the subject or not ; for instance, that the just is not entirely good, for in that case good would be predicable of anything that happens justly ; but to be justly put to death is not desirable.

Another topic is derived from relative terms. For if to have done rightly or justly may be predicated of one, then to have suffered similarly may be

---

[b] *Cf.* i. 13. 2 note.   [c] Authorship unknown.
   [d] Euripides, *Thyestes* (Frag. 396, *T.G.F.*).

πεπονθέναι, καὶ εἰ κελεῦσαι, καὶ τὸ πεποιηκέναι,
οἷον ὡς ὁ τελώνης Διομέδων περὶ τῶν τελῶν "εἰ
γὰρ μηδ' ὑμῖν αἰσχρὸν τὸ πωλεῖν, οὐδ' ἡμῖν τὸ
ὠνεῖσθαι." καὶ εἰ τῷ πεπονθότι τὸ καλῶς ἢ
δικαίως ὑπάρχει, καὶ τῷ ποιήσαντι, καὶ εἰ τῷ
ποιήσαντι, καὶ τῷ πεπονθότι. ἔστι δ' ἐν τούτῳ
παραλογίσασθαι· εἰ γὰρ δικαίως ἔπαθέν τι, δικαίως
πέπονθεν, ἀλλ' ἴσως οὐχ ὑπὸ σοῦ. διὸ δεῖ σκοπεῖν
χωρὶς εἰ ἄξιος ὁ παθὼν παθεῖν καὶ ὁ ποιήσας
1397 b ποιῆσαι, εἶτα χρῆσθαι ὁποτέρως ἁρμόττει· ἐνίοτε
γὰρ διαφωνεῖ τὸ τοιοῦτον καὶ οὐδὲν κωλύει, ὥσπερ
ἐν τῷ Ἀλκμαίωνι τῷ Θεοδέκτου

μητέρα δὲ τὴν σὴν οὔ τις ἐστύγει βροτῶν;

φησὶ δ' ἀποκρινόμενος "ἀλλὰ διαλαβόντα χρὴ
σκοπεῖν." ἐρομένης δὲ τῆς Ἀλφεσιβοίας πῶς,
ὑπολαβών φησι

τὴν μὲν θανεῖν ἔκριναν, ἐμὲ δὲ μὴ κτανεῖν.

καὶ οἷον ἡ περὶ Δημοσθένους δίκη καὶ τῶν ἀπο-
κτεινάντων Νικάνορα· ἐπεὶ γὰρ δικαίως ἐκρίθησαν
ἀποκτεῖναι, δικαίως ἔδοξεν ἀποθανεῖν. καὶ περὶ τοῦ
Θήβησιν ἀποθανόντος, περὶ οὗ ἐκέλευσε κρῖναι εἰ
δίκαιος ἦν ἀποθανεῖν, ὡς οὐκ ἄδικον ὂν τὸ ἀποκτεῖναι
τὸν δικαίως ἀποθανόντα.

---

[a] The argument is that if there was no disgrace in selling
the right of farming the taxes, there could be none in
purchasing this right.

[b] Pupil of Plato and Isocrates, great friend of Aristotle,
the author of fifty tragedies and also of an "Art" of Rhetoric.
Alcmaeon murdered his mother Eriphyle. Alphesiboea, his
wife, says to him, Was not your mother hated? To this he
replied, Yes, but there is a distinction; they said she deserved to die, but not at my hands.

predicated of the other ; there is the same relation
between having ordered and having carried out, as
Diomedon the tax-gatherer said about the taxes, " If
selling is not disgraceful for you, neither is buying
disgraceful for us." [a]   And if rightly or justly can be
predicated of the sufferer, it can equally be predicated
of the one who inflicts suffering ; if of the latter,
then also of the former.   However, in this there is
room for a fallacy.   For if a man has suffered justly,
he has suffered justly, but perhaps not at your hands.
Wherefore one must consider separately whether the
sufferer deserves to suffer, and whether he who inflicts
suffering is the right person to do so, and then make
use of the argument either way ; for sometimes
there is a difference in such a case, and nothing
prevents [its being argued], as in the *Alcmaeon* of
Theodectes [b] :

> And did no one of mortals loathe thy mother ?

Alcmaeon replied : " We must make a division before
we examine the matter."   And when Alphesiboea
asked " How ? ", he rejoined,

> Their decision was that she should die, but that it was not
> for me to kill her.

Another example may be found in the trial of
Demosthenes and those who slew Nicanor.[c]   For
since it was decided that they had justly slain him,
it was thought that he had been justly put to death.
Again, in the case of the man who was murdered at
Thebes, when the defendants demanded that the
judges should decide whether the murdered man
deserved to die, since a man who deserved it could
be put to death without injustice.

[c] Nothing is known of this trial.

299

ARISTOTLE

4 Ἄλλος ἐκ τοῦ μᾶλλον καὶ ἧττον, οἷον " εἰ μηδ᾽
οἱ θεοὶ πάντα ἴσασι, σχολῇ οἵ γε ἄνθρωποι·"
τοῦτο γάρ ἐστιν, εἰ ᾧ μᾶλλον ἂν ὑπάρχοι μὴ
ὑπάρχει, δῆλον ὅτι οὐδ᾽ ᾧ ἧττον. τὸ δ᾽ ὅτι τοὺς
πλησίον τύπτει ὅς γε καὶ τὸν πατέρα, ἐκ τοῦ, εἰ
τὸ ἧττον ὑπάρχει, καὶ τὸ μᾶλλον ὑπάρχει, καθ᾽
ὁπότερον ἂν δέῃ δεῖξαι, εἴθ᾽ ὅτι ὑπάρχει εἴθ᾽ ὅτι
5 οὔ. ἔτι εἰ μήτε μᾶλλον μήτε ἧττον· ὅθεν εἴρηται

καὶ σὸς μὲν οἰκτρὸς παῖδας ἀπολέσας πατήρ·
Οἰνεὺς δ᾽ ἄρ᾽ οὐχὶ κλεινὸν ἀπολέσας γόνον;

καὶ ὅτι, εἰ μηδὲ Θησεὺς ἠδίκησεν, οὐδ᾽ Ἀλέξανδρος, καὶ εἰ μηδ᾽ οἱ Τυνδαρίδαι, οὐδ᾽ Ἀλέξανδρος,
καὶ εἰ Πάτροκλον Ἕκτωρ, καὶ Ἀχιλλέα Ἀλέξανδρος. καὶ εἰ μηδ᾽ οἱ ἄλλοι τεχνῖται φαῦλοι, οὐδ᾽
οἱ φιλόσοφοι. καὶ εἰ μηδ᾽ οἱ στρατηγοὶ φαῦλοι,
ὅτι ἡττῶνται πολλάκις, οὐδ᾽ οἱ σοφισταί. καὶ
ὅτι " εἰ δεῖ τὸν ἰδιώτην τῆς ὑμετέρας δόξης ἐπι-
μελεῖσθαι, καὶ ὑμᾶς τῆς τῶν Ἑλλήνων."

6 Ἄλλος ἐκ τοῦ τὸν χρόνον σκοπεῖν, οἷον ὡς
Ἰφικράτης ἐν τῇ πρὸς Ἁρμόδιον, ὅτι " εἰ πρὶν
ποιῆσαι ἠξίουν τῆς εἰκόνος τυχεῖν ἐὰν ποιήσω,

---

[a] The argument is that since men beat their fathers less
commonly than they do their neighbours, if they beat their
fathers they will also beat their neighbours, and the Paris
ms. in a longer form of the argument has an explanatory
addition to this effect, inserting after ὑπάρχει the words τοὺς
γὰρ πατέρας ἧττον τύπτουσιν ἢ τοὺς πλησίον.
  In a similar passage in the *Topics* (ii. 10) εἰκός (or δοκοῦν)
is inserted after μᾶλλον and ἧττον. Welldon suggests that
here also the reading should be τὸ ἧττον εἰκός and τὸ μᾶλλον
εἰκός (Grote, *Aristotle*, p. 294).
[b] From the *Meleager* of Antiphon (*T.G.F.* p. 885).

Another topic is derived from the more and less.
For instance, if not even the gods know everything,
hardly can men; for this amounts to saying that if
a predicate, which is more probably affirmable of one
thing, does not belong to it, it is clear that it does
not belong to another of which it is less probably
affirmable. And to say that a man who beats his
father also beats his neighbours, is an instance of
the rule that, if the less exists, the more also exists.[a]
Either of these arguments may be used, according
as it is necessary to prove either that a predicate is
affirmable or that it is not. Further, if there is no
question of greater or less; whence it was said,

Thy father deserves to be pitied for having lost his children;
is not Oeneus then equally to be pitied for having lost an
illustrious offspring ? [b]

Other instances are : if Theseus did no wrong,[c]
neither did Alexander (Paris) ; if the sons of
Tyndareus did no wrong, neither did Alexander ;
and if Hector did no wrong in slaying Patroclus,
neither did Alexander in slaying Achilles ; if no other
professional men are contemptible, then neither are
philosophers ; if generals are not despised because
they are frequently defeated,[d] neither are the
sophists ; or, if it behoves a private citizen to take
care of your reputation, it is your duty to take care
of that of Greece.

Another topic is derived from the consideration
of time. Thus Iphicrates, in his speech against
Harmodius, says : " If, before accomplishing anything, I had demanded the statue from you in the

___

[c] In carrying off Helen.

[d] The Paris ms. has θανατοῦνται, " are put to death."

ἔδοτε ἄν· ποιήσαντι δ' ἆρ' οὐ δώσετε; μὴ τοίνυν
μέλλοντες μὲν ὑπισχνεῖσθε, παθόντες δ' ἀφαιρεῖσθε."

1398 a καὶ πάλιν πρὸς τὸ Θηβαίους διεῖναι Φίλιππον εἰς
τὴν Ἀττικήν, ὅτι " εἰ πρὶν βοηθῆσαι εἰς Φωκεῖς
ἠξίου, ὑπέσχοντο ἄν· ἄτοπον οὖν εἰ διότι προεῖτο
καὶ ἐπίστευσε μὴ διήσουσιν."

7   "Ἄλλος ἐκ τῶν εἰρημένων καθ' αὑτοὺς πρὸς τὸν
εἰπόντα· διαφέρει δὲ ὁ τρόπος, οἷον ἐν τῷ Τεύκρῳ·
ᾧ ἐχρήσατο Ἰφικράτης πρὸς Ἀριστοφῶντα, ἐπ-
ερόμενος εἰ προδοίη ἂν τὰς ναῦς ἐπὶ χρήμασιν· οὐ
φάσκοντος δὲ " εἶτα " εἶπεν " σὺ μὲν ὢν Ἀριστο-
φῶν οὐκ ἂν προδοίης, ἐγὼ δ' ὢν Ἰφικράτης;
δεῖ δ' ὑπάρχειν μᾶλλον ἂν δοκοῦντα ἀδικῆσαι
ἐκεῖνον· εἰ δὲ μή, γελοῖον ἂν φανείη, εἰ πρὸς
Ἀριστείδην κατηγοροῦντα τοῦτό τις εἴπειεν, ἀλλὰ
πρὸς ἀπιστίαν τοῦ κατηγόρου· ὅλως γὰρ βούλεται ὁ
κατηγορῶν βελτίων εἶναι τοῦ φεύγοντος· τοῦτ' οὖν
ἐξελέγχειν ἀεί. καθόλου δ' ἄτοπός ἐστιν, ὅταν τις
ἐπιτιμᾷ ἄλλοις ἃ αὐτὸς ποιεῖ ἢ ποιήσειεν ἄν, ἢ προτρέπῃ ποιεῖν ἃ αὐτὸς μὴ ποιεῖ μηδὲ ποιήσειεν ἄν.

---

[a] Fragment of a speech of Lysias. It was proposed to
put up a statue to the famous Athenian general Iphicrates
in honour of his defeat of the Spartans (392 B.C.). This was
later opposed by Harmodius, probably a descendant of the
tyrannicide. The speech, which is considered spurious, was
called ἡ περὶ τῆς εἰκόνος.

[b] Or, " the ways of doing this are various " (Jebb).

[c] The illustration is lost or perhaps purposely omitted as
well known. The *Teucer* was a tragedy of Sophocles.

[d] It would be absurd to use such an argument against
the accusation of a "just man" like Aristides, and to pretend that he is more likely to have committed the crime. It

event of my success, you would have granted it ; will you then refuse it, now that I have succeeded ? Do not therefore make a promise when you expect something, and break it when you have received it." [a] Again, to persuade the Thebans to allow Philip to pass through their territory into Attica, they were told that " if he had made this request before helping them against the Phocians, they would have promised ; it would be absurd, therefore, if they refused to let him through now, because he had thrown away his opportunity and had trusted them."

Another topic consists in turning upon the opponent what has been said against ourselves ; and this is an excellent method.[b] For instance, in the *Teucer* [c] . . . and Iphicrates employed it against Aristophon, when he asked him whether he would have betrayed the fleet for a bribe ; when Aristophon said no, " Then," retorted Iphicrates, " if you, Aristophon, would not have betrayed it, would I, Iphicrates, have done so ? " But the opponent must be a man who seems the more likely to have committed a crime ; otherwise, it would appear ridiculous, if anyone were to make use of such an argument in reference to such an opponent, for instance, as Aristides [d] ; it should only be used to discredit the accuser. For in general the accuser aspires to be better than the defendant ; accordingly, it must always be shown that this is not the case. And generally, it is ridiculous for a man to reproach others for what he does or would do himself, or to encourage others to do what he does not or would not do himself.

must only be used when the opponent's character is suspect, and lends itself to such a retort.

8 Ἄλλος ἐξ ὁρισμοῦ, οἷον ὅτι τὸ δαιμόνιον οὐδέν
ἐστιν ἀλλ᾽ ἢ θεὸς ἢ θεοῦ ἔργον· καίτοι ὅστις οἴεται
θεοῦ ἔργον εἶναι, τοῦτον ἀνάγκη οἴεσθαι καὶ θεοὺς
εἶναι. καὶ ὡς Ἰφικράτης, ὅτι γενναιότατος ὁ
βέλτιστος· καὶ γὰρ Ἁρμοδίῳ καὶ Ἀριστογείτονι
οὐδὲν πρότερον ὑπῆρχε γενναῖον πρὶν γενναῖόν τι
πρᾶξαι. καὶ ὅτι συγγενέστερος αὐτός· "τὰ γοῦν
ἔργα συγγενέστερά ἐστι τὰ ἐμὰ τοῖς Ἁρμοδίου
καὶ Ἀριστογείτονος ἢ τὰ σά." καὶ ὡς ἐν τῷ
Ἀλεξάνδρῳ, ὅτι πάντες ἂν ὁμολογήσειαν τοὺς μὴ
κοσμίους οὐχ ἑνὸς σώματος ἀγαπᾶν ἀπόλαυσιν. καὶ
δι᾽ ὃ Σωκράτης οὐκ ἔφη βαδίζειν ὡς Ἀρχέλαον·
ὕβριν γὰρ ἔφη εἶναι τὸ μὴ δύνασθαι ἀμύνασθαι
ὁμοίως εὖ παθόντα, ὥσπερ καὶ κακῶς. πάντες
γὰρ οὗτοι ὁρισάμενοι καὶ λαβόντες τὸ τί ἐστι,
συλλογίζονται περὶ ὧν λέγουσιν.

9 Ἄλλος ἐκ τοῦ ποσαχῶς, οἷον ἐν τοῖς τοπικοῖς
περὶ τοῦ ὀρθῶς.

10 Ἄλλος ἐκ διαιρέσεως, οἷον εἰ πάντες τριῶν
ἕνεκεν ἀδικοῦσιν· ἢ τοῦδε γὰρ ἕνεκα ἢ τοῦδε ἢ
τοῦδε· καὶ διὰ μὲν τὰ δύο ἀδύνατον, διὰ δὲ τὸ
τρίτον οὐδ᾽ αὐτοί φασιν.

---

a The reference is obviously to Socrates, who claimed that
a *daimonion* (a certain divine principle that acted as his
internal monitor) checked his action in many cases. When
accused of not believing in the gods, he was able to prove,
by his definition of the *daimonion*, that he was no atheist.
Similarly, Iphicrates, by his definition of γενναῖος and συγ-
γενής could refute the allegation that he was ignoble and
show that his deeds were more akin to those of Harmodius
and Aristogiton than to those of his opponents. Paris could
say that he was not intemperate, because he was satisfied
with Helen alone. Lastly, Socrates refused an invitation

Another topic is derived from definition. For instance, that the *daimonion* [a] is nothing else than a god or the work of a god; but he who thinks it to be the work of a god necessarily thinks that gods exist. When Iphicrates desired to prove that the best man is the noblest, he declared that there was nothing noble attaching to Harmodius and Aristogiton, before they did something noble; and, " I myself am more akin to them than you; at any rate, my deeds are more akin to theirs than yours." And as it is said in the *Alexander* [b] that it would be generally admitted that men of disorderly passions are not satisfied with the enjoyment of one woman's person alone. Also, the reason why Socrates refused to visit Archelaus, declaring that it was disgraceful not to be in a position to return a favour as well as an injury.[c] In all these cases, it is by definition and the knowledge of what the thing is in itself that conclusions are drawn upon the subject in question.

Another topic is derived from the different significations of a word, as explained in the *Topics*, where the correct use of these terms has been discussed.[d]

Another, from division. For example, " There are always three motives for wrongdoing; two are excluded from consideration as impossible; as for the third, not even the accusers assert it."

to visit Archelaus, king of Macedonia, because he would be unable to return the benefits received, which would imply his being put to shame, and make the invitation a kind of insult.

[b] Of Polycrates.

[c] " Just as it is to requite them with evil " (Jebb).

[d] Supplying [λελέκται] περὶ τοῦ ὀρθῶς [χρῆσθαι αὐτοῖς]. Others render: " in reference to the use of the word ὀρθῶς " (but ὀρθῶς does not occur in the passage in the *Topics*, i. 15). A suggested reading is περὶ τούτου ὀρθῶς εἴρηται.

11 "Αλλος ἐξ ἐπαγωγῆς, οἷον ἐκ τῆς Πεπαρηθίας,
1398 b ὅτι περὶ τῶν τέκνων αἱ γυναῖκες πανταχοῦ δι-
ορίζουσι τἀληθές· τοῦτο μὲν γὰρ Ἀθήνησι Μαντίᾳ
τῷ ῥήτορι ἀμφισβητοῦντι πρὸς τὸν υἱὸν ἡ μήτηρ
ἀπέφηνεν, τοῦτο δὲ Θήβησιν Ἰσμηνίου καὶ Στίλ-
βωνος ἀμφισβητούντων ἡ Δωδωνὶς ἀπέδειξεν
Ἰσμηνίου τὸν υἱόν, καὶ διὰ τοῦτο Θετταλίσκον
Ἰσμηνίου ἐνόμιζον. καὶ πάλιν ἐκ τοῦ νόμου τοῦ
Θεοδέκτου, εἰ τοῖς κακῶς ἐπιμεληθεῖσι τῶν
ἀλλοτρίων ἵππων οὐ παραδιδόασι τοὺς οἰκείους,
οὐδὲ τοῖς ἀνατρέψασι τὰς ἀλλοτρίας ναῦς· οὐκοῦν
εἰ ὁμοίως ἐφ' ἁπάντων, καὶ τοῖς κακῶς φυλάξασι
τὴν ἀλλοτρίαν οὐ χρηστέον ἐστὶν εἰς τὴν οἰκείαν
σωτηρίαν. καὶ ὡς Ἀλκιδάμας, ὅτι πάντες τοὺς
σοφοὺς τιμῶσιν· Πάριοι γοῦν Ἀρχίλοχον καίπερ
βλάσφημον ὄντα τετιμήκασι, καὶ Χῖοι Ὅμηρον
οὐκ ὄντα πολιτικόν, καὶ Μυτιληναῖοι Σαπφὼ καίπερ
γυναῖκα οὖσαν, καὶ Λακεδαιμόνιοι Χίλωνα τῶν
γερόντων ἐποίησαν ἥκιστα φιλολόγοι ὄντες, καὶ
Ἰταλιῶται Πυθαγόραν, καὶ Λαμψακηνοὶ Ἀναξ-
αγόραν ξένον ὄντα ἔθαψαν καὶ τιμῶσιν ἔτι καὶ
νῦν . . . ὅτι Ἀθηναῖοι τοῖς Σόλωνος νόμοις χρησά-
μενοι εὐδαιμόνησαν καὶ Λακεδαιμόνιοι τοῖς Λυ-
κούργου, καὶ Θήβησιν ἅμα οἱ προστάται φιλόσοφοι
ἐγένοντο καὶ εὐδαιμόνησεν ἡ πόλις.

---

[a] Mantias had one legitimate son Mantitheus and two
illegitimate by a certain Plangon. Mantias at first refused
to acknowledge the latter as his sons, until the mother
declared they were.

[b] The name of the mother; or simply, "the woman of
Dodona," like "the woman of Peparethus."

[c] Others read πολίτην, "although he was not their fellow-
citizen" (but Chios was one of the claimants to his birthplace).

Another, from induction. For instance, from the case of the woman of Peparethus, it is argued that in matters of parentage women always discern the truth; similarly, at Athens, when Mantias the orator was litigating with his son, the mother declared the truth;[a] and again, at Thebes, when Ismenias and Stilbon were disputing about a child, Dodonis[b] declared that Ismenias was its father, Thettaliscus being accordingly recognized as the son of Ismenias. There is another instance in the "law" of Theodectes: "If we do not entrust our own horses to those who have neglected the horses of others, or our ships to those who have upset the ships of others; then, if this is so in all cases, we must not entrust our own safety to those who have failed to preserve the safety of others." Similarly, in order to prove that men of talent are everywhere honoured, Alcidamas said: "The Parians honoured Archilochus, in spite of his evil-speaking; the Chians Homer, although he had rendered no public services;[c] the Mytilenaeans Sappho, although she was a woman; the Lacedaemonians, by no means a people fond of learning, elected Chilon one of their senators; the Italiotes honoured Pythagoras, and the Lampsacenes buried Anaxagoras, although he was a foreigner, and still hold him in honour. . . .[d] The Athenians were happy as long as they lived under the laws of Solon, and the Lacedaemonians under those of Lycurgus; and at Thebes, as soon as those who had the conduct of affairs became philosophers,[e] the city flourished."

[d] Something has fallen out, what follows being intended to prove that the best rulers for a state are the philosophers.

[e] Epaminondas and Pelopidas. One would rather expect, "as soon as philosophers had the conduct of affairs."

12 Ἄλλος ἐκ κρίσεως περὶ τοῦ αὐτοῦ ἢ ὁμοίου ἢ
ἐναντίου, μάλιστα μὲν εἰ πάντες καὶ ἀεί, εἰ δὲ μή,
ἀλλ᾽ οἵ γε πλεῖστοι, ἢ σοφοί, ἢ πάντες ἢ οἱ πλεῖστοι,
ἢ ἀγαθοί. ἢ εἰ αὐτοὶ οἱ κρίνοντες, ἢ οὓς ἀποδέχονται οἱ κρίνοντες, ἢ οἷς μὴ οἷόν τε ἐναντίον
κρίνειν, οἷον τοῖς κυρίοις, ἢ οἷς μὴ καλὸν τὰ ἐναντία κρίνειν, οἷον θεοῖς ἢ πατρὶ ἢ διδασκάλοις,
ὥσπερ τὸ εἰς Μιξιδημίδην εἶπεν Αὐτοκλῆς, εἰ
ταῖς μὲν σεμναῖς θεαῖς ἱκανῶς εἶχεν ἐν Ἀρείῳ
πάγῳ δοῦναι δίκην, Μιξιδημίδῃ δ᾽ οὔ. ἢ ὥσπερ
Σαπφώ, ὅτι τὸ ἀποθνήσκειν κακόν· οἱ θεοὶ γὰρ
οὕτω κεκρίκασιν· ἀπέθνησκον γὰρ ἄν. ἢ ὡς
Ἀρίστιππος πρὸς Πλάτωνα ἐπαγγελτικώτερόν τι
εἰπόντα, ὡς ᾤετο· '' ἀλλὰ μὴν ὅ γ᾽ ἑταῖρος ἡμῶν,''
ἔφη, '' οὐθὲν τοιοῦτον,'' λέγων τὸν Σωκράτην.
καὶ Ἡγήσιππος ἐν Δελφοῖς ἠρώτα τὸν θεόν,
πρότερον κεχρημένος Ὀλυμπίασιν, εἰ αὐτῷ ταὐτὰ
1899 a δοκεῖ ἅπερ τῷ πατρί, ὡς αἰσχρὸν ὂν τἀναντία
εἰπεῖν. καὶ περὶ τῆς Ἑλένης ὡς Ἰσοκράτης
ἔγραψεν ὅτι σπουδαία, εἴπερ Θησεὺς ἔκρινεν· καὶ
περὶ Ἀλεξάνδρου, ὃν αἱ θεαὶ προέκριναν, καὶ περὶ
Εὐαγόρου, ὅτι σπουδαῖος, ὥσπερ Ἰσοκράτης φησίν·

ᵃ Athenian ambassador to Sparta (371 B.C.), whose ag-
gressive policy he attacked. His argument is that, if the
Eumenides could agree without any loss of dignity to stand
their trial before the Areopagus, as described in Aeschylus,
surely Mixidemides could do the same. Nothing is known
of Mixidemides, but it is clear that he refused to submit
his case to it, when charged with some offence.

ᵇ The story is told of Agesipolis (which others read here)
in Xenophon, *Hellenica*, iv. 7. 2. The Argives, when a
Lacedaemonian army threatened to invade their territory,
were in the habit of alleging that it was festival time, when
there should be a holy truce. This obviously left the door

Another topic is that from a previous judgement in regard to the same or a similar or contrary matter, if possible when the judgement was unanimous or the same at all times ; if not, when it was at least that of the majority, or of the wise, either all or most, or of the good ; or of the judges themselves or of those whose judgement they accept, or of those whose judgement it is not possible to contradict, for instance, those in authority, or of those whose judgement it is unseemly to contradict, for instance, the gods, a father, or instructors ; as Autocles [a] said in his attack on Mixidemides, " If the awful goddesses were content to stand their trial before the Areopagus, should not Mixidemides ? " Or Sappho, " Death is an evil ; the gods have so decided, for otherwise they would die." Or as Aristippus, when in his opinion Plato had expressed himself too presumptuously, said, " Our friend at any rate never spoke like that," referring to Socrates. Hegesippus,[b] after having first consulted the oracle at Olympia, asked the god at Delphi whether his opinion was the same as his father's, meaning that it would be disgraceful to contradict him. Helen was a virtuous woman, wrote Isocrates, because Theseus so judged ; the same applies to Alexander (Paris), whom the goddesses chose before others. Evagoras was virtuous, as Isocrates

open to fraud, so Agesipolis (one of the Spartan kings) consulted the oracle of Zeus at Olympia to ask whether he was to respect such a truce. The reply of the oracle was that he might decline a truce fraudulently demanded. To confirm this, Agesipolis put the same question to Apollo : " Is your opinion as to the truce the same as that of your father (Zeus) ? " " Certainly," answered Apollo. Agesipolis thereupon invaded Argos. The point is that really Apollo had little choice, since it would have been disgraceful for the son to contradict the father.

Κόνων γοῦν δυστυχήσας, πάντας τοὺς ἄλλους
παραλιπών, ὡς Εὐαγόραν ἦλθεν.

13 Ἄλλος ἐκ τῶν μερῶν, ὥσπερ ἐν τοῖς τοπικοῖς,
ποία κίνησις ἡ ψυχή· ἤδε γὰρ ἢ ἤδε. παράδειγμα
ἐκ τοῦ Σωκράτους τοῦ Θεοδέκτου· " εἰς ποῖον
ἱερὸν ἠσέβηκεν; τίνας θεῶν οὐ τετίμηκεν ὧν ἡ
πόλις νομίζει; "

14 Ἄλλος, ἐπειδὴ ἐπὶ τῶν πλείστων συμβαίνει ὥσθ'
ἕπεσθαί τι τῷ αὐτῷ ἀγαθὸν καὶ κακόν, ἐκ τοῦ
ἀκολουθοῦντος προτρέπειν ἢ ἀποτρέπειν καὶ κατηγορεῖν ἢ ἀπολογεῖσθαι καὶ ἐπαινεῖν ἢ ψέγειν.
οἷον τῇ παιδεύσει τὸ φθονεῖσθαι ἀκολουθεῖ κακόν,
τὸ δὲ σοφὸν εἶναι ἀγαθόν· οὐ τοίνυν δεῖ παιδεύεσθαι,
φθονεῖσθαι γὰρ οὐ δεῖ· δεῖ μὲν οὖν παιδεύεσθαι,
σοφὸν γὰρ εἶναι δεῖ. ὁ τόπος οὗτός ἐστιν ἡ
Καλλίππου τέχνη προσλαβοῦσα καὶ τὸ δυνατὸν
καὶ τἆλλα, ὡς εἴρηται.

15 Ἄλλος, ὅταν περὶ δυοῖν καὶ ἀντικειμένοιν ἢ
προτρέπειν ἢ ἀποτρέπειν δέῃ, καὶ τῷ πρότερον
εἰρημένῳ τρόπῳ ἐπὶ ἀμφοῖν χρῆσθαι. διαφέρει
δέ, ὅτι ἐκεῖ μὲν τὰ τυχόντα ἀντιτίθεται, ἐνταῦθα
δὲ τἀναντία. οἷον ἱέρεια οὐκ εἴα τὸν υἱὸν δημ-
ηγορεῖν· ἐὰν μὲν γάρ, ἔφη, τὰ δίκαια λέγῃς, οἱ
ἄνθρωποί σε μισήσουσιν, ἐὰν δὲ τὰ ἄδικα, οἱ θεοί.
δεῖ μὲν οὖν δημηγορεῖν· ἐὰν μὲν γὰρ τὰ δίκαια

---

^a After his defeat at Aegospotami (405 b.c.) the Athenian
general Conon, fearing for his life, took refuge with
Evagoras, king of Cyprus—a proof, according to Aristotle,
of the goodness of the latter.

^b If the genus can be affirmed of any subject, then one or
other of the species, which make up the genus, must also be
predicable of it. If the proposition to be maintained is,

310

says, for at any rate Conon^a in his misfortune, passing over everyone else, sought his assistance.

Another topic is that from enumerating the parts, as in the *Topics* : What kind of movement is the soul ? for it must be this or that.^b There is an instance of this in the *Socrates* of Theodectes : " What holy place has he profaned ? Which of the gods recognized by the city has he neglected to honour ? "

Again, since in most human affairs the same thing is accompanied by some bad or good result, another topic consists in employing the consequence to exhort or dissuade, accuse or defend, praise or blame. For instance, education is attended by the evil of being envied, and by the good of being wise ; therefore we should not be educated, for we should avoid being envied ; nay rather, we *should* be educated, for we should be wise. This topic is identical with the " Art " of Callippus, when you have also included the topic of the possible and the others which have been mentioned.

Another topic may be employed when it is necessary to exhort or dissuade in regard to two opposites, and one has to employ the method previously stated in the case of both. But there is this difference, that in the former case things of any kind whatever are opposed, in the latter opposites. For instance, a priestess refused to allow her son to speak in public ; " For if," said she, " you say what is just, men will hate you ; if you say what is unjust, the gods will." On the other hand, " you *should*

the soul is moved, it is necessary to examine whether any of the different kinds of motion (increase, decrease, decay, change of place, generation, alteration) can be predicated of the soul. If not, the generic predicate is not applicable, and the proposition is refuted.

λέγῃς, οἱ θεοί σε φιλήσουσιν, ἐὰν δὲ τὰ ἄδικα,
οἱ ἄνθρωποι. τουτὶ δ' ἐστὶ ταὐτὸ τῷ λεγομένῳ
τὸ ἕλος πρίασθαι καὶ τοὺς ἅλας· καὶ ἡ βλαίσωσις
τοῦτ' ἐστίν, ὅταν δυοῖν ἐναντίοιν ἑκατέρῳ ἀγαθὸν
καὶ κακὸν ἕπηται, ἐναντία ἑκάτερα ἑκατέροις.

16 Ἄλλος, ἐπειδὴ οὐ ταὐτὰ φανερῶς ἐπαινοῦσι
καὶ ἀφανῶς, ἀλλὰ φανερῶς μὲν τὰ δίκαια καὶ τὰ
καλὰ ἐπαινοῦσι μάλιστα, ἰδίᾳ δὲ τὰ συμφέροντα
μᾶλλον βούλονται, ἐκ τούτων πειρᾶσθαι συνάγειν
θάτερον· τῶν γὰρ παραδόξων οὗτος ὁ τόπος κυριώ-
τατός ἐστιν.

17 Ἄλλος ἐκ τοῦ ἀνάλογον ταῦτα συμβαίνειν· οἷον
ὁ Ἰφικράτης τὸν υἱὸν αὐτοῦ νεώτερον ὄντα τῆς
ἡλικίας, ὅτι μέγας ἦν, λειτουργεῖν ἀναγκαζόντων,
εἶπεν ὅτι εἰ τοὺς μεγάλους τῶν παίδων ἄνδρας
νομίζουσι, τοὺς μικροὺς τῶν ἀνδρῶν παῖδας εἶναι
1399 b ψηφιοῦνται. καὶ Θεοδέκτης ἐν τῷ νόμῳ, ὅτι
πολίτας μὲν ποιεῖσθε τοὺς μισθοφόρους, οἷον
Στράβακα καὶ Χαρίδημον διὰ τὴν ἐπιείκειαν·
φυγάδας δ' οὐ ποιήσετε τοὺς ἐν τοῖς μισθοφόροις
ἀνήκεστα διαπεπραγμένους;

18 Ἄλλος ἐκ τοῦ τὸ συμβαῖνον ἐὰν ᾖ ταὐτόν, ὅτι
καὶ ἐξ ὧν συμβαίνει ταυτά· οἷον Ξενοφάνης ἔλεγεν
ὅτι ὁμοίως ἀσεβοῦσιν οἱ γενέσθαι φάσκοντες τοὺς

---

[a] The bad with the good. The exact meaning of
βλαίσωσις (see Glossary) has not been satisfactorily explained.
In the definition given of the retortion of a dilemma, the two
opposite things would be speaking truth or untruth; the two
opposite consequences, pleasing men and pleasing God.

[b] e.g. a man may say that an honourable death should be
preferred to a pleasant life, and honest poverty to ill-acquired
wealth, whereas really he wishes the opposite. "If then his
words are in accordance with his real wishes, he must be
confronted with his public statements; if they are in accord-

speak in public; for if you say what is just, the gods will love you, if you say what is unjust, men will." This is the same as the proverb, " To buy the swamp with the salt " [a]; and retorting a dilemma on its proposer takes place when, two things being opposite, good and evil follow on each, the good and evil being opposite like the things themselves.

Again, since men do not praise the same things in public and in secret, but in public chiefly praise what is just and beautiful, and in secret rather wish for what is expedient, another topic consists in endeavouring to infer its opposite from one or other of these statements.[b] This topic is the most weighty of those that deal with paradox.

Another topic is derived from analogy in things. For instance, Iphicrates, when they tried to force his son to perform public services because he was tall, although under the legal age, said : " If you consider tall boys men, you must vote that short men are boys." Similarly, Theodectes in his " law," [c] says : " Since you bestow the rights of citizenship upon mercenaries such as Strabax and Charidemus on account of their merits, will you not banish those of them who have wrought such irreparable misfortunes ? "

Another topic consists in concluding the identity of antecedents from the identity of results.[d] Thus Xenophanes said : " There is as much impiety in

ance with the latter, he must be confronted with his secret wishes. In either case he must fall into paradox, and contradict either his publicly expressed or secret opinions " (*Sophistici Elenchi*, ii. 12, Poste's translation).

[c] This " law " (already mentioned in 11) is said to have been an oration on the legal position of mercenaries.

[d] Cause and effect.

θεοὺς τοῖς ἀποθανεῖν λέγουσιν· ἀμφοτέρως γὰρ
συμβαίνει μὴ εἶναι τοὺς θεούς ποτε. καὶ ὅλως
δὲ τὸ συμβαῖνον ἐξ ἑκατέρου λαμβάνειν ὡς ταὐτὸ
ἀεί· " μέλλετε δὲ κρίνειν οὐ περὶ Ἰσοκράτους ἀλλὰ
περὶ ἐπιτηδεύματος, εἰ χρὴ φιλοσοφεῖν." καὶ ὅτι
τὸ διδόναι γῆν καὶ ὕδωρ δουλεύειν ἐστίν, καὶ τὸ
μετέχειν τῆς κοινῆς εἰρήνης ποιεῖν τὸ προσ-
ταττόμενον. ληπτέον δ' ὁπότερον ἂν ᾖ χρήσιμον.

19 Ἄλλος ἐκ τοῦ μὴ ταὐτὸ τοὺς αὐτοὺς ἀεὶ αἱρεῖσθαι
ὕστερον ἢ πρότερον, ἀλλ' ἀνάπαλιν, οἷον τόδε τὸ
ἐνθύμημα, " εἰ φεύγοντες μὲν ἐμαχόμεθα ὅπως
κατέλθωμεν, κατελθόντες δὲ φευξόμεθα ὅπως μὴ
μαχώμεθα." ὁτὲ μὲν γὰρ τὸ μένειν ἀντὶ τοῦ
μάχεσθαι ᾑροῦντο, ὁτὲ δὲ τὸ μὴ μάχεσθαι ἀντὶ
τοῦ μὴ μένειν.

20 Ἄλλος τὸ οὗ ἕνεκ' ἂν εἴη ἢ γένοιτο, τούτου
ἕνεκα φάναι εἶναι ἢ γεγενῆσθαι, οἷον εἰ δοίη ἄν
τις τινὶ ἵν' ἀφελόμενος λυπήσῃ. ὅθεν καὶ τοῦτ'
εἴρηται,

πολλοῖς ὁ δαίμων οὐ κατ' εὔνοιαν φέρων
μεγάλα δίδωσιν εὐτυχήματ', ἀλλ' ἵνα
τὰς συμφορὰς λάβωσιν ἐπιφανεστέρας.

καὶ τὸ ἐκ τοῦ Μελεάγρου τοῦ Ἀντιφῶντος,

---

[a] Isocrates, *Antidosis*, 173.
[b] The peace concluded between the Greeks (although the
Lacedaemonians held aloof) and Alexander the Great after
the death of Philip of Macedon (336 B.C.).
[c] Lysias, xxxiv. 11.
[d] *i.e.* after their return, they preferred to leave the city
rather than fight. This is Cope's explanation, but the
meaning of the clause ὁτὲ μὲν . . . ᾑροῦντο is then somewhat obscure. A more suitable interpretation would be:
" At one time they preferred to return from exile at the
price of fighting; at another, not to fight, at the price of

asserting that the gods are born as in saying that
they die ; for either way the result is that at some
time or other they did not exist." And, generally
speaking, one may always regard as identical the
results produced by one or other of any two things :
" You are about to decide, not about Isocrates alone,
but about education generally, whether it is right to
study philosophy." *a* And, " to give earth and water
is slavery," and " to be included in the common
peace *b* implies obeying orders." Of two alternatives, you should take that which is useful.

Another topic is derived from the fact that the
same men do not always choose the same thing
before and after, but the contrary. The following
enthymeme is an example : " If, when in exile, we
fought to return to our country [it would be mon-
strous] if, now that we have returned, we were to
return to exile to avoid fighting " ! *c* This amounts
to saying that at one time they preferred to hold
their ground at the price of fighting ; at another,
not to fight at the price of not remaining.*d*

Another topic consists in maintaining that the
cause of something which is or has been is something
which would generally, or possibly might, be the cause
of it ; for example, if one were to make a present
of something to another, in order to cause him pain
by depriving him of it. Whence it has been said :

It is not from benevolence that the deity bestows great
blessings upon many, but in order that they may suffer
more striking calamities.*e*

And these verses from the *Meleager* of Antiphon :

being exiled a second time (St. Hilaire)," but one does not
see how this can be got out of the Greek.
    e The author is unknown.

οὐχ ἵνα κτάνωσι θῆρ᾽, ὅπως δὲ μάρτυρες
ἀρετῆς γένωνται Μελεάγρῳ πρὸς Ἑλλάδα.

καὶ τὸ ἐκ τοῦ Αἴαντος τοῦ Θεοδέκτου, ὅτι ὁ
Διομήδης προείλετο Ὀδυσσέα οὐ τιμῶν, ἀλλ᾽ ἵνα
ἥττων ᾖ ὁ ἀκολουθῶν· ἐνδέχεται γὰρ τούτου ἕνεκα
ποιῆσαι.

21 Ἄλλος κοινὸς καὶ τοῖς ἀμφισβητοῦσι καὶ τοῖς
συμβουλεύουσι, σκοπεῖν τὰ προτρέποντα καὶ ἀποτρέποντα, καὶ ὧν ἕνεκα καὶ πράττουσι καὶ φεύγου-
σιν· ταῦτα γάρ ἐστιν ἃ ἐὰν μὲν ὑπάρχῃ δεῖ πράττειν
[ἐὰν δὲ μὴ ὑπάρχῃ, μὴ πράττειν], οἷον εἰ δυνατὸν
καὶ ῥᾴδιον καὶ ὠφέλιμον ἢ αὐτῷ ἢ φίλοις, ἢ βλαβερὸν ἐχθροῖς καὶ ἐπιζήμιον, ἢ ἐλάττων ἡ ζημία
τοῦ πράγματος. καὶ προτρέπονται δ᾽ ἐκ τούτων
καὶ ἀποτρέπονται ἐκ τῶν ἐναντίων. ἐκ δὲ τῶν
400 a αὐτῶν τούτων καὶ κατηγοροῦσι καὶ ἀπολογοῦνται·
ἐκ μὲν τῶν ἀποτρεπόντων ἀπολογοῦνται, ἐκ δὲ
τῶν προτρεπόντων κατηγοροῦσιν. ἔστι δ᾽ ὁ τόπος
οὗτος ὅλη τέχνη ἥ τε Παμφίλου καὶ ἡ Καλλίππου.

22 Ἄλλος ἐκ τῶν δοκούντων μὲν γίγνεσθαι ἀ-
πίστων δέ, ὅτι οὐκ ἂν ἔδοξαν, εἰ μὴ ἦν ἢ ἐγγὺς
ἦν. καὶ ὅτι μᾶλλον· ἢ γὰρ τὰ ὄντα ἢ τὰ εἰκότα ὑπο-
λαμβάνουσιν· εἰ οὖν ἄπιστον καὶ μὴ εἰκός, ἀληθὲς
ἂν εἴη· οὐ γὰρ διά γε τὸ εἰκὸς καὶ πιθανὸν δοκεῖ
οὕτως. οἷον Ἀνδροκλῆς ἔλεγεν ὁ Πιτθεὺς κατ-

---

[a] Frag. 2 (*T.G.F.* p. 792).
[b] *Iliad*, x. 218 ; cp. *T.G.F.* p. 801.
[c] By pointing out what is likely to deter a man from committing a crime, and *vice versa*.
[d] The argument is : we accept either that which really is, or that which is probable ; if then a statement is made which

Not in order to slay the monster, but that they may be witnesses to Greece of the valour of Meleager.[a]

And the following remark from the *Ajax* of Theodectes, that Diomedes chose Odysseus before all others,[b] not to do him honour, but that his companion might be his inferior; for this may have been the reason.

Another topic common to forensic and deliberative rhetoric consists in examining what is hortatory and dissuasive, and the reasons which make men act or not. Now, these are the reasons which, if they exist, determine us to act, if not, not; for instance, if a thing is possible, easy, or useful to ourselves or our friends, or injurious and prejudicial to our enemies, or if the penalty is less than the profit. From these grounds we exhort, and dissuade from their contraries. It is on the same grounds that we accuse and defend; for what dissuades serves for defence,[c] what persuades, for accusation. This topic comprises the whole " Art " of Pamphilus and Callippus.

Another topic is derived from things which are thought to happen but are incredible, because it would never have been thought so, if they had not happened or almost happened. And further, these things are even more likely to be true; for we only believe in that which is, or that which is probable : if then a thing is incredible and not probable, it will be true; for it is not because it is probable and credible that we think it true.[d] Thus, Androcles [e] of

is incredible and improbable, we assume that it would not have been made, unless it was true.

[e] Athenian demagogue and opponent of Alcibiades, for whose banishment he was chiefly responsible. When the Four Hundred were set up, he was put to death. Pitthus was an Athenian deme or parish.

ηγορῶν τοῦ νόμου, ἐπεὶ ἐθορύβησαν αὐτῷ εἰπόντι
" δέονται οἱ νόμοι νόμου τοῦ διορθώσοντος· καὶ
γὰρ οἱ ἰχθύες ἁλός, καίτοι οὐκ εἰκὸς οὐδὲ πιθανὸν
ἐν ἄλμῃ τρεφομένους δεῖσθαι ἁλός, καὶ τὰ στέμφυλα
ἐλαίου· καίτοι ἄπιστον, ἐξ ὧν ἔλαιον γίγνεται, ταῦτα
δεῖσθαι ἐλαίου."

23 "Αλλος ἐλεγκτικός, τὸ τὰ ἀνομολογούμενα σκοπεῖν, εἴ τι ἀνομολογούμενον ἐκ πάντων καὶ χρόνων
καὶ πράξεων καὶ λόγων, χωρὶς μὲν ἐπὶ τοῦ ἀμφισβητοῦντος, οἷον " καὶ φησὶ μὲν φιλεῖν ὑμᾶς,
συνώμοσε δὲ τοῖς τριάκοντα," χωρὶς δ' ἐπ' αὐτοῦ,
" καὶ φησὶ μὲν εἶναί με φιλόδικον, οὐκ ἔχει δὲ
ἀποδεῖξαι δεδικασμένον οὐδεμίαν δίκην," χωρὶς
δ' ἐπ' αὐτοῦ καὶ τοῦ ἀμφισβητοῦντος, " καὶ οὗτος
μὲν οὐ δεδάνεικε πώποτ' οὐδέν, ἐγὼ δὲ καὶ πολλοὺς
λέλυμαι ὑμῶν."

24 "Αλλος τοῖς προδιαβεβλημένοις καὶ ἀνθρώποις
καὶ πράγμασιν, ἢ δοκοῦσι,[a] τὸ λέγειν τὴν αἰτίαν
τοῦ παραδόξου· ἔστι γάρ τι δι' ὃ φαίνεται. οἷον
ὑποβεβλημένης τινὸς τὸν αὑτῆς υἱὸν διὰ τὸ ἀσπά-
ζεσθαι ἐδόκει συνεῖναι τῷ μειρακίῳ, λεχθέντος
δὲ τοῦ αἰτίου ἐλύθη ἡ διαβολή· καὶ οἷον ἐν τῷ Αἴαντι
τῷ Θεοδέκτου Ὀδυσσεὺς λέγει πρὸς τὸν Αἴαντα,
διότι ἀνδρειότερος ὢν τοῦ Αἴαντος οὐ δοκεῖ.

25 "Αλλος ἀπὸ τοῦ αἰτίου, ἄν τε ὑπάρχῃ, ὅτι ἔστι,
κἂν μὴ ὑπάρχῃ, ὅτι οὐκ ἔστιν· ἅμα γὰρ τὸ αἴτιον
καὶ οὗ αἴτιον, καὶ ἄνευ αἰτίου οὐθέν ἐστιν. οἷον
Λεωδάμας ἀπολογούμενος ἔλεγε, κατηγορήσαντος
Θρασυβούλου ὅτι ἦν στηλίτης γεγονὼς ἐν τῇ

---

[a] Understanding διαβεβλῆσθαι. Others read μὴ (for ἢ)
δοκοῦσι, " when there seems no reason to suspect them."

Pitthus, speaking against the law, being shouted at when he said "the laws need a law to correct them," went on, "and fishes need salt, although it is neither probable nor credible that they should, being brought up in brine; similarly, pressed olives need oil, although it is incredible that what produces oil should itself need oil."

Another topic, appropriate to refutation, consists in examining contradictories, whether in dates, actions, or words, first, separately in the case of the adversary, for instance, "he says that he loves you, and yet he conspired with the Thirty;" next, separately in your own case, "he says that I am litigious, but he cannot prove that I have ever brought an action against anyone"; lastly, separately in the case of your adversary and yourself together: "he has never yet lent anything, but I have ransomed many of you."

Another topic, when men or things have been attacked by slander, in reality or in appearance,[a] consists in stating the reason for the false opinion; for there must be a reason for the supposition of guilt. For example, a woman embraced her son in a manner that suggested she had illicit relations with him, but when the reason was explained, the slander was quashed. Again, in the *Ajax* of Theodectes, Odysseus explains to Ajax why, although really more courageous than Ajax, he is not considered to be so.

Another topic is derived from the cause. If the cause exists, the effect exists; if the cause does not exist, the effect does not exist; for the effect exists with the cause, and without cause there is nothing. For example, Leodamas, when defending himself against the accusation of Thrasybulus that his name

ARISTOTLE

ἀκροπόλει, ἀλλ' ἐκκόψαι ἐπὶ τῶν τριάκοντα, οὐκ
ἐνδέχεσθαι ἔφη· μᾶλλον γὰρ ἂν πιστεύειν αὐτῷ
τοὺς τριάκοντα ἐγγεγραμμένης τῆς ἔχθρας πρὸς
τὸν δῆμον.

26   Ἄλλος, εἰ ἐνεδέχετο βέλτιον ἄλλως ἢ ἐνδέχεται
ὧν ἢ συμβουλεύει ἢ πράττει ἢ πέπραχε σκοπεῖν·
1400 b φανερὸν γὰρ ὅτι εἰ μὴ οὕτως ἔχει, οὐ πέπραχεν·
οὐδεὶς γὰρ ἑκὼν τὰ φαῦλα καὶ γιγνώσκων προαιρεῖται. ἔστι δὲ τοῦτο ψεῦδος· πολλάκις γὰρ
ὕστερον γίγνεται δῆλον πῶς ἦν πρᾶξαι βέλτιον,
πρότερον δὲ ἄδηλον.

27   Ἄλλος, ὅταν τι ἐναντίον μέλλῃ πράττεσθαι τοῖς
πεπραγμένοις, ἅμα σκοπεῖν· οἷον Ξενοφάνης Ἐλεά-
ταις ἐρωτῶσιν εἰ θύωσι τῇ Λευκοθέᾳ καὶ θρηνῶσιν,
ἢ μή, συνεβούλευεν, εἰ μὲν θεὸν ὑπολαμβάνουσι,
μὴ θρηνεῖν, εἰ δ' ἄνθρωπον, μὴ θύειν.

28   Ἄλλος τόπος τὸ ἐκ τῶν ἁμαρτηθέντων κατηγορεῖν ἢ ἀπολογεῖσθαι, οἷον ἐν τῇ Καρκίνου
Μηδείᾳ οἱ μὲν κατηγοροῦσιν ὅτι τοὺς παῖδας ἀπ-
έκτεινεν, οὐ φαίνεσθαι γοῦν αὐτούς· ἥμαρτε γὰρ
ἡ Μήδεια περὶ τὴν ἀποστολὴν τῶν παίδων· ἡ δ'

---

[a] The names of traitors were inscribed on a brazen pillar
in the Acropolis. Leodamas supported the oligarchical,
Thrasybulus the democratical party. In answer to the
charge that he had had his name removed from the pillar
when his party came into power, Leodamas replied that,
if he had been originally posted as an enemy of the people
and a hater of democracy, he would have preferred to keep
the record, as likely to increase the confidence of the Thirty
in him, than to have it erased, even though it branded him
as a traitor.

[b] If a person has not taken the better course, when he
had the chance of doing so, he cannot be guilty.

[c] Leucothea was the name of the deified Ino. She was
the daughter of Cadmus and the wife of Athamas king of

had been posted in the Acropolis [a] but that he had erased it in the time of the Thirty, declared that it was impossible, for the Thirty would have had more confidence in him if his hatred against the people had been graven on the stone.

Another topic consists in examining whether there was or is another better course than that which is advised, or is being, or has been, carried out. For it is evident that, if this has not been done,[b] a person has not committed a certain action ; because no one, purposely or knowingly, chooses what is bad. However, this argument may be false ; for often it is not until later that it becomes clear what was the better course, which previously was uncertain.

Another topic, when something contrary to what has already been done is on the point of being done, consists in examining them together. For instance, when the people of Elea asked Xenophanes if they ought to sacrifice and sing dirges to Leucothea,[c] or not, he advised them that, if they believed her to be a goddess they ought not to sing dirges, but if they believed her to be a mortal, they ought not to sacrifice to her.

Another topic consists in making use of errors committed, for purposes of accusation or defence. For instance, in the *Medea* of Carcinus,[d] some accuse Medea of having killed her children,—at any rate, they had disappeared ; for she had made the mistake of sending them out of the way. Medea herself

Thebes. The latter went mad and, in order to escape from him. Ino threw herself into the sea with her infant son Melicertes. Both became marine deities.

[d] Tragic poet, contemporary of Aristophanes (*T.G.F.* p. 798).

ἀπολογεῖται ὅτι οὐκ ἂν τοὺς παῖδας ἀλλὰ τὸν
Ἰάσονα ἂν ἀπέκτεινεν· τοῦτο γὰρ ἥμαρτεν ἂν μὴ
ποιήσασα, εἴπερ καὶ θάτερον ἐποίησεν. ἔστι δ᾽
ὁ τόπος οὗτος τοῦ ἐνθυμήματος καὶ τὸ εἶδος ὅλη
ἡ πρότερον Θεοδώρου τέχνη.

29 Ἄλλος ἀπὸ τοῦ ὀνόματος, οἷον ὡς ὁ Σοφοκλῆς

σαφῶς Σιδηρὼ καὶ φοροῦσα τοὔνομα,

καὶ ὡς ἐν τοῖς τῶν θεῶν ἐπαίνοις εἰώθασι λέγειν,
καὶ ὡς Κόνων Θρασύβουλον θρασύβουλον ἐκάλει,
καὶ Ἡρόδικος Θρασύμαχον " ἀεὶ θρασύμαχος
εἶ," καὶ Πῶλον " ἀεὶ σὺ πῶλος εἶ," καὶ Δράκοντα
τὸν νομοθέτην, ὅτι οὐκ ἀνθρώπου οἱ νόμοι ἀλλὰ
δράκοντος· χαλεποὶ γάρ. καὶ ὡς ἡ Εὐριπίδου
Ἑκάβη εἰς τὴν Ἀφροδίτην

καὶ τοὔνομ᾽ ὀρθῶς ἀφροσύνης ἄρχει θεᾶς.

καὶ ὡς Χαιρήμων

Πενθεὺς ἐσομένης συμφορᾶς ἐπώνυμος.

30 Εὐδοκιμεῖ δὲ μᾶλλον τῶν ἐνθυμημάτων τὰ
ἐλεγκτικὰ τῶν ἀποδεικτικῶν διὰ τὸ συναγωγὴν
μὲν ἐναντίων εἶναι ἐν μικρῷ τὸ ἐλεγκτικὸν ἐνθύμημα, παρ᾽ ἄλληλα δὲ φανερὰ εἶναι τῷ ἀκροατῇ

---

[a] An early edition, afterwards enlarged. It must have
contained something more than the topic of "errors" to be
of any use.

[b] Sophocles, *Tyro*, Frag. 597 (*T.G.F.*). The reference is
to Sidero (σίδηρος, iron), the cruel stepmother of Tyro.

[c] Thompson's rendering (Introd. to his ed. of Plato's
Gorgias, p. 5). "Colt" refers to Polus's skittishness and
frisking from one subject to another.

[d] *Troades*, 990.

pleads that she would have slain, not her children, but her husband Jason; for it would have been a mistake on her part not to have done this, if she had done the other. This topic and kind of enthymeme is the subject of the whole of the first " Art " of Theodorus.[a]

Another topic is derived from the meaning of a name. For instance, Sophocles says,

Certainly thou art iron, like thy name.[b]

This topic is also commonly employed in praising the gods. Conon used to call Thrasybulus " the man bold in counsel," and Herodicus said of Thrasymachus, " Thou art ever bold in fight," and of Polus, " Thou art ever Polus (colt) by name and colt by nature," [c] and of Draco the legislator that his laws were not those of a man, but of a dragon, so severe were they. Hecuba in Euripides [d] speaks thus of Aphro-dite :

And rightly does the name of the goddess begin like the word aphro-syne (folly) ;

and Chaeremon [e] of Pentheus,

Pentheus named after his unhappy future.

Enthymemes that serve to refute are more popular than those that serve to demonstrate, because the former is a conclusion of opposites [f] in a small compass, and things in juxtaposition are always clearer to the

[e] Frag. 4 (*T.G.F.*). The name Pentheus is from πένθος (sorrow).

[f] "Admitting the apparent correctness of the opposing argument, we may prove the contradictory of its conclusion by an unassailable argument of our own, which is then called an elenchus " (Thomson, *Laws of Thought*, § 127).

ARISTOTLE

μᾶλλον. πάντων δὲ καὶ τῶν ἐλεγκτικῶν καὶ τῶν
δεικτικῶν συλλογισμῶν θορυβεῖται μάλιστα τὰ
τοιαῦτα ὅσα ἀρχόμενα προορῶσι μὴ τῷ ἐπιπολῆς
εἶναι (ἅμα γὰρ καὶ αὐτοὶ ἐφ' αὑτοῖς χαίρουσι
προαισθανόμενοι), καὶ ὅσων τοσοῦτον ὑστερίζου-
σιν ὥσθ' ἅμα εἰρημένων γνωρίζειν.

24. Ἐπεὶ δ' ἐνδέχεται τὸν μὲν εἶναι συλλογισμόν, τὸν δὲ μὴ εἶναι μὲν φαίνεσθαι δέ, ἀνάγκη καὶ
ἐνθύμημα τὸ μὲν εἶναι ἐνθύμημα, τὸ δὲ μὴ εἶναι
φαίνεσθαι δέ, ἐπείπερ τὸ ἐνθύμημα συλλογισμός τις.

2 Τόποι δ' εἰσὶ τῶν φαινομένων ἐνθυμημάτων εἷς
1401 a μὲν ὁ παρὰ τὴν λέξιν, καὶ τούτου ἓν μὲν μέρος,
ὥσπερ ἐν τοῖς διαλεκτικοῖς, τὸ μὴ συλλογισάμενον
συμπερασματικῶς τὸ τελευταῖον εἰπεῖν, οὐκ ἄρα
τὸ καὶ τό, ἀνάγκη ἄρα τὸ καὶ τό. καὶ τοῖς ἐν-
θυμήμασι τὸ συνεστραμμένως καὶ ἀντικειμένως
εἰπεῖν φαίνεται ἐνθύμημα· ἡ γὰρ τοιαύτη λέξις
χώρα ἐστὶν ἐνθυμήματος. καὶ ἔοικε τὸ τοιοῦτον
εἶναι παρὰ τὸ σχῆμα τῆς λέξεως. ἔστι δὲ εἰς τὸ
τῇ λέξει συλλογιστικῶς λέγειν χρήσιμον τὸ συλλογισμῶν πολλῶν κεφάλαια λέγειν, ὅτι τοὺς μὲν
ἔσωσε, τοῖς δ' ἑτέροις ἐτιμώρησε, τοὺς δ' Ἕλληνας
ἠλευθέρωσεν· ἕκαστον μὲν γὰρ τούτων ἐξ ἄλλων
ἀπεδείχθη, συντεθέντων δὲ φαίνεται καὶ ἐκ τούτων
τι γίγνεσθαι.

Ἕν δὲ τὸ παρὰ τὴν ὁμωνυμίαν, ὡς τὸ φάναι
σπουδαῖον εἶναι μῦν, ἀφ' οὗ γ' ἐστὶν ἡ τιμιωτάτη
πασῶν τελετή· τὰ γὰρ μυστήρια πασῶν τιμιωτάτη

---

[a] Isocrates, *Evagoras*, 65-69.
[b] Or equivocation, in which a single term has a double
meaning.

audience. But of all syllogisms, whether refutative or demonstrative, those are specially applauded, the result of which the hearers foresee as soon as they are begun, and not because they are superficial (for as they listen they congratulate themselves on anticipating the conclusion); and also those which the hearers are only so little behind that they understand what they mean as soon as they are delivered.

24. But as it is possible that some syllogisms may be real, and others not real but only apparent, there must also be real and apparent enthymemes, since the enthymeme is a kind of syllogism.

Now, of the topics of apparent enthymemes one is that of diction, which is of two kinds. The first, as in Dialectic, consists in ending with a conclusion syllogistically expressed, although there has been no syllogistic process, " therefore it is neither this nor that," " so it must be this or that " ; and similarly in rhetorical arguments a concise and antithetical statement is supposed to be an enthymeme ; for such a style appears to contain a real enthymeme. This fallacy appears to be the result of the form of expression. For the purpose of using the diction to create an impression of syllogistic reasoning it is useful to state the heads of several syllogisms : " He saved some, avenged others, and freed the Greeks " ; [a] for each of these propositions has been proved by others, but their union appears to furnish a fresh conclusion.

The second kind of fallacy of diction is homonymy.[b] For instance, if one were to say that the mouse is an important animal, since from it is derived the most honoured of all religious festivals, namely, the

ARISTOTLE

τελετή. ἢ εἴ τις κύνα ἐγκωμιάζων τὸν ἐν τῷ οὐρανῷ συμπαραλαμβάνει ἢ τὸν Πᾶνα, ὅτι Πίνδαρος ἔφησεν

> ὦ μάκαρ, ὅν τε μεγάλας θεοῦ κύνα παντοδαπὸν
> καλέουσιν Ὀλύμπιοι.

ἢ ὅτι τὸ μηδένα εἶναι κύνα ἀτιμότατόν ἐστιν, ὥστε τὸ κύνα δῆλον ὅτι τίμιον. καὶ τὸ κοινωνικὸν φάναι τὸν Ἑρμῆν εἶναι μάλιστα τῶν θεῶν· μόνος γὰρ καλεῖται κοινὸς Ἑρμῆς. καὶ τὸ τὸν λόγον εἶναι σπουδαιότατον, ὅτι οἱ ἀγαθοὶ ἄνδρες οὐ χρημάτων ἀλλὰ λόγου εἰσὶν ἄξιοι· τὸ γὰρ λόγου ἄξιον οὐχ ἁπλῶς λέγεται.

3 Ἄλλος τὸ διῃρημένον συντιθέντα λέγειν ἢ τὸ συγκείμενον διαιροῦντα· ἐπεὶ γὰρ ταὐτὸν δοκεῖ εἶναι οὐκ ὂν ταὐτὸν πολλάκις, ὁπότερον χρησιμώτερον, τοῦτο δεῖ ποιεῖν. ἔστι δὲ τοῦτο Εὐθυδήμου λόγος, οἷον τὸ εἰδέναι ὅτι τριήρης ἐν Πειραιεῖ ἐστίν· ἕκαστον γὰρ οἶδεν. καὶ τὸν τὰ στοιχεῖα

ᵃ Deriving μυστήρια (μύειν, to close the lips) from μῦς (mouse).

ᵇ A fragment from the *Parthenia* (songs sung by maidens to the accompaniment of the flute). Pan is called "the dog of Cybele," the great nature-goddess of the Greeks, as being always in attendance on her, being himself a nature-god. The fact that Pindar calls Pan "dog" is taken as a glorification of that animal.

ᶜ κοινὸς Ἑρμῆς is a proverbial expression meaning "halves!" When anyone had a stroke of luck, such as finding a purse full of money in the street, anyone with him expected to go halves. Hermes was the god of luck, and such a find was called ἑρμαῖον. κοινωνικός is taken to mean (1) liberal to others, or (2) sociable.

ᵈ λόγος: (1) speech ; (2) account, esteem.

326

mysteries [a]; or if, in praising the dog, one were to include the dog in heaven (Sirius), or Pan, because Pindar said,[b]

O blessed one, whom the Olympians call dog of the Great Mother, taking every form,

or were to say that the dog is an honourable animal, since to be without a dog is most dishonourable. And to say that Hermes is the most sociable of the gods, because he alone is called common ; [c] and that words are most excellent, since good men are considered worthy, not of riches but of consideration ; for λόγου ἄξιος has a double meaning.[d]

Another fallacy consists in combining what is divided or dividing what is combined. For since a thing which is not the same as another often appears to be the same, one may adopt the more convenient alternative. Such was the argument of Euthydemus, to prove, for example, that a man knows that there is a trireme in the Piraeus, because he knows the existence of two things, the Piraeus and the trireme ; [e] or that, when one knows the letters, one also knows

[e] Very obscure and no explanation is satisfactory. The parallel passage in *Sophistici elenchi* (20. 6) is : " Do you being in Sicily now know that there are triremes in the Piraeus ? " The ambiguity lies in the position of " now," whether it is to be taken with " in Sicily " or with " in the Piraeus." At the moment when a man is in Sicily he cannot know that there are at this time triremes in the Piraeus ; but being in Sicily he can certainly know of the ships in the Piraeus, which should be there, but are now in Sicily (Kirchmann). St. Hilaire suggests that the two clauses are : Do you now, being in Sicily, see the triremes which are in the Piraeus ? and, Did you when in Sicily, see the triremes which are now in the Piraeus ? The fallacy consists in the two facts (being in the Piraeus and the existence of triremes in Sicily), true separately, being untrue combined.

ἐπιστάμενον ὅτι τὸ ἔπος οἶδεν· τὸ γὰρ ἔπος τὸ
αὐτό ἐστιν. καὶ ἐπεὶ τὸ δὶς τοσοῦτον νοσῶδες,
μηδὲ τὸ ἓν φάναι ὑγιεινὸν εἶναι· ἄτοπον γὰρ εἰ
τὰ δύο ἀγαθὰ ἓν κακόν ἐστιν. οὕτω μὲν οὖν ἐλεγ-
κτικόν, ὧδε δὲ δεικτικόν· οὐ γάρ ἐστιν ἓν ἀγαθὸν
δύο κακά. ὅλος δὲ ὁ τόπος παραλογιστικός. πάλιν
τὸ Πολυκράτους εἰς Θρασύβουλον, ὅτι τριάκοντα
τυράννους κατέλυσεν· συντίθησι γάρ. ἢ τὸ ἐν τῷ
Ὀρέστῃ τῷ Θεοδέκτου· ἐκ διαιρέσεως γάρ ἐστιν.

δίκαιόν ἐστιν, ᾗ τις ἂν κτείνῃ πόσιν,

ἀποθνήσκειν ταύτην, καὶ τῷ πατρί γε τιμωρεῖν
τὸν υἱόν· οὐκοῦν καὶ ταῦτα πέπρακται· συντεθέντα
1401 b γὰρ ἴσως οὐκέτι δίκαιον. εἴη δ' ἂν καὶ παρὰ τὴν
ἔλλειψιν· ἀφαιρεῖται γὰρ τὸ ὑπὸ τίνος.

4 Ἄλλος δὲ τόπος τὸ δεινώσει κατασκευάζειν ἢ
ἀνασκευάζειν. τοῦτο δ' ἐστὶν ὅταν, μὴ δείξας ὅτι
ἐποίησεν, αὐξήσῃ τὸ πρᾶγμα· ποιεῖ γὰρ φαίνεσθαι
ἢ ὡς οὔτε πεποίηκεν, ὅταν ὁ τὴν αἰτίαν ἔχων αὔξῃ,
ἢ ὡς πεποίηκεν, ὅταν ὁ κατηγορῶν ὀργίζηται. οὔκουν ἐστὶν ἐνθύμημα· παραλογίζεται γὰρ ὁ ἀκροατὴς
ὅτι ἐποίησεν ἢ οὐκ ἐποίησεν, οὐ δεδειγμένου.

5 Ἄλλος τὸ ἐκ σημείου· ἀσυλλόγιστον γὰρ καὶ
τοῦτο. οἷον εἴ τις λέγοι " ταῖς πόλεσι συμφέρουσιν
οἱ ἐρῶντες· ὁ γὰρ Ἁρμοδίου καὶ Ἀριστογείτονος

---

[a] Thrasybulus deposed the thirty individuals and put
down the single tyranny which they composed ; he then
claimed a thirtyfold reward, as having put down thirty
tyrannies.
   [b] Frag. 5 (*T.G.F.*).

the word made of them, for word and letters are the same thing. Further, since twice so much is unwholesome, one may argue that neither is the original amount wholesome ; for it would be absurd that two halves separately should be good, but bad combined. In this way the argument may be used for refutation, in another way for demonstration, if one were to say, one good thing cannot make two bad things. But the whole topic is fallacious. Again, one may quote what Polycrates said of Thrasybulus, that he deposed thirty tyrants,*a* for here he combines them ; or the example of the fallacy of division in the *Orestes* of Theodectes *b* : " It is just that a woman who has killed her husband " should be put to death, and that the son should avenge the father ; and this in fact is what has been done. But if they are combined, perhaps the act ceases to be just. The same might also be classed as an example of the fallacy of omission ; for the name of the one who should put the woman to death is not mentioned.

Another topic is that of constructing or destroying by exaggeration, which takes place when the speaker, without having proved that any crime has actually been committed, exaggerates the supposed fact ; for it makes it appear either that the accused is not guilty, when he himself exaggerates it, or that he is guilty, when it is the accuser who is in a rage. Therefore there is no enthymeme ; for the hearer falsely concludes that the accused is guilty or not, although neither has been proved.

Another fallacy is that of the sign, for this argument also is illogical. For instance, if one were to say that those who love one another are useful to States, since the love of Harmodius and Aristogiton

ἔρως κατέλυσε τὸν τύραννον "Ἵππαρχον." ἢ εἴ τις λέγοι ὅτι κλέπτης Διονύσιος· πονηρὸς γάρ· ἀσυλλόγιστον γὰρ καὶ τοῦτο· οὐ γὰρ πᾶς πονηρὸς κλέπτης, ἀλλ' ὁ κλέπτης πᾶς πονηρός.

6 "Ἄλλος διὰ τὸ συμβεβηκός, οἷον ὃ λέγει Πολυκράτης εἰς τοὺς μῦς, ὅτι ἐβοήθησαν διατραγόντες τὰς νευράς. ἢ εἴ τις φαίη τὸ ἐπὶ δεῖπνον κληθῆναι τιμιώτατον· διὰ γὰρ τὸ μὴ κληθῆναι ὁ Ἀχιλλεὺς ἐμήνισε τοῖς Ἀχαιοῖς ἐν Τενέδῳ· ὁ δ' ὡς ἀτιμαζόμενος ἐμήνισεν, συνέβη δὲ τοῦτο ἐπὶ τοῦ μὴ κληθῆναι.

7 "Ἄλλος τὸ παρὰ τὸ ἑπόμενον, οἷον ἐν τῷ Ἀλεξάνδρῳ, ὅτι μεγαλόψυχος· ὑπεριδὼν γὰρ τὴν πολλῶν ὁμιλίαν ἐν τῇ Ἴδῃ διέτριβε καθ' αὑτόν· ὅτι γὰρ οἱ μεγαλόψυχοι τοιοῦτοι, καὶ οὗτος μεγαλόψυχος δόξειεν ἄν. καὶ ἐπεὶ καλλωπιστὴς καὶ νύκτωρ πλανᾶται, μοιχός· τοιοῦτοι γάρ. ὅμοιον δὲ καὶ ὅτι ἐν τοῖς ἱεροῖς οἱ πτωχοὶ καὶ ᾄδουσι καὶ ὀρχοῦνται, καὶ ὅτι τοῖς φυγάσιν ἔξεστιν οἰκεῖν ὅπου ἂν θέλωσιν· ὅτι γὰρ τοῖς δοκοῦσιν εὐδαιμονεῖν ὑπάρχει ταῦτα, καὶ οἷς ταῦτα ὑπάρχει, δόξαιεν ἂν εὐδαιμονεῖν.

ᵃ Herodotus, ii. 141. The story was that, when Sennacherib invaded Egypt, a host of field-mice devoured all the quivers, bowstrings and leather shield-holders of the Assyrians. Apollo was called Smintheus (σμίνθος, mouse) and was represented on coins with a mouse in his hand, either as the mouse-slayer and protector of crops, or because the animal was sacred to him. The story, alluded to elsewhere, was of Greek, not of Egyptian origin. Similar

overthrew the tyrant Hipparchus; or that Dionysius is a thief, because he is a rascal; for here again the argument is inconclusive; not every rascal is a thief although every thief is a rascal.

Another fallacy is derived from accident; for instance, when Polycrates says of the mice, that they rendered great service by gnawing the bowstrings.[a] Or if one were to say that nothing is more honourable than to be invited to a dinner, for because he was not invited Achilles was wroth with the Achaeans at Tenedos; whereas he was really wroth because he had been treated with disrespect, but this was an accident due to his not having been invited.[b]

Another fallacy is that of the Consequence.[c] For instance, in the *Alexander* (Paris) it is said that Paris was high-minded, because he despised the companionship of the common herd and dwelt on Ida by himself; for because the high-minded are of this character, Paris also might be thought high-minded. Or, since a man pays attention to dress and roams about at night, he is a libertine, because libertines are of this character. Similarly, the poor sing and dance in the temples, exiles can live where they please; and since these things belong to those who are apparently happy, those to whom they belong may also be thought happy. But there is a difference in condi-

panegyrics on ridiculous things or animals included pots, counters, salt, flies, bees, and such subjects as death, sleep, and food.

[b] Sophocles, *The Gathering of the Greeks* (*T.G.F.* p. 161), a satyric drama. His not being invited was a mere accident of the disrespect.

[c] Assuming a proposition to be convertible, when it is not; it does not follow, assuming that all the high-minded dwell by themselves, that all who dwell by themselves are high-minded.

ARISTOTLE

διαφέρει δὲ τῷ πῶς· διὸ καὶ εἰς τὴν ἔλλειψιν
ἐμπίπτει.

8 Ἄλλος παρὰ τὸ ἀναίτιον ὡς αἴτιον, οἷον τῷ ἅμα
ἢ μετὰ τοῦτο γεγονέναι· τὸ γὰρ μετὰ τοῦτο ὡς
διὰ τοῦτο λαμβάνουσι, καὶ μάλιστα οἱ ἐν ταῖς
πολιτείαις, οἷον ὡς ὁ Δημάδης τὴν Δημοσθένους
πολιτείαν πάντων τῶν κακῶν αἰτίαν· μετ᾽ ἐκείνην
γὰρ συνέβη ὁ πόλεμος.

9 Ἄλλος παρὰ τὴν ἔλλειψιν τοῦ πότε καὶ πῶς,
οἷον ὅτι δικαίως Ἀλέξανδρος ἔλαβε τὴν Ἑλένην·
αἵρεσις γὰρ αὐτῇ ἐδόθη παρὰ τοῦ πατρός. οὐ γὰρ
ἀεὶ ἴσως, ἀλλὰ τὸ πρῶτον· καὶ γὰρ ὁ πατὴρ μέχρι
1402 a τούτου κύριος. ἢ εἴ τις φαίη τὸ τύπτειν τοὺς
ἐλευθέρους ὕβριν εἶναι· οὐ γὰρ πάντως, ἀλλ᾽ ὅταν
ἄρχῃ χειρῶν ἀδίκων.

10 Ἔτι ὥσπερ ἐν τοῖς ἐριστικοῖς, παρὰ τὸ ἁπλῶς
καὶ μὴ ἁπλῶς, ἀλλὰ τί, γίγνεται φαινόμενος
συλλογισμός· οἷον ἐν μὲν τοῖς διαλεκτικοῖς, ὅτι
ἐστὶ τὸ μὴ ὂν ὄν· ἔστι γὰρ τὸ μὴ ὂν μὴ ὄν. καὶ ὅτι
ἐπιστητὸν τὸ ἄγνωστον· ἔστι γὰρ ἐπιστητὸν τὸ
ἄγνωστον ὅτι ἄγνωστον. οὕτω καὶ ἐν τοῖς ῥητορικοῖς ἐστι φαινόμενον ἐνθύμημα παρὰ τὸ μὴ ἁπλῶς
εἰκός, ἀλλὰ τί εἰκός. ἔστι δὲ τοῦτο οὐ καθόλου,
ὥσπερ καὶ Ἀγάθων λέγει

ᵃ The poor want to get money ; the rich dance and sing
to amuse themselves, or to show that they can do as they
like. Exiles can certainly live where they like in a foreign
land, but would prefer to live in their own country ; the rich,
who are not exiles, travel to amuse themselves.

ᵇ The first " is " means " has a real, absolute existence " ;
the second " is " merely expresses the identity of the terms of
the proposition, and is particular ; but the sophistical reasoner
takes it in the same sense as the first. The same applies to
the argument about the unknown.

tions ;[a] wherefore this topic also falls under the head of omission.

Another fallacy consists of taking what is not the cause for the cause, as when a thing has happened at the same time as, or after, another ; for it is believed that what happens after is produced by the other, especially by politicians. Thus, Demades declared that the policy of Demosthenes was the cause of all the evils that happened, since it was followed by the war.

Another fallacy is the omission of when and how. For instance, Alexander (Paris) had a right to carry off Helen, for the choice of a husband had been given her by her father. But (this was a fallacy), for it was not, as might be thought, for all time, but only for the first time ; for the father's authority only lasts till then. Or, if one should say that it is wanton outrage to beat a free man ; for this is not always the case, but only when the assailant gives the first blow.

Further, as in sophistical disputations, an apparent syllogism arises as the result of considering a thing first absolutely, and then not absolutely, but only in a particular case. For instance, in Dialectic, it is argued that that which is not *is*, for that which is not *is* that which is not [b]; also, that the unknown can be known, for it can be known of the unknown that it is unknown. Similarly, in Rhetoric, an apparent enthymeme may arise from that which is not absolutely probable but only in particular cases. But this is not to be understood absolutely, as Agathon says :

τάχ' ἄν τις εἰκὸς αὐτὸ τοῦτ' εἶναι λέγοι,
βροτοῖσι πολλὰ τυγχάνειν οὐκ εἰκότα.

γίγνεται γὰρ τὸ παρὰ τὸ εἰκός, ὥστε εἰκὸς καὶ τὸ
παρὰ τὸ εἰκός. εἰ δὲ τοῦτο, ἔσται τὸ μὴ εἰκὸς
εἰκός. ἀλλ' οὐχ ἁπλῶς, ἀλλ' ὥσπερ καὶ ἐπὶ τῶν
ἐριστικῶν τὸ κατὰ τί καὶ πρὸς τί καὶ πῆ οὐ προσ-
τιθέμενα ποιεῖ τὴν συκοφαντίαν, καὶ ἐνταῦθα
παρὰ τὸ εἰκὸς εἶναι μὴ ἁπλῶς ἀλλὰ τί εἰκός.
11 ἔστι δ' ἐκ τούτου τοῦ τόπου ἡ Κόρακος τέχνη
συγκειμένη· ἄν τε γὰρ μὴ ἔνοχος ᾖ τῇ αἰτίᾳ, οἷον
ἀσθενὴς ὢν αἰκίας φεύγῃ· οὐ γὰρ εἰκός· κἂν ἔνοχος
ὤν, οἷον ἂν ἰσχυρὸς ὤν· οὐ γὰρ εἰκός, ὅτι εἰκὸς
ἔμελλε δόξειν. ὁμοίως δὲ καὶ ἐπὶ τῶν ἄλλων· ἢ
γὰρ ἔνοχον ἀνάγκη ἢ μὴ ἔνοχον εἶναι τῇ αἰτίᾳ·
φαίνεται μὲν οὖν ἀμφότερα εἰκότα, ἔστι δὲ τὸ μὲν
εἰκός, τὸ δὲ οὐχ ἁπλῶς ἀλλ' ὥσπερ εἴρηται. καὶ
τὸ τὸν ἥττω δὲ λόγον κρείττω ποιεῖν τοῦτ' ἐστίν.
καὶ ἐντεῦθεν δικαίως ἐδυσχέραινον οἱ ἄνθρωποι
τὸ Πρωταγόρου ἐπάγγελμα· ψεῦδός τε γάρ ἐστι, καὶ
οὐκ ἀληθὲς ἀλλὰ φαινόμενον εἰκός, καὶ ἐν οὐδεμιᾷ
τέχνῃ ἀλλ' ἐν ῥητορικῇ καὶ ἐριστικῇ. καὶ περὶ
μὲν ἐνθυμημάτων καὶ τῶν ὄντων καὶ τῶν φαινομένων εἴρηται.

25. Περὶ δὲ λύσεως ἐχόμενόν ἐστι τῶν εἰρημένων εἰπεῖν. ἔστι δὲ λύειν ἢ ἀντισυλλογισάμενον
2 ἢ ἔνστασιν ἐνεγκόντα. τὸ μὲν οὖν ἀντισυλλογί-

---

[a] This utterance of Protagoras gave particular offence as
apparently implying that the weaker cause was really
identical with the worse, so that to support it was to support
injustice. But, considering the high moral character ascribed
to Protagoras, it seems more probable to take the formula as
a statement of the aim of all ancient orators—how to over-
come stronger arguments by arguments weaker in themselves.

One might perhaps say that this very thing is probable, that many things happen to men that are not probable ;

for that which is contrary to probability nevertheless does happen, so that that which is contrary to probability is probable. If this is so, that which is improbable will be probable. But not absolutely ; but as, in the case of sophistical disputations, the argument becomes fallacious when the circumstances, reference, and manner are not added, so here it will become so owing to the probability being not probable absolutely but only in particular cases. The "Art" of Corax is composed of this topic. For if a man is not likely to be guilty of what he is accused of, for instance if, being weak, he is accused of assault and battery, his defence will be that the crime is not probable ; but if he is likely to be guilty, for instance, if he is strong, it may be argued again that the crime is not probable, for the very reason that it was bound to appear so. It is the same in all other cases ; for a man must either be likely to have committed a crime or not. Here, both the alternatives appear equally probable, but the one is really so, the other not probable absolutely, but only in the conditions mentioned. And this is what "making the worse appear the better argument" means. Wherefore men were justly disgusted with the promise of Protagoras *a* ; for it is a lie, not a real but an apparent probability, not found in any art except Rhetoric and Sophistic. So much for real or apparent enthymemes.

25. Next to what has been said we must speak of refutation. An argument may be refuted either by a counter-syllogism *b* or by bringing an objection.

b In which the contrary of an opponent's conclusion is proved.

ARISTOTLE

ζεσθαι δῆλον ὅτι ἐκ τῶν αὐτῶν τόπων ἐνδέχεται
ποιεῖν· οἱ μὲν γὰρ συλλογισμοὶ ἐκ τῶν ἐνδόξων,
3 δοκοῦντα δὲ πολλὰ ἐναντία ἀλλήλοις ἐστίν. αἱ δ'
ἐνστάσεις φέρονται καθάπερ καὶ ἐν τοῖς τοπικοῖς,
τετραχῶς· ἢ γὰρ ἐξ ἑαυτοῦ ἢ ἐκ τοῦ ὁμοίου ἢ ἐκ
4 τοῦ ἐναντίου ἢ ἐκ τῶν κεκριμένων. λέγω δὲ ἀφ'
1402 b ἑαυτοῦ μέν, οἷον εἰ περὶ ἔρωτος εἴη τὸ ἐνθύμημα
ὡς σπουδαῖος, ἡ ἔνστασις διχῶς· ἢ γὰρ καθόλου
εἰπόντα ὅτι πᾶσα ἔνδεια πονηρόν, ἢ κατὰ μέρος
ὅτι οὐκ ἂν ἐλέγετο Καύνιος ἔρως, εἰ μὴ ἦσαν καὶ
5 πονηροὶ ἔρωτες. ἀπὸ δὲ τοῦ ἐναντίου ἔνστασις
φέρεται, οἷον εἰ τὸ ἐνθύμημα ἦν ὅτι ὁ ἀγαθὸς ἀνὴρ
πάντας τοὺς φίλους εὖ ποιεῖ, ἀλλ' οὐδ' ὁ μοχθηρὸς
6 κακῶς. ἀπὸ δὲ τοῦ ὁμοίου, εἰ ἦν τὸ ἐνθύμημα
ὅτι οἱ κακῶς πεπονθότες ἀεὶ μισοῦσιν, ὅτι ἀλλ'
7 οὐδ' οἱ εὖ πεπονθότες ἀεὶ φιλοῦσιν. αἱ δὲ κρίσεις
αἱ ἀπὸ τῶν γνωρίμων ἀνδρῶν, οἷον εἴ τις ἐνθύμημα
εἶπεν ὅτι τοῖς μεθύουσι δεῖ συγγνώμην ἔχειν,
ἀγνοοῦντες γὰρ ἁμαρτάνουσιν, ἔνστασις ὅτι οὔκουν
ὁ Πιττακὸς αἰνετός· οὐ γὰρ ἂν μείζους ζημίας
ἐνομοθέτησεν ἐάν τις μεθύων ἁμαρτάνῃ.
8 Ἐπεὶ δὲ τὰ ἐνθυμήματα λέγεται ἐκ τεττάρων,
τὰ δὲ τέτταρα ταῦτ' ἐστὶν εἰκὸς παράδειγμα
τεκμήριον σημεῖον, ἔστι δὲ τὰ μὲν ἐκ τῶν ὡς ἐπὶ
τὸ πολὺ ἢ ὄντων ἢ δοκούντων συνηγμένα ἐνθυμή-

---

a i.e. the *opponent's* enthymeme.
b Love is regarded as a desire, and therefore as bad as any other desire. It is here included under the general head of want.
c Incest : Ovid, *Metamorphoses*, ix. 454.
d The contrary of " good men do good to all their friends " is " bad men do harm to all their friends," but this is not
336

It is clear that the same topics may furnish counter-syllogisms ; for syllogisms are derived from probable materials and many probabilities are contrary to one another. An objection is brought, as shown in the *Topics*, in four ways : it may be derived either from itself,[a] or from what is similar, or from what is contrary, or from what has been decided. In the first case, if for instance the enthymeme was intended to prove that love is good, two objections might be made ; either the general statement that all want [b] is bad, or in particular. that Caunian love [c] would not have become proverbial, unless some forms of love had been bad. An objection from what is contrary is brought if, for instance, the enthymeme is that the good man does good to all his friends ; it may be objected : But the bad man does not do harm [to all his friends].[d] An objection from what is similar is brought, if the enthymeme is that those who have been injured always hate, by arguing that those who have been benefited do not always love. The fourth kind of objection is derived from the former decisions of well-known men. For instance, if the enthymeme is that one should make allowance for those who are drunk, for their offence is the result of ignorance, it may be objected that Pittacus then is unworthy of commendation, otherwise he would not have laid down severer punishment for a man who commits an offence when drunk.

Now the material of enthymemes is derived from four sources—probabilities, examples, necessary signs, and signs. Conclusions are drawn from probabilities, when based upon things which most commonly occur

always true. Jebb gives the objection as : " No, the bad man does not do evil to all his enemies."

ματα ἐκ τῶν εἰκότων, τὰ δὲ δι᾽ ἐπαγωγῆς διὰ τοῦ
ὁμοίου, ἢ ἑνὸς ἢ πλειόνων, ὅταν λαβὼν τὸ καθόλου
εἶτα συλλογίσηται τὰ κατὰ μέρος διὰ παραδείγματος, τὰ δὲ δι᾽ ἀναγκαίου καὶ ὄντος διὰ τεκμηρίου,
τὰ δὲ διὰ τοῦ καθόλου ἢ τοῦ ἐν μέρει ὄντος, ἐάν
τε ὂν ἐάν τε μή, διὰ σημείων, τὸ δὲ εἰκὸς οὐ τὸ
ἀεὶ ἀλλὰ τὸ ὡς ἐπὶ τὸ πολύ, φανερὸν ὅτι τὰ τοιαῦτα
μὲν τῶν ἐνθυμημάτων ἀεί ἐστι λύειν φέροντα ἔν-
9 στασιν, ἡ δὲ λύσις φαινομένη ἀλλ᾽ οὐκ ἀληθὴς ἀεί·
οὐ γὰρ ὅτι οὐκ εἰκός, λύει ὁ ἐνιστάμενος, ἀλλ᾽ ὅτι
10 οὐκ ἀναγκαῖον. διὸ καὶ ἀεί ἐστι πλεονεκτεῖν ἀπολογούμενον μᾶλλον ἢ κατηγοροῦντα διὰ τοῦτον
τὸν παραλογισμόν· ἐπεὶ γὰρ ὁ μὲν κατηγορῶν
δι᾽ εἰκότων ἀποδείκνυσιν, ἔστι δὲ οὐ ταὐτὸ λῦσαι
ἢ ὅτι οὐκ εἰκὸς ἢ ὅτι οὐκ ἀναγκαῖον, ἀεὶ δ᾽ ἔχει
ἔνστασιν τὸ ὡς ἐπὶ τὸ πολύ· οὐ γὰρ ἂν ἦν εἰκὸς
ἀλλ᾽ ἀεὶ καὶ ἀναγκαῖον· ὁ δὲ κριτὴς οἴεται, ἂν
οὕτω λυθῇ, ἢ οὐκ εἰκὸς εἶναι ἢ οὐχ αὑτῷ κριτέον,
παραλογιζόμενος, ὥσπερ ἐλέγομεν· οὐ γὰρ ἐκ
τῶν ἀναγκαίων δεῖ αὐτὸν μόνον κρίνειν, ἀλλὰ καὶ
ἐκ τῶν εἰκότων· τοῦτο γάρ ἐστι τὸ γνώμῃ τῇ
ἀρίστῃ κρίνειν. οὔκουν ἱκανὸν ἂν λύσῃ ὅτι οὐκ
ἀναγκαῖον, ἀλλὰ δεῖ λύειν ὅτι οὐκ εἰκός. τοῦτο
δὲ συμβήσεται, ἐὰν ᾖ ἡ ἔνστασις μᾶλλον ὡς ἐπὶ
11 τὸ πολύ. ἐνδέχεται δὲ εἶναι τοιαύτην διχῶς, ἢ

---

a Translating ἀεί inserted by Vahlen before ὄντος.
b That is, if the argument is shown to be not "necessary."
c The important point in the conclusion drawn is that the
judge thinks it is not his business to decide, because the
argument is not necessary, whereas his duty is to decide, not
about things that are necessary but about things that are
probable.

or seem to occur; from examples, when they are the result of induction from one or more similar cases, and when one assumes the general and then concludes the particular by an example; from necessary signs, when based upon that which is necessary and ever [a] exists; from signs, when their material is the general or the particular, whether true or not. Now, the probable being not what occurs invariably but only for the most part, it is evident that enthymemes of this character can always be refuted by bringing an objection. But the objection is often only apparent, not real; for he who brings the objection endeavours to show, not that the argument is not probable, but that it is not necessary. Wherefore, by the employment of this fallacy, the defendant always has an advantage over the accuser. For since the latter always bases his proof upon probabilities, and it is not the same thing to show that an argument is not probable as to show that it is not necessary, and that which is only true for the most part is always liable to objection (otherwise it would not be probable, but constant and necessary),— then the judge thinks, if the refutation is made in this manner,[b] either that the argument is not probable, or that it is not for him to decide,[c] being deceived by the fallacy, as we have just indicated. For his judgement must not rest upon necessary arguments alone, but also upon probabilities; for this is what is meant by deciding according to the best of one's judgement. It is therefore not enough to refute an argument by showing that it is not necessary; it must also be shown that it is not probable. This will be attained if the objection itself is specially based upon what happens generally. This may take

ARISTOTLE

τῷ χρόνῳ ἢ τοῖς πράγμασιν, κυριώτατα δέ, εἰ
1403 a ἀμφοῖν· εἰ γὰρ τὰ πλεονάκις οὕτω, τοῦτ᾽ ἐστὶν
εἰκὸς μᾶλλον.

12 Λύεται δὲ καὶ τὰ σημεῖα καὶ τὰ διὰ σημείου
ἐνθυμήματα εἰρημένα, κἂν ᾖ ὑπάρχοντα, ὥσπερ
ἐλέχθη ἐν τοῖς πρώτοις· ὅτι γὰρ ἀσυλλόγιστόν
ἐστι πᾶν σημεῖον, δῆλον ἡμῖν ἐκ τῶν ἀναλυτικῶν.
13 πρὸς δὲ τὰ παραδειγματώδη ἡ αὐτὴ λύσις καὶ τὰ
εἰκότα· ἐάν τε γὰρ ἔχωμέν τι οὐχ οὕτω, λέλυται,
ὅτι οὐκ ἀναγκαῖον, εἰ καὶ τὰ πλείω ἢ πλεονάκις
ἄλλως· ἐάν τε καὶ τὰ πλείω καὶ τὰ πλεονάκις
οὕτω, μαχετέον, ἢ ὅτι τὸ παρὸν οὐχ ὅμοιον ἢ οὐχ
14 ὁμοίως ἢ διαφοράν γέ τινα ἔχει. τὰ δὲ τεκμήρια
καὶ τεκμηριώδη ἐνθυμήματα κατὰ μὲν τὸ ἀσυλλόγιστον οὐκ ἔσται λῦσαι (δῆλον δὲ καὶ τοῦθ᾽ ἡμῖν
ἐκ τῶν ἀναλυτικῶν), λείπεται δ᾽ ὡς οὐχ ὑπάρχει
τὸ λεγόμενον δεικνύναι. εἰ δὲ φανερὸν καὶ ὅτι
ὑπάρχει καὶ ὅτι τεκμήριον, ἄλυτον ἤδη γίγνεται
τοῦτο· πάντα γὰρ γίγνεται ἀποδείξει ἤδη φανερά.

26. Τὸ δ᾽ αὔξειν καὶ μειοῦν οὐκ ἔστιν ἐνθυμήματος στοιχεῖον· τὸ γὰρ αὐτὸ λέγω στοιχεῖον
καὶ τόπον· ἔστι γὰρ στοιχεῖον καὶ τόπος, εἰς ὃ

a χρόνῳ . . . πράγμασιν. If χρόνῳ be taken to mean the
date, there are the following alternatives. The date may be
questioned, the facts admitted ; both date and facts may be
questioned ; both date and facts may be admitted, but
circumstances may have altered (a pound was worth twenty
shillings in 1914, not in 1924). Others take χρόνῳ to mean
the greater number of times the same fact has occurred,
πράγμασι the more numerous facts that increase probability.
But χρόνῳ can hardly bear this meaning (see Jebb's note).
b i. 2. 18 ; or, "at the beginning," i.e. of this book.
c Anal. priora, ii. 27.
d On the other side, in the opponent's favour.

place in two ways, from consideration either of the time or of the facts.[a] The strongest objections are those in which both are combined; for a thing is more probable, the greater the number of similar cases.

Signs and enthymemes based upon signs, even if true, may be refuted in the manner previously stated [b]; for it is clear from the *Analytics* [c] that no sign can furnish a logical conclusion. As for enthymemes derived from examples, they may be refuted in the same manner as probabilities. For if we have a single fact that contradicts the opponent's example, the argument is refuted as not being necessary, even though examples, more in number and of more common occurrence, are otherwise [d]; but if the majority and greater frequency of examples is on the side of the opponent, we must contend either that the present example is not similar to those cited by him, or that the thing did not take place in the same way, or that there is some difference. But necessary signs and the enthymemes derived from them cannot be refuted on the ground of not furnishing a logical conclusion, as is clear from the *Analytics* [c]; the only thing that remains is to prove that the thing alleged is non-existent. But if it is evident that it is true and that it is a necessary sign, the argument at once becomes irrefutable; for, by means of demonstration, everything at once becomes clear.[e]

26. Amplification and depreciation are not elements of enthymeme (for I regard element and topic as identical), since element (or topic) is a head under

[e] That is, "when the *tekmērion* is converted into a syllogism." For *tekmērion* see i. 2. 16.

πολλὰ ἐνθυμήματα ἐμπίπτει. τὸ δ' αὔξειν καὶ
μειοῦν ἐστιν ἐνθυμήματα πρὸς τὸ δεῖξαι ὅτι μέγα
ἢ μικρόν, ὥσπερ καὶ ὅτι ἀγαθὸν ἢ κακὸν ἢ δίκαιον
2 ἢ ἄδικον καὶ τῶν ἄλλων ὁτιοῦν. ταῦτα δ' ἐστὶ
πάντα περὶ ἃ οἱ συλλογισμοὶ καὶ τὰ ἐνθυμήματα·
ὥστ' εἰ μηδὲ τούτων ἕκαστον ἐνθυμήματος τόπος,
3 οὐδὲ τὸ αὔξειν καὶ μειοῦν. οὐδὲ τὰ λυτικὰ ἐνθυμήματα εἶδός τι ἐστιν ἄλλο τῶν κατασκευαστικῶν·
δῆλον γὰρ ὅτι λύει μὲν ἢ δείξας ἢ ἔνστασιν ἐνεγκών,
ἀνταποδεικνύουσι δὲ τὸ ἀντικείμενον, οἷον εἰ
ἔδειξεν ὅτι γέγονεν, οὗτος ὅτι οὐ γέγονεν, εἰ δ'
ὅτι οὐ γέγονεν, οὗτος ὅτι γέγονεν. ὥστε αὕτη
μὲν οὐκ ἂν εἴη ἡ διαφορά· τοῖς αὐτοῖς γὰρ χρῶνται
ἀμφότεροι· ὅτι γὰρ οὐκ ἔστιν ἢ ἔστιν, ἐνθυμήματα
4 φέρουσιν· ἡ δ' ἔνστασις οὐκ ἔστιν ἐνθύμημα, ἀλλὰ
καθάπερ ἐν τοῖς τοπικοῖς τὸ εἰπεῖν δόξαν τινὰ ἐξ
ἧς ἔσται δῆλον ὅτι οὐ συλλελόγισται ἢ ὅτι ψεῦδός
5 τι εἴληφεν. ἐπεὶ δὲ δὴ τρία ἐστὶν ἃ δεῖ πραγματευθῆναι περὶ τὸν λόγον, ὑπὲρ μὲν παραδειγμάτων καὶ γνωμῶν καὶ ἐνθυμημάτων καὶ ὅλως τῶν
περὶ τὴν διάνοιαν, ὅθεν τε εὐπορήσομεν καὶ ὡς
1403 b αὐτὰ λύσομεν, εἰρήσθω ἡμῖν τοσαῦτα, λοιπὸν δὲ
διελθεῖν περὶ λέξεως καὶ τάξεως.

---

[a] "Intellectual capacity, as evinced in language (or
actions), and seen when the actors argue or make an appeal
to the feelings of others, in other words, when they reason or
plead with one of the other *dramatis personae* in the same
sort of way as a rhetor might do" (Bywater on the *Poetics*,
2, 1450 a 6, where the text is speaking of the διάνοια of the
actors in a play).

which several enthymemes are included, but they are enthymemes which serve to show that a thing is great or small, just as others serve to show that it is good or bad, just or unjust, or anything else. All these are the materials of syllogisms and enthymemes; so that if none of these is a topic of enthymeme, neither is amplification or depreciation. Nor are enthymemes by which arguments are refuted of a different kind from those by which they are established; for it is clear that demonstration or bringing an objection is the means of refutation. By the first the contrary of the adversary's conclusion is demonstrated; for instance, if he has shown that a thing has happened, his opponent shows that it has not; if he has shown that a thing has not happened, he shows that it has. This, therefore, will not be the difference between them; for both employ the same arguments; they bring forward enthymemes to show that the thing is or that it is not. And the objection is not an enthymeme, but, as I said in the *Topics*, it is stating an opinion which is intended to make it clear that the adversary's syllogism is not logical, or that he has assumed some false premise. Now, since there are three things in regard to speech, to which special attention should be devoted, let what has been said suffice for examples, maxims, enthymemes, and what concerns the intelligence ^a generally; for the sources of a supply of arguments and the means of refuting them. It only remains to speak of style and arrangement.

Γ

1. Ἐπειδὴ τρία ἐστὶν ἃ δεῖ πραγματευθῆναι περὶ τὸν λόγον, ἓν μὲν ἐκ τίνων αἱ πίστεις ἔσονται, δεύτερον δὲ περὶ τὴν λέξιν, τρίτον δὲ πῶς χρὴ τάξαι τὰ μέρη τοῦ λόγου, περὶ μὲν τῶν πίστεων εἴρηται, καὶ ἐκ πόσων, ὅτι ἐκ τριῶν εἰσί, καὶ ταῦτα ποῖα, καὶ διὰ τί τοσαῦτα μόνα· ἢ γὰρ τῷ αὐτοί τι πεπονθέναι οἱ κρίνοντες, ἢ τῷ ποιούς τινας ὑπολαμβάνειν τοὺς λέγοντας, ἢ τῷ ἀποδεδεῖχθαι πείθονται πάντες. εἴρηται δὲ καὶ τὰ ἐνθυμήματα, πόθεν δεῖ πορίζεσθαι· ἔστι γὰρ τὰ μὲν εἴδη τῶν ἐνθυμημάτων, τὰ δὲ τόποι.

2 Περὶ δὲ τῆς λέξεως ἐχόμενόν ἐστιν εἰπεῖν· οὐ γὰρ ἀπόχρη τὸ ἔχειν ἃ δεῖ λέγειν, ἀλλ' ἀνάγκη καὶ ταῦτα ὡς δεῖ εἰπεῖν, καὶ συμβάλλεται πολλὰ

3 πρὸς τὸ φανῆναι ποιόν τινα τὸν λόγον. τὸ μὲν οὖν πρῶτον ἐζητήθη κατὰ φύσιν, ὅπερ πέφυκε πρῶτον, αὐτὰ τὰ πράγματα ἐκ τίνων ἔχει τὸ πιθανόν· δεύτερον δὲ τὸ ταῦτα τῇ λέξει διαθέσθαι· τρίτον δὲ τούτων, ὃ δύναμιν μὲν ἔχει μεγίστην, οὔπω δ' ἐπικεχείρηται, τὰ περὶ τὴν ὑπόκρισιν, καὶ γὰρ εἰς τὴν τραγικὴν καὶ ῥαψῳδίαν ὀψὲ παρῆλθεν· ὑπεκρίνοντο γὰρ αὐτοὶ τὰς τραγῳδίας

344

BOOK III

1. There are three things which require special attention in regard to speech : first, the sources of proofs ; secondly, style ; and thirdly, the arrangement of the parts of the speech. We have already spoken of proofs and stated that they are three in number, what is their nature, and why there are only three ; for in all cases persuasion is the result either of the judges themselves being affected in a certain manner, or because they consider the speakers to be of a certain character, or because something has been demonstrated. We have also stated the sources from which enthymemes should be derived —some of them being special, the others general commonplaces.

We have therefore next to speak of style ; for it is not sufficient to know what one ought to say, but one must also know how to say it, and this largely contributes to making the speech appear of a certain character. In the first place, following the natural order, we investigated that which first presented itself—what gives things themselves their persuasiveness ; in the second place, their arrangement by style ; and in the third place, delivery, which is of the greatest importance, but has not yet been treated of by any one. In fact, it only made its appearance late in tragedy and rhapsody, for at first the poets

οἱ ποιηταὶ τὸ πρῶτον. δῆλον οὖν ὅτι καὶ περὶ
τὴν ῥητορικήν ἐστι τὸ τοιοῦτον ὥσπερ καὶ περὶ
τὴν ποιητικήν· ὅπερ ἕτεροί τινες ἐπραγματεύθησαν
4 καὶ Γλαύκων ὁ Τήϊος. ἔστι δὲ αὐτὴ μὲν ἐν τῇ
φωνῇ, πῶς αὐτῇ δεῖ χρῆσθαι πρὸς ἕκαστον πάθος,
οἷον πότε μεγάλῃ καὶ πότε μικρᾷ καὶ πότε μέσῃ,
καὶ πῶς τοῖς τόνοις, οἷον ὀξείᾳ καὶ βαρείᾳ καὶ
μέσῃ, καὶ ῥυθμοῖς τίσι πρὸς ἕκαστον. τρία γάρ
ἐστι περὶ ὧν σκοποῦσιν· ταῦτα δ' ἐστὶ μέγεθος
ἁρμονία ῥυθμός. τὰ μὲν οὖν ἆθλα σχεδὸν ἐκ τῶν
ἀγώνων οὗτοι λαμβάνουσιν, καὶ καθάπερ ἐκεῖ
μεῖζον δύνανται νῦν τῶν ποιητῶν οἱ ὑποκριταί,
καὶ κατὰ τοὺς πολιτικοὺς ἀγῶνας διὰ τὴν μοχ-
5 θηρίαν τῶν πολιτειῶν. οὔπω δὲ σύγκειται τέχνη
περὶ αὐτῶν, ἐπεὶ καὶ τὸ περὶ τὴν λέξιν ὀψὲ προ-
ῆλθεν· καὶ δοκεῖ φορτικὸν εἶναι, καλῶς ὑπολαμ-
1404 a βανόμενον. ἀλλ' ὅλης οὔσης πρὸς δόξαν τῆς
πραγματείας τῆς περὶ τὴν ῥητορικήν, οὐκ ὀρθῶς
ἔχοντος, ἀλλ' ὡς ἀναγκαίου τὴν ἐπιμέλειαν ποιητέον, ἐπεὶ τό γε δίκαιον μηδὲν πλείω ζητεῖν περὶ
τὸν λόγον ἢ ὡς μήτε λυπεῖν μήτε εὐφραίνειν·
δίκαιον γὰρ αὐτοῖς ἀγωνίζεσθαι τοῖς πράγμασιν,
ὥστε τἆλλα ἔξω τοῦ ἀποδεῖξαι περίεργα ἐστίν·
ἀλλ' ὅμως μέγα δύναται, καθάπερ εἴρηται, διὰ
6 τὴν τοῦ ἀκροατοῦ μοχθηρίαν. τὸ μὲν οὖν τῆς
λέξεως ὅμως ἔχει τι μικρὸν ἀναγκαῖον ἐν πάσῃ
διδασκαλίᾳ· διαφέρει γάρ τι πρὸς τὸ δηλῶσαι

ᵃ Since the authors of tragedies acted their own plays,
there was no need for professional actors, nor for instruction
in the art of delivery or acting. This explains why no attempt
had been made to deal with the question. Similarly, the
rhapsodists (reciters of epic poems) were at first as a rule the
composers of the poems themselves.

themselves acted their tragedies.[a] It is clear, therefore, that there is something of the sort in rhetoric
as well as in poetry, and it has been dealt with by
Glaucon of Teos among others. Now delivery is a
matter of voice, as to the mode in which it should
be used for each particular emotion; when it should
be loud, when low, when intermediate; and how the
tones, that is, shrill, deep, and intermediate, should
be used; and what rhythms are adapted to each
subject. For there are three qualities that are considered,—volume, harmony, rhythm. Those who use
these properly nearly always carry off the prizes in
dramatic contests, and as at the present day actors
have greater influence on the stage than the poets,
it is the same in political[b] contests, owing to the
corruptness of our forms of government. But no
treatise has yet been composed on delivery, since
the matter of style itself only lately came into
notice; and rightly considered it is thought vulgar.[c]
But since the whole business of Rhetoric is to influence opinion,[d] we must pay attention to it,
not as being right, but necessary; for, as a matter
of right, one should aim at nothing more in a speech
than how to avoid exciting pain or pleasure. For
justice should consist in fighting the case with the
facts alone, so that everything else that is beside
demonstration is superfluous; nevertheless, as we
have just said, it is of great importance owing to the
corruption of the hearer. However, in every system
of instruction there is some slight necessity to pay
attention to style; for it does make a difference, for

[b] In the law courts and public assembly.

[c] Cope prefers: "is thought vulgar, and rightly so
considered."

[d] Or, "is concerned with appearance."

ὡδὶ ἢ ὡδὶ εἰπεῖν· οὐ μέντοι τοσοῦτον, ἀλλ' ἅπαντα
φαντασία ταῦτ' ἐστὶ καὶ πρὸς τὸν ἀκροατήν· διὸ
οὐδεὶς οὕτω γεωμετρεῖν διδάσκει.

7 Ἐκείνη μὲν οὖν ὅταν ἔλθῃ ταὐτὸ ποιήσει τῇ
ὑποκριτικῇ, ἐγκεχειρήκασι δὲ ἐπ' ὀλίγον περὶ
αὐτῆς εἰπεῖν τινές, οἷον Θρασύμαχος ἐν τοῖς ἐλέοις·
καὶ ἔστι φύσεως τὸ ὑποκριτικὸν εἶναι, καὶ ἀτεχνό-
τερον, περὶ δὲ τὴν λέξιν ἔντεχνον. διὸ καὶ τοῖς
τοῦτο δυναμένοις γίνεται πάλιν ἆθλα, καθάπερ
καὶ τοῖς κατὰ τὴν ὑπόκρισιν ῥήτορσιν· οἱ γὰρ
γραφόμενοι λόγοι μεῖζον ἰσχύουσι διὰ τὴν λέξιν
ἢ διὰ τὴν διάνοιαν.

8 Ἤρξαντο μὲν οὖν κινῆσαι τὸ πρῶτον, ὥσπερ
πέφυκεν, οἱ ποιηταί· τὰ γὰρ ὀνόματα μιμήματα
ἐστίν, ὑπῆρξε δὲ καὶ ἡ φωνὴ πάντων μιμητικώ-
τατον τῶν μορίων ἡμῖν· διὸ καὶ αἱ τέχναι συν-
έστησαν, ἥ τε ῥαψῳδία καὶ ἡ ὑποκριτικὴ καὶ ἄλλαι
9 γε. ἐπεὶ δ' οἱ ποιηταὶ λέγοντες εὐήθη διὰ τὴν
λέξιν ἐδόκουν πορίσασθαι τὴν δόξαν, διὰ τοῦτο
ποιητικὴ πρώτη ἐγένετο λέξις, οἷον ἡ Γοργίου.
καὶ νῦν ἔτι οἱ πολλοὶ τῶν ἀπαιδεύτων τοὺς τοιούτους οἴονται διαλέγεσθαι κάλλιστα. τοῦτο δ' οὐκ
ἔστιν, ἀλλ' ἑτέρα λόγου καὶ ποιήσεως λέξις ἐστίν.
δηλοῖ δὲ τὸ συμβαῖνον· οὐδὲ γὰρ οἱ τὰς τραγῳδίας
ποιοῦντες ἔτι χρῶνται τὸν αὐτὸν τρόπον, ἀλλ'
ὥσπερ καὶ ἐκ τῶν τετραμέτρων εἰς τὸ ἰαμβεῖον
μετέβησαν διὰ τὸ τῷ λόγῳ τοῦτο τῶν μέτρων

ᵃ *i.e.* style, delivery, and acting, which are of no use to
serious students.
ᵇ A treatise on Pathos.

the purpose of making a thing clear, to speak in this or that manner; still, the difference is not so very great, but all these things[a] are mere outward show for pleasing the hearer; wherefore no one teaches geometry in this way.

Now, when delivery comes into fashion, it will have the same effect as acting. Some writers have attempted to say a few words about it, as Thrasymachus, in his *Eleoi*[b]; and in fact, a gift for acting is a natural talent and depends less upon art, but in regard to style it is artificial. Wherefore people who excel in this in their turn obtain prizes, just as orators who excel in delivery; for written speeches owe their effect not so much to the sense as to the style.

The poets, as was natural, were the first to give an impulse to style; for words are imitations, and the voice also, which of all our parts is best adapted for imitation, was ready to hand; thus the arts of the rhapsodists, actors, and others, were fashioned. And as the poets, although their utterances were devoid of sense, appeared to have gained their reputation through their style, it was a poetical style that first came into being, as that of Gorgias.[c] Even now the majority of the uneducated think that such persons express themselves most beautifully, whereas this is not the case, for the style of prose is not the same as that of poetry. And the result proves it; for even the writers of tragedies do not employ it in the same manner, but as they have changed from the tetrametric to the iambic metre, because the latter, of all other metres, most nearly resembles

[c] Of Leontini in Sicily, Greek sophist and rhetorician (see Introduction).

ARISTOTLE

ὁμοιότατον εἶναι τῶν ἄλλων, οὕτω καὶ τῶν ὀνομάτων ἀφείκασιν ὅσα παρὰ τὴν διάλεκτόν ἐστιν,
οἷς οἱ πρῶτον ἐκόσμουν, καὶ ἔτι νῦν οἱ τὰ ἐξάμετρα
ποιοῦντες· διὸ γελοῖον μιμεῖσθαι τούτους οἳ αὐτοὶ
10 οὐκέτι χρῶνται ἐκείνῳ τῷ τρόπῳ. ὥστε φανερὸν
ὅτι οὐχ ἅπαντα ὅσα περὶ λέξεώς ἐστιν εἰπεῖν, ἀκριβο-
λογητέον ἡμῖν, ἀλλ' ὅσα περὶ τοιαύτης οἵας λέγομεν.
περὶ δ' ἐκείνης εἴρηται ἐν τοῖς περὶ ποιητικῆς.

1404 b   2. Ἔστω οὖν ἐκεῖνα τεθεωρημένα, καὶ ὡρίσθω
λέξεως ἀρετὴ σαφῆ εἶναι· σημεῖον γὰρ ὅτι ὁ λόγος,
ἐὰν μὴ δηλοῖ, οὐ ποιήσει τὸ ἑαυτοῦ ἔργον· καὶ
μήτε ταπεινὴν μήτε ὑπὲρ τὸ ἀξίωμα, ἀλλὰ πρέ-
πουσαν· ἡ γὰρ ποιητικὴ ἴσως οὐ ταπεινή, ἀλλ'
2 οὐ πρέπουσα λόγῳ. τῶν δ' ὀνομάτων καὶ ῥημάτων
σαφῆ μὲν ποιεῖ τὰ κύρια, μὴ ταπεινὴν δὲ ἀλλὰ
κεκοσμημένην τἆλλα ὀνόματα ὅσα εἴρηται ἐν τοῖς
περὶ ποιητικῆς· τὸ γὰρ ἐξαλλάξαι ποιεῖ φαίνεσθαι
σεμνοτέραν· ὥσπερ γὰρ πρὸς τοὺς ξένους οἱ
ἄνθρωποι καὶ πρὸς τοὺς πολίτας, τὸ αὐτὸ πά-
3 σχουσι καὶ πρὸς τὴν λέξιν. διὸ δεῖ ποιεῖν ξένην
τὴν διάλεκτον· θαυμασταὶ γὰρ τῶν ἀπόντων εἰσίν,
ἡδὺ δὲ τὸ θαυμαστόν. ἐπὶ μὲν οὖν τῶν μέτρων
πολλά τε ποιεῖ τοῦτο, καὶ ἁρμόττει ἐκεῖ· πλέον
γὰρ ἐξέστηκε περὶ ἃ καὶ περὶ οὓς ὁ λόγος· ἐν δὲ

ᵃ *i.e.* the poetic style. See *Poetics*, 22, where the choice
of words and the extent to which out-of-the-way words and
phrases may be used in poetry is discussed.

ᵇ " Nouns and verbs " is a conventional expression for all
the parts of speech. Cp. Horace, *Ars Poetica*, 240, " non ego
inornata et dominantia nomina solum | verbaque," where
dominantia is a literal adaptation of κύρια (see Glossary), the
usual Latin equivalent for which is *propria*.

ᶜ Ch. 21.

ᵈ It is impossible to find a satisfactory English equivalent

350

prose, they have in like manner discarded all such words as differ from those of ordinary conversation, with which the early poets used to adorn their writings, and which even now are employed by the writers of hexameters. It is therefore ridiculous to imitate those who no longer employ that manner of writing. Consequently, it is evident that we need not enter too precisely into all questions of style, but only those which concern such a style as we are discussing. As for the other kind of style,[a] it has already been treated in the *Poetics*.

2. Let this suffice for the consideration of these points. In regard to style, one of its chief merits may be defined as perspicuity. This is shown by the fact that the speech, if it does not make the meaning clear, will not perform its proper function ; neither must it be mean, nor above the dignity of the subject, but appropriate to it ; for the poetic style may be is not mean, but it is not appropriate to prose. Of nouns and verbs it is the proper ones that make style perspicuous [b] ; all the others which have been spoken of in the *Poetics* [c] elevate and make it ornate ; for departure from the ordinary makes it appear more dignified. In this respect men feel the same in regard to style as in regard to foreigners and fellow-citizens. Wherefore we should give our language a " foreign [d] air " ; for men admire what is remote, and that which excites admiration is pleasant. In poetry many things conduce to this and there it is appropriate ; for the subjects and persons spoken of are more out of the common. But

for the terms ξένος, ξενικός, τὸ ξενίζον, as applied to style. "Foreign" does not really convey the idea, which is rather that of something opposed to "home-like,"—out-of-the-way, as if from "abroad." Jebb suggests "distinctive."

τοῖς ψιλοῖς λόγοις πολλῷ ἐλάττοσιν· ἡ γὰρ ὑπόθεσις
ἐλάττων, ἐπεὶ καὶ ἐνταῦθα, εἰ δοῦλος καλλιεποῖτο
ἢ λίαν νέος, ἀπρεπέστερον, ἢ περὶ λίαν μικρῶν·
ἀλλ' ἔστι καὶ ἐν τούτοις ἐπισυστελλόμενον καὶ
4 αὐξανόμενον τὸ πρέπον. διὸ δεῖ λανθάνειν ποιοῦν-
τας, καὶ μὴ δοκεῖν λέγειν πεπλασμένως ἀλλὰ
πεφυκότως· τοῦτο γὰρ πιθανόν, ἐκεῖνο δὲ τοὐναν-
τίον· ὡς γὰρ πρὸς ἐπιβουλεύοντα διαβάλλονται,
καθάπερ πρὸς τοὺς οἴνους τοὺς μεμιγμένους, καὶ
οἷον ἡ Θεοδώρου φωνὴ πέπονθε πρὸς τὴν τῶν
ἄλλων ὑποκριτῶν· ἡ μὲν γὰρ τοῦ λέγοντος ἔοικεν
5 εἶναι, αἱ δ' ἀλλότριαι. κλέπτεται δ' εὖ, ἐάν τις
ἐκ τῆς εἰωθυίας διαλέκτου ἐκλέγων συντιθῇ· ὅπερ
Εὐριπίδης ποιεῖ καὶ ὑπέδειξε πρῶτος.

Ὄντων δ' ὀνομάτων καὶ ῥημάτων ἐξ ὧν ὁ λόγος
συνέστηκεν, τῶν δὲ ὀνομάτων τοσαῦτ' ἐχόντων
εἴδη ὅσα τεθεώρηται ἐν τοῖς περὶ ποιήσεως,
τούτων γλώτταις μὲν καὶ διπλοῖς ὀνόμασι καὶ
πεποιημένοις ὀλιγάκις καὶ ὀλιγαχοῦ χρηστέον
(ὅπου δέ, ὕστερον ἐροῦμεν, τό τε διὰ τί εἴρηται·
6 ἐπὶ τὸ μεῖζον γὰρ ἐξαλλάττει τοῦ πρέποντος.) τὸ
δὲ κύριον καὶ τὸ οἰκεῖον καὶ μεταφορὰ μόναι
χρήσιμοι πρὸς τὴν τῶν ψιλῶν λόγων λέξιν. σημεῖον
δέ, ὅτι τούτοις μόνοις πάντες χρῶνται· πάντες γὰρ
μεταφοραῖς διαλέγονται καὶ τοῖς οἰκείοις καὶ τοῖς
κυρίοις· ὥστε δῆλον ὡς ἂν εὖ ποιῇ τις, ἔσται τε
ξενικὸν καὶ λανθάνειν ἐνδέχεται καὶ σαφηνιεῖ.

---

[a] Cp. Horace, *Ars Poetica*, 46, where it is said that the choice and use of words requires subtlety and care, skill in making an old word new by clever combination (*callida iunctura*) being especially praised. [b] Chs. 3 and 7.

in prose such methods are appropriate in much fewer instances, for the subject is less elevated ; and even in poetry, if fine language were used by a slave or a very young man, or about quite unimportant matters, it would be hardly becoming ; for even here due proportion consists in contraction and amplification as the subject requires. Wherefore those who practise this artifice must conceal it and avoid the appearance of speaking artificially instead of naturally ; for that which is natural persuades, but the artificial does not. For men become suspicious of one whom they think to be laying a trap for them, as they are of mixed wines. Such was the case with the voice of Theodorus as contrasted with that of the rest of the actors ; for his seemed to be the voice of the speaker, that of the others the voice of some one else. Art is cleverly concealed when the speaker chooses his words from ordinary language *a* and puts them together like Euripides, who was the first to show the way.

Nouns and verbs being the components of speech, and nouns being of the different kinds which have been considered in the *Poetics*, of these we should use strange, compound, or coined words only rarely and in few places. We will state later *b* in what places they should be used ; the reason for this has already been mentioned, namely, that it involves too great a departure from suitable language. Proper and appropriate words and metaphors are alone to be employed in the style of prose ; this is shown by the fact that no one employs anything but these. For all use metaphors in conversation, as well as proper and appropriate words ; wherefore it is clear that, if a speaker manages well, there will be some-

7 αὕτη δ' ἦν ἡ τοῦ ῥητορικοῦ λόγου ἀρετή. τῶν δ'
ὀνομάτων τῷ μὲν σοφιστῇ ὁμωνυμίαι χρήσιμοι
(παρὰ ταύτας γὰρ κακουργεῖ), τῷ ποιητῇ δὲ
1405 a συνωνυμίαι. λέγω δὲ κύριά τε καὶ συνώνυμα,
οἷον τὸ πορεύεσθαι καὶ τὸ βαδίζειν· ταῦτα γὰρ
ἀμφότερα καὶ κύρια καὶ συνώνυμα ἀλλήλοις.

Τί μὲν οὖν τούτων ἕκαστόν ἐστι, καὶ πόσα εἴδη
μεταφορᾶς, καὶ ὅτι τοῦτο πλεῖστον δύναται καὶ
ἐν ποιήσει καὶ ἐν λόγοις, εἴρηται, καθάπερ ἐλέ-
8 γομεν, ἐν τοῖς περὶ ποιητικῆς· τοσούτῳ δ' ἐν
λόγῳ δεῖ μᾶλλον φιλοπονεῖσθαι περὶ αὐτῶν, ὅσῳ
ἐξ ἐλαττόνων βοηθημάτων ὁ λόγος ἐστὶ τῶν
μέτρων. καὶ τὸ σαφὲς καὶ τὸ ἡδὺ καὶ τὸ ξενικὸν
ἔχει μάλιστα ἡ μεταφορά. καὶ λαβεῖν οὐκ ἔστιν
9 αὐτὴν παρ' ἄλλου. δεῖ δὲ καὶ τὰ ἐπίθετα καὶ τὰς
μεταφορὰς ἁρμοττούσας λέγειν. τοῦτο δ' ἔσται
ἐκ τοῦ ἀνάλογον· εἰ δὲ μή, ἀπρεπὲς φανεῖται διὰ
τὸ παράλληλα τὰ ἐναντία μάλιστα φαίνεσθαι.
ἀλλὰ δεῖ σκοπεῖν, ὡς νέῳ φοινικίς, οὕτω γέροντι
10 τί· οὐ γὰρ ἡ αὐτὴ πρέπει ἐσθής. καὶ ἐάν τε
κοσμεῖν βούλῃ, ἀπὸ τῶν βελτιόνων τῶν ἐν ταὐτῷ
γένει φέρειν τὴν μεταφοράν, ἐάν τε ψέγειν, ἀπὸ
τῶν χειρόνων. λέγω δ' οἷον, ἐπεὶ τὰ ἐναντία ἐν
τῷ αὐτῷ γένει, τὸ φάναι τὸν μὲν πτωχεύοντα
εὔχεσθαι, τὸν δὲ εὐχόμενον πτωχεύειν, ὅτι ἄμφω
αἰτήσεις, τὸ εἰρημένον ἐστὶ ποιεῖν· ὡς καὶ Ἰφικράτης

---

[a] This is a parenthetical note. [b] Chs. 21, 22.
[c] The different kinds of words.
[d] *Poetics*, 22. 9 : " for this alone cannot be borrowed from another."
[e] Begging (as a beggar does) and praying (as a priest might) are both forms of asking, and by substituting one for the other, you can amplify or depreciate.

354

thing " foreign " about his speech, while possibly the art may not be detected, and his meaning will be clear. And this, as we have said, is the chief merit of rhetorical language. (In regard to nouns, homonyms are most useful to the sophist, for it is by their aid that he employs captious arguments, and synonyms to the poet. Instances of words that are both proper and synonymous are " going " and " walking " : for these two words are proper and have the same meaning.)[a]

It has already been stated, as we have said, in the *Poetics*,[b] what each of these things[c] is, how many kinds of metaphor there are, and that it is most important both in poetry and in prose. But the orator must devote the greater attention to them in prose, since the latter has fewer resources than verse. It is metaphor above all that gives perspicuity, pleasure, and a foreign air, and it cannot be learnt from anyone else ;[d] but we must make use of metaphors and epithets that are appropriate. This will be secured by observing due proportion ; otherwise there will be a lack of propriety, because it is when placed in juxtaposition that contraries are most evident. We must consider, as a red cloak suits a young man, what suits an old one ; for the same garment is not suitable for both. And if we wish to ornament our subject, we must derive our metaphor from the better species under the same genus ; if to depreciate it, from the worse. Thus, to say (for you have two opposites belonging to the same genus) that the man who begs prays, or that the man who prays begs (for both are forms of asking)[e] is an instance of doing this ; as, when

Καλλίαν μητραγύρτην ἀλλ' οὐ δαδοῦχον. ὁ δ'
ἔφη ἀμύητον αὐτὸν εἶναι· οὐ γὰρ ἂν μητραγύρτην
αὐτὸν καλεῖν, ἀλλὰ δαδοῦχον· ἄμφω γὰρ περὶ
θεόν, ἀλλὰ τὸ μὲν τίμιον τὸ δὲ ἄτιμον. καὶ ὁ μὲν
διονυσοκόλακας, αὐτοὶ δ' αὑτοὺς τεχνίτας καλοῦσιν·
ταῦτα δ' ἄμφω μεταφορά, ἡ μὲν ῥυπαινόντων ἡ
δὲ τοὐναντίον. καὶ οἱ μὲν λησταὶ αὑτοὺς ποριστὰς
καλοῦσι νῦν· διὸ ἔξεστι λέγειν τὸν ἀδικήσαντα μὲν
ἁμαρτάνειν, τὸν δ' ἁμαρτάνοντα ἀδικῆσαι, καὶ τὸν
κλέψαντα καὶ λαβεῖν καὶ πορθῆσαι. τὸ δὲ ὡς ὁ
Τήλεφος Εὐριπίδου φησί,

κώπης ἀνάσσειν, κἀποβὰς εἰς Μυσίαν

ἀπρεπές, ὅτι μεῖζον τὸ ἀνάσσειν ἢ κατ' ἀξίαν· οὐ
11 κέκλεπται οὖν. ἔστι δὲ καὶ ἐν ταῖς συλλαβαῖς
ἁμαρτία, ἐὰν μὴ ἡδείας ᾖ σημεῖα φωνῆς, οἷον
Διονύσιος προσαγορεύει ὁ χαλκοῦς ἐν τοῖς ἐλεγείοις

κραυγὴν Καλλιόπης

τὴν ποίησιν, ὅτι ἄμφω φωναί· φαύλη δὲ ἡ μεταφορὰ ταῖς ἀσήμοις φωναῖς.

---

a See i. 7. 32.
b Head of a distinguished Athenian family which held
the office of torch-bearer at the Eleusinian mysteries. A
man of notoriously dissipated character, he took some part
in politics.
c The δαδοῦχος or hereditary torch-bearer ranked next to
the hierophant or chief priest. In addition to holding the
torch during the sacrifices, he took part in the recitation of
the ritual and certain purificatory ceremonies. The
μητραγύρται or mendicant priests collected alms on behalf of
various deities, especially the great Mother Cybele (whence
their name). They included both men and women of
profligate character, addicted to every kind of lewdness.

Iphicrates [a] called Callias [b] a mendicant priest instead of a torch-bearer, Callias replied that Iphicrates himself could not be initiated, otherwise he would not have called him mendicant priest but torch-bearer [c]; both titles indeed have to do with a divinity, but the one is honourable, the other dishonourable. And some call actors flatterers of Dionysus, whereas they call themselves "artists." Both these names are metaphors, but the one is a term of abuse, the other the contrary. Similarly, pirates now call themselves purveyors [d]; and so it is allowable to say that the man who has committed a crime has "made a mistake," that the man who has "made a mistake" is "guilty of crime," and that one who has committed a theft has either "taken" or "ravaged." The saying in the *Telephus* of Euripides,

> Ruling over the oar and having landed in Mysia,

is inappropriate, because the word "ruling" exceeds the dignity of the subject, and so the artifice can be seen. Forms of words also are faulty, if they do not express an agreeable sound; for instance, Dionysius the Brazen [e] in his elegiacs speaks of poetry as

> the scream of Calliope;

both are sounds, but the metaphor is bad, because the sounds have no meaning.[f]

[d] *Cf.* "'convey' the wise it call" (*Merry Wives*, I. iii.). Either the euphemistic or unfavourable application of the term may be adopted.

[e] According to Athenaeus, xv. p. 669, he was a poet and rhetorician who recommended the Athenians to use bronze money.

[f] A scream is neither articulate nor agreeable, like the sound of poetry, although both are voices or sound, and to that extent the metaphor is correct.

357

12 Ἔτι δὲ οὐ πόρρωθεν δεῖ, ἀλλ' ἐκ τῶν συγγενῶν
καὶ τῶν ὁμοειδῶν μεταφέρειν τὰ ἀνώνυμα ὠνο-
μασμένως, ὃ λεχθὲν δῆλόν ἐστιν ὅτι συγγενές,
1405 b οἷον ἐν τῷ αἰνίγματι τῷ εὐδοκιμοῦντι

ἄνδρ' εἶδον πυρὶ χαλκὸν ἐπ' ἀνέρι κολλήσαντα·

ἀνώνυμον γὰρ τὸ πάθος, ἔστι δ' ἄμφω πρόσθεσί;
τις· κόλλησιν τοίνυν εἶπε τὴν τῆς σικύας προσβολήν.
καὶ ὅλως ἐκ τῶν εὖ ᾐνιγμένων ἔστι μεταφορὰς
λαβεῖν ἐπιεικεῖς· μεταφοραὶ γὰρ αἰνίττονται, ὥστε
13 δῆλον ὅτι εὖ μετενήνεκται. καὶ ἀπὸ καλῶν·
κάλλος δὲ ὀνόματος τὸ μέν, ὥσπερ Λικύμνιος
λέγει, ἐν τοῖς ψόφοις ἢ τῷ σημαινομένῳ, καὶ
αἶσχος δὲ ὡσαύτως. ἔτι δὲ τρίτον, ὃ λύει τὸν
σοφιστικὸν λόγον· οὐ γὰρ ὡς ἔφη Βρύσων οὐθένα
αἰσχρολογεῖν, εἴπερ τὸ αὐτὸ σημαίνει τόδε ἀντὶ
τοῦ τόδε εἰπεῖν· τοῦτο γάρ ἐστι ψεῦδος· ἔστι γὰρ
ἄλλο ἄλλου κυριώτερον καὶ ὡμοιωμένον μᾶλλον
καὶ οἰκειότερον τῷ ποιεῖν τὸ πρᾶγμα πρὸ ὀμμάτων.
ἔτι οὐχ ὁμοίως ἔχον σημαίνει τόδε καὶ τόδε, ὥστε
καὶ οὕτως ἄλλο ἄλλου κάλλιον καὶ αἴσχιον θετέον·
ἄμφω μὲν γὰρ τὸ καλὸν καὶ τὸ αἰσχρὸν σημαί-
νουσιν, ἀλλ' οὐχ ᾗ καλὸν ἢ οὐχ ᾗ αἰσχρόν· ἢ
ταῦτα μέν, ἀλλὰ μᾶλλον καὶ ἧττον. τὰς δὲ μεταφορὰς ἐντεῦθεν οἰστέον, ἀπὸ καλῶν ἢ τῇ φωνῇ
ἢ τῇ δυνάμει ἢ τῇ ὄψει ἢ ἄλλῃ τινὶ αἰσθήσει.
διαφέρει δ' εἰπεῖν, οἷον ῥοδοδάκτυλος ἠὼς μᾶλλον
ἢ φοινικοδάκτυλος, ἢ ἔτι φαυλότερον ἐρυθρο-
δάκτυλος.

ᵃ Athenaeus, p. 452.
ᵇ Rhetorician and sophist of Heraclea in Pontus.

Further, metaphors must not be far-fetched, but we must give names to things that have none by deriving the metaphor from what is akin and of the same kind, so that, as soon as it is uttered, it is clearly seen to be akin, as in the famous enigma,

I saw a man who glued bronze with fire upon another.

There was no name for what took place, but as in both cases there is a kind of application, he called the application of the cupping-glass " gluing." [a] And, generally speaking, clever enigmas furnish good metaphors ; for metaphor is a kind of enigma, so that it is clear that the transference is clever. Metaphors should also be derived from things that are beautiful, the beauty of a word consisting, as Licymnius says, in its sound or sense, and its ugliness in the same. There is a third condition, which refutes the sophistical argument ; for it is not the case, as Bryson [b] said, that no one ever uses foul language, if the meaning is the same whether this or that word is used ; this is false ; for one word is more proper than another, more of a likeness, and better suited to putting the matter before the eyes. Further, this word or that does not signify a thing under the same conditions ; thus for this reason also it must be admitted that one word is fairer or fouler than the other. Both, indeed, signify what is fair or foul, but not *qua* fair or foul ; or if they do, it is in a greater or less degree. Metaphors therefore should be derived from what is beautiful either in sound, or in signification, or to sight, or to some other sense. For it does make a difference, for instance, whether one says " rosy-fingered morn," rather than " purple-fingered," or, what is still worse, " red-fingered."

14 Καὶ ἐν τοῖς ἐπιθέτοις ἔστι μὲν τὰς ἐπιθέσεις ποιεῖσθαι ἀπὸ φαύλου ἢ αἰσχροῦ, οἷον ὁ μητροφόντης, ἔστι δ᾽ ἀπὸ τοῦ βελτίονος, οἷον ὁ πατρὸς ἀμύντωρ· καὶ ὁ Σιμωνίδης, ὅτε μὲν ἐδίδου μισθὸν ὀλίγον αὐτῷ ὁ νικήσας τοῖς ὀρεῦσιν, οὐκ ἤθελε ποιεῖν ὡς δυσχεραίνων εἰς ἡμιόνους ποιεῖν, ἐπεὶ δ᾽ ἱκανὸν ἔδωκεν, ἐποίησε

χαίρετ᾽ ἀελλοπόδων θύγατρες ἵππων·

καίτοι καὶ τῶν ὄνων θυγατέρες ἦσαν. ἔτι τὸ
15 αὐτὸ ὑποκορίζεσθαι. ἔστι δ᾽ ὁ ὑποκορισμός, ὃς ἔλαττον ποιεῖ καὶ τὸ κακὸν καὶ τὸ ἀγαθόν, ὥσπερ καὶ ὁ Ἀριστοφάνης σκώπτει ἐν τοῖς Βαβυλωνίοις, ἀντὶ μὲν χρυσίου χρυσιδάριον, ἀντὶ δ᾽ ἱματίου ἱματιδάριον, ἀντὶ δὲ λοιδορίας λοιδορημάτιον καὶ νοσημάτιον. εὐλαβεῖσθαι δὲ δεῖ καὶ παρατηρεῖν ἐν ἀμφοῖν τὸ μέτριον.

3. Τὰ δὲ ψυχρὰ ἐν τέτταρσι γίγνεται κατὰ τὴν λέξιν, ἔν τε τοῖς διπλοῖς ὀνόμασιν, οἷον Λυκόφρων τὸν πολυπρόσωπον οὐρανὸν τῆς μεγαλοκορύφου γῆς καὶ ἀκτὴν δὲ στενοπόρον, καὶ ὡς Γοργίας ὠνόμαζε, πτωχόμουσος κόλαξ, ἐπιορκήσαντας καὶ
1406 a κατευορκήσαντας. καὶ ὡς Ἀλκιδάμας "μένους μὲν τὴν ψυχὴν πληρουμένην, πυρίχρων δὲ τὴν ὄψιν γιγνομένην," καὶ "τελεσφόρον ᾠήθη τὴν προθυμίαν αὐτῶν γενήσεσθαι," καὶ "τελεσφόρον τὴν πειθὼ τῶν λόγων κατέστησεν," καὶ "κυανό-

---

ᵃ Euripides, *Orestes*, 1588. In the preceding line Menelaus accuses Orestes as a matricide and ready to heap murder on murder, to which Orestes replies, you should rather call me the avenger of my father Agamemnon, who had been murdered by his wife Clytaemnestra, the mother

As for epithets, they may be applied from what is vile or disgraceful, for instance, " the matricide," or from what is more honourable, for instance, " the avenger of his father." [a]   When the winner in a mule-race offered Simonides a small sum, he refused to write an ode, as if he thought it beneath him to write on half-asses ; but when he gave him a sufficient amount, he wrote,

> Hail, daughters of storm-footed steeds ! [b]

and yet they were also the daughters of asses. Further, the use of diminutives amounts to the same. It is the diminutive which makes the good and the bad appear less, as Aristophanes in the *Babylonians* jestingly uses " goldlet, cloaklet, affrontlet, disease-let " instead of " gold, cloak, affront, disease." But one must be careful to observe the due mean in their use as well as in that of epithets.

3. Frigidity of style arises from four causes : first, the use of compound words, as when Lycophron [c] speaks of " the many-faced sky of the mighty-topped earth," " narrow-passaged shore " ; and Gorgias of " a begging-poet flatterer," " those who commit perjury and those who swear right solemnly.[d] " And as Alcidamas says, " the soul full of anger and the face fire-coloured," " he thought that their zeal would be end-accomplishing," " he made persuasive words end-accomplishing," and " the azure-coloured

---

of Orestes. " Matricide " and "avenger of his father " show the good and bad sides of the deed of Orestes.

[b] Frag. 7 (*P.L.G.* iii. p. 390).   The winner of the mule-race was Anaxilaus of Rhegium.

[c] A sophist, not the poet (author of the obscure *Alexander* or *Cassandra*), who was later than Aristotle.

[d] Lobeck conjectured κατεπιορκήσαντας, " who commit out-and-out perjury."

χρων τὸ τῆς θαλάττης ἔδαφος·" πάντα γὰρ ταῦτα
ποιητικὰ διὰ τὴν δίπλωσιν φαίνεται.

2 Μία μὲν οὖν αὕτη αἰτία, μία δὲ τὸ χρῆσθαι
γλώτταις, οἷον Λυκόφρων Ξέρξην πέλωρον ἄνδρα,
καὶ Σκίρων σίννις ἀνήρ, καὶ Ἀλκιδάμας ἄθυρμα
τῇ ποιήσει, καὶ τὴν τῆς φύσεως ἀτασθαλίαν, καὶ
ἀκράτῳ τῆς διανοίας ὀργῇ τεθηγμένον.

3 Τρίτον δ' ἐν τοῖς ἐπιθέτοις τὸ ἢ μακροῖς ἢ
ἀκαίροις ἢ πυκνοῖς χρῆσθαι· ἐν μὲν γὰρ ποιήσει
πρέπει γάλα λευκὸν εἰπεῖν, ἐν δὲ λόγῳ τὰ μὲν
ἀπρεπέστερα, τὰ δέ, ἂν ᾖ κατακορῆ, ἐξελέγχει
καὶ ποιεῖ φανερὸν ὅτι ποίησίς ἐστιν· ἐπεὶ δεῖ γε
χρῆσθαι αὐτοῖς· ἐξαλλάττει γὰρ τὸ εἰωθός, καὶ
ξενικὴν ποιεῖ τὴν λέξιν. ἀλλὰ δεῖ στοχάζεσθαι
τοῦ μετρίου, ἐπεὶ μεῖζον ποιεῖ κακὸν τοῦ εἰκῇ
λέγειν· ἡ μὲν γὰρ οὐκ ἔχει τὸ εὖ, ἡ δὲ τὸ κακῶς.
διὸ τὰ Ἀλκιδάμαντος ψυχρὰ φαίνεται· οὐ γὰρ
ἡδύσματι χρῆται ἀλλ' ὡς ἐδέσματι τοῖς ἐπιθέτοις,
οὕτω πυκνοῖς καὶ μείζοσι καὶ ἐπιδήλοις, οἷον οὐχ
ἱδρῶτα ἀλλὰ τὸν ὑγρὸν ἱδρῶτα, καὶ οὐκ εἰς Ἴσθμια
ἀλλ' εἰς τὴν τῶν Ἰσθμίων πανήγυριν, καὶ οὐχὶ νόμους
ἀλλὰ τοὺς τῶν πόλεων βασιλεῖς νόμους, καὶ οὐ
δρόμῳ ἀλλὰ δρομαίᾳ τῇ τῆς ψυχῆς ὁρμῇ, καὶ
οὐχὶ μουσεῖον ἀλλὰ τὸ τῆς φύσεως παραλαβὼν
μουσεῖον, καὶ σκυθρωπὸν τὴν φροντίδα τῆς ψυχῆς,
καὶ οὐ χάριτος ἀλλὰ πανδήμου χάριτος δημιουργός,

---

[a] Sciron and Sinnis were both robbers slain by Theseus,
but Lycophron turns Sinnis into a γλῶττα, using it adjectiv-
ally = "destructive"; *cf.* σίνος, "harm"; σίντης = σίννις.

[b] The meaning of παραλαβών is quite obscure: various
renderings are "having taken to himself," "received,"
"grasped," "inherited." The word μουσεῖον, originally a
haunt of the Muses, came to mean a school of art or literature.

floor of the sea," for all these appear poetical because they are compound.

This is one cause of frigidity ; another is the use of strange words ; as Lycophron calls Xerxes " a monster of a man," Sciron " a human scourge[a] " ; and Alcidamas says " plaything in poetry," " the audaciousness of nature," " whetted with unmitigated wrath of thought."

A third cause is the use of epithets that are either long or unseasonable or too crowded ; thus, in poetry it is appropriate to speak of white milk, but in prose it is less so ; and if epithets are employed to excess, they reveal the art and make it evident that it is poetry. And yet such may be used to a certain extent, since it removes the style from the ordinary and gives a " foreign " air. But one must aim at the mean, for neglect to do so does more harm than speaking at random ; for a random style lacks merit, but excess is vicious. That is why the style of Alcidamas appears frigid ; for he uses epithets not as a seasoning but as a regular dish, so crowded, so long, and so glaring are they. For instance, he does not say " sweat " but " damp sweat " ; not " to the Isthmian games " but " to the solemn assembly of the Isthmian games " ; not " laws," but " the laws, the rulers of states " ; not " running," but " with a race-like impulse of the soul " ; not " museum," but " having taken up the museum of nature "[b]; and " the scowling anxiety of the soul"; " creator," not " of favour," but " all-popular favour"; and " dis-

The fault appears to consist in the addition of τῆς φύσεως, but it is difficult to see why. Cope confesses his inability to understand the passage. Jebb translates : " he does not say, 'having taken to himself a school of the Muses,' but 'to *Nature's* school of the Muses.'"

καὶ οἰκονόμος τῆς τῶν ἀκουόντων ἡδονῆς, καὶ οὐ
κλάδοις ἀλλὰ τοῖς τῆς ὕλης κλάδοις ἀπέκρυψεν,
καὶ οὐ τὸ σῶμα παρήμπισχεν ἀλλὰ τὴν τοῦ σώματος
αἰσχύνην, καὶ ἀντίμιμον τὴν τῆς ψυχῆς ἐπιθυμίαν
(τοῦτο δ' ἅμα καὶ διπλοῦν καὶ ἐπίθετον, ὥστε
ποίημα γίνεται), καὶ οὕτως ἔξεδρον τὴν τῆς
μοχθηρίας ὑπερβολήν. διὸ ποιητικῶς λέγοντες
τῇ ἀπρεπείᾳ τὸ γελοῖον καὶ τὸ ψυχρὸν ἐμποιοῦσι,
καὶ τὸ ἀσαφὲς διὰ τὴν ἀδολεσχίαν· ὅταν γὰρ
γιγνώσκοντι ἐπεμβάλλῃ, διαλύει τὸ σαφὲς τῷ
ἐπισκοτεῖν· οἱ δ' ἄνθρωποι τοῖς διπλοῖς χρῶνται,
ὅταν ἀνώνυμον ᾖ καὶ ὁ λόγος εὐσύνθετος, οἷον τὸ
χρονοτριβεῖν· ἀλλ' ἂν πολύ, πάντως ποιητικόν. διὸ
1406 b χρησιμωτάτη ἡ διπλῆ λέξις τοῖς διθυραμβοποιοῖς·
οὗτοι γὰρ ψοφώδεις· αἱ δὲ γλῶτται τοῖς ἐποποιοῖς·
σεμνὸν γὰρ καὶ αὔθαδες· ἡ μεταφορὰ δὲ τοῖς ἰαμ-
βείοις· τούτοις γὰρ νῦν χρῶνται, ὥσπερ εἴρηται.

4   Καὶ ἔτι τέταρτον τὸ ψυχρὸν ἐν ταῖς μεταφοραῖς
γίγνεται· εἰσὶ γὰρ καὶ μεταφοραὶ ἀπρεπεῖς, αἱ μὲν
διὰ τὸ γελοῖον (χρῶνται γὰρ καὶ οἱ κωμῳδοποιοὶ
μεταφοραῖς), αἱ δὲ διὰ τὸ σεμνὸν ἄγαν καὶ τραγικόν·
ἀσαφεῖς δέ, ἂν πόρρωθεν. οἷον Γοργίας "χλωρὰ
καὶ ἄναιμα τὰ πράγματα". "σὺ δὲ ταῦτα αἰσχρῶς
μὲν ἔσπειρας, κακῶς δὲ ἐθέρισας·" ποιητικῶς
γὰρ ἄγαν. καὶ ὡς Ἀλκιδάμας τὴν φιλοσοφίαν

ᵃ On this passage Thompson (*Gorgias*, p. 179) says:
"The metaphor of reaping and sowing is a mere commonplace . . . but 'pallid and bloodless affairs' is a phrase
which would need apology even from a modern." On the
other hand, it is difficult to see what objection there is to
calling the *Odyssey* "a beautiful mirror of human life."
Another reading is ἔναιμα, which Cope translates "events

penser of the pleasure of the hearers "; " he hid,"
not " with branches," but " with the branches of the
forest "; " he covered," not " his body," but " the
nakedness of his body." He also calls desire
" counter-initiative " of the soul "—an expression
which is at once compound and an epithet, so that
it becomes poetry—and " the excess of his depravity
so beyond all bounds." Hence those who employ
poetic language by their lack of taste make the
style ridiculous and frigid, and such idle chatter produces obscurity ; for when words are piled upon one
who already knows, it destroys perspicuity by a
cloud of verbiage. People use compound words,
when a thing has no name and the word is easy to
combine, as χρονοτριβεῖν, to pass time ; but if the
practice is abused, the style becomes entirely poetical.
This is why compound words are especially employed
by dithyrambic poets, who are full of noise ; strange
words by epic poets, for they imply dignity and
self-assertion ; metaphor to writers of iambics, who
now employ them, as we have stated.

The fourth cause of frigidity of style is to be found
in metaphors ; for metaphors also are inappropriate,
some because they are ridiculous—for the comic
poets also employ them—others because they are too
dignified and somewhat tragic ; and if they are far-
fetched, they are obscure, as when Gorgias says :
" Affairs pale and bloodless " [a]; " you have sown
shame and reaped misfortune " ; for this is too much
like poetry. And as Alcidamas calls philosophy " a

fresh with the blood in them." If the two extracts are taken
together, it is suggested (apparently by the editor of Cope's
notes) that the sense may be: "things green and unripe
(flushed with sap), and this was the crop which you . . .,"
the adjectives referring to green and unripe stalks of corn.

ἐπιτείχισμα τῶν νόμων, καὶ τὴν Ὀδύσσειαν καλὸν
ἀνθρωπίνου βίου κάτοπτρον, καὶ "οὐδὲν τοιοῦτον
ἄθυρμα τῇ ποιήσει προσφέρων·" ἅπαντα γὰρ
ταῦτα ἀπίθανα διὰ τὰ εἰρημένα. τὸ δὲ Γοργίου
εἰς τὴν χελιδόνα, ἐπεὶ κατ' αὐτοῦ πετομένη ἀφῆκε
τὸ περίττωμα, ἄριστα τῶν τραγικῶν· εἶπε γὰρ
"Αἰσχρόν γε ὦ Φιλομήλα." ὄρνιθι μὲν γάρ, εἰ
ἐποίησεν, οὐκ αἰσχρόν, παρθένῳ δὲ αἰσχρόν. εὖ
οὖν ἐλοιδόρησεν εἰπὼν ὃ ἦν, ἀλλ' οὐχ ὃ ἔστιν.

4. Ἔστι δὲ καὶ ἡ εἰκὼν μεταφορά· διαφέρει
γὰρ μικρόν· ὅταν μὲν γὰρ εἴπῃ τὸν Ἀχιλλέα

> ὡς δὲ λέων ἐπόρουσεν,

εἰκών ἐστιν, ὅταν δὲ "λέων ἐπόρουσε," μεταφορά·
διὰ γὰρ τὸ ἄμφω ἀνδρείους εἶναι, προσηγόρευσε
2 μετενέγκας λέοντα τὸν Ἀχιλλέα. χρήσιμον δὲ ἡ
εἰκὼν καὶ ἐν λόγῳ, ὀλιγάκις δέ· ποιητικὸν γάρ.
οἰστέαι δὲ ὥσπερ αἱ μεταφοραί· μεταφοραὶ γάρ
3 εἰσι διαφέρουσαι τῷ εἰρημένῳ. εἰσὶ δ' εἰκόνες
οἷον ἣν Ἀνδροτίων εἰς Ἰδριέα, ὅτι ὅμοιος τοῖς ἐκ
τῶν δεσμῶν κυνιδίοις· ἐκεῖνά τε γὰρ προσπίπτοντα
δάκνει, καὶ Ἰδριέα λυθέντα ἐκ τῶν δεσμῶν εἶναι
χαλεπόν. καὶ ὡς Θεοδάμας εἴκαζεν Ἀρχίδαμον
Εὐξένῳ γεωμετρεῖν οὐκ ἐπισταμένῳ ἐν τῷ ἀνάλογον·
ἔσται γὰρ καὶ ὁ Εὔξενος Ἀρχίδαμος γεωμετρικός.
καὶ τὸ ἐν τῇ πολιτείᾳ τῇ Πλάτωνος, ὅτι οἱ τοὺς

---

[a] Or, "a barrier against the laws." This is the general
meaning of ἐπιτείχισμα, a border fortress commanding an
enemy's country.

[b] Compare *Iliad*, xxii. 164 ἐνάντιον ὦρτο λέων ὥς.

[c] Pupil of Isocrates and historical writer. Idrieus was a
prince of Caria, who had been imprisoned.

[d] Meaning that there was no difference between Euxenus

bulwark of the laws," [a] and the *Odyssey* " a beautiful
mirror of human life," and " introducing no such
plaything in poetry." All these expressions fail to
produce persuasion, for the reasons stated. As for
what Gorgias said to the swallow which, flying over
his head, let fall her droppings upon him, it was in
the best tragic style. He exclaimed, " Fie, for
shame, Philomela ! " ; for there would have been
nothing in this act disgraceful for a bird, whereas it
would have been for a young lady. The reproach
therefore was appropriate, addressing her as she was,
not as she is.

4. The simile also is a metaphor ; for there is very
little difference. When the poet says of Achilles,[b]

he rushed on like a lion,

it is a simile ; if he says, " a lion, he rushed on," it
is a metaphor ; for because both are courageous, he
transfers the sense and calls Achilles a lion. The
simile is also useful in prose, but should be less
frequently used, for there is something poetical about
it. Similes must be used like metaphors, which only
differ in the manner stated. The following are examples of similes. Androtion [c] said of Idrieus that
he was like curs just unchained ; for as they attack
and bite, so he when loosed from his bonds was
dangerous. Again, Theodamas likened Archidamus
to a Euxenus ignorant of geometry, by proportion ; [d]
for Euxenus " will be Archidamus acquainted with
geometry." Again, Plato in the *Republic* [e] compares
without a knowledge of geometry and Archidamus with a
knowledge of geometry. The proportion of geometrical
knowledge will remain the same, so that Archidamus can
be called an ungeometrical Euxenus, and Euxenus a geometrical Archidamus (see note [a] on p. 370 for " by proportion ").

[e] 469 D.

ARISTOTLE

τεθνεῶτας σκυλεύοντες ἐοίκασι τοῖς κυνιδίοις, ἃ
τοὺς λίθους δάκνει τοῦ βάλλοντος οὐχ ἁπτόμενα.
καὶ ἡ εἰς τὸν δῆμον, ὅτι ὅμοιος ναυκλήρῳ ἰσχυρῷ
μὲν ὑποκώφῳ δέ. καὶ ἡ εἰς τὰ μέτρα τῶν ποιητῶν,
ὅτι ἔοικε τοῖς ἄνευ κάλλους ὡραίοις· οἱ μὲν γὰρ
1407 a ἀπανθήσαντες, τὰ δὲ διαλυθέντα οὐχ ὅμοια φαίνεται.
καὶ ἡ Περικλέους εἰς Σαμίους, ἐοικέναι αὐτοὺς
τοῖς παιδίοις ἃ τὸν ψωμὸν δέχεται μέν, κλαίοντα
δέ. καὶ εἰς Βοιωτούς, ὅτι ὅμοιοι τοῖς πρίνοις·
τούς τε γὰρ πρίνους ὑφ' αὑτῶν κατακόπτεσθαι,
καὶ τοὺς Βοιωτοὺς πρὸς ἀλλήλους μαχομένους.
καὶ ὁ Δημοσθένης τὸν δῆμον, ὅτι ὅμοιός ἐστι τοῖς
ἐν τοῖς πλοίοις ναυτιῶσιν. καὶ ὡς ὁ Δημοκράτης
εἴκασε τοὺς ῥήτορας ταῖς τίτθαις αἳ τὸ ψώμισμα
καταπίνουσαι τῷ σιάλῳ τὰ παιδία παραλείφουσιν.
καὶ ὡς Ἀντισθένης Κηφισόδοτον τὸν λεπτὸν
λιβανωτῷ εἴκασεν, ὅτι ἀπολλύμενος εὐφραίνει.
πάσας γὰρ ταύτας καὶ ὡς εἰκόνας καὶ ὡς μεταφορὰ
ἔξεστι λέγειν· ὥστε ὅσαι ἂν εὐδοκιμῶσιν ὡς
μεταφοραὶ λεχθεῖσαι, δῆλον ὅτι αὗται καὶ εἰκόνες
ἔσονται, καὶ αἱ εἰκόνες μεταφοραὶ λόγου δεόμεναι.
4 ἀεὶ δὲ δεῖ τὴν μεταφορὰν τὴν ἐκ τοῦ ἀνάλογον
ἀνταποδιδόναι καὶ ἐπὶ θάτερα τῶν ὁμογενῶν· οἷον

ᵃ 488 A.   ᵇ 601 B.
ᶜ If metrical restrictions have been removed and they are
read as prose.

368

those who strip the dead to curs, which bite stones, but do not touch those who throw them; he also says that the people is like a ship's captain who is vigorous, but rather deaf;ᵃ that poets' verses resemble those who are in the bloom of youth but lack beauty;ᵇ for neither the one after they have lost their bloom, nor the others after they have been broken up,ᶜ appear the same as before.   Pericles said that the Samians were like children who cry while they accept the scraps.ᵈ   He also compared the Boeotians to holm-oaks; for just as these are beaten down by knocking against each other,ᵉ so are the Boeotians by their civil strife. Demosthenes compared the people to passengers who are seasick.ᶠ Democrates said that orators resembled nurses who gulp down the morsel and rub the babies' lips with the spittle.ᵍ   Antisthenes likened the skinny Cephisodotus to incense, for he also gives pleasure by wasting away.   All such expressions may be used as similes or metaphors, so that all that are approved as metaphors will obviously also serve as similes which are metaphors without the details.   But in all cases the metaphor from proportion should be reciprocal and applicable to either of the two things of the same genus; for instance, if the goblet is the

---

ᵈ Meaning that they did not appreciate the benefits received from the Athenians, who conquered the islands (440 B.C.).

ᵉ Or, " are cut down by axes, the handles of which are made of their own wood."

ᶠ It is disputed whether Demosthenes is the orator or the Athenian general in the Peloponnesian War.   The point of the comparison is that in a democracy the general instability of political conditions makes the people sick of the existing state of things and eager for a change.

ᵍ Aristophanes, *Knights*, 715-718.

εἰ ἡ φιάλη ἀσπὶς Διονύσου, καὶ τὴν ἀσπίδα ἁρμόττει
λέγεσθαι φιάλην Ἄρεος.

5. Ὁ μὲν οὖν λόγος συντίθεται ἐκ τούτων.
ἔστι δ᾽ ἀρχὴ τῆς λέξεως τὸ ἑλληνίζειν· τοῦτο δ᾽
2 ἐστὶν ἐν πέντε, πρῶτον μὲν ἐν τοῖς συνδέσμοις,
ἂν ἀποδιδῷ τις ὡς πεφύκασι πρότεροι καὶ ὕστεροι
γίγνεσθαι ἀλλήλων, οἷον ἔνιοι ἀπαιτοῦσιν, ὥσπερ
ὁ μέν καὶ ὁ ἐγὼ μέν ἀπαιτεῖ τὸν δέ καὶ τὸν ὁ δέ.
δεῖ δὲ ἕως μέμνηται ἀνταποδιδόναι ἀλλήλοις, καὶ
μήτε μακρὰν ἀπαρτᾶν μήτε σύνδεσμον πρὸ συνδέσμου ἀποδιδόναι τοῦ ἀναγκαίου· ὀλιγαχοῦ γὰρ
ἁρμόττει. " ἐγὼ δ᾽, ἐπεί μοι εἶπεν (ἦλθε γὰρ
Κλέων δεόμενός τε καὶ ἀξιῶν) ἐπορευόμην παραλαβὼν αὐτούς." ἐν τούτοις γὰρ πολλοὶ πρὸ τοῦ
ἀποδοθησομένου συνδέσμου προεμβέβληνται σύνδεσμοι. ἐὰν δὲ πολὺ τὸ μεταξὺ γένηται τοῦ
3 ἐπορευόμην, ἀσαφές. ἐν μὲν δὴ τὸ εὖ ἐν τοῖς
συνδέσμοις, δεύτερον δὲ τὸ τοῖς ἰδίοις ὀνόμασι
4 λέγειν καὶ μὴ τοῖς περιέχουσιν. τρίτον, μὴ
ἀμφιβόλοις· ταῦτα δέ, ἂν μὴ τἀναντία προαιρῆται.
ὅπερ ποιοῦσιν, ὅταν μηθὲν μὲν ἔχωσι λέγειν,
προσποιῶνται δέ τι λέγειν· οἱ γὰρ τοιοῦτοι ἐν

---

a As the shield is to Ares, so is the goblet to Dionysus.
Proportion is defined (*Ethics*, v. 3. 8) as "an equality of
ratios, implying four terms at the least," and the proportional
metaphor is one in which the second term is to the first as
the fourth is to the third; for then one can by metaphor
substitute the fourth for the second, or the second for the
fourth.   Let A be Dionysus, B a goblet, C Ares, D a shield.
Then by the definition, the goblet is to Dionysus as the shield

shield of Dionysus, then the shield may properly be called the goblet of Ares.[a]

5. Such then are the elements of speech. But purity, which is the foundation of style, depends upon five rules. First, connecting particles should be introduced in their natural order, before or after, as they require; thus, μέν and ἐγὼ μέν require to be followed by δέ and ὁ δέ. Further, they should be made to correspond whilst the hearer still recollects; they should not be put too far apart, nor should a clause be introduced before the necessary connexion[b]; for this is rarely appropriate. For instance, "As for me, I, after he had told me—for Cleon came begging and praying—set out, taking them with me." For in this phrase several connecting words have been foisted in before the one which is to furnish the apodosis; and if the interval between "I" and "set out" is too great, the result is obscurity. The first rule therefore is to make a proper use of connecting particles; the second, to employ special, not generic terms. The third consists in avoiding ambiguous terms, unless you deliberately intend the opposite, like those who, having nothing to say, yet pretend to say something; such people accomplish this by the use of verse, after the

is to Ares. The metaphor consists in transferring to the goblet the name belonging to its analogue the shield. Sometimes an addition is made by way of explanation of the word in its new sense, and the goblet may be described as the shield of Dionysus and the shield as the goblet of Ares. The shield and the goblet both come under the same genus, being characteristics of a deity, and can therefore be reciprocally transferred (*Poetics*, 21. 4).

[b] The apodosis. ἀποδιδόναι is used in the sense of introducing a clause answering to the πρότασις, and ἀπόδοσις for this answering clause.

ποιήσει λέγουσι ταῦτα, οἷον Ἐμπεδοκλῆς· φενακίζει
γὰρ τὸ κύκλῳ πολὺ ὄν, καὶ πάσχουσιν οἱ ἀκροαταὶ
ὅπερ οἱ πολλοὶ παρὰ τοῖς μάντεσιν· ὅταν γὰρ
λέγωσιν ἀμφίβολα, συμπαρανεύουσιν.

Κροῖσος Ἅλυν διαβὰς μεγάλην ἀρχὴν καταλύσει.

καὶ διὰ τὸ ὅλως ἔλαττον εἶναι ἁμάρτημα, διὰ τῶν
1407 b γενῶν τοῦ πράγματος λέγουσιν οἱ μάντεις· τύχοι
γὰρ ἄν τις μᾶλλον ἐν τοῖς ἀρτιασμοῖς ἄρτια ἢ
περισσὰ εἰπὼν μᾶλλον ἢ πόσα ἔχει, καὶ τὸ ὅτι
ἔσται ἢ τὸ πότε, διὸ οἱ χρησμολόγοι οὐ προσ-
ορίζονται τὸ πότε. ἅπαντα δὴ ταῦτα ὅμοια· ὥστ'
5 ἂν μὴ τοιούτου τινὸς ἕνεκα, φευκτέον. τέταρτον,
ὡς Πρωταγόρας τὰ γένη τῶν ὀνομάτων διήρει,
ἄρρενα καὶ θήλεα καὶ σκεύη· δεῖ γὰρ ἀποδιδόναι
6 καὶ ταῦτα ὀρθῶς· " ἡ δ' ἐλθοῦσα καὶ διαλεχθεῖσα
ᾤχετο." πέμπτον, ἐν τῷ τὰ πολλὰ καὶ ὀλίγα καὶ
ἐν ὀρθῶς ὀνομάζειν· " οἱ δ' ἐλθόντες ἔτυπτόν με."

Ὅλως δὲ δεῖ εὐανάγνωστον εἶναι τὸ γεγραμμένον καὶ εὔφραστον· ἔστι δὲ τὸ αὐτό. ὅπερ οἱ
πολλοὶ σύνδεσμοι οὐκ ἔχουσιν οὐδ' ἃ μὴ ῥᾴδιον

---

a Of Agrigentum (c. 490-430), poet, philosopher, and
physician. Among other legends connected with him, he is
said to have thrown himself into the crater of Etna, so that
by suddenly disappearing he might be thought to be a god.
His chief work was a poem called Nature, praised by
Lucretius. The principles of things are the four elements,
fire, air, water, and earth, which are unalterable and in-
destructible. Love and hate, alternately prevailing, regulate
the periods of the formation of the world. The existing
fragments corroborate Aristotle's statement.

b Herodotus, i. 53, 91. Croesus consulted the Delphian
oracle whether he should attack Cyrus the Persian or not.

manner of Empedocles.[a] For the long circumlocution takes in the hearers, who find themselves affected like the majority of those who listen to the soothsayers. For when the latter utter their ambiguities, they also assent; for example,

Croesus, by crossing the Halys, shall ruin a mighty dominion.[b]

And as there is less chance of making a mistake when speaking generally, diviners express themselves in general terms on the question of fact; for, in playing odd or even, one is more likely to be right if he says " even " or " odd " than if he gives a definite number, and similarly one who says " it will be " than if he states " when." This is why soothsayers do not further define the exact time. All such ambiguities are alike, wherefore they should be avoided, except for some such reason.[c] The fourth rule consists in keeping the genders distinct—masculine, feminine, and neuter,[d] as laid down by Protagoras; these also must be properly introduced: "She, having come (*fem.*) and having conversed (*fem.*) with me, went away." The fifth rule consists in observing number, according as many, few, or one are referred to: " They, having come (*pl.*), began to beat (*pl.*) me."

Generally speaking, that which is written should be easy to read or easy to utter, which is the same thing. Now, this is not the case when there is a number of connecting particles, or when the punctua-

Encouraged by the ambiguous oracle, he did so, but was utterly defeated.

[c] The deliberate intention to mislead.

[d] σκεύη, "inanimate things," the classification probably being male, female, and inanimate, not the grammatical one of masculine, feminine, and neuter.

διαστίξαι, ὥσπερ τὰ Ἡρακλείτου. τὰ γὰρ Ἡρακλείτου διαστίξαι ἔργον διὰ τὸ ἄδηλον εἶναι
ποτέρῳ πρόσκειται, τῷ ὕστερον ἢ τῷ πρότερον,
οἷον ἐν τῇ ἀρχῇ αὐτοῦ τοῦ συγγράμματος· φησὶ
γὰρ " τοῦ λόγου τοῦδ' ἐόντος ἀεὶ ἀξύνετοι ἄνθρωποι
γίγνονται" ἄδηλον γὰρ τὸ ἀεί, πρὸς ὁποτέρῳ
7 διαστίξαι. ἔτι δὲ ποιεῖ σολοικίζειν τὸ μὴ ἀποδιδόναι, ἐὰν μὴ ἐπιζευγνύῃς ἀμφοῖν ὃ ἁρμόττει·
οἷον ἢ ψόφον ἢ χρῶμα, τὸ μὲν ἰδών οὐ κοινόν, τὸ
δ' αἰσθόμενος κοινόν. ἀσαφῆ δὲ καὶ ἂν μὴ προθεὶς
εἴπῃς, μέλλων πολλὰ μεταξὺ ἐμβάλλειν· οἷον
" ἔμελλον γὰρ διαλεχθεὶς ἐκείνῳ τάδε καὶ τάδε
καὶ ὧδε πορεύεσθαι," ἀλλὰ μὴ " ἔμελλον γὰρ
διαλεχθεὶς πορεύεσθαι, εἶτα τάδε καὶ τάδε καὶ
ὧδε ἐγένετο."

6. Εἰς ὄγκον δὲ τῆς λέξεως συμβάλλεται τάδε,
τὸ λόγῳ χρῆσθαι ἀντ' ὀνόματος, οἷον μὴ κύκλον,
ἀλλ' ἐπίπεδον τὸ ἐκ τοῦ μέσου ἴσον. εἰς δὲ συν-
2 τομίαν τὸ ἐναντίον, ἀντὶ τοῦ λόγου ὄνομα. καὶ
ἐὰν αἰσχρὸν ἢ ἀπρεπές· ἐὰν μὲν ἐν τῷ λόγῳ ᾖ
αἰσχρόν, τοὔνομα λέγειν, ἐὰν δ' ἐν τῷ ὀνόματι,
3 τὸν λόγον. καὶ μεταφοραῖς δηλοῦν καὶ τοῖς
4 ἐπιθέτοις, εὐλαβούμενον τὸ ποιητικόν. καὶ τὸ ἐν

---

[a] Heraclitus of Ephesus (c. 535-475). His chief work
was on Nature. From the harshness of his language and
the carelessness of his style he was called ὁ σκοτεινός (the
obscure). According to him, fire was the origin of all
things; all things become fire, and then fire becomes all
other things. All things are in a constant state of flux; all
is the same and yet not the same. Knowledge is founded
upon sensual perception, but only the gods possess knowledge in perfection.

tion is hard, as in the writings of Heraclitus.[a] For it is hard, since it is uncertain to which word another belongs, whether to that which follows or that which precedes; for instance, at the beginning of his composition he says : " Of this reason which exists [b] always men are ignorant," where it is uncertain whether " always " should go with " which exists " or with " are ignorant." Further, a solecism results from not appropriately connecting or joining two words with a word which is equally suitable to both. For instance, in speaking of " sound " and " colour," the word " seeing " should not be used, for it is not suitable to both, whereas " perceiving " is. It also causes obscurity, if you do not say at the outset what you mean, when you intend to insert a number of details in the middle ; for instance, if you say : " I intended after having spoken to him thus and thus and in this way to set out " instead of " I intended to set out after having spoken to him," and then this or that happened, in this or that manner.

6. The following rules contribute to loftiness of style. Use of the description instead of the name of a thing ; for instance, do not say " circle," but " a plane figure, all the points of which are equidistant from the centre." But for the purpose of conciseness the reverse—use the name instead of the description. You should do the same to express anything foul or indecent ; if the foulness is in the description, use the name ; if in the name, the description. Use metaphors and epithets by way of illustration, taking care, however, to avoid what is too poetical. Use

[b] Or, "although this reason exists for ever men are born . . . without understanding " (Welldon).

πολλὰ ποιεῖν, ὅπερ οἱ ποιηταὶ ποιοῦσιν· ἑνὸς ὄντος
λιμένος ὅμως λέγουσι

λιμένας εἰς Ἀχαϊκούς
καὶ
δέλτου μὲν αἵδε πολύθυροι διαπτυχαί.

5 καὶ μὴ ἐπιζευγνύναι, ἀλλ' ἑκατέρῳ ἑκάτερον,
"τῆς γυναικὸς τῆς ἡμετέρας." ἐὰν δὲ συντόμως,
6 τοὐναντίον "τῆς ἡμετέρας γυναικός." καὶ μετὰ
συνδέσμου λέγειν· ἐὰν δὲ συντόμως, ἄνευ μὲν
1408 a συνδέσμου, μὴ ἀσύνδετα δέ, οἷον "πορευθεὶς καὶ
7 διαλεχθείς," "πορευθεὶς διελέχθην." καὶ τὸ Ἀντι-
μάχου χρήσιμον, ἐξ ὧν μὴ ἔχει λέγειν, ὃ ἐκεῖνος
ποιεῖ ἐπὶ τοῦ Τευμησσοῦ,

ἔστι τις ἠνεμόεις ὀλίγος λόφος·

αὔξεται γὰρ οὕτως εἰς ἄπειρον. ἔστι δὲ τοῦτο
καὶ ἐπὶ ἀγαθῶν καὶ κακῶν, ὅπως οὐκ ἔχει, ὁποτέρως
ἂν ᾖ χρήσιμον. ὅθεν καὶ τὰ ὀνόματα οἱ ποιηταὶ
φέρουσι, τὸ ἄχορδον καὶ τὸ ἄλυρον μέλος· ἐκ τῶν
στερήσεων γὰρ ἐπιφέρουσιν· εὐδοκιμεῖ γὰρ τοῦτο
ἐν ταῖς μεταφοραῖς λεγόμενον ταῖς ἀνάλογον, οἷον
τὸ φάναι τὴν σάλπιγγα εἶναι μέλος ἄλυρον.

7. Τὸ δὲ πρέπον ἕξει ἡ λέξις, ἐὰν ᾖ παθητική
τε καὶ ἠθικὴ καὶ τοῖς ὑποκειμένοις πράγμασιν
2 ἀνάλογον. τὸ δ' ἀνάλογόν ἐστιν, ἐὰν μήτε περὶ
εὐόγκων αὐτοκαβδάλως λέγηται μήτε περὶ εὐτελῶν
σεμνῶς, μηδ' ἐπὶ τῷ εὐτελεῖ ὀνόματι ἐπῇ κόσμος·

---

[a] Euripides, *Iphig. Taur.* 727.
[b] In Boeotia. The quotation is from the *Thebaid* of
Antimachus of Claros (*c.* 450 B.C.). The Alexandrians
placed him next to Homer among the epic poets. In his
eulogy of the little hill, he went on to attribute to it all the

the plural for the singular, after the manner of the poets, who, although there is only one harbour, say

> to Achaean harbours,

and,

> Here are the many-leaved folds of the tablet.[a]

You should avoid linking up, but each word should have its own article : τῆς γυναικὸς τῆς ἡμετέρας. But for conciseness, the reverse : τῆς ἡμετέρας γυναικός. Employ a connecting particle or for conciseness omit it, but avoid destroying the connexion ; for instance " having gone and having conversed with him," or, " having gone, I cónversed with him." Also the practice of Antimachus is useful, that of describing a thing by the qualities it does not possess ; thus, in speaking of the hill Teumessus,[b] he says,

> There is a little wind-swept hill ;

for in this way amplification may be carried on *ad infinitum*. This method may be applied to things good and bad, in whichever way it may be useful. Poets also make use of this in inventing words, as a melody " without strings " or " without the lyre " ; for they employ epithets from negations, a course which is approved in proportional metaphors, as for instance, to say that the sound of the trumpet is a melody without the lyre.

7. Propriety of style will be obtained by the expression of emotion and character, and by proportion to the subject matter. Style is proportionate to the subject matter when neither weighty matters are treated offhand, nor trifling matters with dignity, and no embellishment is attached to an ordinary

good qualities it did *not* possess, a process which could obviously be carried on *ad infinitum*.

ARISTOTLE

εἰ δὲ μή, κωμῳδία φαίνεται, οἷον ποιεῖ Κλεοφῶν·
ὁμοίως γὰρ ἔνια ἔλεγε καὶ εἰ εἴπειεν ἂν " πότνια
3 συκῆ." παθητικὴ δέ, ἐὰν μὲν ᾖ ὕβρις, ὀργιζομένου λέξις, ἐὰν δὲ ἀσεβῆ καὶ αἰσχρά, δυσχεραί-
νοντος καὶ εὐλαβουμένου καὶ λέγειν, ἐὰν δὲ ἐπ-
αινετά, ἀγαμένως, ἐὰν δὲ ἐλεεινά, ταπεινῶς, καὶ
4 ἐπὶ τῶν ἄλλων δὲ ὁμοίως. πιθανοῖ δὲ τὸ πρᾶγμα
καὶ ἡ οἰκεία λέξις· παραλογίζεται γὰρ ἡ ψυχὴ ὡς
ἀληθῶς λέγοντος, ὅτι ἐπὶ τοῖς τοιούτοις οὕτως
ἔχουσιν, ὥστ᾽ οἴονται, εἰ καὶ μὴ οὕτως ἔχει, ὡς
ὁ λέγων, τὰ πράγματα οὕτως ἔχειν, καὶ συν-
ομοιοπαθεῖ ὁ ἀκούων ἀεὶ τῷ παθητικῶς λέγοντι,
5 κἂν μηθὲν λέγῃ. διὸ πολλοὶ καταπλήττουσι τοὺς
ἀκροατὰς θορυβοῦντες.
6 Καὶ ἠθικὴ δὲ αὕτη ἡ ἐκ τῶν σημείων δεῖξις,
ὅτι ἀκολουθεῖ ἡ ἁρμόττουσα ἑκάστῳ γένει καὶ
ἕξει. λέγω δὲ γένος μὲν καθ᾽ ἡλικίαν, οἷον παῖς
ἢ ἀνὴρ ἢ γέρων, καὶ γυνὴ ἢ ἀνήρ, καὶ Λάκων ἢ
Θετταλός, ἕξεις δέ, καθ᾽ ἃς ποιός τις τῷ βίῳ·
7 οὐ γὰρ καθ᾽ ἅπασαν ἕξιν οἱ βίοι ποιοί τινες. ἐὰν
οὖν καὶ τὰ ὀνόματα οἰκεῖα λέγῃ τῇ ἕξει, ποιήσει
τὸ ἦθος· οὐ γὰρ ταὐτὰ οὐδ᾽ ὡσαύτως ἀγροῖκος
ἂν καὶ πεπαιδευμένος εἴπειεν. πάσχουσι δέ τι
οἱ ἀκροαταὶ καὶ ᾧ κατακόρως χρῶνται οἱ λογογράφοι, "τίς δ᾽ οὐκ οἶδεν;" "ἅπαντες ἴσασιν." ὁμο-

---

a By some identified with the tragic poet spoken of in the
Poetics, 2. His manner of expression, due to the wish to
use fine language, was ridiculous owing to its being out of
harmony with the subject. Others consider that he was not
a poet at all but an orator. πότνια was a title of respect,
applied to females, whether they were goddesses or ordinary
women.

378

word ; otherwise there is an appearance of comedy, as in the poetry of Cleophon,[a] who used certain expressions that reminded one of saying " madam fig." Style expresses emotion, when a man speaks with anger of wanton outrage ; with indignation and reserve, even in mentioning them, of things foul or impious ; with admiration of things praiseworthy ; with lowliness of things pitiable ; and so in all other cases. Appropriate style also makes the fact appear credible ; for the mind of the hearer is imposed upon [b] under the impression that the speaker is speaking the truth, because, in such circumstances, his feelings are the same, so that he thinks (even if it is not the case as the speaker puts it) that things are as he represents them ; and the hearer always sympathizes with one who speaks emotionally, even though he really says nothing. This is why speakers often confound their hearers by mere noise.

Character also may be expressed by the proof from signs, because to each class and habit there is an appropriate style. I mean class in reference to age —child, man, or old man ; to sex—man or woman ; to country—Lacedaemonian or Thessalian. I call habits those moral states which form a man's character in life ; for not all habits do this. If then anyone uses the language appropriate to each habit, he will represent the character ; for the uneducated man will not say the same things in the same way as the educated. But the hearers also are impressed in a certain way by a device employed *ad nauseam* by writers of speeches :[c] " Who does not know ? " " Everybody knows " ; for the hearer agrees, because

---

[b] Or, " draws a wrong conclusion."

[c] Alluding to Isocrates.

λογεῖ γὰρ ὁ ἀκούων αἰσχυνόμενος, ὅπως μετέχῃ
οὗπερ καὶ οἱ ἄλλοι πάντες.

8 Τὸ δ' εὐκαίρως ἢ μὴ εὐκαίρως χρῆσθαι κοινὸν
9 ἁπάντων τῶν εἰδῶν ἐστίν. ἄκος δ' ἐπὶ πάσῃ
1408 b ὑπερβολῇ τὸ θρυλούμενον· δεῖ γὰρ αὐτὸν αὑτῷ
προεπιπλήττειν· δοκεῖ γὰρ ἀληθὲς εἶναι, ἐπεὶ οὐ
10 λανθάνει γε ὃ ποιεῖ τὸν λέγοντα. ἔτι τοῖς ἀνάλογον μὴ πᾶσιν ἅμα χρήσασθαι· οὕτω γὰρ κλέπτεται
ὁ ἀκροατής. λέγω δὲ οἷον ἐὰν τὰ ὀνόματα σκληρὰ
ᾖ, μὴ καὶ τῇ φωνῇ καὶ τῷ προσώπῳ καὶ τοῖς
ἁρμόττουσιν· εἰ δὲ μή, φανερὸν γίνεται ἕκαστον
ὅ ἐστιν. ἐὰν δὲ τὸ μὲν τὸ δὲ μή, λανθάνει ποιῶν
τὸ αὐτό. ἐὰν οὖν τὰ μαλακὰ σκληρῶς καὶ τὰ
σκληρὰ μαλακῶς λέγηται, ἀπίθανον γίγνεται.

11 Τὰ δὲ ὀνόματα τὰ διπλᾶ καὶ τὰ ἐπίθετα πλείω
καὶ τὰ ξένα μάλιστα ἁρμόττει λέγοντι παθητικῶς·
συγγνώμη γὰρ ὀργιζομένῳ κακὸν φάναι οὐρανό-
μηκες ἢ πελώριον εἰπεῖν. καὶ ὅταν ἔχῃ ἤδη τοὺς
ἀκροατὰς καὶ ποιήσῃ ἐνθουσιάσαι ἢ ἐπαίνοις ἢ
ψόγοις ἢ ὀργῇ ἢ φιλίᾳ, οἷον καὶ Ἰσοκράτης ποιεῖ
ἐν τῷ πανηγυρικῷ ἐπὶ τέλει, "φήμη δὲ καὶ γνώμη "
καὶ " οἵ τινες ἔτλησαν." φθέγγονταί τε γὰρ τὰ
τοιαῦτα ἐνθουσιάζοντες, ὥστε καὶ ἀποδέχονται
δῆλον ὅτι ὁμοίως ἔχοντες. διὸ καὶ τῇ ποιήσει
ἥρμοσεν· ἔνθεον γὰρ ἡ ποίησις. ἢ δὴ οὕτω δεῖ,

ᵃ Or, " to all the special rules given above."

ᵇ The exaggeration should be brought forward first, by
way of forestalling the objection, and accompanied by some
limiting phrase. Quintilian (*Inst. Orat.* viii. 3. 37) gives
as examples: "so to say," "if I may be allowed to say so."

ᶜ Adaptation of voice, features, etc., to the subject.

ᵈ § 186, where μνήμη is the reading, translated "name"
above (lit. memory) for the sake of the jingle, which also

he is ashamed to appear not to share what is a matter of common knowledge.

The opportune or inopportune use of these devices applies to all kinds of Rhetoric.[a] But whenever one has gone too far, the remedy may be found in the common piece of advice—that he should rebuke himself in advance ;[b] then the excess seems true, since the orator is obviously aware of what he is doing. Further, one ought not to make use of all kinds of correspondence[c] together ; for in this manner the hearer is deceived. I mean, for instance, if the language is harsh, the voice, features, and all things connected should not be equally harsh ; otherwise what each really is becomes evident. But if you do this in one instance and not in another, the art escapes notice, although the result is the same. If mild sentiments are harshly expressed or harsh sentiments mildly, the speech lacks persuasiveness.

Compound words, a number of epithets, and " foreign " words especially, are appropriate to an emotional speaker ; for when a man is enraged it is excusable for him to call an evil " high-as-heaven " or " stupendous." He may do the same when he has gripped his audience and filled it with enthusiasm, either by praise, blame, anger, or friendliness, as Isocrates does at the end of his *Panegyricus*[d] : " Oh, the fame and the name!" and " In that they endured." For such is the language of enthusiastic orators, and it is clear that the hearers accept what they say in a sympathetic spirit. Wherefore this style is appropriate to poetry ; for there is something inspired in poetry. It should therefore be used either in this

appears in the Greek of Isocrates. All the mss. of Aristotle give γνώμην here, which shows that it is a misquotation.

ἢ μετ' εἰρωνείας, ὅπερ Γοργίας ἐποίει καὶ τὰ ἐν
τῷ Φαίδρῳ.

8. Τὸ δὲ σχῆμα τῆς λέξεως δεῖ μήτε ἔμμετρον
εἶναι μήτε ἄρρυθμον· τὸ μὲν γὰρ ἀπίθανον (πε-
πλάσθαι γὰρ δοκεῖ) καὶ ἅμα καὶ ἐξίστησιν· προσ-
έχειν γὰρ ποιεῖ τῷ ὁμοίῳ, πότε πάλιν ἥξει.
ὥσπερ οὖν τῶν κηρύκων προλαμβάνουσι τὰ παιδία
τὸ "τίνα αἱρεῖται ἐπίτροπον ὁ ἀπελευθερούμενος;
2 Κλέωνα." τὸ δὲ ἄρρυθμον ἀπέραντον, δεῖ δὲ
πεπεράνθαι μέν, μὴ μέτρῳ δέ· ἀηδὲς γὰρ καὶ
ἄγνωστον τὸ ἄπειρον. περαίνεται δὲ ἀριθμῷ πάντα·
ὁ δὲ τοῦ σχήματος τῆς λέξεως ἀριθμὸς ῥυθμός
3 ἐστιν, οὗ καὶ τὰ μέτρα τμήματα. διὸ ῥυθμὸν δεῖ
ἔχειν τὸν λόγον, μέτρον δὲ μή· ποίημα γὰρ ἔσται.
ῥυθμὸν δὲ μὴ ἀκριβῶς· τοῦτο δὲ ἔσται, ἐὰν μέχρι
του ᾖ.

4 Τῶν δὲ ῥυθμῶν ὁ μὲν ἡρῷος σεμνὸς ἀλλὰ
λεκτικῆς ἁρμονίας δεόμενος, ὁ δ' ἴαμβος αὐτή

_____

ᵃ 238 D, 241 E. In the first of these passages Socrates
attributes his unusual flow of words to the inspiration of the
nymphs, and tells Phaedrus not to wonder if he seems to be
in a divine fury, for he is not far from breaking out into
dithyrambs. An example of the irony (a term implying a
certain amount of contempt (ii. 2. 25)) of Gorgias is given in
the *Politics* (iii. 2). When asked how a person comes to be
a citizen, he answers: "as those are mortars which have been
made by mortar-makers, so those are Larissaeans who have
been made by artisans (δημιουργούς); for some of these were
Larissa-makers (δημιουργούς). There is a play on the double
meaning of δημιουργός, (1) artisan, (2) magistrate, *lit.* people-
maker. Larissa-makers means makers of Larissaeans in
such numbers that they might be regarded as makers of
Larissa itself. It has also been suggested that λαρισοποιούς
may mean "kettle-makers," from λάρισα "a kettle," so

way or when speaking ironically, after the manner
of Gorgias, or of Plato in the *Phaedrus*.[a]

8. The form of diction should be neither metrical
nor without rhythm. If it is metrical, it lacks persuasiveness, for it appears artificial, and at the same
time it distracts the hearer's attention, since it sets
him on the watch for the recurrence of such and
such a cadence; just as, when the public criers ask,
" Whom does the emancipated [b] choose for his
patron ? " the children shout " Cleon." If it is
without rhythm, it is unlimited, whereas it ought to
be limited (but not by metre); for that which is
unlimited is unpleasant and unknowable. Now all
things are limited by number, and the number
belonging to the form of diction is rhythm, of which
the metres are divisions.[c] Wherefore prose must be
rhythmical, but not metrical, otherwise it will be a
poem. Nor must this rhythm be rigorously carried
out, but only up to a certain point.

Of the different rhythms the heroic is dignified,
but lacking the harmony of ordinary conversation ;
the iambic is the language of the many, wherefore

called from having been first made at Larissa, but this seems
unnecessary. The point is that Gorgias maintained that all
were citizens who were made so by the magistrates, that
citizenship was a manufactured article (see W. L. Newman's
note on the passage, and W. H. Thompson's Appendix to
his edition of Plato's *Gorgias*).

[b] He did not generally possess full rights of citizenship.
The point of the illustration is that the hearer looks for the
cadence just as confidently as, when a freedman is asked what
patron he selects, every one expects him to say "Cleon."

[c] Bywater's emendation for τμητά of the MSS. Aristotle
seems to be referring to the Pythagorean theory that
"number" is the regulating force in all things, and in giving
shape to language "number" is rhythm, which reduces a
formless mass of words to order.

ἐστιν ἡ λέξις ἡ τῶν πολλῶν· διὸ μάλιστα πάντων τῶν μέτρων ἰαμβεῖα φθέγγονται λέγοντες. δεῖ δὲ σεμνότητα γενέσθαι καὶ ἐκστῆσαι. ὁ δὲ τροχαῖος
1409 a κορδακικώτερος· δηλοῖ δὲ τὰ τετράμετρα· ἔστι γὰρ τροχερὸς ῥυθμὸς τὰ τετράμετρα. λείπεται δὲ παιάν, ᾧ ἐχρῶντο μὲν ἀπὸ Θρασυμάχου ἀρξάμενοι, οὐκ εἶχον δὲ λέγειν τίς ἦν.

Ἔστι δὲ τρίτος ὁ παιάν, καὶ ἐχόμενος τῶν εἰρημένων· τρία γὰρ πρὸς δύ᾽ ἐστίν, ἐκείνων δὲ ὁ μὲν ἓν πρὸς ἕν, ὁ δὲ δύο πρὸς ἕν. ἔχεται δὲ τῶν λόγων τούτων ὁ ἡμιόλιος· οὗτος δ᾽ ἐστὶν ὁ παιάν.
5 οἱ μὲν οὖν ἄλλοι διά τε τὰ εἰρημένα ἀφετέοι, καὶ διότι μετρικοί· ὁ δὲ παιὰν ληπτέος· ἀπὸ μόνου γὰρ οὐκ ἔστι μέτρον τῶν ῥηθέντων ῥυθμῶν, ὥστε μάλιστα λανθάνειν. νῦν μὲν οὖν χρῶνται τῷ ἑνὶ παιᾶνι καὶ ἀρχόμενοι, δεῖ δὲ διαφέρειν τὴν τελευτὴν
6 τῆς ἀρχῆς. ἔστι δὲ παιᾶνος δύο εἴδη ἀντικείμενα ἀλλήλοις, ὧν τὸ μὲν ἐν ἀρχῇ ἁρμόττει, ὥσπερ καὶ χρῶνται· οὗτος δ᾽ ἐστὶν οὗ ἄρχει μὲν ἡ μακρά, τελευτῶσι δὲ τρεῖς βραχεῖαι,

> Δαλογενὲς εἴτε Λυκίαν

καὶ

> χρυσεοκόμα Ἕκατε παῖ Διός.

ἕτερος δ᾽ ἐξ ἐναντίας, οὗ βραχεῖαι ἄρχουσι τρεῖς, ἡ δὲ μακρὰ τελευταία·

> μετὰ δὲ γᾶν ὕδατά τ᾽ ὠκεανὸν ἠφάνισε νύξ.

---

[a] The heroic rhythm (dactyls, spondees, and anapaests) is as 1 to 1, two short syllables being equal to one long; trochaic and iambic 2 to 1 on the same principle; paean, 3 to 2 (three shorts and one long), being the mean between the other two. [b] Understanding καὶ τελευτῶντες.
[c] All three attributed to Simonides (Frag. 26 B: *P.L.G.*).

of all metres it is most used in common speech;
but speech should be dignified and calculated to
rouse the hearer. The trochaic is too much like the
cordax; this is clear from the tetrameters, which
form a tripping rhythm. There remains the paean,
used by rhetoricians from the time of Thrasymachus, although they could not define it.

The paean is a third kind of rhythm closely related
to those already mentioned; for its proportion is
3 to 2, that of the others 1 to 1 and 2 to 1, with
both of which the paean, whose proportion is 1½ to 1,
is connected.[a] All the other metres then are to be
disregarded for the reasons stated, and also because
they are metrical; but the paean should be retained,
because it is the only one of the rhythms mentioned
which is not adapted to a metrical system, so that
it is most likely to be undetected. At the present
day one kind of paean alone is employed, at the
beginning as well as at the end;[b] the end, however,
ought to differ from the beginning. Now there are
two kinds of paeans, opposed to each other. The
one is appropriate at the beginning, where in fact it
is used. It begins with a long syllable and ends with
three short:

Δᾱλŏγĕνĕ̆ς | ε̆ἴτε Λῠκῐ|αν ("O Delos-born, or it may be
Lycia"),

and

Χρῡσĕŏκŏμ|ᾱ ῞ Εκᾰτĕ | παῖ Δῐŏς ("Golden-haired far-darter,
son of Zeus").

The other on the contrary begins with three short
syllables and ends with one long one:

μĕτᾰ δὲ γᾶν | ῠ̔δᾰτᾰ τ' ὡ|κĕᾰνŏν ἠ̆|φᾰνῑσε ° νῠ́ξ ("after earth
and waters, night obscured ocean").

385

ARISTOTLE

οὗτος δὲ τελευτὴν ποιεῖ· ἡ γὰρ βραχεῖα διὰ τὸ
ἀτελὴς εἶναι ποιεῖ κολοβόν. ἀλλὰ δεῖ τῇ μακρᾷ
ἀποκόπτεσθαι καὶ δήλην εἶναι τὴν τελευτήν, μὴ
διὰ τὸν γραφέα, μηδὲ διὰ τὴν παραγραφήν, ἀλλὰ
7 διὰ τὸν ῥυθμόν. ὅτι μὲν οὖν εὔρυθμον δεῖ εἶναι
τὴν λέξιν καὶ μὴ ἄρρυθμον, καὶ τίνες εὔρυθμον
ποιοῦσι ῥυθμοὶ καὶ πῶς ἔχοντες, εἴρηται.

9. Τὴν δὲ λέξιν ἀνάγκη εἶναι ἢ εἰρομένην καὶ
τῷ συνδέσμῳ μίαν, ὥσπερ αἱ ἐν τοῖς διθυράμβοις
ἀναβολαί, ἢ κατεστραμμένην καὶ ὁμοίαν ταῖς τῶν
ἀρχαίων ποιητῶν ἀντιστρόφοις. ἡ μὲν οὖν εἰρο-
2 μένη λέξις ἡ ἀρχαία ἐστίν· "'Ηροδότου Θουρίου
ἥδ' ἱστορίης ἀπόδειξις·" ταύτῃ γὰρ πρότερον μὲν
ἅπαντες, νῦν δὲ οὐ πολλοὶ χρῶνται. λέγω δὲ
εἰρομένην, ἣ οὐδὲν ἔχει τέλος καθ' αὑτήν, ἂν μὴ
τὸ πρᾶγμα λεγόμενον τελειωθῇ. ἔστι δὲ ἀηδὲς
διὰ τὸ ἄπειρον· τὸ γὰρ τέλος πάντες βούλονται
καθορᾶν. διόπερ ἐπὶ τοῖς καμπτῆρσιν ἐκπνέουσι
καὶ ἐκλύονται· προορῶντες γὰρ τὸ πέρας οὐ κάμ-
3 νουσι πρότερον. ἡ μὲν οὖν εἰρομένη τῆς λέξεώς
ἐστιν ἥδε, κατεστραμμένη δὲ ἡ ἐν περιόδοις· λέγω
δὲ περίοδον λέξιν ἔχουσαν ἀρχὴν καὶ τελευτὴν
1409 b αὐτὴν καθ' αὑτὴν καὶ μέγεθος εὐσύνοπτον. ἡδεῖα
δ' ἡ τοιαύτη καὶ εὐμαθής, ἡδεῖα μὲν διὰ τὸ ἐναντίως
ἔχειν τῷ ἀπεράντῳ, καὶ ὅτι ἀεί τι οἴεται ἔχειν ὁ
ἀκροατὴς [καὶ] πεπεράνθαι τι αὐτῷ· τὸ δὲ μηδὲν
προνοεῖν εἶναι μηδὲ ἀνύειν ἀηδές. εὐμαθὴς δέ, ὅτι
εὐμνημόνευτος. τοῦτο δέ, ὅτι ἀριθμὸν ἔχει ἡ

---

[a] A dash below the first word of a line, indicating the end
of a sentence.

[b] καμπτῆρες, properly the turning-point of the δίαυλος or
double course, is here used for the goal itself.

This is a suitable ending, for the short syllable, being incomplete, mutilates the cadence. But the period should be broken off by a long syllable and the end should be clearly marked, not by the scribe nor by a punctuation mark,[a] but by the rhythm itself. That the style should be rhythmical and not unrhythmical, and what rhythms and what arrangement of them make it of this character, has now been sufficiently shown.

9. The style must be either continuous and united by connecting particles, like the dithyrambic preludes, or periodic, like the antistrophes of the ancient poets. The continuous style is the ancient one; for example, "This is the exposition of the investigation of Herodotus of Thurii." It was formerly used by all, but now is used only by a few. By a continuous style I mean that which has no end in itself and only stops when the sense is complete. It is unpleasant, because it is endless, for all wish to have the end in sight. That explains why runners, just when they have reached the goal,[b] lose their breath and strength, whereas before, when the end is in sight, they show no signs of fatigue. Such is the continuous style. The other style consists of periods, and by period I mean a sentence that has a beginning and end in itself and a magnitude that can be easily grasped. What is written in this style is pleasant and easy to learn, pleasant because it is the opposite of that which is unlimited, because the hearer at every moment thinks he is securing something for himself and that some conclusion has been reached; whereas it is unpleasant neither to foresee nor to get to the end of anything. It is easy to learn, because it can be easily retained in the memory. The reason is that

ἐν περιόδοις λέξις, ὃ πάντων εὐμνημονευτότατον.
διὸ καὶ τὰ μέτρα πάντες μνημονεύουσι μᾶλλον τῶν
4 χύδην· ἀριθμὸν γὰρ ἔχει ᾧ μετρεῖται. δεῖ δὲ τὴν
περίοδον καὶ τῇ διανοίᾳ τετελειῶσθαι, καὶ μὴ
διακόπτεσθαι ὥσπερ τὰ Σοφοκλέους ἰαμβεῖα,

Καλυδὼν μὲν ἥδε γαῖα Πελοπίας χθονός·

τοὐναντίον γὰρ ἔστιν ὑπολαβεῖν τῷ διαιρεῖσθαι,
ὥσπερ καὶ ἐπὶ τοῦ εἰρημένου τὴν Καλυδῶνα εἶναι
τῆς Πελοποννήσου.
5 Περίοδος δὲ ἡ μὲν ἐν κώλοις, ἡ δ' ἀφελής. ἔστι
δ' ἐν κώλοις μὲν λέξις ἡ τετελειωμένη τε καὶ
διῃρημένη καὶ εὐανάπνευστος, μὴ ἐν τῇ διαιρέσει
ὥσπερ ἡ εἰρημένη περίοδος, ἀλλ' ὅλη. κῶλον δ'
ἐστὶ τὸ ἕτερον μόριον ταύτης. ἀφελῆ δὲ λέγω τὴν
6 μονόκωλον. δεῖ δὲ καὶ τὰ κῶλα καὶ τὰς περιόδους
μήτε μυούρους εἶναι μήτε μακράς. τὸ μὲν γὰρ
μικρὸν προσπταίειν πολλάκις ποιεῖ τὸν ἀκροατήν·
ἀνάγκη γάρ, ὅταν ἔτι ὁρμῶν ἐπὶ τὸ πόρρω καὶ τὸ
μέτρον, οὗ ἔχει ἐν ἑαυτῷ ὅρον, ἀντισπασθῇ παυσα-
μένου, οἷον προσπταίειν γίγνεσθαι διὰ τὴν ἀντί-
κρουσιν. τὰ δὲ μακρὰ ἀπολείπεσθαι ποιεῖ, ὥσπερ
οἱ ἐξωτέρω ἀποκάμπτοντες τοῦ τέρματος· ἀπο-
λείπουσι γὰρ καὶ οὗτοι τοὺς συμπεριπατοῦντας.
ὁμοίως δὲ καὶ αἱ περίοδοι αἱ μακραὶ οὖσαι λόγος

ᵃ τῶν χύδην : lit. what is poured forth promiscuously :
in flowing, unfettered language (Liddell and Scott).
ᵇ Really from the *Meleager* of Euripides, Frag. 515
(*T.G.F.*). The break in the sense comes after γαῖα, Πελοπίας
χθονός really belonging to the next line : ἐν ἀντιπόρθμοις πέδι'
ἔχουσ' εὐδαίμονα. As it stands in the text, the line implies
that Calydon was in Peloponnesus, which of course it was
not. The meaning then is : "This is the land of Calydon,

the periodic style has number, which of all things is the easiest to remember ; that explains why all learn verse with greater facility than prose,[a] for it has number by which it can be measured. But the period must be completed with the sense and not stop short, as in the iambics of Sophocles,[b]

This is Calydon, territory of the land of Pelops ;

for by a division of this kind it is possible to suppose the contrary of the fact, as in the example, that Calydon is in Peloponnesus.

A period may be composed of clauses, or simple. The former is a complete sentence, distinct in its parts and easy to repeat in a breath, not divided like the period in the line of Sophocles above, but when it is taken as a whole.[c] By clause I mean one of the two parts of this period, and by a simple period one that consists of only one clause. But neither clauses nor periods should be curtailed or too long. If too short, they often make the hearer stumble ; for when he is hurrying on towards the measure of which he already has a definite idea, if he is checked by the speaker stopping, a sort of stumble is bound to occur in consequence of the sudden stop. If too long, they leave the hearer behind, as those who do not turn till past the ordinary limit leave behind those who are walking with them. Similarly long periods assume the proportions of a speech and

with its fertile plains in the country over against Peloponnesus " (on the opposite side of the strait, near the mouth of the Corinthian gulf).

[c] It does not consist in simply dividing off any words from the context as the speaker pleases, but the parts of the sentence as a whole are properly constructed and distinguished and the sense also is complete.

γίνεται καὶ ἀναβολῇ ὅμοιον. ὥστε γίνεται ὃ
ἔσκωψε Δημόκριτος ὁ Χῖος εἰς Μελανιππίδην
ποιήσαντα ἀντὶ τῶν ἀντιστρόφων ἀναβολάς,

οἷ τ' αὐτῷ κακὰ τεύχει ἀνὴρ ἄλλῳ κακὰ τεύχων,
ἡ δὲ μακρὰ ἀναβολὴ τῷ ποιήσαντι κακίστη·

ἁρμόττει γὰρ τὸ τοιοῦτον καὶ εἰς τοὺς μακρο-
κώλους λέγειν. αἵ τε λίαν βραχύκωλοι οὐ περίοδος
γίγνεται· προπετῆ οὖν ἄγει τὸν ἀκροατήν.

7   Τῆς δὲ ἐν κώλοις λέξεως ἡ μὲν διῃρημένη ἐστὶν
ἡ δὲ ἀντικειμένη, διῃρημένη μὲν οἷον " πολλάκις
ἐθαύμασα τῶν τὰς πανηγύρεις συναγόντων καὶ
τοὺς γυμνικοὺς ἀγῶνας καταστησάντων," ἀντικειμένη δέ, ἐν ᾗ ἑκατέρῳ τῷ κώλῳ ἢ πρὸς
ἐναντίῳ ἐναντίον σύγκειται ἢ ταὐτὸ ἐπέζευκται
τοῖς ἐναντίοις, οἷον " ἀμφοτέρους δ' ὤνησαν, καὶ
τοὺς ὑπομείναντας καὶ τοὺς ἀκολουθήσαντας· τοῖς
μὲν γὰρ πλείω τῆς οἴκοι προσεκτήσαντο, τοῖς
δὲ ἱκανὴν τὴν οἴκοι κατέλιπον." ἐναντία ὑπομονὴ
ἀκολούθησις, ἱκανὸν πλεῖον. " ὥστε καὶ τοῖς
χρημάτων δεομένοις καὶ τοῖς ἀπολαῦσαι βουλομένοις." ἀπόλαυσις κτήσει ἀντίκειται. καὶ ἔτι
" συμβαίνει πολλάκις ἐν ταύταις καὶ τοὺς φρο-
νίμους ἀτυχεῖν καὶ τοὺς ἄφρονας κατορθοῦν."
" εὐθὺς μὲν τῶν ἀριστείων ἠξιώθησαν, οὐ πολὺ
δὲ ὕστερον τὴν ἀρχὴν τῆς θαλάττης ἔλαβον."
" πλεῦσαι μὲν διὰ τῆς ἠπείρου, πεζεῦσαι δὲ διὰ

ᵃ A well-known musician.
ᵇ Of Melos. He wrote rambling dithyrambic *preludes*
without strophic correspondence. Others take ἀναβολή to
mean an entire *ode*.

resemble dithyrambic preludes. This gives rise to what Democritus of Chios [a] jokingly rebuked in Melanippides,[b] who instead of antistrophes composed dithyrambic preludes :

A man does harm to himself in doing harm to another, and a long prelude is most deadly to one who composes it ; [c]

for these verses may be applied to those who employ long clauses. Again, if the clauses are too short, they do not make a period, so that the hearer himself is carried away headlong.

The clauses of the periodic style are divided or opposed ; divided, as in the following sentence : " I have often wondered at those who gathered together the general assemblies and instituted the gymnastic contests ";[d] opposed, in which, in each of the two clauses, one contrary is brought close to another, or the same word is coupled with both contraries ; for instance, " They were useful to both, both those who stayed and those who followed ; for the latter they gained in addition greater possessions than they had at home, for the former they left what was sufficient in their own country. Here " staying behind," " following," " sufficient," " more " are contraries. Again : " to those who need money and those who wish to enjoy it " ; where " enjoying " is contrary to " acquiring." Again : " It often happens in these vicissitudes that the wise are unsuccessful, while fools succeed " : " At once they were deemed worthy of the prize of valour and not long after won the command of the sea " : " To sail over the mainland, to go by land over the

---

[c] Hesiod, *Works and Days*, 265. The second line is a parody of 266, ἡ δὲ κακὴ βουλὴ τῷ βουλεύσαντι κακίστη.

[d] The beginning of Isocrates' *Panegyricus*.

τῆς θαλάττης, τὸν μὲν Ἑλλήσποντον ζεύξας, τὸν
δ᾽ Ἄθω διορύξας.'' '' καὶ φύσει πολίτας ὄντας
νόμῳ τῆς πόλεως στέρεσθαι.'' ''οἱ μὲν γὰρ
αὐτῶν κακῶς ἀπώλοντο, οἱ δ᾽ αἰσχρῶς ἐσώθησαν.''
'' ἰδίᾳ μὲν τοῖς βαρβάροις οἰκέταις χρῆσθαι, κοινῇ
δὲ πολλοὺς τῶν συμμάχων περιορᾶν δουλεύοντας.''
'' ἢ ζῶντας ἕξειν ἢ τελευτήσαντας καταλείψειν.''
καὶ ὃ εἰς Πειθόλαόν τις εἶπε καὶ Λυκόφρονα ἐν
τῷ δικαστηρίῳ, '' οὗτοι δ᾽ ὑμᾶς οἴκοι μὲν ὄντες
ἐπώλουν, ἐλθόντες δ᾽ ὡς ὑμᾶς ἐώνηνται.'' ἅπαντα
8 γὰρ ταῦτα ποιεῖ τὸ εἰρημένον. ἡδεῖα δ᾽ ἐστὶν ἡ
τοιαύτη λέξις, ὅτι τἀναντία γνωριμώτατα καὶ
παράλληλα μᾶλλον γνώριμα, καὶ ὅτι ἔοικε συλ-
λογισμῷ· ὁ γὰρ ἔλεγχος συναγωγὴ τῶν ἀντι-
κειμένων ἐστίν.

9 Ἀντίθεσις μὲν οὖν τὸ τοιοῦτόν ἐστιν, παρίσωσις
δ᾽ ἐὰν ἴσα τὰ κῶλα, παρομοίωσις δ᾽ ἐὰν ὅμοια
τὰ ἔσχατα ἔχῃ ἑκάτερον τὸ κῶλον. ἀνάγκη δὲ
ἢ ἐν ἀρχῇ ἢ ἐπὶ τελευτῆς ἔχειν. καὶ ἀρχὴ μὲν
ἀεὶ τὰ ὀνόματα, ἡ δὲ τελευτὴ τὰς ἐσχάτας συλλαβὰς
ἢ τοῦ αὐτοῦ ὀνόματος πτώσεις ἢ τὸ αὐτὸ ὄνομα.

ᵃ '' To dwell with us '' (Jebb). The point seems to be
that the barbarian domestics were in a comfortable position
as compared with those of the allies who were reduced to
slavery; and there is a contrast between the desire of getting
servants for private convenience, while in a matter affecting
public life indifference was shown.
  ᵇ All the above quotations are from the *Panegyricus*:
1, 35, 41, 48, 72, 89, 105, 149, 181, 186, with slight variations.
The last quotation is part of the sentence of which the
beginning appears in 7. 11 above. The whole runs: '' And
how great must we consider the fame and the name and the

sea, bridging over the Hellespont and digging through Athos " : " And that, though citizens by nature, they were deprived of the rights of citizenship by law " : " For some of them perished miserably, others saved themselves disgracefully " : " Privately to employ barbarians as servants,[a] but publicly to view with indifference many of the allies reduced to slavery " : " Either to possess it while living or to leave it behind when dead." [b] And what some one said against Pitholaus and Lycophron [c] in the law-court : " These men, who used to sell you when they were at home, having come to you have bought you." All these passages are examples of antithesis. This kind of style is pleasing, because contraries are easily understood and even more so when placed side by side, and also because antithesis resembles a syllogism ; for refutation is a bringing together of contraries.

Such then is the nature of antithesis ; equality of clauses is parisosis ; the similarity of the final syllables of each clause paromoiosis. This must take place at the beginning or end of the clauses. At the beginning the similarity is always shown in entire words ; at the end, in the last syllables, or the inflexions of one and the same word, or the repetition of the same word. For instance, at the

glory which those who have highly distinguished themselves in such deeds of valour will either have when living or will leave behind after their death."

[c] They murdered Alexander, tyrant of Pherae, being in-stigated by their sister, his wife. Nothing is known of the case referred to. According to Cope, the meaning is : " When they were at Pherae, they used to sell you as slaves, but now they have come to buy you " (referring to bribery in court). Others take ὠνεῖσθαι in a passive sense : " they have been bought," i.e. have had to sell themselves to you.

ARISTOTLE

ἐν ἀρχῇ μὲν τὰ τοιαῦτα " ἀγρὸν γὰρ ἔλαβεν ἀργὸν
παρ᾽ αὐτοῦ,"[a]

δωρητοί τ᾽ ἐπέλοντο παράρρητοί τ᾽ ἐπέεσσιν·[b]

ἐπὶ τελευτῆς δὲ " ᾠήθησαν αὐτὸν παιδίον τετοκέναι, ἀλλ᾽ αὐτοῦ αἴτιον γεγονέναι," " ἐν πλείσταις
δὲ φροντίσι καὶ ἐν ἐλαχίσταις ἐλπίσιν." πτῶσις
δὲ ταὐτοῦ " ἄξιος δὲ σταθῆναι χαλκοῦς, οὐκ ἄξιος
ὢν χαλκοῦ." ταὐτὸ δ᾽ ὄνομα " σὺ δ᾽ αὐτὸν καὶ
ζῶντα ἔλεγες κακῶς καὶ νῦν γράφεις κακῶς."
1410 b ἀπὸ συλλαβῆς δὲ " τί ἂν ἔπαθες δεινόν, εἰ ἄνδρ᾽
εἶδες ἀργόν;" ἔστι δὲ ἅμα πάντα ἔχειν ταὐτό,
καὶ ἀντίθεσιν εἶναι ταὐτὸ καὶ πάρισον καὶ ὁμοιο-
τέλευτον. αἱ δ᾽ ἀρχαὶ τῶν περιόδων σχεδὸν ἐν
10 τοῖς Θεοδεκτείοις ἐξηρίθμηνται. εἰσὶ δὲ καὶ
ψευδεῖς ἀντιθέσεις, οἷον καὶ Ἐπίχαρμος ἐποίει,

τόκα μὲν ἐν τήνων ἐγὼν ἦν, τόκα δὲ παρὰ τήνοις
ἐγών.

10. Ἐπεὶ δὲ διώρισται περὶ τούτων, πόθεν
λέγεται τὰ ἀστεῖα καὶ τὰ εὐδοκιμοῦντα λεκτέον.
ποιεῖν μὲν οὖν ἐστὶ τοῦ εὐφυοῦς ἢ τοῦ γεγυμνα-
2 σμένου, δεῖξαι δὲ τῆς μεθόδου ταύτης. εἴπωμεν
οὖν καὶ διαριθμησώμεθα· ἀρχὴ δ᾽ ἔστω ἡμῖν αὕτη.
τὸ γὰρ μανθάνειν ῥᾳδίως ἡδὺ φύσει πᾶσιν ἐστί,

---

[a] Aristophanes, Frag. 649 (Kock, *Com. Att. Frag.* i. 1880).
[b] *Iliad*, ix. 526.
[c] The text is obviously corrupt.
[d] See Introduction.
[e] Roemer's text has ἀρεταί (excellences).
[f] There is no real antithesis, the sense of both clauses being the same.

394

beginning: Ἀγρὸν γὰρ ἔλαβεν ἀργὸν παρ' αὐτοῦ,[a] "for he received from him land untilled";

δωρητοί τ' ἐπέλοντο παράρρητοί τ' ἐπέεσσιν,[b] "they were ready to accept gifts and to be persuaded by words;"

at the end: ᾠήθησαν αὐτὸν παιδίον τετοκέναι, ἀλλ' αὐτοῦ αἴτιον γεγονέναι,[c] "they thought that he was the father of a child, but that he was the cause of it"; ἐν πλείσταις δὲ φροντίσι καὶ ἐν ἐλαχίσταις ἐλπίσιν, "in the greatest anxiety and the smallest hopes." Inflexions of the same word: ἄξιος δὲ σταθῆναι χαλκοῦς, οὐκ ἄξιος ὢν χαλκοῦ, "worthy of a bronze statue, not being worth a brass farthing." Repetition of a word: σὺ δ' αὐτὸν καὶ ζῶντα ἔλεγες κακῶς καὶ νῦν γράφεις κακῶς, "while he lived you spoke ill of him, now he is dead you write ill of him." Resemblance of one syllable: τί ἂν ἔπαθες δεινόν, εἰ ἄνδρ' εἶδες ἀργόν, "what ill would you have suffered, if you had seen an idle man?" All these figures may be found in the same sentence at once—antithesis, equality of clauses, and similarity of endings. In the *Theodectea*[d] nearly all the beginnings[e] of periods have been enumerated. There are also false antitheses, as in the verse of Epicharmus:

τόκα μὲν ἐν τήνων ἐγὼν ἦν, τόκα δὲ παρὰ τήνοις ἐγών, "at one time I was in their house, at another I was with them."[f]

10. Having settled these questions, we must next state the sources of smart and popular sayings. They are produced either by natural genius or by practice; to show what they are is the function of this inquiry. Let us therefore begin by giving a full list of them, and let our starting-point be the following. Easy learning is naturally pleasant to all, and words mean

τὰ δὲ ὀνόματα σημαίνει τι, ὥστε ὅσα τῶν ὀνομάτων ποιεῖ ἡμῖν μάθησιν, ἥδιστα. αἱ μὲν οὖν
γλῶτται ἀγνῶτες, τὰ δὲ κύρια ἴσμεν. ἡ δὲ μεταφορὰ ποιεῖ τοῦτο μάλιστα· ὅταν γὰρ εἴπῃ τὸ γῆρας
καλάμην, ἐποίησε μάθησιν καὶ γνῶσιν διὰ τοῦ
3 γένους· ἄμφω γὰρ ἀπηνθηκότα. ποιοῦσι μὲν οὖν
καὶ αἱ τῶν ποιητῶν εἰκόνες τὸ αὐτό· διόπερ ἂν εὖ,
ἀστεῖον φαίνεται. ἔστι γὰρ ἡ εἰκών, καθάπερ
εἴρηται πρότερον, μεταφορὰ διαφέρουσα προσθέσει·
διὸ ἧττον ἡδύ, ὅτι μακροτέρως· καὶ οὐ λέγει ὡς
τοῦτο ἐκεῖνο· οὔκουν οὐδὲ ζητεῖ τοῦτο ἡ ψυχή.
4 ἀνάγκη δὴ καὶ λέξιν καὶ ἐνθυμήματα ταῦτ' εἶναι
ἀστεῖα, ὅσα ποιεῖ ἡμῖν μάθησιν ταχεῖαν. διὸ
οὔτε τὰ ἐπιπόλαια τῶν ἐνθυμημάτων εὐδοκιμεῖ
(ἐπιπόλαια γὰρ λέγομεν τὰ παντὶ δῆλα, καὶ ἃ
μηδὲν δεῖ ζητῆσαι), οὔτε ὅσα εἰρημένα ἀγνοούμενα
ἐστίν, ἀλλ' ὅσων ἢ ἅμα λεγομένων ἡ γνῶσις
γίνεται, καὶ εἰ μὴ πρότερον ὑπῆρχεν, ἢ μικρὸν
ὑστερίζει ἡ διάνοια· γίγνεται γὰρ οἷον μάθησις,
ἐκείνως δὲ οὐδέτερον.
5 Κατὰ μὲν οὖν τὴν διάνοιαν τοῦ λεγομένου τὰ
τοιαῦτα εὐδοκιμεῖ τῶν ἐνθυμημάτων, κατὰ δὲ τὴν
λέξιν τῷ μὲν σχήματι, ἐὰν ἀντικειμένως λέγηται,

---

[a] *Odyssey*, xiv. 213 ἀλλ' ἔμπης καλάμην γέ σ' ὀίομαι
εἰσορόωντα | γιγνώσκειν. The words are those of Odysseus,
whom Athene had changed into an old beggar, to Eumaeus,
his faithful swineherd, in whose house he was staying un-
recognized.

[b] προσθέσει: the addition of the particle of comparison
ὡς. προθέσει (the reading of the Paris ms.) would mean,
(1) " manner of setting forth" (Cope), or (2) " a metaphor,
with a preface " (Jebb) (but the meaning of this is not clear).
The simile only says that one thing *resembles* another, not

something, so that all words which make us learn something are most pleasant. Now we do not know the meaning of strange words, and proper terms we know already. It is metaphor, therefore, that above all produces this effect; for when Homer [a] calls old age stubble, he teaches and informs us through the genus ; for both have lost their bloom. The similes of the poets also have the same effect ; wherefore, if they are well constructed, an impression of smartness is produced. For the simile, as we have said, is a metaphor differing only by the addition of a word, [b] wherefore it is less pleasant because it is longer ; it does not say that this *is* that, so that the mind does not even examine this. Of necessity, therefore, all style and enthymemes that give us rapid information are smart. This is the reason why superficial enthymemes, meaning those that are obvious to all and need no mental effort, and those which, when stated, are not understood, are not popular, but only those which are understood the moment they are stated, or those of which the meaning, although not clear at first, comes a little later ; for from the latter a kind of knowledge results, from the former neither the one nor the other. [c]

In regard to the meaning of what is said, then, such enthymemes are popular. As to style, popularity of form is due to antithetical statement ; for

like the metaphor, that it *is* another ; since the speaker does not say this, the result is that the mind of the hearer does not go into the matter, and so the chance of instruction, of acquiring some information, is lost.

[c] The meaning is : the two kinds of enthymemes mentioned last do convey some information, whereas the superficial enthymemes teach nothing, either at once, or a little later, when reflection has made the meaning clear.

οἷον '' καὶ τὴν τοῖς ἄλλοις κοινὴν εἰρήνην νομι-
ζόντων τοῖς αὑτῶν ἰδίοις πόλεμον·'' ἀντίκειται
6 πόλεμος εἰρήνῃ. τοῖς δ' ὀνόμασιν, ἐὰν ἔχῃ μεταφοράν, καὶ ταύτην μήτ' ἀλλοτρίαν, χαλεπὸν γὰρ
συνιδεῖν, μήτ' ἐπιπόλαιον, οὐδὲν γὰρ ποιεῖ πάσχειν.
ἔτι εἰ πρὸ ὀμμάτων ποιεῖ· ὁρᾶν γὰρ δεῖ τὰ πραττόμενα μᾶλλον ἢ μέλλοντα. δεῖ ἄρα τούτων
στοχάζεσθαι τριῶν, μεταφορᾶς ἀντιθέσεως ἐν-
εργείας.

7   Τῶν δὲ μεταφορῶν τεττάρων οὐσῶν εὐδοκιμοῦσι
1411 a μάλιστα αἱ κατ' ἀναλογίαν, ὥσπερ Περικλῆς ἔφη
τὴν νεότητα τὴν ἀπολομένην ἐν τῷ πολέμῳ οὕτως
ἠφανίσθαι ἐκ τῆς πόλεως ὥσπερ εἴ τις τὸ ἔαρ ἐκ
τοῦ ἐνιαυτοῦ ἐξέλοι. καὶ Λεπτίνης περὶ Λακεδαιμονίων, οὐκ ἐᾶν περιιδεῖν τὴν Ἑλλάδα ἑτερόφθαλμον
γενομένην. καὶ Κηφισόδοτος σπουδάζοντος Χάρητος εὐθύνας δοῦναι περὶ τὸν Ὀλυνθιακὸν πόλεμον
ἠγανάκτει, φάσκων εἰς πνῖγμα τὸν δῆμον ἔχοντα
τὰς εὐθύνας πειρᾶσθαι δοῦναι. καὶ παρακαλῶν

---

[a] Isocrates, *Philippus*, 73.

[b] In the *Poetics* (21) metaphor and its four classes are
defined : " Metaphor consists in assigning to a thing the
name of something else ; and this may take place either
from genus to species, or from species to genus, or from
species to species, or proportionally.   An instance of a
metaphor from genus to species is 'here stands my ship,'
for 'standing' is a genus, 'being moored' a species ; from
species to genus : 'Odysseus truly has wrought a myriad
good deeds,' for 'myriad' is a specific large number, used
for the generic 'multitude' ;   from species to species :
'having drawn off the life with the bronze' and 'having cut
it with the unyielding bronze,' where 'drawn off' is used in
the sense of 'cut,' and 'cut' in the sense of 'drawn off,' both
being species of 'taking away.' "   For the proportional
metaphor see note on 4. 4 above.

instance, " accounting the peace that all shared
to be a war against their private interests," [a] where
" war " is opposed to " peace " ; as to words, they
are popular if they contain metaphor, provided it be
neither strange, for then it is difficult to take in at
a glance, nor superficial, for then it does not impress
the hearer ; further, if they set things " before the
eyes " ; for we ought to see what is being done
rather than what is going to be done. We ought
therefore to aim at three things—metaphor, antithesis, actuality.

Of the four kinds of metaphor [b] the most popular are
those based on proportion. Thus, Pericles said that
the youth that had perished during the war had disappeared from the State as if the year had lost its
springtime.[c] Leptines, speaking of the Lacedaemonians, said that he would not let the Athenians
stand by and see Greece deprived of one of her eyes.
When Chares was eager to have his accounts for the
Olynthian war examined, Cephisodotus indignantly
exclaimed that, now he had the people by the throat,
he was trying to get his accounts examined [d] ; on
another occasion also he exhorted the Athenians to

---

[c] i. 7. 34.

[d] εὔθυνα was the technical term for the examination of
accounts to which all public officers had to submit when
their term of office expired. Cephisodotus and Chares were
both Athenian generals. "Having the people by the throat "
may refer to the condition of Athens financially and his unsatisfactory conduct of the war. But the phrase εἰς πνῖγμα
τὸν δῆμον ἔχοντα is objected to by Cope, who reads ἀγαγόντα
and translates: "that he drove the people into a fit of
choking by his attempts to offer his accounts for scrutiny
in this way," i.e. he tried to force his accounts down their
throats, and nearly choked them. Another reading
suggested is ἄγχοντα (throttling so as to choke).

ARISTOTLE

ποτὲ τοὺς Ἀθηναίους εἰς Εὔβοιαν ἐπισιτισομένους
ἔφη δεῖν ἐξιέναι τὸ Μιλτιάδου ψήφισμα. καὶ
Ἰφικράτης σπεισαμένων Ἀθηναίων πρὸς Ἐπί-
δαυρον καὶ τὴν παραλίαν ἠγανάκτει, φάσκων
αὐτοὺς τὰ ἐφόδια τοῦ πολέμου παρηρῆσθαι. καὶ
Πειθόλαος τὴν Πάραλον ῥόπαλον τοῦ δήμου,
Σηστὸν δὲ τηλίαν τοῦ Πειραιέως. καὶ Περικλῆς
τὴν Αἴγιναν ἀφελεῖν ἐκέλευσε τὴν λήμην τοῦ
Πειραιέως. καὶ Μοιροκλῆς οὐθὲν ἔφη πονηρό-
τερος εἶναι, ὀνομάσας τινὰ τῶν ἐπιεικῶν· ἐκεῖνον
μὲν γὰρ ἐπιτρίτων τόκων πονηρεύεσθαι, αὐτὸν
δὲ ἐπιδεκάτων. καὶ τὸ Ἀναξανδρίδου ἰαμβεῖον
ὑπὲρ τῶν θυγατέρων πρὸς τὸν γάμον ἐγχρονι-
ζουσῶν,

ὑπερήμεροί μοι τῶν γάμων αἱ παρθένοι.

καὶ τὸ Πολυεύκτου εἰς ἀποπληκτικόν τινα Σπεύσ-
ιππον, τὸ μὴ δύνασθαι ἡσυχίαν ἄγειν ὑπὸ τῆς
τύχης ἐν πεντεσυρίγγῳ νόσῳ δεδεμένον. καὶ
Κηφισόδοτος τὰς τριήρεις ἐκάλει μύλωνας ποικί-
λους, ὁ Κύων δὲ τὰ καπηλεῖα τὰ Ἀττικὰ φιδίτια.

---

[a] This may refer to a decree of Miltiades which was so
speedily carried out that it became proverbial. The expedition was undertaken to assist Euboea against Thebes.

[b] By making peace, Iphicrates said that the Athenians
had deprived themselves of the opportunity of attacking and
plundering a weak maritime city, and so securing provisions
for the war. The word ἐφόδια properly means provisions
for a journey and travelling expenses.

[c] The Paralus and Salaminia were the two sacred galleys
which conveyed state prisoners.

[d] It commanded the trade of the Euxine.

[e] Moerocles was a contemporary of Demosthenes, and an
anti-Macedonian in politics. He seems to have been a
money-grubber and was once prosecuted for extortion. The

400

set out for Euboea without delay " and provision
themselves there, like the decree of Miltiades.ᵃ "
After the Athenians had made peace with Epidaurus
and the maritime cities, Iphicrates indignantly declared " that they had deprived themselves of provisions for the war." ᵇ Pitholaus called the Paralus ᶜ
" the bludgeon of the people," and Sestos " the corn-
chest ᵈ of the Piraeus." Pericles recommended that
Aegina, " the eyesore of the Piraeus," should be removed. Moerocles, mentioning a very "respectable"
person by name, declared that he was as much a
scoundrel as himself ; for whereas that honest man
played the scoundrel at 33 per cent. he himself was
satisfied with 10 per cent.ᵉ And the iambic of
Anaxandrides,ᶠ on girls who were slow to marry,

> My daughters are " past the time " of marriage.

And the saying of Polyeuctus ᵍ upon a certain
paralytic named Speusippus, " that he could not keep
quiet, although Fortune had bound him in a five-
holed pillory of disease." Cephisodotus called the
triremes " parti-coloured mills," ʰ and [Diogenes] the
Cynic used to say that the taverns ⁱ were " the

degree of the respectability (or rather, the swindling
practices) of each is calculated by their respective profits.
ᶠ Poet of the Middle Comedy : Frag. 68 (Kock, *Com.
Att. Frag.* ii.). The metaphor in ὑπερήμεροι is from those
who failed to keep the term of payment of a fine or debt.
Cope translates : " I find (μοι) the young ladies are . . ."
ᵍ Athenian orator, contemporary of Demosthenes.
ʰ As grinding down the tributary states. They differed
from ordinary mills in being gaily painted.
ⁱ Contrasted with the Spartan " messes," which were of
a plain and simple character, at which all the citizens dined
together. The tavern orgies, according to Diogenes, represented these at Athens.

ARISTOTLE

Αἰσίων δέ, ὅτι εἰς Σικελίαν τὴν πόλιν ἐξέχεαν·
τοῦτο γὰρ μεταφορὰ καὶ πρὸ ὀμμάτων. καὶ
" ὥστε βοῆσαι τὴν Ἑλλάδα"· καὶ τοῦτο τρόπον
τινὰ μεταφορὰ καὶ πρὸ ὀμμάτων. καὶ ὥσπερ
Κηφισόδοτος εὐλαβεῖσθαι ἐκέλευε μὴ πολλὰς ποιή-
σωσι τὰς συνδρομάς. καὶ Ἰσοκράτης πρὸς τοὺς
συντρέχοντας ἐν ταῖς πανηγύρεσιν. καὶ οἷον ἐν
τῷ ἐπιταφίῳ, διότι ἄξιον ἦν ἐπὶ τῷ τάφῳ τῷ τῶν
ἐν Σαλαμῖνι τελευτησάντων κείρασθαι τὴν Ἑλλάδα
ὡς συγκαταθαπτομένης τῇ ἀρετῇ αὐτῶν τῆς
ἐλευθερίας· εἰ μὲν γὰρ εἶπεν ὅτι ἄξιον δακρῦσαι
συγκαταθαπτομένης τῆς ἀρετῆς, μεταφορὰ καὶ
πρὸ ὀμμάτων, τὸ δὲ " τῇ ἀρετῇ τῆς ἐλευθερίας"
ἀντίθεσίν τινα ἔχει. καὶ ὡς Ἰφικράτης εἶπεν
" ἡ γὰρ ὁδός μοι τῶν λόγων διὰ μέσων τῶν
Χάρητι πεπραγμένων ἐστίν." μεταφορὰ κατ᾽
ἀναλογίαν, καὶ τὸ διὰ μέσου πρὸ ὀμμάτων ποιεῖ.
καὶ τὸ φάναι παρακαλεῖν τοὺς κινδύνους τοῖς
κινδύνοις βοηθήσοντας, πρὸ ὀμμάτων μεταφορά.
καὶ Λυκολέων ὑπὲρ Χαβρίου " οὐδὲ τὴν ἱκετηρίαν
αἰσχυνθέντες αὐτοῦ, τὴν εἰκόνα τὴν χαλκῆν"·
μεταφορὰ γὰρ ἐν τῷ παρόντι, ἀλλ᾽ οὐκ ἀεί, ἀλλὰ
πρὸ ὀμμάτων· κινδυνεύοντος γὰρ αὐτοῦ ἱκετεύει
ἡ εἰκών, τὸ ἄψυχον δὴ ἔμψυχον, τὸ ὑπόμνημα
τῶν τῆς πόλεως ἔργων. καὶ " πάντα τρόπον
μικρὸν φρονεῖν μελετῶντες"· τὸ γὰρ μελετᾶν

---

a Athenian orator, opponent of Demosthenes.
b Referring to the disastrous Sicilian expedition.
c *Philippus*, 12. Both συνδρομάς and συντρέχοντας refer to
the collecting of a mob in a state of excitement.
d The statue of Chabrias, erected after one of his victories,
represented him as kneeling on the ground, the position

messes " of Attica. Aesion [a] used to say that they
had "drained" the State into Sicily, [b] which is a
metaphor and sets the thing before the eyes. His
words " so that Greece uttered a cry " are also in a
manner a metaphor and a vivid one. And again,
as Cephisodotus bade the Athenians take care not
to hold their "concourses" too often ; and in the
same way Isocrates, who spoke of those " who rush
together" in the assemblies. [c] And as Lysias says
in his Funeral Oration, that it was right that
Greece should cut her hair at the tomb of those who
fell at Salamis, since her freedom was buried along
with their valour. If the speaker had said that it
was fitting that Greece should weep, her valour
being buried with them, it would have been a
metaphor and a vivid one, whereas " freedom " by
the side of " valour " produces a kind of antithesis.
And as Iphicrates said, " The path of my words leads
through the centre of the deeds of Chares " ; here
the metaphor is proportional and the words " through
the centre " create vividness. Also, to say that one
" calls upon dangers to help against dangers " is a
vivid metaphor. And Lycoleon on behalf of Chabrias
said, " not even reverencing the suppliant attitude of
his statue of bronze," [d] a metaphor for the moment,
not for all time, but still vivid ; for when Chabrias is in
danger, the statue intercedes for him, the inanimate
becomes animate, the memorial of what he has done
for the State. And " in every way studying poor-
ness of spirit," [e] for " studying " a thing implies to

which he had ordered his soldiers to take up when awaiting
the enemy. The statue was in the agora and could be seen
from the court. Lycoleon points to it, and bases his appeal
on its suppliant attitude.

[e] Isocrates, *Panegyricus*, 151.

αὔξειν τι ἐστίν. καὶ ὅτι τὸν νοῦν ὁ θεὸς φῶς
ἀνῆψεν ἐν τῇ ψυχῇ· ἄμφω γὰρ δηλοῖ τι. " οὐ γὰρ
διαλυόμεθα τοὺς πολέμους, ἀλλ' ἀναβαλλόμεθα·"
ἄμφω γάρ ἐστι μέλλοντα, καὶ ἡ ἀναβολὴ καὶ ἡ
τοιαύτη εἰρήνη. καὶ τὸ τὰς συνθήκας φάναι
" τρόπαιον εἶναι πολὺ κάλλιον τῶν ἐν τοῖς πολέμοις
γινομένων· τὰ μὲν γὰρ ὑπὲρ μικρῶν καὶ μιᾶς
τύχης, αὗται δ' ὑπὲρ παντὸς τοῦ πολέμου"· ἄμφω
γὰρ νίκης σημεῖα. ὅτι καὶ αἱ πόλεις τῷ ψόγῳ
τῶν ἀνθρώπων μεγάλας εὐθύνας διδόασιν· ἡ γὰρ
εὔθυνα βλάβη τις δικαία ἐστίν.

11. Ὅτι μὲν οὖν τὰ ἀστεῖα ἐκ μεταφορᾶς τε
τῆς ἀνάλογον λέγεται καὶ τῷ πρὸ ὀμμάτων ποιεῖν,
εἴρηται. λεκτέον δὲ τί λέγομεν πρὸ ὀμμάτων,
2 καὶ τί ποιοῦσι γίγνεται τοῦτο. λέγω δὴ πρὸ
ὀμμάτων ταῦτα ποιεῖν, ὅσα ἐνεργοῦντα σημαίνει.
οἷον τὸν ἀγαθὸν ἄνδρα φάναι εἶναι τετράγωνον
μεταφορά· ἄμφω γὰρ τέλεια, ἀλλ' οὐ σημαίνει
ἐνέργειαν. ἀλλὰ τὸ " ἀνθοῦσαν ἔχοντος τὴν ἀκμήν"
ἐνέργεια, καὶ τὸ " σὲ δ' ὥσπερ ἄφετον" ἐνέργεια,
καὶ

τοὐντεῦθεν οὖν Ἕλληνες ἄξαντες ποσίν

τὸ ἄξαντες ἐνέργεια καὶ μεταφορά. καὶ ὡς

---

[a] Metaphor from species to genus (p. 398, n.), "studying"
being a species of "increasing." As a rule one studies to
increase some good quality, not a bad one.
[b] Ibid. 172.　　　[c] Ibid. 180 (apparently from memory).
[d] εὔθυνα (see note on p. 399) further implies the punishment for an unsatisfactory statement of accounts.
[e] Simonides, Frag. 5 (P.L.G. ii.). Both a good man and
a square are complete as far as they go, but they do not
express actuality.　　　[f] Isocrates, Philippus, 10.
[g] Ibid. 127. This speech is an appeal to Philip to lead
the Greeks against Persia. As a sacred animal could roam

increase it.[a] And that "reason is a light that God has kindled in the soul," for both the words reason and light make something clear. " For we do not put an end to wars, but put them off,"[b] for both ideas refer to the future—putting off and a peace of such a kind. And again, it is a metaphor to say that such a treaty is " a trophy far more splendid than those gained in war ; for the latter are raised in memory of trifling advantages and a single favour of fortune, but the former commemorates the end of the whole war " ;[c] for both treaty and trophy are signs of victory. Again, that cities also render a heavy account to the censure of men ; for rendering an account [d] is a sort of just punishment.

11. We have said that smart sayings are derived from proportional metaphor and expressions which set things before the eyes. We must now explain the meaning of " before the eyes," and what must be done to produce this. I mean that things are set before the eyes by words that signify actuality. For instance, to say that a good man is " four-square "[e] is a metaphor, for both these are complete, but the phrase does not express actuality, whereas " of one having the prime of his life in full bloom "[f] does ; similarly, " thee, like a sacred animal ranging at will "[g] expresses actuality, and in

Thereupon the Greeks shooting forward with their feet[h]

the word " shooting " contains both actuality and

where it pleased within the precincts of its temple, so Philip could claim the whole of Greece as his fatherland, while other descendants of Heracles (whom Isocrates calls the author of Philip's line) were tied down and their outlook narrowed by the laws and constitution of the city in which they dwelt.

[h] Euripides, *Iphig. Aul.* 80, with δορί for ποσίν.

κέχρηται Ὅμηρος πολλαχοῦ τῷ τὰ ἄψυχα ἔμψυχα
3 λέγειν διὰ τῆς μεταφορᾶς. ἐν πᾶσι δὲ τῷ ἐνέργειαν ποιεῖν εὐδοκιμεῖ, οἷον ἐν τοῖσδε,

αὖτις ἐπὶ δάπεδόνδε κυλίνδετο λᾶας ἀναιδής,

καὶ

ἔπτατ' ὀϊστός,

καὶ

ἐπιπτέσθαι μενεαίνων,

καὶ

1412 a ἐν γαίῃ ἵσταντο λιλαιόμενα χροὸς ἆσαι,

καὶ

αἰχμὴ δὲ στέρνοιο διέσσυτο μαιμώωσα.

ἐν πᾶσι γὰρ τούτοις διὰ τὸ ἔμψυχα εἶναι ἐνεργοῦντα φαίνεται· τὸ ἀναισχυντεῖν γὰρ καὶ μαιμᾶν
καὶ τἆλλα ἐνέργεια. ταῦτα δὲ προσῆψε διὰ τῆς
κατ' ἀναλογίαν μεταφορᾶς· ὡς γὰρ ὁ λίθος πρὸς
τὸν Σίσυφον, ὁ ἀναισχυντῶν πρὸς τὸν ἀναισχυν-
4 τούμενον. ποιεῖ δὲ καὶ ἐν ταῖς εὐδοκιμούσαις
εἰκόσιν ἐπὶ τῶν ἀψύχων ταῦτα·

κυρτά, φαληριόωντα· πρὸ μέν τ' ἄλλ', αὐτὰρ ἐπ'
ἄλλα·

κινούμενα γὰρ καὶ ζῶντα ποιεῖ πάντα, ἡ δ' ἐνέργεια
κίνησις.

5 Δεῖ δὲ μεταφέρειν, καθάπερ εἴρηται πρότερον,
ἀπὸ οἰκείων καὶ μὴ φανερῶν, οἷον καὶ ἐν φιλο-
σοφίᾳ τὸ ὅμοιον καὶ ἐν πολὺ διέχουσι θεωρεῖν
εὐστόχου, ὥσπερ Ἀρχύτας ἔφη ταὐτὸν εἶναι
διαιτητὴν καὶ βωμόν· ἐπ' ἄμφω γὰρ τὸ ἀδικού-

ᵃ *Odyssey*, xi. 598, with ἔπειτα πέδονδε for ἐπὶ δάπεδόνδε.

metaphor. And as Homer often, by making use of metaphor, speaks of inanimate things as if they were animate ; and it is to creating actuality in all such cases that his popularity is due, as in the following examples :

Again the ruthless stone rolled down to the plain.[a]
The arrow flew.[b]
[The arrow] eager to fly [towards the crowd].[c]
[The spears] were buried in the ground, longing to take their fill of flesh.[d]
The spear-point sped eagerly through his breast.[e]

For in all these examples there is appearance of actuality, since the objects are represented as animate : " the shameless stone," " the eager spear-point," and the rest express actuality. Homer has attached these attributes by the employment of the proportional metaphor ; for as the stone is to Sisyphus, so is the shameless one to the one who is shamelessly treated. In his popular similes also he proceeds in the same manner with inanimate things :

Arched, foam-crested, some in front, others behind ;[f]

for he gives movement and life to all, and actuality is movement.

As we have said before, metaphors should be drawn from objects which are proper to the object, but not too obvious ; just as, for instance, in philosophy it needs sagacity to grasp the similarity in things that are apart. Thus Archytas said that there was no difference between an arbitrator and an altar, for the wronged betakes itself to one or the other.

[b] *Iliad*, xiii. 587.　　[c] *Ibid.* iv. 126.　　[d] *Ibid.* xi. 574.
[e] *Ibid.* xv. 541.
[f] *Ibid.* xiii. 799. The reference is to the " boiling waves of the loud-roaring sea."

ARISTOTLE

μενον καταφεύγει. ἢ εἴ τις φαίη ἄγκυραν καὶ
κρεμάθραν τὸ αὐτὸ εἶναι· ἄμφω γὰρ ταὐτό τι,
ἀλλὰ διαφέρει τῷ ἄνωθεν καὶ κάτωθεν. καὶ τὸ
"ὡμαλίσθαι τὰς πόλεις" ἐν πολὺ διέχουσι ταὐτό, ἐν
ἐπιφανείᾳ καὶ δυνάμεσι τὸ ἴσον.

6 Ἔστι δὲ καὶ τὰ ἀστεῖα τὰ πλεῖστα διὰ μεταφορᾶς καὶ ἐκ τοῦ προεξαπατᾶν· μᾶλλον γὰρ
γίγνεται δῆλον ὅτι ἔμαθε παρὰ τὸ ἐναντίως ἔχειν,
καὶ ἔοικε λέγειν ἡ ψυχὴ "ὡς ἀληθῶς, ἐγὼ δ'
ἥμαρτον." καὶ τῶν ἀποφθεγμάτων δὲ τὰ ἀστεῖά
ἐστιν ἐκ τοῦ μὴ ὃ φησι λέγειν, οἷον τὸ τοῦ Στησιχόρου, ὅτι οἱ τέττιγες ἑαυτοῖς χαμόθεν ᾄσονται.
καὶ τὰ εὖ ᾐνιγμένα διὰ τὸ αὐτὸ ἡδέα· μάθησις
γάρ, καὶ λέγεται μεταφορά. καὶ ὃ λέγει Θεόδωρος,
τὸ καινὰ λέγειν. γίγνεται δέ, ὅταν παράδοξον ᾖ,
καὶ μή, ὡς ἐκεῖνος λέγει, πρὸς τὴν ἔμπροσθεν
δόξαν, ἀλλ' ὥσπερ οἱ ἐν τοῖς γελοίοις τὰ παρα-
πεποιημένα. ὅπερ δύναται καὶ τὰ παρὰ γράμμα
σκώμματα· ἐξαπατᾷ γάρ. καὶ ἐν τοῖς μέτροις·
οὐ γὰρ ὥσπερ ὁ ἀκούων ὑπέλαβεν·

ᵃ The anchor keeps a ship steady *below*, the pot-hook is
above, and the pot hangs down from it.

ᵇ Cope, retaining ἀνωμαλίσθαι (as if from ἀνομαλίζειν,
aequalitatem restituere Bonitz, *cf.* ἀνομάλωσις) says: "the
widely dissimilar things here compared are the areas of
properties and the state offices and privileges, which are to
be alike equalized," translating: "And the re-equalization
of cities, when the same principle is applied to things standing wide apart, viz. to surface (area) and powers (functions,
offices)." (ἀν- is not negative, but = re.) But the passage
quoted by Victorius from Isocrates, *Philippus*, § 40: "for I
know that all the cities of Greece have been placed on the
same level (ὡμαλίσθαι) by misfortunes" suggests this as a

Similarly, if one were to say that an anchor and a
pot-hook hung up were identical; for both are the
same sort of thing, but they differ in this—that one
is hung up above and the other below.[a] And if one
were to say " the cities have been reduced to the
same level," this amounts to the same in the case
of things far apart—the equality of " levelling " in
regard to superficies and resources.[b]

Most smart sayings are derived from metaphor,
and also from misleading the hearer beforehand.[c]
For it becomes more evident to him that he has
learnt something, when the conclusion turns out
contrary to his expectation, and the mind seems to
say, " How true it is ! but I missed it." And smart
apophthegms arise from not meaning what one says,
as in the apophthegm of Stesichorus, that " the
grasshoppers will sing to themselves from the
ground."[d] And clever riddles are agreeable for the
same reason ; for something is learnt, and the expression is also metaphorical. And what Theodorus
calls " novel expressions " arise when what follows
is paradoxical, and, as he puts it, not in accordance
with our previous expectation ; just as humorists
make use of slight changes in words. The same
effect is produced by jokes that turn on a change
of letter ; for they are deceptive. These novelties
occur in poetry as well as in prose ; for instance,
the following verse does not finish as the hearer
expected :

preferable reading here, ὡμαλίσθαι meaning (1) have been
levelled to the ground (although the Lexica give no instance
of this use), (2) reduced to the same level of weakness.

[c] προεξαπατᾶν. Or, reading προσεξαπατᾶν, " by adding de-
ception."

[d] See ii. 21. 8.

ἔστειχε δ' ἔχων ὑπὸ ποσσὶ χίμεθλα·

ὁ δ' ᾤετο πέδιλα ἐρεῖν. τούτου δ' ἅμα λεγομένου
δεῖ δῆλον εἶναι. τὰ δὲ παρὰ γράμμα ποιεῖ οὐχ ὃ
λέγει λέγειν, ἀλλ' ὃ μεταστρέφει ὄνομα, οἷον τὸ
Θεοδώρου εἰς Νίκωνα τὸν κιθαρῳδόν " θράττει "
προσποιεῖται γὰρ λέγειν τὸ " θράττει σε " καὶ
ἐξαπατᾷ· ἄλλο γὰρ λέγει· διὸ μαθόντι ἡδύ, ἐπεὶ
1412 b εἰ μὴ ὑπολαμβάνει Θρᾷκα εἶναι, οὐ δόξει ἀστεῖον
7 εἶναι. καὶ τὸ " βούλει αὐτὸν πέρσαι." δεῖ δὲ
ἀμφότερα προσηκόντως λεχθῆναι. οὕτω δὲ καὶ
τὰ ἀστεῖα, οἷον τὸ φάναι Ἀθηναίοις τὴν τῆς
θαλάττης ἀρχὴν μὴ ἀρχὴν εἶναι τῶν κακῶν·
ὄνασθαι γάρ. ἢ ὥσπερ Ἰσοκράτης τὴν ἀρχὴν τῇ
πόλει ἀρχὴν εἶναι τῶν κακῶν. ἀμφοτέρως γὰρ ὃ
οὐκ ἄν ᾠήθη τις ἐρεῖν, τοῦτ' εἴρηται, καὶ ἐγνώσθη
ὅτι ἀληθές· τό τε γὰρ τὴν ἀρχὴν φάναι ἀρχὴν εἶναι
οὐθὲν σοφόν· ἀλλ' οὐχ οὕτω λέγει ἀλλ' ἄλλως,
8 καὶ ἀρχὴν οὐχ ὃ εἶπεν ἀπόφησιν, ἀλλ' ἄλλως. ἐν
ἅπασι δὲ τούτοις, ἐὰν προσηκόντως τὸ ὄνομα ἐνέγκῃ
ὁμωνυμίᾳ ἢ μεταφορᾷ, τότε τὸ εὖ. οἷον " Ἀνά-

---

^a According to Cope, θρᾶττ' εἶ, " you are no better than
a Thracian slave-girl."

^b There is obviously a play on πέρσαι (aor. 1 infin. of
πέρθω) and Πέρσαι (Persians), but no satisfactory interpretation of the joke has been suggested.

^c The paradoxical and verbal. "Suitably" may refer
to the manner of delivery; to being used at the proper time;
or to taking care that the word is one that may be used in
the two senses.

^d *Philippus*, 61; *De Pace*, 101. The point in the illus-
trations lies in the use of ἀρχή, first in the sense of "empire,"
then in that of "beginning." It could be said that the

And he strode on, under his feet—chilblains,

whereas the hearer thought he was going to say "sandals." This kind of joke must be clear from the moment of utterance. Jokes that turn on the word are produced, not by giving it the proper meaning, but by perverting it; for instance, when Theodorus said to Nicon, the player on the cithara, "you are troubled" (θράττει); for while pretending to say "something troubles you," he deceives us; for he means something else.[a] Therefore the joke is only agreeable to one who understands the point; for if one does not know that Nicon is a Thracian, he will not see any joke in it. Similarly, "you wish to destroy him (πέρσαι)." [b] Jokes of both these kinds [c] must be suitably expressed. Similar instances are such witticisms as saying that "the empire of the sea" was not "the beginning of misfortunes" for the Athenians, for they benefited by it; or, with Isocrates,[d] that "empire" was "the beginning of misfortunes for the city"; in both cases that which one would not have expected to be said is said, and recognized as true. For, in the second example, to say that "empire is empire" shows no cleverness, but this is not what he means, but something else; in the first, the ἀρχή which is negatived is used in a different sense. In all these cases, success is attained when a word is appropriately applied, either by homonym or by metaphor. For example, in the phrase Anaschetos (Bearable) is Unbearable,[e] there

---

"empire" of the sea was or was not "the beginning of misfortunes" for Athens; for at first it was highly beneficial to them, but in the end brought disaster, and thus was the "beginning" of evil.

[e] Usually translated, "There is no bearing Baring."

ARISTOTLE

σχετος οὐκ ἀνασχετός·" ὁμωνυμίαν ἀπέφησεν,
ἀλλὰ προσηκόντως, εἰ ἀηδής. καὶ

οὐκ ἂν γένοιο μᾶλλον ἢ ξένος ξένος·

ἢ οὐ μᾶλλον ἢ σὲ δεῖ, τὸ αὐτό. καὶ "οὐ δεῖ τὸν
ξένον ξένον ἀεὶ εἶναι·" ἀλλότριον γὰρ καὶ τοῦτο.
τὸ αὐτὸ καὶ τὸ Ἀναξανδρίδου τὸ ἐπαινούμενον,

καλόν γ' ἀποθανεῖν πρὶν θανάτου δρᾶν ἄξιον·

ταὐτὸν γάρ ἐστι τῷ εἰπεῖν ἄξιον γὰρ ἀποθανεῖν μὴ
ὄντα ἄξιον ἀποθανεῖν, ἢ ἄξιόν γ' ἀποθανεῖν μὴ
θανάτου ἄξιον ὄντα, ἢ μὴ ποιοῦντα θανάτου ἄξια.
9 τὸ μὲν οὖν εἶδος τὸ αὐτὸ τῆς λέξεως τούτων· ἀλλ'
ὅσῳ ἂν ἐλάττονι καὶ ἀντικειμένως λεχθῇ, τοσούτῳ
εὐδοκιμεῖ μᾶλλον. τὸ δ' αἴτιον ὅτι ἡ μάθησις διὰ
μὲν τὸ ἀντικεῖσθαι μᾶλλον, διὰ δὲ τὸ ἐν ὀλίγῳ
10 θᾶττον γίνεται. δεῖ δ' ἀεὶ προσεῖναι ἢ τὸ πρὸς
ὃν λέγεται ἢ τὸ ὀρθῶς λέγεσθαι, εἰ τὸ λεγόμενον
ἀληθὲς καὶ μὴ ἐπιπόλαιον· ἔστι γὰρ ταῦτα χωρὶς
ἔχειν, οἷον "ἀποθνήσκειν δεῖ μηθὲν ἁμαρτάνοντα"·
ἀλλ' οὐκ ἀστεῖον. "τὴν ἀξίαν δεῖ γαμεῖν τὸν
ἄξιον·" ἀλλ' οὐκ ἀστεῖον. ἀλλ' ἐὰν ἅμα ἄμφω
ἔχῃ· "ἄξιόν γ' ἀποθανεῖν μὴ ἄξιον ὄντα τοῦ
ἀποθανεῖν." ὅσῳ δ' ἂν πλείω ἔχῃ, τοσούτῳ
ἀστειότερον φαίνεται, οἷον εἰ καὶ τὰ ὀνόματα

---

[a] Kock, *C.A.F.* iii. 209, p. 448. In the two first examples
"stranger" refers to a distant and reserved manner, as we
say "don't make yourself a stranger"; in the third ξένος is
apparently to be taken in the sense of "alien." Cope
translates: "for that too is of a different kind" (foreign,
alien to the two others; ἀλλότριον, belonging to something or
somebody else, opposed to οἰκεῖον). But the whole passage
is obscure.

is a contradiction of the homonym, which is only appropriate, if Anaschetus is an unbearable person. And, "Thou shalt not be more of a stranger than a stranger," or "not more than you should be," which is the same thing. And again,

> The stranger must not always be a stranger,

for here too the word repeated is taken in a different sense.[a] It is the same with the celebrated verse of Anaxandrides,

> It is noble to die before doing anything that deserves death ;[b]

for this is the same as saying that "it is worthy to die when one does not deserve to die," or, that "it is worthy to die when one is not worthy of death," or, "when one does nothing that is worthy of death." Now the form of expression of these sayings is the same ; but the more concisely and antithetically they are expressed, the greater is their popularity. The reason is that antithesis is more instructive and conciseness gives knowledge more rapidly. Further, in order that what is said may be true and not superficial, it must always either apply to a particular person or be suitably expressed ; for it is possible for it to have one quality and not the other. For instance, "One ought to die guiltless of any offence," "The worthy man should take a worthy woman to wife." There is no smartness in either of these expressions, but there will be if both conditions are fulfilled : "It is worthy for a man to die, when he is not worthy of death." The more special qualities the expression possesses, the smarter it appears ; for instance, if the words contain a metaphor, and a

---

[b] Kock, *C.A.F.* ii. Frag. 64, p. 163.

ARISTOTLE

μεταφορὰ εἴη καὶ μεταφορὰ τοιαδὶ καὶ ἀντίθεσις
καὶ παρίσωσις, καὶ ἔχοι ἐνέργειαν.

11 Εἰσὶ δὲ καὶ αἱ εἰκόνες, ὥσπερ εἴρηται καὶ ἐν τοῖς
ἄνω, ἀεὶ εὐδοκιμοῦσαι τρόπον τινὰ μεταφοραί.
ἀεὶ γὰρ ἐκ δυοῖν λέγονται, ὥσπερ ἡ ἀνάλογον
μεταφορά· οἷον ἡ ἀσπὶς φαμέν ἐστι φιάλη Ἄρεος,
1413 a καὶ τόξον φόρμιγξ ἄχορδος. οὕτω μὲν οὖν λέγουσιν
οὐχ ἁπλοῦν, τὸ δ᾽ εἰπεῖν τὸ τόξον φόρμιγγα ἢ τὴν
12 ἀσπίδα φιάλην ἁπλοῦν. καὶ εἰκάζουσι δὲ οὕτως,
οἷον πιθήκῳ αὐλητήν, λύχνῳ ψακαζομένῳ μύωπα·
13 ἄμφω γὰρ συνάγεται. τὸ δὲ εὖ ἐστὶν ὅταν μεταφορὰ ᾖ· ἔστι γὰρ εἰκάσαι τὴν ἀσπίδα φιάλη Ἄρεος
καὶ τὸ ἐρείπιον ῥάκει οἰκίας, καὶ τὸν Νικήρατον
φάναι Φιλοκτήτην εἶναι δεδηγμένον ὑπὸ Πράτυος,
ὥσπερ εἴκασε Θρασύμαχος ἰδὼν τὸν Νικήρατον
ἡττημένον ὑπὸ Πράτυος ῥαψῳδοῦντα, κομῶντα
δὲ καὶ αὐχμηρὸν ἔτι. ἐν οἷς μάλιστα ἐκπίπτουσιν
οἱ ποιηταί, ἐὰν μὴ εὖ, καὶ ἐὰν εὖ, εὐδοκιμοῦσιν.
λέγω δ᾽ ὅταν ἀποδιδῶσιν,

ὥσπερ σέλινον οὖλα τὰ σκέλη φορεῖ,

ὥσπερ Φιλάμμων ζυγομαχῶν τῷ κωρύκῳ.

καὶ τὰ τοιαῦτα πάντ᾽ εἰκόνες εἰσίν. αἱ δ᾽ εἰκόνες
ὅτι μεταφοραί, εἴρηται πολλάκις.

---

[a] Or, reading αἱ for ἀεί, "approved similes are. . . ."

[b] In the simple metaphor "goblet" is substituted for
"shield," but sometimes additions are made to the word as
differently applied, such as "of Ares" and "without strings."
These additions, besides involving greater detail (a characteristic of the simile), distinctly bring out the contrast of the
two terms and make a simile, whereas the metaphor simply
transfers the meaning.

[c] In posture.

414

metaphor of a special kind, antithesis, and equality of clauses, and actuality.

Similes also, as said above, are always in a manner approved metaphors;[a] since they always consist of two terms, like the proportional metaphor, as when we say, for instance, that the shield is the goblet of Ares, and the bow a lyre without strings. But such an expression is not simple, but when we call the bow a lyre, or the shield a goblet, it is.[b] And similes may be formed as follows : a flute-player resembles an ape,[c] a short-sighted man a spluttering lamp ; for in both cases there is contraction.[d] But they are excellent when there is a proportional metaphor ; for it is possible to liken a shield to the goblet of Ares and a ruin to the rag of a house ; to say that Niceratus is a Philoctetes bitten by Pratys, to use the simile of Thrasymachus, when he saw Niceratus, defeated by Pratys in a rhapsodic competition, still dirty with his hair uncut.[e] It is herein that poets are especially condemned if they fail, but applauded if they succeed. I mean, for instance, when they introduce an answering clause :[f]

> He carries his legs twisted like parsley,

or again,

> Like Philammon punching the leather sack.

All such expressions are similes, and similes, as has been often said, are metaphors of a kind.

[d] Contraction of eyelids and flame.
[e] Like Philoctetes on Lemnos after he had been bitten by the snake.
[f] When the concluding corresponds with the introductory expression. This "answering clause" is called apodosis (p. 371), not restricted, as in modern usage, to the conclusion of a conditional sentence.

14 Καὶ αἱ παροιμίαι μεταφοραὶ ἀπ' εἴδους ἐπ' εἶδός εἰσιν· οἷον ἄν τις ὡς ἀγαθὸν πεισόμενος αὐτὸς ἐπαγάγηται, εἶτα βλαβῇ, ὡς ὁ Καρπάθιός φησι τὸν λαγώ· ἄμφω γὰρ τὸ εἰρημένον πεπόνθασιν. ὅθεν μὲν οὖν τὰ ἀστεῖα λέγεται καὶ διότι, σχεδὸν εἴρηται τὸ αἴτιον.

15 Εἰσὶ δὲ καὶ εὐδοκιμοῦσαι ὑπερβολαὶ μεταφοραί, οἷον εἰς ὑπωπιασμένον " ᾠήθητε δ' ἂν αὐτὸν εἶναι συκαμίνων κάλαθον"· ἐρυθρὸν γάρ τι τὸ ὑπώπιον, ἀλλὰ τὸ πολὺ σφόδρα. τὸ δὲ ὥσπερ τὸ καὶ τό, ὑπερβολὴ τῇ λέξει διαφέρουσα.

ὥσπερ Φιλάμμων ζυγομαχῶν τῷ κωρύκῳ·

ᾠήθης δ' ἂν αὐτὸν Φιλάμμωνα εἶναι μαχόμενον τῷ κωρύκῳ.

ὥσπερ σέλινον οὖλα τὰ σκέλη φορεῖν·

ᾠήθης δ' ἂν οὐ σκέλη ἀλλὰ σέλινα ἔχειν οὕτως οὖλα.

16 εἰσὶ δὲ ὑπερβολαὶ μειρακιώδεις· σφοδρότητα γὰρ δηλοῦσιν. διὸ ὀργιζόμενοι λέγουσι μάλιστα·

οὐδ' εἴ μοι τόσα δοίη ὅσα ψάμαθός τε κόνις τε.
κούρην δ' οὐ γαμέω Ἀγαμέμνονος Ἀτρείδαο,
οὐδ' εἰ χρυσείη Ἀφροδίτῃ κάλλος ἐρίζοι,
ἔργα δ' Ἀθηναίῃ.

1413 b χρῶνται δὲ μάλιστα τούτῳ οἱ Ἀττικοὶ ῥήτορες. διὸ πρεσβυτέρῳ λέγειν ἀπρεπές.

---

[a] Or, "he says it is a case of the Carpathian and the hare." An inhabitant of the island of Carpathus introduced a brace of hares, which so multiplied that they devoured all the crops and ruined the farmers (like the rabbits in Australia).
[b] *Iliad*, ix. 385.
[c] This must be taken as a parenthetical remark, if it is Aristotle's at all.

416

Proverbs also are metaphors from species to species. If a man, for instance, introduces into his house something from which he expects to benefit, but afterwards finds himself injured instead, it is as the Carpathian[a] says of the hare; for both have experienced the same misfortunes. This is nearly all that can be said of the sources of smart sayings and the reasons which make them so.

Approved hyperboles are also metaphors. For instance, one may say of a man whose eye is all black and blue, "you would have thought he was a basket of mulberries," because the black eye is something purple, but the great quantity constitutes the hyperbole. Again, when one says "like this or that" there is a hyperbole differing only in the wording :

> Like Philammon punching the leather sack,

or, "you would have thought that he was Philammon fighting the sack";

> Carrying his legs twisted like parsley,

or, "you would have thought that he had no legs, but parsley, they being so twisted." There is something youthful about hyperboles; for they show vehemence. Wherefore those who are in a passion most frequently make use of them :

Not even were he to offer me gifts as many in number as the sand and dust . . . but a daughter of Agamemnon, son of Atreus, I will not wed, not even if she rivalled golden Aphrodite in beauty, or Athene in accomplishments.[b]

(Attic orators are especially fond of hyperbole.[c]) Wherefore[d] it is unbecoming for elderly people to make use of them.

[d] Because they are boyish.

12. Δεῖ δὲ μὴ λεληθέναι ὅτι ἄλλη ἑκάστῳ γένει ἁρμόττει λέξις. οὐ γὰρ ἡ αὐτὴ γραφικὴ καὶ ἀγωνιστική, οὐδὲ δημηγορικὴ καὶ δικανική. ἄμφω δὲ ἀνάγκη εἰδέναι· τὸ μὲν γάρ ἐστιν ἑλληνίζειν ἐπίστασθαι, τὸ δὲ μὴ ἀναγκάζεσθαι κατασιωπᾶν, ἄν τι βούληται μεταδοῦναι τοῖς ἄλλοις, ὅπερ 2 πάσχουσιν οἱ μὴ ἐπιστάμενοι γράφειν. ἔστι δὲ λέξις γραφικὴ μὲν ἡ ἀκριβεστάτη, ἀγωνιστικὴ δὲ ἡ ὑποκριτικωτάτη. ταύτης δὲ δύο εἴδη· ἡ μὲν γὰρ ἠθικὴ ἡ δὲ παθητική. διὸ καὶ οἱ ὑποκριταὶ τὰ τοιαῦτα τῶν δραμάτων διώκουσι, καὶ οἱ ποιηταὶ τοὺς τοιούτους. βαστάζονται δὲ οἱ ἀναγνωστικοί, οἷον Χαιρήμων (ἀκριβὴς γὰρ ὥσπερ λογογράφος) καὶ Λικύμνιος τῶν διθυραμβοποιῶν. καὶ παραβαλλόμενοι οἱ μὲν τῶν γραφικῶν ἐν τοῖς ἀγῶσι στενοὶ φαίνονται, οἱ δὲ τῶν ῥητόρων εὖ λεχθέντες ἰδιωτικοὶ ἐν ταῖς χερσίν. αἴτιον δ᾽ ὅτι ἐν τῷ ἀγῶνι ἁρμόττει· διὸ καὶ τὰ ὑποκριτικὰ ἀφηρημένης τῆς ὑποκρίσεως οὐ ποιοῦντα τὸ αὑτῶν ἔργον φαίνεται εὐήθη, οἷον τά τε ἀσύνδετα καὶ τὸ πολλάκις τὸ αὐτὸ εἰπεῖν ἐν τῇ γραφικῇ ὀρθῶς ἀποδοκιμάζεται, ἐν δὲ ἀγωνιστικῇ καὶ οἱ ῥήτορες χρῶνται· ἔστι 3 γὰρ ὑποκριτικά. ἀνάγκη δὲ μεταβάλλειν τὸ αὐτὸ λέγοντας· ὅπερ ὡς προοδοποιεῖ τῷ ὑποκρίνεσθαι· "οὗτός ἐστιν ὁ κλέψας ὑμῶν, οὗτός ἐστιν ὁ ἐξαπατήσας, οὗτος ὁ τὸ ἔσχατον προδοῦναι ἐπιχειρήσας." οἷον καὶ Φιλήμων ὁ ὑποκριτὴς ἐποίει ἐν

---

[a] See 2. 13 of this book.

[b] What follows, to the end of § 3, is of the nature of a parenthesis, not immediately connected with the subject of the chapter.

[c] The variation in the form of the expression suggests a similar variation in the form of the delivery or declamation.

12. But we must not lose sight of the fact that a different style is suitable to each kind of Rhetoric. That of written compositions is not the same as that of debate; nor, in the latter, is that of public speaking the same as that of the law courts. But it is necessary to be acquainted with both; for the one requires a knowledge of good Greek, while the other prevents the necessity of keeping silent when we wish to communicate something to others, which happens to those who do not know how to write. The style of written compositions is most precise, that of debate is most suitable for delivery. Of the latter there are two kinds, ethical and emotional; this is why actors are always running after plays of this character, and poets after suitable actors. However, poets whose works are only meant for reading are also popular, as Chaeremon, who is as precise as a writer of speeches, and Licymnius [a] among dithyrambic poets. When compared, the speeches of writers appear meagre in public debates, while those of the rhetoricians, however well delivered, are amateurish when read. The reason is that they are only suitable to public debates; hence speeches suited for delivery, when delivery is absent, do not fulfil their proper function and appear silly. For instance, asyndeta and frequent repetition of the same word are rightly disapproved in written speech, but in public debate even rhetoricians make use of them, for they lend themselves to acting.[b] (But one must vary the expression when one repeats the same thing, for this as it were paves the way for declamation:[c] as, "This is he who robbed you, this is he who deceived you, this is he who at last attempted to betray you." This is what Philemon the actor

419

ARISTOTLE

τε τῇ Ἀναξανδρίδου γεροντομανίᾳ, ὅτε λέγει
" Ῥαδάμανθυς καὶ Παλαμήδης," καὶ ἐν τῷ προλόγῳ τῶν Εὐσεβῶν τὸ " ἐγώ·" ἐὰν γάρ τις τὰ
τοιαῦτα μὴ ὑποκρίνηται, γίνεται " ὁ τὴν δοκὸν
φέρων."

4 Καὶ τὰ ἀσύνδετα ὡσαύτως· " ἦλθον, ἀπήντησα,
ἐδεόμην·" ἀνάγκη γὰρ ὑποκρίνεσθαι καὶ μὴ ὡς
ἓν λέγοντα τῷ αὐτῷ ἤθει καὶ τόνῳ εἰπεῖν. ἔτι
ἔχει ἴδιόν τι τὰ ἀσύνδετα· ἐν ἴσῳ γὰρ χρόνῳ πολλὰ
δοκεῖ εἰρῆσθαι· ὁ γὰρ σύνδεσμος ἓν ποιεῖ τὰ πολλά,
ὥστ' ἐὰν ἐξαιρεθῇ, δῆλον ὅτι τοὐναντίον ἔσται τὸ
ἓν πολλά. ἔχει οὖν αὔξησιν· " ἦλθον, διελέχθην,
1414ᵃ ἱκέτευσα·" πολλὰ δοκεῖ ὑπεριδεῖν ὅσα εἶπεν.
τοῦτο δὲ βούλεται ποιεῖν καὶ Ὅμηρος ἐν τῷ

Νιρεὺς αὖ Σύμηθεν,
Νιρεὺς Ἀγλαΐης,
Νιρεὺς ὃς κάλλιστος.

περὶ οὗ γὰρ πολλὰ εἴρηται, ἀνάγκη καὶ πολλάκις
εἰρῆσθαι· εἰ οὖν καὶ πολλάκις, καὶ πολλὰ δοκεῖ,
ὥστε ηὔξησεν ἅπαξ μνησθεὶς διὰ τὸν παραλογισμόν,

ᵃ The meaning of this has not been satisfactorily explained.
On the face of it, it seems to mean that the excellence of
Philemon's delivery consisted in his way of declaiming
passages in which the same words were repeated. Philemon
is not to be confused with the writer of the New Comedy,
the rival and contemporary of Menander.

ᵇ Used of a stiff, ungraceful speaker.

ᶜ Spengel's reading here is: πολλὰ δοκεῖ· " ὑπερεῖδεν ὅσα
εἶπον," πολλὰ δοκεῖ being parenthetical, and ὑπερεῖδεν ὅσα
420

did in *The Old Man's Folly* of Anaxandrides, when he
says " Rhadamanthus and Palamedes," and when he
repeats the word " I " in the prologue to *The Pious.*[a]
For unless such expressions are varied by action, it
is a case of " the man who carries the beam "[b] in
the proverb.)

It is the same with asyndeta : " I came, I met, I
entreated." For here delivery is needed, and the
words should not be pronounced with the same tone
and character, as if there was only one clause.
Further, asyndeta have a special characteristic ; for
in an equal space of time many things appear to be
said, because the connecting particle makes many
things one, so that, if it be removed, it is clear that
the contrary will be the case, and that the one will
become many. Therefore an asyndeton produces
amplification : thus, in " I came, I conversed, I
besought," the hearer seems to be surveying many
things, all that the speaker said.[c] This also is
Homer's intention in the passage

> Nireus, again, from Syme . . .,
> Nireus son of Aglaïa . . .,
> Nireus, the most beautiful . . . ;[d]

for it is necessary that one of whom much has been
said should be often mentioned ; if then the name is
often mentioned, it seems as if much has been said[e] ;
so that, by means of this fallacy, Homer has increased

εἶπον part of the quotation. Jebb translates: " I came, I
spoke to him, I besought " (these seem *many* things); " he
disregarded all I said " (which certainly gives a more natural
sense to ὑπερεῖδεν).

[d] *Iliad*, ii. 671 ff.

[e] Cope translates: " they think that, if the name is often
repeated, there *must be a great deal to say* about its owner " ;
but can this be got out of the Greek (εἰρῆσθαι)?

καὶ μνήμην πεποίηκεν, οὐδαμοῦ ὕστερον αὐτοῦ
λόγον ποιησάμενος.

5 Ἡ μὲν οὖν δημηγορικὴ λέξις καὶ παντελῶς ἔοικε
τῇ σκιαγραφίᾳ· ὅσῳ γὰρ ἂν πλείων ᾖ ὁ ὄχλος,
πορρωτέρω ἡ θέα, διὸ τὰ ἀκριβῆ περίεργα καὶ
χείρω φαίνεται ἐν ἀμφοτέροις· ἡ δὲ δικανικὴ ἀκρι-
βεστέρα. ἔτι δὲ μᾶλλον ἡ ἐνὶ κριτῇ· ἐλάχιστον
γὰρ ἐστιν ῥητορικῆς· εὐσύνοπτον γὰρ μᾶλλον τὸ
οἰκεῖον τοῦ πράγματος καὶ τὸ ἀλλότριον, καὶ ὁ
ἀγὼν ἄπεστιν, ὥστε καθαρὰ ἡ κρίσις. διὸ οὐχ
οἱ αὐτοὶ ἐν πᾶσι τούτοις εὐδοκιμοῦσι ῥήτορες·
ἀλλ᾽ ὅπου μάλιστα ὑποκρίσεως, ἐνταῦθα ἥκιστα
ἀκρίβεια ἔνι. τοῦτο δέ, ὅπου φωνῆς, καὶ μάλιστα
ὅπου μεγάλης.

Ἡ μὲν οὖν ἐπιδεικτικὴ λέξις γραφικωτάτη·
6 τὸ γὰρ ἔργον αὐτῆς ἀνάγνωσις· δευτέρα δὲ ἡ
δικανική. τὸ δὲ προσδιαιρεῖσθαι τὴν λέξιν, ὅτι
ἡδεῖαν δεῖ καὶ μεγαλοπρεπῆ, περίεργον· τί γὰρ
μᾶλλον ἢ σώφρονα καὶ ἐλευθέριον καὶ εἴ τις ἄλλη
ἤθους ἀρετή; τὸ γὰρ ἡδεῖαν εἶναι ποιήσει δῆλον
ὅτι τὰ εἰρημένα, εἴπερ ὀρθῶς ὥρισται ἡ ἀρετὴ τῆς
λέξεως· τίνος γὰρ ἕνεκα δεῖ σαφῆ καὶ μὴ ταπεινὴν
εἶναι ἀλλὰ πρέπουσαν; ἄν τε γὰρ ἀδολεσχῇ, οὐ

ᵃ Intended to produce the effect of finished work at a
distance before a large number of spectators.

ᵇ The meaning apparently is that there is no discussion,
as might be the case when there were several judges, so
that the decision is clear and unbiased. ἀγών and ἀγωνιστική
λέξις are terms used for debate (e.g. in the law courts) and
the style suited to it (cf. § 1). Cope's editor refers to Cicero,
Ad Atticum, i. 16. 8 "remoto illo studio contentionis, quem
vos [you Athenians] ἀγῶνα appellatis." Jebb translates: "the

the reputation of Nireus, though he only mentions him in one passage ; he has perpetuated his memory, although he never speaks of him again.

The deliberative style is exactly like a rough sketch,[a] for the greater the crowd, the further off is the point of view ; wherefore in both too much refinement is a superfluity and even a disadvantage. But the forensic style is more finished, and more so before a single judge, because there is least opportunity of employing rhetorical devices, since the mind more readily takes in at a glance what belongs to the subject and what is foreign to it ; there is no discussion,[b] so the judgement is clear. This is why the same orators do not excel in all these styles ; where action is most effective, there the style is least finished, and this is a case in which voice, especially a loud one, is needed.

The epideictic style is especially suited to written compositions, for its function is reading ;[c] and next to it comes the forensic style. It is superfluous to make the further distinction that style should be pleasant or magnificent. Why so, any more than temperate, liberal, or anything else that indicates moral virtue ? For it is evident that, if virtue of style has been correctly defined, what we have said will suffice to make it pleasant. For why, if not to please, need it be clear, not mean, but appropriate ? If it be too diffuse, or too concise, it will not be

turmoil is absent, so that the judgement is serene " (in a note, " unclouded ").

[c] This does not seem to agree with the general view. Funeral orations of the nature of panegyrics, for instance, were certainly meant to be spoken ; but the ἔργον or proper function of an epideictic may be said to consist in reading, in its being agreeable to read. Its τέλος or end is to be read.

σαφής, οὐδὲ ἂν σύντομος. ἀλλὰ δῆλον ὅτι τὸ μέσον
ἁρμόττει. καὶ τὸ ἡδεῖαν τὰ εἰρημένα ποιήσει, ἂν
εὖ μιχθῇ, τὸ εἰωθὸς καὶ ξενικόν, καὶ ὁ ῥυθμός, καὶ
τὸ πιθανὸν ἐκ τοῦ πρέποντος. περὶ μὲν οὖν τῆς
λέξεως εἴρηται, καὶ κοινῇ περὶ ἁπάντων καὶ ἰδίᾳ
περὶ ἕκαστον γένος· λοιπὸν δὲ περὶ τάξεως εἰπεῖν.

13. Ἔστι δὲ τοῦ λόγου δύο μέρη· ἀναγκαῖον
γὰρ τό τε πρᾶγμα εἰπεῖν περὶ οὗ, καὶ τότ' ἀποδεῖξαι.
διὸ εἰπόντα μὴ ἀποδεῖξαι ἢ ἀποδεῖξαι μὴ προειπόντα ἀδύνατον· ὅ τε γὰρ ἀποδεικνύων τι ἀποδείκνυσι, καὶ ὁ προλέγων ἕνεκα τοῦ ἀποδεῖξαι
2 προλέγει. τούτων δὲ τὸ μὲν πρόθεσίς ἐστι τὸ δὲ
πίστις, ὥσπερ ἂν εἴ τις διέλοι ὅτι τὸ μὲν πρόβλημα
3 τὸ δὲ ἀπόδειξις. νῦν δὲ διαιροῦσι γελοίως· διήγησις
γάρ που τοῦ δικανικοῦ μόνου λόγου ἐστίν, ἐπιδεικτικοῦ δὲ καὶ δημηγορικοῦ πῶς ἐνδέχεται
εἶναι διήγησιν οἵαν λέγουσιν, ἢ τὰ πρὸς τὸν ἀντί-
1414 b δικον, ἢ ἐπίλογον τῶν ἀποδεικτικῶν; προοίμιον
δὲ καὶ ἀντιπαραβολὴ καὶ ἐπάνοδος ἐν ταῖς δημη-
γορίαις τότε γίνεται, ὅταν ἀντιλογία ᾖ. καὶ γὰρ
ἡ κατηγορία καὶ ἡ ἀπολογία πολλάκις, ἀλλ' οὐχ
ᾗ συμβουλή· ἀλλ' ὁ ἐπίλογος ἔτι οὐδὲ δικανικοῦ
παντός, οἷον ἐὰν μικρὸς ὁ λόγος, ἢ τὸ πρᾶγμα

ᵃ The generally accepted divisions are: προοίμιον (exordium),
διήγησις (narrative), πίστις (proof), ἐπίλογος (peroration).
(διήγησις is a species of πρόθεσις, which is used instead of it
just before.) Aristotle objects that it is (as a rule) only the
forensic speech which requires a regular διήγησις, a full and
detailed statement of what has happened before. In
epideictic and demonstrative (deliberative) speeches, the

clear ; but it is plain that the mean is most suitable.
What we have said will make the style pleasant, if
it contains a happy mixture of proper and " foreign "
words, of rhythm, and of persuasiveness resulting
from propriety. This finishes what we had to say
about style ; of all the three kinds of Rhetoric in
general, and of each of them in particular. It only
remains to speak of arrangement.

13. A speech has two parts. It is necessary to
state the subject, and then to prove it. Wherefore
it is impossible to make a statement without proving
it, or to prove it without first putting it forward ;
for both he who proves proves something, and he
who puts something forward does so in order to
prove it. The first of these parts is the statement
of the case, the second the proof, a similar division
to that of problem and demonstration. But the
division now generally made is absurd ; for narrative
only belongs in a manner to forensic speech, but in
epideictic or deliberative speech how is it possible that
there should be narrative as it is defined, or a refutation; or an epilogue in demonstrative speeches ? [a]
In deliberative speeches, again, exordium, comparison, and recapitulation are only admissible when
there is a conflict of opinion. For both accusation
and defence are often found in deliberative, but not
qua deliberative speech. And further, the epilogue
does not even belong to every forensic speech, for
instance, when it is short, or the matter is easy to

object of which is to prove something, there is no need of
another existing division called the refutation of the adversary,
and in the demonstrative there can be no room for an epilogue,
which is not a summary of *proofs and arguments.* Thus
the necessary divisions of a speech are really only two:
πρόθεσις and πίστις, or at most four.

ARISTOTLE

εὐμνημόνευτον· συμβαίνει γὰρ τοῦ μήκους ἀφαιρεῖσθαι.

4 Ἀναγκαῖα ἄρα μόρια πρόθεσις καὶ πίστις. ἴδια
μὲν οὖν ταῦτα, τὰ δὲ πλεῖστα προοίμιον πρόθεσις
πίστις ἐπίλογος· τὰ γὰρ πρὸς τὸν ἀντίδικον τῶν
πίστεών ἐστι, καὶ ἡ ἀντιπαραβολὴ αὔξησις τῶν
αὐτοῦ, ὥστε μέρος τι τῶν πίστεων· ἀποδείκνυσι
γάρ τι ὁ ποιῶν τοῦτο, ἀλλ' οὐ τὸ προοίμιον, οὐδ'
5 ὁ ἐπίλογος, ἀλλ' ἀναμιμνήσκει. ἔσται οὖν, ἄν
τις τὰ τοιαῦτα διαιρῇ, ὅπερ ἐποίουν οἱ περὶ Θεό-
δωρον, διήγησις ἕτερον καὶ ἐπιδιήγησις καὶ προ-
διήγησις καὶ ἔλεγχος καὶ ἐπεξέλεγχος. δεῖ δὲ
εἶδός τι λέγοντα καὶ διαφορὰν ὄνομα τίθεσθαι.
εἰ δὲ μή, γίνεται κενὸν καὶ ληρῶδες, οἷον Λικύμνιος
ποιεῖ ἐν τῇ τέχνῃ, ἐπούρωσιν ὀνομάζων καὶ ἀπο-
πλάνησιν καὶ ὄζους.

14. Τὸ μὲν οὖν προοίμιόν ἐστιν ἀρχὴ λόγου,
ὅπερ ἐν ποιήσει πρόλογος καὶ ἐν αὐλήσει προαύλιον·
πάντα γὰρ ἀρχαὶ ταῦτ' εἰσί, καὶ οἷον ὁδοποίησις
τῷ ἐπιόντι. τὸ μὲν οὖν προαύλιον ὅμοιον τῷ τῶν
ἐπιδεικτικῶν προοιμίῳ· καὶ γὰρ οἱ αὐληταί, ὅ τι
ἂν εὖ ἔχωσιν αὐλῆσαι, τοῦτο προαυλήσαντες
συνῆψαν τῷ ἐνδοσίμῳ, καὶ ἐν τοῖς ἐπιδεικτικοῖς
λόγοις δεῖ οὕτω γράφειν· ὅ τι γὰρ ἂν βούληται
εὐθὺ εἰπόντα ἐνδοῦναι καὶ συνάψαι. ὅπερ πάντες
ποιοῦσιν. παράδειγμα τὸ τῆς Ἰσοκράτους Ἑλένης

_____

ᵃ i.e. its use is to recall the main facts briefly (§ 4 end),
which in a short speech is needless.
ᵇ Plato, *Phaedrus*, 266 ᴅ, where the additional kinds of
narrative are omitted, and their place taken by πίστωσις and
ἐπιπίστωσις (confirmation of the proof).

426

recollect; for in the epilogue what happens is that there is a reduction of length.[a]

So then the necessary parts of a speech are the statement of the case and proof. These divisions are appropriate to every speech, and at the most the parts are four in number—exordium, statement, proof, epilogue; for refutation of an opponent is part of the proofs, and comparison is an amplification of one's own case, and therefore also part of the proofs; for he who does this proves something, whereas the exordium and the epilogue are merely aids to memory. Therefore, if we adopt all such divisions we shall be following Theodorus[b] and his school, who distinguished narrative, additional narrative, and preliminary narrative, refutation and additional refutation. But one must only adopt a name to express a distinct species or a real difference; otherwise, it becomes empty and silly, like the terms introduced by Licymnius in his "Art," where he speaks of "being wafted along," "wandering from the subject,"[c] and "ramifications.'

14. The exordium is the beginning of a speech, as the prologue in poetry and the prelude in flute-playing; for all these are beginnings, and as it were a paving the way for what follows. The prelude resembles the exordium of epideictic speeches; for as flute-players begin by playing whatever they can execute skilfully and attach it to the key-note, so also in epideictic speeches should be the composition of the exordium; the speaker should say at once whatever he likes, give the key-note and then attach the main subject. And all do this, an example being the exordium of the *Helen* of Isocrates; for

[c] Or, " diverting the judge's attention."

προοίμιον· οὐθὲν γὰρ οἰκεῖον ὑπάρχει τοῖς ἐριστικοῖς καὶ Ἑλένῃ. ἅμα δὲ καὶ ἐὰν ἐκτοπίσῃ,
ἁρμόττει μὴ ὅλον τὸν λόγον ὁμοειδῆ εἶναι.

2 Λέγεται δὲ τὰ τῶν ἐπιδεικτικῶν προοίμια ἐξ
ἐπαίνου ἢ ψόγου· οἷον Γοργίας μὲν ἐν τῷ Ὀλυμ-
πικῷ λόγῳ '' ὑπὸ πολλῶν ἄξιοι θαυμάζεσθαι, ὦ
ἄνδρες Ἕλληνες·'' ἐπαινεῖ γὰρ τοὺς τὰς πανηγύρεις συνάγοντας· Ἰσοκράτης δὲ ψέγει, ὅτι τὰς
μὲν τῶν σωμάτων ἀρετὰς δωρεαῖς ἐτίμησαν, τοῖς
3 δ' εὖ φρονοῦσιν οὐθὲν ἆθλον ἐποίησαν. καὶ ἀπὸ
συμβουλῆς, οἷον ὅτι δεῖ τοὺς ἀγαθοὺς τιμᾶν, διὸ
καὶ αὐτὸς Ἀριστείδην ἐπαινεῖ, ἢ τοὺς τοιούτους
οἳ μήτε εὐδοκιμοῦσι μήτε φαῦλοι, ἀλλ' ὅσοι
1415 a ἀγαθοὶ ὄντες ἄδηλοι, ὥσπερ Ἀλέξανδρος ὁ
4 Πριάμου· οὗτος γὰρ συμβουλεύει. ἔτι δ' ἐκ τῶν
δικανικῶν προοιμίων· τοῦτο δ' ἐστὶν ἐκ τῶν πρὸς
τὸν ἀκροατήν, εἰ περὶ παραδόξου λόγος ἢ περὶ
χαλεποῦ ἢ περὶ τεθρυλημένου πολλοῖς, ὥστε
συγγνώμην ἔχειν, οἷον Χοιρίλος

        νῦν δ' ὅτε πάντα δέδασται.

τὰ μὲν οὖν τῶν ἐπιδεικτικῶν λόγων προοίμια ἐκ
τούτων, ἐξ ἐπαίνου, ἐκ ψόγου, ἐκ προτροπῆς, ἐξ
ἀποτροπῆς, ἐκ·τῶν πρὸς τὸν ἀκροατήν· δεῖ δὲ ἢ
ξένα ἢ οἰκεῖα εἶναι τὰ ἐνδόσιμα τῷ λόγῳ.

5 Τὰ δὲ τοῦ δικανικοῦ προοίμια δεῖ λαβεῖν ὅτι

ᵃ The subject of the oration was the praise of Helen, but
Isocrates took the opportunity of attacking the sophists.
This exemplifies his skill in the introduction of matter not
strictly proper to, or in common with, the subject. The
key-note is Helen; but the exordium is an attack on the
Eristics, with special allusion to the Cynics and Megarians.
    ᵇ Of Samos, epic poet, author of a poem on the Persian

the eristics and Helen have nothing in common.[a]
At the same time, even if the speaker wanders from
the point, this is more appropriate than that the
speech should be monotonous.

In epideictic speeches, the sources of the exordia
are praise and blame, as Gorgias, in the *Olympiacus*,
says, " Men of Greece, you are worthy to be admired
by many," where he is praising those who instituted
the solemn assemblies.   Isocrates on the other hand
blames them because they rewarded bodily excellences, but instituted no prize for men of wisdom.
Exordia may also be derived from advice, for instance,
" one should honour the good," wherefore the speaker
praises Aristides, or such as are neither famous nor
worthless, but who, although they are good, remain
obscure, as Alexander, son of Priam ; for this is a
piece of advice.   Again, they may be derived from
forensic exordia, that is to say, from appeals to the
hearer, if the subject treated is paradoxical, difficult,
or commonly known, in order to obtain indulgence,
like Choerilus [b]:

But now when all has been allotted.

These then are the sources of epideictic exordia—
praise, blame, exhortation, dissuasion, appeals to the
hearer.   And these exordia [c] may be either foreign
or intimately connected with the speech.

As for the exordia of the forensic speech, it must

war, from which this half-line and the context preserved in
the Scholiast are taken.   He complains that whereas the
poets of olden times had plenty to write about, the field of
poetry being as yet untilled, it was now all apportioned, and
he, the last of the poets, was left behind, unable to find " a
new chariot for the race-course of his song."

[c] ἐνδόσιμα here = προοίμια.

ταὐτὸ δύναται ὅπερ τῶν δραμάτων οἱ πρόλογοι
καὶ τῶν ἐπῶν τὰ προοίμια· τὰ μὲν γὰρ τῶν δι-
θυράμβων ὅμοια τοῖς ἐπιδεικτικοῖς·

δ
διὰ σὲ καὶ τεὰ δῶρα εἴτε σκῦλα.

6 ἐν δὲ τοῖς λόγοις καὶ ἔπεσι δεῖγμά ἐστι τοῦ λόγου,
ἵνα προειδῶσι περὶ οὗ ἦν ὁ λόγος καὶ μὴ κρέμηται
ἡ διάνοια· τὸ γὰρ ἀόριστον πλανᾷ· ὁ δοὺς οὖν
ὥσπερ εἰς τὴν χεῖρα τὴν ἀρχὴν ποιεῖ ἐχόμενον
ἀκολουθεῖν τῷ λόγῳ. διὰ τοῦτο

μῆνιν ἄειδε θεά,

ἄνδρα μοι ἔννεπε μοῦσα,

ἥγεό μοι λόγον ἄλλον, ὅπως Ἀσίας ἀπὸ γαίης
ἦλθεν ἐς Εὐρώπην πόλεμος μέγας.

καὶ οἱ τραγικοὶ δηλοῦσι περὶ τὸ δρᾶμα, κἂν μὴ
εὐθὺς ὥσπερ Εὐριπίδης, ἀλλ' ἐν τῷ προλόγῳ γέ
που, ὥσπερ καὶ Σοφοκλῆς

ἐμοὶ πατὴρ ἦν Πόλυβος.

καὶ ἡ κωμῳδία ὡσαύτως. τὸ μὲν οὖν ἀναγκαιό-
τατον ἔργον τοῦ προοιμίου καὶ ἴδιον τοῦτο, δηλῶσαι
τί ἐστι τὸ τέλος οὗ ἕνεκα ὁ λόγος. διόπερ ἂν
δῆλον ᾖ καὶ μικρὸν τὸ πρᾶγμα, οὐ χρηστέον
7 προοιμίῳ. τὰ δὲ ἄλλα εἴδη οἷς χρῶνται, ἰατρεύ-

ᵃ A parenthetical remark to the effect that epideictic
exordia are different. Those of a forensic speech are like
prologues and epic exordia, but it is different with epideictic,
which may be wild, high-flown, as in the example given from
an unknown author.

ᵇ That is, forensic speeches. δράμασι has been suggested
for λόγοις.

ᶜ *Iliad*, i. 1.   ᵈ *Odyssey*, i. 1.

be noted that they produce the same effect as dramatic prologues and epic exordia (for those of dithyrambs resemble epideictic exordia :

> For thee and thy presents or spoils).[a]

But in speeches [b] and epic poems the exordia provide a sample of the subject, in order that the hearers may know beforehand what it is about, and that the mind may not be kept in suspense, for that which is undefined leads astray ; so then he who puts the beginning, so to say, into the hearer's hand enables him, if he holds fast to it, to follow the story. Hence the following exordia :

> Sing the wrath, O Muse.[c]
> Tell me of the man, O Muse.[d]
> Inspire me with another theme, how from the land of Asia a great war crossed into Europe.[e]

Similarly, tragic poets make clear the subject of their drama, if not at the outset, like Euripides, at least somewhere in the prologue, like Sophocles,

> My father was Polybus.[f]

It is the same in comedy. So then the most essential and special function of the exordium is to make clear what is the end or purpose of the speech ; wherefore it should not be employed, if the subject is quite clear or unimportant. All the other forms of exordia in use are only remedies,[g] and are common to all three

[e] From Choerilus (§ 4).
[f] Sophocles, *Oed. Tyr.* 774. But this can hardly be called the prologue.
[g] That is, special remedies in the case of the hearers suffering from " inattention, unfavourable disposition, and the like " (Cope).

ARISTOTLE

ματα καὶ κοινά. λέγεται δὲ ταῦτα ἔκ τε τοῦ
λέγοντος καὶ τοῦ ἀκροατοῦ καὶ τοῦ πράγματος
καὶ τοῦ ἐναντίου. περὶ αὑτοῦ μὲν καὶ τοῦ ἀντι-
δίκου, ὅσα περὶ διαβολὴν λῦσαι καὶ ποιῆσαι.
ἔστι δὲ οὐχ ὁμοίως· ἀπολογουμένῳ μὲν γὰρ
πρῶτον τὰ πρὸς διαβολήν, κατηγοροῦντι δ' ἐν τῷ
ἐπιλόγῳ. δι' ὃ δέ, οὐκ ἄδηλον· τὸν μὲν γὰρ
ἀπολογούμενον, ὅταν μέλλῃ εἰσάξειν αὑτόν, ἀναγκαῖον ἀνελεῖν τὰ κωλύοντα, ὥστε λυτέον πρῶτον
τὴν διαβολήν· τῷ δὲ διαβάλλοντι ἐν τῷ ἐπιλόγῳ
διαβλητέον, ἵνα μνημονεύσωσι μᾶλλον.

Τὰ δὲ πρὸς τὸν ἀκροατὴν ἔκ τε τοῦ εὔνουν
ποιῆσαι καὶ ἐκ τοῦ ὀργίσαι, καὶ ἐνίοτε δὲ ἐκ τοῦ
προσεκτικὸν ἢ τοὐναντίον· οὐ γὰρ ἀεὶ συμφέρει
ποιεῖν προσεκτικόν, διὸ πολλοὶ εἰς γέλωτα πειρῶνται προάγειν. εἰς δὲ εὐμάθειαν ἅπαντα ἀνάξει,
ἐάν τις βούληται, καὶ τὸ ἐπιεικῆ φαίνεσθαι· προσ-
1415 b ἔχουσι γὰρ μᾶλλον τούτοις. προσεκτικοὶ δὲ τοῖς
μεγάλοις, τοῖς ἰδίοις, τοῖς θαυμαστοῖς, τοῖς ἡδέσιν·
διὸ δεῖ ἐμποιεῖν ὡς περὶ τοιούτων ὁ λόγος. ἐὰν
δὲ μὴ προσεκτικούς, ὅτι μικρόν, ὅτι οὐδὲν πρὸς
ἐκείνους, ὅτι λυπηρόν.

8 Δεῖ δὲ μὴ λανθάνειν ὅτι πάντα ἔξω τοῦ λόγου
τὰ τοιαῦτα· πρὸς φαῦλον γὰρ ἀκροατὴν καὶ τὰ
ἔξω τοῦ πράγματος ἀκούοντα, ἐπεὶ ἂν μὴ τοιοῦτος
432

branches of Rhetoric. These are derived from the speaker, the hearer, the subject, and the opponent. From the speaker and the opponent, all that helps to destroy or create prejudice. But this must not be done in the same way ; for the defendant must deal with this at the beginning, the accuser in the epilogue. The reason is obvious. The defendant, when about to introduce himself, must remove all obstacles, so that he must first clear away all prejudice ; the accuser must create prejudice in the epilogue, that his hearers may have a livelier recollection of it.

The object of an appeal to the hearer is to make him well disposed or to arouse his indignation, and sometimes to engage his attention or the opposite ; for it is not always expedient to engage his attention, which is the reason why many speakers try to make their hearers laugh. As for rendering the hearers tractable, everything will lead up to it if a person wishes, including the appearance of respectability, because respectable persons command more attention. Hearers pay most attention to things that are important, that concern their own interests, that are astonishing, that are agreeable ; wherefore one should put the idea into their heads that the speech deals with such subjects. To make his hearers inattentive, the speaker must persuade them that the matter is unimportant, that it does not concern them, that it is painful.

But we must not lose sight of the fact that all such things are outside the question, for they are only addressed to a hearer whose judgement is poor and who is ready to listen to what is beside the case ; for if he is not a man of this kind, there is no need

ᾖ, οὐθὲν δεῖ προοιμίου, ἀλλ' ἢ ὅσον τὸ πρᾶγμα εἰπεῖν κεφαλαιωδῶς, ἵνα ἔχῃ ὥσπερ σῶμα κεφαλήν. 9 ἔτι τὸ προσεκτικοὺς ποιεῖν πάντων τῶν μερῶν κοινόν, ἐὰν δέῃ· πανταχοῦ γὰρ ἀνιᾶσι μᾶλλον ἢ ἀρχόμενοι. διὸ γελοῖον ἐν ἀρχῇ τάττειν, ὅτε μάλιστα πάντες προσέχοντες ἀκροῶνται. ὥστε ὅπου ἂν ᾖ καιρός, λεκτέον "καί μοι προσέχετε τὸν νοῦν· οὐθὲν γὰρ μᾶλλον ἐμὸν ἢ ὑμέτερον" καὶ "ἐρῶ γὰρ ὑμῖν οἷον οὐδεπώποτε" ἀκηκόατε δεινὸν ἢ οὕτω θαυμαστόν. τοῦτο δ' ἐστίν, ὥσπερ ἔφη Πρόδικος, ὅτε νυστάζοιεν οἱ ἀκροαταί, παρ-10 εμβάλλειν τῆς πεντηκονταδράχμου αὐτοῖς. ὅτι δὲ πρὸς τὸν ἀκροατὴν οὐχ ᾗπερ ἀκροατής, δῆλον· πάντες γὰρ ἢ διαβάλλουσιν ἢ φόβους ἀπολύονται ἐν τοῖς προοιμίοις.

ἄναξ, ἐρῶ μὲν οὐχ ὅπως σπουδῆς ὕπο.

τί φροιμιάζῃ;

καὶ οἱ πονηρὸν τὸ πρᾶγμα ἔχοντες ἢ δοκοῦντες· πανταχοῦ γὰρ βέλτιον διατρίβειν ἢ ἐν τῷ πράγματι. διὸ οἱ δοῦλοι οὐ τὰ ἐρωτώμενα λέγουσιν ἀλλὰ τὰ 11 κύκλῳ, καὶ προοιμιάζονται. πόθεν δ' εὔνους δεῖ ποιεῖν, εἴρηται, καὶ τῶν ἄλλων ἕκαστον τῶν τοιούτων. ἐπεὶ δ' εὖ λέγεται

---

[a] i.e. to claim the hearer's attention at the beginning, for every one is keen to listen then, but later on attention slackens.

[b] The hearer qua hearer should be unbiased, but in fact

of an exordium, except just to make a summary statement of the subject, so that, like a body, it may have a head. Further, engaging the hearers' attention is common to all parts of the speech, if necessary ; for attention slackens everywhere else rather than at the beginning. Accordingly, it is ridiculous to put this[a] at the beginning, at a time when all listen with the greatest attention. Wherefore, when the right moment comes, one must say, " And give me your attention, for it concerns you as much as myself"; and, " I will tell you such a thing as you have never yet " heard of, so strange and wonderful. This is what Prodicus used to do ; whenever his hearers began to nod, he would throw in a dash of his fifty-drachma lecture. But it is clear that one does not speak thus to the hearer *qua* hearer ; [b] for all in their exordia endeavour either to arouse prejudice or to remove their own apprehensions :

O prince, I will not say that with haste [I have come breathless].[c]

Why this preamble ? [d]

This is what those also do who have, or seem to have, a bad case ; for it is better to lay stress upon anything rather than the case itself. That is why slaves never answer questions directly but go all round them, and indulge in preambles. We have stated[e] how the hearer's goodwill is to be secured and all other similar states of mind. And since it is rightly said,

hearers often suffer from the defects referred to in § 7, for which certain forms of exordia are remedies.

[c] Sophocles, *Antigone*, 223.
[d] Euripides, *Iphig. Taur.* 1162.   [e] ii. 1. 7, 8.

δός μ᾽ ἐς Φαίηκας φίλον ἐλθεῖν ἠδ᾽ ἐλεεινόν,

τούτων δεῖ δύο στοχάζεσθαι.

Ἐν δὲ τοῖς ἐπιδεικτικοῖς οἴεσθαι δεῖ ποιεῖν συνεπαινεῖσθαι τὸν ἀκροατήν, ἢ αὐτὸν ἢ γένος ἢ ἐπιτηδεύματ᾽ αὐτοῦ ἢ ἁμῶς γέ πως· ὃ γὰρ λέγει Σωκράτης ἐν τῷ ἐπιταφίῳ, ἀληθές, ὅτι οὐ χαλεπὸν Ἀθηναίους ἐν Ἀθηναίοις ἐπαινεῖν ἀλλ᾽ ἐν Λακεδαιμονίοις.

12 Τὰ δὲ τοῦ δημηγορικοῦ ἐκ τῶν τοῦ δικανικοῦ λόγου ἐστίν, φύσει δ᾽ ἥκιστα ἔχει· καὶ γὰρ καὶ περὶ οὗ ἴσασι, καὶ οὐδὲν δεῖται τὸ πρᾶγμα προοιμίου, ἀλλ᾽ ἢ δι᾽ αὐτὸν ἢ τοὺς ἀντιλέγοντας, ἢ ἐὰν μὴ ἡλίκον βούλει ὑπολαμβάνωσιν, ἀλλ᾽ ἢ μεῖζον ἢ ἔλαττον. διὸ ἢ διαβάλλειν ἢ ἀπολύεσθαι ἀνάγκη, καὶ ἢ αὐξῆσαι ἢ μειῶσαι. τούτων δὲ ἕνεκα προοιμίου δεῖται, ἢ κόσμου χάριν, ὡς αὐτοκάβδαλα 1416 a φαίνεται, ἐὰν μὴ ἔχῃ. τοιοῦτον γὰρ τὸ Γοργίου ἐγκώμιον εἰς Ἠλείους· οὐδὲν γὰρ προεξαγκωνίσας οὐδὲ προανακινήσας εὐθὺς ἄρχεται " Ἦλις πόλις εὐδαίμων."

15. Περὶ δὲ διαβολῆς ἓν μὲν τὸ ἐξ ὧν ἄν τις ὑπόληψιν δυσχερῆ ἀπολύσαιτο· οὐθὲν γὰρ διαφέρει εἴτε εἰπόντος τινὸς εἴτε μή, ὥστε τοῦτο καθόλου. 2 ἄλλος τρόπος ὥστε πρὸς τὰ ἀμφισβητούμενα ἀπαντᾶν, ἢ ὡς οὐκ ἔστιν, ἢ ὡς οὐ βλαβερόν, ἢ οὐ τούτῳ, ἢ ὡς οὐ τηλικοῦτον ἢ οὐκ ἄδικον ἢ οὐ μέγα

---

[a] *Odyssey*, vii. 327. [b] See i. 9. 30.
[*] Another reading is τόπος (topic) and so throughout.

Grant that on reaching the Phaeacians I may find friendship or compassion,[a]

the orator should aim at exciting these two feelings.

In epideictic exordia, one must make the hearer
believe that he shares the praise, either himself, or
his family, or his pursuits, or at any rate in some
way or other. For Socrates says truly in his Funeral
Oration that " it is easy to praise Athenians in the
presence of Athenians, but not in the presence of
Lacedaemonians." [b]

Deliberative oratory borrows its exordia from
forensic, but naturally they are very uncommon in
it. For in fact the hearers are acquainted with the
subject, so that the case needs no exordium, except
for the orator's own sake, or on account of his
adversaries, or if the hearers attach too much or too
little importance to the question according to his
idea. Wherefore he must either excite or remove
prejudice, and magnify or minimize the importance
of the subject. Such are the reasons for exordia ; or
else they merely serve the purpose of ornament, since
their absence makes the speech appear offhand. For
such is the encomium on the Eleans, in which Gorgias,
without any preliminary sparring or movements,
starts off at once, " Elis, happy city."

15. One way of removing prejudice is to make use
of the arguments by which one may clear oneself from
disagreeable suspicion ; for it makes no difference
whether this suspicion has been openly expressed or
not ; and so this may be taken as a general rule.
Another way [c] consists in contesting the disputed
points, either by denying the fact or its harmfulness,
at least to the plaintiff ; or by asserting that its
importance is exaggerated ; or that it is not unjust

ἢ οὐκ αἰσχρὸν ἢ οὐκ ἔχον μέγεθος· περὶ γὰρ τοιούτων ἡ ἀμφισβήτησις, ὥσπερ Ἰφικράτης πρὸς Ναυσι-
κράτην· ἔφη γὰρ ποιῆσαι ὃ ἔλεγε καὶ βλάψαι, ἀλλ᾽
οὐκ ἀδικεῖν. ἢ ἀντικαταλλάττεσθαι ἀδικοῦντα, εἰ
βλαβερὸν ἀλλὰ καλόν, εἰ λυπηρὸν ἀλλ᾽ ὠφέλιμον
ἤ τι ἄλλο τοιοῦτον.

3   Ἄλλος τρόπος ὡς ἐστὶν ἁμάρτημα ἢ ἀτύχημα
ἢ ἀναγκαῖον, οἷον Σοφοκλῆς ἔφη τρέμειν οὐχ ὡς
ὁ διαβάλλων ἔφη, ἵνα δοκῇ γέρων, ἀλλ᾽ ἐξ ἀνάγκης·
οὐ γὰρ ἑκόντι εἶναι αὐτῷ ἔτη ὀγδοήκοντα. καὶ
ἀντικαταλλάττεσθαι τὸ οὗ ἕνεκα, ὅτι οὐ βλάψαι
ἐβούλετο, ἀλλὰ τόδε, καὶ οὐ τοῦτο ὃ διεβάλλετο
ποιῆσαι, συνέβη δὲ βλαβῆναι· '' δίκαιον δὲ μισεῖν,
εἰ ὅπως τοῦτο γένηται ἐποίουν.''

4   Ἄλλος, εἰ ἐμπεριείληπται ὁ διαβάλλων, ἢ νῦν
5 ἢ πρότερον, ἢ αὐτὸς ἢ τῶν ἐγγύς. ἄλλος, εἰ ἄλλοι
ἐμπεριλαμβάνονται, οὓς ὁμολογοῦσι μὴ ἐνόχους
εἶναι τῇ διαβολῇ, οἷον εἰ ὅτι καθάριος μοιχός, καὶ
ὁ δεῖνα καὶ ὁ δεῖνα ἄρα.

6   Ἄλλος, εἰ ἄλλους διέβαλεν, ἢ ἄλλος αὐτούς,
ἢ ἄνευ διαβολῆς ὑπελαμβάνοντο ὥσπερ αὐτὸς νῦν,
οἳ πεφήνασιν οὐκ ἔνοχοι.

ᵃ Sophocles had two sons, Iophon and Ariston, by different
wives; the latter had a son named Sophocles. Iophon,
jealous of the affection shown by Sophocles to this grandson,
summoned him before the *phratores* (a body which had some
jurisdiction in family affairs) on the ground that his age
rendered him incapable of managing his affairs. In reply
to the charge, Sophocles read the famous choric ode on
Attica from the *Oedipus Coloneus*, beginning Εὔιππου, ξένε,
τᾶσδε | χώρας (668 ff.), and was acquitted. The story in this
form is probably derived from some comedy, which introduced the case on the stage (see Jebb's Introd. to the tragedy).

ᵇ In the reading in the text, αὐτούς must apparently refer

at all, or only slightly so ; or neither disgraceful nor
important. These are the possible points of dispute :
as Iphicrates, in answer to Nausicrates, admitted
that he had done what the prosecutor alleged and
inflicted damage, but denied that he had been guilty
of wrongdoing. Again, one may strike the balance,
when guilty of wrongdoing, by maintaining that
although the action was injurious it was honourable,
painful but useful, or anything else of the kind.

Another method consists in saying that it was a
case of error, misfortune, or necessity ; as, for example, Sophocles said that he trembled, not, as the
accuser said, in order to appear old, but from necessity, for it was against his wish that he was eighty
years of age.[a] One may also substitute one motive
for another, and say that one did not mean to injure
but to do something else, not that of which one was
accused, and that the wrongdoing was accidental :
" I should deserve your hatred, had I acted so as to
bring this about."

Another method may be employed if the accuser,
either himself or one closely related to him has been
involved in a similar charge, either now or formerly ;
or, if others are involved who are admittedly not
exposed to the charge ; for instance, if it is argued
that so-and-so is an adulterer, because he is a dandy,
then so-and-so must be.

Again, if the accuser has already similarly accused
others, or himself been accused by others ;[b] or if
others, without being formally accused, have been
suspected as you are now, and their innocence has
been proved.

to the defendant, and one would rather expect αὐτόν. Spengel's
suggested ἢ ἄλλος ἢ αὐτός for ἢ ἄλλος αὐτούς: "if he (i.e. the
adversary) or another has similarly accused others."

7   "Αλλος ἐκ τοῦ ἀντιδιαβάλλειν τὸν διαβάλλοντα·
ἄτοπον γὰρ εἰ ὃς αὐτὸς ἄπιστος, οἱ τούτου λόγοι
ἔσονται πιστοί.

8   "Αλλος, εἰ γέγονε κρίσις, ὥσπερ Εὐριπίδης πρὸς
Ὑγιαίνοντα ἐν τῇ ἀντιδόσει κατηγοροῦντα ὡς
ἀσεβής, ὅς γ' ἐποίησε κελεύων ἐπιορκεῖν

ἡ γλῶσσ' ὀμώμοχ', ἡ δὲ φρὴν ἀνώμοτος.

ἔφη γὰρ αὐτὸν ἀδικεῖν τὰς ἐκ τοῦ Διονυσιακοῦ
ἀγῶνος κρίσεις εἰς τὰ δικαστήρια ἄγοντα· ἐκεῖ
γὰρ αὐτῶν δεδωκέναι λόγον ἢ δώσειν, εἰ βούλεται
κατηγορεῖν.

9   "Αλλος ἐκ τοῦ διαβολῆς κατηγορεῖν, ἡλίκον, καὶ
τοῦτο ὅτι ἄλλας κρίσεις ποιεῖ, καὶ ὅτι οὐ πιστεύει
τῷ πράγματι.

1416 b   Κοινὸς δ' ἀμφοῖν ὁ τόπος τὸ σύμβολα λέγειν,
οἷον ἐν τῷ Τεύκρῳ ὁ Ὀδυσσεὺς ὅτι οἰκεῖος τῷ
Πριάμῳ· ἡ γὰρ Ἡσιόνη ἀδελφή· ὁ δὲ ὅτι ὁ πατὴρ
ἐχθρὸς τῷ Πριάμῳ, ὁ Τελαμών, καὶ ὅτι οὐ κατεῖπε
τῶν κατασκόπων.

---

[a] When a citizen was called upon to perform a "liturgy" or public service (*e.g.* the equipment of a chorus), if he thought that one richer than himself had been passed over he could summon him and compel him to exchange properties.

[b] *Hippolytus*, 612. This well-known verse is three times parodied in Aristophanes (*Thesmophoriazusae*, 275; *Frogs*, 101, 1471). In the first passage, the sense is reversed: Euripides has dressed up a certain Mnesilochus as a woman in order that he may attend the Thesmophorian assembly. Mnesilochus first requires Euripides to take an oath that he will help him out of any trouble that may arise. Euripides takes an oath by all the gods, whereupon Mnesilochus says to Euripides: "Remember that it was your mind that swore, but not your tongue."

When Euripides was engaged in a lawsuit, his adversary quoted the line, implying that even on oath Euripides could

Another method consists in counter-attacking the accuser ; for it would be absurd to believe the words of one who is himself unworthy of belief.

Another method is to appeal to a verdict already given, as Euripides did in the case about the exchange of property ;[a] when Hygiaenon accused him of impiety as having advised perjury in the verse,

> My tongue hath sworn, but my mind is unsworn,[b]

Euripides replied that his accuser did wrong in transferring the decisions of the court of Dionysus to the law courts ; for he had already rendered an account of what he had said there,[c] or was still ready to do so, if his adversary desired to accuse him.

Another method consists in attacking slander, showing how great an evil it is, and this because it alters the nature of judgements,[d] and that it does not rely on the real facts of the case.

Common to both parties is the topic of tokens, as, in the *Teucer*,[e] Odysseus reproaches Teucer with being a relative of Priam, whose sister his mother Hesione was ; to which Teucer replied that his father Telamon was the enemy of Priam, and that he himself did not denounce the spies.[f]

not be believed ; Euripides replied that his adversary had no right to bring before the law courts a matter which had already been settled by the theatrical judges.

[c] In the great Dionysiac theatre.

[d] Or, "makes extraneous points the subject of decision" (Cope), "raises false issues" (Jebb).

[e] Of Sophocles.

[f] Who had been sent to Troy by the Greeks to spy upon the Trojans. It seems that he was afterwards accused of treachery, the *token* being the fact that Teucer was a near connexion of Priam ; to which he replied with another *token* that his father was an enemy of Priam, and further, when the Greek spies were in Troy, he never betrayed them.

10 Ἄλλος τῷ διαβάλλοντι, τὸ ἐπαινοῦντι μικρὸν
μακρῶς ψέξαι μέγα συντόμως, ἢ πολλὰ ἀγαθὰ
προθέντα, ὃ εἰς τὸ πρᾶγμα προφέρει ἓν ψέξαι.
τοιοῦτοι δὲ οἱ τεχνικώτατοι καὶ ἀδικώτατοι· τοῖς
ἀγαθοῖς γὰρ βλάπτειν πειρῶνται, μιγνύντες αὐτὰ
τῷ κακῷ.

Κοινὸν δὲ τῷ διαβάλλοντι καὶ τῷ ἀπολυομένῳ,
ἐπειδὴ τὸ αὐτὸ ἐνδέχεται πλειόνων ἕνεκα πραχθῆναι, τῷ μὲν διαβάλλοντι κακοηθιστέον ἐπὶ τὸ
χεῖρον ἐκλαμβάνοντι, τῷ δὲ ἀπολυομένῳ ἐπὶ τὸ
βέλτιον· οἷον ὅτι ὁ Διομήδης τὸν Ὀδυσσέα προείλετο, τῷ μὲν ὅτι διὰ τὸ ἄριστον ὑπολαμβάνειν
τὸν Ὀδυσσέα, τῷ δ' ὅτι οὔ, ἀλλὰ διὰ τὸ μόνον μὴ
ἀνταγωνιστεῖν ὡς φαῦλον. καὶ περὶ μὲν διαβολῆς
εἰρήσθω τοσαῦτα.

16. Διήγησις δ' ἐν μὲν τοῖς ἐπιδεικτικοῖς ἐστὶν
οὐκ ἐφεξῆς ἀλλὰ κατὰ μέρος· δεῖ μὲν γὰρ τὰς
πράξεις διελθεῖν ἐξ ὧν ὁ λόγος· σύγκειται γὰρ
ἔχων ὁ λόγος τὸ μὲν ἄτεχνον (οὐθὲν γὰρ αἴτιος ὁ
λέγων τῶν πράξεων) τὸ δ' ἐκ τῆς τέχνης· τοῦτο
δ' ἐστὶν ἢ ὅτι ἔστι δεῖξαι, ἐὰν ᾖ ἄπιστον, ἢ ὅτι
2 ποιόν, ἢ ὅτι ποσόν, ἢ καὶ ἅπαντα. διὰ δὲ τοῦτ'
ἐνίοτε οὐκ ἐφεξῆς δεῖ διηγεῖσθαι πάντα, ὅτι
δυσμνημόνευτον τὸ δεικνύναι οὕτως. ἐκ μὲν οὖν

---

a Jebb refers τοιοῦτοι to the accusers, translating τεχνικοί
" artistic," certainly the commoner meaning.

b Involving a continuous succession of proofs.

442

Another method, suitable for the accuser, is to praise something unimportant at great length, and to condemn something important concisely; or, putting forward several things that are praiseworthy in the opponent, to condemn the one thing that has an important bearing upon the case. Such methods [a] are most artful and unfair; for by their use men endeavour to make what is good in a man injurious to him, by mixing it up with what is bad.

Another method is common to both accuser and defender. Since the same thing may have been done from several motives, the accuser must disparage it by taking it in the worse sense, while the defender must take it in the better sense. For instance, when Diomedes chose Odysseus for his companion, it may be said on the one hand that he did so because he considered him to be the bravest of men, on the other, that it was because Odysseus was the only man who was no possible rival for him, since he was a poltroon. Let this suffice for the question of prejudice.

16. In the epideictic style the narrative should not be consecutive, but disjointed; for it is necessary to go through the actions which form the subject of the speech. For a speech is made up of one part that is inartificial (the speaker being in no way the author of the actions which he relates), and of another that does depend upon art. The latter consists in showing that the action did take place, if it be incredible, or that it is of a certain kind, or of a certain importance, or all three together. This is why it is sometimes right not to narrate all the facts consecutively, because a demonstration of this kind [b] is difficult to remember. From some facts a man

ARISTOTLE

τούτων ἀνδρεῖος, ἐκ δὲ τῶνδε σοφὸς ἢ δίκαιος.
καὶ ἀπλούστερος ὁ λόγος οὗτος, ἐκεῖνος δὲ ποικίλος
3 καὶ οὐ λιτός. δεῖ δὲ τὰς μὲν γνωρίμους ἀνα-
μιμνήσκειν· διὸ οἱ πολλοὶ οὐδὲν δέονται διηγήσεως,
οἷον εἰ θέλεις Ἀχιλλέα ἐπαινεῖν· ἴσασι γὰρ πάντες
τὰς πράξεις, ἀλλὰ χρῆσθαι αὐταῖς δεῖ. ἐὰν δὲ
4 Κριτίαν, δεῖ· οὐ γὰρ πολλοὶ ἴσασιν. . . . νῦν δὲ
γελοίως τὴν διήγησίν φασι δεῖν εἶναι ταχεῖαν.
καίτοι ὥσπερ ὁ τῷ μάττοντι ἐρομένῳ πότερον
σκληρὰν ἢ μαλακὴν μάξῃ, "τί δ';" ἔφη, "εὖ
ἀδύνατον;" καὶ ἐνταῦθα ὁμοίως· δεῖ γὰρ μὴ
μακρῶς διηγεῖσθαι ὥσπερ οὐδὲ προοιμιάζεσθαι
μακρῶς, οὐδὲ τὰς πίστεις λέγειν· οὐδὲ γὰρ ἐνταῦθά
ἐστι τὸ εὖ ἢ τὸ ταχὺ ἢ τὸ συντόμως, ἀλλὰ τὸ
μετρίως· τοῦτο δ' ἐστὶ τὸ λέγειν ὅσα δηλώσει
1417 a τὸ πρᾶγμα, ἢ ὅσα ποιήσει ὑπολαβεῖν γεγονέναι ἢ
βεβλαφέναι ἢ ἠδικηκέναι, ἢ τηλικαῦτα ἡλίκα
5 βούλει· τῷ δὲ ἐναντίῳ τὰ ἐναντία. παραδιηγεῖσθαι
δὲ ὅσα εἰς τὴν σὴν ἀρετὴν φέρει, οἷον "ἐγὼ δ'
ἐνουθέτουν ἀεὶ τὰ δίκαια λέγων, μὴ τὰ τέκνα
ἐγκαταλείπειν." ἢ θατέρου κακίαν· "ὁ δ' ἀπεκρί-
νατό μοι ὅτι οὗ ἂν ᾖ αὐτός, ἔσται ἄλλα παιδία·"
ὃ τοὺς ἀφισταμένους Αἰγυπτίους ἀποκρίνασθαί
φησιν ὁ Ἡρόδοτος. ἢ ὅσα ἡδέα τοῖς δικασταῖς.
6 Ἀπολογουμένῳ δὲ ἐλάττων ἡ διήγησις, αἱ δ'

---

[a] Something has been lost here, as is shown by the transition from epideictic to forensic Rhetoric. All the mss. have a gap, which in several of them is filled by introducing the passage ἔστι δ' ἔπαινος . . . μετατεθῇ (i. 9. 33-37).
[b] ii. 30. The story was that a number of Egyptian soldiers had revolted and left in a body for Ethiopia. Their king Psammetichus begged them not to desert their wives

444

may be shown to be courageous, from others wise or just. Besides, a speech of this kind is simpler, whereas the other is intricate and not plain. It is only necessary to recall famous actions; wherefore most people have no need of narrative—for instance, if you wish to praise Achilles; for everybody knows what he did, and it is only necessary to make use of it. But if you wish to praise Critias, narrative is necessary, for not many people know what he did....[a]

But at the present day it is absurdly laid down that the narrative should be rapid. And yet, as the man said to the baker when he asked whether he was to knead bread hard or soft, "What! is it impossible to knead it well?" so it is in this case; for the narrative must not be long, nor the exordium, nor the proofs either. For in this case also propriety does not consist either in rapidity or conciseness, but in a due mean; that is, one must say all that will make the facts clear, or create the belief that they have happened or have done injury or wrong, or that they are as important as you wish to make them. The opposite party must do the opposite. And you should incidentally narrate anything that tends to show your own virtue, for instance, " I always recommended him to act rightly, not to forsake his children "; or the wickedness of your opponent, for instance, " but he answered that, wherever he might be, he would always find other children," an answer attributed by Herodotus [b] to the Egyptian rebels; or anything which is likely to please the dicasts.

In defence, the narrative need not be so long; for

and children, to which one of them made answer (τῶν δέ τινα λέγεται δέξαντα τὸ αἰδοῖον εἰπεῖν, ἔνθα ἂν τοῦτο ᾖ, ἔσεσθαι αὐτοῖσι ἐνθαῦτα καὶ τέκνα καὶ γυναῖκας).

ἀμφισβητήσεις ἢ μὴ γεγονέναι ἢ μὴ βλαβερὸν
εἶναι ἢ μὴ ἄδικον ἢ μὴ τηλικοῦτον, ὥστε περὶ τὸ
ὁμολογούμενον οὐ διατριπτέον, ἐὰν μή τι εἰς
ἐκεῖνο συντείνῃ, οἷον εἰ πέπρακται, ἀλλ᾿ οὐκ
7 ἄδικον. ἔτι πεπραγμένα δεῖ λέγειν, ὅσα μὴ
πραττόμενα ἢ οἶκτον ἢ δείνωσιν φέρει. παράδειγμα ὁ ᾿Αλκίνου ἀπόλογος, ὅτι πρὸς τὴν Πηνε-
λόπην ἐν ἑξήκοντα ἔπεσι πεποίηται. καὶ ὡς
Φάϋλλος τὸν κύκλον, καὶ ὁ ἐν τῷ Οἰνεῖ πρόλογος.
8 ᾿Ηθικὴν δὲ χρὴ τὴν διήγησιν εἶναι. ἔσται δὲ
τοῦτο, ἂν εἰδῶμεν τί ἦθος ποιεῖ· ἓν μὲν δὴ τὸ
προαίρεσιν δηλοῦν, ποιὸν δὲ τὸ ἦθος τῷ ποιὰν
ταύτην· ἡ δὲ προαίρεσις ποιὰ τῷ τέλει. διὰ τοῦτο
οὐκ ἔχουσιν οἱ μαθηματικοὶ λόγοι ἤθη, ὅτι οὐδὲ
προαίρεσιν· τὸ γὰρ οὗ ἕνεκα οὐκ ἔχουσιν. ἀλλ᾿
οἱ Σωκρατικοί· περὶ τοιούτων γὰρ λέγουσιν.
9 ἄλλα ἠθικὰ τὰ ἑπόμενα ἑκάστῳ ἤθει, οἷον ὅτι
ἅμα λέγων ἐβάδιζεν· δηλοῖ γὰρ θρασύτητα καὶ
ἀγροικίαν ἤθους. καὶ μὴ ὡς ἀπὸ διανοίας λέγειν,
ὥσπερ οἱ νῦν, ἀλλ᾿ ὡς ἀπὸ προαιρέσεως. "ἐγὼ
δ᾿ ἐβουλόμην· καὶ προειλόμην γὰρ τοῦτο· ἀλλ᾿
εἰ μὴ ὠνήμην, βέλτιον." τὸ μὲν γὰρ φρονίμου
τὸ δὲ ἀγαθοῦ· φρονίμου μὲν γὰρ ἐν τῷ τὸ ὠφέλιμον
διώκειν, ἀγαθοῦ δ᾿ ἐν τῷ τὸ καλόν. ἂν δ᾿ ἄπιστον
ᾖ, τότε τὴν αἰτίαν ἐπιλέγειν, ὥσπερ Σοφοκλῆς
ποιεῖ παράδειγμα τὸ ἐκ τῆς ᾿Αντιγόνης, ὅτι μᾶλλον

---

[a] *Odyssey*, xxiii. 264-284, 310-343. The title referred to
the narrative in Books ix.-xii. It became proverbial for a
long-winded story.

[b] He apparently summarized it.

[c] Of Euripides. It was apparently very compact.

the points at issue are either that the fact has not
happened or that it was neither injurious nor wrong
nor so important as asserted, so that one should not
waste time over what all are agreed upon, unless
anything tends to prove that, admitting the act, it
is not wrong. Again, one should only mention such
past things as are likely to excite pity or indignation
if described as actually happening; for instance,
the story of Alcinous, because in the presence of
Penelope it is reduced to sixty lines,[a] and the way
in which Phaÿllus dealt with the epic cycle,[b] and the
prologue to the *Oeneus*.[c]

And the narrative should be of a moral character,
and in fact it will be so, if we know what effects
this. One thing is to make clear our moral purpose;
for as is the moral purpose, so is the character, and
as is the end, so is the moral purpose. For this
reason mathematical treatises have no moral character, because neither have they moral purpose; for
they have no moral end. But the Socratic dialogues
have; for they discuss such questions. Other ethical
indications are the accompanying peculiarities of each
individual character; for instance, "He was talking
and walking on at the same time," which indicates
effrontery and boorishness. Nor should we speak as
if from the intellect, after the manner of present-day
orators, but from moral purpose: "But I wished it,
and I preferred it; and even if I profited nothing, it
is better." The first statement indicates prudence,
the second virtue; for prudence consists in the
pursuit of what is useful, virtue in that of what is
honourable. If anything of the kind seems incredible, then the reason must be added; of this
Sophocles gives an example, where his Antigone says

447

τοῦ ἀδελφοῦ ἐκήδετο ἢ ἀνδρὸς ἢ τέκνων· τὰ μὲν
γὰρ ἂν γενέσθαι ἀπολόμενα,

μητρὸς δ' ἐν ᾅδου καὶ πατρὸς βεβηκότων
οὐκ ἔστ' ἀδελφὸς ὅς τις ἂν βλάστοι ποτέ.

ἐὰν δὲ μὴ ἔχῃς αἰτίαν, ἀλλ' ὅτι οὐκ ἀγνοεῖς ἄπιστα
λέγων, ἀλλὰ φύσει τοιοῦτος εἶ· ἀπιστοῦσι γὰρ
ἄλλο τι πράττειν ἑκόντα πλὴν τὸ συμφέρον.

10   Ἔτι ἐκ τῶν παθητικῶν λέγειν, διηγούμενον
καὶ τὰ ἑπόμενα καὶ ἃ ἴσασι, καὶ τὰ ἰδίᾳ ἢ αὑτῷ
ἢ ἐκείνῳ προσόντα· " ὁ δ' ᾤχετό με ὑποβλέψας."

1417 b καὶ ὡς περὶ Κρατύλου Αἰσχίνης, ὅτι διασίζων
καὶ τοῖν χεροῖν διασείων· πιθανὰ γάρ, διότι σύμβολα γίνεται ταῦτα ἃ ἴσασιν ἐκείνων ὧν οὐκ ἴσασιν.
πλεῖστα δὲ τοιαῦτα λαβεῖν ἐξ Ὁμήρου ἔστιν.

ὣς ἄρ' ἔφη, γρηῢς δὲ κατέσχετο χερσὶ πρόσωπα·

οἱ γὰρ δακρύειν ἀρχόμενοι ἐπιλαμβάνονται τῶν
ὀφθαλμῶν. καὶ εὐθὺς εἰσάγαγε σεαυτὸν ποιόν
τινα, ἵνα ὡς τοιοῦτον θεωρῶσι καὶ τὸν ἀντίδικον·
λανθάνων δὲ ποίει. ὅτι δὲ ῥᾴδιον, ὁρᾶν δεῖ ἐκ
τῶν ἀπαγγελλόντων· περὶ ὧν γὰρ μηθὲν ἴσμεν,
ὅμως λαμβάνομεν ὑπόληψίν τινα.

11   Πολλαχοῦ δὲ δεῖ διηγεῖσθαι, καὶ ἐνίοτε οὐκ ἐν

ᵃ *Antigone*, 911-912, where the mss. have κεκευθότοιν
instead of Aristotle's βεβηκότων.

ᵇ Whereas this man makes his temperament responsible
for the strange things he does; he is built that way and
cannot help it.

ᶜ Supposed to be Aeschines called Socraticus from his
intimate friendship with Socrates. A philosopher and writer
of speeches for the law courts, he had a great reputation
as an orator.

that she cared more for her brother than for her husband or children; for the latter can be replaced after they are gone,

but when father and mother are in the grave, no brother can ever be born.[a]

If you have no reason, you should at least say that you are aware that what you assert is incredible, but that it is your nature; for no one believes that a man ever does anything of his own free will except from motives of self-interest.[b]

Further, the narrative should draw upon what is emotional by the introduction of such of its accompaniments as are well known, and of what is specially characteristic of either yourself or of the adversary: " And he went off looking grimly at me "; and as Aeschines [c] says of Cratylus, that he hissed violently and violently shook his fists. Such details produce persuasion because, being known to the hearer, they become tokens of what he does not know. Numerous examples of this may be found in Homer:

Thus she spoke, and the aged nurse covered her face with her hands; [d]

for those who are beginning to weep lay hold on their eyes. And you should at once introduce yourself and your adversary as being of a certain character, that the hearers may regard you or him as such; but do not let it be seen. That this is easy is perfectly clear [e] from the example of messengers; we do not yet know what they are going to say, but nevertheless we have an inkling of it.

Again, the narrative should be introduced in several

---

[d] *Odyssey*, xix. 361.
[e] δεῖ (omitted by others) = " one cannot help seeing."

ἀρχῇ. ἐν δὲ δημηγορίᾳ ἥκιστα διήγησίς ἐστιν,
ὅτι περὶ τῶν μελλόντων οὐθεὶς διηγεῖται· ἀλλ'
ἐάν περ διήγησις ᾖ, τῶν γενομένων ἔσται, ἵν'
ἀναμνησθέντες ἐκείνων βέλτιον βουλεύσωνται περὶ
τῶν ὕστερον. ἢ διαβάλλοντες, ἢ ἐπαινοῦντες. ἀλλὰ
τότε οὐ τὸ τοῦ συμβούλου ποιεῖ ἔργον. ἂν δ' ᾖ
ἄπιστον, ὑπισχνεῖσθαί [τε] καὶ αἰτίαν λέγειν εὐθύς,
καὶ διατάττειν οἷς βούλονται, οἷον ἡ Ἰοκάστη ἡ
Καρκίνου ἐν τῷ Οἰδίποδι ἀεὶ ὑπισχνεῖται πυνθα-
νομένου τοῦ ζητοῦντος τὸν υἱόν. καὶ ὁ Αἵμων
ὁ Σοφοκλέους.

17. Τὰς δὲ πίστεις δεῖ ἀποδεικτικὰς εἶναι·
ἀποδεικνύναι δὲ χρή, ἐπεὶ περὶ τεττάρων ἡ ἀμφισβήτησις, περὶ τοῦ ἀμφισβητουμένου φέροντα τὴν
ἀπόδειξιν· οἷον εἰ ὅτι οὐ γέγονεν ἀμφισβητεῖ, ἐν
τῇ κρίσει δεῖ τούτου μάλιστα τὴν ἀπόδειξιν φέρειν,
εἰ δ' ὅτι οὐκ ἔβλαψεν, τούτου, καὶ ὅτι οὐ τοσόνδε
ἢ ὅτι δικαίως, ὡσαύτως καὶ εἰ περὶ τοῦ γενέσθαι
2 τοῦτο ἡ ἀμφισβήτησις. μὴ λανθανέτω δ' ὅτι
ἀναγκαῖον ἐν ταύτῃ τῇ ἀμφισβητήσει μόνῃ τὸν

---

[a] Omitting τε. The difficulty is διατάττειν, which can
apparently only mean " arrange." Jebb retains τε, and
reads ὡς for οἷς: " the speaker must make himself responsible for the fact . . . and marshal his reasons in a way
acceptable to the hearers." The old Latin translation *vadiare
quibus volunt* suggested to Roemer διαιτηταῖς, " to the
arbitrators they approve."

[b] According to Jebb, Jocasta tells the inquirer incredible
things about her son, and pledges her word for the facts.
Cope says: "promises (to do something or other to satisfy
him)."

[c] *Antigone*, 683-723. On this Cope remarks: "This last
example must be given up as hopeless; there is nothing in
the extant play which could be interpreted as required here."

places, sometimes not at all at the beginning. In deliberative oratory narrative is very rare, because no one can narrate things to come ; but if there is narrative, it will be of things past, in order that, being reminded of them, the hearers may take better counsel about the future. This may be done in a spirit either of blame or of praise ; but in that case the speaker does not perform the function of the deliberative orator. If there is anything incredible, you should immediately promise both to give a reason for it at once and to submit it to the judgement of any whom the hearers approve ; [a] as, for instance, Jocasta in the *Oedipus* of Carcinus [b] is always promising, when the man who is looking for her son makes inquiries of her ; and similarly Haemon in Sophocles.[c]

17. Proofs should be demonstrative, and as the disputed points are four, the demonstration should bear upon the particular point disputed ; for instance, if the fact is disputed, proof of this must be brought at the trial before anything else ; or if it is maintained that no injury has been done ; or that the act was not so important as asserted ; or was just, then this must be proved, the three last questions being matters of dispute just as the question of fact. But do not forget that it is only in the case of a dispute as to this question of fact that one of

According to Jebb, the "incredibility" consists in the fact that Haemon, although in love with Antigone, and strongly opposed to the sentence pronounced upon her by his father Creon, still remains loyal to the latter. Haemon explains the reason in lines 701-3, where he says that he prizes his father's welfare more than anything else, for a father's good name and prosperity is the greatest ornament for children, as is the son's for the father.

ἕτερον εἶναι πονηρόν· οὐ γάρ ἐστιν ἄγνοια αἰτία,
ὥσπερ ἂν εἴ τινες περὶ τοῦ δικαίου ἀμφισβητοῖεν,
ὥστ᾿ ἐν τούτῳ χρονιστέον, ἐν δὲ τοῖς ἄλλοις οὔ.

3 Ἐν δὲ τοῖς ἐπιδεικτικοῖς τὸ πολύ, ὅτι καλὰ καὶ
ὠφέλιμα, ἡ αὔξησις ἔσται· τὰ γὰρ πράγματα δεῖ
πιστεύεσθαι· ὀλιγάκις γὰρ καὶ τούτων ἀποδείξεις
φέρουσιν, ἐὰν ἄπιστα ᾖ ἢ ἐὰν ἄλλος αἰτίαν ἔχῃ.

4 Ἐν δὲ τοῖς δημηγορικοῖς ἢ ὡς οὐκ ἔσται ἀμφι-
σβητήσειεν ἄν τις, ἢ ὡς ἔσται μὲν ἃ κελεύει, ἀλλ᾿
οὐ δίκαια ἢ οὐκ ὠφέλιμα ἢ οὐ τηλικαῦτα. δεῖ
δὲ καὶ ὁρᾶν εἴ τι ψεύδεται ἐκτὸς τοῦ πράγματος·
τεκμήρια γὰρ ταῦτα φαίνεται καὶ τῶν ἄλλων ὅτι
418 a ψεύδεται.

5 Ἔστι δὲ τὰ μὲν παραδείγματα δημηγορικώτατα,
τὰ δ᾿ ἐνθυμήματα δικανικώτερα· ἡ μὲν γὰρ περὶ
τὸ μέλλον, ὥστ᾿ ἐκ τῶν γενομένων ἀνάγκη παραδείγματα λέγειν, ἡ δὲ περὶ ὄντων ἢ μὴ ὄντων,
οὗ μᾶλλον ἀπόδειξίς ἐστι καὶ ἀνάγκη· ἔχει γὰρ
6 τὸ γεγονὸς ἀνάγκην. οὐ δεῖ δὲ ἐφεξῆς λέγειν τὰ

---

^a Aristotle's argument is as follows. But it must not be
forgotten that it is only in a dispute as to this question of
fact that one of the two parties must necessarily be a rogue.
For ignorance is not the cause (of there being a dispute
about the fact, *e.g.* "you hit me," "no, I didn't," where
both know the truth), as it might be in a dispute on what
was right or wrong, so that this is the topic on which you
should spend some time (*i.e.* because here you can prove or
disprove that A is πονηρός).

The passage is generally taken to mean that when it is a
question of fact it is universally true that one of the dis-
putants must be a rogue. Cope alone among editors makes
any comment. In his note he says: "all that is meant is
that there is a certain class of cases which fall under this

the two parties must necessarily [a] be a rogue; for ignorance is not the cause, as it might be if a question of right or wrong were the issue; so that in this case one should spend time on this topic, but not in the others.

In epideictic speeches, amplification is employed, as a rule, to prove that things are honourable or useful; for the facts must be taken on trust, since proofs of these are rarely given, and only if they are incredible or the responsibility is attributed to another.[b]

In deliberative oratory, it may be maintained either that certain consequences will not happen, or that what the adversary recommends will happen, but that it will be unjust, inexpedient, or not so important as supposed. But one must also look to see whether he makes any false statements as to things outside the issue; for these look like evidence that he makes misstatements about the issue itself as well.

Examples are best suited to deliberative oratory and enthymemes to forensic. The first is concerned with the future, so that its examples must be derived from the past; the second with the question of the existence or non-existence of facts, in which demonstrative and necessary proofs are more in place; for the past involves a kind of necessity.[c] One should not introduce a series of enthymemes continuously

issue, in which this topic may be safely used." For instance, A may on justifiable grounds charge B with theft; B denies it, and he may be innocent, although the evidence is strongly against him. In such a case, neither of the parties is necessarily πονηρός.

[b] Or, reading ἄλλως, " if there is some other reason."

[c] It is irrevocable, and it is possible to discuss it with some degree of certainty, whereas the future is quite uncertain, and all that can be done is to draw inferences from the past.

ἐνθυμήματα, ἀλλ' ἀναμιγνύναι· εἰ δὲ μή, κατα-
βλάπτει ἄλληλα. ἔστι γὰρ καὶ τοῦ ποσοῦ ὅρος·

ὦ φίλ', ἐπεὶ τόσα εἶπες ὅσ' ἂν πεπνυμένος ἀνήρ,

7 ἀλλ' οὐ τοιαῦτα. καὶ μὴ περὶ πάντων ἐνθυμήματα
ζητεῖν· εἰ δὲ μή, ποιήσεις ὅπερ ἔνιοι ποιοῦσι τῶν
φιλοσοφούντων, οἳ συλλογίζονται τὰ γνωριμώτερα
8 καὶ πιστότερα ἢ ἐξ ὧν λέγουσιν. καὶ ὅταν πάθος
ποιῇς, μὴ λέγε ἐνθύμημα· ἢ γὰρ ἐκκρούσει τὸ
πάθος ἢ μάτην εἰρημένον ἔσται τὸ ἐνθύμημα·
ἐκκρούουσι γὰρ αἱ κινήσεις ἀλλήλας αἱ ἅμα, καὶ
ἢ ἀφανίζουσιν ἢ ἀσθενεῖς ποιοῦσιν. οὐδ' ὅταν
ἠθικὸν τὸν λόγον, οὐ δεῖ ἐνθύμημά τι ζητεῖν ἅμα·
οὐ γὰρ ἔχει οὔτε ἦθος οὔτε προαίρεσιν ἡ ἀπόδειξις.
9 Γνώμαις δὲ χρηστέον καὶ ἐν διηγήσει καὶ ἐν
πίστει· ἠθικὸν γάρ. "καὶ ἐγὼ δέδωκα, καὶ ταῦτ'
εἰδὼς ὡς οὐ δεῖ πιστεύειν." ἐὰν δὲ παθητικῶς,
"καὶ οὐ μεταμέλει μοι καίπερ ἠδικημένῳ· τούτῳ
μὲν γὰρ περίεστι τὸ κέρδος, ἐμοὶ δὲ τὸ δίκαιον."
10 Τὸ δὲ δημηγορεῖν χαλεπώτερον τοῦ δικάζεσθαι,
εἰκότως, διότι περὶ τὸ μέλλον· ἐκεῖ δὲ περὶ τὸ
γεγονός, ὃ ἐπιστητὸν ἤδη καὶ τοῖς μάντεσιν, ὡς
ἔφη Ἐπιμενίδης ὁ Κρής· ἐκεῖνος γὰρ περὶ τῶν
ἐσομένων οὐκ ἐμαντεύετο, ἀλλὰ περὶ τῶν γεγονό-

but mix them up; otherwise they destroy one
another, For there is a limit of quantity; thus,

Friend, since thou hast said as much as a wise man would
say,[a]

where Homer does not say τοιαῦτα (such things as),
but τόσα (as many things as). Nor should you try
to find enthymemes about everything; otherwise
you will be imitating certain philosophers, who draw
conclusions that are better known and more plausible
than the premises from which they are drawn.[b] And
whenever you wish to arouse emotion, do not use an
enthymeme, for it will either drive out the emotion
or it will be useless; for simultaneous movements
drive each other out, the result being their mutual
destruction or weakening. Nor should you look for
an enthymeme at the time when you wish to give
the speech an ethical character; for demonstration
involves neither moral character nor moral purpose.

Moral maxims, on the other hand, should be used
in both narrative and proof; for they express moral
character; for instance, " I gave him the money and
that although I knew that one ought not to trust."
Or, to arouse emotion : " I do not regret it, although
I have been wronged; his is the profit, mine the
right."

Deliberative speaking is more difficult than
forensic, and naturally so, because it has to do with
the future; whereas forensic speaking has to do with
the past, which is already known, even by diviners,
as Epimenides the Cretan said; for he used to
divine, not the future, but only things that were past

[a] *Odyssey*, iv. 204.
[b] For this passage see i. 2. 12-13. The meaning is that it
is absurd to prove what every one knows already.

τῶν μὲν ἀδήλων δέ. καὶ ὁ νόμος ὑπόθεσις ἐν τοῖς
δικανικοῖς· ἔχοντα δὲ ἀρχὴν ῥᾷον εὑρεῖν ἀπόδειξιν.
καὶ οὐκ ἔχει πολλὰς διατριβάς, οἷον πρὸς ἀντίδικον
ἢ περὶ αὑτοῦ, ἢ παθητικὸν ποιεῖν. ἀλλ' ἥκιστα
πάντων, ἐὰν μὴ ἐξίστηται. δεῖ οὖν ἀποροῦντα
τοῦτο ποιεῖν ὅπερ οἱ Ἀθήνησι ῥήτορες ποιοῦσι
καὶ Ἰσοκράτης· καὶ γὰρ συμβουλεύων κατηγορεῖ,
οἷον Λακεδαιμονίων μὲν ἐν τῷ πανηγυρικῷ,
Χάρητος δ' ἐν τῷ συμμαχικῷ.

11   Ἐν δὲ τοῖς ἐπιδεικτικοῖς δεῖ τὸν λόγον ἐπεισοδιοῦν ἐπαίνοις, οἷον Ἰσοκράτης ποιεῖ· ἀεὶ γάρ
τινα εἰσάγει. καὶ ὃ ἔλεγε Γοργίας, ὅτι οὐχ
ὑπολείπει αὐτὸν ὁ λόγος, τοῦτό ἐστιν· εἰ γὰρ
Ἀχιλλέα λέγει, Πηλέα ἐπαινεῖ, εἶτα Αἰακόν, εἶτα
τὸν θεόν, ὁμοίως δὲ καὶ ἀνδρίαν, ἢ τὰ καὶ τὰ
12 ποιεῖ ἢ τοιόνδε ἐστίν. ἔχοντα μὲν οὖν ἀποδείξεις
1418 b καὶ ἠθικῶς λεκτέον καὶ ἀποδεικτικῶς, ἐὰν δὲ μὴ
ἔχῃς ἐνθυμήματα, ἠθικῶς· καὶ μᾶλλον τῷ ἐπιεικεῖ
ἁρμόττει χρηστὸν φαίνεσθαι ἢ τὸν λόγον ἀκριβῆ.
13   Τῶν δὲ ἐνθυμημάτων τὰ ἐλεγκτικὰ μᾶλλον
εὐδοκιμεῖ τῶν δεικτικῶν, ὅτι ὅσα ἔλεγχον ποιεῖ,

---

[a] The remark of Epimenides is by many editors interpreted as a sarcasm upon the fraternity of soothsayers, who
pretended to be able to *foretell the future*. But how is this
to be got out of the Greek? The point is perhaps something like : "it is easy enough to talk about the past, for
even soothsayers know it." What Aristotle says here is that
Epimenides practised a different kind of divination, relating
to the obscure phenomena of the past. The following is an
instance. After the followers of Cylon, who tried to make
himself tyrant of Athens (*c.* 632) had been put to death by
the Alcmaeonid archon Megacles, in violation of the terms
of surrender, a curse rested upon the city and it was devastated by a pestilence. On the advice of the oracle,

456

but obscure.[a] Further, the law is the subject in forensic speaking; and when one has a starting-point, it is easier to find a demonstrative proof. Deliberative speaking does not allow many opportunities for lingering—for instance, attacks on the adversary, remarks about oneself, or attempts to arouse emotion. In this branch of Rhetoric there is less room for these than in any other, unless the speaker wanders from the subject. Therefore, when at a loss for topics, one must do as the orators at Athens, amongst them Isocrates, for even when deliberating, he brings accusations against the Lacedaemonians, for instance, in the *Panegyricus*,[b] and against Chares in the *Symmachikos* (On the Peace).[c]

Epideictic speeches should be varied with laudatory episodes, after the manner of Isocrates, who is always bringing somebody in. This is what Gorgias meant when he said that he was never at a loss for something to say; for, if he is speaking of Peleus, he praises Achilles, then Aeacus, then the god; similarly courage, which does this and that,[d] or is of such a kind. If you have proofs, then, your language must be both ethical and demonstrative; if you have no enthymemes, ethical only. In fact, it is more fitting that a virtuous man should show himself good than that his speech should be painfully exact.

Refutative enthymemes are more popular than demonstrative, because, in all cases of refutation, it

---

Epimenides was summoned from Crete, and by certain rites and sacrifices purified the city and put a stop to the pestilence.
  [b] 110–114.   [c] 27.
  [d] He enumerates all the deeds that proceed from courage. Another reading is ἢ τὰ καὶ τά, ποιεῖ δ τοιόνδε ἐστίν, *i.e.* when praising courage, and this or that, he is employing a method of the kind mentioned.

ARISTOTLE

μᾶλλον δῆλον ὅτι συλλελόγισται· παράλληλα γὰρ
14 μᾶλλον τἀναντία γνωρίζεται. τὰ δὲ πρὸς τὸν
ἀντίδικον οὐχ ἕτερόν τι εἶδος, ἀλλὰ τῶν πίστεων
ἔστι τὰ μὲν λῦσαι ἐνστάσει τὰ δὲ συλλογισμῷ.
δεῖ δὲ καὶ ἐν συμβουλῇ καὶ ἐν δίκῃ ἀρχόμενον μὲν
λέγειν τὰς ἑαυτοῦ πίστεις πρότερον, ὕστερον δὲ
πρὸς τἀναντία ἀπαντᾶν λύοντα καὶ προδιασύροντα.
ἂν δὲ πολύχους ᾖ ἡ ἐναντίωσις, πρότερον τὰ
ἐναντία, οἷον ἐποίησε Καλλίστρατος ἐν τῇ Μεσ-
σηνιακῇ ἐκκλησίᾳ· ἃ γὰρ ἐροῦσι προανελὼν οὕτως
15 τότε αὐτὸς εἶπεν. ὕστερον δὲ λέγοντα πρῶτον
τὰ πρὸς τὸν ἐναντίον λόγον λεκτέον, λύοντα καὶ
ἀντισυλλογιζόμενον, καὶ μάλιστα ἂν εὐδοκιμηκότα
ᾖ· ὥσπερ γὰρ ἄνθρωπον προδιαβεβλημένον οὐ
δέχεται ἡ ψυχή, τὸν αὐτὸν τρόπον οὐδὲ λόγον,
ἐὰν ὁ ἐναντίος εὖ δοκῇ εἰρηκέναι. δεῖ οὖν χώραν
ποιεῖν ἐν τῷ ἀκροατῇ τῷ μέλλοντι λόγῳ· ἔσται
δέ, ἂν ἀνέλῃς. διὸ ἢ πρὸς πάντα ἢ τὰ μέγιστα ἢ
τὰ εὐδοκιμοῦντα ἢ τὰ εὐέλεγκτα μαχεσάμενον
οὕτω τὰ αὑτοῦ πιστὰ ποιητέον.

---

a There is no difference in form between the demonstrative
and refutative enthymeme, but the latter draws opposite
conclusions; and opposites are always more striking when
they are brought together, and a parallel drawn between
them. It is then easy to see where the fallacy lies. *Cf.* ii.
23. 30 : "Refutative enthymemes are more effective (popular)
than demonstrative, because they bring opposites together in
a small compass, which are more striking (clearer) to the
hearer from being put side by side."
458

is clearer that a logical conclusion has been reached ; for opposites are more noticeable when placed in juxtaposition.[a] The refutation of the opponent is not a particular kind of proof ; his arguments should be refuted partly by objection, partly by counter-syllogism.[b] In both deliberative and forensic rhetoric he who speaks first should state his own proofs and afterwards meet the arguments of the opponent, refuting or pulling them to pieces beforehand. But if the opposition is varied,[c] these arguments should be dealt with first, as Callistratus did in the Messenian assembly ; in fact, it was only after he had first refuted what his opponents were likely to say that he put forward his own proofs. He who replies should first state the arguments against the opponent's speech, refuting and answering it by syllogisms, especially if his arguments have met with approval. For as the mind is ill-disposed towards one against whom prejudices have been raised beforehand, it is equally so towards a speech, if the adversary is thought to have spoken well. One must therefore make room in the hearer's mind for the speech one intends to make ; and for this purpose you must destroy the impression made by the adversary. Wherefore it is only after having combated all the arguments, or the most important, or those which are plausible, or most easy to refute, that you should substantiate your own case :

[b] In the translation τῶν πίστεων is taken with ἔστι : it is the business of, the proper function of, proofs. Others take it with τὰ μὲν . . . τὰ δέ : some . . . other (of the opponent's arguments).

[c] If the opponent's arguments are numerous and strong, by reason of the varied nature of the points dealt with.

ταῖς θεαῖσι πρῶτα σύμμαχος γενήσομαι.
ἐγὼ γὰρ Ἥραν . . .

ἐν τούτοις ἥψατο πρῶτον τοῦ εὐηθεστάτου.
16 Περὶ μὲν οὖν πίστεων ταῦτα. εἰς δὲ τὸ ἦθος,
ἐπειδὴ ἔνια περὶ αὑτοῦ λέγειν ἢ ἐπίφθονον ἢ
μακρολογίαν ἢ ἀντιλογίαν ἔχει, καὶ περὶ ἄλλου ἢ
λοιδορίαν ἢ ἀγροικίαν, ἕτερον χρὴ λέγοντα ποιεῖν,
ὅπερ Ἰσοκράτης ποιεῖ ἐν τῷ Φιλίππῳ καὶ ἐν τῇ
ἀντιδόσει, καὶ ὡς Ἀρχίλοχος ψέγει· ποιεῖ γὰρ τὸν
πατέρα λέγοντα περὶ τῆς θυγατρὸς ἐν τῷ ἰάμβῳ

χρημάτων δ' ἄελπτον οὐθέν ἐστιν οὐδ' ἀπώμοτον,

καὶ τὸν Χάρωνα τὸν τέκτονα ἐν τῷ ἰάμβῳ οὗ ἡ
ἀρχὴ

οὔ μοι τὰ Γύγεω.

καὶ ὡς Σοφοκλῆς τὸν Αἵμονα ὑπὲρ τῆς Ἀντιγόνης
17 πρὸς τὸν πατέρα ὡς λεγόντων ἑτέρων. δεῖ δὲ

---

[a] Euripides, *Troades*, 969-971. Hecuba had advised
Menelaus to put Helen to death; she defends herself at
length, and is answered by Hecuba in a reply of which these
words form part. Her argument is that none of the three
goddesses who contended for the prize of beauty on Mt. Ida
would have been such fools as to allow Argos and Athens to
become subject to Troy as the result of the contest, which
was merely a prank.

[b] 4-7. Isocrates says that *his friends* thought very highly
of one of his addresses, as likely to bring peace.

[c] 132-139, 141-149. Here again Isocrates puts compli-
ments on his composition into the mouth of an imaginary
friend.

[d] Archilochus (*c.* 650) of Paros was engaged to Neobule,
the daughter of Lycambes. Her father broke off the engagement, whereupon Archilochus pursued father and
daughter with furious and scurrilous abuse. It is here said

I will first defend the goddesses, for I [do not think] that Hera . . .[a]

in this passage the poet has first seized upon the weakest argument.

So much concerning proofs. In regard to moral character, since sometimes, in speaking of ourselves, we render ourselves liable to envy, to the charge of prolixity, or contradiction, or, when speaking of another, we may be accused of abuse or boorishness, we must make another speak in our place, as Isocrates does in the *Philippus* [b] and in the *Antidosis*.[c] Archilochus uses the same device in censure ; for in his iambics he introduces the father speaking as follows of his daughter :

There is nothing beyond expectation, nothing that can be sworn impossible,[d]

and the carpenter Charon in the iambic verse beginning

I [care not for the wealth] of Gyges ; [e]

Sophocles, also,[f] introduces Haemon, when defending Antigone against his father, as if quoting the opinion

that, instead of attacking the daughter directly, he represented her as being attacked by her father. The meaning of ἄελπτον is not clear. It may be a general statement : the unexpected often happens ; or, there is nothing so bad that you may not expect it. B. St. Hilaire translates : " There is nothing that money cannot procure," meaning that the father was prepared to sell his daughter (Frag. 74).

[e] The line ends : τοῦ πολυχρύσου μέλει. Archilochus represents Charon the carpenter as expressing his own disapproval of the desire for wealth and of the envy caused by others possessing it.

[f] Here again, Haemon similarly puts his own feelings as to Creon's cruel treatment of Antigone into the mouth of the people of the city, and refers to popular rumour.

καὶ μεταβάλλειν τὰ ἐνθυμήματα καὶ γνώμας
ποιεῖν ἐνίοτε, οἷον " χρὴ δὲ τὰς διαλλαγὰς ποιεῖν
τοὺς νοῦν ἔχοντας εὐτυχοῦντας· οὕτω γὰρ ἂν
μέγιστα πλεονεκτοῖεν." ἐνθυμηματικῶς δέ " εἰ
γὰρ δεῖ, ὅταν ὠφελιμώταται ὦσι καὶ πλεον-
εκτικώταται αἱ καταλλαγαί, τότε καταλλάττεσθαι,
εὐτυχοῦντας δεῖ καταλλάττεσθαι."

18. Περὶ δὲ ἐρωτήσεως, εὔκαιρόν ἐστι ποιεῖσθαι
1419 a μάλιστα μὲν ὅταν τὸ ἕτερον εἰρηκὼς ᾖ, ὥστε ἑνὸς
προσερωτηθέντος συμβαίνει τὸ ἄτοπον· οἷον Περικλῆς Λάμπωνα ἐπήρετο περὶ τῆς τελετῆς τῶν τῆς
σωτείρας ἱερῶν, εἰπόντος δὲ ὅτι οὐχ οἷόν τε
ἀτέλεστον ἀκούειν, ἤρετο εἰ οἶδεν αὐτός, φάσκον-
2 τος δὲ " καὶ πῶς ἀτέλεστος ὤν;" δεύτερον δὲ
ὅταν τὸ μὲν φανερὸν ᾖ, τὸ δὲ ἐρωτήσαντι δῆλον ᾖ
ὅτι δώσει· πυθόμενον γὰρ δεῖ τὴν μίαν πρότασιν
μὴ προσερωτᾶν τὸ φανερόν, ἀλλὰ τὸ συμπέρασμα
εἰπεῖν, οἷον Σωκράτης Μελήτου οὐ φάσκοντος
αὐτὸν θεοὺς νομίζειν [ἤρετο] εἰ δαιμόνιόν τι λέγοι,
ὁμολογήσαντος δὲ ἤρετο εἰ οὐχ οἱ δαίμονες ἤτοι θεῶν
παῖδες εἶεν ἢ θεῖόν τι, φήσαντος δὲ " ἔστιν οὖν,"
3 ἔφη, " ὅστις θεῶν μὲν παῖδας οἴεται εἶναι, θεοὺς

---

a The words ὅταν . . . ᾖ have been variously translated:
(1) when one of the two alternatives has already been stated ;
(2) when the opponent has stated what is different from the
fact ; (3) when the opponent has already conceded so much,
" made one admission " (Jebb).

b Reading ἤρετο.

of others. One should also sometimes change enthymemes into moral maxims ; for instance, " Sensible men should become reconciled when they are prosperous ; for in this manner they will obtain the greatest advantages," which is equivalent to the enthymeme : " If men should become reconciled whenever it is most useful and advantageous, they should be reconciled in a time of prosperity."

18. In regard to interrogation, its employment is especially opportune, when the opponent has already stated the opposite, so that the addition of a question makes the result an absurdity [a] ; as, for instance, when Pericles interrogated Lampon about initiation into the sacred rites of the saviour goddess. On Lampon replying that it was not possible for one who was not initiated to be told about them, Pericles asked him if he himself was acquainted with the rites, and when he said yes, Pericles further asked, " How can that be, seeing that you are uninitiated ? " Again, interrogation should be employed when one of the two propositions is evident, and it is obvious that the opponent will admit the other if you ask him. But the interrogator, having obtained the second premise by putting a question, should not make an additional question of what is evident, but should state the conclusion. For instance, Socrates, when accused by Meletus of not believing in the gods, asked [b] whether he did not say that there was a divine something ; and when Meletus said yes, Socrates went on to ask if divine beings were not either children of the gods or something godlike. When Meletus again said yes, Socrates rejoined, " Is there a man, then, who can admit that the children of the gods exist without at the same time admitting

ARISTOTLE

δὲ οὔ;" ἔτι ὅταν μέλλῃ ἢ ἐναντία λέγοντα δείξειν
4 ἢ παράδοξον. τέταρτον δέ, ὅταν μὴ ἐνῇ ἀλλ' ἢ
σοφιστικῶς ἀποκρινάμενον λῦσαι· ἐὰν γὰρ οὕτως
ἀποκρίνηται, ὅτι ἔστι μὲν ἔστι δ' οὔ, ἢ τὰ μὲν τὰ
δ' οὔ, ἢ πῇ μὲν πῇ δ' οὔ, θορυβοῦσιν ὡς ἀποροῦντος.
ἄλλως δὲ μὴ ἐγχειρεῖν· ἐὰν γὰρ ἐνστῇ, κεκρατῆσθαι
δοκεῖ· οὐ γὰρ οἷόν τε πολλὰ ἐρωτᾶν διὰ τὴν ἀ-
σθένειαν τοῦ ἀκροατοῦ. διὸ καὶ τὰ ἐνθυμήματα
ὅτι μάλιστα συστρέφειν δεῖ.
5 Ἀποκρίνασθαι δὲ δεῖ πρὸς μὲν τὰ ἀμφίβολα
διαιροῦντα λόγῳ καὶ μὴ συντόμως, πρὸς δὲ τὰ
δοκοῦντα ἐναντία τὴν λύσιν φέροντα εὐθὺς τῇ
ἀποκρίσει, πρὶν ἐπερωτῆσαι τὸ ἐπιὸν ἢ συλλογίσα-
σθαι· οὐ γὰρ χαλεπὸν προορᾶν ἐν τίνι ὁ λόγος.
φανερὸν δ' ἡμῖν ἔστω ἐκ τῶν τοπικῶν καὶ τοῦτο
6 καὶ αἱ λύσεις. καὶ συμπεραινόμενον, ἐὰν ἐρώτημα
ποιῇ τὸ συμπέρασμα, τὴν αἰτίαν εἰπεῖν· οἷον
Σοφοκλῆς ἐρωτώμενος ὑπὸ Πεισάνδρου εἰ ἔδοξεν
αὐτῷ ὥσπερ καὶ τοῖς ἄλλοις προβούλοις, καταστῆσαι τοὺς τετρακοσίους, ἔφη. "τί δέ; οὐ
πονηρά σοι ταῦτα ἐδόκει εἶναι;" ἔφη. "οὐκοῦν

ᵃ For the first of the quibbles Sandys refers to Aristophanes, *Acharnians*, 396, where Cephisophon, being asked
if Euripides was indoors, replies, "Yes and no, if you understand me"; and he gives the explanation, his mind is outside,
collecting scraps of poetry, while he himself is upstairs
(ἀναβάδην, unless it means "with his legs up") composing
a tragedy. The reference in the second instance is to the
adversary being reduced to such a position that he cannot
answer without having recourse to sophistical divisions
and distinctions, which seem to imply uncertainty. Aristotle
himself is fond of such "cautiously limited judgements"
(Gomperz).
   The translation is that of the reading ἀποροῦντος, a con-
jecture of Spengel's. The audience will be ready to express

that the gods exist ? " Thirdly, when it is intended
to show that the opponent either contradicts himself
or puts forward a paradox. Further, when the
opponent can do nothing else but answer the question
by a sophistical solution ; for if he answers, " Partly
yes, and partly no," " Some are, but some are not,"
" In one sense it is so, in another not," the hearers
cry out against him as being in a difficulty.[a] In other
cases interrogation should not be attempted ; for if
the adversary raises an objection, the interrogator
seems to be defeated ; for it is impossible to ask a
number of questions, owing to the hearer's weakness.
Wherefore also we should compress our enthymemes
as much as possible.

Ambiguous questions should be answered by defining them by a regular explanation, and not too
concisely ; those that appear likely to make us contradict ourselves should be solved at once in the
answer, before the adversary has time to ask the
next question or to draw a conclusion ; for it is not
difficult to see the drift of his argument. Both this,
however, and the means of answering will be sufficiently clear from the *Topics*.[b] If a conclusion is
put in the form of a question, we should state the
reason for our answer. For instance, Sophocles[c]
being asked by Pisander whether he, like the rest
of the Committee of Ten, had approved the setting
up of the Four Hundred, he admitted it. " What
then ? " asked Pisander, " did not this appear to
you to be a wicked thing ? " Sophocles admitted it.

its disapproval of his shuffling answers, which are evidence
of his perplexity.   The ordinary reading ἀποροῦντες attributes
the " perplexity " to the hearers.   Or, " the hearers, thinking
he is puzzled, *applaud us* [the interrogator] " (Jebb).
  [b] viii. 4.   [c] Cp. i. 14. 3.

σὺ ταῦτα ἔπραξας τὰ πονηρά;" "ναί," ἔφη· "οὐ
γὰρ ἦν ἄλλα βελτίω." καὶ ὡς ὁ Λάκων εὐθυνό-
μενος τῆς ἐφορίας, ἐρωτώμενος εἰ δοκοῦσιν αὐτῷ
δικαίως ἀπολωλέναι ἅτεροι, ἔφη. ὁ δὲ "οὐκοῦν
σὺ τούτοις ταὐτὰ ἔθου;" καὶ ὃς ἔφη. "οὐκοῦν
δικαίως ἄν," ἔφη, "καὶ σὺ ἀπόλοιο;" "οὐ
δῆτα," ἔφη· "οἱ μὲν γὰρ χρήματα λαβόντες ταῦτα
ἔπραξαν, ἐγὼ δ' οὔ, ἀλλὰ γνώμῃ." διὸ οὔτ'
ἐπερωτᾶν δεῖ μετὰ τὸ συμπέρασμα, οὔτε τὸ συμ-
1419 b πέρασμα ἐπερωτᾶν, ἐὰν μὴ τὸ πολὺ περιῇ τοῦ
ἀληθοῦς.

7   Περὶ δὲ τῶν γελοίων, ἐπειδή τινα δοκεῖ χρῆσιν
ἔχειν ἐν τοῖς ἀγῶσι, καὶ δεῖν ἔφη Γοργίας τὴν
μὲν σπουδὴν διαφθείρειν τῶν ἐναντίων γέλωτι
τὸν δὲ γέλωτα σπουδῇ, ὀρθῶς λέγων, εἴρηται
πόσα εἴδη γελοίων ἐστὶν ἐν τοῖς περὶ ποιητικῆς,
ὧν τὸ μὲν ἁρμόττει ἐλευθέρῳ τὸ δ' οὔ. ὅπως οὖν
τὸ ἁρμόττον αὑτῷ λήψεται. ἔστι δ' ἡ εἰρωνεία
τῆς βωμολοχίας ἐλευθεριώτερον· ὁ μὲν γὰρ αὑτοῦ
ἕνεκα ποιεῖ τὸ γελοῖον, ὁ δὲ βωμολόχος ἑτέρου.

19. Ὁ δ' ἐπίλογος σύγκειται ἐκ τεττάρων, ἔκ
τε τοῦ πρὸς ἑαυτὸν κατασκευάσαι εὖ τὸν ἀκροατὴν
καὶ τὸν ἐναντίον φαύλως, καὶ ἐκ τοῦ αὐξῆσαι καὶ
ταπεινῶσαι, καὶ ἐκ τοῦ εἰς τὰ πάθη τὸν ἀκροατὴν
καταστῆσαι, καὶ ἐξ ἀναμνήσεως. πέφυκε γὰρ
μετὰ τὸ ἀποδεῖξαι αὐτὸν μὲν ἀληθῆ τὸν δὲ ἐναντίον
ψευδῆ, οὕτω τὸ ἐπαινεῖν καὶ ψέγειν καὶ ἐπιχαλ-
κεύειν. δυοῖν δὲ θατέρου δεῖ στοχάζεσθαι, ἢ ὅτι
τούτοις ἀγαθὸς ἢ ὅτι ἁπλῶς, ὁ δ' ὅτι κακὸς τούτοις

ᵃ The chapters are lost (cp. i. 11. 29).
ᵇ Or, " mould the hearers to one's will " (L. and S.).

" So then you did what was wicked ? "   " Yes, for
there was nothing better to be done." The Lacedaemonian, who was called to account for his ephoralty,
being asked if he did not think that the rest of his
colleagues had been justly put to death, answered
yes. " But did not you pass the same measures as
they did ? " " Yes." " Would not you, then, also
be justly put to death ? " " No ; for my colleagues
did this for money ; I did not, but acted according
to my conscience." For this reason we should not
ask any further questions after drawing the conclusion, nor put the conclusion itself as a question,
unless the balance of truth is unmistakably in our
favour.

As for jests, since they may sometimes be useful
in debates, the advice of Gorgias was good—to confound the opponents' earnest with jest and their jest
with earnest. We have stated in the *Poetics* [a] how
many kinds of jests there are, some of them becoming
a gentleman, others not. You should therefore
choose the kind that suits you. Irony is more
gentlemanly than buffoonery ; for the first is employed on one's own account, the second on that of
another.

19. The epilogue is composed of four parts : to
dispose the hearer favourably towards oneself and
unfavourably towards the adversary ; to amplify and
depreciate ; to excite the emotions of the hearer ;
to recapitulate. For after you have proved that you
are truthful and that the adversary is false, the
natural order of things is to praise ourselves, blame
him, and put the finishing touches.[b] One of two
things should be aimed at, to show that you are
either relatively or absolutely good and the adversary

ARISTOTLE

ἢ ὅτι ἁπλῶς. ἐξ ὧν δὲ δὴ τοιούτους κατασκευάζειν
δεῖ, εἴρηνται οἱ τόποι πόθεν σπουδαίους δεῖ κατα-
2 σκευάζειν καὶ φαύλους. τὸ δὲ μετὰ τοῦτο δεδειγ-
μένων ἤδη αὔξειν ἐστὶ κατὰ φύσιν ἢ ταπεινοῦν·
δεῖ γὰρ τὰ πεπραγμένα ὁμολογεῖσθαι, εἰ μέλλει
τὸ ποσὸν ἐρεῖν· καὶ γὰρ ἡ τῶν σωμάτων αὔξησις
ἐκ προϋπαρχόντων ἐστίν. ὅθεν δὲ δεῖ αὔξειν καὶ
3 ταπεινοῦν, ἔκκεινται οἱ τόποι πρότερον. μετὰ
δὲ ταῦτα, δήλων ὄντων καὶ οἷα καὶ ἡλίκα, εἰς τὰ
πάθη ἄγειν τὸν ἀκροατήν· ταῦτα δ᾽ ἐστὶν ἔλεος
καὶ δείνωσις καὶ ὀργὴ καὶ μῖσος καὶ φθόνος καὶ
ζῆλος καὶ ἔρις. εἴρηνται δὲ καὶ τούτων οἱ τόποι
4 πρότερον. ὥστε λοιπὸν ἀναμνῆσαι τὰ προειρη-
μένα. τοῦτο δὲ ἁρμόττει ποιεῖν οὕτως ὥσπερ
φασὶν ἐν τοῖς προοιμίοις, οὐκ ὀρθῶς λέγοντες·
ἵνα γὰρ εὐμαθῆ ᾖ, κελεύουσι πολλάκις εἰπεῖν.
ἐκεῖ μὲν οὖν δεῖ τὸ πρᾶγμα εἰπεῖν, ἵνα μὴ λανθάνῃ
περὶ οὗ ἡ κρίσις, ἐνταῦθα δὲ δι᾽ ὧν δέδεικται
κεφαλαιωδῶς.

5 Ἀρχὴ δέ, διότι ἃ ὑπέσχετο ἀποδέδωκεν· ὥστε
ἅ τε καὶ δι᾽ ὃ λεκτέον. λέγεται δὲ ἐξ ἀντιπαρα-
βολῆς τοῦ ἐναντίου. παραβάλλειν δὲ ἢ ὅσα περὶ
τὸ αὐτὸ ἄμφω εἶπον, ἢ μὴ καταντικρύ. "ἀλλ᾽
οὗτος μὲν τάδε περὶ τούτου, ἐγὼ δὲ ταδί, καὶ διὰ
1420 a ταῦτα." ἢ ἐξ εἰρωνείας, οἷον "οὗτος γὰρ τάδ᾽
εἶπεν, ἐγὼ δὲ τάδε. καὶ τί ἂν ἐποίει, εἰ τάδε
ἔδειξεν, ἀλλὰ μὴ ταδί;" ἢ ἐξ ἐρωτήσεως· "τί

---

i. 9.　　　　^b ii. 19.　　　　^c ii. 1-11.

either relatively or absolutely bad. The topics which serve to represent men as good or bad have already been stated.[a] After this, when the proof has once been established, the natural thing is to amplify or depreciate ; for it is necessary that the facts should be admitted, if it is intended to deal with the question of degree ; just as the growth of the body is due to things previously existing. The topics of amplification and depreciation have been previously set forth.[b] Next, when the nature and importance of the facts are clear, one should rouse the hearer to certain emotions—pity, indignation, anger, hate, jealousy, emulation, and quarrelsomeness. The topics of these also have been previously stated,[c] so that all that remains is to recapitulate what has been said. This may appropriately be done at this stage in the way certain rhetoricians wrongly recommend for the exordium, when they advise frequent repetition of the points, so that they may be easily learnt. In the exordium we should state the subject, in order that the question to be decided may not escape notice, but in the epilogue we should give a summary statement of the proofs.

We should begin by saying that we have kept our promise, and then state what we have said and why. Our case may also be closely compared with our opponent's ; and we may either compare what both of us have said on the same point, or without direct comparison : " My opponent said so-and-so, and I said so-and-so on this point and for these reasons." Or ironically, as for instance, " He said this and I answered that ; what would he have done, if he had proved this, and not simply that ? " Or by interrogation : " What is there that has not been proved ? "

469

οὐ δέδεικται;" ἢ "οὗτος τί ἔδειξεν;" ἢ δὴ
οὕτως ἐκ παραβολῆς, ἢ κατὰ φύσιν, ὡς ἐλέχθη,
οὕτω τὰ αὑτοῦ, καὶ πάλιν, ἐὰν βούλῃ, χωρὶς τὰ
6 τοῦ ἐναντίου λόγου. τελευτῇ δὲ τῆς λέξεως
ἁρμόττει ἡ ἀσύνδετος, ὅπως ἐπίλογος ἀλλὰ μὴ
λόγος ᾖ· " εἴρηκα, ἀκηκόατε, ἔχετε, κρίνατε."

---

^a Reading τελευτῇ, a conjecture of Victorius. With
τελευτή, the sense will be: "as a conclusion, the asyndetic
style is appropriate."
^b It is generally supposed that this example of a suitable

or, " What has my opponent proved ? " We may, therefore, either sum up by comparison, or in the natural order of the statements, just as they were made, our own first, and then again, separately, if we so desire, what has been said by our opponent. To the conclusion of the speech [a] the most appropriate style is that which has no connecting particles, in order that it may be a peroration, but not an oration : " I have spoken ; you have heard ; you know the facts ; now give your decision." [b]

peroration is an echo of the conclusion of the speech of Lysias *Against Eratosthenes.*

SELECT GLOSSARY

OF TECHNICAL AND OTHER TERMS

[As a rule, only the meanings of words in Aristotle's "Rhetoric" are noticed, without reference to later rhetoricians.]

ἀγωνιστικός (i. 5. 14) : "fit for athletic contests"; (iii. 12. 1) of style: "suited to debate" (ἀγών), including both deliberative and forensic speeches. It is opposed to γραφική, the style of compositions meant to be read.

ἀκρίβεια (iii. 12. 5), ἀκριβολογία (i. 5. 15), ἀκριβής (iii. 17. 12) : of style, "precise," "nicely finished," "highly correct"; of statements, "exact," "closely reasoned."

ἀποπλάνησις (iii. 13. 5) : throwing dust in the eyes of the judge and diverting his attention from what is unfavourable ; unless it is taken in a neuter sense, wandering from the subject, "digression."

ἁρμονία (iii. 1. 4) : lit. joining ; here, pitch or tone, accent, modulation of the voice.

ἀρχή . . . αἴτιον (i. 7. 12) : the latter (cause) precedes the former (first principle or beginning). "In a plant, the seed is the ἀρχή, the power of vegetation the αἴτιον."

ἄτεχνοι (i. 2. 2 ; 15. 1) ; of proofs, those which are independent of art, being already in existence and ready for use ; ἔντεχνοι are those which have to be invented by the orator: *alias esse probationes quas extra dicendi rationem acciperet orator, alias quas ex causa traheret ipse et quodammodo gigneret ; ideoque illas ἀτέχνους, inartificiales, has ἐντέχνους, artificiales, vocaret* (Quint. *Inst. Orat.* v. 1. 8).

αὔξησις (i. 9. 39), αὐξητικά (i. 9. 38), αὔξειν (ii. 18. 4) : "amplification." Its object is to increase the rhetorical effect and importance of a statement by intensifying the circumstances of an object or action.

αὐτοκαβδάλως (iii. 7. 2) : "off-hand, lightly, at random ;"

472

GLOSSARY

αὐτοκάβδαλος (iii. 14. 11) is used of a hastily built ship by the poet Lycophron (see note on iii. 3. 1). It is said to be properly applied to badly kneaded meal.

ἀφελής (iii. 9. 5): "simple," the equivalent of ἁπλοῦς or μονόκωλος as applied to the period; that is, consisting of only one κῶλον (member, clause) as opposed to the complex, which allowed more than one, but was not supposed to exceed four κῶλα.

βλαίσωσις (ii. 23. 15): retortion of a dilemma upon the proposer of it: a form of enthymeme in which, from each of two contraries, some good or evil follows, each contrary to the other. The adj. βλαισός is translated (1) bow-legged, or (2) bandy-legged; but the connexion of this with the examples given is obscure. Cope suggests that the word properly means "straddling of the legs"; "legs irregularly diverging" (Welldon).

γλῶττα (iii. 3. 2): an obsolete, foreign, or dialectal word, in any way out of the common, which needs to be explained.

γνώμη (ii. 21. 2): a moral maxim or sentiment; a general (not particular) statement relating to the conduct of life. Maxims are to enthymemes as premises are to syllogisms, not in the case of every enthymeme, but only those that deal with the actions and passions of ordinary life.

γραφικὴ λέξις (iii. 12. 1): "suited for writing," "literary," opposed to ἀγωνιστικὴ λ.

δεῖγμα (iii. 14. 6): "sample, pattern"; the prologue or proem in an epic poem or drama, so called from its giving a sample of what is to follow, thus making the hearer acquainted with the nature of the subject to be treated of.

δεικτικὰ ἐνθυμήματα (ii. 22. 14): direct arguments (as opposed e.g. to the *reductio ad absurdum*), the object of which is to demonstrate or explain: they are opposed to ἐλεγκτικὰ ἐ., the object of which is refutation; δεῖξις (iii. 7. 6): "method of proof."

δείνωσις (ii. 21. 10): "exaggeration," "intensification," defined by Longinus as a form of αὔξησις; also "indignation," or the arousing of this feeling. Cicero (*De inventione*, i. 53. 100) describes it as a form of speech whereby intense hatred of a person or disgust at anything is aroused.

διαίρεσις (ii. 23. 10): distribution or division into parts or

473

GLOSSARY

heads, dealing with the different bearings of the case; in *Poetics* (1461 a 23) it is more or less equivalent to punctuation, although it includes every kind of break. διαιρεῖν τῷ λόγῳ (iii. 18. 5) is used of giving a detailed explanation, as opposed to συντόμως, one that is concise.

διαλεκτική (i. 1. 1): logical discussion, properly by way of question and answer; here and elsewhere in Aristotle, the logic of probabilities, as opposed to strict demonstration or scientific proof (ἀπόδειξις). The premises of the latter being incontrovertibly true, the conclusions drawn from them must be equally true. The premises of the dialectic syllogism and the rhetorical enthymeme on the other hand are only probable, such as *appear* to be true to certain persons, and therefore the conclusions drawn from them can only be probable.

Rhetoric is here stated to be a counterpart of, not absolutely identical with, Dialectic (Cicero, *Orator*, 114, *quasi* ex altera parte respondere *dialecticae*), since there are points of difference as well as resemblance between them. Elsewhere it is called an offshoot, or likeness, of Dialectic. Both are, theoretically, of universal application (although practically Rhetoric is limited to Politics in the widest sense, including the ethical sciences) and deal with material which to a certain extent is within the knowledge of all and belongs to no separate science. Neither has any special first principles, like those of a particular science, which cannot be transferred to another.

Dialectic proceeds by question and answer, whereas Rhetoric sets forth its ideas in a continuous speech, addressed, not to a select audience, but to a miscellaneous crowd with the object of persuading them to embrace a certain opinion. While the dialectical syllogism leads to general conclusions, the rhetorical, dealing rather with individual questions, leads to particular conclusions; for instance, whether punishment is to be inflicted in a particular case.

Both take either side of a question and are ready to prove either a negative or affirmative, whereas the conclusions of demonstrative proof are universal and necessary, and cannot be used to support one view or its opposite indifferently.

διάνοια (i. 13. 17; iii. 10. 4, 5): "meaning," "intention";

474

GLOSSARY

(ii. 26. 5; iii. 1. 7): "thought," the logical or inventive part of Rhetoric; (iii. 16. 9): "intellectual capacity," contrasted with the moral purpose.

διαστίζειν (iii. 5. 6): "to punctuate" (see διαίρεσις).

διατριβή (iii. 17. 10): opportunity for dwelling on a subject (*commoratio*); occasion for digression.

διηρημένη (iii. 9. 7): disjointed (of style), in which the members or clauses of a period are marked off by a connecting particle.

δύναμις: (1) power, strength, of body or authority: (2) faculty, natural capacity, cleverness: (3) potentiality, virtual existence or action, as opposed to ἐνέργεια, actuality, actual existence or action.

ἐγκώμιον (i. 9. 33): eulogy of achievements, bodily or mental, distinguished from ἔπαινος, praise of virtuous qualities.

εἶδος: (1) form, appearance; (2) particular kind, sort: (3) species, as contrasted with genus: (4) "special topics."

εἰκός (i. 2. 15): probability, a proposition in contingent matter, which is true in the greater number of cases (Envious men hate those whom they envy), but not in all. Its relation to the conclusion to be drawn is that of the universal to the particular.

εἰκών (iii. 4. 3): a metaphor with the addition of the particle of comparison "as," "like." Quintilian, *Inst. Orat.* viii. 6. 8, 9 *metaphora est brevior similitudo, eoque distat, quod illa comparatur rei, quam volumus exprimere, haec pro ipsa re dicitur.*

εἰρομένη λέξις (iii. 9. 1): continuous, running style (lit. strung together), such as that of Herodotus, in which the only connexion is that of the σύνδεσμοι; the sentences resemble straight lines which may be produced indefinitely, keeping an uninterrupted course.

ἐνδόσιμον (iii. 14. 1): the key-note in music; (iii. 14. 4) the key-note in a speech, almost the same as προοίμιον.

ἐνέργεια (iii. 11. 2): actualization, vividness, representing things inanimate as animate (see δύναμις).

ἐνθύμημα (i. 2. 8): an enthymeme (lit. thought, argument) in the *Rhetoric* is a rhetorical syllogism, that is, it is drawn from probable premises and is therefore not a strictly demonstrative proof. The use of the term for a syllogism in which one of the premises is suppressed is due to a misunderstanding of the word ἀτελής [unless

475

GLOSSARY

this is an interpolation], "incomplete," in *Anal. Priora*, ii. 29 [27]. 2, which refers to its logical value, not to its form. In the same treatise Aristotle defines an enthymeme as a syllogism from probabilities or signs (see R. C. Seaton in *Classical Review*, June, 1914).

ἔνστασις (ii. 25. 1): in logic, an objection directed not against an opponent's conclusion, but to the proposition advanced by him. This being universal if his conclusion is to be universal, the objection may be universal or particular. The establishment of the denial of one particular is sufficient to destroy the universal.

ἔντεχνοι πίστεις (i. 2. 2): see ἄτεχνοι πίστεις.

ἕξις (ii. 12. 2): a formed and permanent habit of mind, the result of πρᾶξις; it tends to the production of certain actions and is bound to produce them, unless external circumstances prevent it.

ἔπαινος (i. 9. 33): see ἐγκώμιον.

ἐπεισοδιοῦν (iii. 17. 11): to introduce an ἐπεισόδιον or accessory incident.

ἐπιεικής, ἐπιείκεια (i. 2. 4): goodness ; (i. 13. 13): reasonable treatment, equity.

ἐπίθετον (iii. 2. 14 ; iii. 3. 3): not limited to adjectives, but used for any strengthening, descriptive, or ornamental addition (*e.g.* Tydides).

ἐπίλογος (iii. 13. 3): peroration, winding-up of a speech, in which the chief points are recapitulated.

ἐπιστήμη (i. 1. 1), ἐπιστητός (ii. 24. 10): science, that which can be scientifically known, opposed to τέχνη, a system or set of rules, and to ἐμπειρία, experience, knack, without knowledge of principles.

ἐποικοδομεῖν (i. 7. 31): "building up of one phrase upon another, one rising above another step by step like the rounds of a ladder, κλῖμαξ " (Cope). They are so arranged that the last important word of one is repeated as the first of the next, as in Romans, v. 3-4 Tribulation worketh patience, and patience experience, and experience hope. " Climax " is hardly a suitable rendering, which in modern popular language generally implies the highest point, culmination.

ἐρώτησις (iii. 18. 1): a question put to the adversary, which only requires a simple affirmative or negative answer, opposed to πεῦσις or πύσμα, which needs an explanation.

476

GLOSSARY

εὐήθης (ii. 12. 7): good-natured, simple, opposed to κακοήθης; (iii. 1. 9; 12. 2): of speeches and style, foolish, lacking force, empty.

εὔογκος (iii. 7. 2): lit. bulky: of style, "weighty," "important," opposed to εὐτελής, "cheap," "poor," "meagre."

εὐφυής (i. 6. 29): possessed of good natural gifts, as distinct from powers that are the result of practice and study.

ἦθος: originally, a man's natural bent, his habitual temper or disposition, moral character; it furnishes an indirect proof (1) from the character of the speaker, who wants to convince his hearers of his own virtue (i. 2. 3); (2) from the characters of the different forms of government (i. 8. 6) and the various conditions of men (ii. 12-17), to which different language and methods of conciliation are suitable; in style (iii. 7. 6; 16. 8, 9), from exhibiting a knowledge of and due regard for the characteristics of individuals.

ἰατρεύματα (iii. 14. 7): "correctives," "antidotes" to the listlessness and indifference of the hearer, of general application, capable of being used in any part of a speech.

ἴδια ὀνόματα (iii. 5. 3): "specific," opposed to περιέχοντα, "general" terms.

κατασκευάζειν (ii. 24. 4): "to construct" an argument, opposed to ἀνασκευάζειν, ἀναιρεῖν, "to demolish"; (ii. 2. 27; iii. 19. 1) "to put into a certain frame of mind"; κατασκευαστικός (ii. 26. 3): "constructive."

κατεστραμμένη λέξις (iii. 9. 3): "close" or periodic style, in which the period, as distinguished from sentences in the εἰρομένη λ., resembles a circular line, which returns and ends at a certain point.

κύριος (i. 1. 11; i. 8. 1, 2; 15. 9, 21): "authoritative," "effective"; (i. 3. 4) "opportune," "appropriate"; (iii. 2. 2) of words, "established," "vernacular," used in their natural sense, opposed to "foreign," figurative, or archaic words, in fact, to any that are unusual or out of the common.

κῶλον (iii. 9. 5): "member," "clause," a subdivision of the period.

λεκτικός (iii. 8. 4): belonging to the language of ordinary life and conversation.

λιτός (iii. 16. 2): lit. smooth; of style, "plain," "unadorned."

λόγος: "speech," "oration"; (iii. 6. 1) "description," "de-

477

GLOSSARY

finition," opposed to ὄνομα, the noun or term ; (iii. 2. 7) prose ; (ii. 20. 2) "story," "fable"; (ii. 2. 18) "account," "consideration" (λόγῳ ἐν μηδένι εἶναι).

μαλακός (i. 10. 4): "effeminate"; (ii. 17. 4) "mild," "unimpassioned"; (ii. 22. 10) of reasoning, "slack," "loose."

μέγεθος (i. 5. 13): "stature,"; (iii. 1. 4) of style, "grandeur."

μειοῦν (ii. 18. 4): "to extenuate," "depreciate," opposed to αὔξειν, αὔξησις.

μείουρος, μύουρος (iii. 9. 6): "docked," "curtailed," of a clause or period which seems to end too soon.

μειρακιώδης (iii. 11. 16): of style, characterized by youthful force and vehemence and therefore not becoming to the old. In other rhetorical writers, "puerile."

μείωσις (μειοῦν, ii. 18. 4 ; 26. 1): "depreciation," "extenuation," opposed to αὔξησις, αὔξειν.

μετανάστης (ii. 2. 6): "immigrant," "vagrant," opposed to a native. It appears to be the same as the later μέτοικος (resident alien): cp. *Politics*. iii. 5. 9, where ἀτίμητος is explained as "having no share of office." It might also mean "of no value," one whom anybody could kill with impunity (see Leaf on *Iliad*. ix. 648).

μεταφορά (iii. 10. 7): "transference," "metaphor." "Metaphor is the application to a thing of a name that belongs to something else, the transference taking place from genus to species, from species to genus, from species to species, or proportionally" (*Poetics*, 21).

μέτρον : "metre," "measure": see ῥυθμός.

μονόκωλος (iii. 9. 5): of a period, consisting of only one clause or member.

νόμος : sometimes used in the sense of "convention," as opposed to φύσις.

ὄγκος (iii. 6. 1): "weight," "importance," "dignity." It also has the sense of "bombast" (Longinus, iii. 4).

οἰκεῖος (i. 5. 7): "one's own," that which one can dispose of as one wishes ; (i. 4. 12), that which is peculiar to something. as to a form of government ; (iii. 2. 6 ; 7. 4): of style and the use of words, "appropriate," much the same as κύριος.

ὁμωνυμία (ii. 24. 2 ; iii. 2. 7): the use of words in an equivocal sense and such words themselves, *i.e.* those that have the same sound but a different sense.

ὄνομα : as a general term, includes nouns, adjectives, articles,

478

GLOSSARY

and pronouns; as a special term, "noun" opposed to "verb."

πάθος, πάσχειν (ii. 16. 1, 2): mental condition or affection generally; (ii. 1. 8; iii. 17. 8), "passion," "emotion"; (i. 2. 1) "quality," "property" of things; (i. 9. 15) "suffering"; (iii. 7. 3) a pathetic style; so παθητικὴ λέξις and παθητικῶς λέγειν.

παραβολή (iii. 19. 5): "placing side by side," "comparison"; (ii. 20. 4) "illustration."

παράδειγμα (ii. 20. 1, 2): "example," "instance," including both the historical (παραβολή) and the fictitious (λόγος); (i. 2. 8) proof from example, "rhetorical induction," contrasted with ἐνθύμημα.

παράλογος (i. 13. 16): "beyond calculation," "unexpected;" παραλογίζεσθαι (i. 14. 1), "to cheat," "defraud"; (ii. 24. 4) "to reason falsely, or be led astray by false reasoning" (also in an active sense); παραλογιστικός (i. 9. 29), "fallacious," παραλογισμός (iii. 12. 4), "fallacy."

παρίσωσις (iii. 9. 9): "balancing of clauses;" πάρισος, of a clause, "exactly balanced."

παρομοίωσις (iii. 9. 9): "making like," "assimilation" of sounds at the beginning or end of clauses.

πεποιημένον ὄνομα (iii. 2. 5): a word coined or invented for the occasion.

περίοδος (iii. 9. 3): a complete sentence, composed of several clauses, from one full stop to another; π. τῆς γῆς (i. 4. 13): a traveller's description of the countries visited by him.

περιπέτεια (i. 11. 24): sudden change or reverse of fortune In tragedy, the word implies "a complete change or reversal of situation within the limits of a single scene or act" (Bywater on *Poetics*, 10).

πίστις (i. 14. 5): pledge of good faith, distinguished from ὅρκος and δεξιά; (i. 1. 11. and elsewhere): means of persuasion, "probable" opposed to "demonstrative" proof.

πρακτικός (i. 6. 11): "able to do," followed by the genitive, unless here it be translated "efficient," "practical," not connected grammatically with τῶν ἀγαθῶν.

πρόθεσις (iii. 13. 2): "setting forth," "statement of the case," like a problem (πρόβλημα) in geometry.

προοίμιον (i. 1. 9; iii. 14. 1): "preamble," "exordium," compared to the πρόλογος in tragedy and comedy, "all that

479

GLOSSARY

part of the play which comes before the first song of the chorus " (*Poetics*, 12. 4).

πρότασις (i. 3. 7): "proposition," "premise" of a syllogism; combined with δόξα, "notion," "popular opinion" as useful for producing persuasion (ii. 1. 1).

πτῶσις (i. 7. 27): used by Aristotle as a general term for the inflexions, not only of a noun, but also of a verb, generally marked by a difference of form; thus, the adjective χαλκοῦς from χαλκός (iii. 9. 9) and the adverb ἀνδρείως from ἀνδρία (i. 7. 27) are instances of "inflexions" (Bywater on *Poetics*, 20. 10).

ῥῆμα: (1) generally, that which is spoken ; (2) grammatically, a verb as opposed to a noun (ὄνομα). The term also appears to be applied to an adjective when used as a predicate.

ῥητορική: see διαλεκτική.

ῥυθμός (iii. 1. 4, 8. 2): "time"; in general, any regular, harmonious movement, in sound or motion, which can be measured by number; thus, it may be applied to the tramp of a body of soldiers, the flapping of birds' wings, the dance, music, and writing, in the last expressed in long and short syllables. " Rhythm consists of certain lengths of time, while metre is determined by the order in which these lengths are placed. Consequently, the one seems to be concerned with quantity, the other with quality [the syllables must be in a certain order] . . . rhythm has unlimited space over which it may range, whereas the spaces of metre are confined ; . . . further, metre is concerned with words alone, while rhythm extends also to the motion of the body " (Quintilian, *Inst. Orat.* ix. 4. 45, Loeb Series translation).

σαφὴς λέξις (iii. 2. 1): "clear," "perspicuous," defined (iii. 12. 6) as the mean between ἀδολεσχία (garrulity, prolixity) and συντομία (excessive conciseness).

σεμνὴ λέξις (iii. 2. 2): "noble," "majestic," "dignified."

σημεῖον (i. 2. 16): "sign," a probable argument as proof of a conclusion. Signs are of two kinds, one having the relation of particular to universal, the other that of universal to particular. τεκμήριον, on the other hand, is a necessary sign, and such signs can be made into a demonstrative syllogism, which cannot be refuted. Thus, " sign " is both a general and special term. As a general

GLOSSARY

term, it embraces the τεκμήρια; as a special term, the two kinds of signs, which are capable of refutation.

σόλοικος (ii. 16. 2): "one who offends against good taste or manners"; also one who speaks incorrectly (σολοικίζειν, iii. 5. 7).

στενός (iii. 12. 2): of style, "thin," "meagre," "jejune."

στοιχεῖον (ii. 22. 13; 26. 1): "element" of an enthymeme, identified by Aristotle with τόπος.

στρογγύλος (ii. 21. 7): "rounded"; of style, "terse," "compact."

συκοφαντία (ii. 24. 10): "false accusation," here used for "sophism," a specious but fallacious argument.

σύμβολον (iii. 15. 9, 16. 10): "sign," "token"; not to be confused with συμβολή (i. 4. 11), "contract." σύμβολον itself elsewhere = mutual covenant.

συνάγειν (i. 2. 13; ii. 22. 3, 15): "to conclude," "draw an inference": (iii. 11. 12) "draw together," "contract."

σύνδεσμος (iii. 5. 2): "connecting particle": it includes the preposition, the copulative conjunctions, and certain particles.

συνεστραμμένως (ii. 24. 2): "twisted up," "compactly" (cp. συστρέφειν, iii. 18. 4).

σύστοιχα (i. 7. 27): "conjugates," "co-ordinates": λέγεται δὲ σύστοιχα μὲν τὰ τοιάδε οἷον τὰ δίκαια καὶ ὁ δίκαιος τῃ δικαιοσύνῃ καὶ τὰ ἀνδρεῖα καὶ ὁ ἀνδρεῖος τῇ ἀνδρίᾳ (Topics, ii. 9. 1).

σχετλιασμός (ii. 21. 10): "passionate complaint" of injustice or ill-fortune: one of the parts of the peroration, in which we endeavour to secure the commiseration of the hearer, the first thing necessary being to put him into a sympathetic and pitying frame of mind (Forcellini, s.v. conquestio).

σχῆμα (ii. 24. 2; iii. 8. 1): "form," "figure" of a speech. It does not correspond to the modern expression "figure of speech," but is an "attitude" or "turn of meaning given to the language when it comes to be actually spoken" . . . "a difference of sense resulting from a difference of some kind in the mode of enunciation" (Bywater, Poetics, 19. 7).

τάξις (iii. 13-19): the arrangement or distribution of the parts of a speech.

ταπεινὴ λέξις (iii. 2. 1): "low," "poor," "mean"; in a moral sense, "base," "vile" (ταπεινότης, ii. 6. 10).

481

GLOSSARY

τεκμήριον (i. 2. 16, 17): see σημεῖον.

τέχνη (i. 1. 3): set of rules, "handbook" of Rhetoric: elsewhere of the "tricks" of rhetoricians ; τεχνολογεῖν (i. 1. 9):
to bring under the rules of art, reduce to a system.

τόπος (ii. 26. 1): lit., a place to look for a store of something,
and the store itself; a heading or department, containing
a number of rhetorical arguments of the same kind (τόπος
εἰς ὃ πολλὰ ἐνθυμήματα ἐμπίπτει). These are all classified
and placed where they can be easily found ready for use.
τόποι are of two kinds : (1) κοινοὶ τόποι ("commonplaces")
or simply τόποι, the topics common to the three kinds of
Rhetoric (i. 2. 21 ; ii. 18. 3–5); (2) εἴδη or ἴδια (i. 2. 21),
specific topics, propositions of limited applicability, chiefly
derived from Ethics and Politics.

ὑπόκρισις (iii. 1. 3): "delivery" of a speech, under which
declamation, gesticulation, expression, and everything
connected with acting are included ; ὑποκριτικὴ λέξις (iii.
12. 2), "style suited for delivery," "lending itself to
acting" ; [τέχνη] (iii. 1. 7): "the art of acting."

χώρα (iii. 17. 15): "room" for our own arguments as well
as those of the adversary in the hearer's mind, "to get a
footing" for what we are going to say ; (ii. 24. 2): the
proper place, province.

ψιλός (iii. 2. 3): "bare," "bald," of prose as opposed to
poetry.

ψυχρός (iii. 3. 1): "cold," "frigid," "insipid." As a noun,
τὸ ψυχρόν means generally any defect of style as opposed
to ἀρετὴ λέξεως.

INDEX OF NAMES

483

INDEX OF NAMES

---

[1] In both these passages it is proposed to read *Prodicus.*

INDEX OF NAMES

485

INDEX OF NAMES

GENERAL INDEX

487

GENERAL INDEX

GENERAL INDEX

489

GENERAL INDEX

490

GENERAL INDEX

491

GENERAL INDEX